Learning to Photograph

Volume 2

Cora Banek, Georg Banek

Learning to Photograph

Volume 2: Visual Concepts and Composition

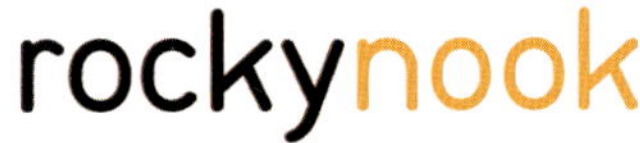

Cora and Georg Banek (www.artepictura.de)

Editor: Gerhard Rossbach
Copyeditor: Jeanne Hansen/Maggie Yates
Translator: David Schlesinger
Layout: Cora Banek
Cover Design: Helmut Kraus, www.exclam.de
Printer: Everbest Printing Co. Ltd through Four Colour Print Group, Louisville, Kentucky
Printed in China

ISBN 978-1-937538-21-7

1st Edition 2013

Rocky Nook Inc.
802 East Cota St., 3rd Floor
Santa Barbara, CA 93103

www.rockynook.com

Title of the German original: Fotografieren lernen, Band 2: Bildgestaltung und Bildsprache
ISBN 978-3-89864-699-4

Library of Congress Cataloging-in-Publication Data

Banek, Cora, 1981-
[Fotografieren lernen. English]
Learning to photograph / by Cora Banek, Georg Banek. -- 1st edition.
volumes cm
Translation of: Fotografieren lernen.
ISBN 978-1-937538-21-7 (softcover : acid-free paper : volume 2)
1. Photography. I. Banek, Georg, 1969- II. Title.
TR146.B2713 2013
770--dc23
2012051146

Distributed by O'Reilly Media
1005 Gravenstein Highway North
Sebastopol, CA 95472

Dear Reader,

If you listen in on conversations between photographers, it would be easy to get the impression that the following statement is true: *eighty percent of photography is technical. The rest is visual design.* Most discourse centers on the technology of photography instead of the design—but it should be exactly the other way around.

There is no shortage of examples showing that photography has less to do with technology than we generally believe. Generations of professional and amateur photographers alike have created superb images with the simplest of tools—images that draw our attention, that capture, move, and inform. Images that, in the best case, stay with us forever. These images are the product of intense perception at the moment of exposure. Visual design is the result of applying learned rules that are recalled in critical fractions of a second. Image design can also, however, last for minutes, hours, or days. In either case, design occurs when a photographer actively brings him- or herself into the process of creating an image. At this critical moment, the photographer becomes part of the photograph.

It's understandable that we talk a lot about technology, especially since the advent of digital photography; it is fascinating and we should know how to use our tools. However, I think it's important to detach ourselves from technology and refocus our attention on what's really crucial and important: the subject and image composition. Cora and Georg Banek deserve thanks and recognition for this book and their efforts to reposition image design in our consciousness as an essential element of successful photographs.

Martin Breutmann
Publisher and editor-in-chief, *fotoforum* magazine

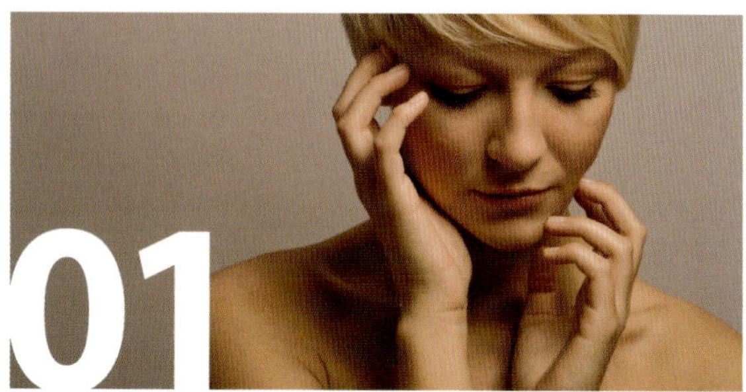

The Basics of Image Design

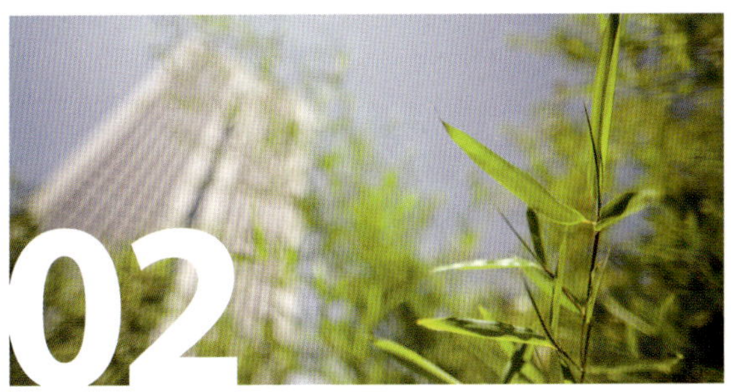

Composition

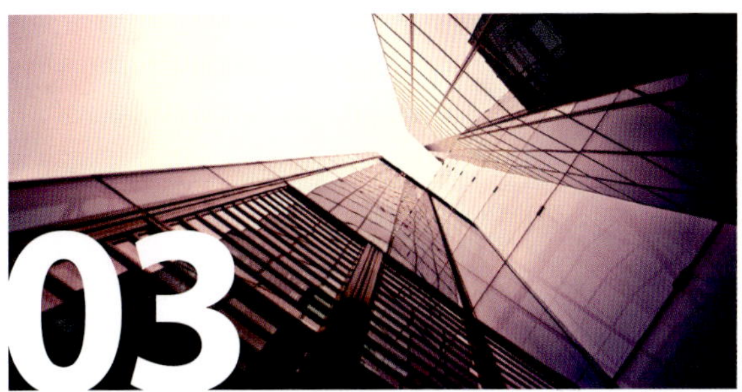

Shapes and Lines

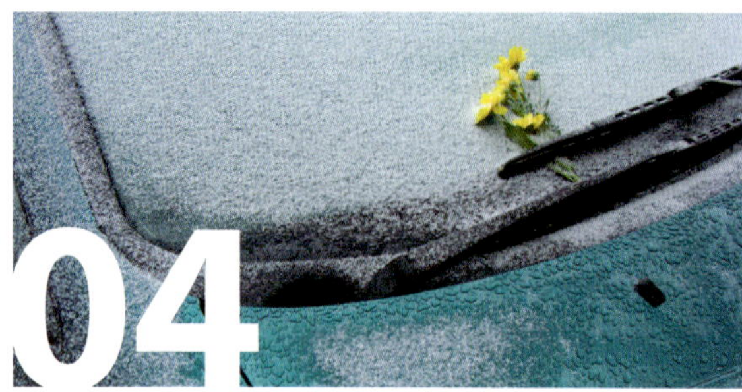

Standpoint and Point of View

Light

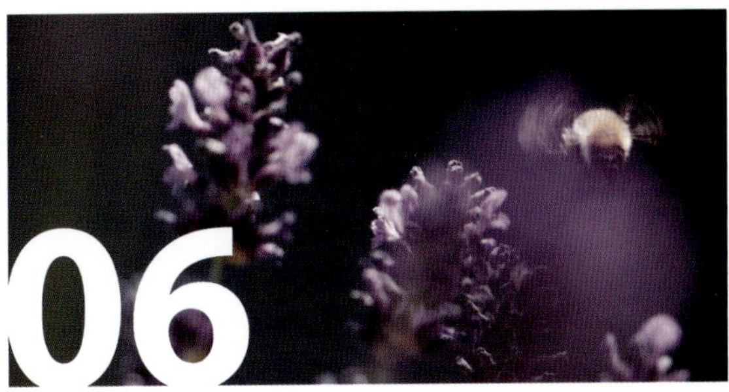

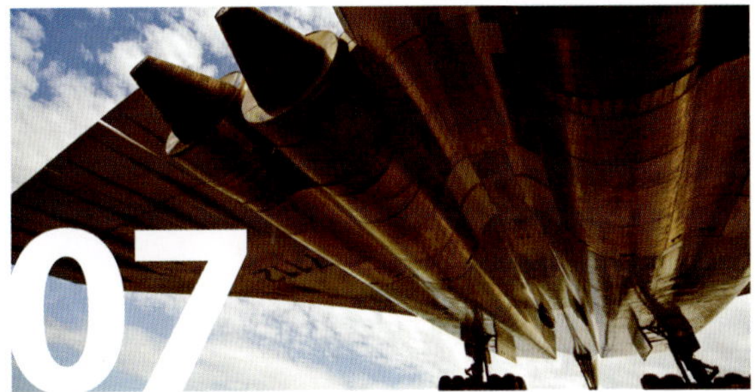

Color and Black-and-White

Sharpness and Blur

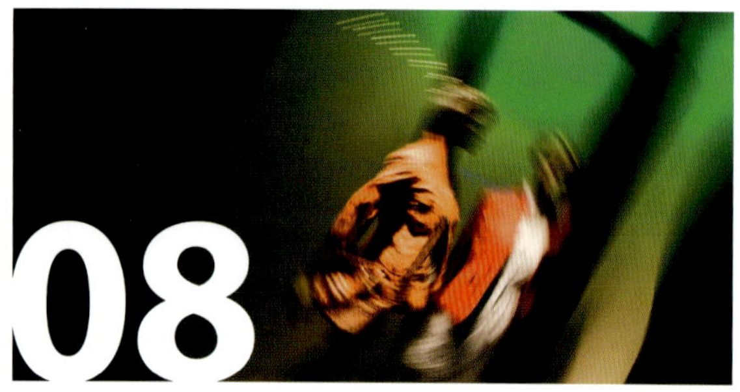

The Overall Effect

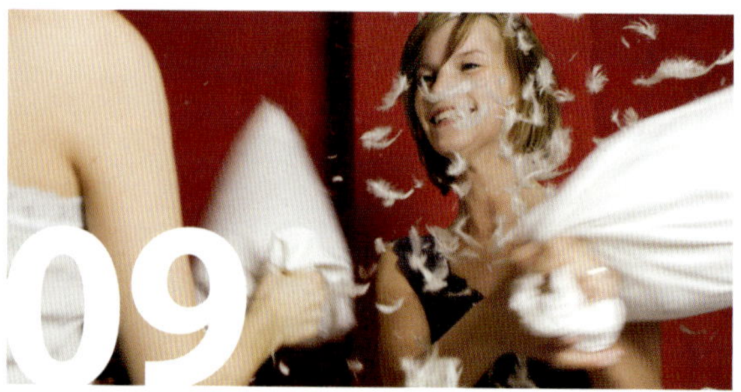

Image Analysis and Evaluation

We're delighted that you are interested in one of the most exciting, versatile, and creative subjects of photography: visual design. Writing a book about this important but often-overlooked subject is of particular concern to us. It is a matter near our hearts—image design is a main focus of our own photography. There are countless resources that address the technology of photography, but often the photo tips or general rules for image design are unsatisfactory. Based on what we've seen, the resources that attempt to impart both an understanding of photographic design elements and practical advice are, at best, insufficient. Because personal taste plays such a large role in this area of photography, most approaches to the topic are general and broad. The lack of resources may also stem from the fact that it is difficult to characterize the relationship between conscious image design and its effect on the viewer.

We can certainly confirm the difficulty of structuring this information: it took us several attempts to organize the basic concepts we wanted to present in this book. When we tried to use the traditional concepts of image design, we found that cause was always being confused with effect, and different themes popped up in several places. Movement, for example, is just as much a stylistic tool as it is an effect of an image. As a design tool it's just one aspect of image sharpness. Similarly, while most people understand that contrast refers to differences in brightness, it also plays a role in colors, shapes, surfaces, and lines. For reasons like this, we didn't limit our discussion of contrast to one chapter—we address it throughout the book, when appropriate.

We start this book with an overview of the basics. What are the variables that influence image design? How do they work together? What impact does human perception have on the process? How does this affect you as a photographer? Next, we focus on six influential aspects of image design: composition; shapes and lines; point of view; light; color and black-and-white; and sharpness and blur. Each of these subject areas has its own chapter where we introduce relevant elements of design, describe their applications, and analyze their effect on the image and the viewer. Consider, for instance, how the application of different formats (portrait, landscape, panorama, or square) can influence the design of an image. Then consider how the resulting photographs might affect the viewer in different ways.

In these six chapters, we discuss the effects of working with each design element individually. When discussing one design method, we keep all others unchanged. This approach is very theoretical, but it's useful to examine what influence particular elements of image design have on the end result. In separate chapters, we examine the overall effect of an image as well as how to analyze and evaluate photographs. This knowledge is a critical foundation for creating quality images, and for assessing your own work and the work of others.

For each of these subjects we show you the relationship between cause and effect, rather than labeling practices as correct or incorrect. We won't tell you, "If you do it this way, your images will turn out well." We are not familiar with your personal taste or your photographic goals, and since we know nothing about the ideas behind your images and the visual language you hope to convey, such judgments aren't possible. With each new exposure, you need to decide for yourself which visual design tools you should employ, and how to use those tools to create results that align with your intention. It may sound complicated and difficult, but with practice it will become second nature, and you'll be rewarded with pleasing images that engage and enthrall viewers.

We hope you enjoy the time you spend reading, creating images, and—last but not least—cultivating your own visual language.

Cora and Georg Banek
kontakt@artepicture.de

"Seeing changes our beliefs. Our beliefs change what we see." Jean Piaget, Swiss developmental psychologist

01 The Basics of Image Design

Before we present the various ways that photographers can utilize visual design to influence their photographs, it makes sense to go over some photographic design basics. This will be helpful for understanding the larger concepts of image design.

In *Learning to Photograph: Volume 1*, we introduced the fundamental process of photography and the factors that influence the resulting image, with a clear emphasis on the technology at hand. A similar introduction from the perspective of image design will show methods photographers can use, and what they can consider when trying to create a desired effect. It's important to know how images are perceived, but also to be familiar with the mechanisms that affect viewers. We explain the entire process of how people perceive images, and why different image design methods produce specific biological reactions.

Your individual personality as a photographer also has a great influence on the design of your images. You alone decide how to depict your subject to achieve a desired effect. The more conscious you are of these decisions, the more control you'll have over how your images affect the viewer.

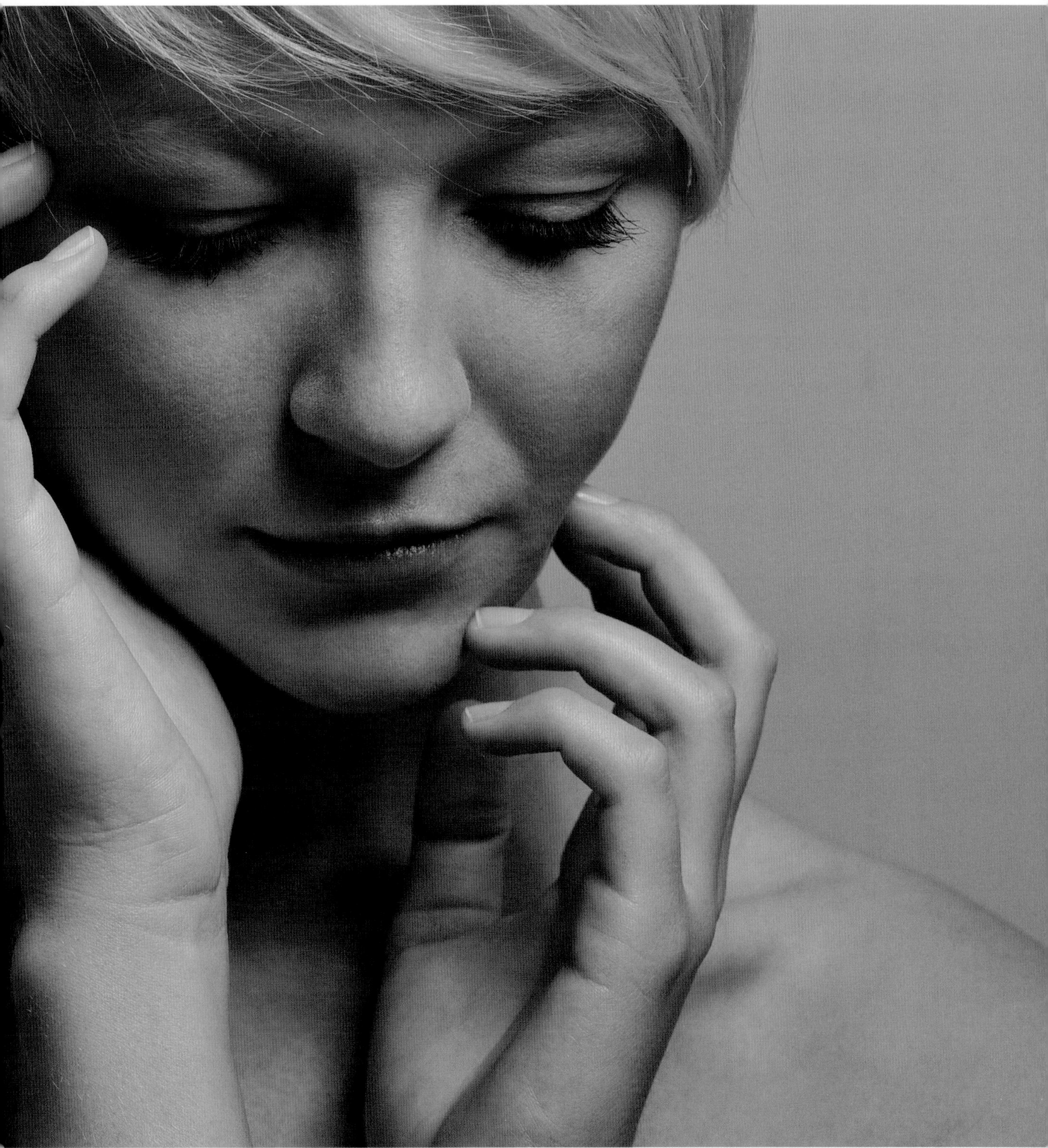

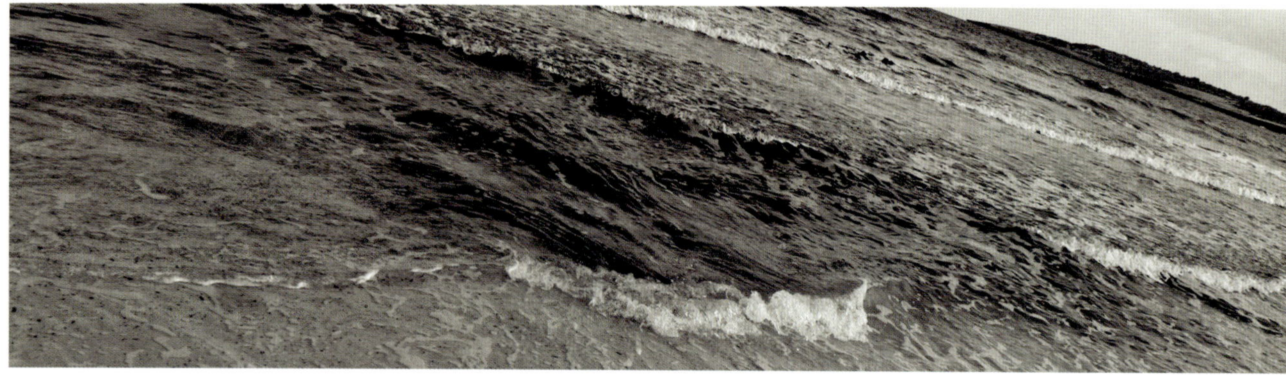

1.1 From Idea to Picture

The personality of the photographer influences what they choose to photograph, edit, and present—they control everything that goes into the production of an image. After that, they have little to no influence over how their work will be interpreted. For this reason, photographers need to do everything they can during shooting and editing to ensure that the final photograph is as close to their intention as possible. A broad understanding of the ways to influence the look of an image, and the possibilities those options offer, help photographers design images with purpose.

Tulips are popular the world over. We know them both as flowers we encounter in our daily lives and as the inspiration for countless photographs. Our familiarity with this beloved front yard regular is deep, but it's always possible to capture tulips in new, visually exciting ways.

The Photographer Designs

You alone decide what to capture in your images and how to do so. There are three factors that determine—whether consciously or subconsciously—how you apply the tools of visual design: your design knowledge, your design ability, and your design desire. **Your design knowledge** is the basic familiarity you have with image design. This foundational knowledge is a combination of conscious and subconscious think-

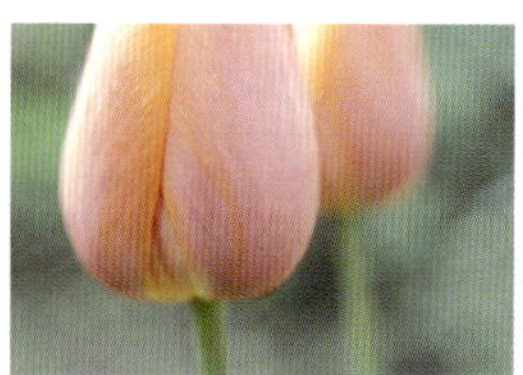
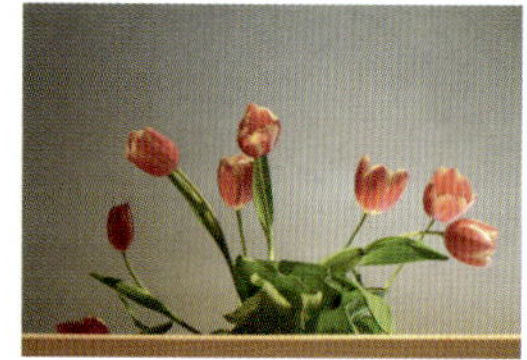
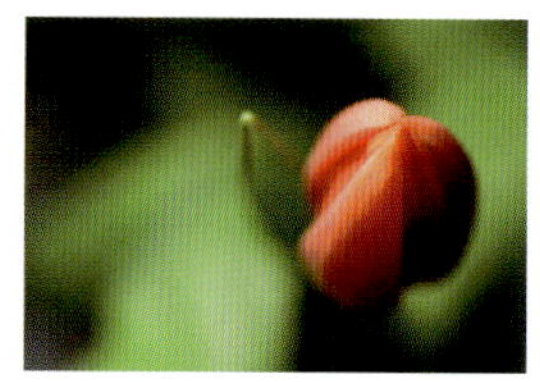
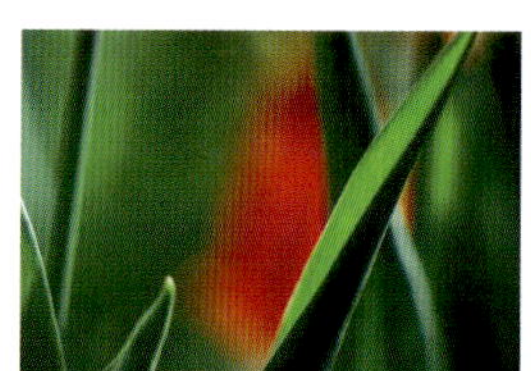
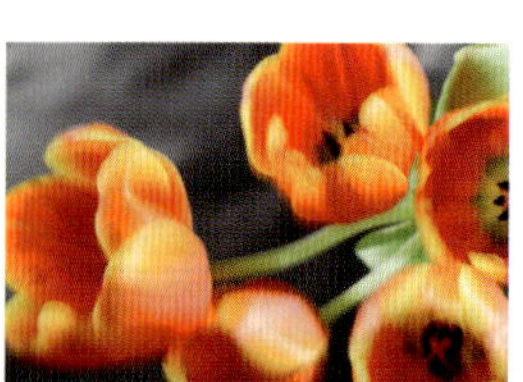
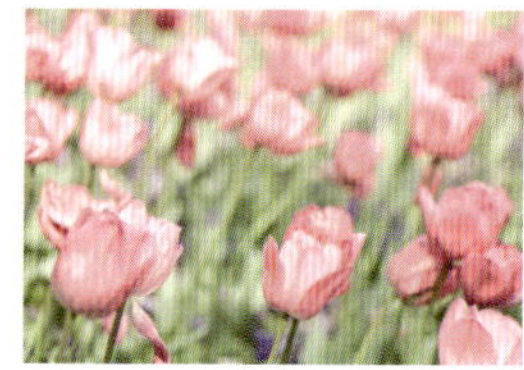
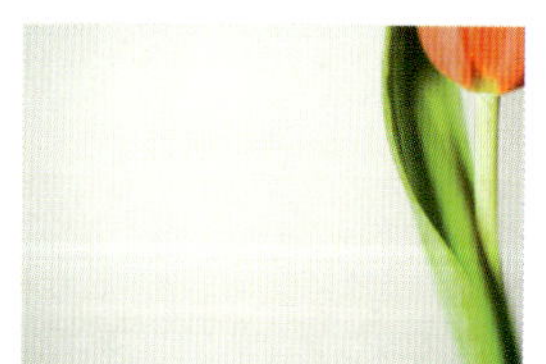
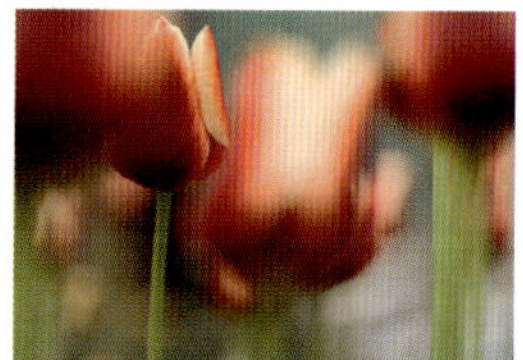

ing. The conscious consideration is built on the practice of analyzing images, reading about visual design, and learning from other photographers. It is important to be familiar with different possibilities for expression, just as it is important to understand the ways in which particular visual design choices produce specific reactions from the viewer. This is the next topic of this book: making clear the effects of specific design choices.

There are many factors that influence the final look of an image and determine how viewers receive it. The most important of these are depicted in this diagram.

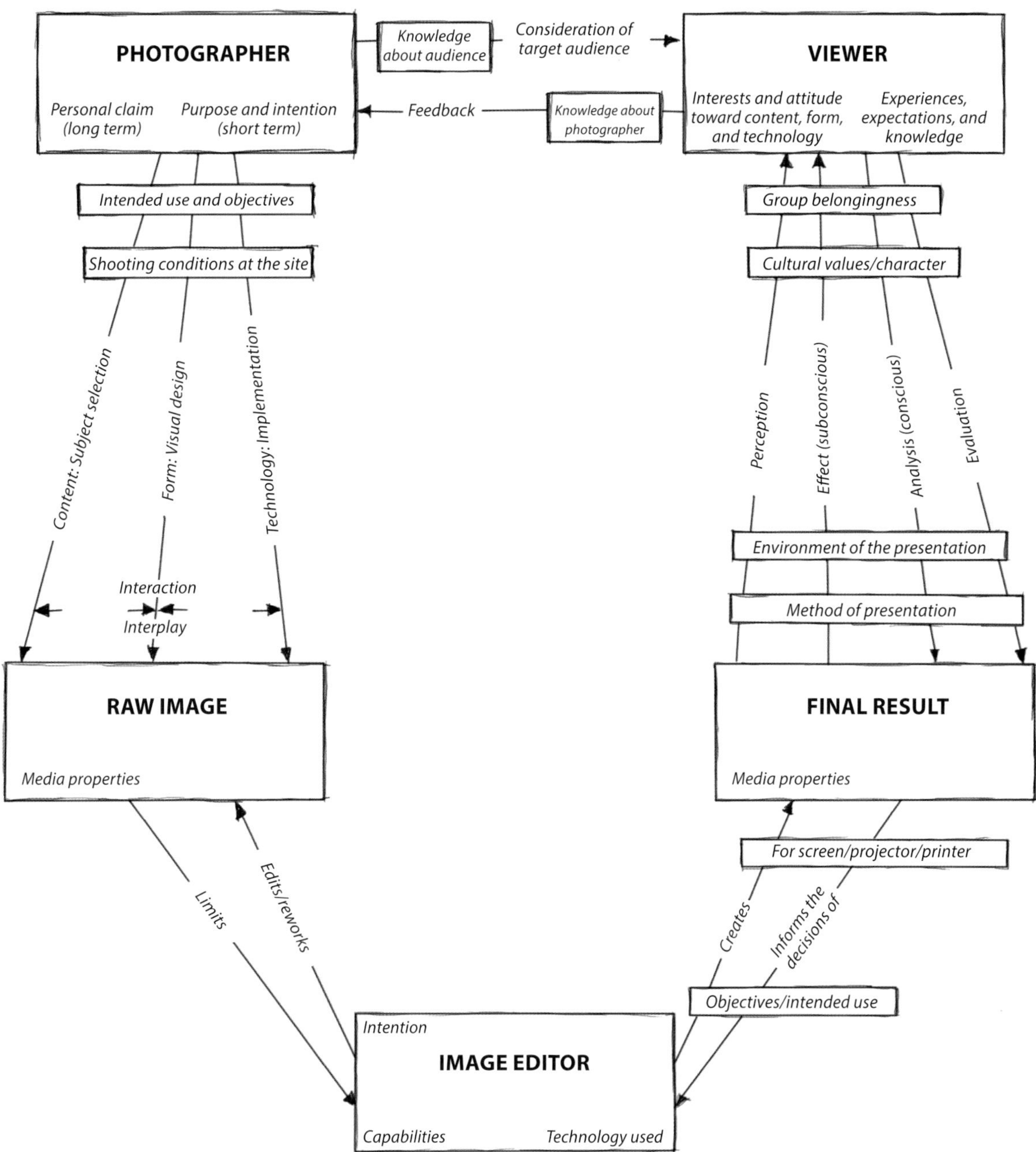

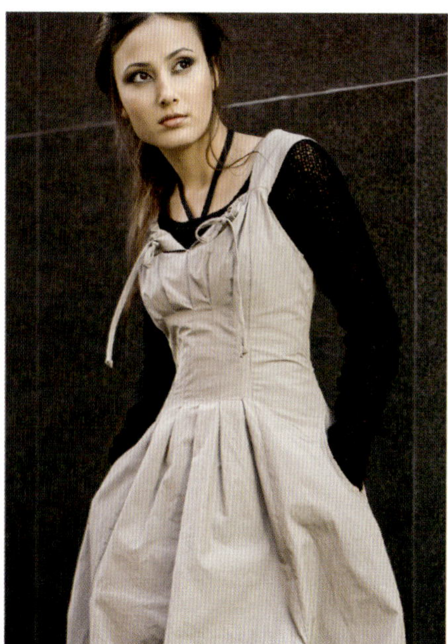

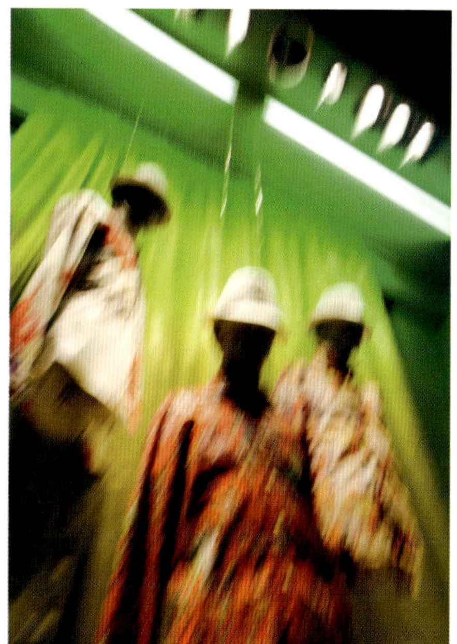

Your personal preferences and photographic priorities play a big role in how your subject comes across in your image. Clothing is featured in both of these images, but while Cora strives for a perfect presentation full of calm and harmony (left), Georg opts to use technical gimmickry and color for a more dynamic exposure (right).

The subconscious choices that influence your image design are based on the images that you have seen in your lifetime and stored away in your memory. The more photos you've seen, and the more diverse the selection of photos you've seen, the broader your design horizon will be. If you primarily see images in the daily newspaper, at the supermarket, or on television, you will naturally develop a different visual style than if you frequent high-quality photography communities on the Internet, read fashion magazines, or visit international art exhibitions. Even the media outlets and websites that you visit can influence your background knowledge about images: there are a wide variety of unique visual languages in popular magazines such as *View, Vogue, Elle*, and *National Geographic*. You can also visit websites such as 1x.com or flickr.com to be inspired by the visual languages of countless individuals.

The second factor is **your design ability**, or your ability to transfer everything you see in your subject to your photograph. This includes your ability to operate your camera and its exposure capabilities. For example, if you know exactly how to select the sharpness of your image by considering the results of your various options in advance (page 183), you'll be able to design your images with much greater control than if you entrusted your exposure settings to your camera's automatic features. Furthermore, aspects of your particular equipment can either help or hinder certain design techniques.

Without a depth-of-field preview button, for example, you won't really be able to examine the effect of your aperture selection while you're shooting—you'll have to wait to examine the image on your computer.

The third factor could be called **your design desire**. Here the emphasis is on your personal taste: your conscious design preferences are based on your individual style, which has developed slowly over time. Just because an element of design is at your disposal doesn't mean you necessarily want to use it to shape all your images.

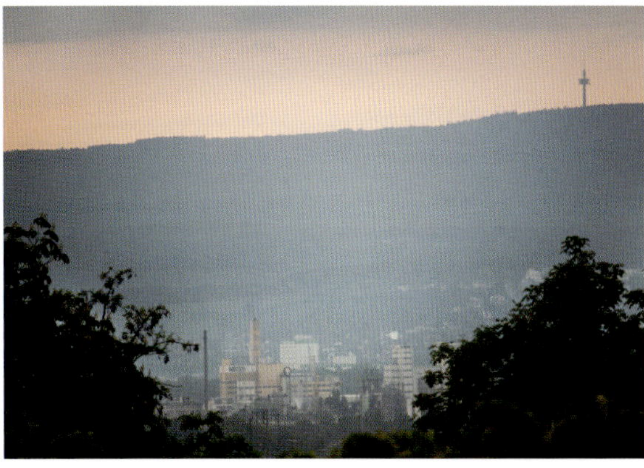

Not every photo is feasible. Sometimes you'll be too far away, you won't have the right equipment with you, or you won't have time to take the perfect picture.

Limitations of Design

There are always external factors that influence the design of an image. The circumstances surrounding some subjects can impose and prevent certain design choices. Some famous attractions even have designated points where most photographers choose to take their pictures because it is too troublesome or inconvenient to find a different vantage point. Other constraints, such as the distance to the subject, fences, regulations, or constrained quarters may prevent you from approaching your subject or finding another perspective. Many photographers attempt to justify images that were shot under less than ideal circumstances rather than choosing a different subject.

Sometimes there are explicit requirements that the photographer must satisfy. If you are shooting for a calendar that is designed to have black-and-white images in portrait format, other colors and formats aren't options. With contract work, there are usually certain constraining aspects that you have to take into consideration. The lead photo for a magazine article, for example, is normally in landscape format and takes up a two-page spread so there's a large, comfortable space for the title and the introductory blurb.

If you've been asked by a newspaper to capture the domino effect of bricks set up throughout the city, you might have specific assignments: documenting the setup (left), emphasizing the local color (middle), or revealing the action (right).

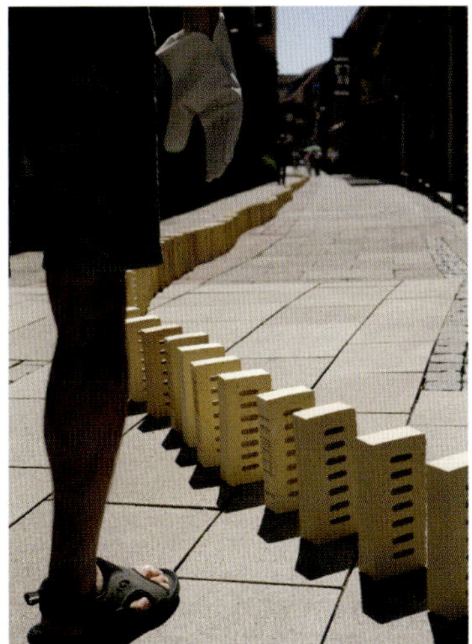

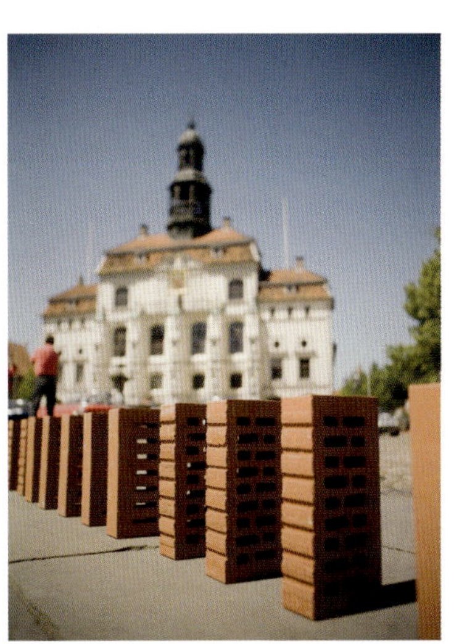

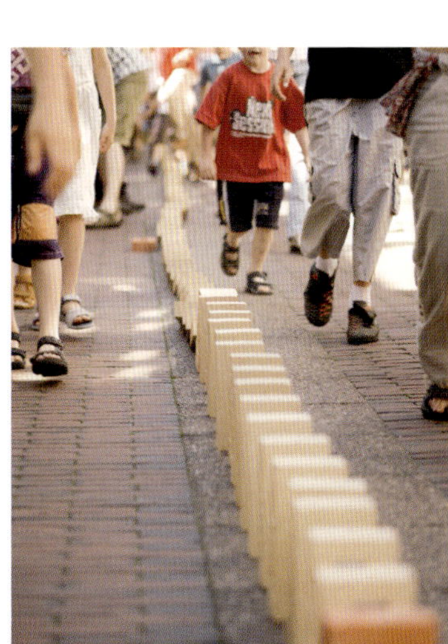

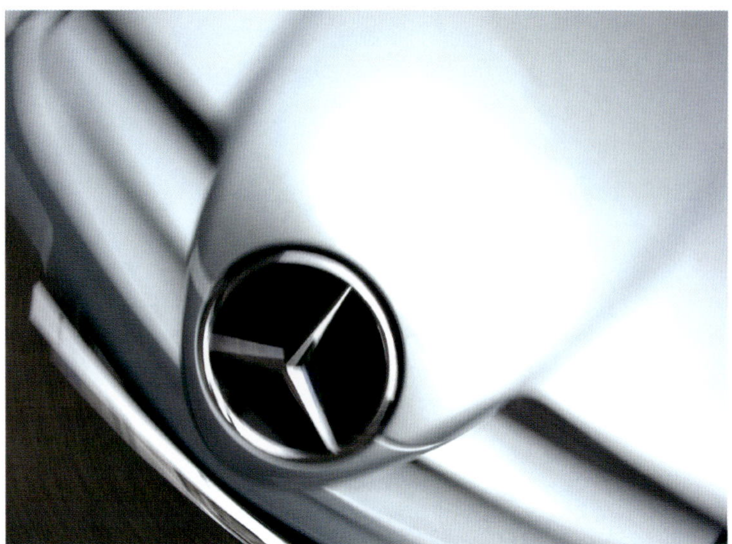

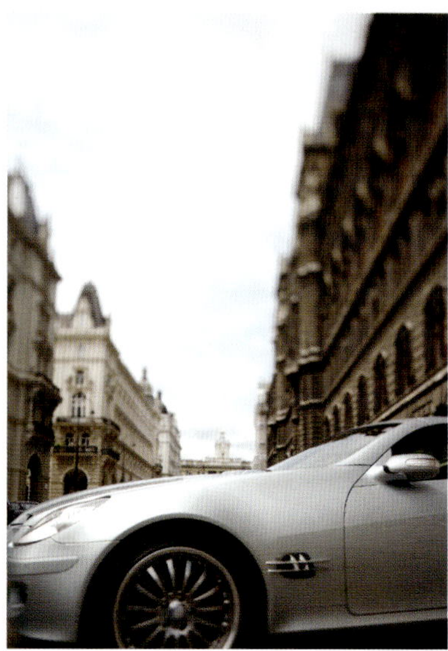

Different photographers depict the same subject in very different ways. This becomes apparent if you go on a photo tour with a group and compare pictures afterwards. The content of the images is identical, but the technical realization is markedly different. On the left, a specific detail is called out. It is shot from above so it fills up the entire frame, and a slow shutter speed was used for the exposure. On the right, a tension-building composition is designed with the subject near the border and the surrounding scene included. A tilt-shift lens is employed to shift the focal plane.

The Design Process

Despite any internal or external influences and constraints, you have the latitude to determine three central aspects of photography: content, form, and technology. Content comprises the subject: what can be seen in the image, the emotions conveyed, and what you intend to show or impart to your audience (page 31). The selection of what to include in an image (page 48), the search for an exciting subject, and the elaborate staging of shots are the most important tasks of photography. These aspects determine whether or not the story the photographer wishes to tell will be interesting or successful.

The form is the visual design, or the method by which the content is presented in the image. This includes the breadth of all design elements, such as the placement of the objects within the image, perspective, sharpness and blur, prevailing contours, and color saturation. The net effect of all design choices should support the visual statement of the image. If you are shooting a soft picture of a mother holding her baby in her arms and smiling intimately, then gaudy neon colors, sharp contrast, or an orientation near the edge of the image frame won't suit your subject nearly as well as a quiet, gentle approach.

Technology allows you to be able to control the design of your images purposefully. It allows you to capture movements in sharp detail, create distorted, blurred representations of reality, or make tiny details appear humongous. Often, an increase in technology leads to an increase in the photographer's comfort or emotional well-being, which can indirectly impact his or her photography. It's important to remember, though, that technology is a means of achieving a goal. More technology, either through better quality equipment or the ability to design your images a certain way, doesn't necessarily translate to an improvement in your photography.

The Balance of Content, Form, and Technology

Naturally, these three factors are not separate from one another, but have strong interaction. In general, the content is the foremost concern, because the subject of a photo is essential to the story, the idea, or the intended message you wish to impart. The form should complement the content of the image, either through harmony or contrast. The technology is the foundation of the process.

In each of these areas, photographers must make a slew of conscious and subconscious decisions about how to create their picture. These decisions, however, may leave a great deal to chance when it comes to the camera's automatic functions, especially with point-and-shoot cameras or in the world of Lomography (page 54). The more you know and the more aspects of the process you're capable of controlling, the more consciously and intentionally you can influence the final product. This means you'll be able to consistently create the results you planned in advance, rather than leaving it to chance.

The Role of Image Editing

After you've taken the photograph, it is first saved as an undeveloped image either on film or as a RAW file. The image you see on your camera monitor or on your computer screen represents the potential of the RAW data. You see the fully realized image only after the data is developed; at that point, the image contains significantly less information. The development process can happen either automatically, by a software program, or manually, by a person. The analog or digital editing of an image allows you to control a variety of visual design elements, such as color, contrast, cropping, and light, even after the image has been exposed. The image is only considered a final result once it has been edited.

The decision to present an image in full color, desaturated, or in gray tones influences its effect enormously. An image can be changed drastically as a result of post-processing. Extreme processing techniques are capable of completely changing a picture's visual statement.

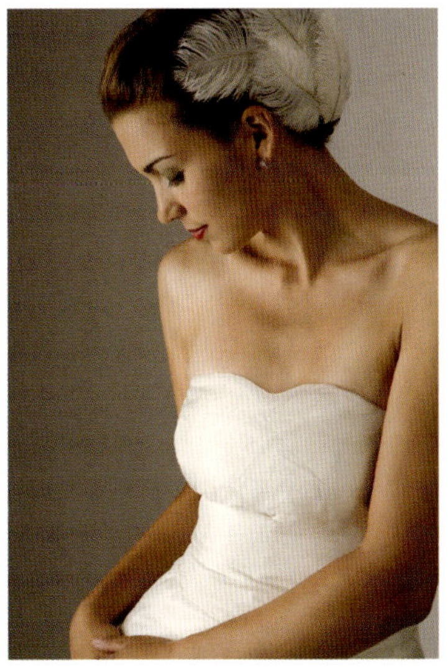

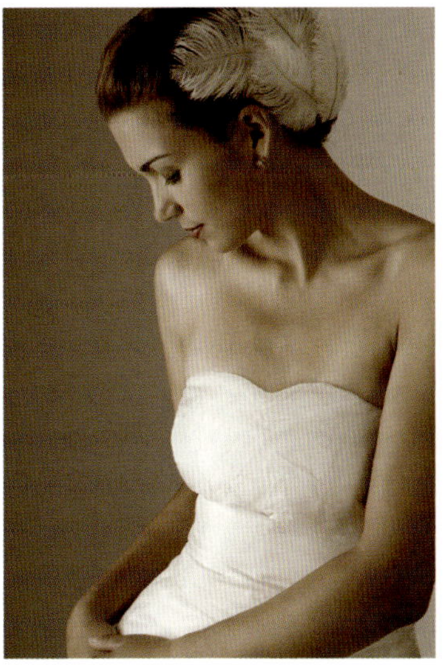

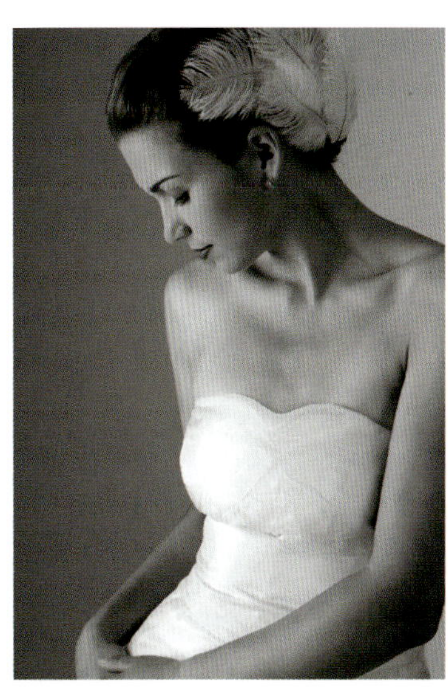

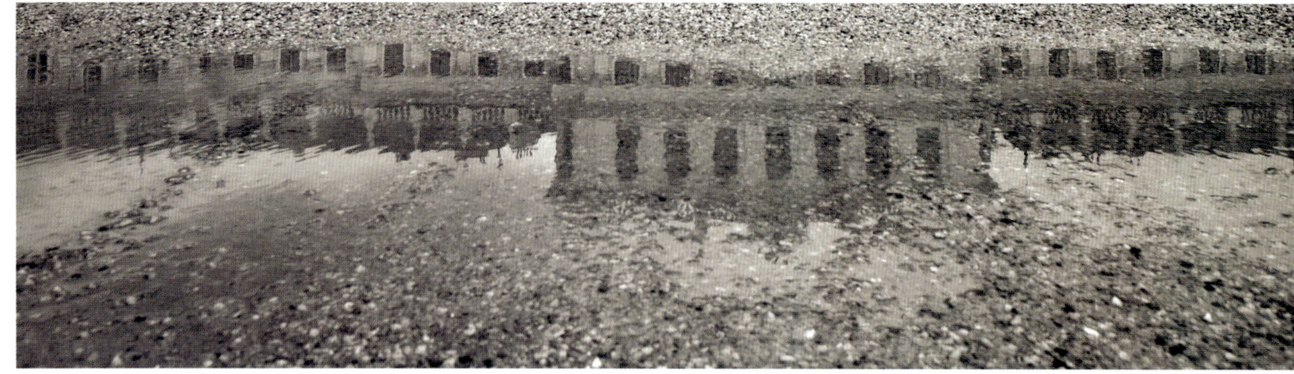

1.2 The Process of Perception

The process of perception is extremely complex—not every detail is perceived at the same time. The longer someone uses a critical eye to study an image, the more they will discover. To take advantage of this process of discovery, photographers should imbue their images with multiple facets.

Viewers need to perceive an image for it to have an effect on them. When people first see a picture, they quickly and subconsciously experience a general gut feeling about whether or not they like it. To form a more purposeful opinion about an image, other factors need to be considered; the image must be subjected to a conscious and targeted analysis. Since photographers can influence these factors, and thus, the opinion of the viewer, with the visual design of their photographs, it is important to understand exactly how people perceive images.

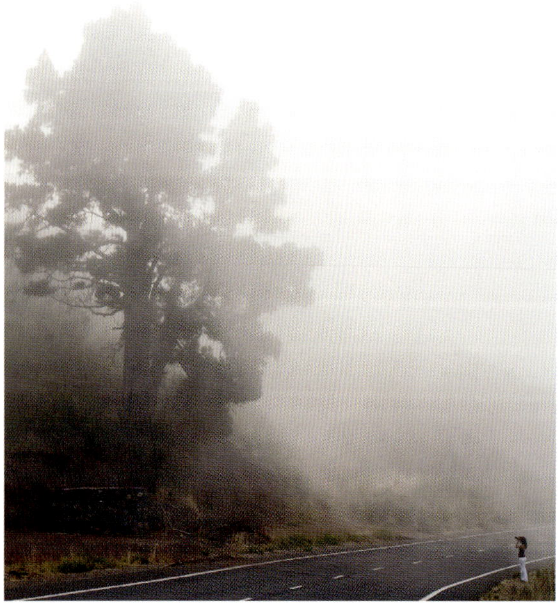

Steps of Perception

There are many scientific studies about how people perceive and understand images, and how pictures affect viewers. Scientific models and explanations give us a good introduction to this process, which we've summarized in the adjacent diagram and will discuss in greater detail in the following paragraphs.

Perception in the Strictest Sense

Perception is the threshold of comprehension. It always begins with a reaction to a central or peripheral stimulus. Only images that we perceive with our eyes and observe for a sufficient amount of time can affect us—sometimes this may only be a fraction of a second.

Subconscious Evaluation

Subconscious evaluation is surprising, vexing, and, at first, sounds unlikely: when looking at an image, the viewer's subconscious spontaneously and involuntarily evaluates the image before the brain has time to fully process the content of the photograph. This mental filtering protects the brain from becoming overwhelmed. It occurs not only with pictures, but also with all the information we encounter in our daily lives. The human brain does not have the capacity to process the massive amount of data it encounters, so our subconscious determines what information we should pay attention to and what information we can disregard.

Here's where it becomes clear just how fast our brain evaluates images: there have been impressive attempts to insert images with incongruous content into films. The images are displayed only momentarily, but despite being registered beneath the conscious level of perception, they created detectable, corresponding feelings in the test subjects, such as hunger, fear, anxiety, or relaxation.

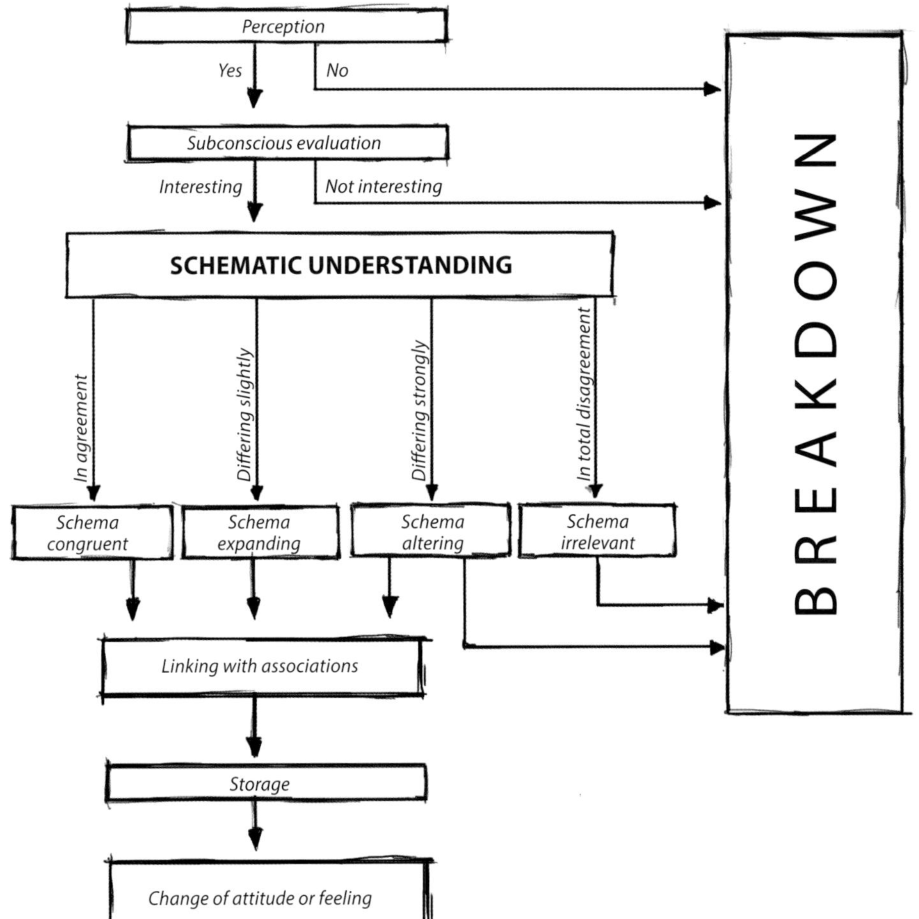

An overview of the step-by-step process of image detection: after perceiving an image, uninteresting pictures are filtered out before the brain can consciously register them or recognize their content. Only when the image is consciously perceived can an it produce an associated emotional effect, and only after it is stored in the memory can it change the viewer's thoughts, attitude, or behavior.

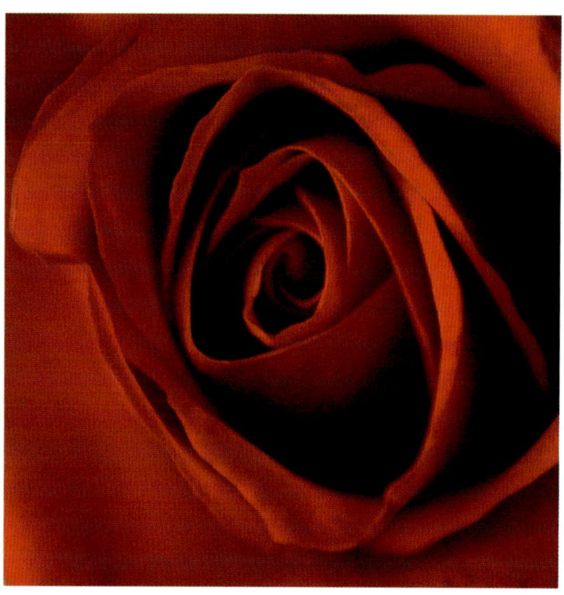

Schematic Understanding

Once the conscious brain begins to determine what is depicted in an image, it executes a schematic process, whereby it compares the image with familiar patterns stored in memory. This comparison process is automatic and works on several levels of comprehension. The brain will recognize objects that are already part of the viewer's schema—the Eiffel Tower, for example, or the face of a familiar person. During the comparison process, the brain draws similarities between an image and related aspects of the viewer's schema, and applies background knowledge to correlating subjects. Viewers can recognize a tree, a table, or an animal, even when they have never seen the particular specimen that is documented in the image.

There is nothing surprising, new, or different about this picture of a rose that you haven't seen in a thousand similar photos. The image is schema congruent for most viewers—the confirmation of a cliché.

- If the image exactly matches our schema, a phenomenon called schema congruity occurs. In other words, everything we see in the image matches with our memory exactly. With schema congruity, we can classify the information immediately and we don't have any reason to continue looking at the image—our perception turns off. The effect of such images strengthens our existing schema. This is how clichés and stereotypes evolve, and how repetitive ad campaigns succeed, even if they're annoying or poorly executed. If the viewer has seen many images within the same schema, they might not remember a single one individually.
- When an image deviates from our schema in even the slightest way, we tend to be surprised and disturbed, which causes us to engage more consciously and purposefully with the image. This mental activation creates increased awareness of and attention to the image; however, this deviation from our expectations, which the brain treats as new and extra information, also leads to an expansion of our schema.
- When what we see differs drastically from our preconceptions, the brain has trouble making sense of it. We must arduously decode the visual information, which often leads to miscomprehension. Such strong disturbances call our own knowledge into question, and can also lead to a change in our schema. This isn't always the case, since we have a tendency to protect our self-created worldview. We may instead reject these images, causing an abrupt cessation of the perception process and any active engagement with the image.
- When an image doesn't resemble anything in our schema at all, it's considered schema irrelevant. This usually results in the process of perception being abandoned. This might be the case, for instance, when we look at completely blurred

or abstract images. Only when there is supplementary motivation, such as when we visit an exhibition or look at the work of a famous artist, do we grant the image the additional attention necessary for critical engagement.

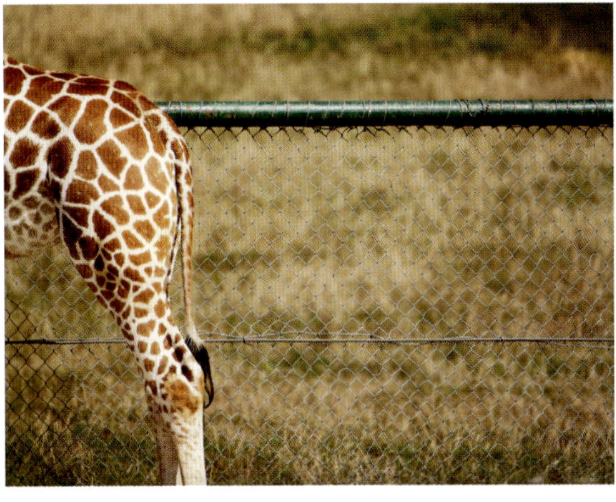

It doesn't take the whole giraffe for you to recognize the animal in the picture. In terms of schematic recognition, the characteristic markings on its coat are as meaningful as its long legs. Schema congruity allows us to recognize the whole, even when we only see a small part of the subject.

The spontaneous evaluation of an image and the initial comparison with our schema determines which images we look at more closely, which ones we process, and which ones we ignore. Our initial reaction influences the way we perceive the image and how it affects us. New or unexpected images capture our attention, and we barely perceive images that are boring or confusing. Novel content and form grabs our attention; conversely, we become overly familiar with and uninterested in well-known subjects.

Our brain can recognize objects much faster than it can read—this is why we look at pictures first. We can detect the subject of an image in only a hundredth of a second. In one or two seconds, we can take in the full subject of a moderately complex photo. In the span of those few seconds, we can glean more meaning from a visual stimulus than we can from reading a few words of text.

This process naturally depends, in an important way, on the knowledge and background the viewer brings to the image. A biologist or a nature photographer can recognize insects in a picture much faster than a city dweller. But the photographer can make it easier or harder for the viewer to recognize and understand the content of an image through various design tools.

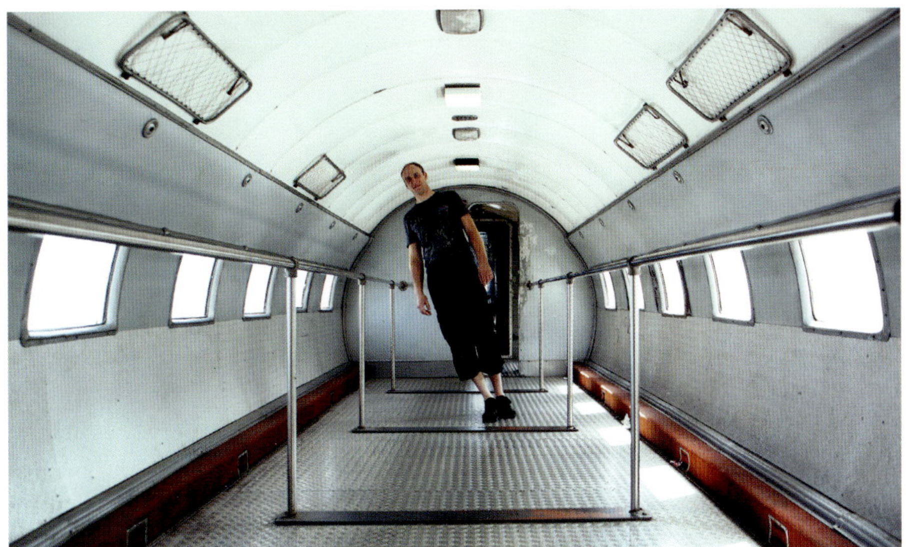

What we see in this image doesn't mesh perfectly with our schema. The space has vertical and horizontal lines of reference, and we expect that a person will stand up straight. Instead, however, the subject is leaning over so far that we expect him to fall. Even after we learn that the airplane itself is off-kilter and the camera is equally slanted, it's still not easy to align the image with our schema.

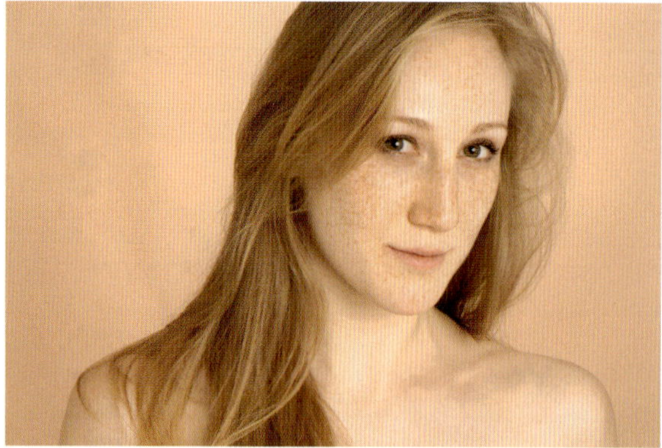

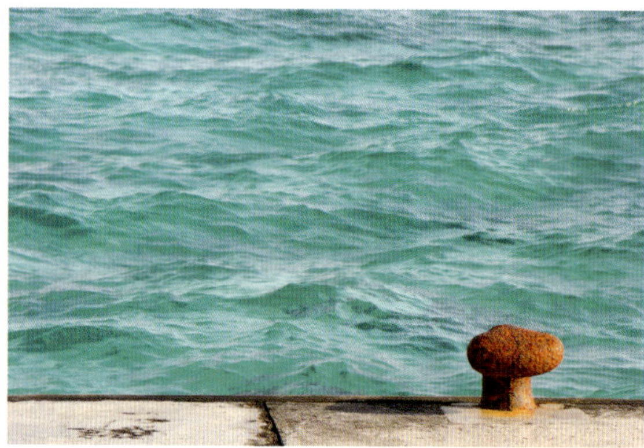

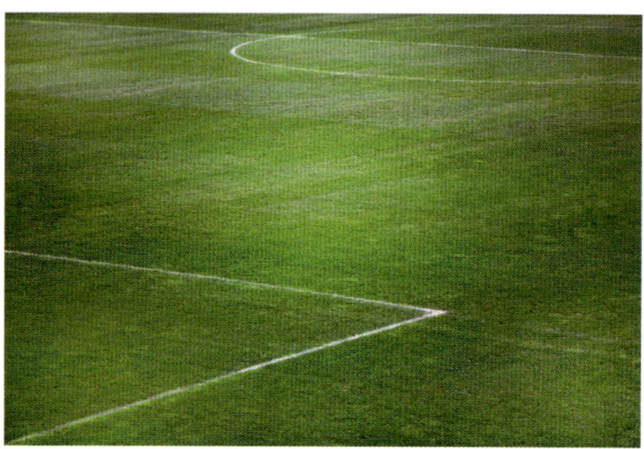

The aspect of an image that first draws your attention depends on several factors. People, faces, and especially eyes are compelling subjects (above left). But shapes and colors that jump out of an image also command attention, such as the rusty bollard set against turquoise water (above right). Uniform images that lack contrast are read from left to right; in this case, the eye follows the slanting lines (below left). In a very bright image, the dark areas stand out and attract the most attention, even when they are overwhelmingly surrounded by signal colors (below right).

Getting into the Picture

Although our subconscious perceives and considers an image in its entirety, conscious observation and decoding of the image happen incrementally. The point of entry for every image isn't the same, but the factors that compel viewers to begin their examination are consistent.

If an image doesn't have a particular attention-grabbing element, viewers will examine it in the same way that they read. Here in the West, that means viewers begin at the top left, move their gaze to the right, drop down to a lower point on the left, and then move right again. However, if an image has a conspicuous center of attraction, viewers will be compelled to settle their gaze at that specific point.

This point of interest can be created through pure form; in general, white or bright areas of an image strongly attract a viewer's attention. In high-key images (page 156), darker areas usually draw the viewer's attention first. Colors can also attract attention—the brighter and the more saturated, the stronger the effect. Neon colors are the most effective, and signal colors (red and yellow) command more attention at every saturation level than green, blue, or violet (page 150).

When people view pictures that have a shallow depth of field, the eye is immediately drawn to the sharpest element (page 185). In small-scale images, certain geometric shapes (page 96), like circles, can also be attention-grabbing. Small, eye-catching features generally exhibit a high degree of contrast in relation to the overall image (page 79). Aside from all this, there are certain subjects that we involuntarily examine first because we have learned through experience that they convey the most important visual information. In a landscape, cityscape, or any other scenery shot, our gaze always gravitates toward a person or a group of people. As social beings, we are naturally wired to be interested in other people. People we recognize and have relationships with are of special interest. The larger the depiction of the person in an image, the stronger the pull is to examine the face, especially the eyes, which function as magnets for our gaze when they are adequately discernible.

Examining the Image

After our initial view of an image, the process of examining the rest of the photo happens erratically—the eye makes jumps from one element to the next, often guided by contour lines (page 82) or attraction to other, less-powerful features. Our eyes rest at each of these optical stopping points to gather information before jumping again to the next stopping point. Scientists refer to these jumps as saccades and the momentary examinations as fixations.

In most cases, the goal of a photographer is to engage the attention of a viewer long enough to have them view the image critically. In addition to exciting subject matter, a creative and cohesive method of guiding the viewer's gaze (page 84) can help achieve this goal. By defining the image frame (page 48) and establishing the perspective for the shot (page 104), you can determine where the optical stopping points will be and establish lines for the viewer's gaze to follow. Viewers can interpret your photo better and faster, and avoid becoming confused; they are more likely to examine your photo longer so they can process it in detail.

Special devices can trace the movement of the eye as it examines a photo. This process is not regular: the eye jumps erratically from one anchor point to another, where it rests just long enough to collect information before jumping to yet another fixation point.

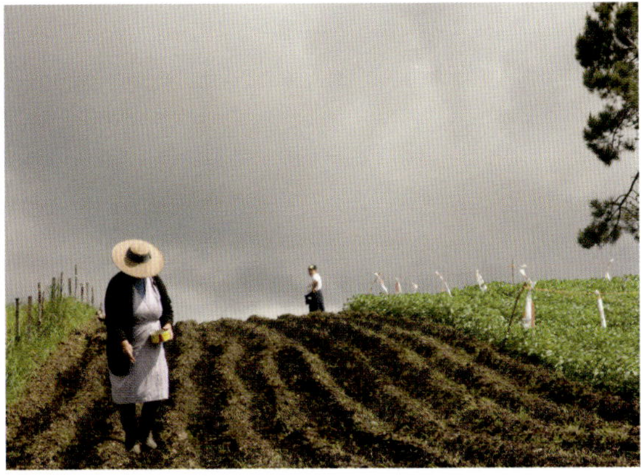

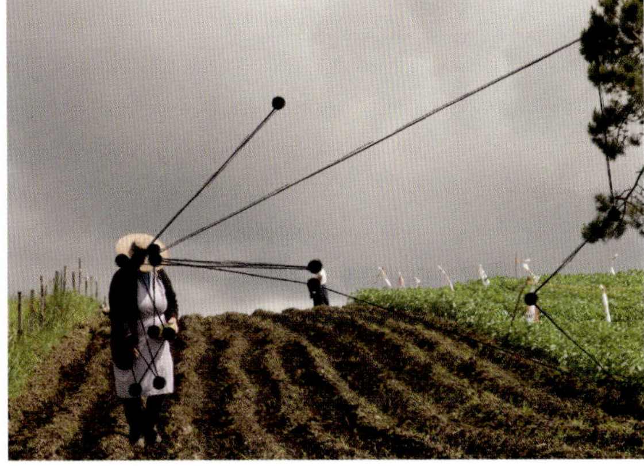

Mental Processing

The thought process begins when the viewer recognizes the subject. At this point, emotional associations are linked to the content of the image before it is saved to memory. This is how images are stored internally and how our schema is reinforced, expanded, or changed.

What viewers get out of an image, how they evaluate it, and what they associate it with depends on several factors. These factors include the viewers' personalities and how the photo is presented. The following points are not the only influences, but they are the most important.

For starters, the viewer's personal preferences can affect their perception of the image in several ways:

- Each viewer will have a different level of interest in the **content of a picture**. Pictures of architecture, flowers, or dragonflies aren't for everyone. Nevertheless, there are certain subjects that usually generate a high level of interest, such as people or dangerous animals. However, even with these subjects, the viewer's level of interest plays an important role.
- When researchers describe the way people examine things, they distinguish between **involvement**, which is a general, but passive interest in something, and **engagement**, which refers to actively seeking information. If I were interested in buying a new car, I would look at pictures of cars with a higher degree of attention than if I merely had a general interest in cars, or if I were restricted to using public transit or a bicycle to get around. Similarly, baby photos of someone in your own family have a much different meaning than photos of babies you don't know.
- Even though a certain method of **image design** might work similarly for most people, it doesn't mean it will work for everyone. One person might like close crops, and someone else might not. The same goes for loud colors, crooked lines, and flat light. Our personal taste is further developed by other images we encounter in our lifetimes.

Whether or not an image appeals to a viewer depends on his or her personal preferences regarding subject matter, design, and technique. A crooked horizon or a crop through someone's face will not sit comfortably with most traditionalists (outside images). An erotic depiction of a woman's leg or a bird's-eye view of a stylish car may catch a viewer's attention, but it also might not (middle images).

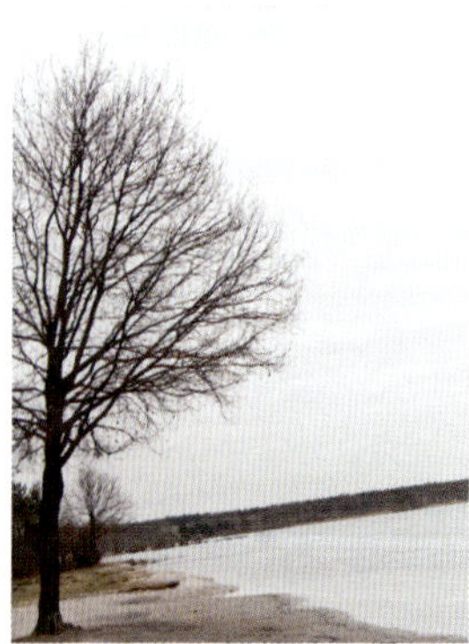
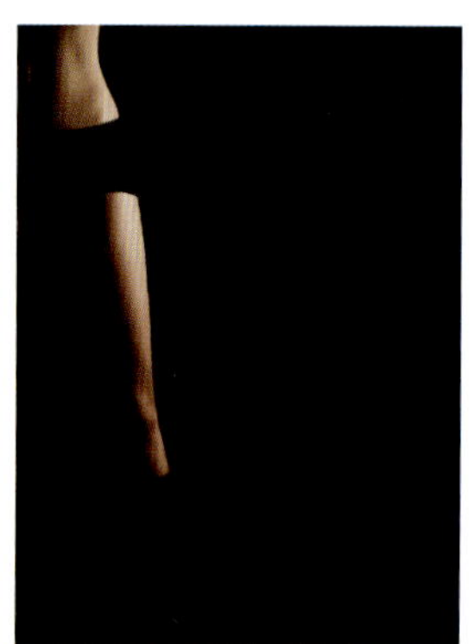
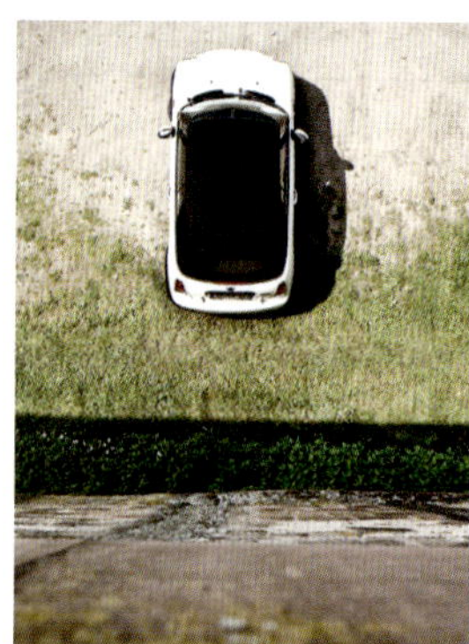
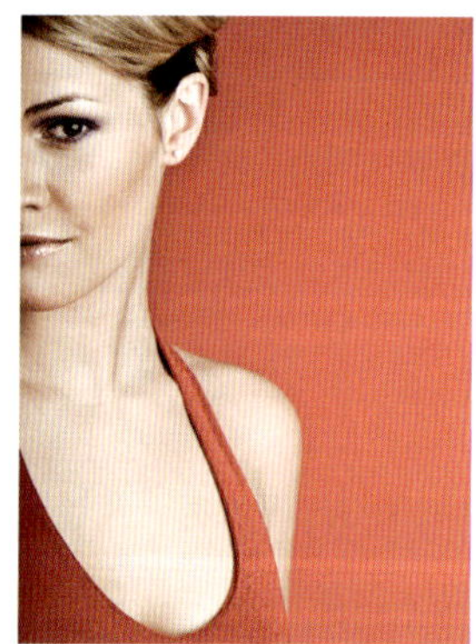

- **Exposure** and **editing techniques** also elicit various reactions from viewers. Viewers who create high dynamic range (HDR) images, panoramas, or 3-D images themselves will be particularly interested in images created with those techniques. One person may be fascinated by images taken with a telephoto lens, but someone else may prefer images taken with a wide-angle lens.

The way viewers understand an image depends on their previous knowledge, which they most likely learned by being a part of a certain social group or class.

Aside from personal taste, there are other social or cultural group affiliations that influence the way individuals see images:

- Simply belonging to a **social group** often has direct effects on which subjects and what type of visual language appeals to people. For example, a nighttime photo of a deer positioned directly in the center of an image will likely be more appealing to viewers in their sixties than to teenagers. Similarly, fans of comic books or science fiction may like a graphic novel type of aesthetic more than fans of classic literature.
- Belonging to a particular **culture** also influences the way viewers respond to visual information. This stems, in part, from the reading direction of a viewer's native language; movements in one direction feel natural, while the opposite direction feels vexing or confusing (page 84). Even individual colors and color combinations (page 146 and 159) affect people differently, depending on their cultural affiliation. Completely conventional scenes from a large Western city may seem foreign and surreal to rice farmers in Asia. Conversely, images from an African desert, a rain forest, or a Chinese fishing village fascinate Westerners and give us a sense of the exotic and unknown.

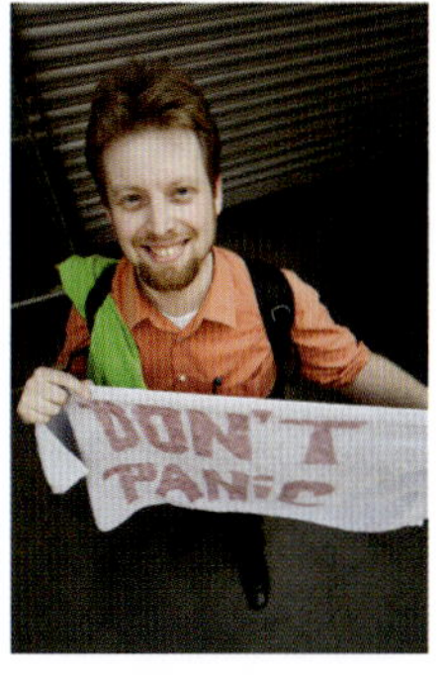

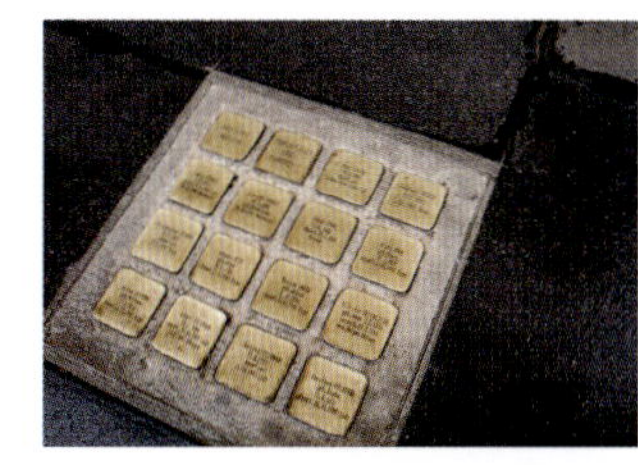

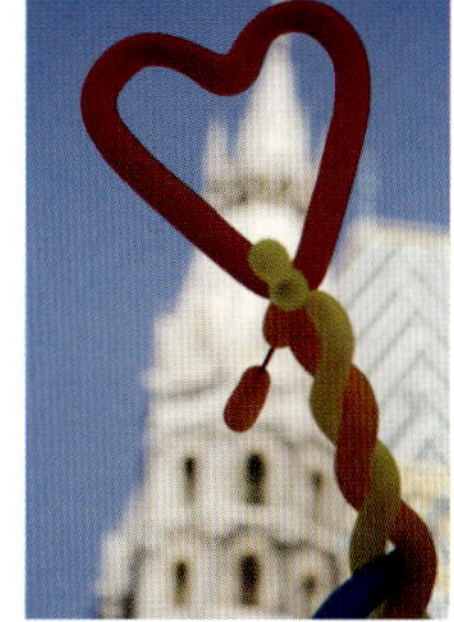

Every fan of science fiction author Douglas Adams will understand the image with the hand towel (above left). Someone familiar with Asian cultures is likely to think of Japanese characters, and a gardener may think of bark beetles (below left). And to make sense of the two images on the right, you need to be familiar with the work of the artist Gunter Demnig—www.stolpersteine.com—(above) and St. Stephen's Cathedral in Vienna (below).

You will consciously or instinctively consider all these preferences and tendencies when you compose and design your images. Doing so will increase the likelihood that viewers will associate specific ideas and concepts with your work. The more critical it is to create images with a specific audience in mind—which is the case in competitions, advertising, and stock photography, for example—the more important it is to take these viewing habits into consideration.

This happens in less formal settings, too; insecure photographers may choose an image and use visual language that will garner the most support on certain photography websites. When you want to shoot strictly for yourself, you can use your own personal taste as your guide—this may agree with what's popular, but it certainly isn't necessary.

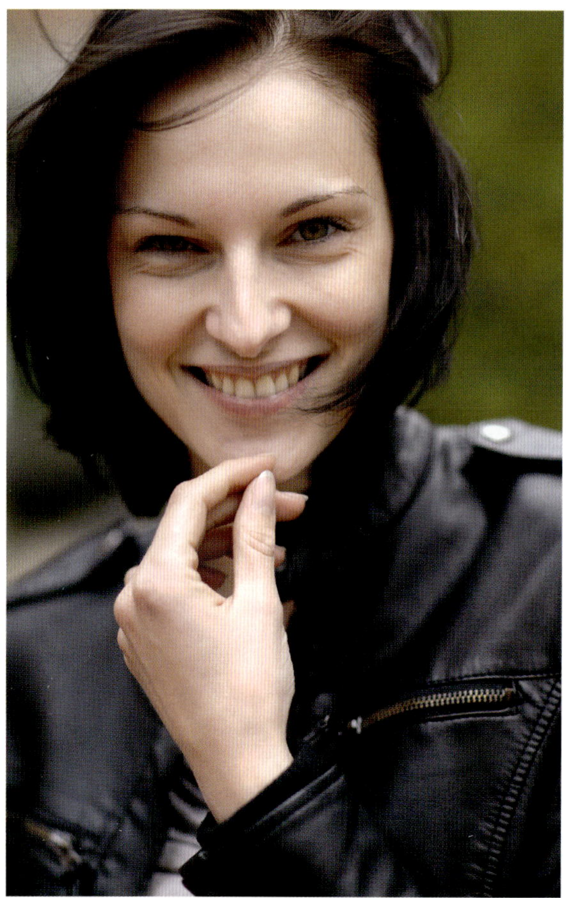

Mirror neurons in the human brain endow people with an astonishing emotional reflex. Observing an emotion in another person inspires the same emotion in us. This empathy response carries over to the world of photography, where a recognizable emotion in a picture can transfer to the viewer—the emotion is literally contagious.

How Photos Work

Understanding the association that viewers make when they look at images shows how photos elicit emotional, instead of rational, responses. Another phenomenon supports this: the human brain has cells called mirror neurons that cause us to feel the same emotions that we observe. If we see another person crying, we have an instinctive response to participate in the emotion. This phenomenon also influences a viewer's response to an image, especially one that showcases human emotion.

The ability to bring forth an empathetic response isn't the only way images trigger specific emotions. Subject matter selection, image design, exposure technique, and post-processing all have the potential to influence the viewer's response. With the right photos, you can influence beliefs and ways of thinking. A picture elicits a response even when it is not consciously perceived. Images affect us on a subconscious level, even if we try to avoid them or defend ourselves against them. This fact about the psychology of perception is often exploited in advertising, politics and business, where much specific thought is given to visual presentations.

Saving Images Internally

After our perceptual apparatus links corresponding associations to an image, both are saved in our memory, where internal visual and emotional pictures are created. Simply viewing an image creates a level of awareness that allows for processing and saving an external message, which is more effective than reading text alone. Not only do we internalize images better and faster than text, but we recall them better and remember them longer—the more concrete the subject, the more noticeable this phenomenon is.

One exciting facet of this process is that both sides of the brain are active while images are stored in the memory. Researchers suggest that images are coded in two ways: on the right side of the brain, images are stored visually and can be recalled as such; on the left side, however, the images are stored as a linguistic code, meaning that they are available as an abstract, symbolic description in words. This dual storage means humans are exceptionally well suited for recalling images.

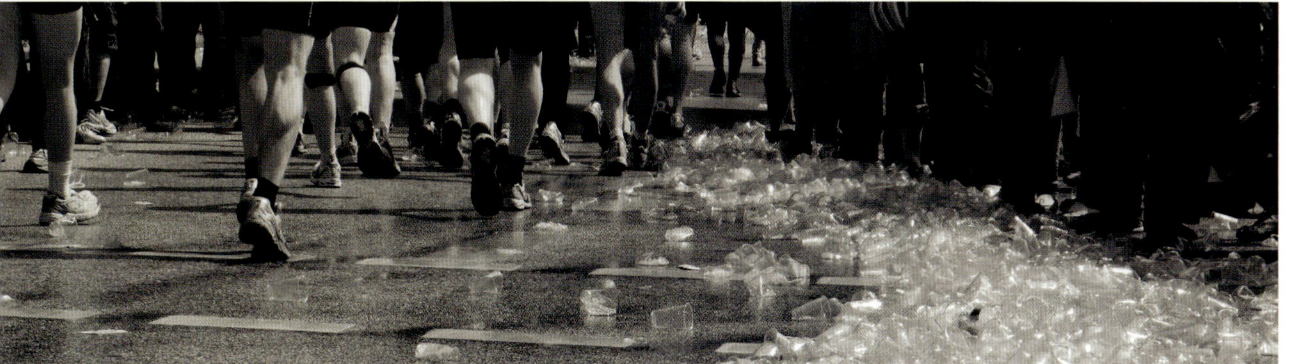

1.3 Designing Images with Purpose

Let's now turn from the process of perceiving images to the process of taking pictures, and consider for a moment what we as photographers can achieve with our pictures and how we can precisely apply and control our methods. Spontaneous and coincidental shots can, of course, elicit a response from viewers, but in this book we are concerned with deliberate photography. To learn how to make our work purposeful, we first need to understand what it is we want to create. In short, we need a clear understanding of our objective!

The goal, or the planned visual effect, differs with every picture. This is exactly what inspires a photographer to pick up a camera and start shooting pictures. There are a variety of objectives you can achieve with a photo; let's consider the many reasons photographers take pictures.

The motivation for shooting doesn't always stem directly from the photographer—especially for weddings, babies, and families. It's usually the people being photographed who want to have the pictures. In these situations, the photographer adopts the motivations of the subjects and adjusts to the intentions and wishes of those in the photo shoot.

Motivation

Every photographer has a personal reason for taking pictures. One person might be interested in learning all the ways to apply the technology of photography, while someone else may have a favorite subject that he or she wants to show others. Some people use photography as a way to meet a variety of people, or to collect image material for creating entirely new worlds through extreme digital post-processing. Some people take pictures for themselves, others do so to share pictures on the Internet, and others do so for money. For one person it's a pleasant pastime, for another it's an indispensable passion. Many people find photography to be a therapeutic

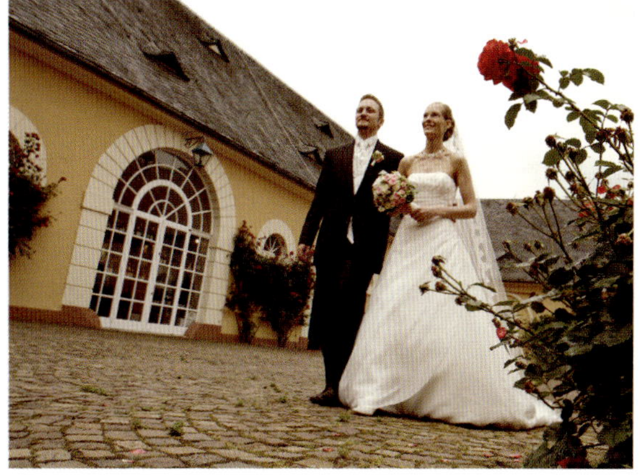

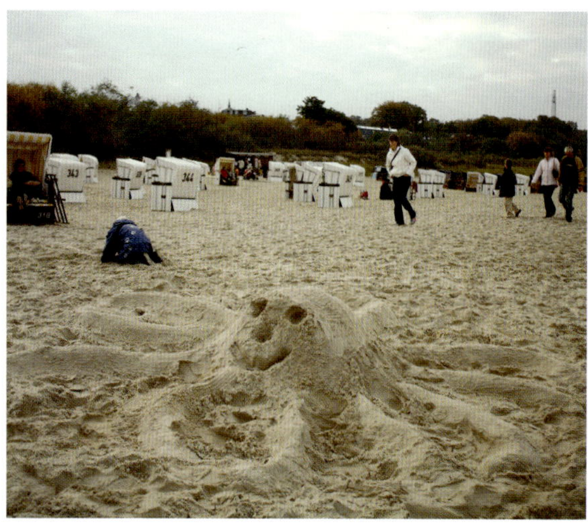

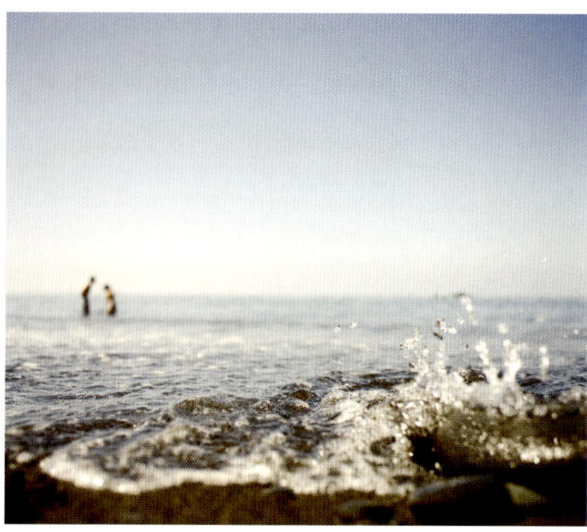

These two pictures depict a vacation but are dramatically different in their intentions. The one on the left is a simple memento that depicts a cute scene. The one on the right, in contrast, attempts to capture a beach vacation symbolically and in an abstract way that might be used in an advertisement.

activity, while others live a part of their sexuality through it. Some want to create art with their camera; others use photos as a diary or a notebook. The most common reason for taking pictures is to capture memories and to share special moments of life with people who weren't there.

Take a minute to remember the original reason you started taking pictures. Then consider whether this original motivation still exists, if other reasons have inspired you, or if your motivation has changed entirely. Be honest with yourself, because your insights will not only help improve your photography and your continued development as a photographer (see *Learning to Photograph Vol.1*), they will also help you avoid several creative blocks that photographers run into from time to time.

Subjects

The motivations for people to take pictures are as diverse as the possible subjects for photography. It's not possible to list everything that we consider worthy of being photographed, and even the classical genres of photography represent only a fraction of the possibilities. Photographers select their subjects for their own reasons and count on finding like-minded people who share their interests.

With that said, don't fall into the trap of thinking that a photographic subject should interest everyone, just because it appeals to you (and a few others). Since you can't please everyone, consider the advice of Viennese photographer Lisette Model: "Never take pictures of something that you don't find interesting!" It's your interest in a subject that inspires you to see it with a critical eye, to search for something exciting, and to develop your picture into something special—to tell your own story.

After all, what is photography other than the visual communication of stories? Just like in a novel or a movie, your subject has multiple dimensions. To one person, your photo may simply represent exactly what it appears to be—two people staring deeply into each other's eyes, for example. To someone else it may be more about the action, the relationship between two people, or the interplay of elements in the image. The picture might convey the intensity of the couple's amorous glance; it may even conjure a wistful remembrance of one's first love. All of these aspects of your subject are embedded in your image.

Nevertheless, you will run into roadblocks with some photographic subjects. Although photographs often have strong symbolic power, they can't precisely depict abstract ideas in the same way that writing can. Everything that you photograph is concrete. Abstract ideas, such as love, can't be captured in a photo. We can only show examples of the idea, such as a carved heart or a couple in love.

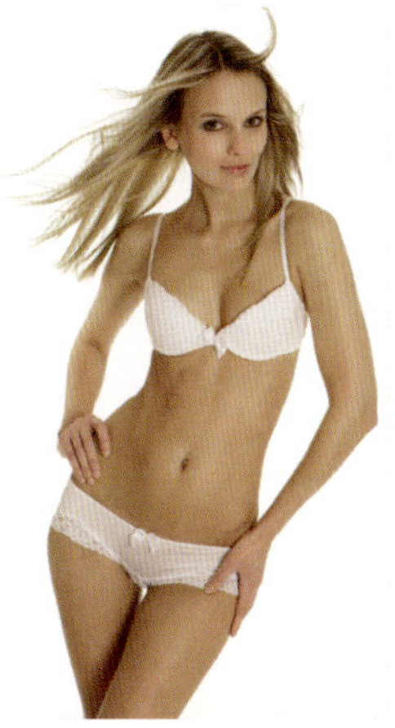

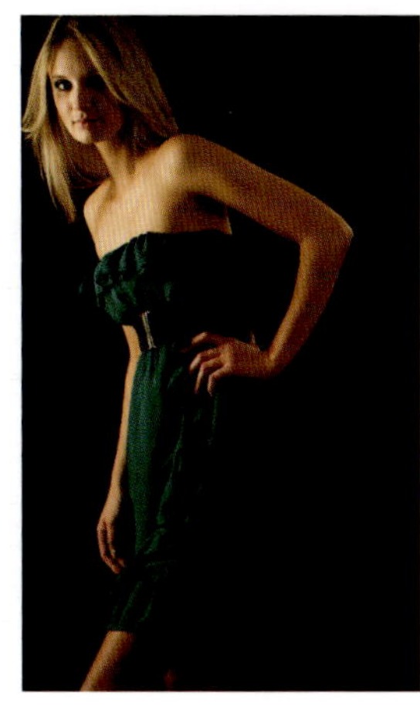

There is a wide range of motivations for taking pictures of people, for example. This is reflected in the two genres depicted here: erotic and fashion photography. Sometimes the methods photographers use to treat their subjects reveal more about the person behind the camera than the subject.

Similarly, photography is not capable of conveying negation. While language has no trouble expressing that two people are not in love, photography only has the option to positively affirm something—two people looking at each other angrily, for example. This characteristic sets photography apart from the abstract symbolism of human language.

Aspirations versus Reality

With all forms of communication, a message must be understood by both the giver and the receiver to effectively convey information. In the same way, photographic language also needs to be understandable and accessible. Sometimes, what you intend to communicate is misunderstood. What you actually communicate isn't always what you set out to show. I can't capture everything I'm able to see in a photograph, and not everything I wish to show is actually in the picture.

Photography—in contrast to language and what we can see with our eyes—has its own peculiarities that we can exploit with the various tools of image design to communicate our message as accurately as possible.

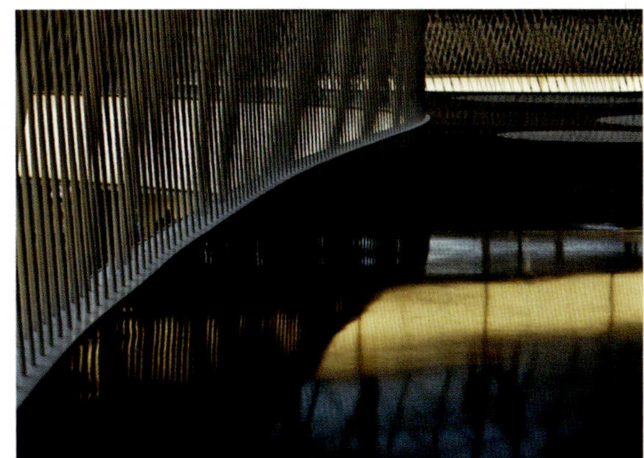

Not every picture turns out the way the photographer intends. Georg waited for this picture until the two silhouettes at the bottom right moved to the correct position. Even so, they are barely perceptible, and the final image is effective in a way that he didn't see while looking through the viewfinder.

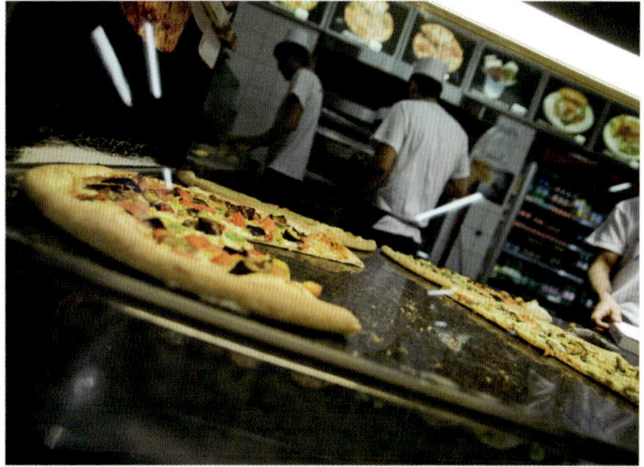

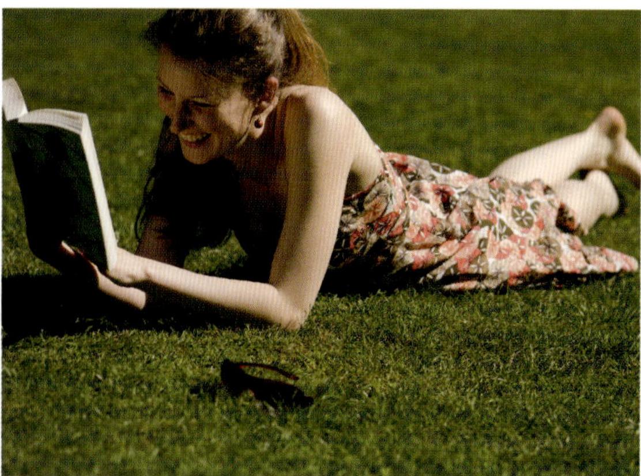

An image can be good or bad, appropriate or inappropriate, at the same time—depending on its intended purpose. The image on the left isn't appropriate for a pizzeria advertisement, but it's an evocative illustration for a report on dining at a train station. The photo on the right could be suitable in a campaign to advocate reading, but it's less effective as a fashion photo because the model's pose conceals her dress almost entirely

Intentions and Goals

The potential intentions of images are just as diverse as the potential uses of language. They may be used to inform, report news, impart knowledge, capture moments and memories, bring forth emotions, change beliefs or values, or manipulate viewers. Pictures should arouse fear or desire; create, change, or reinforce an idea; capture, manipulate, or create entirely new realities; tell stories; inspire confidence; galvanize; communicate feeling; provide orientation; establish identity; recall associations; amuse; or establish connections for viewers, which they may find plausible or vexing. The purpose of every photo depends on where, how, and why it's being displayed in the first place.

Whatever the intention of a photo, one thing is always true: it's all about the activation of the viewer's attention, and the engagement of that attention for as long as it takes for the image to have the intended effect.

An image can be good or bad, appropriate or inappropriate, at the same time—depending on its intended purpose. The image on the left isn't appropriate for a pizzeria advertisement, but it's an evocative illustration for a report on dining at a train station. The photo on the right could be suitable in a campaign to advocate reading, but it's less effective as a fashion photo because the model's pose conceals her dress almost entirely.

Image Design as a Means to a Goal

As with technique, image design is not an end in itself. The design should always be based on the content of the image and should support it in a way that makes the photo accessible. In this regard, image design is a tool to express your idea, your emotions, or your story. In some ways it is similar to language. When we learn a new language, we start with vocabulary and grammar, which in the world of photography, corresponds to basic exposure techniques. Next we practice reading sentences and speaking without making mistakes, which in the language of photography, correlates to image design. We need vocabulary and grammar to understand sentences, and we need language exercises to learn how to have a conversation. But it's not until we converse with new people in new cultures and experience an emotional expansion that the whole effort gains meaning and value.

Language has many purposes; it can be used in text messages, poems, novels, telephone books, and textbooks. It can be molded into a brand or an advertising slogan. It can be used to discuss any topic. It's used to woo men and women, to found cultures, to build organizations, and to support regimes—just to mention a few! Images, likewise, have the same potential for diversity, universality, and power. The content of an image plays the most important role, of course, but it needs to be presented in a way that underscores the message. The design of an image doesn't always have to be pleasant or harmonious, it just needs to support the purpose of the photo.

As a photographer, you determine how to present reality—whether consciously or coincidentally—within the frame of your image, and you choose all the other points of reference for the viewers. In this way you impose your own perspective onto the viewers and force them to see your image in one particular way. You strive to capture their attention and achieve a specific effect. With this in mind, it can be useful to know what tools of design are at your disposal, how to use them, and how the final result will come across to the viewer.

That is exactly the purpose of this book!

One subject, with the same light and the same camera, but with different intentions, can produce dramatically different results. The left picture depicts a bird-of-paradise flower with lively and dynamic colors and multiple facets, and the image on the right shows only a portion of the blossom and emphasizes the visual character of its delicate lines.

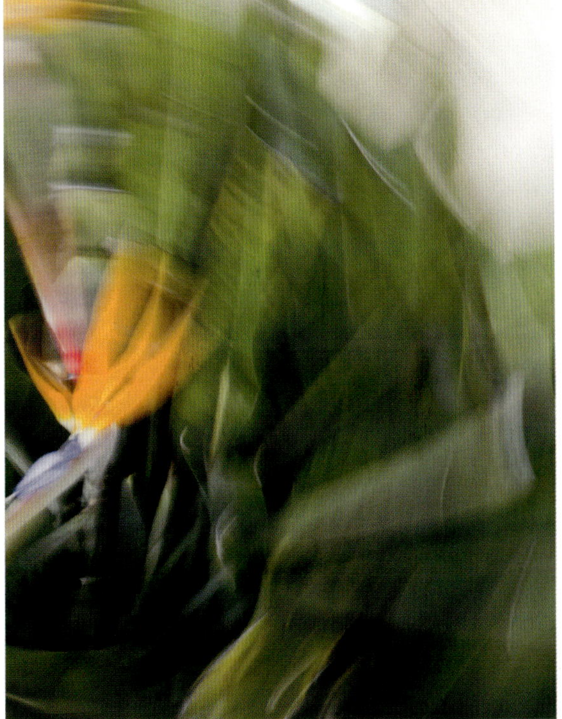

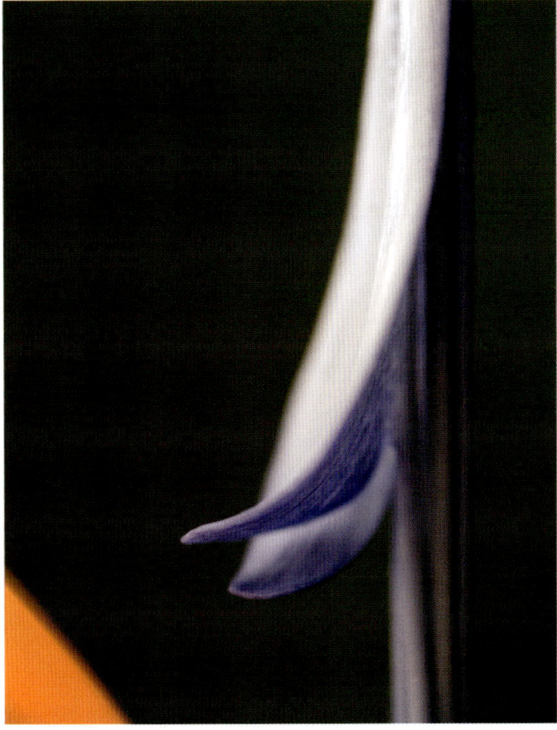

What You'll Find in this Book . . .

There are a lot of design elements that can influence your final image, and each of those elements has further dimensions and options to explore. When all other variables are held constant, every one of these specific characteristics has a particular effect on the image and on the viewer. Examining design elements in this way is somewhat academic, since you'll rarely want to change one element while holding the others constant. But it does allow us to isolate the specific effect of changing one variable or, more accurately, to display with a greater degree of clarity how this change alters the overall effect of an image (page 196).

The effect of certain elements of design will not be universal for everyone; there are a number of influences that alter how an image will perceived. Within the same culture, most elements of image design will have the same result, and within a specific social group, these tools will affect the vast majority of individuals in the same way. Any discrepancies in how design elements affect viewers are usually emphasized by cultural influences—such as the meaning of different colors—rather than purely objective factors like image format.

Many viewers would consider an image like this to be flawed: how can you crop off someone's head? The subject of this shot isn't the person, though, it's the action—drawing a weapon. By making the person anonymous, the image becomes more universal and focused.

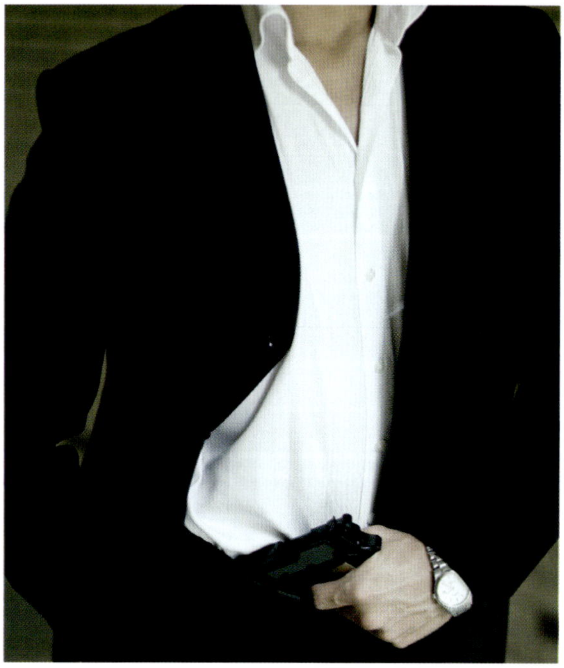

Within these constraints, you can attribute precise qualities to certain design elements: a landscape format is calm, a portrait format is dynamic; red is warm, blue is cold. These general effects apply to all images, both spontaneous and deliberately designed. Many tools of design feature yet another variation—the element of the unplanned, unintended, or erroneous. We don't explicitly discuss this in the first chapters because we want to focus on the elements of design that you can control.

With that in mind, we will introduce different methods of design in the next six chapters and describe their various applications and effects. When necessary, we'll also describe the technical means by which you can achieve these effects. Whenever possible, we will also include illustrative pictures and provide specific applications for individual photographic genres. This will allow us to concentrate on the distinct, fundamental building blocks of image design.

After that, we'll bring all of the design elements together in individual photos. We will discuss how an image's visual message is a combination of the overall effect of a photo and additional influences, such as form and the environment in which the photo is presented. We also include further aspects of image design, such as the analysis and evaluation of images, and suggestions for preparing a successful collection of photos.

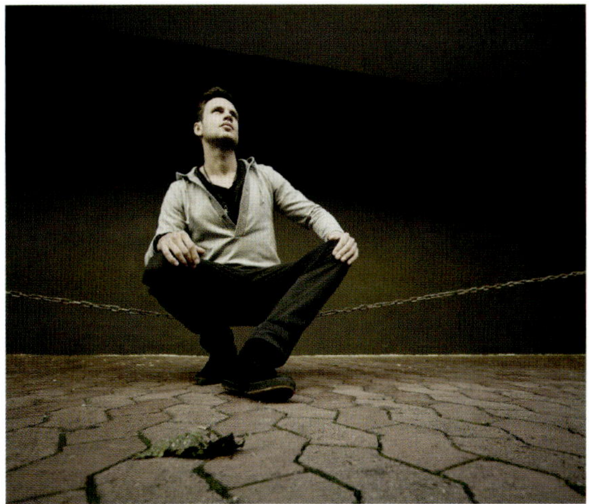

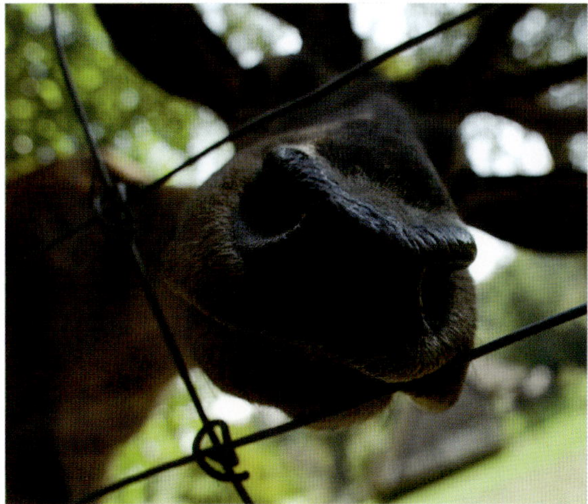

"Never use a wide-angle lens for portraits" and "Never place your subject in the middle of the frame" are just two examples of many so-called design rules that you often hear or read about. There are many images that don't follow these rules but are nevertheless exciting, interesting, and evocative—exactly because they violate these rules. Instead of following broad and arbitrary rules, it makes sense to consider the interplay of the individual image design elements and to apply them purposefully to your subject. This is a more complicated route that entails increased responsibility, but it also means you'll have a larger repertoire at your disposal for designing your images creatively and purposefully.

. . . And What You Won't

You won't find some things in this book, such as the many so-called rules for image design that are the subject of many discussions (and arguments) among photographers. These rules pervade photography literature—usually with the attendant advice to break them. No ominous rules actually exist anywhere, so the tendency to quote them can be vexing because it implies that when you follow (or break) these rules, you will create good images. Such rules are incredibly broad, and can't possibly apply to all images.

Think about this line of reasoning as it relates to writing. In journalistic writing, it's generally a rule to include the most important and recent information at the beginning of an article. Applying this rule to a mystery novel, though, would be the worst thing you could do—it would eliminate the suspense. Whether or not an image is good—or suitable—can only be established in relation to the original intentions of the photographer, or the personal taste of the viewer. We discuss this process in more detail in a later chapter, Image Analysis and Evaluation (page 216).

In this book, we focus instead on the many variables of image design, which we describe in their full complexity, diversity, and interdependence. We won't tell you, "If you do this, you'll have a great picture." Instead we say, "If you do this, it will have this effect under these conditions, and when you do it differently, this will be the result." The decision of what design will work best for your idea is left entirely up to you.

This approach is more complicated, which means it takes longer. But, it will open up a fascinating and diverse network of design possibilities that you can use with an eye toward whatever you're photographing at the moment, and whatever purpose you have for that particular shot. This knowledge will serve you well not only when you shoot, but also when you select, analyze, or conduct a targeted, objective evaluation of images. It will inform every conversation you'll ever have about photography.

"Perfection isn't reached when there's nothing left to add—it's when there's nothing left to remove." Antoine de Saint-Exupéry, French writer

02 Composition

When you shoot a picture, you have a number of decisions to make. You'll make some of these decisions intuitively, but others will require more conscious deliberation. The first and most important choice for a photographer is always what to include in the image—and what to leave out. Everything else rests on this decision. It determines what your subject will be and what fragment of reality the viewer will see. The snippet of reality you choose to capture is highly subjective—photography is not, by nature, an objective medium. Your photos will rarely feature a solitary subject, and what you include with the main subject is very telling. Viewers will see all the elements in relation to one another.

Deciding what elements to include in your image isn't the end of composition; you must also decide how to arrange them. The mental and physical relationship a photographer has with the objects in an image strongly influences how viewers will perceive the photo. The degree to which photographers can move in their shooting space and their level of open-mindedness gives them flexibility to design an image. This close relationship between the content of an image and its design is fundamental to depicting the subject and establishing a visual statement.

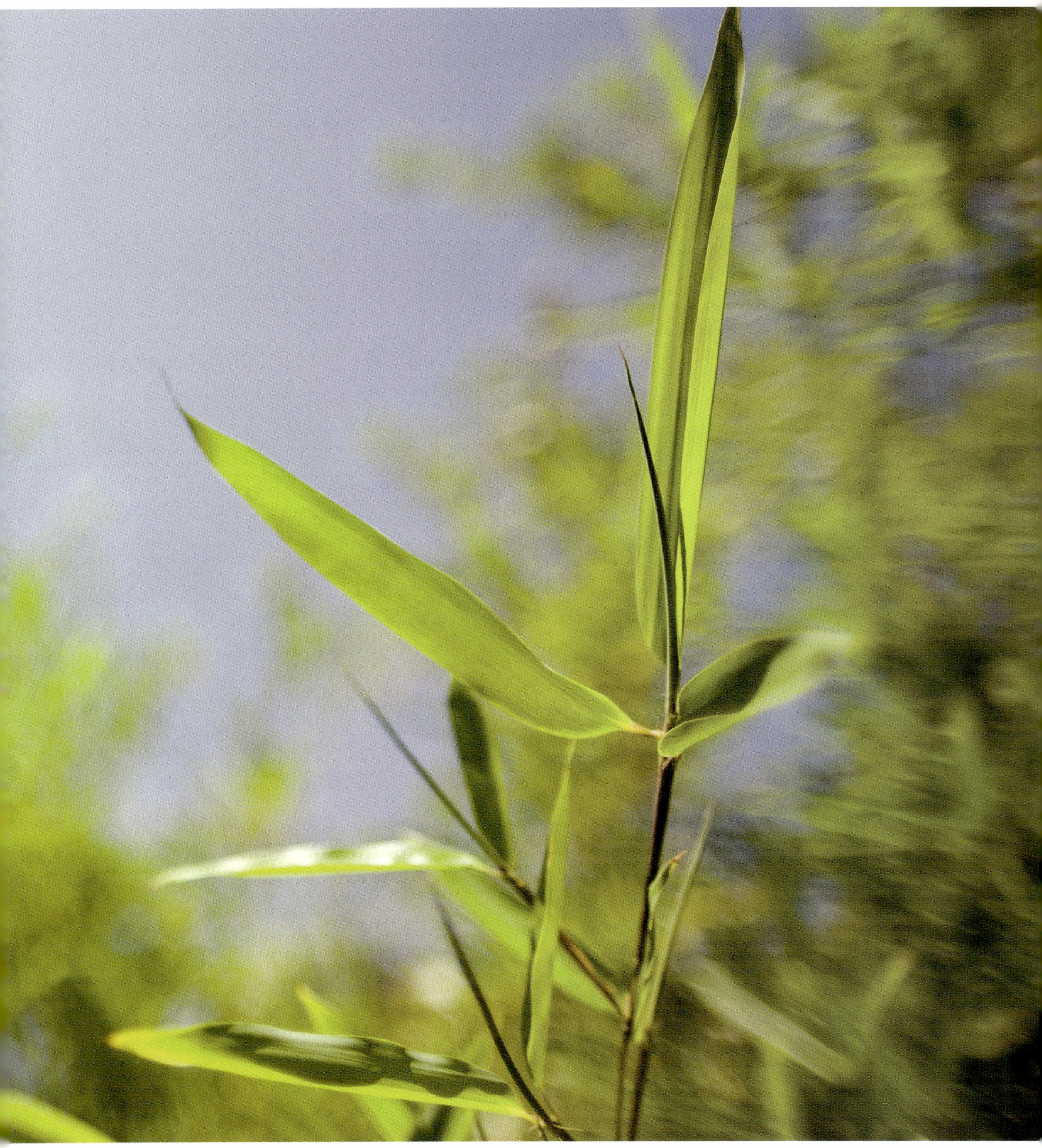

2.1 Image Format

If you're designing your image through the viewfinder of your camera, choosing a format, including selecting an image frame, is one of the first steps of composition (page 48). The fundamental decision between portrait and landscape has strong implications for the final effect of an image. When you choose a format—while shooting or later, on your computer—you are defining the areas in which you can position the elements of your image.

Aspect Ratios

If we ignore images shot with a fisheye lens (page 117), images that are cropped after they're shot, or photos that are mounted with a mat, then all potential image formats use right angles. Choose an aspect ratio and the corresponding portrait or landscape versions; the aspect ratio depends on the camera, and ranges from square or nearly square, to standard rectangular, to panorama formats.

As a rule, the aspect ratio of the exposure is based on the dimensions of the camera's sensor or film, but increasingly more cameras allow photographers to switch between different formats. Keep in mind that changing the image format doesn't change the size of the sensor. It only changes the dimensions of the image, which makes this method nothing more than an irreversible enlargement. Image information is lost, or rather, the full capability of the sensor isn't used. The most common

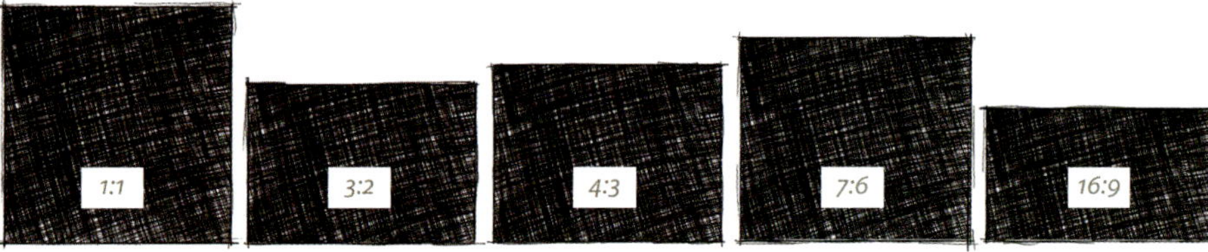

The various aspect ratios of standard photo formats affect images differently. Your camera also helps determine the aspect ratio.

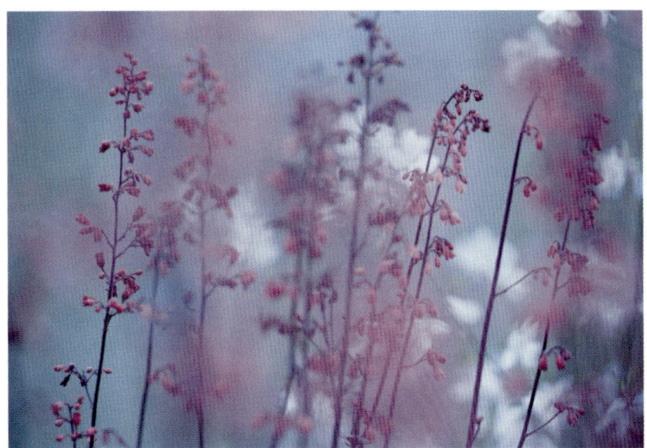

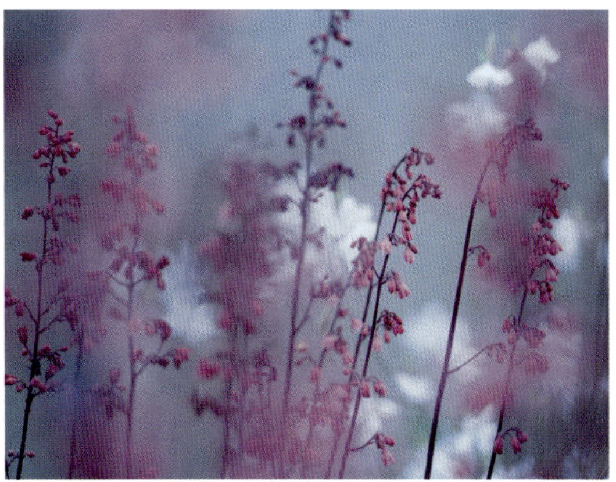

The 35mm format from film photography has an aspect ratio of 3:2 (left). It's trimmer, more elegant, and more pleasant than the plump 4:3 format that is common to most digital compact or cropped-format cameras (right). The prevalence of the latter, however, will eventually change what people consider normal.

aspect ratio has long been 3:2, stemming from 35mm film. It is generally considered to be the correct image format. It's thin, elegant, and almost as balanced as the golden ratio (page 66). However, in the world of digital photography, only a few single-lens reflex (SLR) cameras use this ratio—they are called full-frame cameras.

The somewhat compressed 4:3 format of many compact digital cameras is much more common. This format is slightly condensed and is not as balanced as the standard ratio from 35mm film. It was standard in the 1920s for moving and still images. Now, however, it's experiencing a revival thanks to digital camera sensors.

Somewhat less common, and therefore less familiar, is the 16:9 ratio, which we know primarily from movies. The emphasis on the longer side of the image makes this format very exciting and effective for epic tales.

Historically, a square ratio (1:1) was relatively rare, and gave the impression of high-quality art, partly because of its novelty. Much less familiar, and rarely seen in this age of digital photography, is the 7:6 ratio, which is a large format that conveys a sense of calm and sophistication.

Landscape Format

With the exception of the square format, all aspect ratios can be oriented in a landscape or portrait format when you take a picture, although landscape is much more common. It's no coincidence that the descriptions and dimensions of image formats are based on a landscape orientation, since our eyes are situated next to each other. People see in landscape format, so it feels comfortable and familiar. Landscape photographers primarily use this format because it allows the capture of an expanded horizon.

The relationship between the larger width and the narrow height emphasizes the breadth of the subject and the prominent horizontal lines—especially the horizon (page 85). In fact, the word horizontal is derived from the word horizon. The atmospheres of landscape images range from calm, familiar, and stable, to sedate, passive,

We're used to seeing many subjects in a horizontal orientation, both in photos and in daily life—landscapes, architecture, nature, and travel photos, to name a few. As the name suggests, portrait format is mostly used for portraits. It's somewhat unsettling and surprising for us to see a human portrait shot in a landscape format.

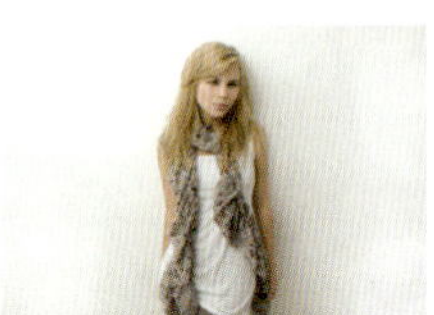

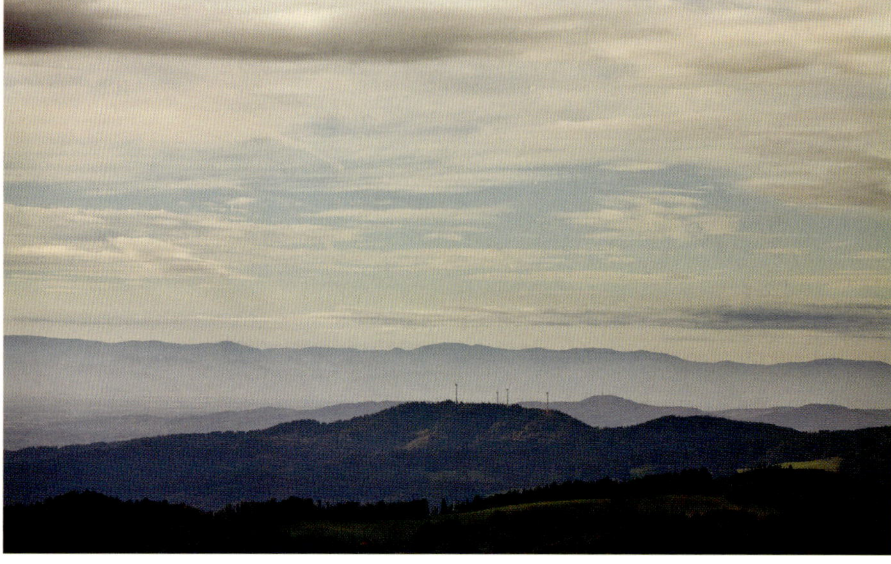

heavy, static, and conservative. The format also creates a free, wide feeling because our eyes can wander left and right without running into any borders.

The landscape format gives the subject these same qualities and emphasizes the subject's horizontal contours. Subjects with horizontal motion are an exception, because the movement tends to visually shorten the format. We're used to seeing subjects with a predominantly vertical orientation, such as people, shot in the portrait format so they can fill the majority of the frame. When the landscape format is used with vertical subjects, it creates an unusual and exciting effect.

Landscape Panorama

Horizontal panoramas create the same atmosphere as a normal landscape format, but to an even greater degree, and in more interesting ways. Because they are less common, panoramas get more attention. A panorama is even less restrictive than a regular-sized landscape photo. Viewers must move their eyes more, and their brains need to work harder to examine a panoramic image.

Horizontal panoramas are most common in landscape photography, both for natural landscapes and city skylines. These are familiar uses of the panoramic format, so when it is used for other subjects, it gets more attention.

The more details that are included in a panorama, the longer it takes for viewers to perceive them all. If the scene is too easily decoded, the format will lose interest just as quickly as it attracted attention. If the image contains too little information, or if the viewer is not partial to the subject, he or she may not be willing to expend the extra visual effort necessary to fully engage with the photo.

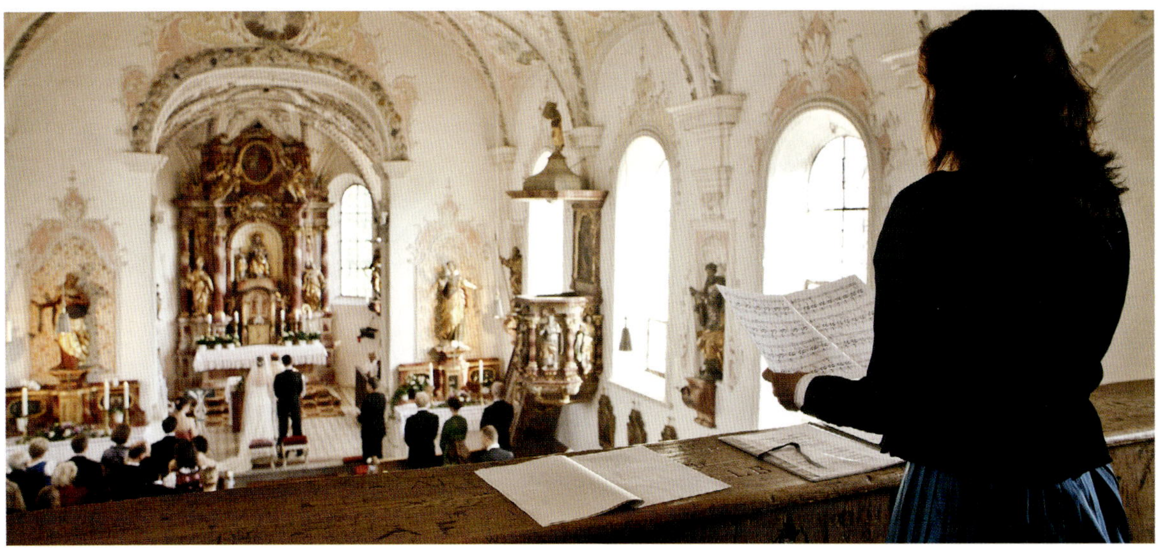

The many details of this scene give the viewer's eyes plenty to feast on as they wander from one side of the frame to the other. This image tells a much more complicated story than what could be captured in a quick glance.

Portrait Format

The portrait format functions as an excerpt of reality because it artificially limits our field of view. It cuts off our peripheral vision (page 113), which leads to heightened awareness of the aspects we can still see. We use peripheral vision to watch for potential danger, so when that part of our vision is cut off, we experience a heightened sense of alertness. The long edge of a rectangle looks longer when it is vertical, which underscores the effect of this format.

Because the portrait format is taller than it is wide, it creates a dynamic, upright sensation that can translate to an unstable feeling. This format can easily be used to create a voyeuristic effect by offering a glimpse through a small gap, such as a keyhole, a window, or a gap in a fence. This gives the exposure a striking, exciting, and interesting effect that is independent of the subject.

The effects of this format depend on the objects within the frame—pictures of people or a standard portrait of a single person come across as agreeable, fitting, and familiar to viewers. This is based on the fact that the human body is narrow and tall,

In the landscape format, the prevailing direction of movement is down; in the portrait format, even with the same subject, the eye tends to be drawn up.

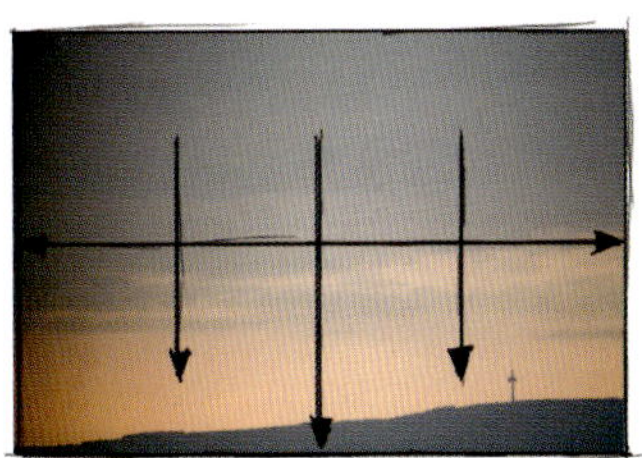

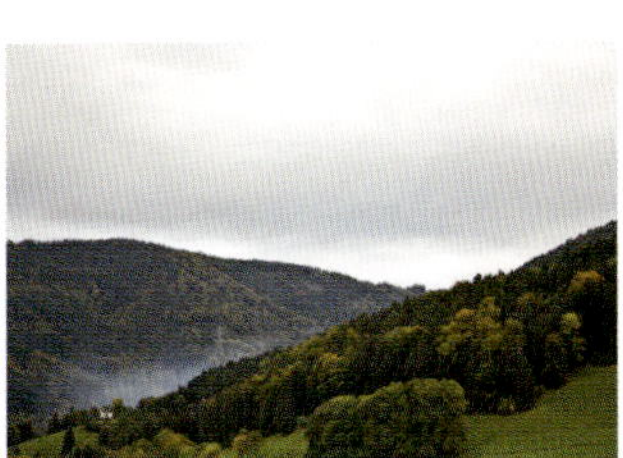

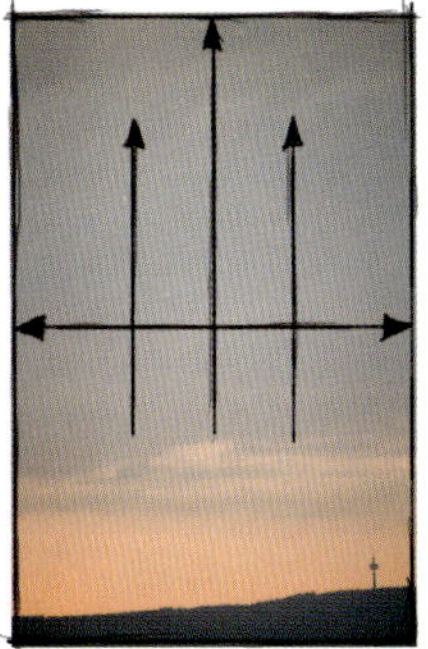

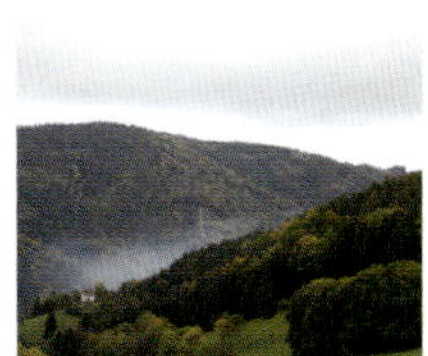

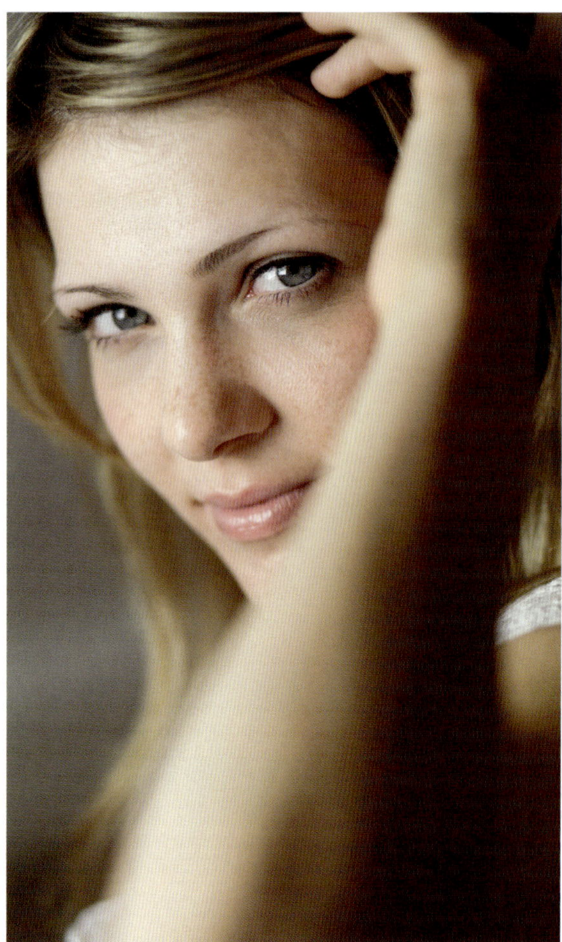

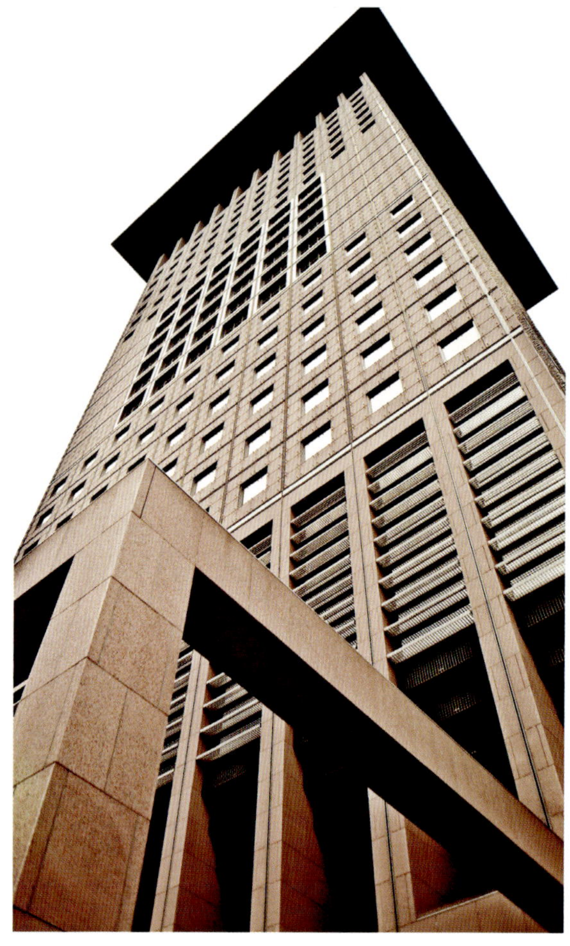

Few subjects are exclusively suited to the portrait format. People are the most common subjects for this format. Other tall subjects that stand by themselves, such as this building, are also predisposed to being shot in the portrait format.

which is why the portrait format is standard for this genre. Other vertical subjects, such as some works of architecture, also lend themselves to the portrait format. Subjects with more width look cropped when they are shot in portrait format—viewers perceive such images as a small segment and are subconsciously driven to know what's beyond the edges (page 58).

Portrait Panorama

A portrait panorama is similar to its horizontal counterpart, but a portrait panorama attracts even more attention because it's exceptionally rare, even for subjects that obviously lend themselves to this treatment. Not many photographers seek out subjects that are suited to an extreme vertical frame; only a few picture books play directly with this effect, such as New York Vertical and Paris Vertical, which exclusively show images in the upright 3:1 ratio. When we think of the word *panorama*, we immediately visualize a wide and short landscape format.

Portrait panoramas always have the look and feel of a narrow strip that's being shown in place of the larger whole, which makes us curious about what appears directly to the right and left of the photograph's border. As a result of the tension created with this format and the natural human preference for a horizontal perspective, our gaze quickly turns away from images composed in this way.

A portrait panorama functions like a single strip of wallpaper—viewers see it as incomplete, and they want to discover what lies on either side of the frame. This format irritates viewers and quickly captures their attention, even if the subject itself is more or less static.

Square Format

The square format—a rectangle with sides of equal length—functions in an artistic and structured way. The strong geometric shape sets itself apart from most portrait and landscape photos. The effect is calm, stable, neutral, and still. The internal movement of an image in this format is balanced and pulls outward toward the four corners. This creates a strong sense of equilibrium for symmetrically positioned elements, but even subjects that are asymmetric exude more calmness in this format, compared to a format without equal sides (page 40). The potential downside is that subjects can be uninteresting, and it can be difficult to find a composition that retains the viewer's attention.

Square images recall exposures in large or medium format and Polaroid cameras; they convey an artistic quality and sophistication. Photographers can leverage this format to bring calmness to an exposure and, at the same time, enhance it. When a square format is used for a black-and-white image, viewers can hardly draw themselves away.

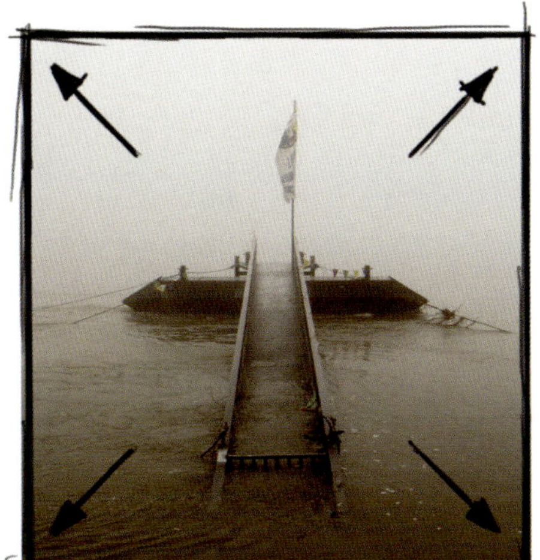

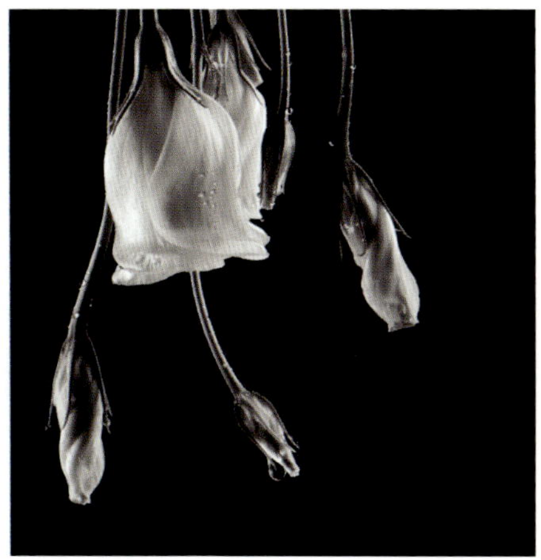

A square is a stylized image format that creates a profound calmness that can border on lifelessness. The forces in the picture on the left are so evenly balanced that the image looks static. At the same time, there's something artistic about the square format, which recalls the use of medium-format film. It complements grayscale images in the realm of fine art photography.

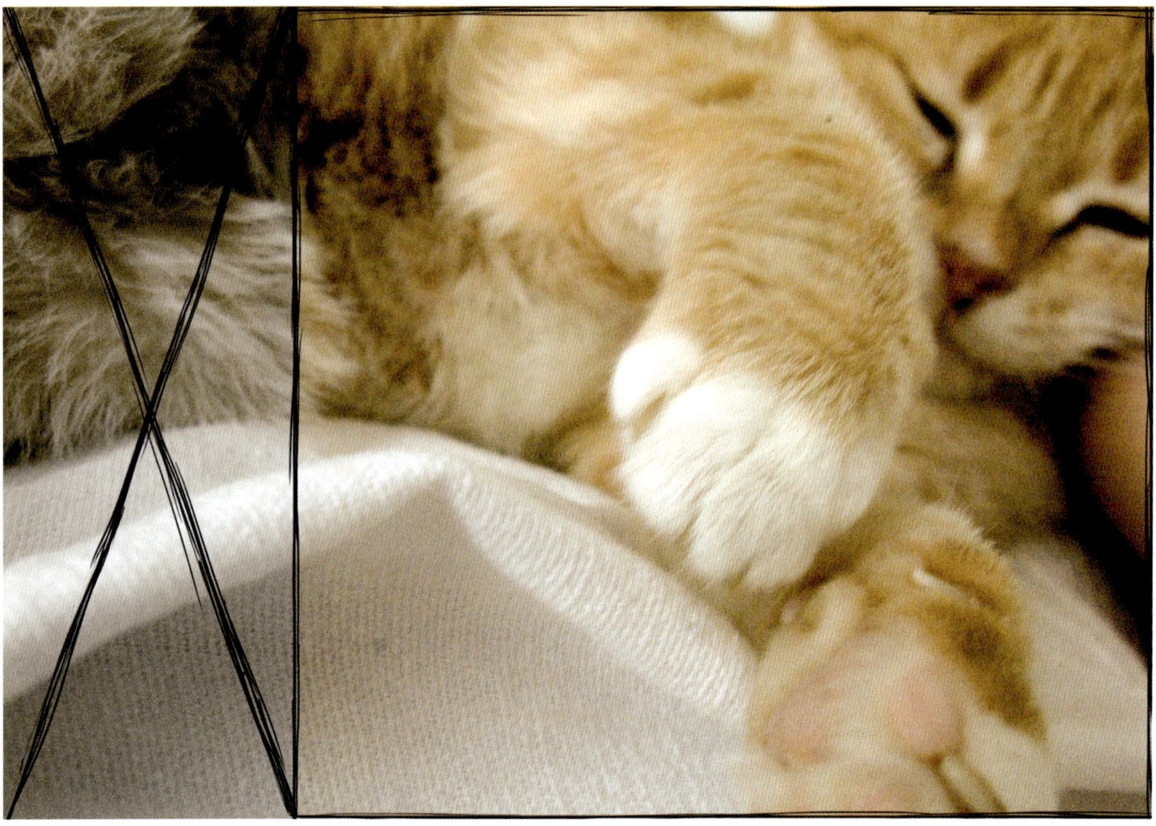

Many times you won't apply the final crop until after you've already captured an image. There are several reasons for this: your viewfinder may not match the exposure area of the image perfectly, or you may not notice an unnecessary or distracting detail until afterward. If you already have a format in mind while you're shooting, though, it's best to set up and shape your exposure with the final frame in mind.

Creating Formats

You can produce standard portrait and landscape formats by holding the camera body vertically or horizontally, respectively.

Panoramas—both portrait and landscape—can be created in three different ways. The first is to use a special panoramic film camera, which exposes a wider area of the negative and omits a narrow strip on the bottom and top of the negative. The second method is to combine multiple individual exposures. You can do this with careful handwork, or you can use special software, either in-camera or on your computer. The third method is to crop your photos after they've already been exposed. As with the first method, this has the disadvantage of wasting image information. Splicing several images together in a montage may require the most effort, but it also produces the best results.

Square-format photos are produced with a medium-format camera or by cropping a photo that was originally shot in portrait or landscape format.

Any time you create a format that deviates from the standard, you'll lose some quality due to the post-exposure crop. For many photographers, however, this is the only affordable option, since it may not be practical to purchase the requisite panorama or medium-format equipment for a first foray into new formats.

The biggest advantage of cropping an image is the ability to tailor the format specifically for your photo and create nonstandard formats. This also allows you to create multiple variations of the same image. Most viewers won't detect small crops and adjustments of the aspect ratio—for example, a change from 4:3 to 3:2. Only someone who examines lots of photos would be able to detect the smallest deviations from common formats. Keep in mind that nontraditional aspect ratios may act as optical stumbling blocks since knowledgeable viewers might subconsciously judge an image as flawed, artificial, or manipulated.

Some cameras allow you to switch between different aspect ratios, usually 4:3, 3:2, 16:9, and 1:1. This dramatically expands your design potential, but it also adds a step because you need to select a new format for each exposure, and you have to remember the current selection.

If you decide to design your images while shooting and only use the viewfinder, it's best to train your eye to make quick judgments. At some point you'll no longer need to crop your images. You'll be able to plan for a specific format and design your image accordingly while shooting. This will reduce your editing work and allow you to retain your highest-quality images. It will also give you the satisfaction of having a quick photographic eye. The exception here is minimal crops that are necessary because the viewfinders of most SLRs don't cover the frame completely, which means you end up with more in your image than you saw in your viewfinder.

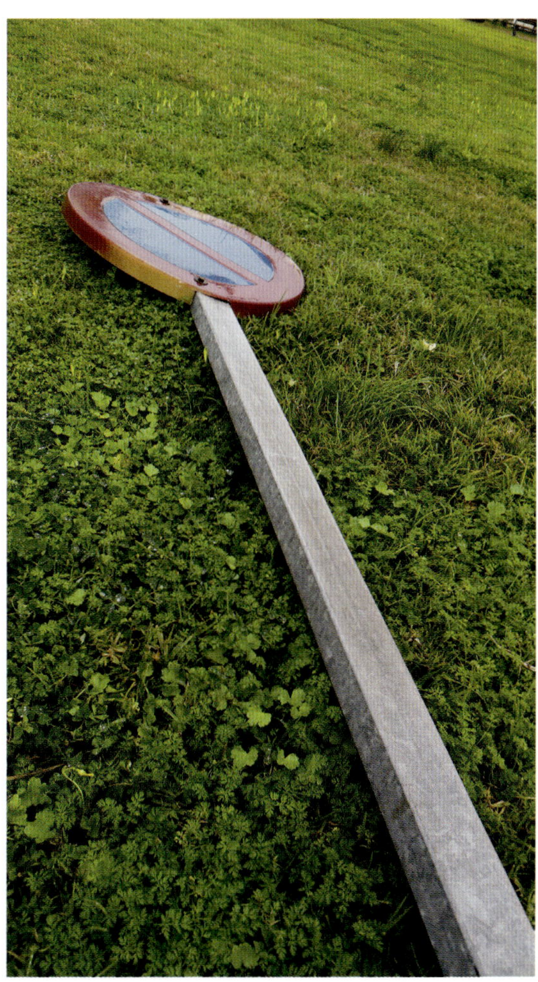

Format Limitations

Many photographers limit themselves to certain frame formats. They think of the limitation as an exciting and interesting challenge to their way of seeing objects, and they depict their subjects with the preselected format in mind. This can be a practical approach for a specific medium, or when you are preparing a gallery of related images (page 225). However, when it comes to design alone, this practice often results in images that would be more effective in other formats. Self-imposed limitations like this prioritize form over content and neglect to consider the unique dimensions of each subject. The format, along with every other element of design, should be selected with the purpose of the photo in mind.

Product or stock photography—the preparation of photos for publications—is an exception to this rule. In this type of photography, photographers must use predetermined formats that correspond to a predefined layout. Stock photographers use the most common aspect ratios and, ideally, take both a portrait and a landscape version of every shot.

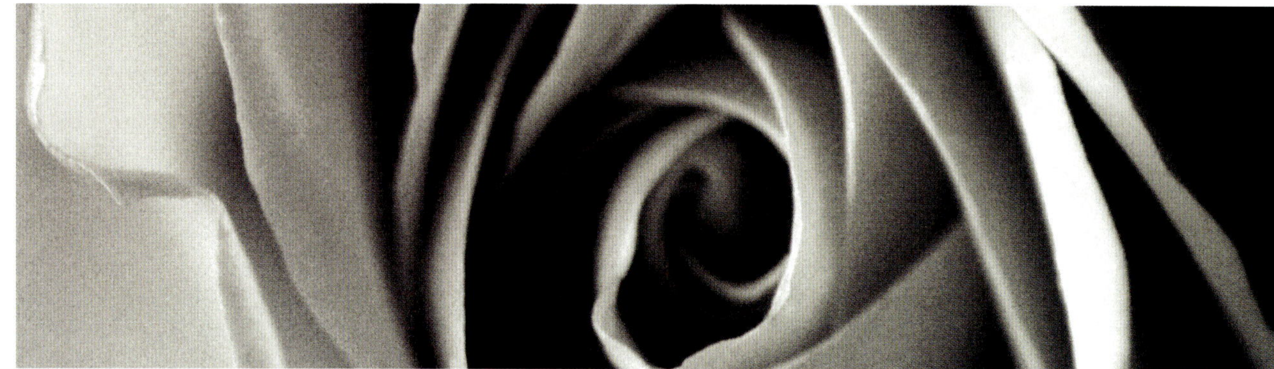

2.2 Image Area

Along with selecting an image format, the most important step in composition is choosing the image area, or the specific bit of reality that you intend to show the viewer. The image border will surround your selection, and the image design will take place within this boundary. This decision does not only concern the form; it also shapes your chosen excerpt of reality by making it visible and accessible. In the truest sense of the word, the photographer grounds the photo with this decision.

When you select the image area, you determine what message your picture conveys. Include details deliberately and avoid trying to cram as much as possible into your frame. It's better to take multiple shots that are purposeful and clear; too many subjects in a picture causes each element to lose its own meaning. When this happens, viewers become confused and lose interest quickly.

Telling Stories

With every picture, a photographer attempts to tell a story that the viewer must interpret from the context, without an explanation. The more clear and concise the story, the easier and more interesting it will be for the viewer. Frequently, though, photos fall short. Photographers can't make up their minds about which details to include because too many objects pique their interest. A man traveling to Paris might be overwhelmed by the Eiffel Tower, the setting sun in the background, the passersby

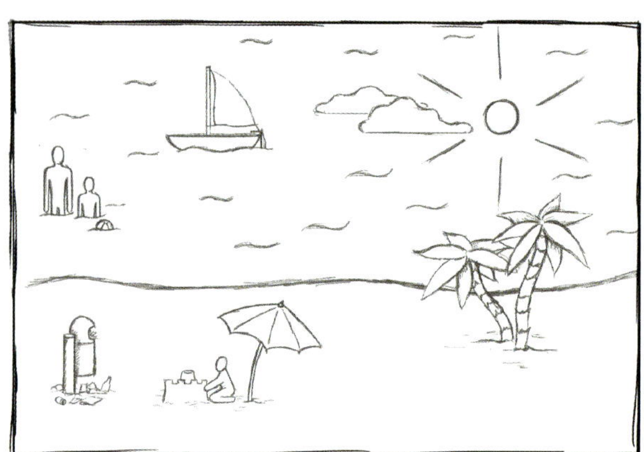

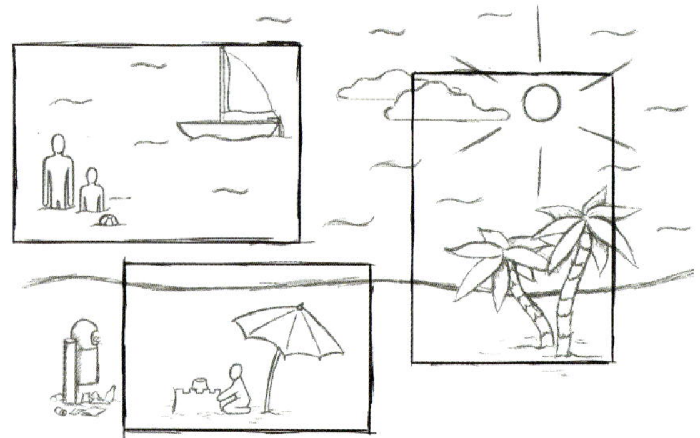

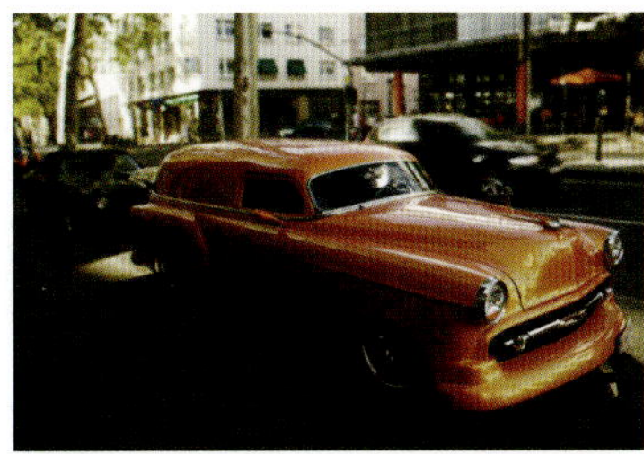
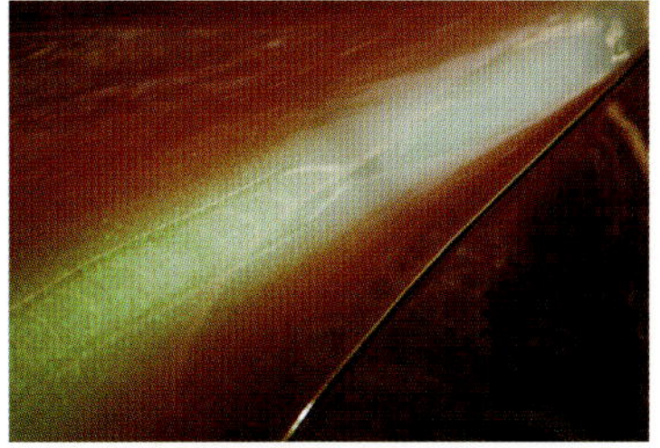
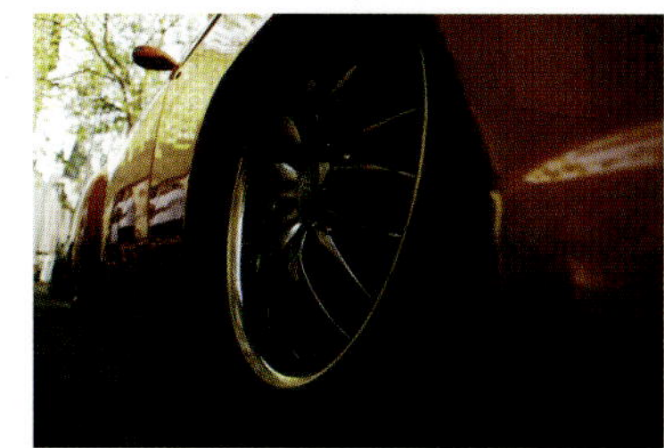
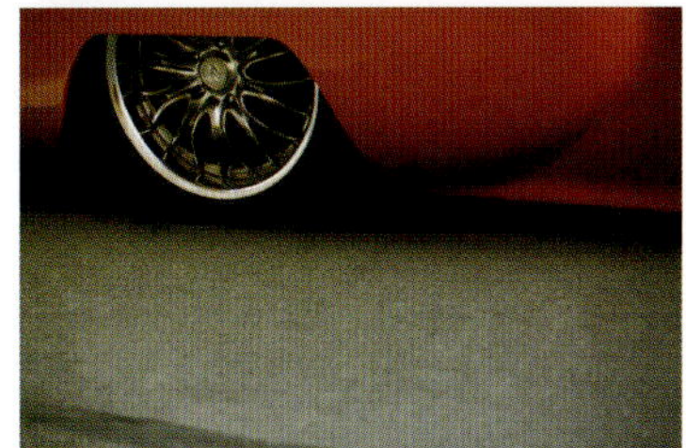
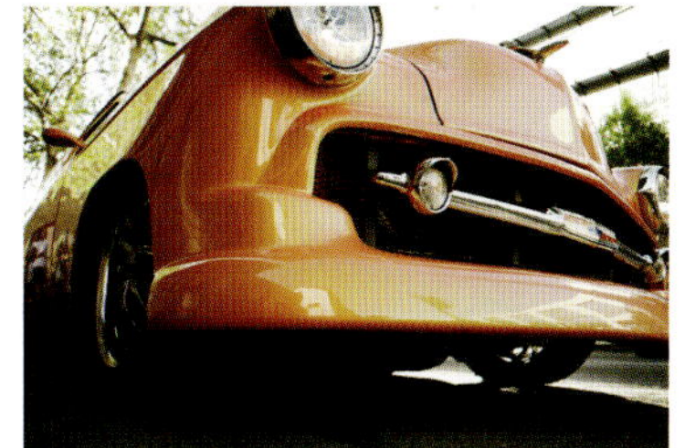
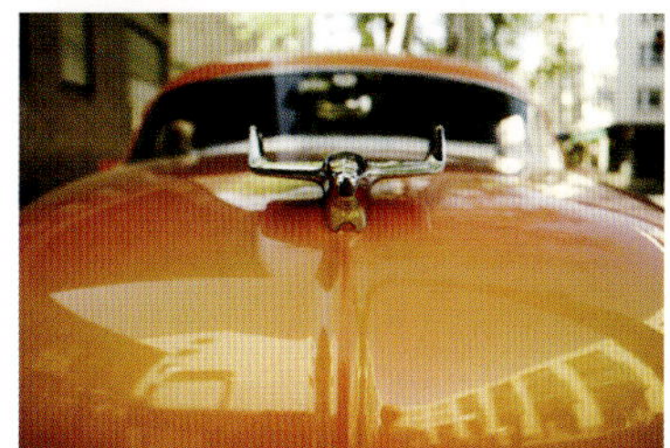
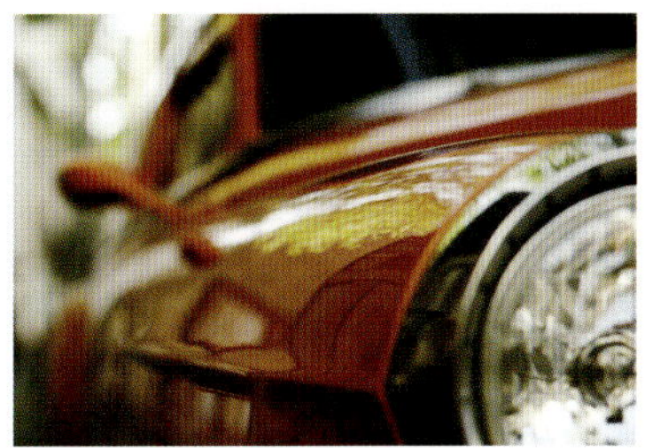
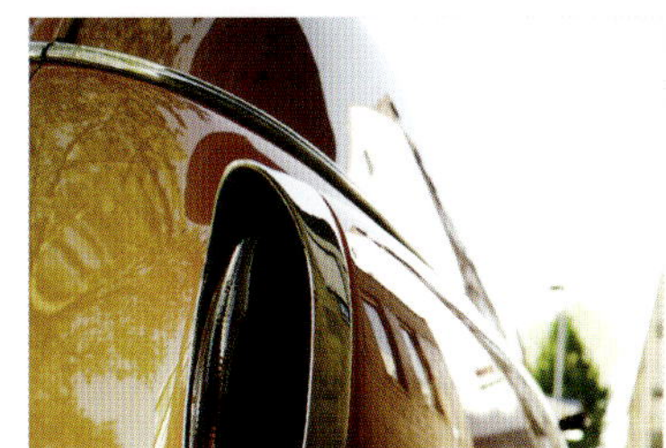
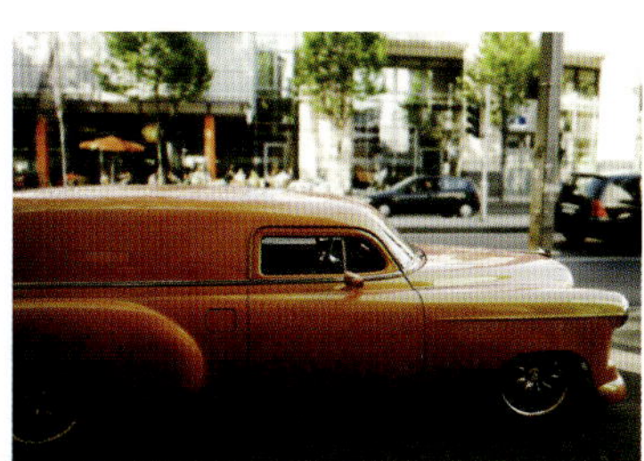

A single subject, such as this stationary vehicle, can provide enough source material for a number of pictures. This requires that you think critically about the subject and that you refuse to be content with your first successful shot. Look your subject over carefully and move all the way around it. Alter the height of your camera and try to shoot from as many different perspectives as possible.

in the foreground, the street musician to the right, the flowers to the left, the travel guide—before he knows it, he crams all these elements into a single frame. The photographer may think this successful because he documented everything in the scene exactly as it was, but we don't perceive everything at once—we process elements in our surroundings one at a time.

At first glance, viewers are greeted by a disorganized confusion of subjects, and they don't know what to look at first. We perceive pictures differently than objects in the real world; all of the elements in a photo compete for our attention at the same time. The fewer points of interest there are in a photo, the more important and prominent each one becomes, regardless of the size of the objects within the frame. As a general rule, less is more. With this particular scene in Paris, three or four exposures that are less cluttered might produce more coherent, harmonious, and conclusive results than one single photo with everything included. When the series is viewed in a sequence, these images could tell the same story as the overloaded one. Each photo should be composed and designed for accessibility—or better yet, framed for accessibility. The art of photography is all about isolating a subject from the real world, or capturing a specific moment or object in time and space. In practice, it means concentrating exclusively on what's essential and leaving out anything that's not!

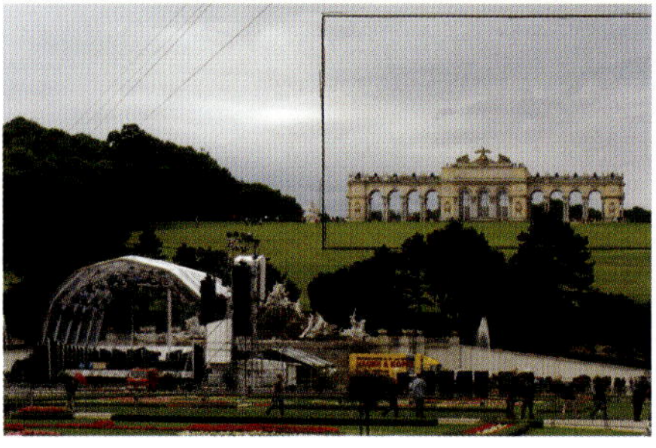

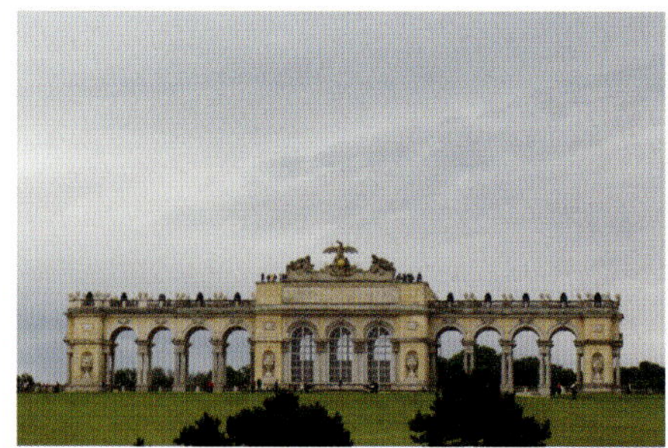

The purpose of the frame is to include and exclude what will appear in your image. Unnecessary objects tend to disturb, distract from, or drown out your main subject and can be left out entirely. By intentionally avoiding the flower bed and the concert stage, we get a clear and focused view of the main subject: the Gloriette in the Schönbrunn Palace Garden, Vienna.

Determining exactly what is essential depends on what you intend to show in your picture. Naturally, there will be more to see in an overview shot than in a close-up (page 52). If you want to isolate a single flower in a large bed of plants, your story is more of a character portrait; if you include the background along with the flower, your story has more characters and it becomes a study of place. Or, if you're at the coast and you capture a portion of the beach along with clear views of a snack stand and a jewelry vendor, your story is more about the commercialization of vacations or typical tourist traps. But if you capture a group of children playing in front of a sand castle while their parents watch, your story is about the family-friendly nature of the beach.

Showing and Not Showing

Since every picture has only a limited amount of space surrounded by a border, viewers automatically assume that everything you include in a photo is critical. It doesn't matter if you included a detail in your photo intentionally or accidentally; the viewer sees what you present. Ideally this presentation is the result of deliberately and consciously answering these questions: what do I want to show? What is my theme? What emphasizes my visual message? Conversely, what do I not want to show? What will unnecessarily disturb or change my meaning?

What you show in your image isn't the only thing that matters; what you don't show is also important. If you edit out superfluous details it's easier for viewers to understand your message and focus their attention on the essential elements in your photo. If you leave too much out, the image may be inaccessible, unclear, or uninteresting. If you're taking pictures at your son's birthday party, for example, snapping a photo of him wearing a party hat will not be enough to make the specific nature of the occasion apparent to viewers. Even if you were to take a photo of him surrounded by gifts, someone might mistake the action for Christmas. But when you bring the birthday cake into the picture, there will be no doubt about what's happening, even if you don't include any other details about the situation. The birthday boy's sister, who is standing nearby and looking off in another direction while twirling her hair, isn't supporting the main purpose of your photo, so she can safely be left out without harming your image.

In most cases you can make the following generalization: the more you reveal, the more concrete a picture becomes; the more you conceal, the more anonymous and universal it becomes. You must walk this line for each photo. Consider and reconsider each element in your image. Is it necessary to my purpose? Does it have to appear in the photo to convey my message? Could I do without it? The more clearly and concretely you understand what you actually want to photograph, the easier it will be for you to make decisions about your image frame.

The selection of an image frame may be used to intentionally deceive or manipulate viewers. This method is often used to influence public opinion. If a photographer documenting a small demonstration outside city hall includes the 20 protestors in addition to the massive empty square behind them, the photo conveys the message that there's a small group. But if the photographer fills the entire frame with protestors so people are cut off at the borders (page 56), it gives the impression that the event was well attended. Similarly, it's no coincidence that when there's an oil spill disaster at sea, the oil company publishes images that show the entire coast, while groups like Greenpeace opt to show small animals covered in oil.

Through the process of selecting your image frame, you can visually link objects that aren't related. The leaves in the foreground of this image didn't fall from the tree that's visible here, especially given that the tree is on the other side of the street, but the subjects function together.

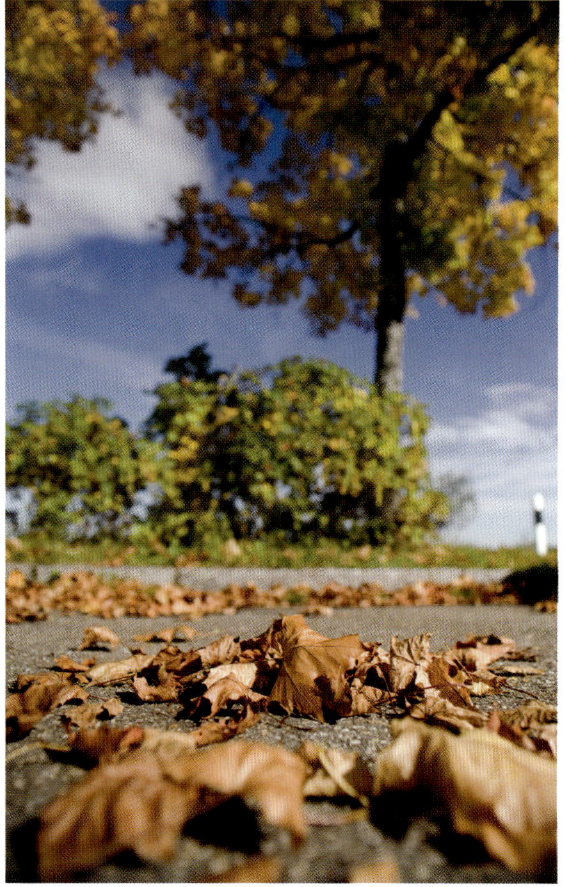

Combining Subjectively

As soon as you settle on the elements that are critical for your picture, you can start to position them within your frame and combine them to support your vision. It's completely up to you which elements to bring together in visual relationships. You might bring several small subjects together to create a general impression for the viewer, or you might choose fewer subjects to highlight their relative importance. The elements you choose to include and how you combine them will shape the fundamental way people see the photo. The point of view can be well-known and familiar, or completely new and unusual—in any case, it's subjective.

Truth and reality are of limited concern to photographers because their objective may be to demonstrate a relationship that someone else hasn't seen before or that may not exist at all in nature. This doesn't only concern the vast possibilities of digital manipulation; it also concerns the selection of the camera's perspective and image frame. Photography is, in some ways, a game of seeing something others don't see.

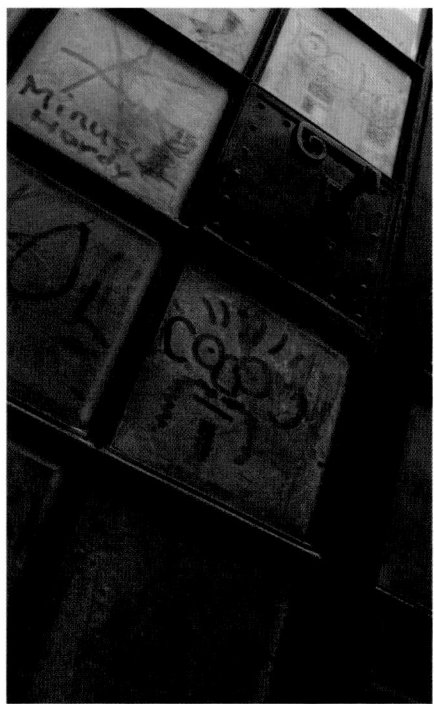

Everyone can see at eye level. From that perspective things look the same as always. It's only when we depart from our standard perception habits and consider other unusual perspectives that we capture unconventional images—a practice worth adopting only if it aligns with your photographic objectives. Selecting one small portion of this larger door and shooting it from below requires some physical—and mental—flexibility.

The Right Perspective

Your image frame is not only established by focal length and angle of view—the physical position of the camera matters, as does your perspective on the subject (page 104). To find the best position for a photograph, move around between shots. Examine your subject from all sides, crouch down, climb on top of something, increase and decrease the distance between your subject and your lens—in other words, use your feet to zoom. Keeping your feet in motion will keep your perspective fresh and your ideas flowing. It's the best way to stumble onto a perspective that you otherwise wouldn't have considered.

For this reason, we recommend against using a tripod while you're getting started with photography, and for subjects that don't require the extra stability. Working with a tripod is too static, rigid, and uncomfortable for quickly trying out new positions for your camera. It impedes your search for the ideal perspective on the subject.

Field Sizes

The language used to describe field size in moviemaking is also useful when discussing the distance between the subject and the camera in still photography. In the following list we'll discuss each field size in the same way that a zoom lens works—starting from far away and moving closer to the subject:

- **Extreme long:** This field size, which shows everything, gives the viewer a broad overview of a scene and is very common in landscape photography. This perspective can lift a viewer up over a river valley, meadow, field, or city to reveal the largest structures in an all-encompassing manner. Of course, even an extreme long shot excludes details because it can only show a limited frame.
- **Long:** A long shot is closer, but still presents an overview. It gives viewers a rough vision of individual elements without making them appear finite. In a shot of a town, viewers would be able to make out individual streets and houses.
- **Medium long:** If the individual elements in the image are recognizable to the viewers, even if the general surroundings still dominate the frame, they're looking as a medium-long shot in this field size. This might mean depicting an individual street or a town square. Nearby details and the sky are still present, but they've been relegated to a supporting role.
- **Full:** This is a close shot. Full shots depict one central element in its entirety along with the nearby surroundings, such as a bicycle or a car parked on the street.
- **Medium:** When an element, such as a bicycle, is cropped, and therefore no longer shown in its entirety, it is in the range of close field sizes. Here, the surroundings are unimportant, and smaller details, such as the basket of flowers and the details of the bicycle itself, are recognizable.
- **Close-up:** If the flowers are so close that it is difficult or impossible for viewers to orient themselves in relation to the surroundings, and the bicycle basket is no longer visible in its entirety, the shot is a close-up.
- **Detail:** A detail shot is even closer. The field size encompasses just a single element, which, in reality, is fairly small. This might be a frame-filling view of a single flower that takes on an anonymous and universal feeling.

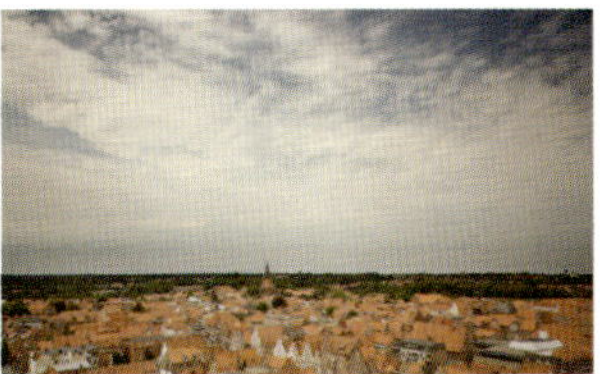
Extreme long

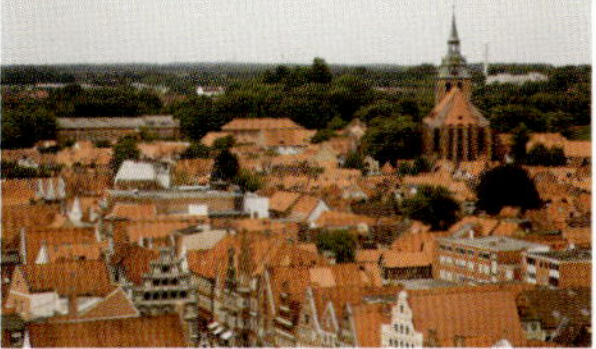
Long

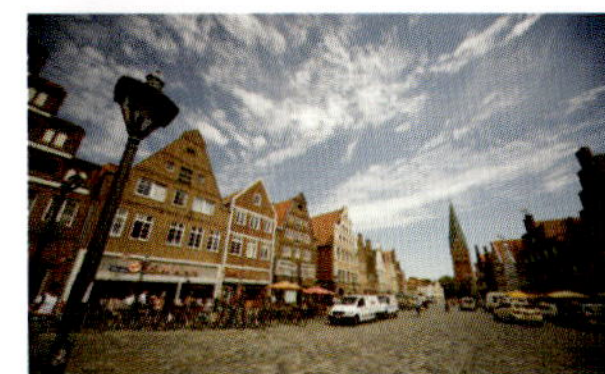
Medium long

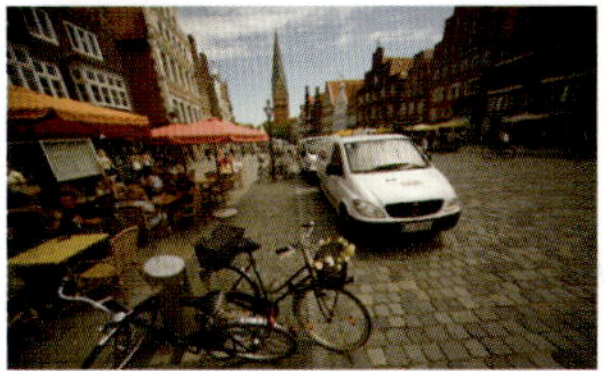
Full

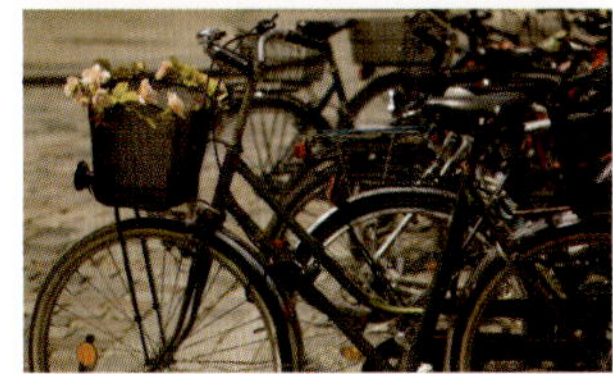
Medium

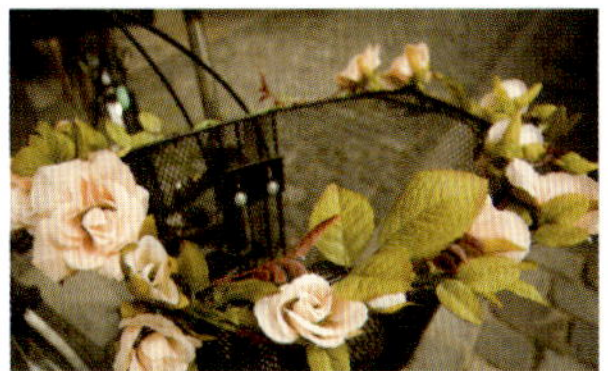
Close-up

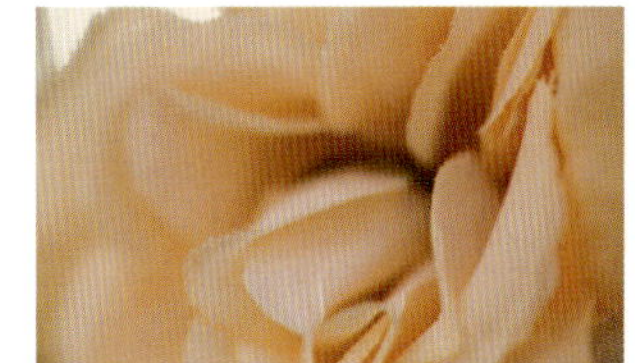
Detail

To shoot the same subject in different field sizes, it's not enough to swap out your focal length or your angle of view while standing in one place. Field sizes have much more to do with how large the subject will be—or how much of it will be shown—in the final image. In this example of a decorated bicycle in the old town of Lüneburg, Germany, the images, from top to bottom, show the different field sizes, from an extreme long shot to a detail shot.

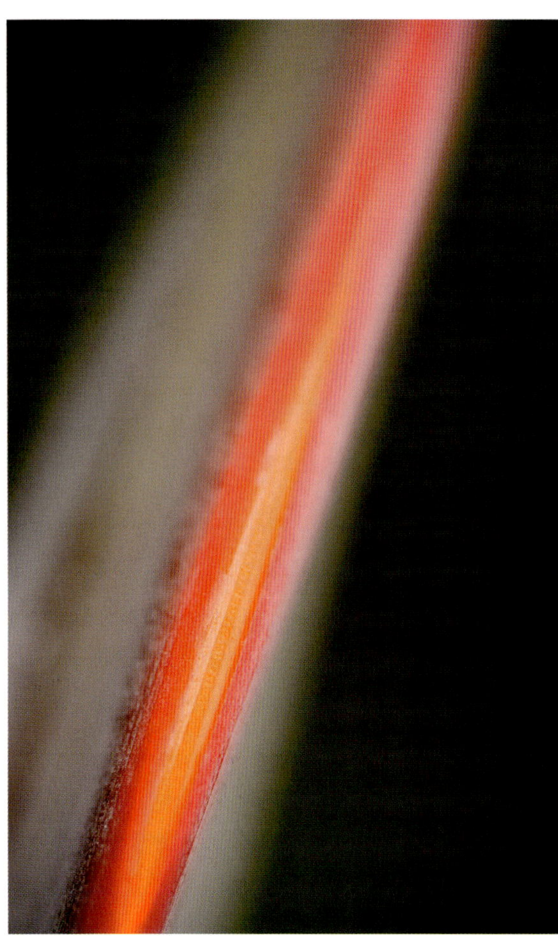

The closer you capture your subject, the more likely you are to obscure its surroundings and the characteristic shapes and forms that make it recognizable. If you do this intentionally, you can create visual puzzles that may force viewers to stay engaged with your photo longer. Or have you already recognized the bird-of-paradise flower?

How Image Borders Work

The image border plays a large role in the effect of an image, regardless of the content. In general, the closer your camera is to the subject—and by extension, the closer the viewer is—the more intimate, immediate, and concrete the resulting photo will be. Greater distance creates more detached images that are often more clearly arranged. When viewers can make out details in the background, they will have an easier time deciphering the subject. Little or no recognizable background produces a more artistic and universal effect.

Your subject can also appear abstract if you are very close to it. You can exploit this trick by using a macro lens to create visual puzzles, which are sure to make your viewers curious.

As soon as we recognize one detail of a subject, we immediately fill in the rest of the visual information, even if we can only see a small fraction of the whole subject. A single characteristic is generally enough to convey the whole story to the viewer—pars pro toto (part for the whole). After seeing a shot of an elephant's trunk, for example, our brain immediately recalls an image of the entire animal. Similarly, if the only visible part of a sunflower is the characteristic arrangement of seeds, we recall the entire flower. On the other hand, when viewers are not familiar with the subject, you can show them substantially larger parts of the whole, and they still won't be able to figure out what is being depicted.

Spontaneous Framing

Coincidence is the dominant factor in one style of snapshot photography called Lomography. The history of this particular type of photography goes back to a Russian camera equipped for purists: the LOMO Compact Automat (LC-A). In Vienna in the 1990s, photographers used this camera to shoot new perspectives of the world with experimental and rudimentary methods.

These photographers did not look through a viewfinder to frame their photos; instead, they shot from the hip. This technique is possible with every camera, and it invites coincidence and chaos into your images because it completely does away with the purposeful selection of an image area. The better you can visualize your results while shooting, the better you can control—or at least somewhat influence—the chaos. Regardless of your freestyle talent, when you use this method, you can assume that your pile of discarded images is going to grow. Taking a quick look at your camera monitor to see what you captured can be a good way to improve your results on a second shot. Similarly, cropping off portions of your images after you've uploaded them to your computer can be an effective way to optimize an unplanned photo or remove a distraction from the frame. As you can imagine, it's not easy to create a truly excellent picture when conventional standards don't take experimental methods into account.

If you do succeed, however, you'll always have access to this newly discovered perspective that you wouldn't have otherwise—not just because you never would have thought of it, but also because our subconscious often prevents us from trying new things. New perspectives are out there, and this can be an effective way to add them to your photographic repertoire. Not everyone will value or care for the results of inviting chance into your exposures, which will often end up slanted. But no one will be able to deny the lively, authentic, and dramatic effect that these images produce.

The image frame is not always deliberately planned—often it's left up to chance rather than a careful look through the viewfinder. This gives images a lively spontaneity that sometimes results in a fresh and authentic quality.

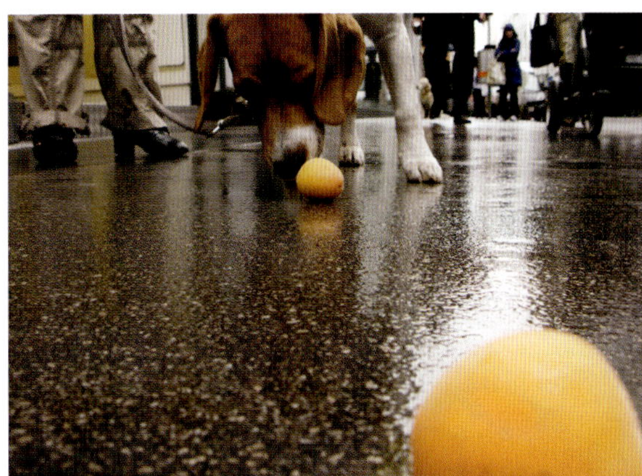

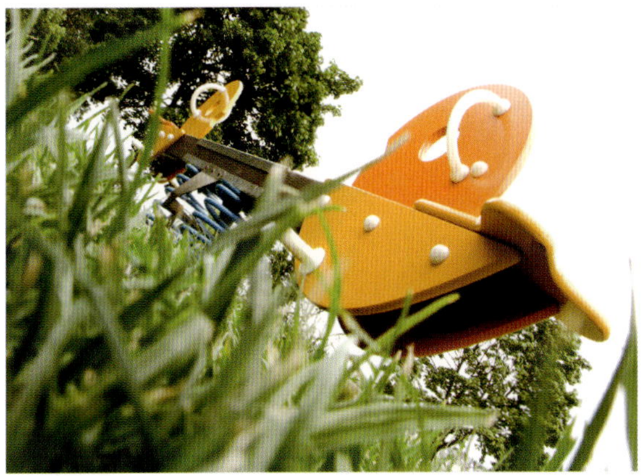

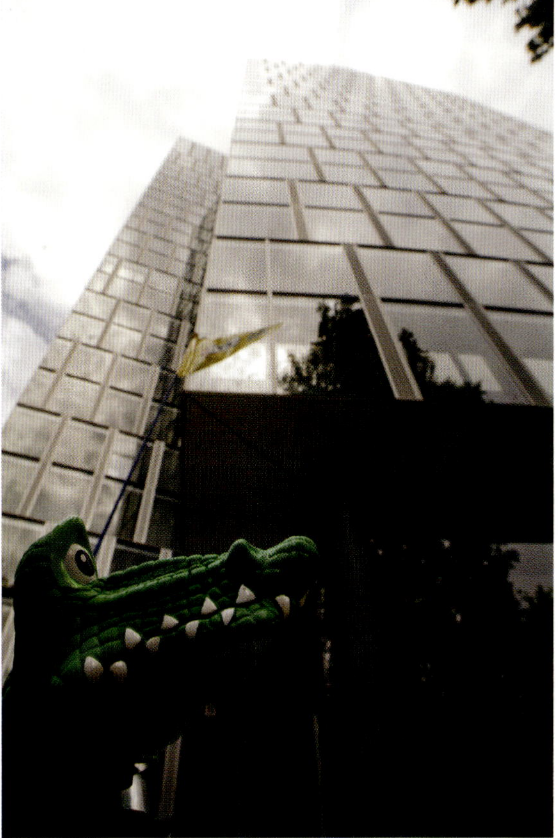

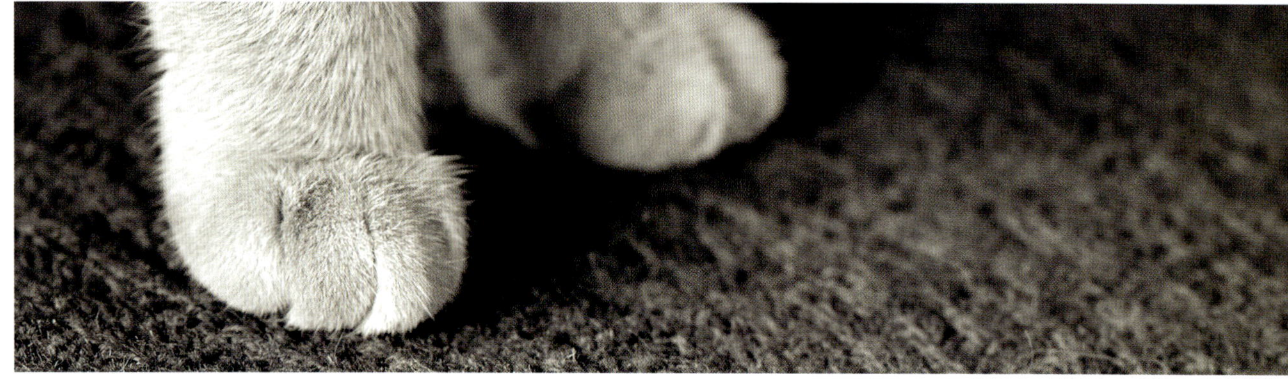

2.3 Cropping

Intentionally cropping or truncating critical elements of your image causes some viewers to scratch their heads, others to get irritated, and others to turn away. Anyone who swears off this design approach, however, is missing out on an exciting way to enhance the intimacy of your photos. Not everything needs to be shown in full to give an image impact—what's not shown often plays an important role.

The human brain is capable of completing and recognizing objects that are only partly shown, so don't hesitate to use an image frame that cuts off a portion of a critical element. This will shift the weight of your image—in this case, from the gecko's body to its face.

Complete Representations

When we talk about how a cropped element can irritate a viewer, we assume that the viewer is expecting the main subject to be complete. This expectation doesn't apply to everything within the border; it only applies to the main subject. Since a photo is only a snippet of reality, not everything in a photo must be represented in full. To cite one example, consider a scene of a house in a large meadow, with a road in the foreground leading up to it and various trees and shrubs surrounding it. Viewers don't expect to see full representations of the entire meadow and road, but they do expect

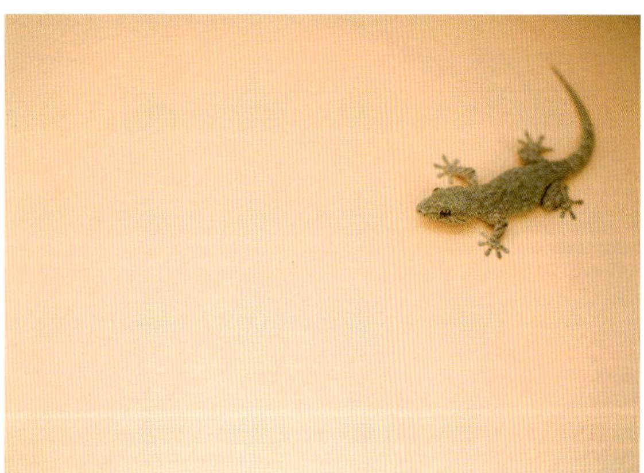

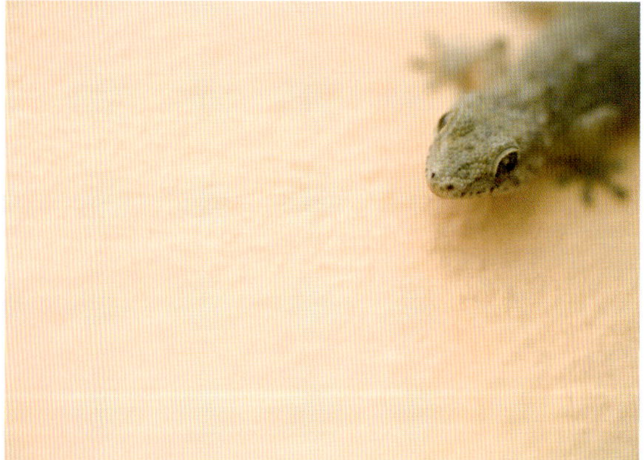

the house, and perhaps the most dominant trees, to appear in their entirety. Deciding not to truncate the house is a design tactic that allows you to emphasize the house in your image. Showing the house in full establishes it as the main subject of the photo.

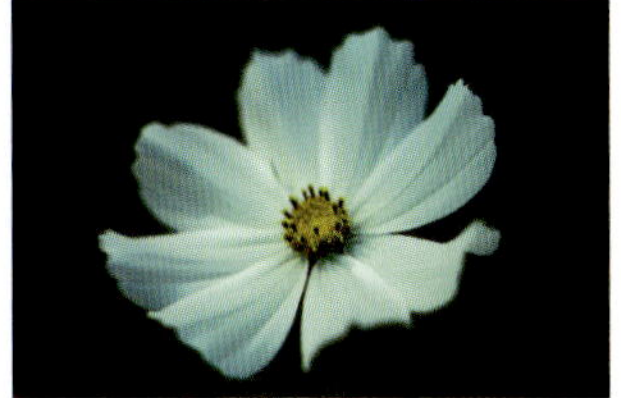

Cropping a small portion of a subject at its top or bottom can anchor it and prevent it from appearing to float around, lost in space.

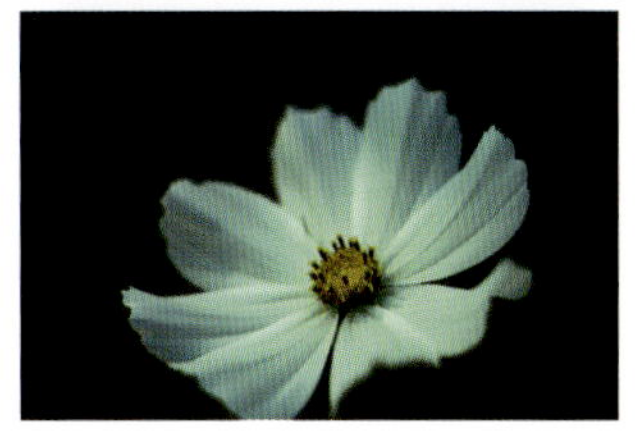

Reducing Visual Dominance

Cropping the subject of an image reduces its visual importance. If a photographer creates an image that splits a house down the middle, that house takes up less area of the final image and allows something else to be the main subject—a detail on the house, the relationship of the house with its surroundings, or a purely visual aspect, such as the colors of the meadow. Cropping through objects limits their visual importance and transfers their emphasis to other, less dominant details. This is particularly noticeable with a picture of someone's face. Cropping out a person's hair reduces the otherwise dominant shape of the head and hair (page 94) and emphasizes the person's eyes, nose, and mouth.

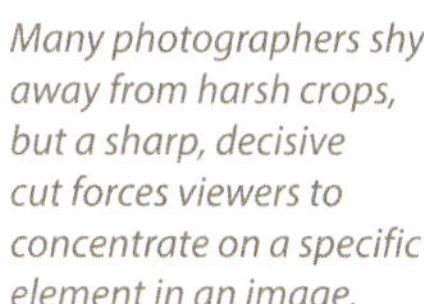

Many photographers shy away from harsh crops, but a sharp, decisive cut forces viewers to concentrate on a specific element in an image.

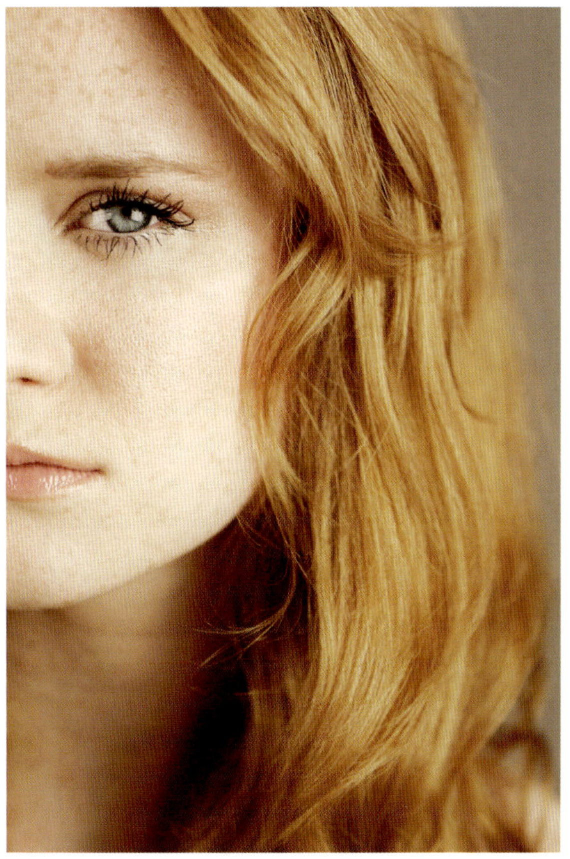

The severity of the crop corresponds to the degree of reduced emphasis. Modest truncations limit the dominance of a subject only minimally and may not even be consciously noticed. This type of treatment creates an optical anchor for objects in front of a uniform surface and prevents them from looking isolated and detached. Harsher, more radical crops produce a noticeable impact and can drastically reduce the relative importance of an object—sometimes to the point of irrelevance.

Creating Closeness

Extreme crops are useful for more than shifting the relative importance of elements within the image frame; they can also produce a noticeable degree of intimacy. Harshly cropped subjects seem closer to the viewer. They make photos feel more open and immediate, and they reduce emotional distance.

This is true of all photography genres, but it's most noticeable in pictures of people. In this part of the world, a socially acceptable distance between two people is about one arm's length. At this distance we can generally see the entire head of the other person. We usually only allow people we know very well—partners, family members, friends—to stand close enough to us that we can't see their entire head, or even their face. People have the same expectation for photos.

You can crop your subjects to simulate a closer proximity between the viewer and the subject. Depending on how the viewer sympathizes with the subject, this will either kindle a heightened fascination because the nearness will be almost palpable, or it will foster discomfort, and the viewer may attempt to establish a safer distance. In either case, the viewer will be emotionally engaged with the photo.

Cropping Off, Not Cropping Out

In addition to increased emotional power, there are other reasons a purposeful crop causes viewers to remain engaged with an image. Viewers know that in reality, the subject is complete, so they imagine the missing parts of the subject. They might imagine that lines, patterns, or structures continue indefinitely, without changing direction or appearance. For this reason it's important not to crop someone's body at

We instinctively try to maintain a minimum distance from people we don't know very well—no one likes to be too close for comfort. In our culture, an acceptable distance is about one arm's length. The head of someone standing at arm's length is usually entirely within our field of perception, and we retain this expectation when we view photographs. Only with close friends and family do we get so close that it's possible to see only the features of someone's face. A close crop puts viewers in the position of experiencing the intimacy of feeling that they know the subject well.

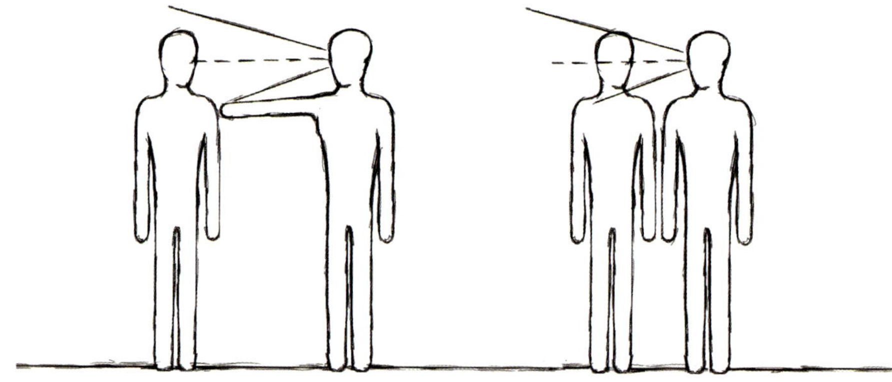

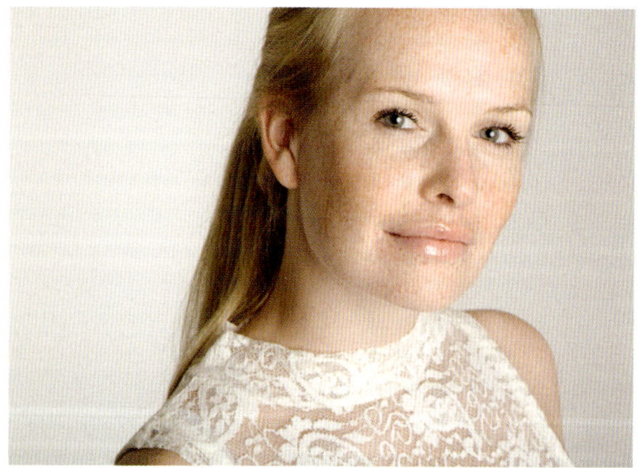

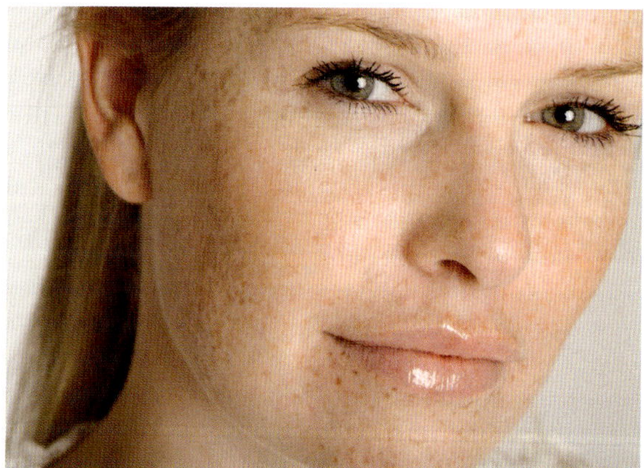

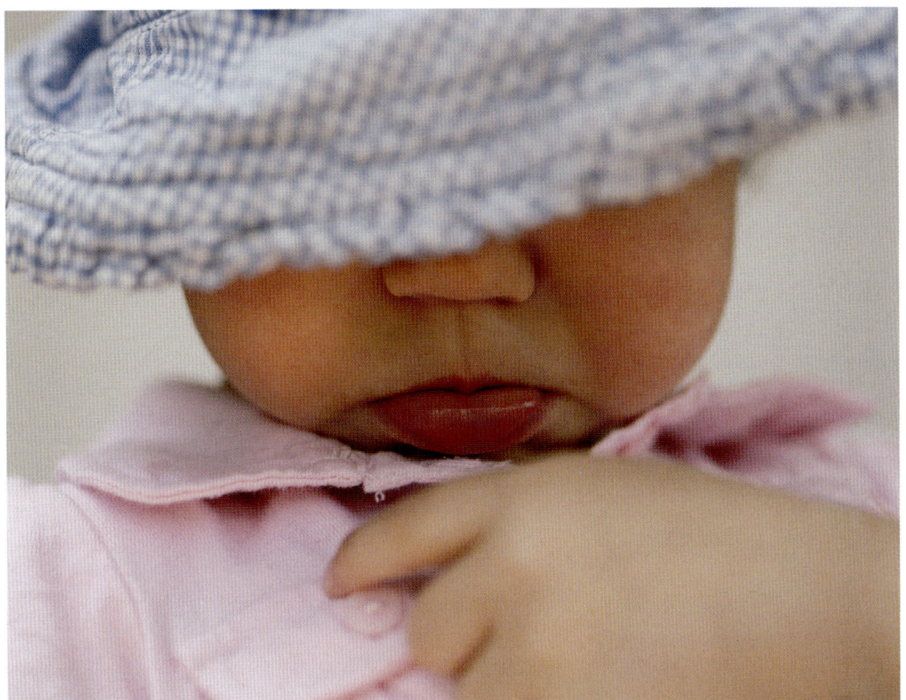

In addition to truncating elements in your photos with the image border, you can also use overlapping internal elements. This baby's hat, for example, creates a harsh crop, obscuring a large portion of the face and giving the image a more anonymous feel.

the widest part; this can be quite unflattering. The difficulty of mentally completing a cropped object depends on the shape and look of the element, and the subject's position within the image area (page 96). A viewer will mentally complete an object regardless of these details; if you crop off part of the main subject, the viewer will spend more time engaged with the image than if you don't crop it at all. Cropping elements of the image is a good way to increase the likelihood that your photo will command attention.

The location of a cropped subject within the image area affects the extent to which this design choice influences the viewer. A crop on the right or top reduces the optical dominance of the subject.

Location Is Everything

There are two basic ways that a subject can be truncated: (1) overlapping it behind another element in the image and (2) extending the subject beyond the border of the image area. The latter option is more pronounced and produces a stronger effect, but the crop doesn't work the same on all four sides of the image. A crop along the bottom edge is often barely noticed unless it's so extreme that essential parts of the subject are split, such as a crop between someone's nose and mouth. But if a logical, distinct portion of a subject is cropped

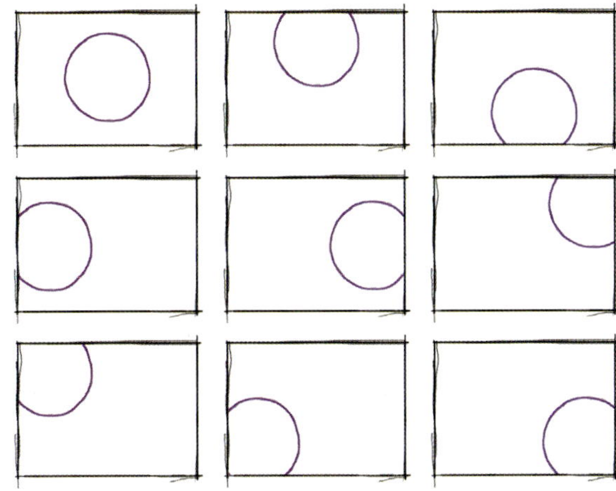

along the bottom edge, it often still appears complete; for example, a crop at stomach level turns a full portrait into a top-half portrait.

Viewers tend to accept crops along the top border as inconspicuous, especially when the objective of the crop is to establish a more intimate tone or to anchor an otherwise ungrounded object. But radically cropping off an integral feature of the main subject will be extremely noticeable.

Crops along the side have a stronger effect. They are more conspicuous and emphasize the side opposite of the crop. When the objective is to have viewers imagine what lies beyond the image border, it's more effective to crop along the right side of the photo because it's faster and more intuitive for viewers to mentally complete an image in the direction of reading. In general, it's easier to imagine geometric shapes beyond the image border as organic and regular patterns than to imagine them as irregular. This is true for all sides of the image.

When an element is cropped on more than one side, the result is added emphasis on the uncropped sides. This increases the feeling of intimacy and closeness.

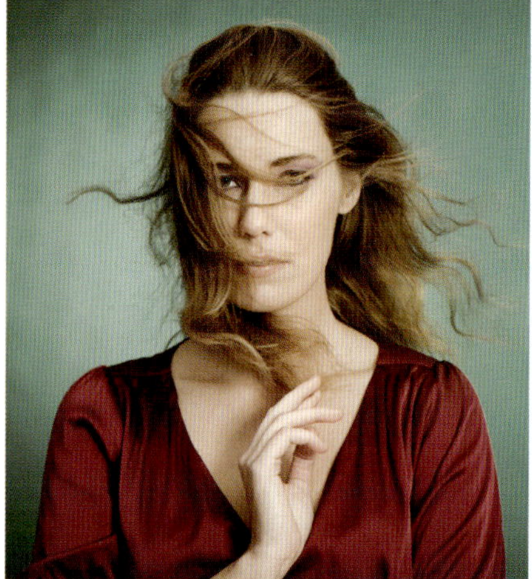

Cropping part of your subject not only reduces its optical significance, it also reduces the importance of the background. With uniform backgrounds, cropping causes the background to split into two smaller, less important areas.

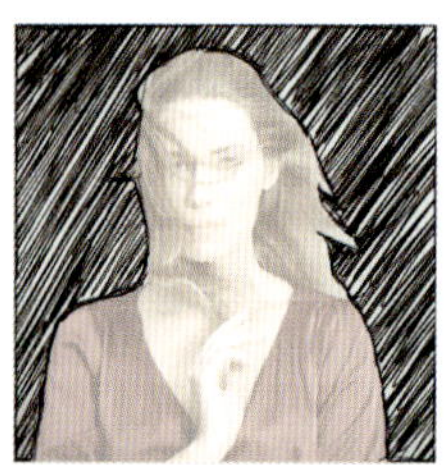

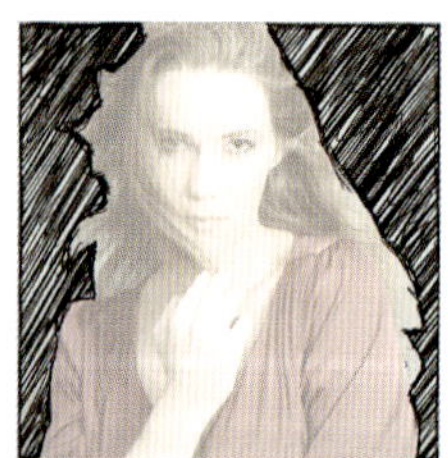

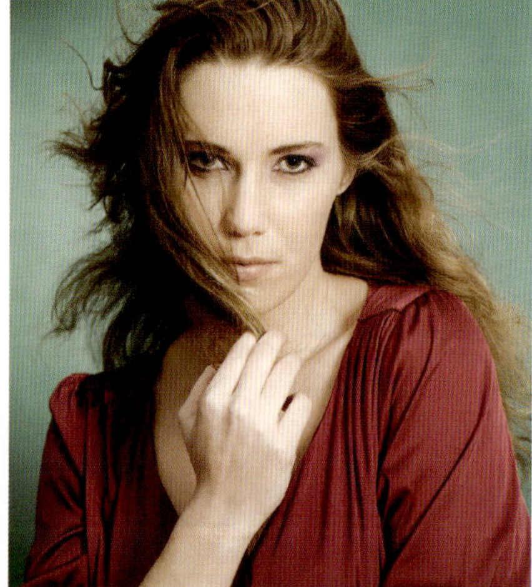

Dividing the Background

Cropping an element along one of the borders influences more than its relative importance; it also affects the importance of the background and surroundings. A crop can reduce the dominance of the background, especially when it has a uniform color or texture. As soon as an element in the foreground spills over the border, the background is divided into two areas. These two smaller, separate areas possess less optical weight than one solid, undivided background. When a crop occurs on more than one side of the image, the background is divided into even smaller parts and becomes less and less noticeable.

The crop doesn't have to be drastic to reduce the emphasis on the background—just barely touching the border will do.

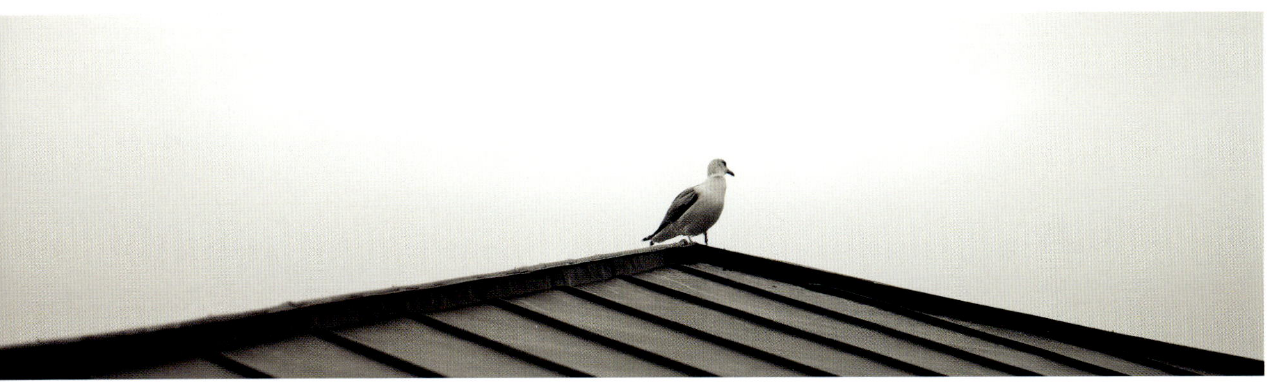

2.4 Arranging Visual Elements

If you have settled on a position for your camera and a specific focal length—and have therefore determined your field size—you have also settled on a specific number of elements to have in your image. Now your work centers on arranging those elements within the image area to produce your intended visual effect or message (page 104). Arranging the important visual elements within your image frame affects more than how organized or chaotic the final picture looks. You're creating your desired effect in a purposeful way by inviting calmness or force, harmony or irritation, torpor or excitement, dimension or flatness.

The foundational units of an image are the visual elements, even if they are very diverse. Here, the two pairs of shoes, the footprints, and the metal block are perceived as a coherent group.

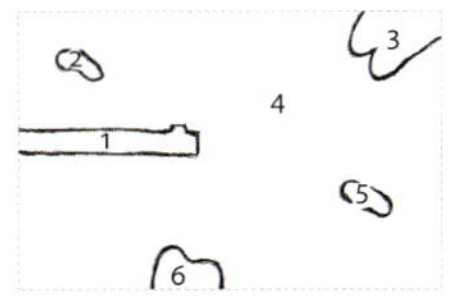

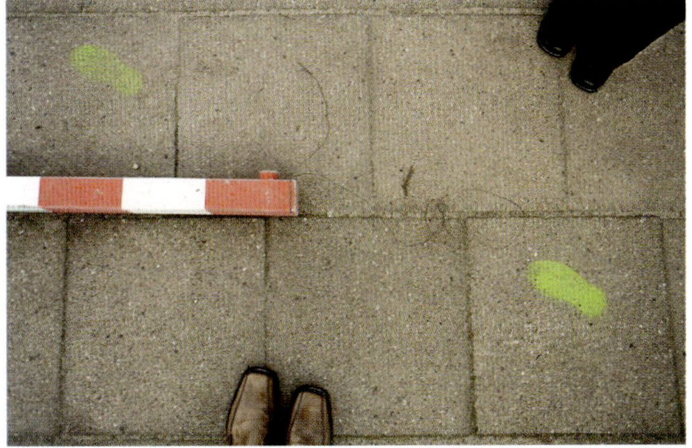

Visual Elements

The elements of an image are the coherent units in a photo that are perceived as separate from their surroundings. Such coherent units can stand out from their surroundings at the content level or the structural level. Visual units related to content stand out as elements in an image because their relationships are understood. A car and its wheels visually appear to be unrelated, but the associations we know from experience allow us to perceive that they belong together. The same goes for someone's head and their body. On the level of shapes and forms, elements run the gamut: points, stripes, surfaces, shapes, or textures (page 76).

What viewers perceive as a distinct element depends on its individual characteristics, the rest of the depicted objects, their respective size relationships, and their arrangement within the image. A small person standing in a large landscape functions as an element; but, if the person fills up the image area, it is perceived as many individual elements—legs, arms, torso, and head. When the person's head alone fills up the area, it can be broken down into the individual elements of eyes, nose, mouth, cheeks, chin, forehead, ears, and hair. A few principles from the psychology of perception can help make sense of how we mentally separate units of meaning.

The Basics of Gestalt Theory

Gestalt psychology was developed in Germany at the beginning of the 20th century to study how the human brain makes sense of complex patterns. The main subject of the investigation was to determine the principles by which we perceive shapes, surfaces, lines, and points. Since these Gestalt principles are applicable to photography, it's worthwhile to consider the following rules that are relevant to two-dimensional still frames to help us design our images more effectively. Becoming familiar with Gestalt principles will help you understand that regardless of how you arrange the individual parts of your image, viewers will perceive other coherent units—or visual elements—jointly and independently from their context.

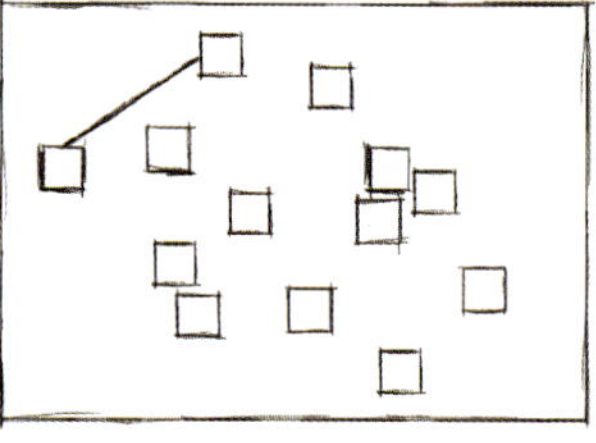

- **The principle of proximity and relatedness:** The closer together that objects appear, the stronger the perceived relationship among them. Distance between objects has the inverse effect. Connections among individual elements lead to them being interpreted jointly.

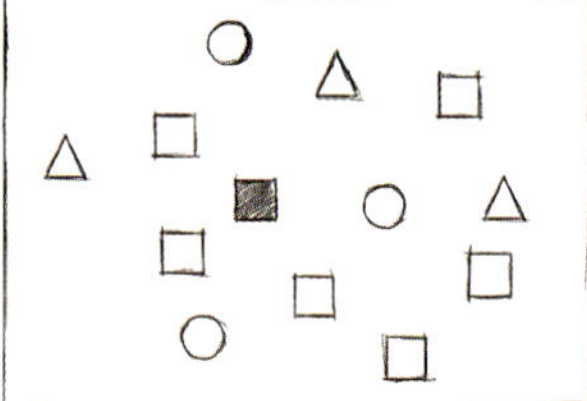

- **The principle of similarity:** Objects that are similar in appearance, whether it be color, shape, or texture, will be perceived as linked. A dissimilarity of appearance separates elements from one another.

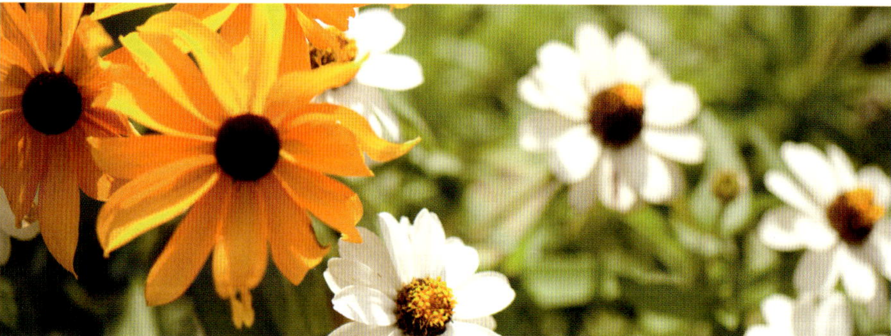

The shapes of all these flowers are nearly identical, but they clearly fall into two different groups based on their closeness, relatedness, similarity, and above all, different colors.

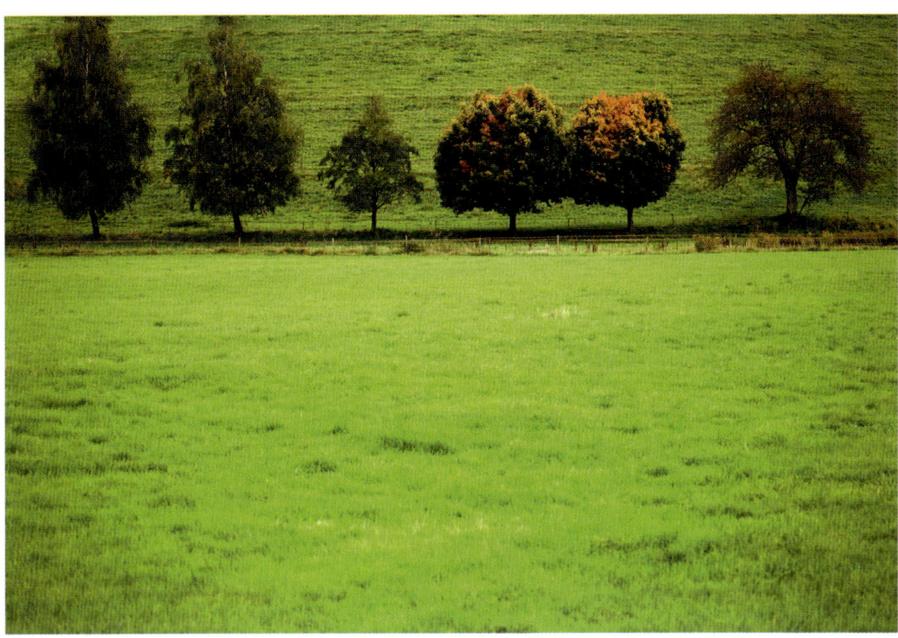

The principle of continuation causes these six trees to function as a coherent unit, despite their dissimilar shapes and colors.

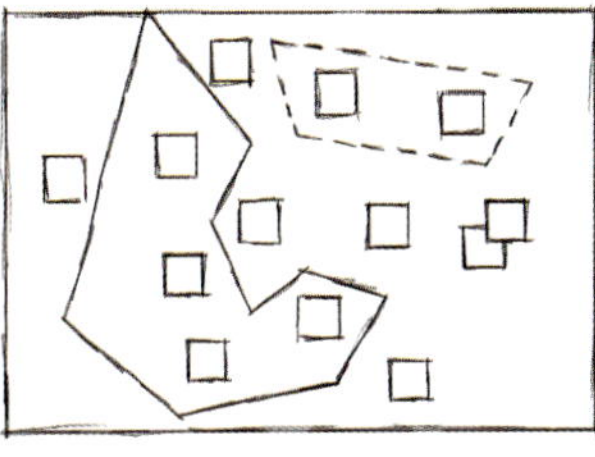

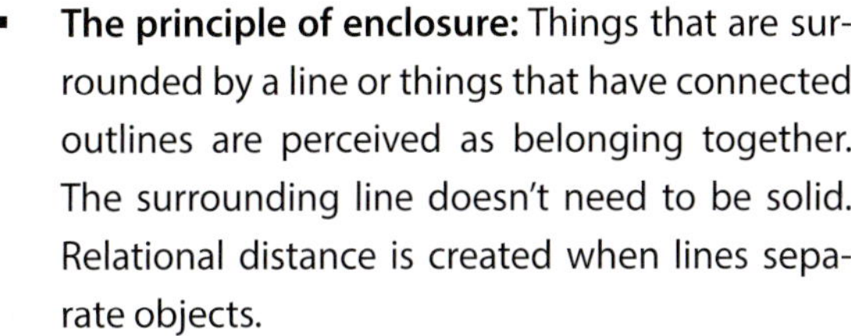

- **The principle of enclosure:** Things that are surrounded by a line or things that have connected outlines are perceived as belonging together. The surrounding line doesn't need to be solid. Relational distance is created when lines separate objects.

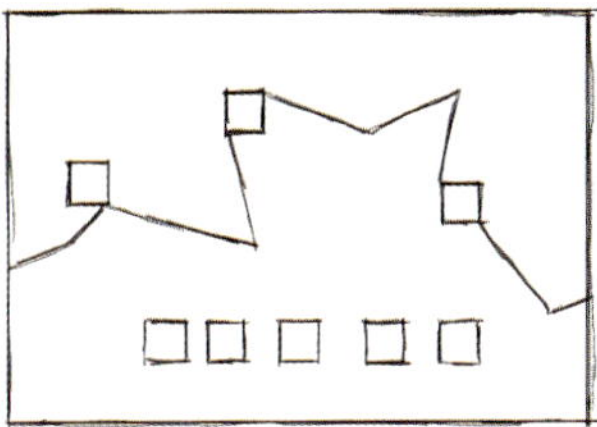

- **The principle of continuation:** Objects on the same line are perceived as related. The line doesn't need to be solid, nor does it need to completely connect the objects. In addition, we perceive lines to be indefinite. When we view a cross, we extend our vision along diagonal lines, rather than converging lines that run to a point.

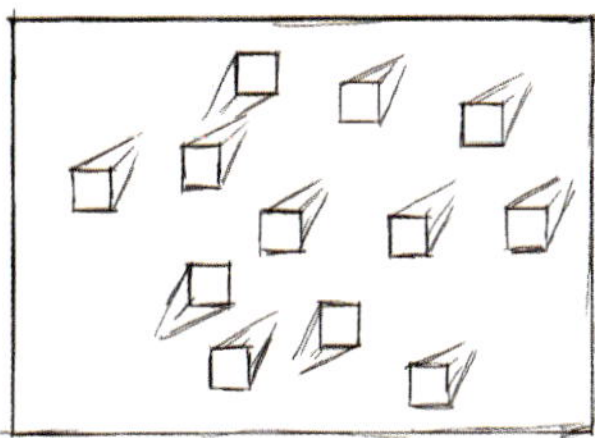

- **The principle of common fate:** Things that move together or in the same direction are perceived as related. Countermovement establishes separation between objects. This applies to objects that have obvious movement in an image. It also applies when viewers know from experience whether an object would be moving and the likely direction of its movement.

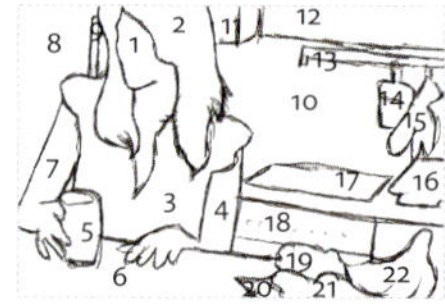

The more elements that appear in an image, the harder the photographer has to work to balance and organize them so the viewer does not get confused and lose interest. A large number of well-balanced subjects can tell a rich story and hold a viewer's attention for a long time.

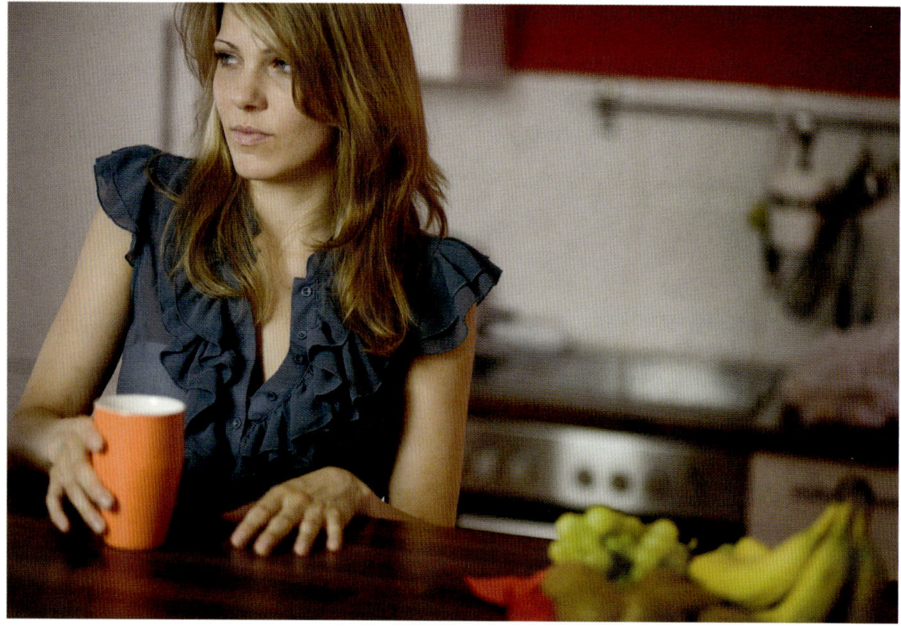

Images with many elements can come across as clearly arranged and structured if the main element is adequately emphasized through position, size, color, and focus. Additional smaller elements complete the image and provide supplementary visual information.

The effects of these principles are stronger when the visual elements are small and numerous; the effects are less obvious when only a few elements are separated within the image area. The most important of these five principles is similarity, which can quickly establish a unit; for example, several trees may be perceived as a grove or a forest. A tree and a house in close proximity, however, will sometimes be processed as a single unit if they are of the same brightness, color, or shape, or if they blend together on some other formal level.

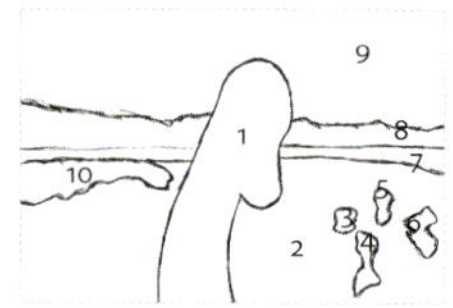

The Quantity of Visual Elements

Separating the coherent units in an image depends on several qualities that relate to the subjects: their level of detail, how easily they can be recognized, their orderliness within the image area, and their familiarity. The total quantity of visual elements within the image—not to be mistaken for the total number of objects in an image—establishes a sense of simplicity or complexity, order or disorder.

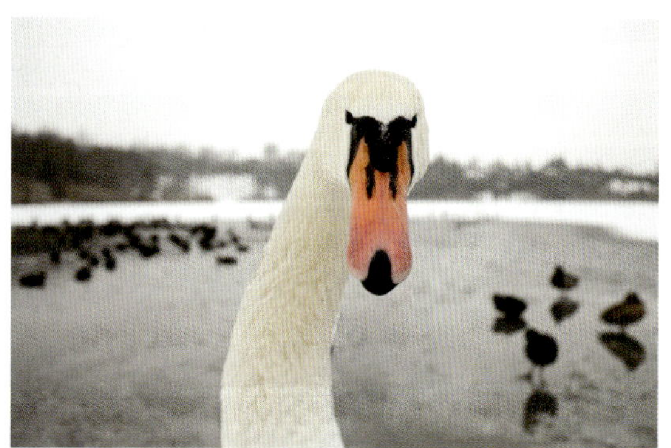

With the objective of providing viewers an interesting level of complexity that captures their attention but does not overwhelm or bore them, the number of visual elements should be manageable. You can't go wrong by employing the motto Less Is More, which is often the best way to create a clear and effective image design.

It's not possible to specify how many visual elements you should use to prevent an image from becoming too sparse. It depends on the subject, your purpose, the viewer's interests, and how the viewer absorbs information. When you shoot an overview of a busy farmers' market, for example, geometric paths through the stands can help organize the people, fruits, vegetables, and awnings into coherent units of sense. If the paths don't have this sort of structure, the details could turn into an incoherent muddle (page 71).

Main and Secondary Elements

Visual elements can be divided into three different groups, depending on their level of importance within an image. Main elements stand out because of what they are or how they look; they play a central role in the visual message of the photograph and are clearly emphasized through their size, placement, focus, alignment, geometric composition, brightness, or color. Not every image has such a clearly defined central element, but it is exceedingly rare to have two or more of such elements that are equally significant.

Secondary elements are the other coherent units that are relevant to an image. They support and complement the main element without distracting from it. Some images lack a main element and have only secondary elements. Typically, such

The comprehensive design of an image determines the main subject and the secondary subjects. In the left image the woman is clearly the main element, but in the right image she is a secondary element. The inverse is true for the house behind the model—in the left image it functions as a secondary element, and in the right image it's the primary element. The design, rather than the subject itself, establishes the significance of the elements within an image.

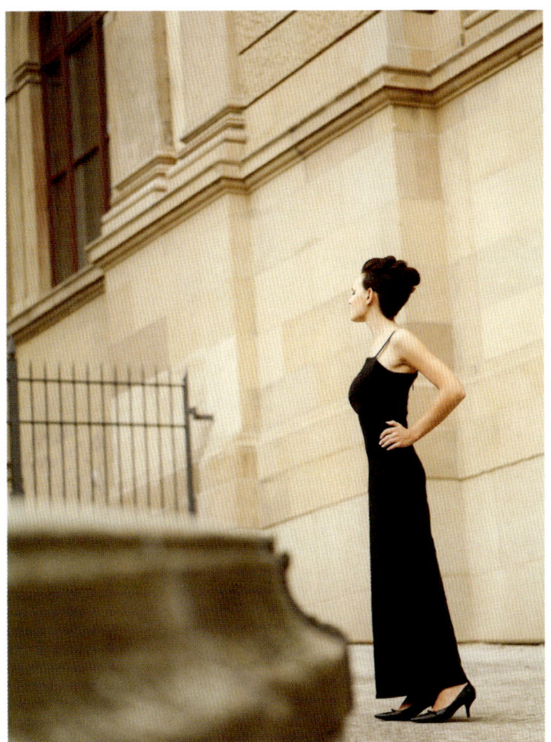

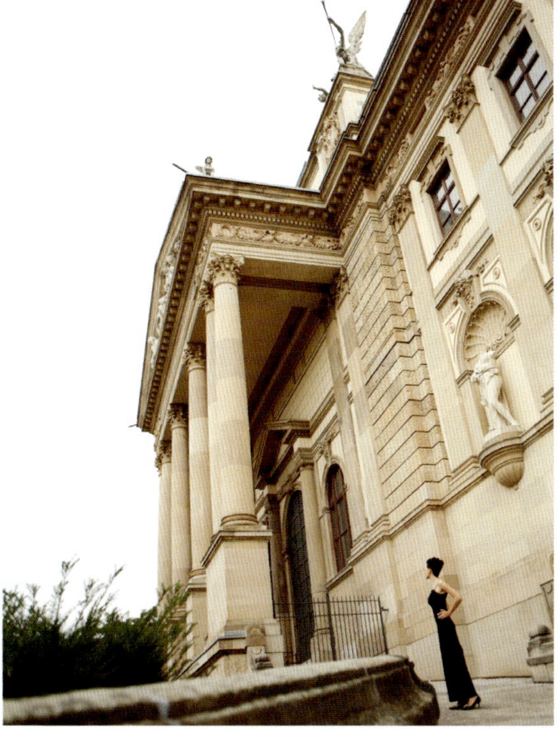

Not every element in an image is meaningful. Some could be removed entirely without detracting from the image. In this example, the people in the background are too small to contribute to the photo in any sort of meaningful way.

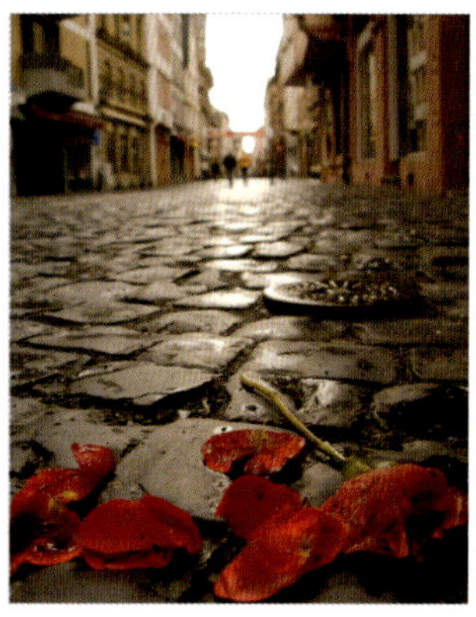

images don't feature structure or order and rely on the sheer variety of depicted elements.

The third group of elements within an image is objects that don't play any significant part in the message. They function as filler and are present but (ideally) not perceived. These objects appear in shots taken on location, when you're documenting an unaltered situation, as opposed to shots that are fully staged. Any time you have complete control over all factors in an image, these nonessential elements should not occur.

When you arrange the various elements within an image, you should make the relative importance of your subjects explicitly clear. The respective sizes of the elements play a role, as do intentional crops and their location on the border.

The Golden Ratio

The most well-known composition is the golden ratio, which refers to a unique division ratio in which the short length is identically proportional to the long length, and the long length is proportional to the sum of both lengths. Discovered in antiquity, the specific ratio is 1:1.618. Proportions that correspond to the golden ratio are considered aesthetic and pleasing. This visual relationship is less useful if you are looking for something dramatic or exciting. The golden ratio is used in the visual arts and architecture to create harmonious designs; it is also often found in the natural world. If you divide the height and width of a photo based on this ratio, you'll end up with four intersections that are ideal locations for the most important element in your image—assuming you wish to create a balanced, pleasant result. This is especially true when the one main element is relatively small in comparison to the full image area (page 78).

Situating your main subject according to the golden ratio is not a photographic cure-all, as many books about so-called rules for photography would have you believe. It creates a harmonious end result, and should be used only when it suits your subject.

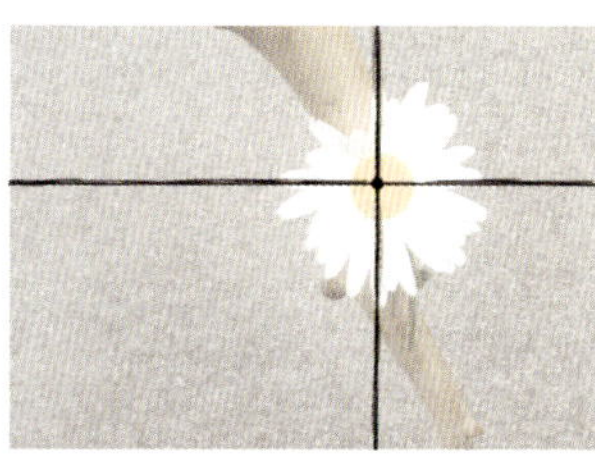

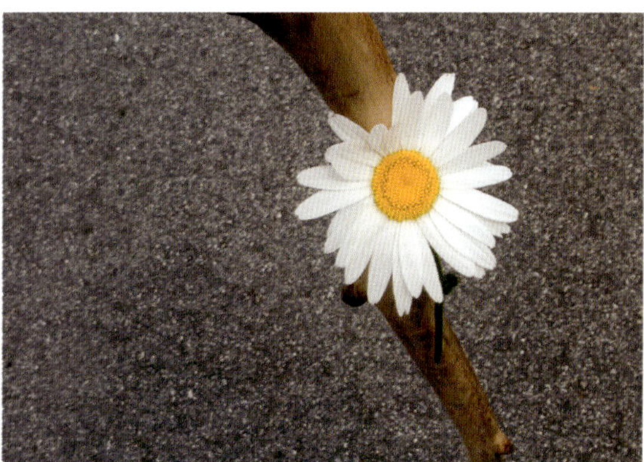

Grid Methods

There are other ways to divide the image area to arrange image elements in a balanced way. The rule of thirds says that dividing the image area into nine equal parts creates intersections that are useful for situating two main or secondary elements in a harmonious manner. Dividing the area into 12 or 16 equal areas creates intersection points that are closer to the edge of the image, thus producing balanced images that are noticeably more dynamic, with specific emphasis on the relationship between the visual elements. If only one element is used with a 16-square grid, the result is much more forceful. Grid methods help photographers establish even distances between elements and help them bring balance to their images.

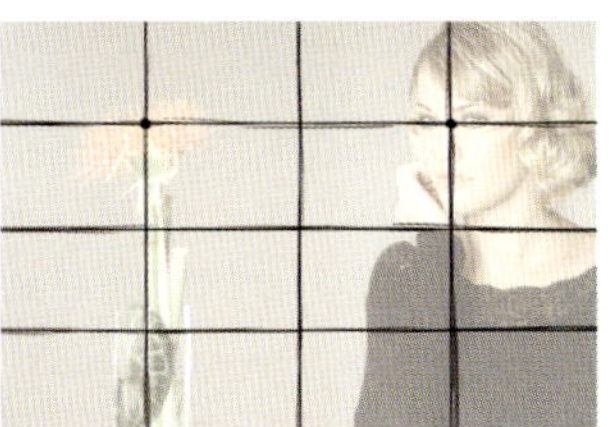

If you situate the key elements in your image along the nodes of a uniform grid, you can create stability and balance in your images. A nine-square grid emphasizes the elements themselves, and a 16-square grid brings out their relationship (or lack thereof) and the space between them.

Symmetry and Asymmetry

Another way to divide an image is to split the image area in half with either a vertical or a horizontal line. The two halves then compete in a balanced, symmetrical construction. Symmetrical arrangements give the impression of extreme balance, intention, and planning; they are associated with order and perfection—and monotony and dullness. The more central the axis of symmetry is (page 68), the stronger the static and stable effect will be. Vertical axes of symmetry divide an image more noticeably and highlight the symmetrical quality of the subject more acutely than horizontal lines of symmetry. The latter are more familiar, common, and less artificial because the viewer sees only horizontal reflections in nature, like a landscape reflected on a body of water.

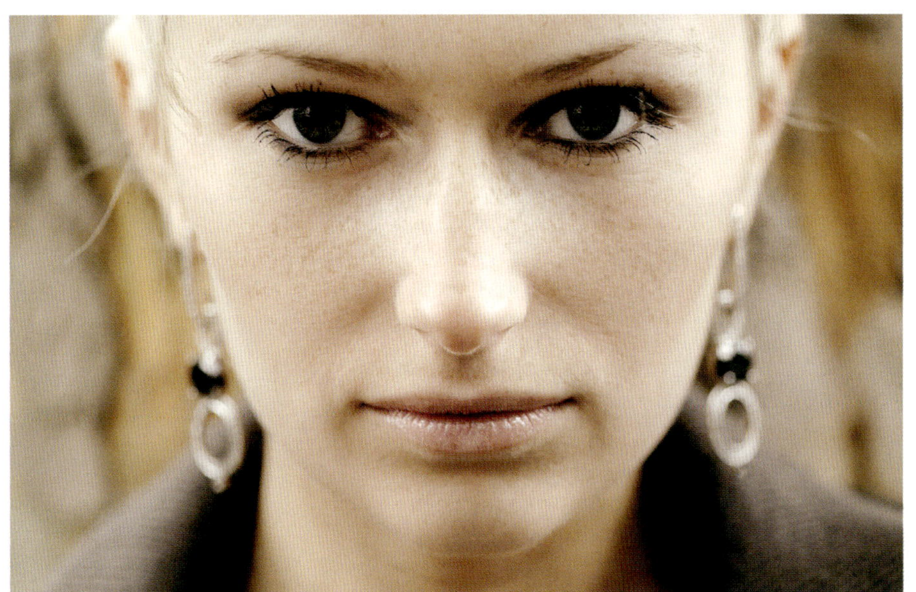

Symmetrical faces are considered especially beautiful, and a symmetrical composition can imbue this beauty with a profound stillness. To keep the viewer engaged, however, the subject itself needs to be interesting.

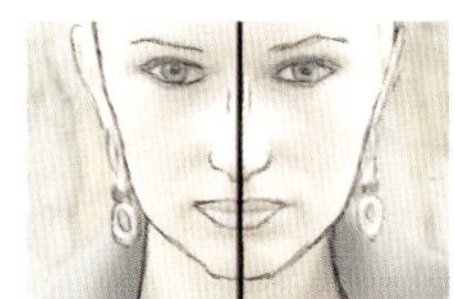

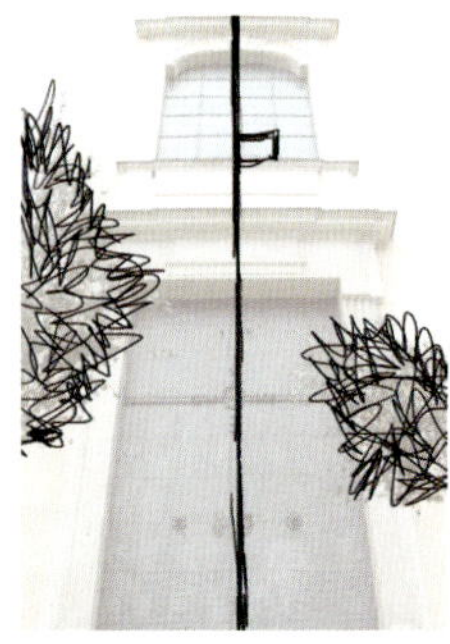

Asymmetrical elements, such as the trees here, break up the otherwise rigid structure of the image. However, the near symmetry is still the main feature of the composition.

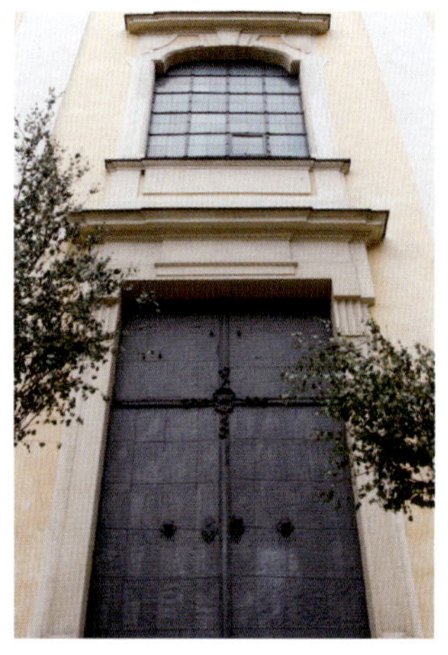

You don't need a subject that is 100 percent symmetrical to give viewers the impression of symmetry. Nearly symmetrical objects with inexact details on either side of the line of symmetry will give images a similar quality, but the closer the image is to purely symmetrical, the more viewers will notice it. Asymmetrical compositions play with the expectations of symmetrical images and intentionally have small departures to disrupt the high degree of perfection. These discrepancies draw the viewer's attention.

Unless you are working with a perfectly symmetrical object or are working in a studio, some degree of asymmetry will likely be present in your image. You can refine the symmetry by choosing a composition that looks symmetrical at first glance, and then intentionally disrupting it by capturing diverging details or by shifting or turning the axis of symmetry, causing one of the sides to have greater weight.

Asymmetry is often thought to be the opposite of symmetry, but this isn't accurate. Asymmetry describes objects that have a partial degree of symmetry or symmetry that is disrupted by irregularities. An irregular composition that has no symmetry establishes an immediately discernible imbalance among various image areas and creates contrast among different image elements. Some subjects are highlighted and emphasized, while others play a less meaningful visual role. In contrast to symmetrical and asymmetrical compositions, an arrangement without symmetry has a chaotic, lively, and dramatic visual effect.

Arranging the Main Element

If you plan to have only one element in your photo, you actually have two elements: the subject itself and the background (page 74). The subject is the main element, and the background is either a secondary element or is entirely insignificant, depending on its nature and the size of the main element. You can position the main subject within the image area based on the horizontal and vertical orientation you want.

Positioning your main subject in the horizontal center of the image area creates a static, lifeless result, but it still draws a high degree of attention. A small shift away

This figure clearly demonstrates how an image changes from static to harmonious when the main element shifts closer to the border.

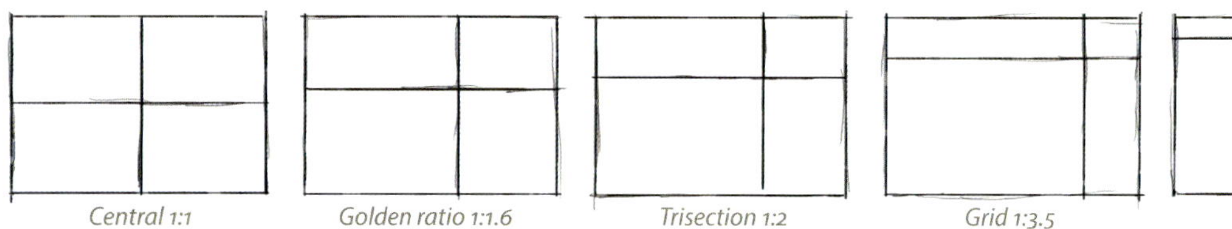

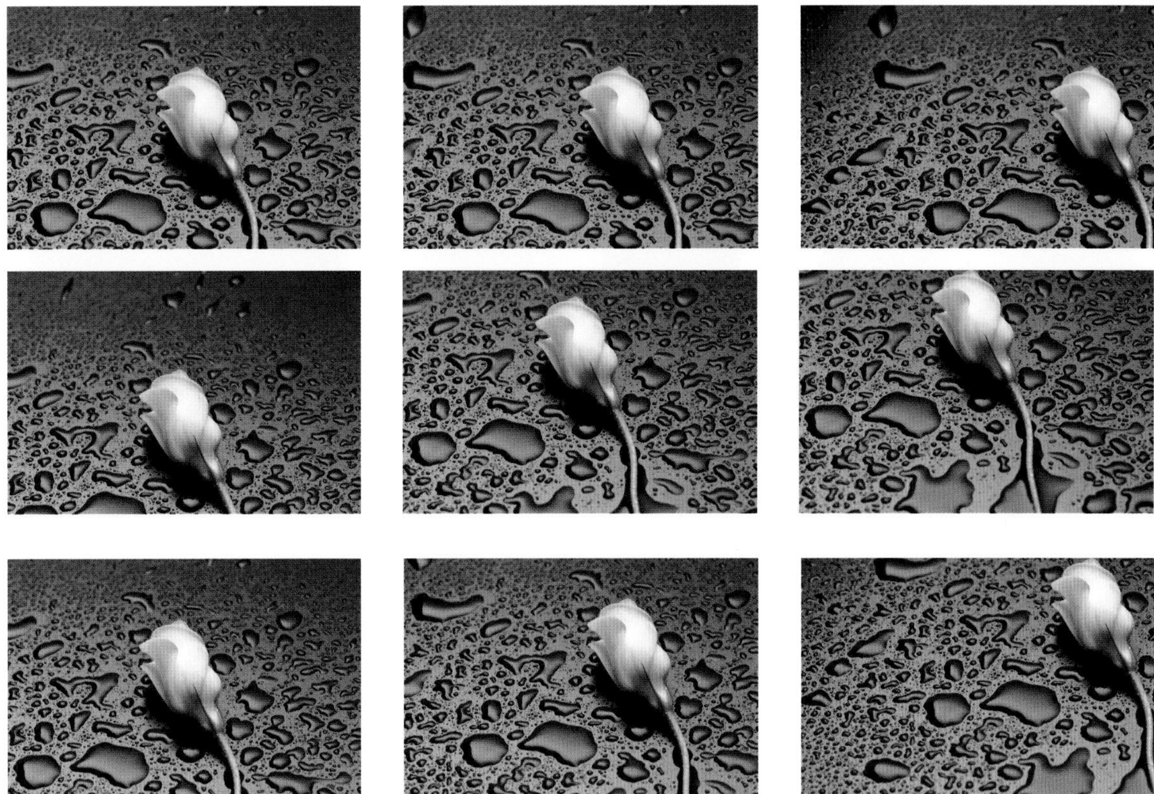

from the center also results in a quiet photo, but it has a slightly jarring asymmetry that creates a bit of life. An arrangement at the golden ratio establishes a harmonious, gentle, and balanced feel. The tension continues to rise as the subject moves closer to the image border. Placing the subject right at the border is a dramatic move that gives a high level of tension to any picture.

The results are similar with the vertical orientation, but a central alignment along the vertical axis tends to be uninteresting, even when the subject is placed in an extreme position. Furthermore, the effect of moving the subject vertically to the point of the golden ratio, and even to the edge of the image, influences the overall effect of the design to a lesser degree.

If the subject is placed on the same horizontal and vertical position—along an intersection of the golden ratio, in the exact center of an image, or in one of the corners—the noticeability of the design choice increases exponentially and the effect of stillness or tension becomes extreme. An offset visual arrangement, such as placing the main subject along the golden ratio for the horizontal axis and in the center of the vertical axis, leads to counteractive effects that reduce the intensity of the composition, but creates a more interesting interaction within the image. Such an arrangement is a simple way to give an image greater compositional depth.

Shifting the main subject horizontally (top row) invites some energy into the picture, but the central vertical positioning keeps this energy in check. The results are similar when the subject is shifted vertically (middle row), even if the increased energy is more noticeable. In combination, however, these two shifts transform the look to harmonious and then to vibrant (bottom row).

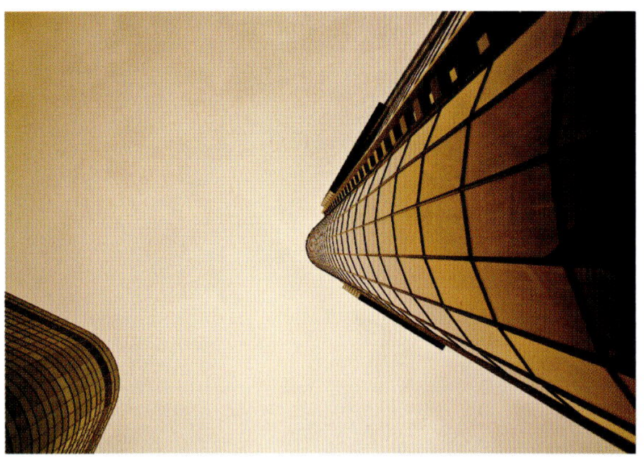

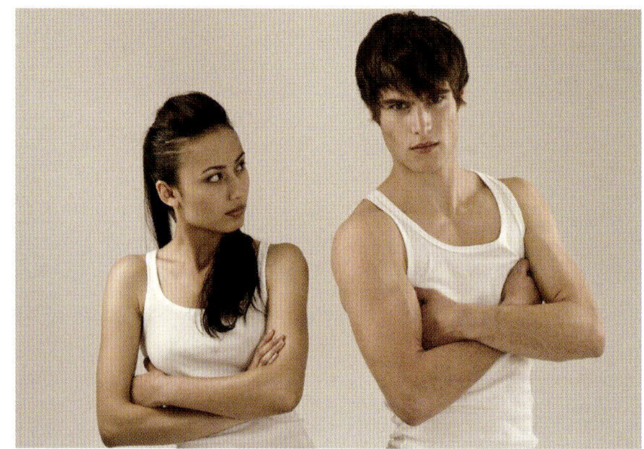

It's rare to find two evenly weighted subjects in the same photo. Usually the relative size, position, color, or a targeted crop adds emphasis to one of the subjects.

Arranging Two Elements

As soon as you bring a second key element into the picture, composition is no longer only about the spatial positioning within the image area. With multiple objects, composition is also about the position of the objects in relation to each other. The two objects inevitably influence each other and reveal a relationship—which is why they appear together in the same photo.

You can arrange two elements so they balance each other or so that one is clearly weighted more than the other. Composing the photo so both elements are equal inevitably means that they compete for the viewer's attention. This is strongest when the composition is symmetrical—when the objects mirror each other in content and form and when they are separated on a horizontal line at, and equidistant from, the center of the image.

A vertical or diagonal composition results when one object appears more dominant than the other. This occurs when objects are different distances from the center of the photo; whichever object is above the other or closer to the center functions as the more dominant feature. Viewers even interpret minor deviations above or below a horizontal alignment as meaningful. In terms of the two objects' positions, the less important of the two is usually lower or closer to the border.

The more similar the elements in a picture are, the easier it is to trace lines of connection between them. The rose, the pepper grinder, and the group in the back cause the eye to move in a triangle.

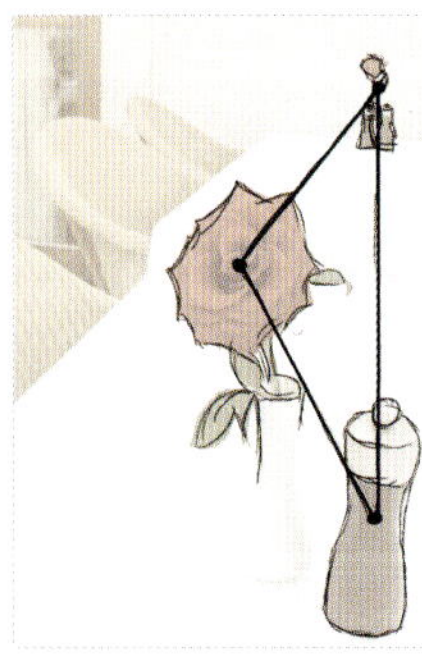

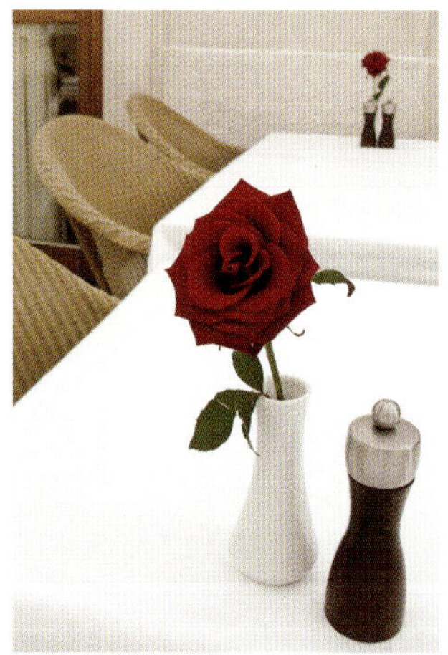

Arranging Multiple Elements

As soon as you have two objects in the same image, they inevitably establish an imaginary line of connection. When more than two elements are featured, this line plays an even more important role. If the objects are placed on a regular grid (page 66), the line becomes even stronger and usually indicates a direction of movement.

Above a certain number of elements, the complexity of the composition increases and the connecting lines become more complicated; they are often interpreted as many lines rather than a single one. It becomes especially important for you to weight your subjects clearly amidst this complexity. When you use a definite grid, establish the main and secondary elements. You can also guide the viewer's perception of the image through other elements of design, such as color, light, or focus.

Busy Scenes

Busy scenes are overview shots with so many elements that it is impossible to distinguish between main and secondary. Every object appears to have the same weight, and the viewer's eye is constantly searching for regularity, patterns, or the center of attraction. Other image design techniques, especially a purposeful geometric composition, can bring order to these busy scenes. If no other design principles are used, the exposure appears two-dimensional and viewers will interpret it as a single, chaotic plane. The eye has no obvious point of entry into the image. In the best-case scenario, the viewer's gaze will wander aimlessly around the photo. In the worst case the viewer won't even bother to engage. This problem often arises when leafless tree branches take up a large area of an image. Small, guiding lines lead in all different directions, and the branches themselves don't convey any critical information. Although these irregular patterns may be fascinating when you see them in nature, they tend to cause confusion when they are captured in a photo. These images are only successful in exceptional cases.

Images that lack clear primary or secondary elements present a challenge for the viewer's gaze, which has to search through a confusing composition. Only if the viewer is particularly interested in your subject matter will he or she take time to engage with such a photo.

When you position a seemingly countless number of subjects, effective arrangement is the first priority. The selection of elements is critical to the success of your photo. When the subjects are similar to one another, such as a pile of leaves, their uniformity gives them structure and allows them to be perceived as a single element (page 61). If the elements are dissimilar, as is often the case with details in nature, the result is usually perceived as an unorganized and chaotic mess. With subjects like these, it's critical that the viewer has a personal interest in the subject matter, otherwise he or she won't engage with the image. This is the case, for example, with group portraits featuring people that the viewer knows—the viewer will find details that will hold his or her attention longer.

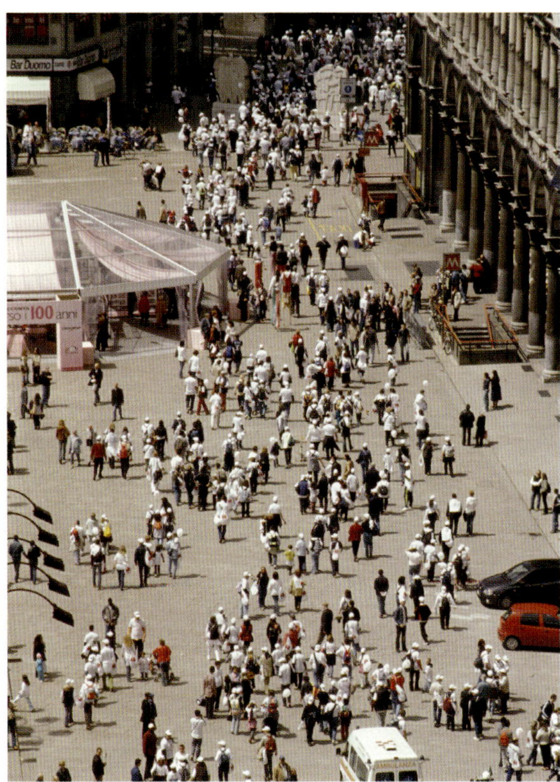

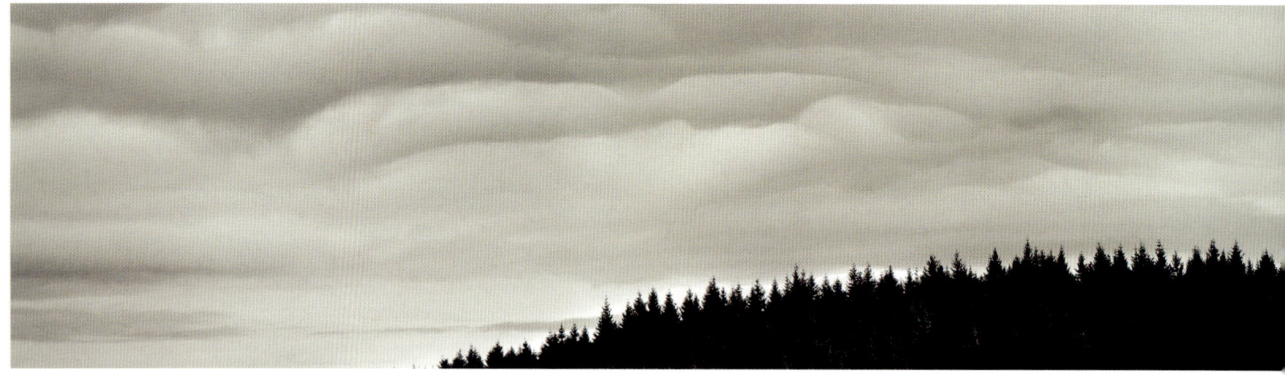

2.5 Visual Levels

The various levels of depth in this image are ambiguous. Determining what belongs on each level is key to the appeal of this exposure.

Arranging visual elements involves more than positioning them within the image area; it also requires the photographer to position the depth of the elements, despite the fact that a photograph doesn't actually have three dimensions. You can create the illusion of depth by using techniques like establishing different visual levels.

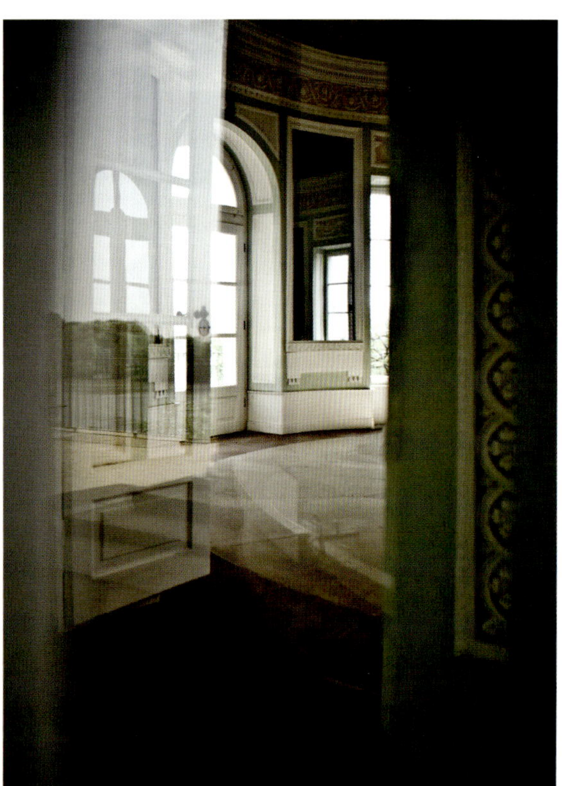

Three, Two, One Level(s)

Visual levels of depth exist as long as viewers can perceive them. These levels involve clearly distinguishable areas that appear to be in front of one another. You can achieve this effect by creating intentional areas of focus and blur, by overlapping objects, or by emphasizing size relationships within the image. Our spatial vision plays a key role in how these design methods establish levels of depth. We're familiar with the decreasing level of focus in front of and behind the in-focus object (page 179), we know that objects are often hidden behind others, and we can interpret information from the relative sizes of objects; for example, we know that a house must be a good distance behind a man if they appear to be the same height (page 105).

The more levels a photo has, the more strongly it will establish the illusion of depth. In general, three levels suffice to convey the depth of an image: foreground, middle ground, and background. The combination of these levels corresponds to our familiar,

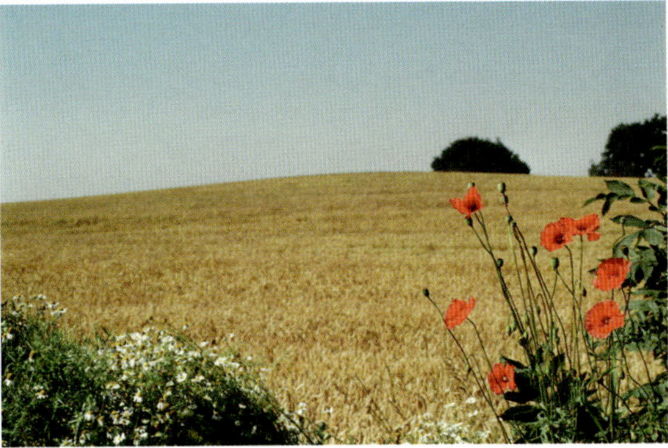

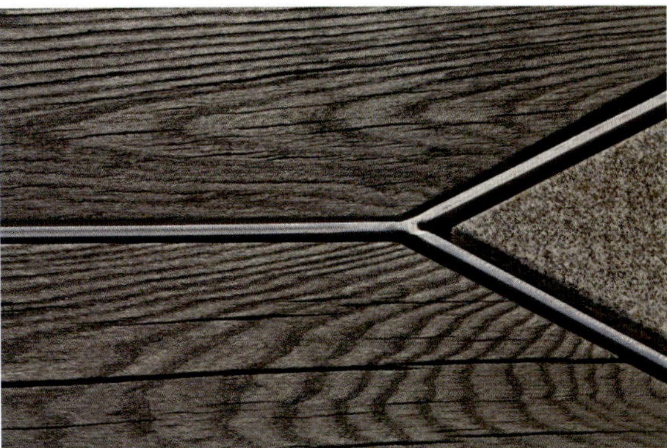

You can clearly see three visual levels in the image on the left: foreground, middle ground, and background. These levels establish a strong sense of depth that is lacking in the image on the right, which appears flat due to its single level of depth.

realistic way of seeing. Conversely, images with only one level of depth come across as two-dimensional and flat. Even if the subject has multiple levels, there's no guarantee that they will show up effectively in an image—tight crops, for example, make it possible to only show one level in the final image.

Foreground

In images that rely on classical composition methods and feature three clear levels, the foreground is the location for all of the visual elements that are supposed to appear in front of the main subject. Blur or harsh crops often reduce the prominence of these elements. Only rarely should the foreground contain the primary subject, and it should make sense to separate the levels behind it.

When a photo only has two levels of depth, the main element is almost always featured in the foreground. Photographers may break this rule when they wish to use small secondary elements, such as accessories in a portrait, to complement the main subject in the background.

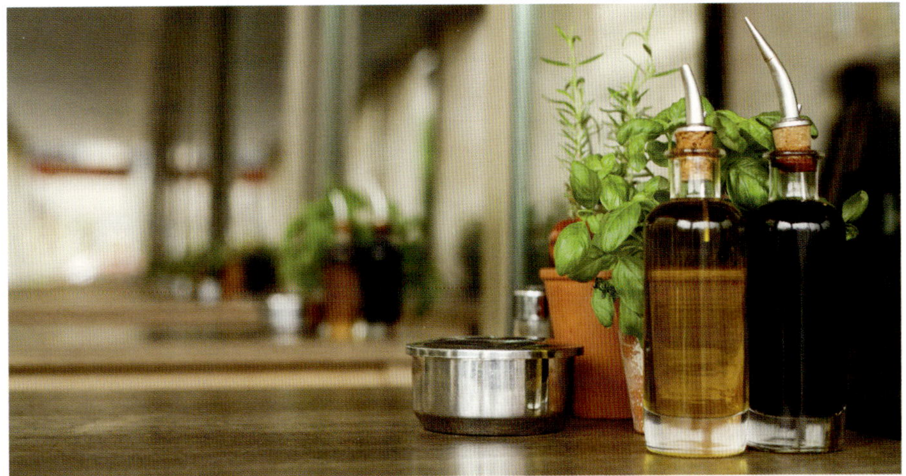

Placing the main subject in the foreground and using the rest of the visual depth to establish context is a very effective image composition. The spatial effect is very similar to how we normally see.

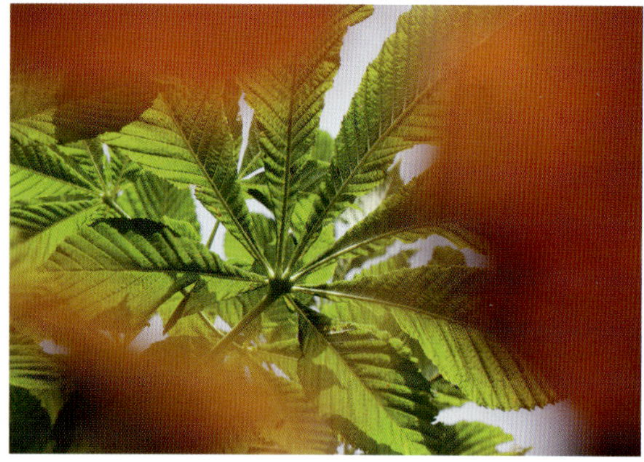

Middle Ground

The middle ground is the range that exists between the foreground and the background—its very existence is defined by the presence of these other two levels of depth. This is usually the location for the main subject, so this level is often in sharp focus while the levels in front of and behind it are often out of focus. The distance of this level is also relative to the other two levels, and it can vary greatly with respect to the position of the camera.

Composing an image by situating the main element in the middle ground and including additional elements in the foreground and background is as classic as it is popular. However, just because this tried-and-true method is a classic, doesn't mean it can't yield unexpected results.

Background

Everything that appears behind the main subject is considered the background, whether it's a backdrop, a uniform structure, or a surface that lacks specific information. This sort of plain surface is often found in studio photography, where the background functions as a sort of canvas for the subject. If the surface is white, black, or gray, it influences the emotional effect of an image through its brightness or darkness. Colorful background surfaces impart much stronger emotional information (page 150).

Exposures snapped outside of a studio generally feature more expressive backgrounds because even uniform structures, such as walls, shrubs, or similar surfaces, convey meaningful visual information. If the background plays a significant role in a photo, it can establish a context or complement the subject through its detail, structure, pattern, shape, and texture.

In some cases the main subject appears in the background, which naturally gives this level of depth added emphasis and reassigns the foreground to a supporting role. It's also possible to completely wipe out the background—either by isolating the subject with a mask or by applying a close crop that reduces an image to one level of depth.

Even a simple background can convey meaningful visual information. A uniform studio backdrop does this strictly through color (right), and a natural background in an uncontrolled environment supports the image with details and texture (left).

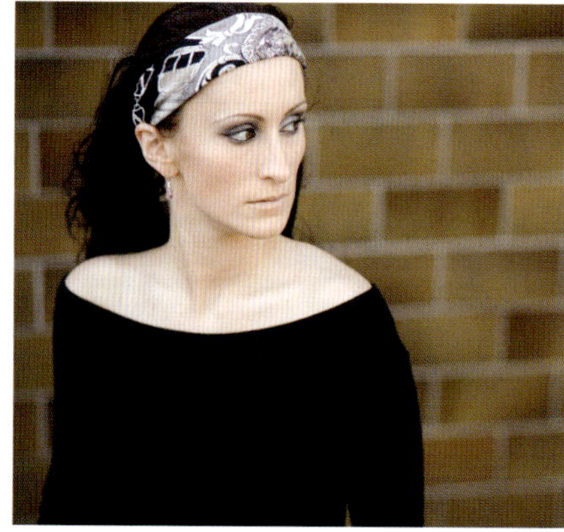

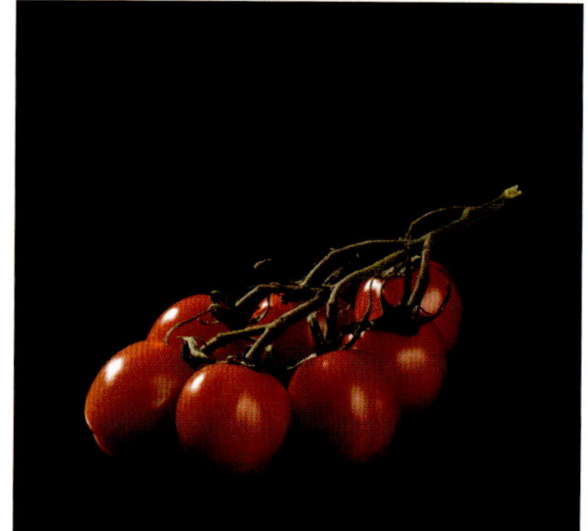

Weighting

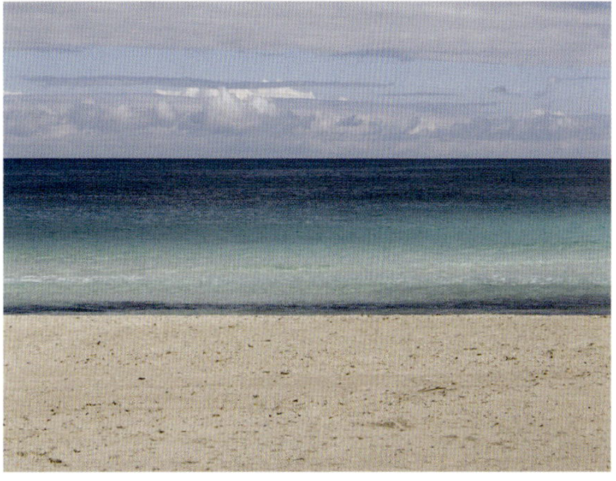

We are used to seeing the different visual levels of an image correspond to the bottom, middle, and top parts of a picture. It's familiar to have the foreground appear at the bottom of the image, the middle ground at the central region of the image, and the background at the top. These areas generally correspond to a third of the total image area. This practice and its familiarity stem from the world of landscape photography, where the distance to the subject makes this sort of composition necessary. Use this division only when you want to balance the weight of the different levels in your image. Be aware: this composition can be monotonous if you don't supplement it with other design accents.

Images that feature an equal emphasis on the three levels of depth come across as ordered and the viewer can engage comfortably with the content, as shown here with the beach, the water, and the sky. However, since this composition doesn't challenge the viewer's perception, it may not keep his or her attention.

It can be much more exciting when you give one visual level more weight than another. This effect can be all the more dramatic when the broadest level of visual depth also contains the main element of your photo, since this weighting gives additional gravity to your primary subject. If, however, you decide to place the main subject in a narrower level, you can create a dramatic interplay between the main element and the largest level of depth (page 72).

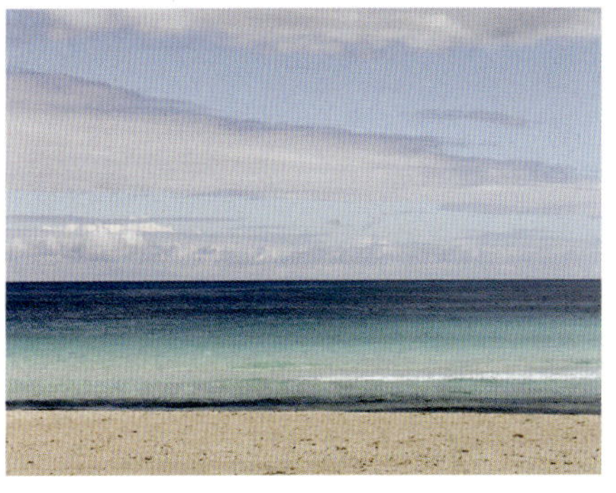

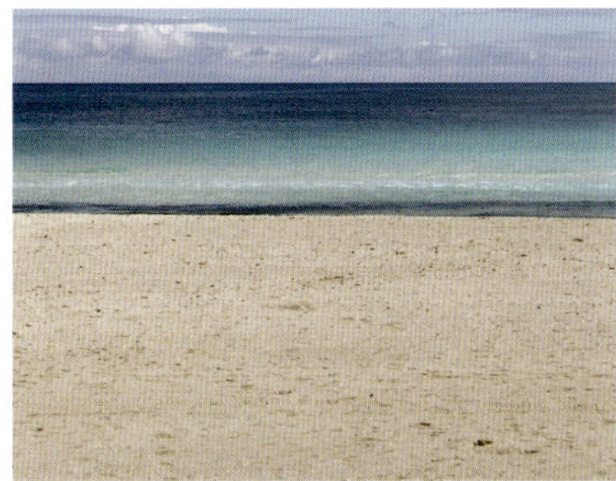

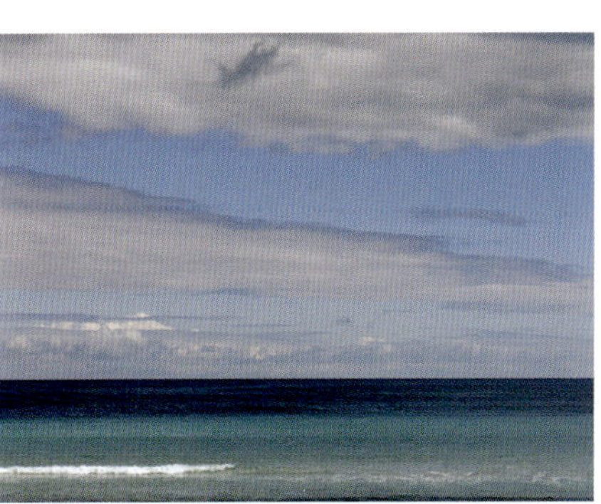

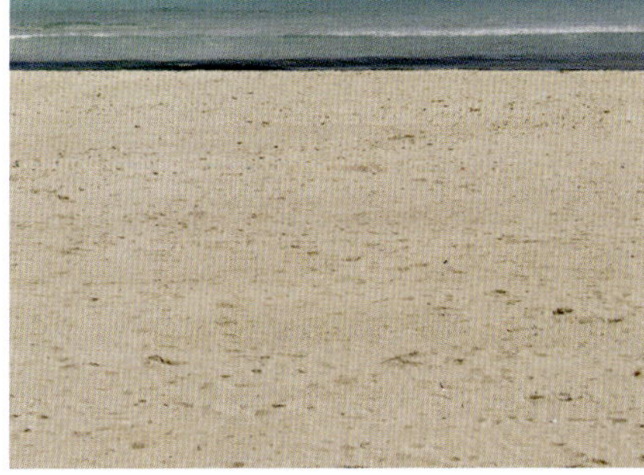

It's much more interesting for the viewer when the different areas of an image are uneven and contrast markedly with one another. You can get a sense of how this affects an image by applying different crops to a photo.

"Small things make perfection, but perfection is no small thing." Henry Royce, British carmaker

03 Shapes and Lines

When photographers talk about image design, the conversation almost reflexively centers on two topics: the golden ratio and prevailing lines. The conversation often never extends beyond these two issues. Aside from the arrangement of subjects, the process of designing with points, lines, shapes, and patterns guides the discussion of image design and the way we perceive the elements of the photograph. Yet shapes and lines are only a small portion of the whole range of design tools.

These graphical design tools are very important for the layout and rhythm of the entire image, partially because photographers use these tools to direct the viewer's gaze. In an exaggerated sense, the photographer can use this element of design to create a well-marked map for a hike along a paved trail or an adventurous backpacking tour through the backcountry. Not every viewer will care for both types of journeys, and the difference between a visual hiking path and aimless wandering often lies in the eye of the beholder.

Aside from this, geometric design establishes other features of the image—the relationships of areas to one another, for example, and the spatial or flat effect of the image. These geometric elements of design are familiar. They are analyzed in detail in the world of painting, where they are better known, which makes carrying them over to the world of photography all the easier. Maybe that's the reason image design often gets reduced to shapes and lines.

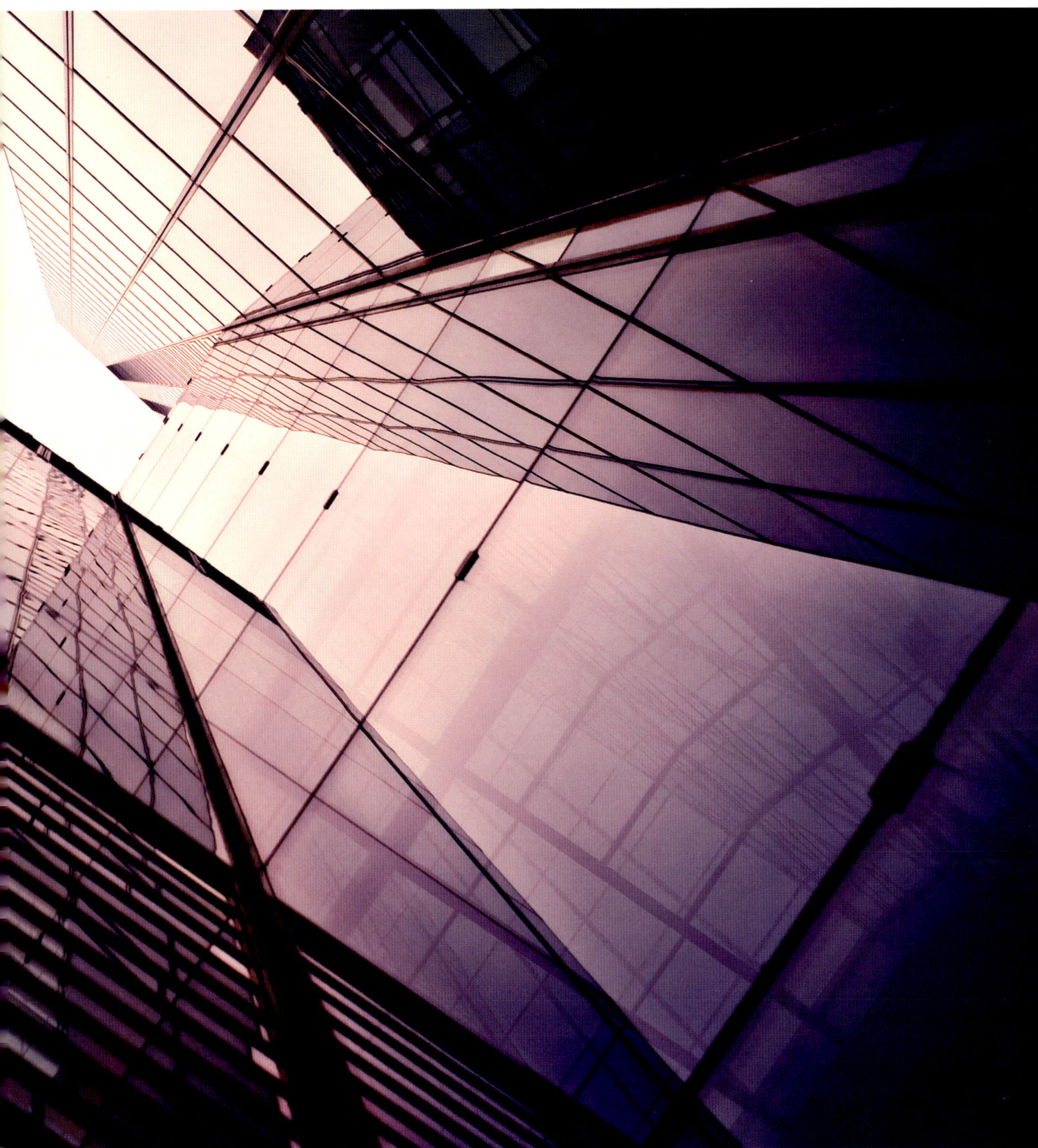

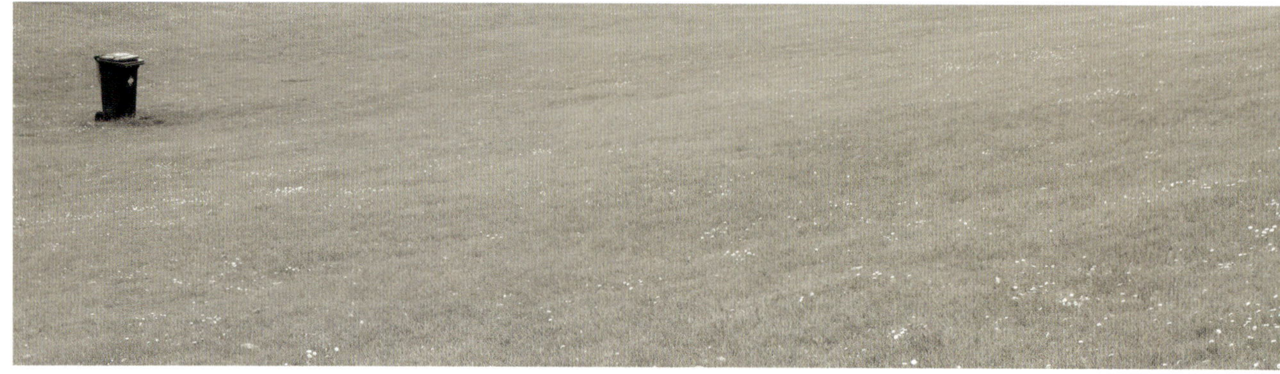

3.1 Points

Points are the smallest of the graphical elements, and they are principally defined by one variable: their size. The umbrella term *point* encompasses more than a dot from the tip of a brush in painting, or the smallest unit in an image editing or graphics program. Instead, a point means any small area—small being relative to what else is in the image—that is clearly separate from the rest of the image and dramatically stands out from its surroundings.

Points are small visual elements that can be perceived as individual units. They don't need to be round, as the image on the right demonstrates. They also don't need to be a single object; the sandals function as a single point even though it is technically made up of two objects.

Appearance

Every conceivable subject—every object, plant, animal, person, building, and so on—can become a point if it appears small with respect to the total image area. The exact moment that a point becomes a larger object within an image is not easy to define. The main characteristics of a point are that it attracts attention, can be perceived in a moment, dominates an image, visually anchors a photo, and has a static effect by itself. Individual points don't impart dynamic qualities, even on a subcon-

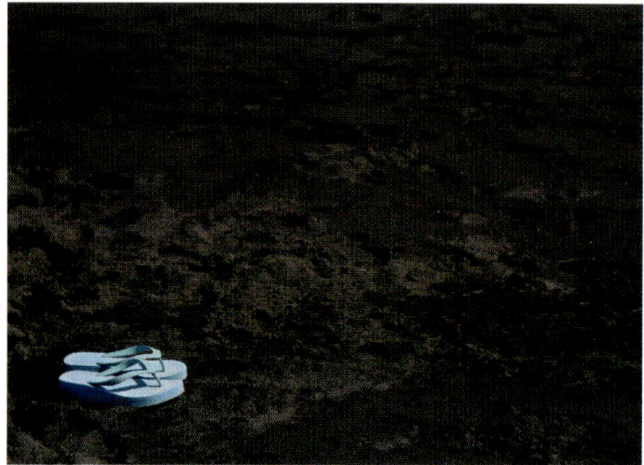

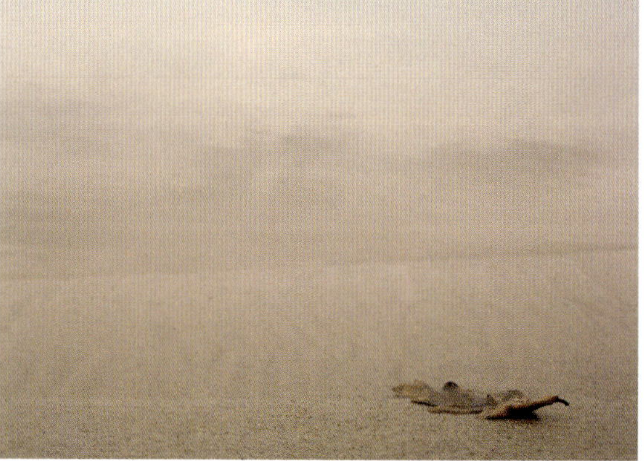

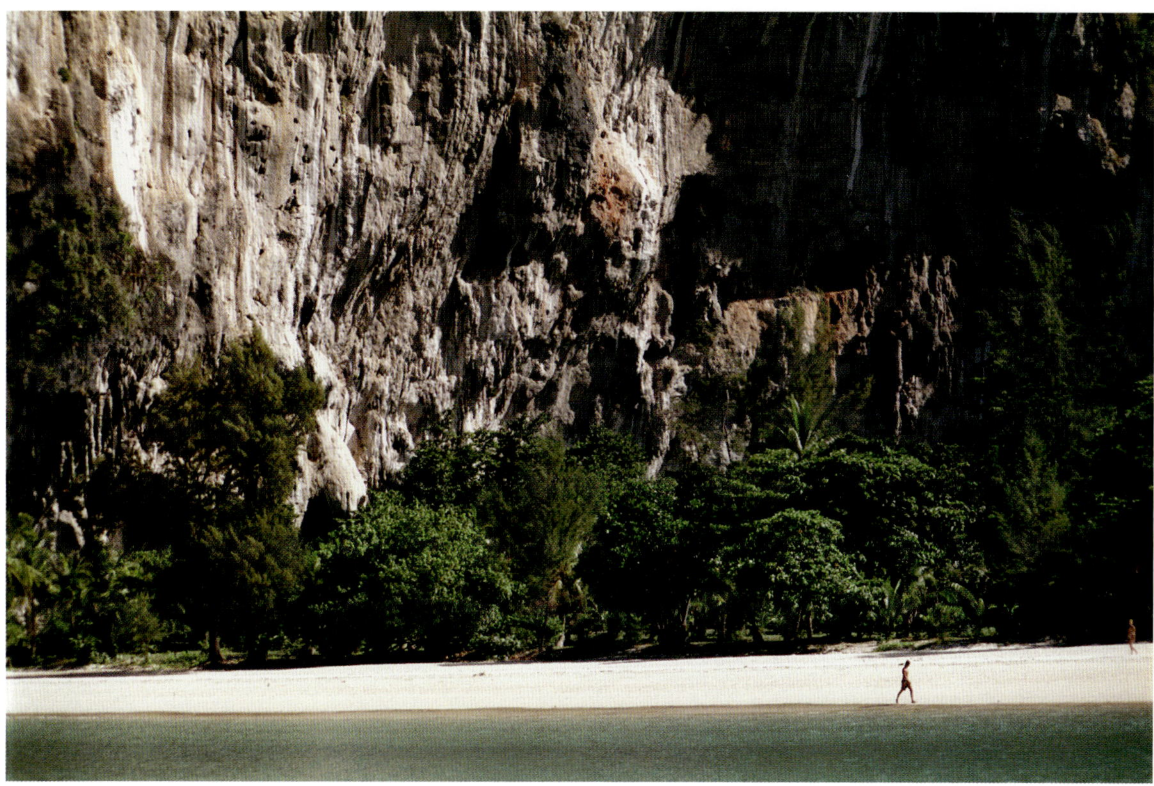

The small figure of a person serves two purposes in this image: a point of reference for the immensity of the surroundings and an attention-grabber. His small, dark shape stands out against the bright sand behind him, making him all the more irresistible to look at. The bright and orange parts of the cliffs also serve as anchor points to pull the viewer's gaze away from the person. This encourages the viewer to actively engage with the whole area of the image by inspecting many elements rather than examining only one small detail.

scious level. They can be any representational or abstract shapes. Despite their small size, the viewer will try to determine what they are. Points are most effective when they are markedly different from their surroundings in terms of brightness or color; that is, when there is a strong contrast between the point and the surrounding area.

Anchors and Attention-Grabbers

If a point plays an important role, especially when it's the most important part of a composition, it should ideally exhibit a stark contrast with its surroundings. If it is obviously emphasized within the image, it will capture the viewer's attention immediately. Visual points have the potential to dominate an image and command the viewer's attention. This is why points are known as anchors and attention-grabbers. People, especially faces, attract the viewer's attention, as do sources of danger, logos, symbols, and familiar attention-grabbers such as traffic lights.

Anchors are points that direct the viewers' gaze within an image (page 27). Viewers immediately settle their gaze on a visual anchor point and then quickly move to the next point. Although anchor points command viewers' immediate attention, they can't retain it for long because they don't deliver much visual information. It's important to have a second visual anchor in the image to keep the viewers engaged.

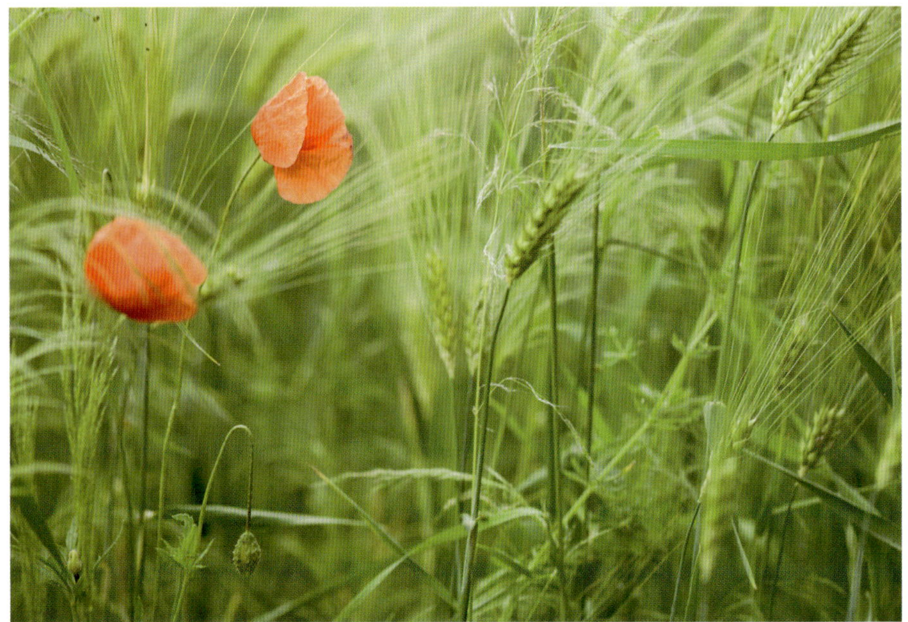

The two poppies markedly contrast with their background and function as two individual points because of their shape and size. Their arrangement in the photo encourages the viewer to create a line from the lower left flower to the upper right flower (because of our direction of reading), even though this line doesn't actually exist. Nonetheless, the relationship between these two distinct points creates a dynamic effect.

Multiple Points

When a photo features multiple points, viewers perceive the distance between the anchors as connected by an imaginary line (page 82). The similarity of the points determines how strongly this connection is felt. The imaginary lines between points work in the same way as actual lines, with an equally strong effect. Multiple points within a single image can give the photo a sense of movement because the viewer's attention follows the progression along the invisible connections from one point to the next. The direction of travel is determined by the dominance of the points; the viewer will focus on the most conspicuous point first, followed by the second most conspicuous point, then the third, and so on.

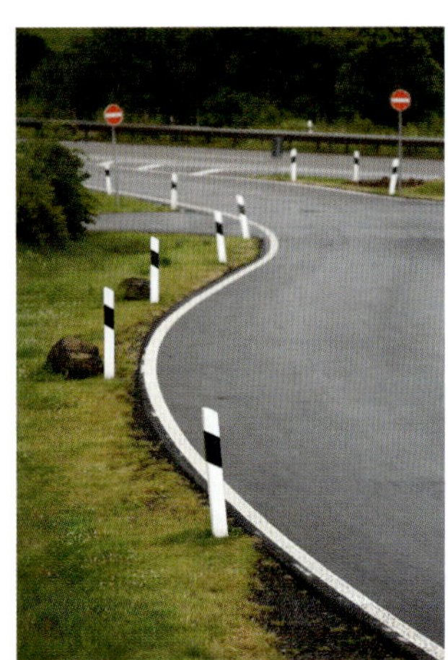

The anchor points in a picture don't always pull the viewer's attention to a part of the image that contains important or interesting visual information. Distracting points in the background break up the natural flow of an image. Keep an eye out for undesirable points in the backgrounds of your images and make frequent use of the depth-of-field preview button to keep them under control.

Distracting Points

The fact that points command attention despite their relatively small size means they can be disadvantageous when they are unimportant or superfluous, like dust, spots on the sensor, light reflections, garbage lying on the ground, or spots on the asphalt. Bright spots on the dark ground, dark spots on the bright ground, loud colors, geometric shapes, and symbols can be disturbing if their potential to attract attention is not controlled. They throw the balance of a photo into disarray.

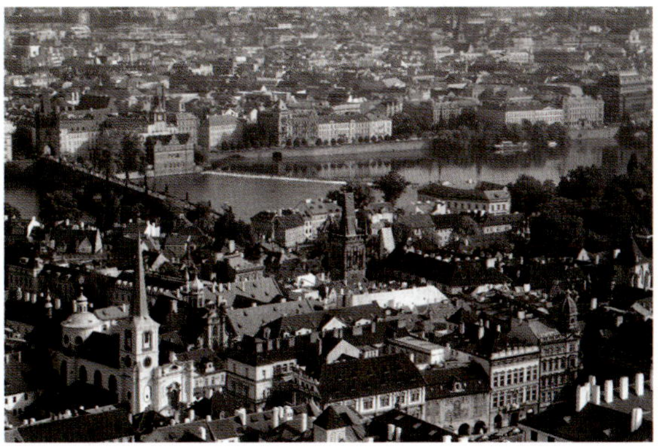

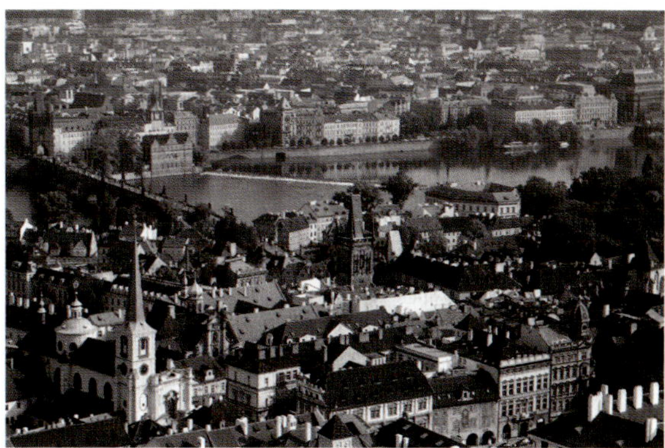

When you shoot images, be on the lookout to make sure that small visual elements don't cause unwanted distractions in your photos. Even if you can remove distracting points with image editing software, you can often eradicate these problems while shooting. Choose a vantage point without disturbing points—especially in the potentially blurry background and near the borders. Conspicuous geometric shapes (page 96) such as traffic signs, loud color on umbrellas, colorfully dressed people, or incidental details, can attract the eye so strongly that viewers will hardly see the main subject in the foreground. If these distracting elements are positioned too close to a border, the attention-grabbing effect can cause the viewer's gaze to move out of the image. Even the smallest high-contrast points have the power to do this.

Light points near the border of an image are especially distracting. They pull the viewer's attention away from the subject and out of the picture entirely (left). If you get rid of these areas by cropping or clone stamping them away, you'll end up with a much calmer result (right).

Invisible Points

Visual points serve as important stepping stones as the viewer begins to engage with a photo. But the visible points within an image are not the only ones that command attention—the invisible ones do, too. Invisible points occur anywhere that lines cross, bend, or touch (page 82), since the human brain naturally continues any perceived line along its current trajectory. This process occurs as long as there are no other image elements or anchor points that obstruct this continuation.

This effect also occurs when multiple lines converge toward one point; the point at which they would meet is subconsciously perceived as though it were actually in the image. Invisible points are not as dominant as visible ones, but they can't be disregarded, especially when they are established as part of formative lines; for example, vanishing lines may converge at a point either within or beyond the image area (page 89).

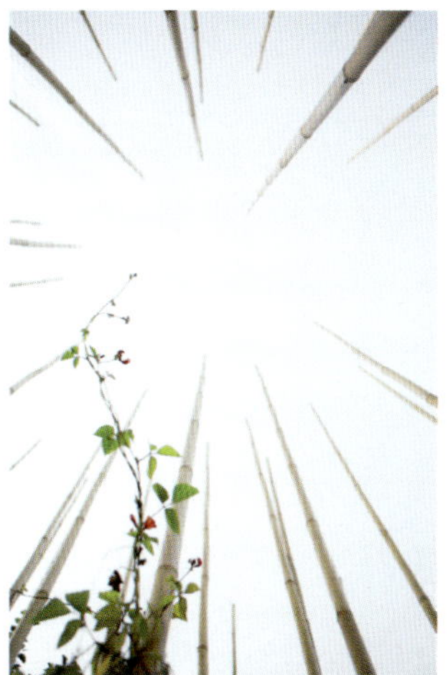

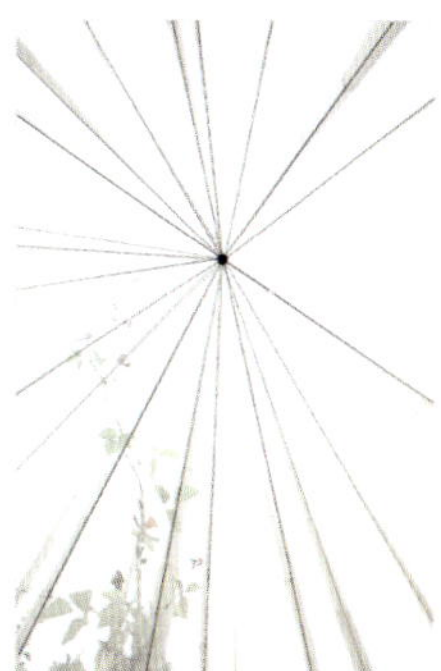

The point of intersection for these bamboo stalks is near the middle of the image. Our gaze instinctively moves to this spot, where it perceives a visual point, even though nothing is actually there.

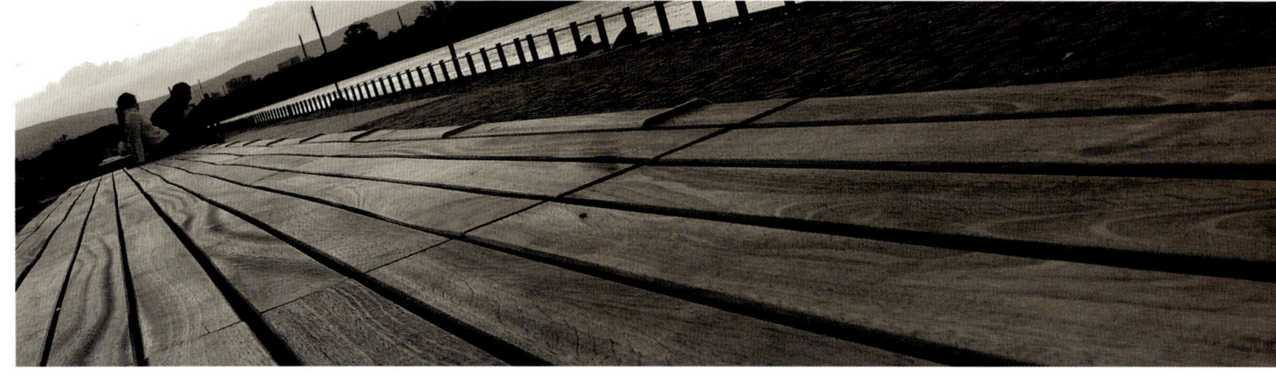

3.2 Lines

In contrast to static points, lines are dynamic because not only do they attract and capture the viewer's eye, they also lead it throughout the image. You might think of lines as the guardrail or the road for the viewer's gaze. Lines stand out for three reasons: first, they are a dominant feature in any picture; second, because of their length; and third, because of their direction. The net effect of all the lines in an image is referred to as linear composition. This particular element of design is one of the most powerful and one of the most likely to result in problematic images.

Appearance

Not all lines are the same. Like with points, some lines are visible and others are imaginary. Lines that are actually present in an image may occur where the contours of objects or creatures overlap, or they may result from long individual elements: tree trunks, branches, plant stems, lampposts, poles, rails, gutters, human bodies, arms, legs, rivers, streets, paths, and so forth.

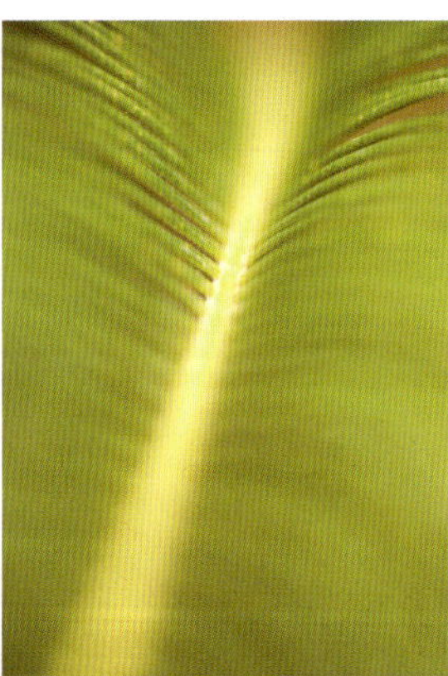

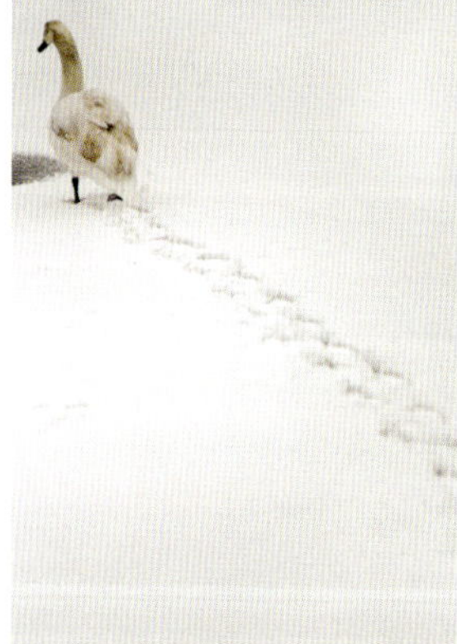

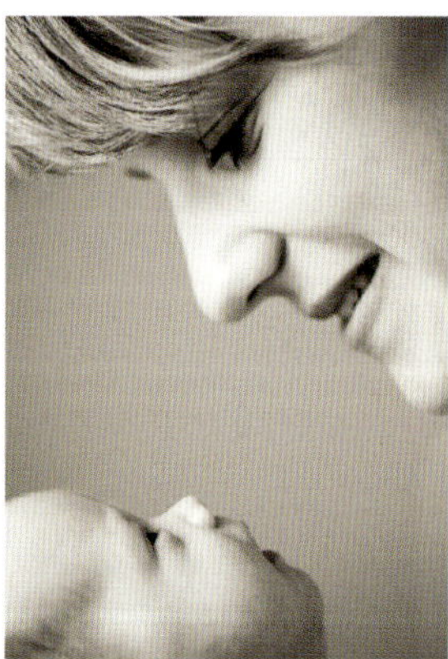

In the image on the left, the lines are actually present. On one hand, they exist because of the contrasting color between the stalk in the middle and the green of the leaf; on the other hand, they are present as a result of the dark spaces between the individual fibers. In the middle image, our brain connects the clues in the snow to create a solid line, even though it is actually individual, unconnected points or footprints. In the right image, the gazes of the mother and child establish an invisible but very strong line that connects their faces.

Partially visible lines don't appear completely solid in an image, either because they are broken up by another visual element or because they are composed of small individual elements. This is how multiple visual points form a line when they are arranged in a row, especially when all of the points are similar in appearance (page 62). The human brain naturally connects these dots instead of perceiving them as individual elements.

The third type of line is the imagined lines. These may arise from the direction of a person's or animal's sight, or they may connect two elements within the image area. Even though these lines are invisible, they function in the same way as actual lines.

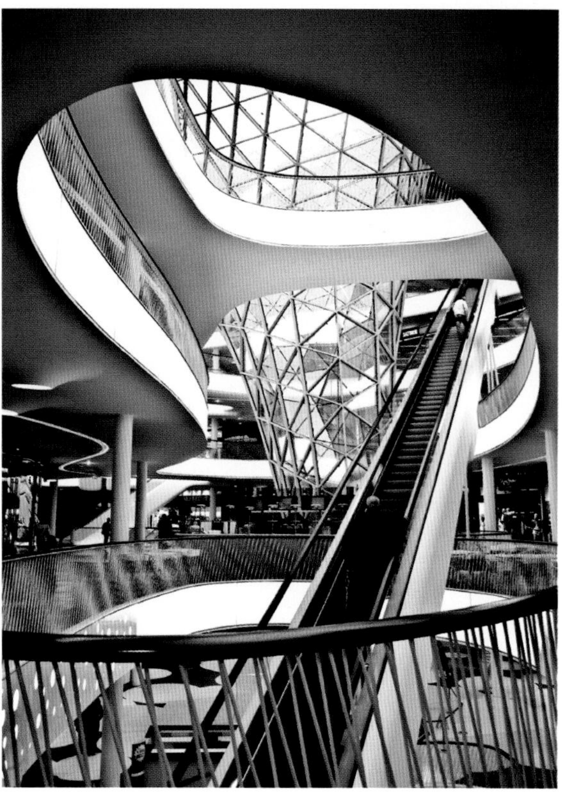

Lines don't have to be straight to direct the viewer's attention—curved lines can also achieve this. This image depicts several main lines and many secondary lines. When lines are too conspicuous they dominate an image, causing viewers to examine the image based on its lines instead of its content.

Linear Composition

Not every line within an image has the same level of significance. The extent to which a line serves as a guardrail for the eye depends on its dominance, which is based on its thickness, color, brightness, texture, and contrast with the immediate surroundings. The prevalence of a line also depends on the total number of lines in the image—the more lines there are, the less significant each one becomes. Longer lines generally have a stronger effect than shorter ones, but when a line is so long that it traverses the entire area of an image, it loses its function as a guide for the viewer's gaze and becomes more of a structural frame or an internal border.

If a prevalent line reaches an image border and has the potential to lead the viewer's gaze out of the photo, you should ideally include an additional feature to prevent the viewer from disengaging with the photo. This can be an area that's more blurry or darker than the rest of the image, a line that runs in the opposite direction, or an interesting element that is positioned near the point in question.

Lines serve purposes other than directing the viewer's gaze. In images with only one main element, managing the lines becomes unimportant, while the character and attention-grabbing capability of the line becomes more significant. In exceptionally busy photos that feature many short lines or lines that move in many different directions, other characteristics, such as the shape and color of the lines, are important because they serve as anchor points for the viewer's attention. If a photo like this does not have resting points, it will come across as chaotic.

If there aren't any lines in an image because it's essentially a composition of surfaces that lack noteworthy contrast, it will function like a pictograph. A lack of lines

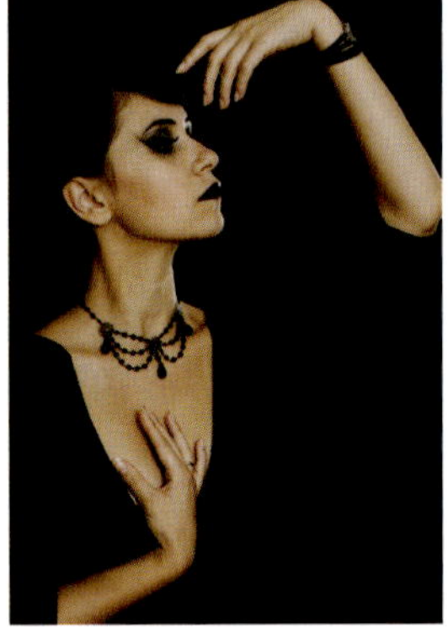
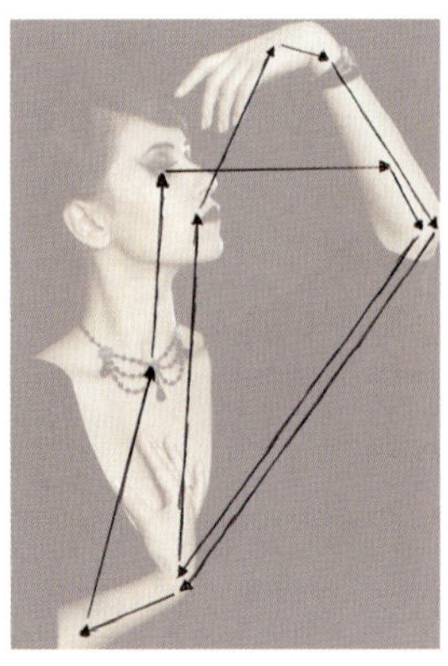
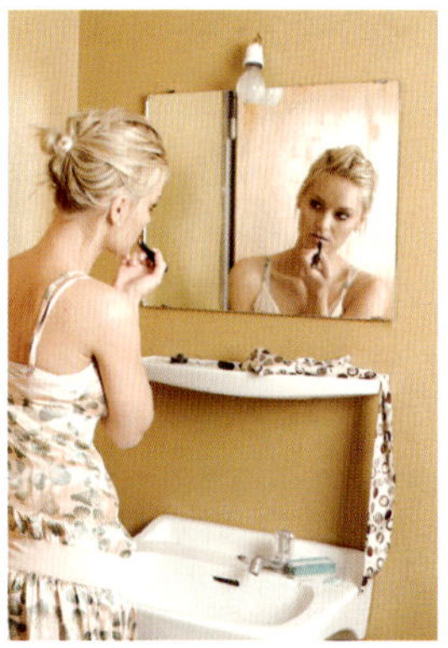
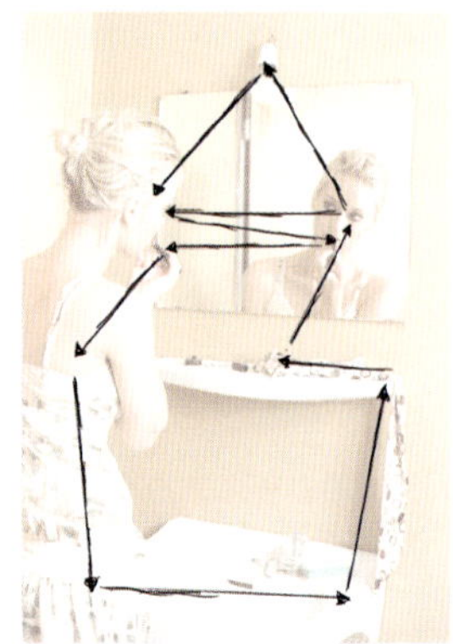

A linear composition that is contained within itself is ideal for complex images of exciting and interesting subjects. Since this composition holds the viewer's gaze within the image, he or she will continue to examine it for a longer period of time.

leads to a flat impression; the image can be perceived quickly and immediately disregarded. Ideally, all the lines will work collectively, independent from the actual content of the image, to lead the viewer's gaze in a way that corresponds to the original idea behind the photo. The clearer and smoother the lines are within an image, the easier it is for the viewer to follow the photographer's intention. If the lines are contained, they will encourage the viewer to engage with an image for a longer time.

Contained Systems of Lines

The goal of a contained system of lines is to keep the viewer's attention focused on the most important parts of the subject and to keep the viewer interested in the image. The photographer strives to contain the movement of an image within itself. If the viewer's gaze is led to the border and out of an image, then the viewer was not engaged with the photo for very long.

In some contexts, however, like in an advertising illustration, the goal of the line arrangement may be to capture the viewer's attention and direct it to a specific object outside the image, such as a product photo, brand, or logo. In these cases a contained system of lines is counterproductive; it's much more common and useful to exploit lines with the purpose of directing the viewer's attention to something outside the photo.

Simple marks on a white background clearly demonstrate the effect that the direction of a dominant line can produce in an image.

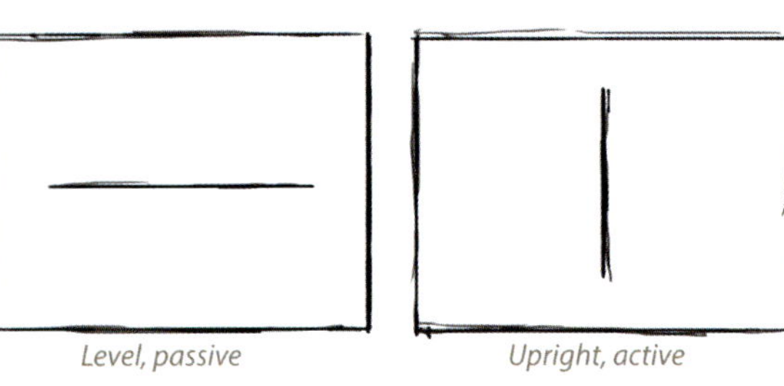

Level, passive

Upright, active

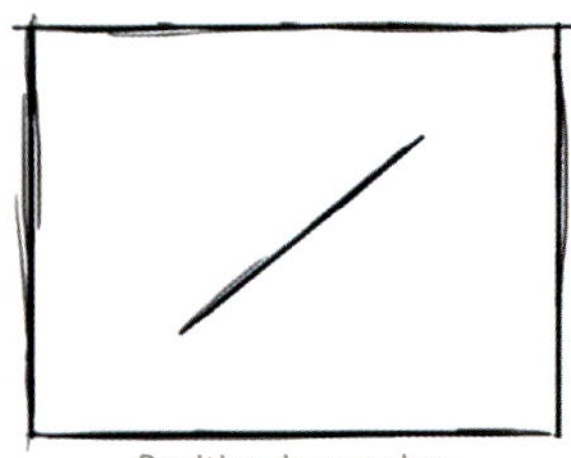

Positive, increasing

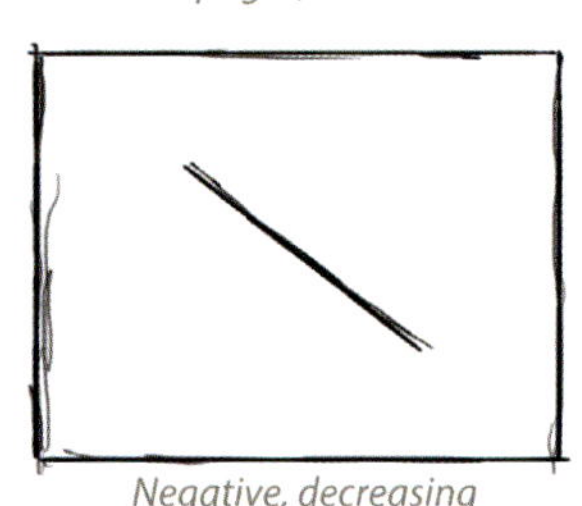

Negative, decreasing

Movement and Countermovement

The viewer's reading direction plays a significant role in the way that individual lines influence them. Here in the West, we read from the top left corner to the bottom right. It's not unusual to first examine a picture at the top left for just this reason. We interpret a line's direction of movement with respect to our standard direction of reading.

This doesn't mean you can't have countermovement in an image, such as a line that zigs and zags or a specific subject moving on its own against our traditional direction of reading, such as a jogger or a moving car. This may result in back-and-forth movement within the image, or it may result in an image that must be viewed in the direction opposite of what we're used to, which can be confusing and unusual. Movement against our reading direction tends to seem slow, and movement with our reading direction tends to seem fast (page 187).

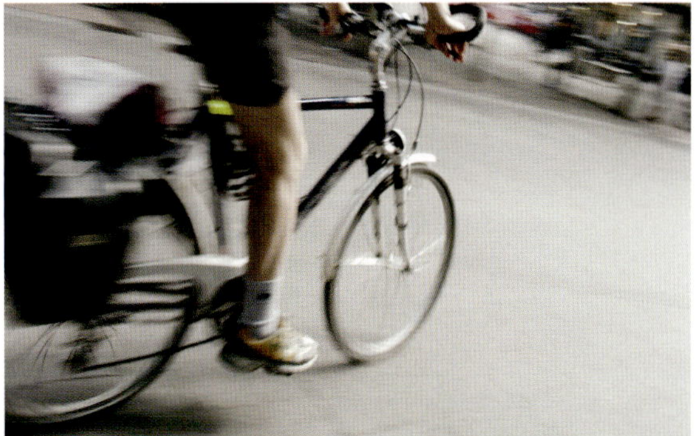

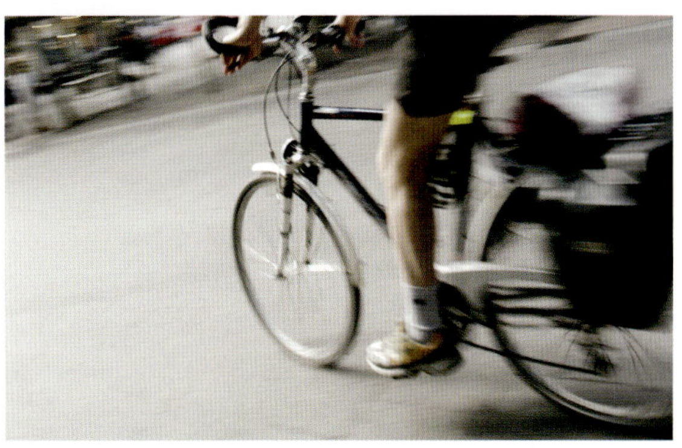

Lines that follow our direction of reading are perceived as especially fast (top). Movements that run against this direction slow down our eyes (below). The motion blur at the border conveys an additional degree of movement.

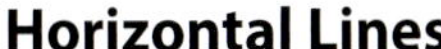

Horizontal Lines

Our view follows a horizontal line from left to right, based on our direction of reading. The stronger a line stands out from the image, the faster we follow it from one end to the other. Additional supporting lines that run parallel to a prevalent horizontal line also accelerate the viewer's visual movement. If the line starts within the image area but ends beyond its border, our view is drawn to the image border. Whether the line extends beyond the left or the right border is significant for the total effect of an image. If the line continues beyond the left border, it serves as a point of entry for the photo. If the line extends beyond the right border, it serves as a point of exit. If both ends of the line are visible within the image area, it is perceived as a whole visual element that conveys a sense of stillness, reliability, stability, and balance, owing to its flat orientation. If both ends are beyond the image border, the horizontal line splits the image area into halves and causes viewers to think about the horizon, even if the content of the photo doesn't have anything to do with nature.

A horizon is the most common and familiar line. It is associated with certain expectations and strongly influences the process of perception. The horizon line divides the image entirely, but not in a disruptive way, as can be the case with many vertical lines

These sketches demonstrate the results of different types of dominant horizontal lines more clearly than photos could.

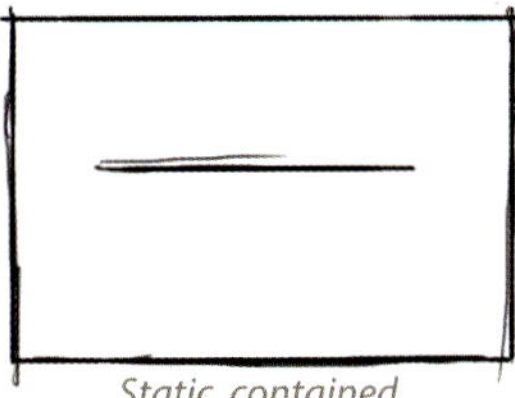

Static, contained

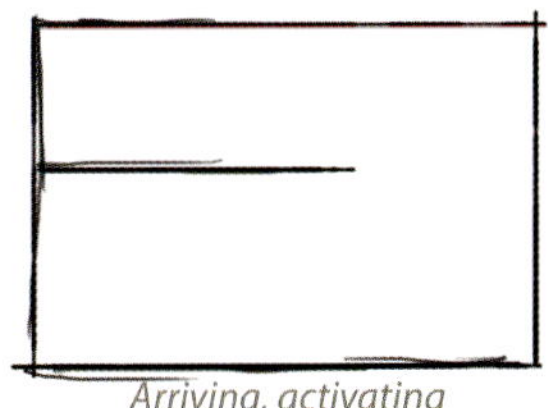

Arriving, activating

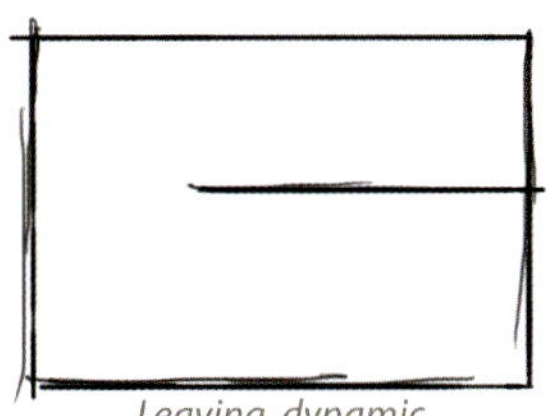

Leaving, dynamic

Divisive, endless

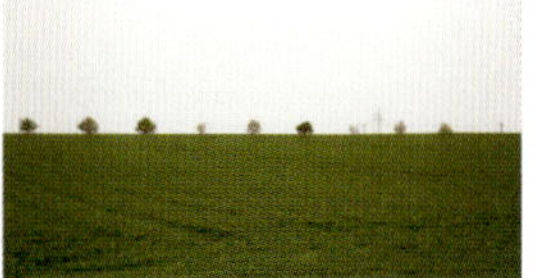
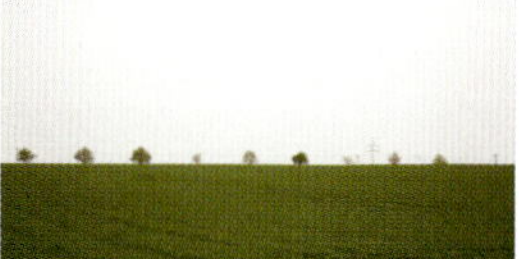

Positioning the important and dominating horizon line assigns a certain weight to the two areas that are created above and below it. This establishes a tension and a contrast between them that is based on how close the horizon is to the top and bottom borders.

(page 87). It creates two different areas of the image: one for the sky and one for the earth. This important line symbolizes distance, width, inaccessibility, and insurmountable separation, all of which we attribute to other horizontal lines, even in non-landscape photos, because of the horizon's ubiquity.

Horizontal lines that traverse the entire image area shift the weight in an image. The larger area, whether it is above or below the horizontal line, carries dramatically more gravity than the smaller area. This means you should carefully determine the exact position of the horizon in your image. A central alignment conveys stillness that may border on dullness; it should be used sparingly because of its overpowering effect. This choice is suitable only when the goal of your visual message is to show the even balance of the two image areas.

The positions between three-fifths and one-third of the vertical height of the image area tend to produce a harmonious image; anything closer to the image border increases the contrast and heightens the tension between the two areas. You can take this so far as to leave only a tiny strip of sky or earth at the top or bottom of your image for a dramatic effect. The landscape format emphasizes the effect of the horizon because of its long horizontal line. This effect is so strong that sometimes the edge of a picture can function as a horizon line, especially if you don't see the expected horizon line. The portrait format tends to reduce the effect of the horizon because the vertical orientation counteracts the width of the horizon line and visually reduces its presence.

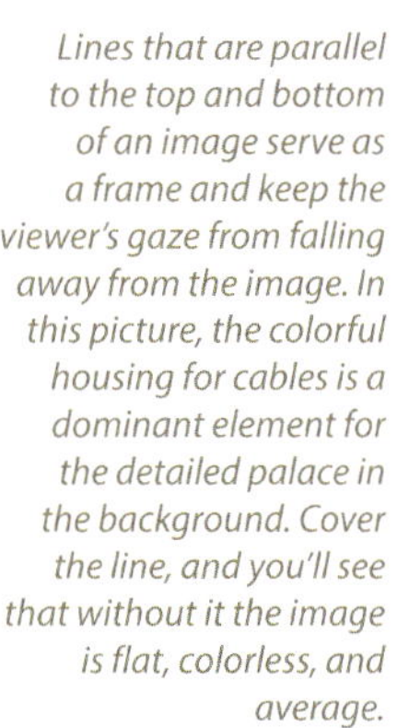

Lines that are parallel to the top and bottom of an image serve as a frame and keep the viewer's gaze from falling away from the image. In this picture, the colorful housing for cables is a dominant element for the detailed palace in the background. Cover the line, and you'll see that without it the image is flat, colorless, and average.

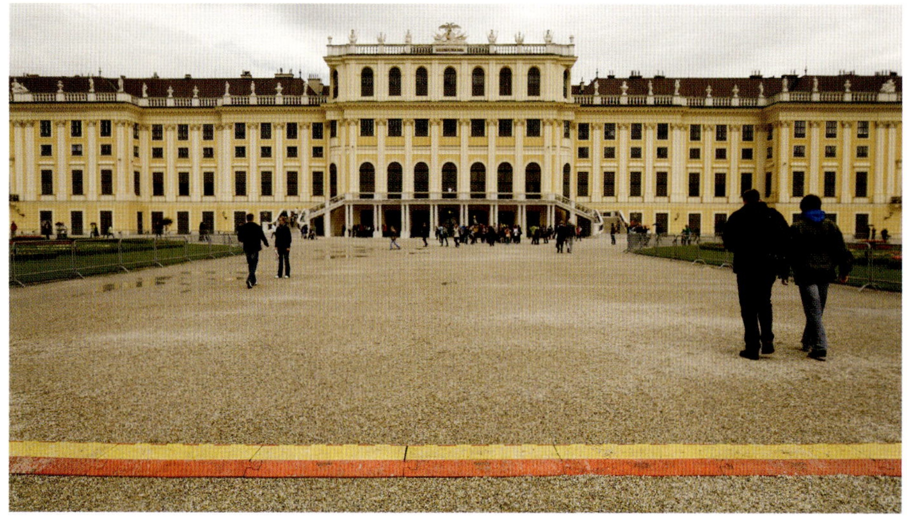

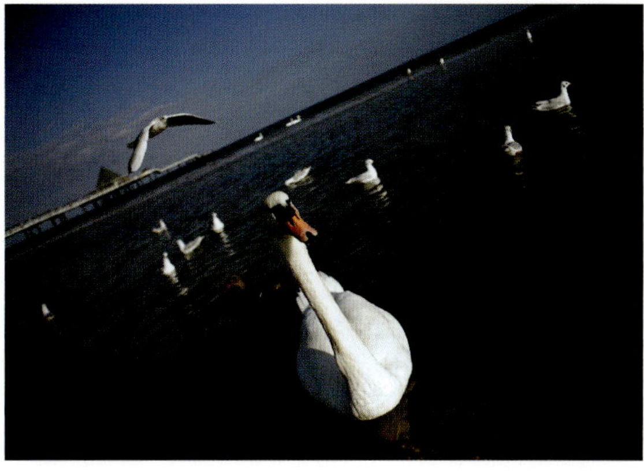

One of the most important expectations about horizontal lines that span the width of an image is their exact levelness; they should be precisely parallel to the horizontal edges of the border. Even though this sort of perfect levelness can be found only at the border between the sky and a large body of water, the expectation is so prevalent that any slant in a horizon is often considered wrong. This especially applies to exposures that capture surfaces of water because people sense that a tilted horizon would cause the water to spill. But even when an uneven horizon is applied to other subjects, many viewers don't care for the intense drama created by this unnatural way of seeing things. Images with uneven horizons are extremely emotional, subjective, and tend to be favored by viewers who are sympathetic to unconventional visual language. Regardless of the viewer, a slanted horizon must serve the subject of an image. This spontaneous and dynamic design method is less suited for a carefully composed photo shoot than it is for a spur-of-the-moment snapshot. Likewise, it lends itself better to sports photography than portraiture.

An uneven horizon line is definitely not everyone's cup of tea. But no one can deny that it establishes a dynamic, spontaneous, and mildly chaotic feel. When used in tandem with other design elements that achieve an opposite effect, you can prevent your image from turning into full-fledged chaos and give the impression that you created the look intentionally.

Vertical Lines

Lines that are perpendicular to the top and bottom edges of an image guide the viewer's attention vertically. In contrast to horizontal lines, the conventional direction of reading plays an insignificant role in how these lines affect how we view the image. The direction of the line is based mostly on the subject. Subjects that reach up or grow follow upward lines, and falling subjects create a sideways or downward movement. The format of the picture also influences the direction of a vertical line. In portrait format, vertical lines move upward; in landscape format, they move downward.

Whether or not a vertical line is completely contained within an image further determines its effect. Viewers will hardly notice if a vertical line extends downward past the bottom border of an image because the bottom border is more clearly perceived as an optical boundary than the other three borders. If a line extends beyond the top of an image, it takes the viewer's attention out of the image with it. In fact, any time

These lines demonstrate the effects of dominant vertical lines. The text below each box describes the effect of each type of vertical line.

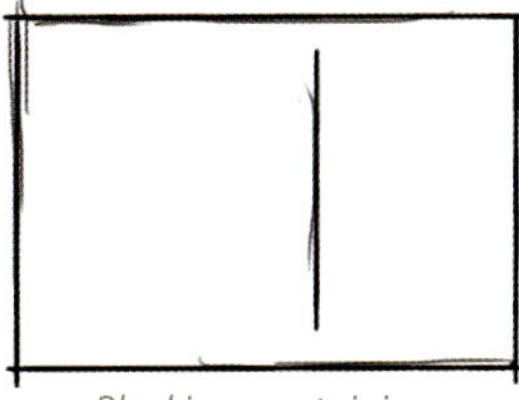

Blocking, containing

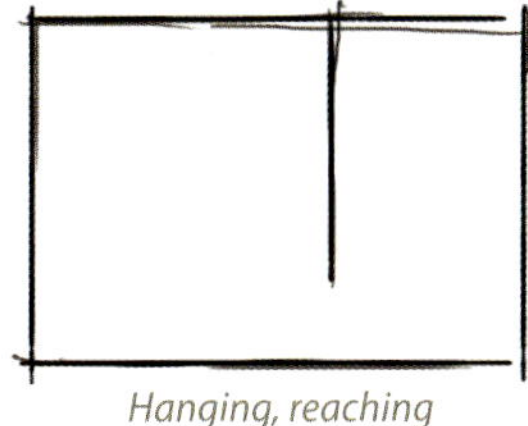

Hanging, reaching

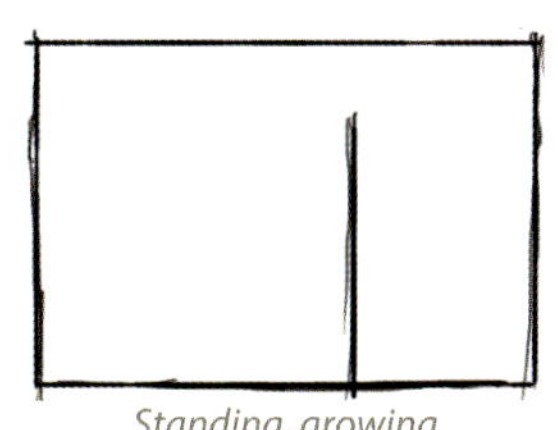

Standing, growing

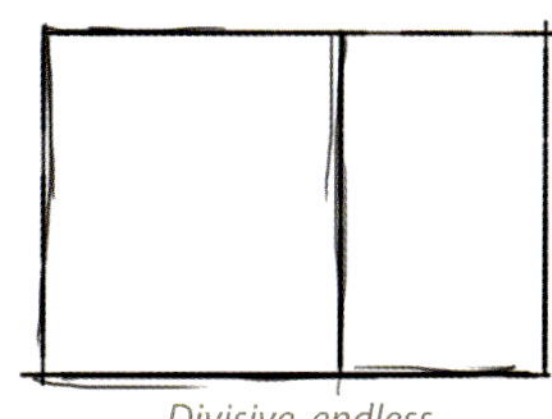

Divisive, endless

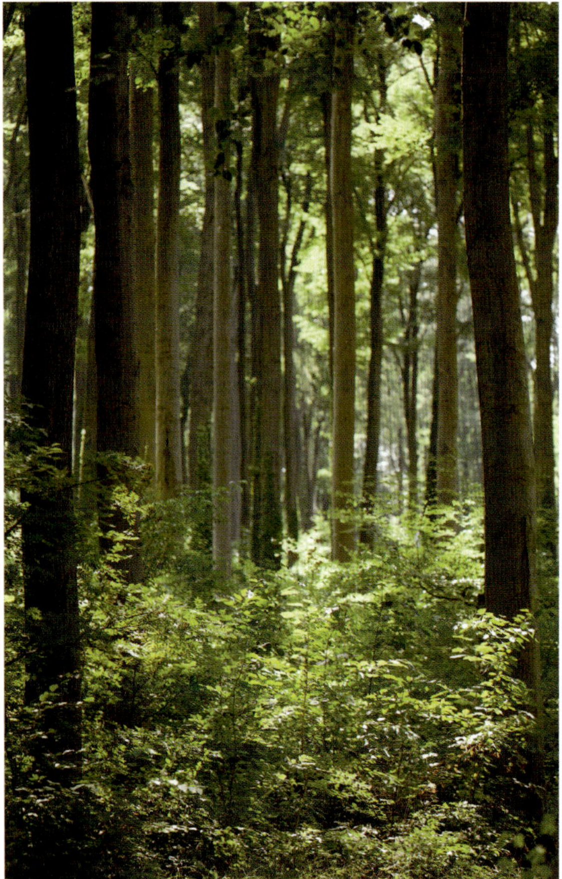

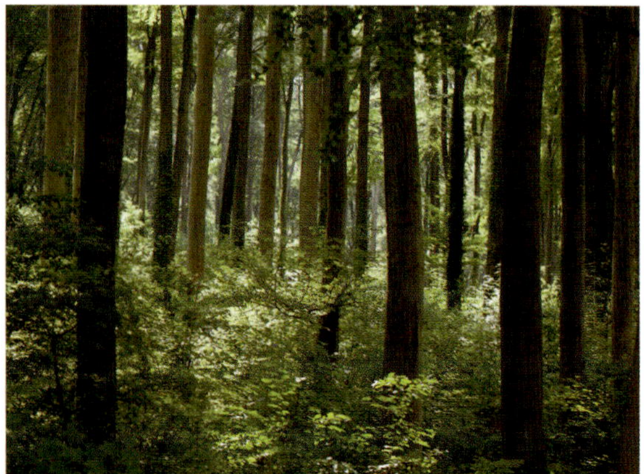

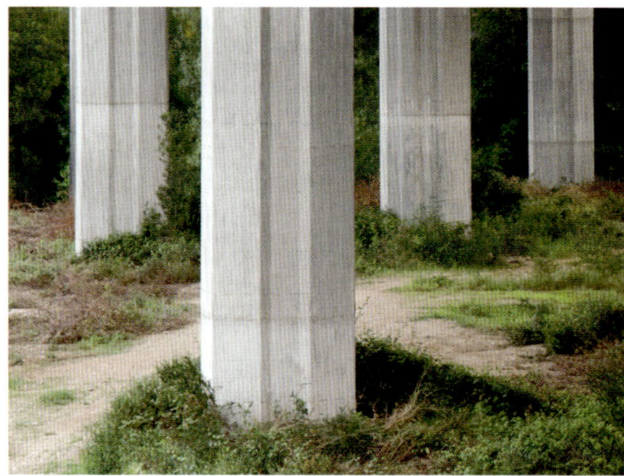

The same vertical lines appear much longer when captured in portrait format than they do in landscape. Vertical lines like the ones shown here—trees, which we know are rooted beneath the ground, and bridge pillars that start within the image but extend upward— strongly guide our interest to the top of the image and beyond.

a vertical line touches the top border, you should take care to establish some sort of attention-grabber that prevents the viewer's eye from exiting the image, or place an alluring and conspicuous element in the bottom half of the photo.

Vertical lines that extend beyond both the top and bottom borders of an image split the image area in two, severing connections between the two sides and causing both to be evaluated on their own. Usually such a line is perceived as disruptive and overpowering, and only rarely does it come across as appealing or purposeful. A purposeful vertical line is achieved most often when there is a strong, accessible, and readily recognizable connection between the content in the two parts of the image. Some examples include identical colors or a representation of two aspects of the same object on either side of the divider, such as one part of a construction site that is completed and another that is still in progress. The presence of multiple vertical lines tends to diminish this divisive effect—a fact that is generally true for all lines.

The relative effects of positioning vertical lines in different places within the image frame are similar to those of horizontal lines. Placing a vertical line at the middle of an

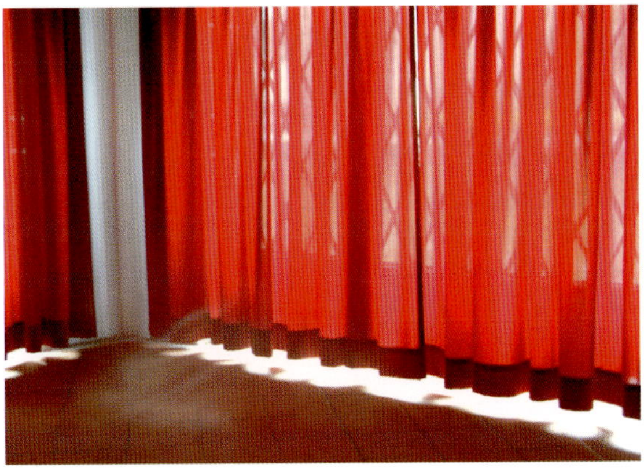

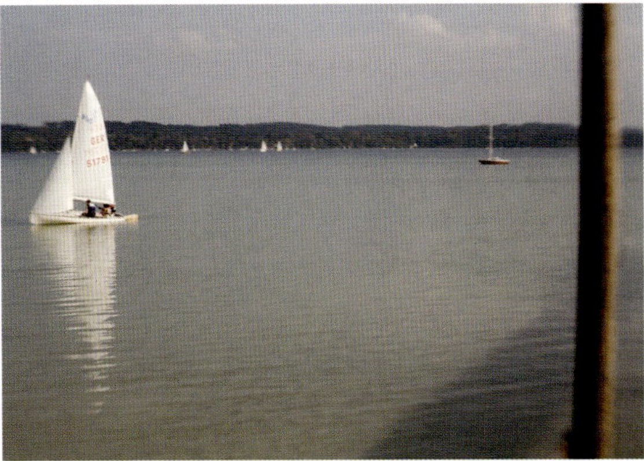

In the image on the left, your gaze starts at the vertical line on the left and wanders in the direction of reading through the rest of the image. Conversely, in the right image the vertical line at the right border serves as a stopping place after you observe the rest of the photo. This start/stop function of vertical lines can overpower other visual elements.

image creates a static effect that quickly becomes boring, placing one at the golden ratio creates a perfectly balanced effect, and putting one near the border creates a suspenseful effect. A vertical line functions as a boundary when it touches the left or right edge of an image; when it is used on the right side it can really bring the viewer's attention to a stop. Vertical lines on both sides of an image create a frame that emphasizes the subject matter between them.

Slanted and Diagonal Lines

All lines that cut through an image at a slant increase the vibrant, dynamic, and unsettled qualities of the photo. They serve as expressways for the eyes and direct the viewer's attention through the image much more quickly than anything else. Lines that move from the bottom left to the top right create a positive impression,

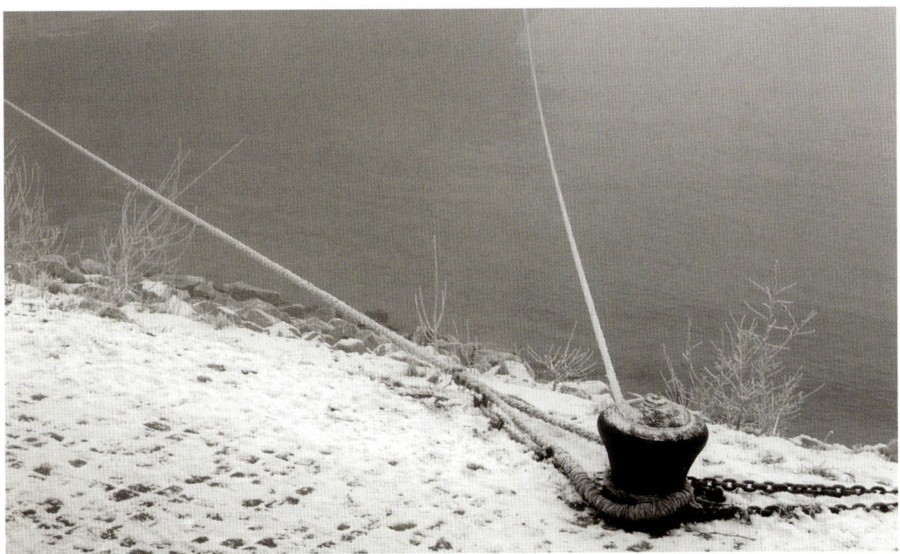

The three dominant, slanted lines of the bank and the ropes create a spatial effect, even though the vanishing point lies in the foreground. When the lines spread outward, the dimensional effect is more powerful.

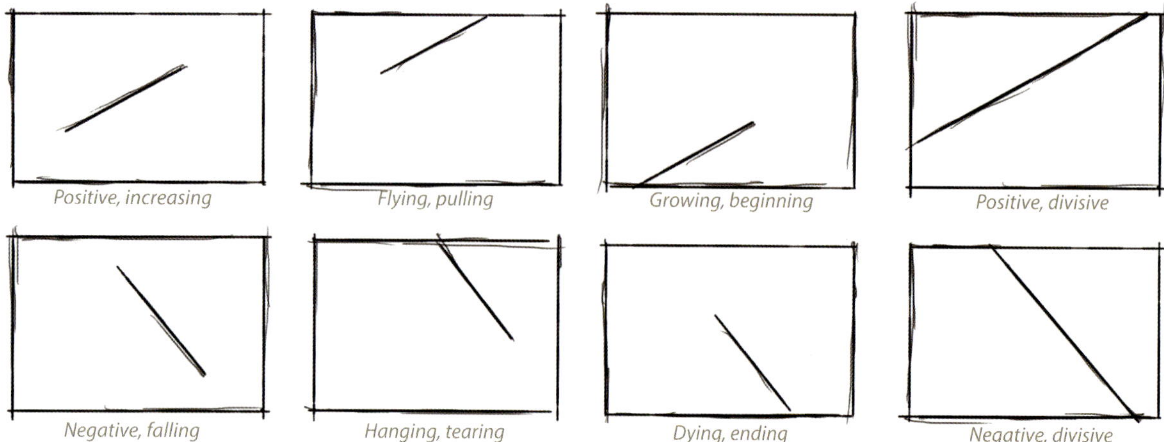

Slanted lines always convey a sense of direction that can create a positive or a negative effect in an image. The angle of the slant corresponds to the extent of the dynamic effect.

and lines that move from the top left to the bottom right create a negative, melancholy, and mournful mood. If the slanted line happens to be a complete diagonal that connects opposite corners of an image, the upward-trending line creates a sense of harmony, and the downward-trending line creates a sense of finality and lifelessness. These emotional impressions are based on the direction that viewers would typically read and are more noticeable in portrait images.

There are two special types of slanted lines. The first is called converging verticals. This is when parallel lines appear to be slanted slightly inward (toward each other)

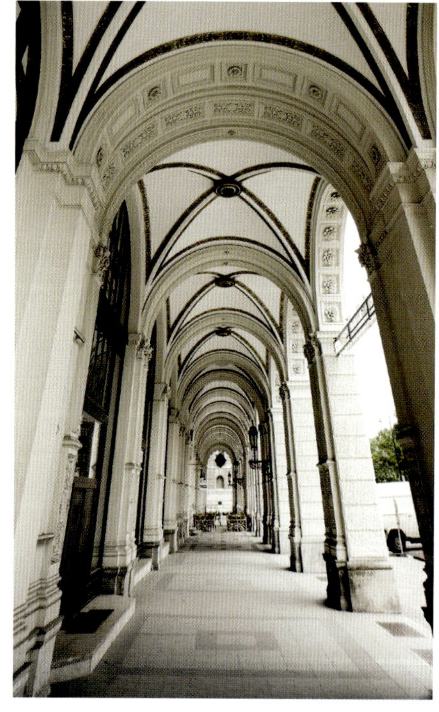

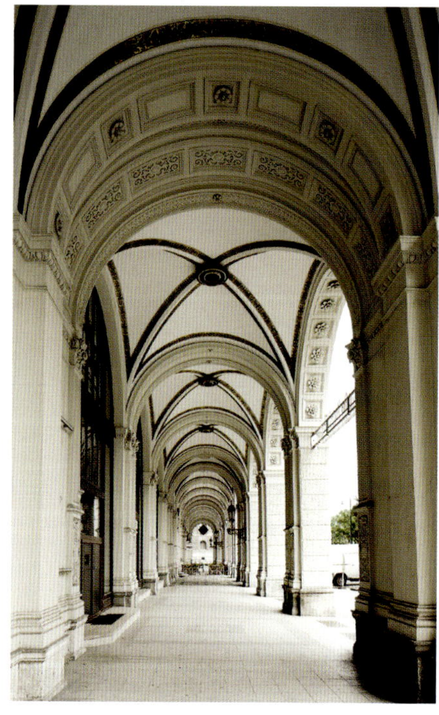

Converging verticals not only give images a strong dimensionality, they also can establish a sense of unrest, subjectivity, and liveliness. When they are applied intentionally, they can bring static buildings to life and give them an optical energy that they wouldn't have otherwise. This comes at the expense of creating an objective, realistic image.

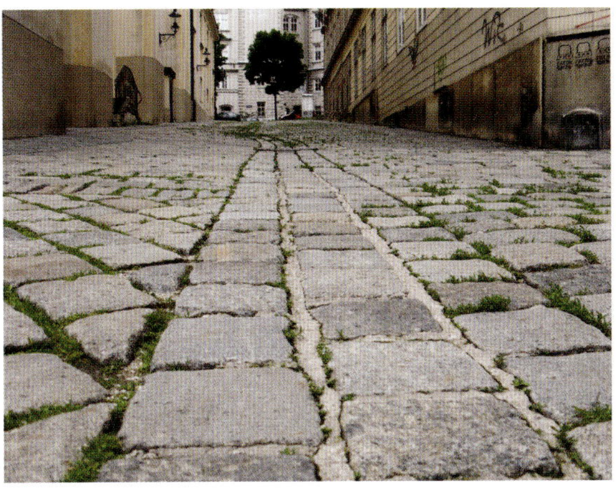

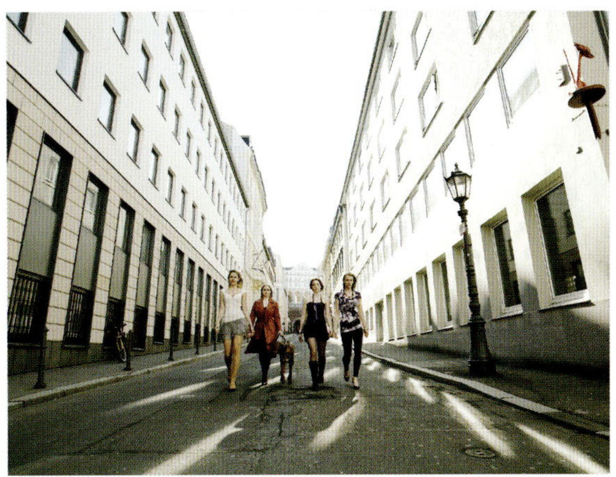

or slightly outward (away from each other) because of the optical effects of the lens. This phenomenon is especially problematic in architectural photography.

The second type of slanted line is vanishing lines, which converge at a single point within the image area or beyond it. The lines give a profound spatial depth to an image. By placing a critical area of an image at or near the vanishing point, photographers can intentionally guide the viewer's gaze, which will always return to that point.

To reduce the general unrest that diagonal lines create, you can compose your photo so they run out to the corners of your image. Doing so grounds them and provides them a stable footing. For many lines that appear within an image, it's enough to let the most important or dominant ones run to the corner to bring the composition under control.

Vanishing lines strongly establish all three dimensions within a photo. In the left image, the lines converge at a point that doesn't contain any critical information. The tree stands in close proximity to this point, though, and serves as the next closest anchor point, causing the viewer's gaze to remain in motion after reaching the vanishing point. Conversely, the right image shows vanishing lines that point toward the subject, where the viewer's gaze stays fixed. There are enough interesting details where the people are located to keep the viewer engaged.

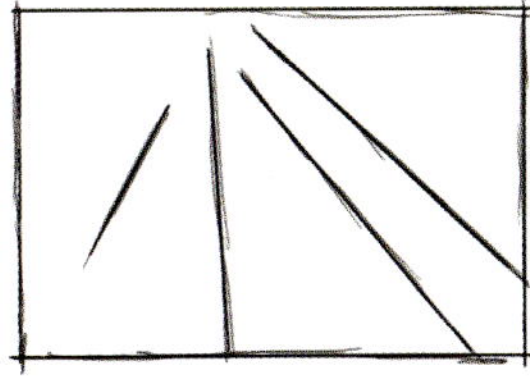

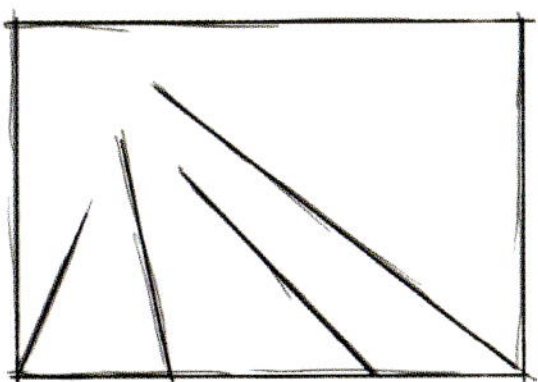

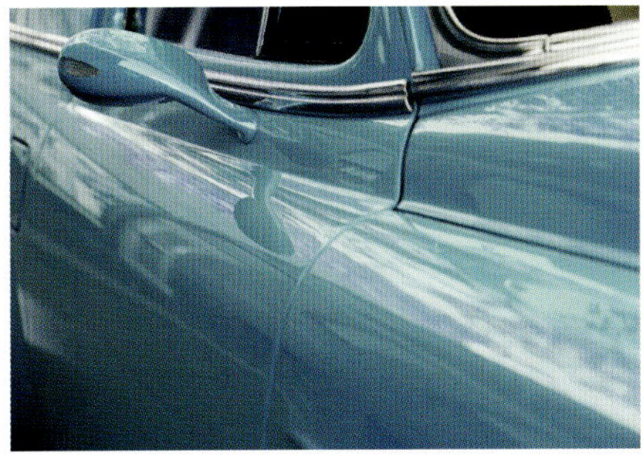

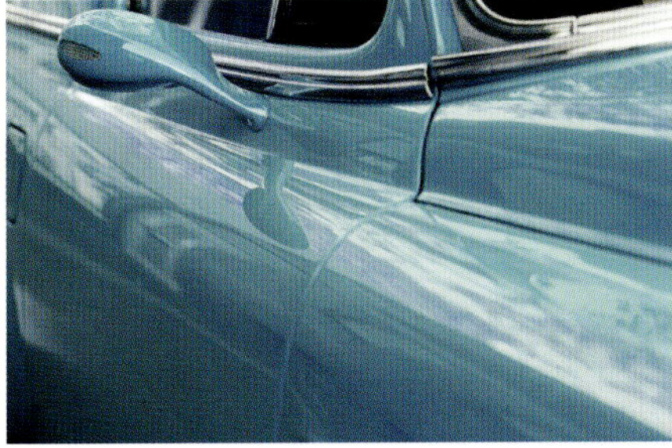

With a viewfinder or monitor that displays the image area in its entirety, you can set up your composition so the slanted lines run to the corners when you first expose your image. This can help you create a tidy and composed shot. If you don't have this ability, applying a crop afterward can naturally produce the same result.

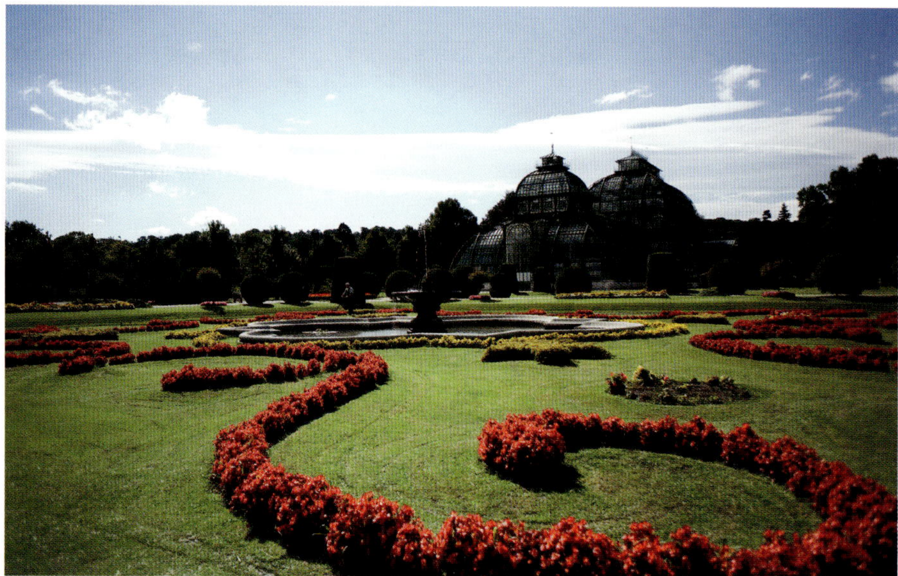

The flourish of flowers captures the viewer's attention in a playful manner and smoothly guides it into the background. This optical journey takes much longer than it would with a straight line. This allows the viewer to take in the whole image area and many of the details along the way. The curved shape of the line suits the flowers much better than if the flowerbeds were in perfectly straight rows.

Curved Lines

Lines that aren't straight generally aren't as effective at directing the viewer's attention within an image unless they form another geometric shape, such as half circles, circles, triangles, or zigzags. In these cases the lines are linked with different shapes or areas, and they give the image a different but equally distinctive effect (page 94).

Curved lines are perceived as organic, natural, and soft. They direct the viewer's gaze slowly and gently through the image. If the line is wave shaped, it can create a dynamic effect despite its lack of geometry.

The Contrast of Lines

Contrasts are always based on differences between two or more items. Contrasting lines indicate that multiple types of lines appear within an image area. This has the potential to intensify, diminish, or alter the various effects of lines.

Contrasting lines can be particularly interesting when they are sporadically set against one another, such as when a few lines move in one direction and one dominant line moves in another direction. The lines don't have to be strictly vertical and horizontal; slanted lines at different slopes also form interesting contrasts. Lines with different characteristics can also produce intriguing contrasts, such as narrow versus wide, focused versus blurry, or short versus long.

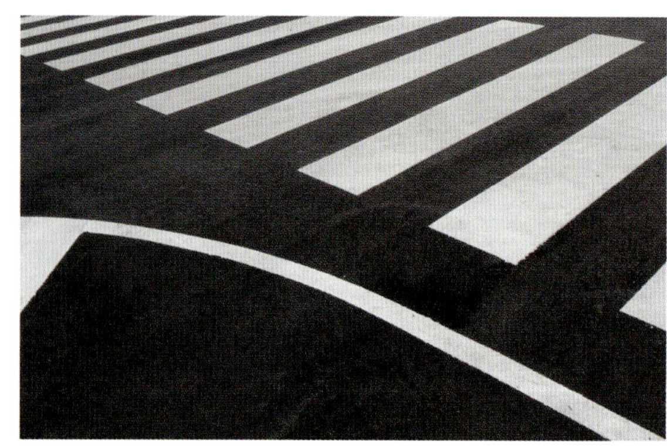

Stripes with a strong bright/dark contrast make up this crosswalk. They attract further attention because they are so regular. This image contrasts the stripes against another shape of lines, the curved line in the foreground

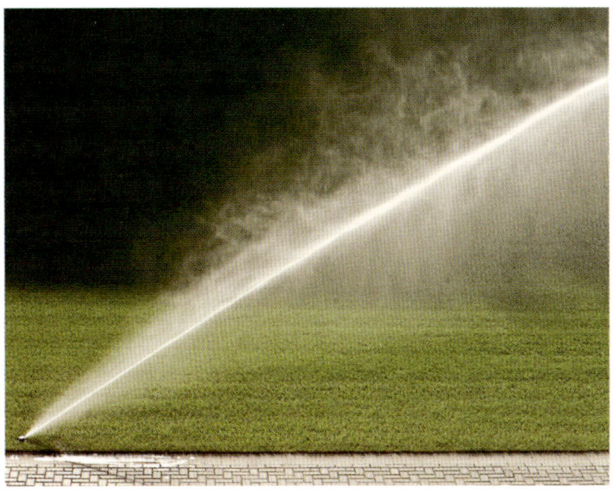

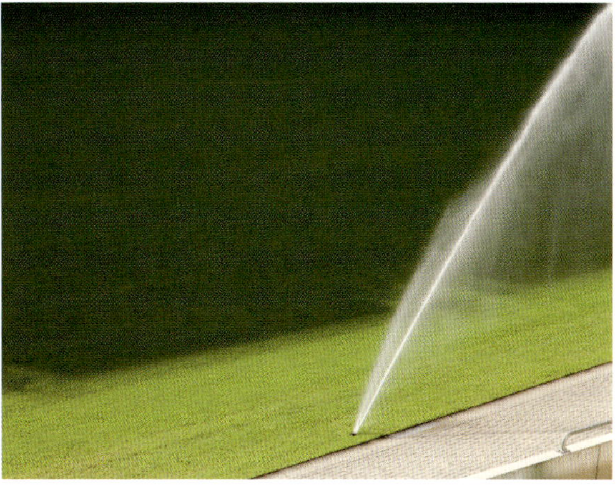

The inclusion of too many different kinds of lines within an image is confusing, and it's difficult for the viewer to decipher the content of the image. A leafless tree is a good example; the trunk and the main branches provide clear main lines, but they don't establish a uniform direction because of their growth pattern. Smaller branches that function as secondary lines add to the confusion because they pull the viewer's gaze in many different directions. To make it worse, the branches and twigs aren't straight lines to begin with.

A confused, unfocused linear design may be responsible for images that do not look good, even if you can't specifically identify what the problem is.

These two images clearly show how various diagonal lines function, depending on their angle and their relationship with other lines. The left image has a two-dimensional effect, despite the main diagonal line. This is because both the bottom line and the shadow in the background are parallel to the bottom edge of the image. The right image includes a steeper angle for the main line, and the other lines are at various degrees of slant, which emphasizes the depth of the scene.

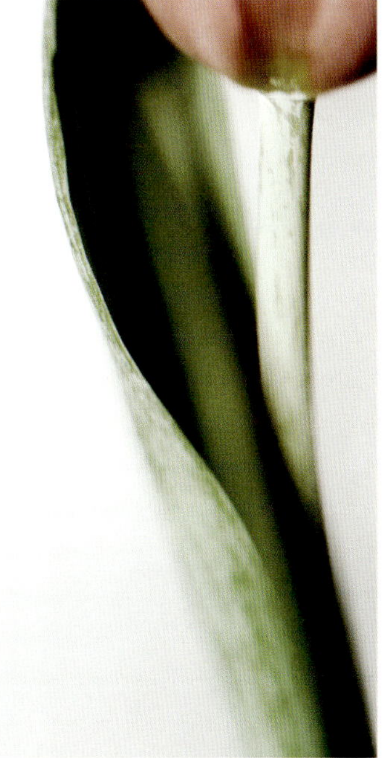

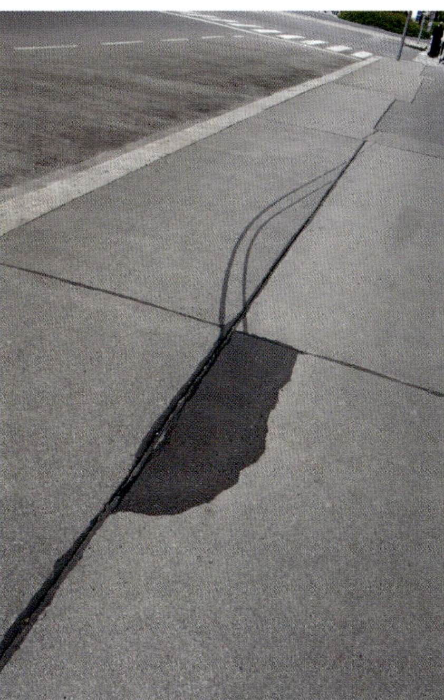

You can emphasize curved lines by combining them with straight lines. This effect is underscored when the curved lines are set against harsh geometric lines, as with the gentle curves of the tulip and the playful, lively tracks of a stroller leading away from a puddle.

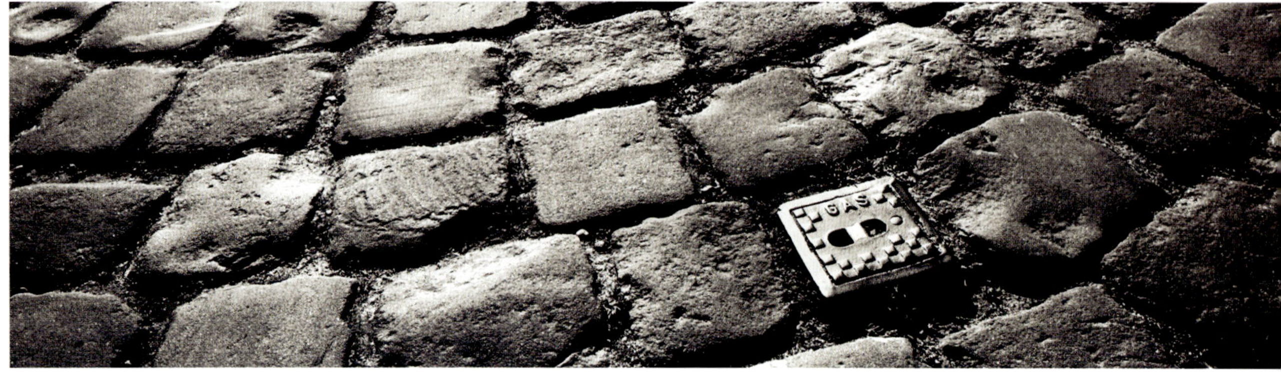

3.3 Shapes

Photographs reduce the three-dimensional world to two dimensions. The result is a combination of various shapes and surfaces that sometimes appear organic and other times appear geometric. The geometric shapes have a great potential for attracting attention. Depending on their objectives, photographers should use this knowledge to exploit or avoid these shapes.

The shape of an element in a photo can take the shape of the object itself, as is the case with the basketball in the photo on the right. We quickly recognize this object and perceive it as a coherent unit. But multiple individual elements, such as each petal in the photo on the left, can give rise to a collective shape when the similarities among the elements are stronger than the similarities with their surroundings.

Appearance

Viewers usually try to decipher all the elements in an image as quickly as possible. This process of perception (page 22) occurs to discern meaning. When we recognize an object, we relate to it based on its context within our lives, not on its formal visual qualities. We see a house as a house, for example, not as a combination of a rectangle (the front) and a triangle (the roof). Despite this, even familiar objects affect us on an abstract level based on their formal qualities. For elements we don't recognize, or that we can't place in a familiar context, the formal qualities are more apparent.

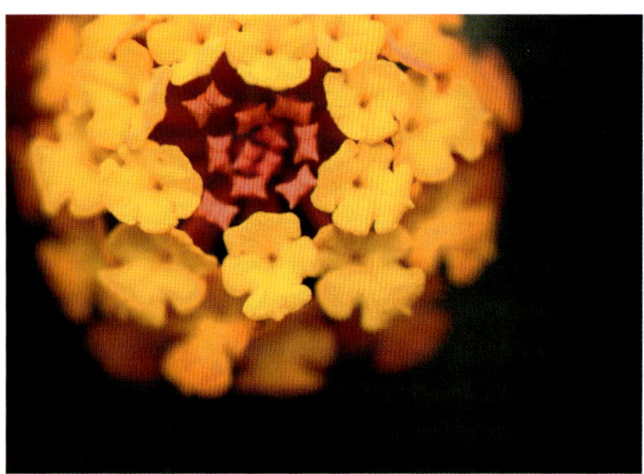

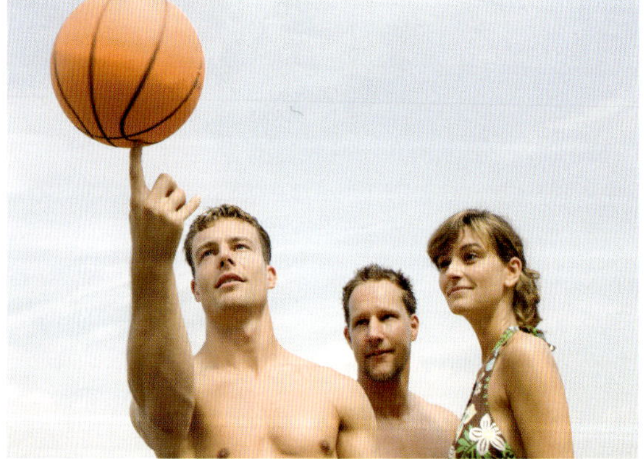

Shapes in an image can arise in several different ways. First, they may be a clear outline or a direct representation of an already existing shape, such as a traffic sign. Second, shapes may result from the perception of multiple objects that have the same or similar color, texture, and brightness as a single entity. Third, repeated points that form a line can be interpreted as a single figure. Fourth, gaps and spaces between visual elements can form shapes, as can certain areas where the background is not blocked by objects in front of them.

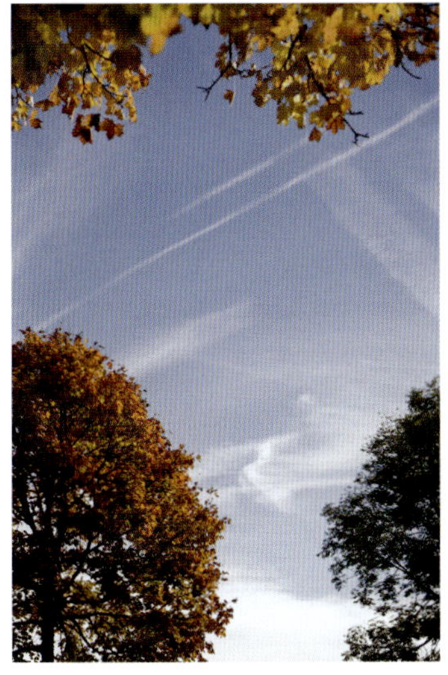

Gaps can create shapes. The blue sky is an expansive shape, but the frame of the trees obscures it. Here, the sky function as a single, irregular area.

These various types of shapes can be divided into two categories: *contour* shapes and *area* shapes. In general, shapes have a stronger visual effect when they are clearly depicted. This means, for example, that a shape resulting from a row of individual points (an indirect contour shape) will be less conspicuous than a solid outline (a contour shape), but not as conspicuous as a shape with a solid area or a uniform texture (an area shape).

If shapes result from a gap, the subject will determine whether the enclosed shape or the outline itself is more dominant.

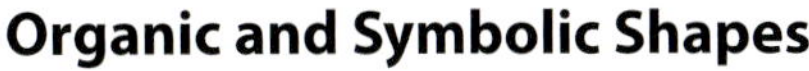

Organic and Symbolic Shapes

Softly shaped visual elements appear natural and pleasant. Viewers tend to not perceive these subjects as actual shapes and instead see them for what they are. Organic shapes don't become conspicuous until they are uniformly structured, form a full surface, or reveal content that commands a high degree of attention, such as a person or a familiar or characteristic animal.

Familiar symbolic shapes—such as a heart, a cross, a yin-yang symbol, warning signs, popular logos, or zodiac signs—also have the potential to elicit a high degree of attention.

Abstract shapes can prompt certain special associations based on the details of their outlines. Waves or curved shapes often give an image a sense of direction by providing it with movement and vitality.

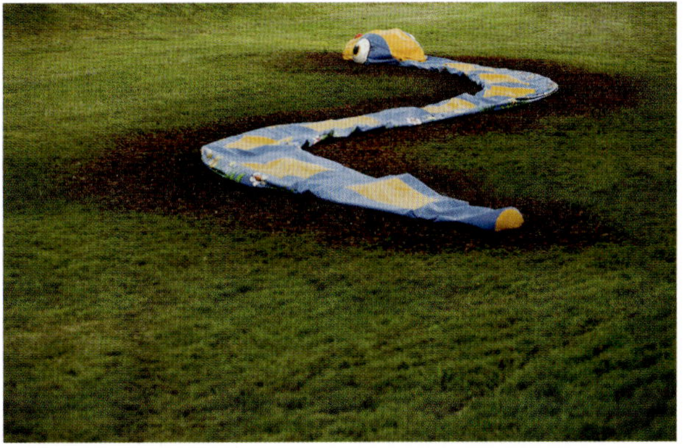

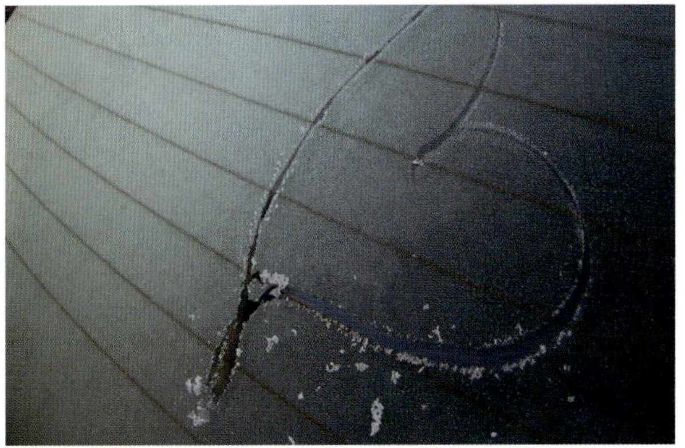

The human eye is especially attuned to drawings and symbols because they represent a type of communication. Viewers will think of a question mark when they see the shape in the top image, and they will recognize a heart in the bottom image, despite the fact that the crop, perspective, lines, and color don't highlight that particular shape.

Geometric Shapes

In comparison to organic shapes, geometric shapes attract much more attention because they have an artificial, man-made appearance. We're so familiar with the most common shapes that it's impossible for us to overlook a circle, triangle, rectangle, square, or any of their variations. The more clear and sharp a shape is within an image, the stronger it will attract the viewer's attention. This magnetism occurs regardless of whether the shape is depicted in its entirety; cropping part of the shape or hiding it behind another object won't diminish its visual appeal. Our perception is especially adept at completing partial circles, and it does so quickly. The same goes for other shapes, such as rectangles, squares, triangles, or stars that are missing a corner.

The complete shape of a circle often attracts the most attention. The pull of a circle is so strong that we notice it first and often never look away. You can use various design elements to reduce the dominance of a circle, such as cropping, overlapping, hiding, or reducing its size. These images demonstrate several examples of how you can integrate a circular shape into your pictures without having it overwhelm the other elements.

Circles and Ovals

Circles, the most conspicuous shape of all, come across as self-contained, closed, complete, and stable. Their effect on an image differs based on their placement. When they appear in the lower half of an image, they create an immobile and heavy feeling; if they are positioned in the top half of an image, they seem light and appear to float. As complete areas, circles punch a hole through an image and suck the viewer's gaze into their center. No other shape, and hardly any other design element, has such as strong pull on the viewer's attention.

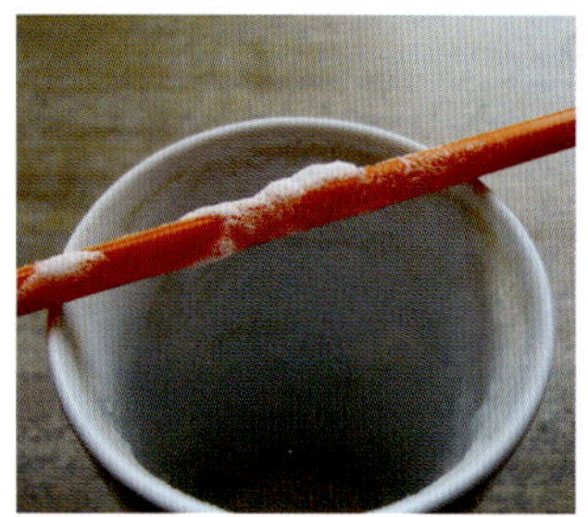

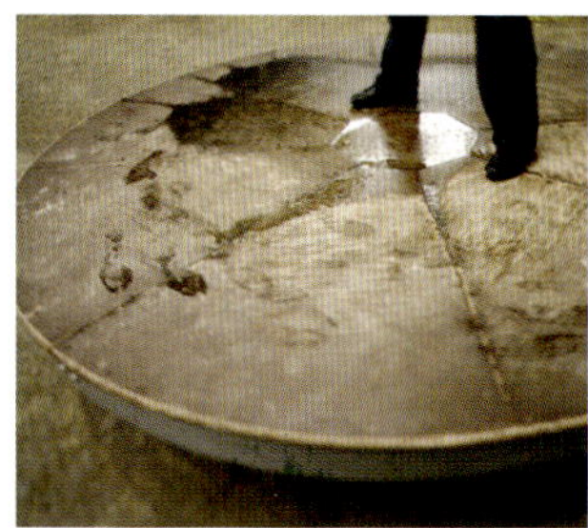

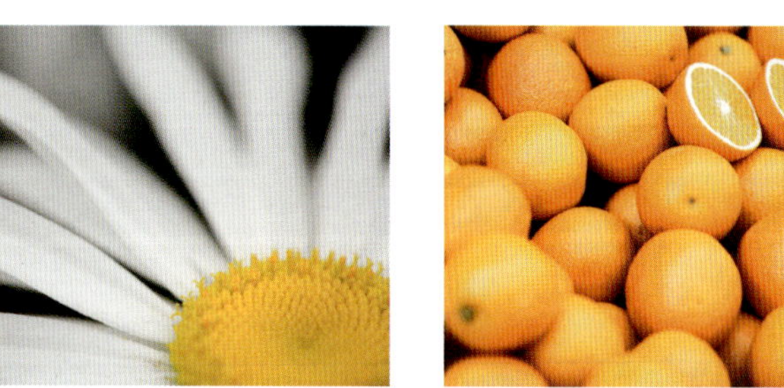

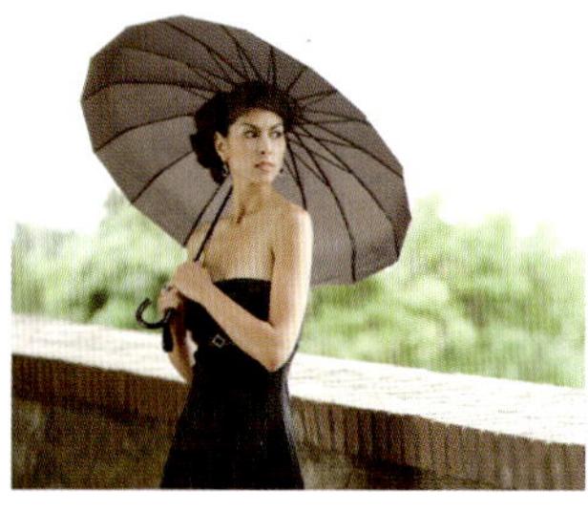

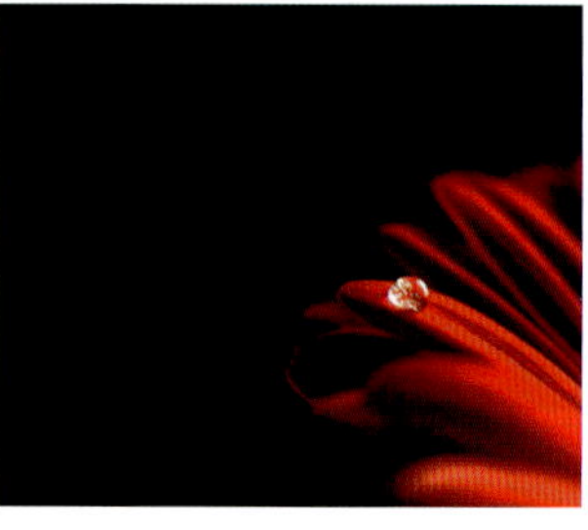

For this reason, you should think twice about placing a complete circle within your image area. If you do, it should contain enough visual information to support the entire image. With a small circle you can successfully pull the viewer's gaze away by placing another attractive element nearby. Another way to reduce at least some of its optical dominance is cropping one or two sides. If the shape in your image is actually an oval and not a perfect circle, it will still attract the viewer's attention—but not with the same intensity as a circle—and will give your image a slightly different dynamic quality.

A quarter circle or pie slice shape functions more like a triangle because of the sharp point created by its converging lines.

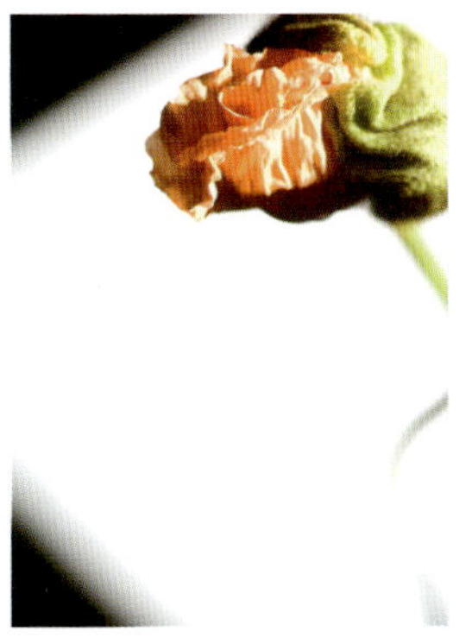
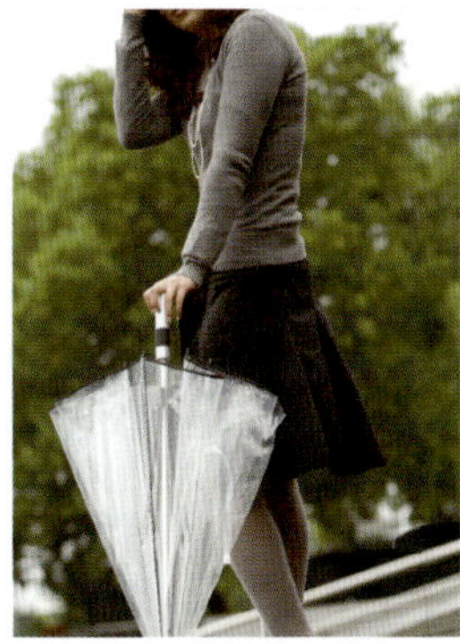
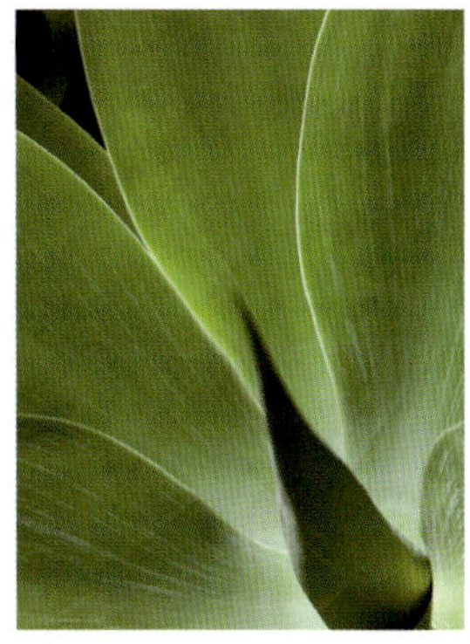
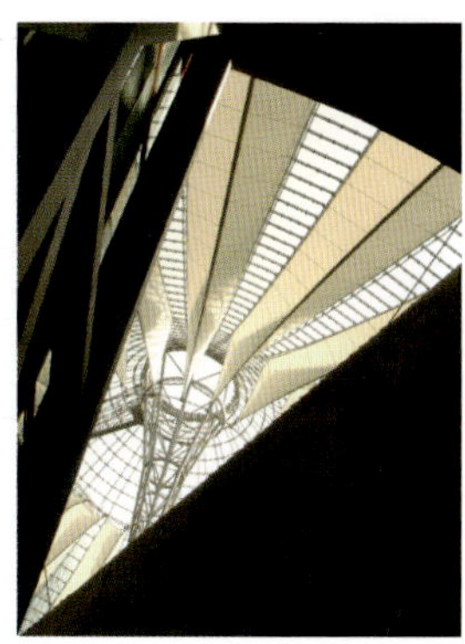

Triangles

A triangle is another extremely powerful shape that produces different effects based on how it is oriented within the image. When the tip of a triangle is pointed down, it appears wobbly and unstable; if the base is down, it seems stable and secure. Equilateral triangles convey a sense of balance because of their perfect symmetry, and isosceles triangles tend to ramp up the energy within an image. If all three sides of the triangle are a different length, the shape forfeits its stable qualities and comes across as a restless element.

Triangles are extremely dynamic elements as long as they are not resting on one of their sides. Even shifting them slightly can turn triangles into unstable shapes that direct the viewer's gaze, and they have the potential to bring plenty of tension and turbulence into an image.

A triangle looks like the head of an arrow. Pointier triangles have an increased capacity for directing the viewer's gaze. An equilateral triangle exhibits this quality only when one of its sides runs parallel to the image border—the point on the opposite side points the way. The arrow effect of triangles is emphasized depending on how much the point is directed to the right or top.

Not every quadrilateral is a rectangle. Rectangles appear in a photo only when the camera is held at a right angle to the object in question and the viewer is looking directly at the subject. When this happens, rectangles have a two-dimensional effect in an image.

Rectangles, Squares, and Diamonds

Rectangles that are parallel to the frame of the image area are as familiar as they are common. As far as shapes go, rectangles are the least conspicuous, and they come into play only when they are depicted in their entirety. Even distorted variations of rectangles are relatively familiar because everyday sights readily demonstrate how changes in perspective can alter rectangles, such as corridors that appear between rows of tall buildings. Squares, however, are something else entirely. Their four equal sides have a more artificial effect, and their perfect symmetry tends to attract a lot of attention.

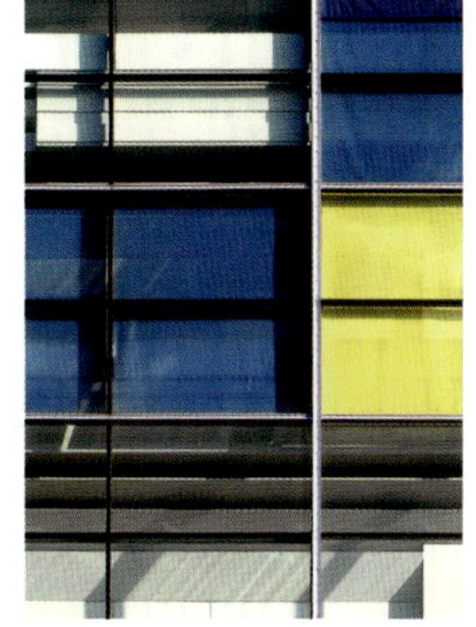
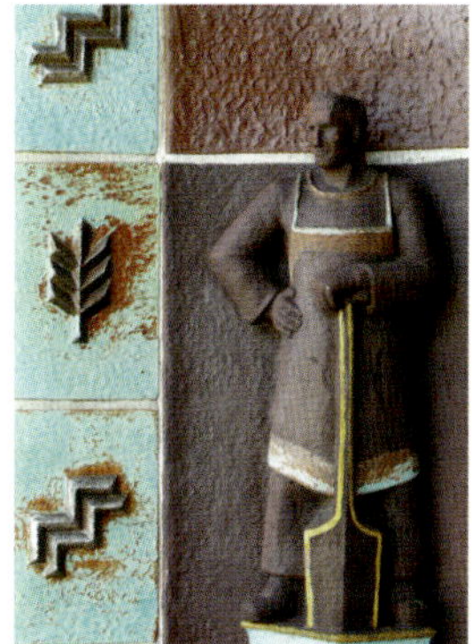

In general, if rectangles and squares have sides that run parallel to the borders of an image, they have a stable and static effect—a quality that can border on monotony and dullness if they are not

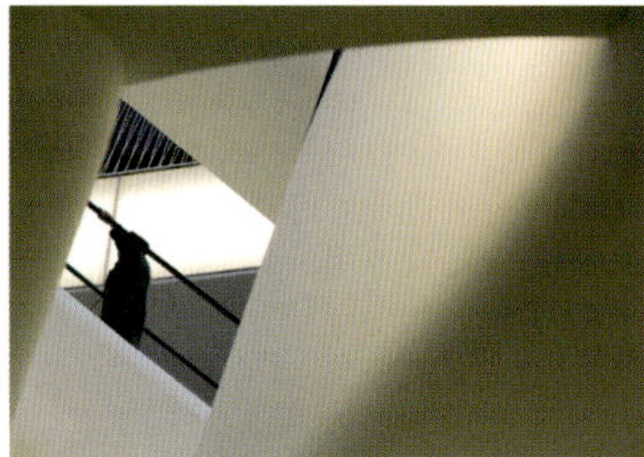

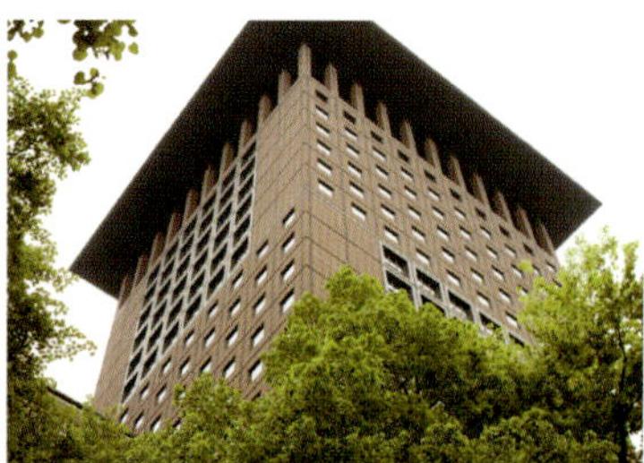

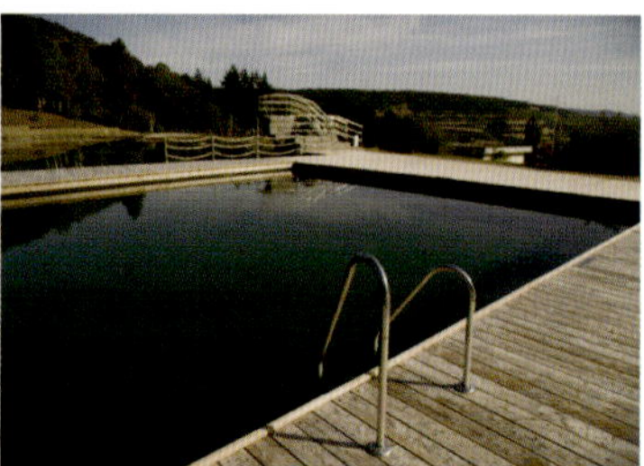

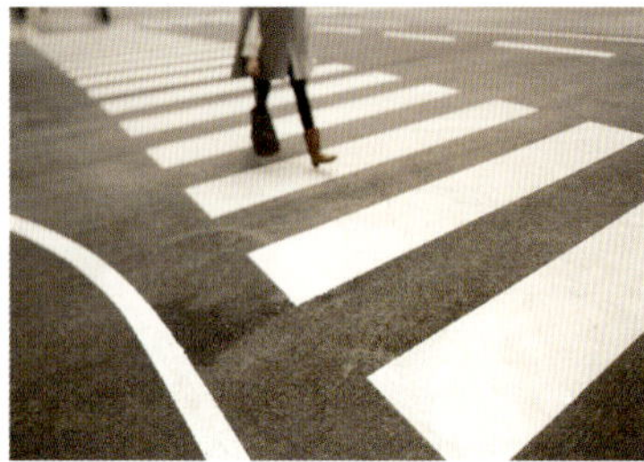

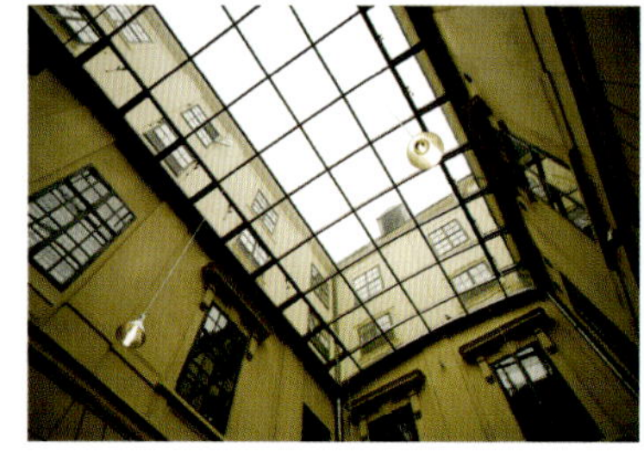

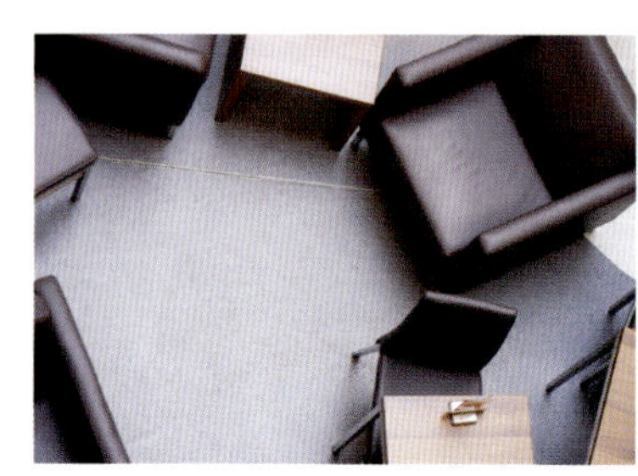

Acute angles cause surfaces that have right angles in reality to look diamond-shaped in an image. Since we know that the subject in question actually has right angles, we see this as a visual distortion and immediately perceive the three-dimensionality of the image. Any shapes standing on a point impart a sense of instability and vitality to an image.

managed carefully. An exception is narrow, tall rectangles that stand upright in an image. Despite their parallel orientation to the border, these shapes can produce a tipsy quality. If a rectangle or a square is rotated so it's standing on a point, its potential to engage the viewer increases. Diamonds are less stable than squares, but more activating, dynamic and exciting. They have a stronger pull on the viewer's attention.

Stars and Crosses

Although they are not exactly geometric shapes, stars and crosses jump out at us. Their precise and familiar look makes them particularly conspicuous. Both shapes give an image a highly dynamic quality. Stars tend to direct the viewer's gaze from a center point outward and then back to the center again. A cross functions as a marker and calls the viewer's attention to a specific point, the intersection of two lines (page 81).

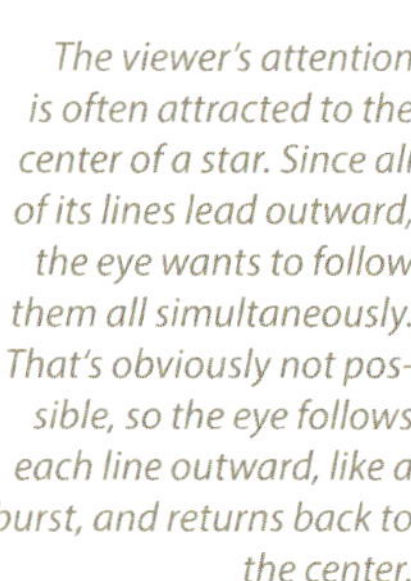

The viewer's attention is often attracted to the center of a star. Since all of its lines lead outward, the eye wants to follow them all simultaneously. That's obviously not possible, so the eye follows each line outward, like a burst, and returns back to the center.

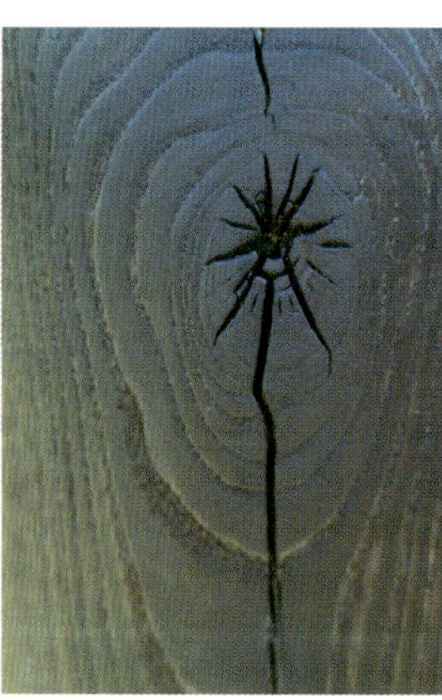

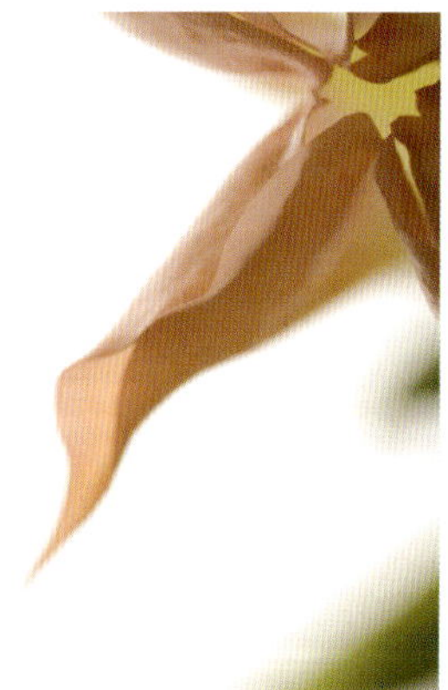

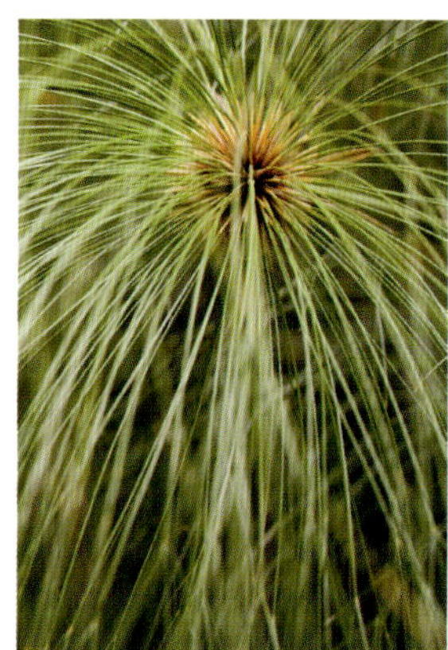

Shapes in a Picture

When you use shapes in your images, you must first consider what you hope to achieve with them. Obvious, solid-area shapes quickly give images a graphic, flat look and feel, but contoured or indirect shapes don't jump out as conspicuously, and they allow you to create a spatial design.

You will encounter situations when a geometric shape is problematic because it's too eye-catching for your purposes. In these cases, your goal should be to reduce the dominance of the shape or to completely avoid it. Clearly recognizable shapes can be especially problematic in large overview shots or in the background of an image because they can detract from your main subject. If you can't avoid them, a radical crop may keep the shape from taking the spotlight.

When different shapes appear within the same image, the results can be appealing. Juxtaposing hard, straight, and angular shapes with soft, round, and organic ones can create a positive visual tension. This is especially true when natural shapes are contrasted with artificial, man-made ones because the image takes on an additional dimension at the content level.

Combining Shapes

If you attempt to combine multiple geometric shapes in an image, the shapes themselves will become the dominant subject. It will also give your picture a very straight, flat, or possibly abstract character. Including multiple variants of the same shape, such as several squares or circles, is so commanding that it reduces all the other elements in the image area. Combining a number of purely geometric shapes with one organic version of the same shape is an interesting possibility (page 79).

Featuring several versions of the same shape tends to amplify the qualities of that particular shape, while diverse shapes highlight the differences among them. In moderation, mixed shapes can produce exciting results, but too many different shapes can quickly create a disorderly look and feel. Shapes can differ not only in appearance, but also in size. Small shapes are less conspicuous than large ones, but a small shape generally wins out over a large contoured shape in terms of its relative visual dominance. Color, brightness, and texture can also help to regulate the weight of different shapes.

Bringing various shapes into a picture invites variety that allows the eye to jump back and forth between elements. Especially when shapes overlap, you can end up with a visual ambiguity that allows you to make several subjects out of one. This variety allows the viewer to stay actively engaged in the image because no one shape is overly dominant.

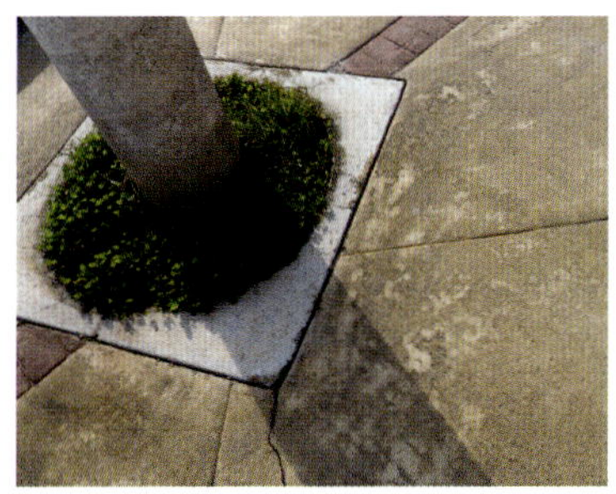

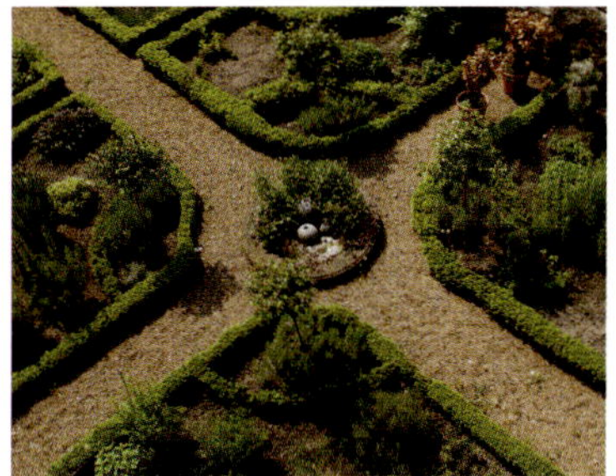

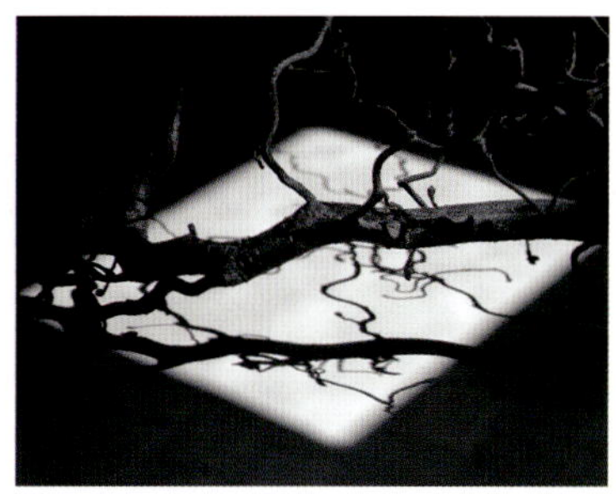

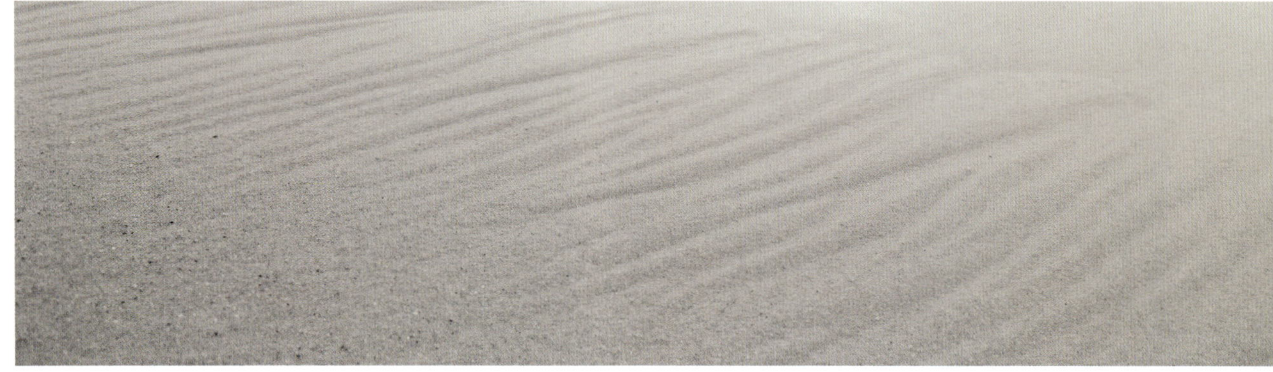

3.4 Structures and Repetition

Structures are the fourth type of graphic element that can influence an image. In contrast to an area with a single color that conveys information only through color and shape, structures can amplify or diminish the dominance of a visual element based on their particular characteristics.

Appearance

Viewers perceive rough structures as individual elements until the brain integrates them into a pattern (left). Structures with smaller elements are perceived as a coherent unit, or a structured area. You might need to use additional elements of design, such as a calculated depth of field, to accentuate them (right).

Structures occur when similar or identical visual elements are repeated. This repetition can include points, lines, shapes, or a combination of these elements. If they are arranged closely enough, they will not be perceived as individual elements—they will be seen as a unified whole and establish the impression of a visual structure.

Structures can be regular or irregular. Regular structures arise as a result of an exact—or nearly exact—aligned and ordered arrangement of elements, and it comes across as artificial. If larger elements are arranged in this manner it is referred to as a sequence. Conversely, irregular structures don't rely on a rigid arrangement; they have an uneven configuration and come across as natural and less prominent.

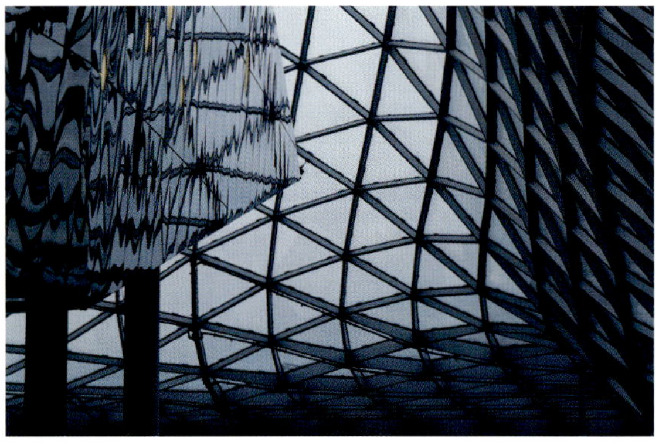

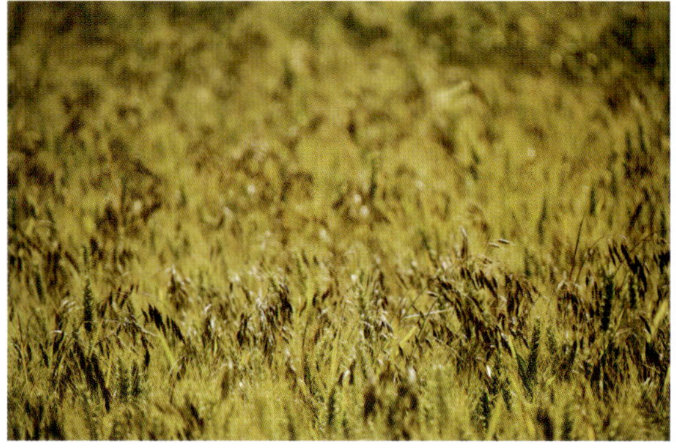

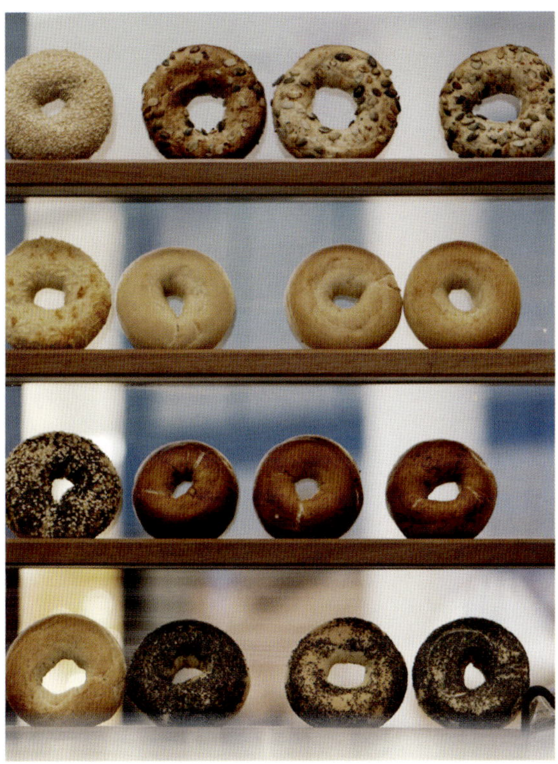

The Effects of Structures

The smaller the basic element of a structure, the easier it is to perceive the area as a unified visual element. With these types of structures, the outside shape of the area is critical for perception. With structures that feature larger base elements, the repetition of the elements is a more interesting visual effect. Rows or sequences of objects that fit strict requirements can give an image an exceptionally organized appearance. If the sequences are parallel to the border of an image, the structure itself will come across as static, fixed, and uniform. If they are slanted, the image will have more life and a clear direction of motion. This is particularly effective when the distances between the individual elements are varied.

Structures can provide details and visual information that can hold the viewer's attention for a long time. Structures tend to open images, instill them with increased excitement, and allow them to have a more dimensional, realistic, and interesting effect.

The repetition of round shapes in the left image establishes a sequence of individual elements, instead of a uniform, coherent structure, because the individual donuts are dissimilar and have inconsistent distances between them. The drops in the right image are the same size and are regularly arranged, which results in a clear pattern or structure.

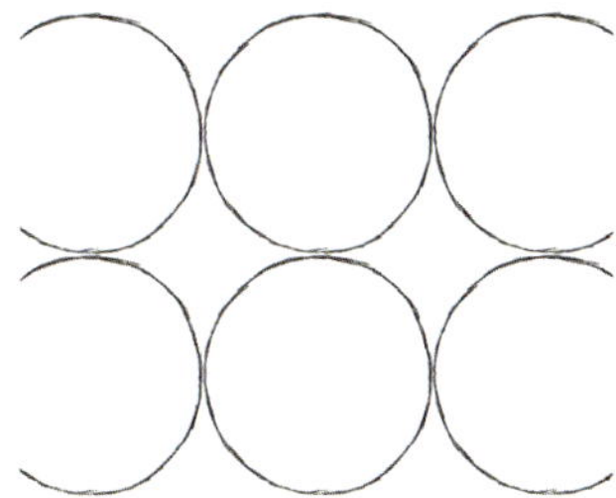

Larger repeated elements are perceived individually—they create a sequence. Smaller elements, however, function as part of a larger structure.

"The satisfaction comes from working next to 500 photographers and coming away with something different." David Burnett, American photojournalist

04 Standpoint and Point of View

The concepts related to this particular element of image design are mostly familiar from everyday speech: standpoint, point of view, and perspective. Just like in everyday life, these photographic terms describe how you look at something and the location from where you view it. The power, force, and endless possibilities of this design element come from these simple variables. In no other area of image design will you be able to express your own subjective viewpoints and creativity as clearly as you can here.

As the term *standpoint* implies, this concept includes a statement about the photographer. Has the photographer discovered a unique vantage point or revealed an unusual perspective of a familiar subject? The ability to see photographically is closely connected to this aspect of image design—not everybody innately possesses this ability, but you can learn it through practice.

After a photographer sees a subject, he or she must *capture* it. This involves the deliberate use of a lens, which both limits and extends our ability to see. We can capture only what the optics allow us to see, and various focal lengths can tremendously extend and clarify our angle of view. It is our responsibility to creatively and purposefully use the peculiarities and exposure characteristics of lenses in a way that best suits our subjects.

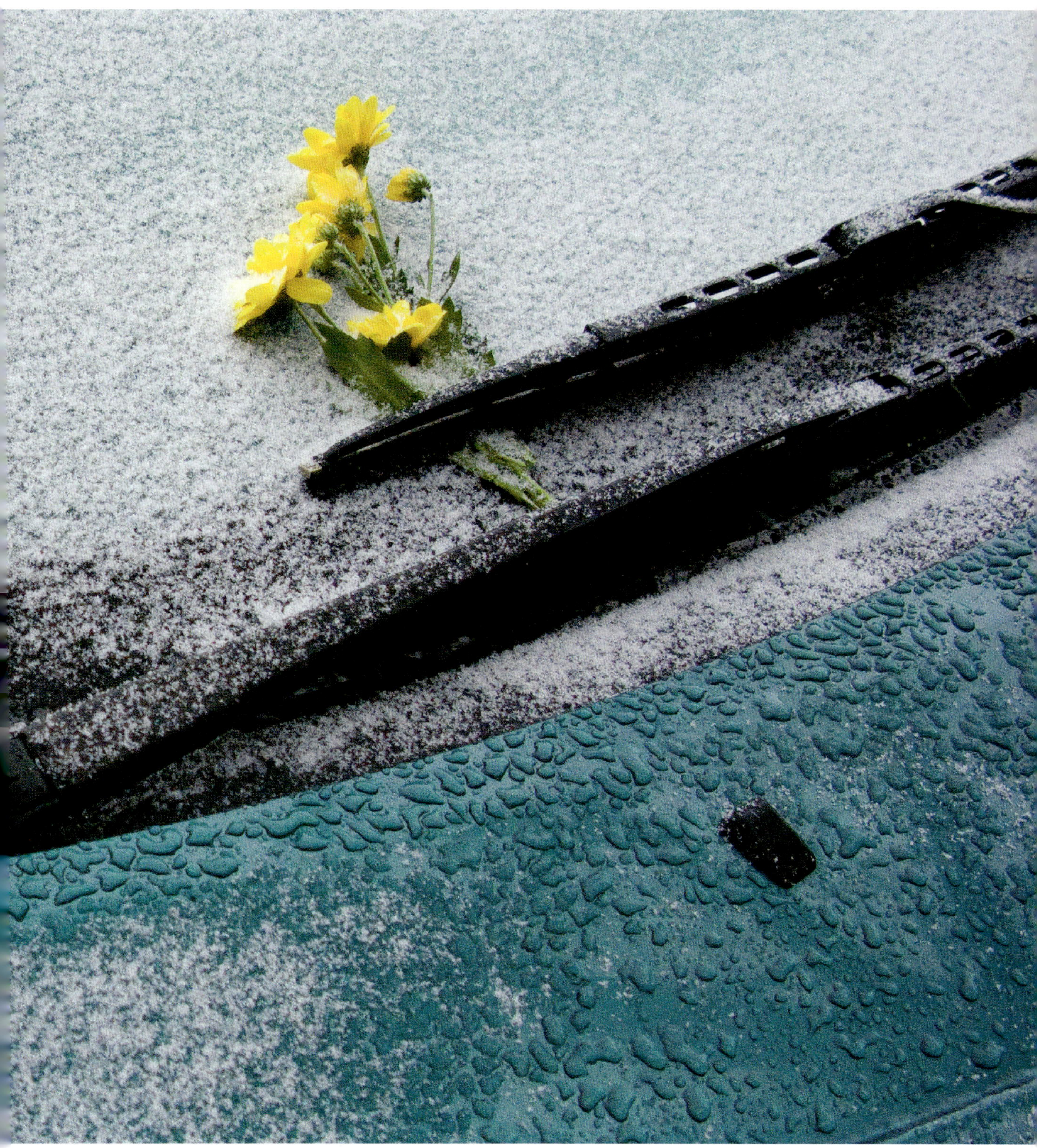

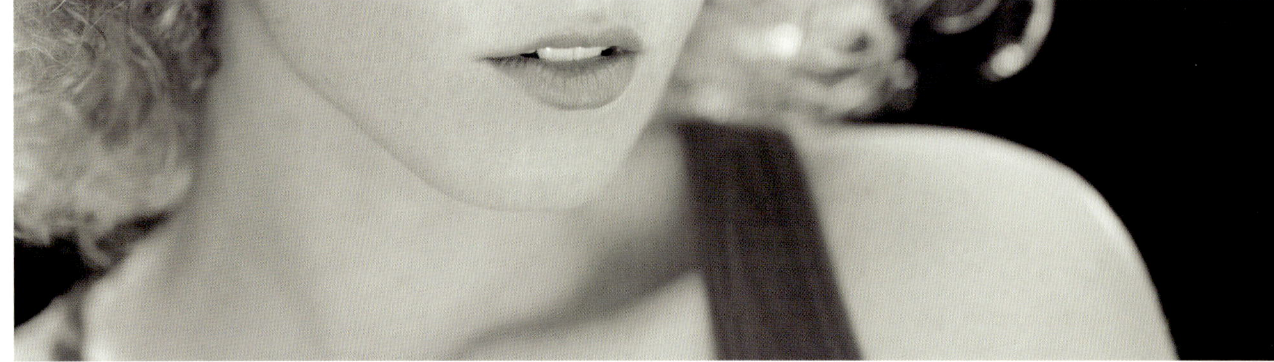

4.1 The Position of the Camera

By selecting the position of your camera, you establish the relationship between your camera and your subject. You define a very subjective and specific piece of reality for the viewer. There are two principal variables to consider when selecting this position: first, the arrangement of elements within the image area, and second, the height of your camera.

Selecting a Vantage Point

No one can tell you where to position your camera—there are no rules or guidelines. You alone can decide if what you see in your viewfinder is worth capturing. It's a good idea to think about this decision and try various viewpoints before you snap your exposure. In other words, don't equate the first good point of view with the

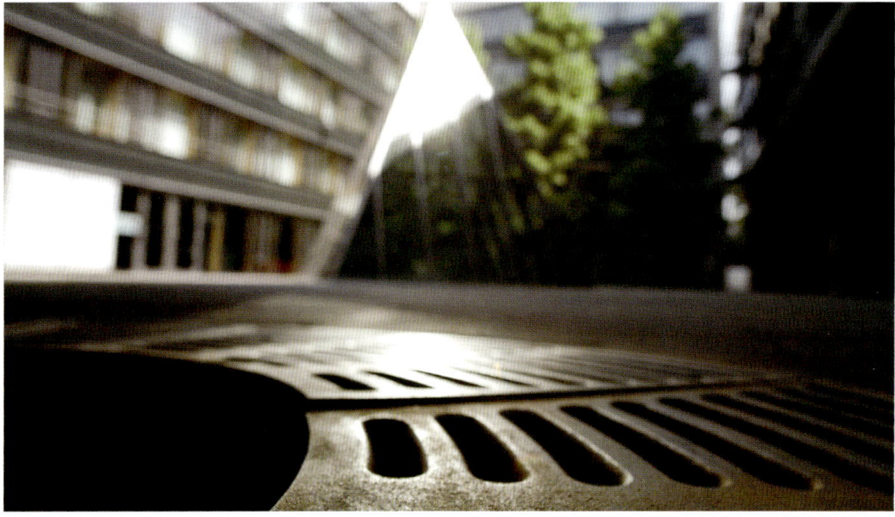

It's easy to capture exciting and attention-grabbing images by just changing your point of view. Bring your camera to unusual places and show viewers a perspective they have not seen before. Who else but a photographer lies down in the middle of the street?

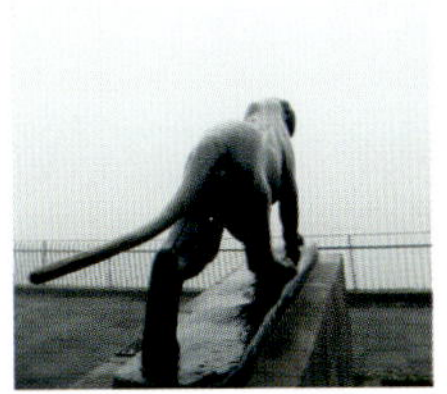
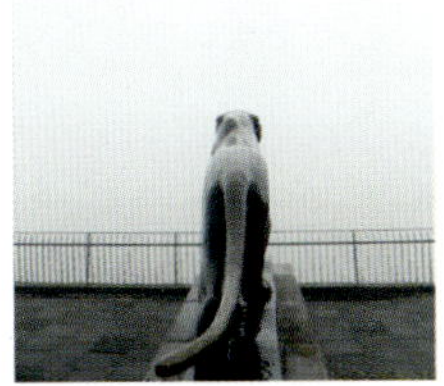
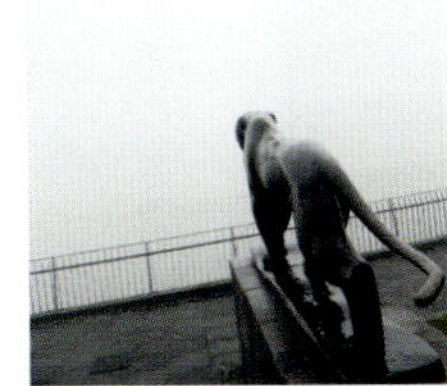
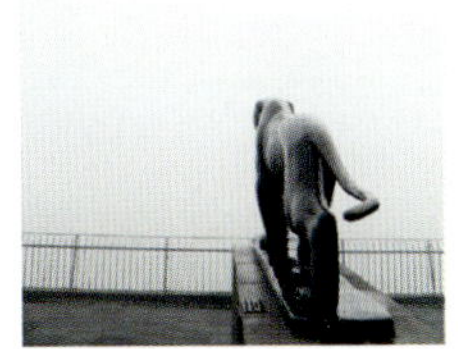
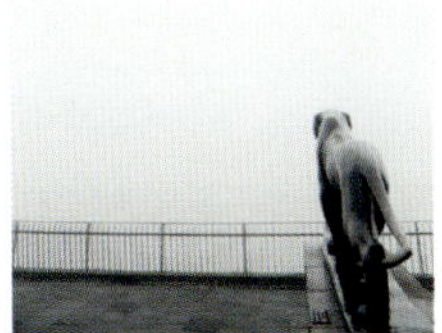

ideal point of view; instead, engage with your subject by moving around it. Examine it from all sides. Sometimes it takes only a few inches to turn a passable shot into a powerfully designed image, and sometimes it takes only a few steps to the side to change a conventional image into something unusual and new. If you always resign yourself to your first idea, you won't make discoveries like these.

It's especially important to try new standpoints when you're working with a zoom lens because it's so easy to adjust your image border with your zoom instead of varying your perspective by repositioning yourself. First decide on a focal length, then move around to find the perfect position—you can make any final adjustments with the zoom after you've found your ideal spot.

When you settle on the ideal position for you and your camera, you also determine who or what to photograph, and from what direction. The way the ambient light influences your shot has a big impact on this (page 129). You also decide which details to include in your deliberately chosen image design. The more consciously you select your standpoint and the more variations of the same subject you try, the faster you will learn to make these minor position adjustments. You'll also train your eye to see subjects more comprehensively.

Engage with your subject as thoroughly as possible to find the perfect point of view for your shot. Take some time to walk around your subject; kneel down or raise your camera above your head—vary your perspective and observe how these decisions influence the resulting photograph.

The closer a subject is to your camera, the larger it appears in the photo. This explains the phenomenon of converging verticals. In a photo, a tree trunk with the same circumference at the top and bottom may seem to have a thinner top, so you end up with a trapezoid shape from the converging vertical lines.

Proportions

The distance between your camera and the subject influences the proportions of the photographic elements. The shorter the distance, the larger the subject appears. Objects that appear larger within the image area come across as more dominant than ones that appear smaller. In short, the larger an object, the more importance it carries, which is especially true for elements that fill up the entire image frame. Altering the size of an object within your image is a design technique that can help you organize and weight your image. This applies mostly

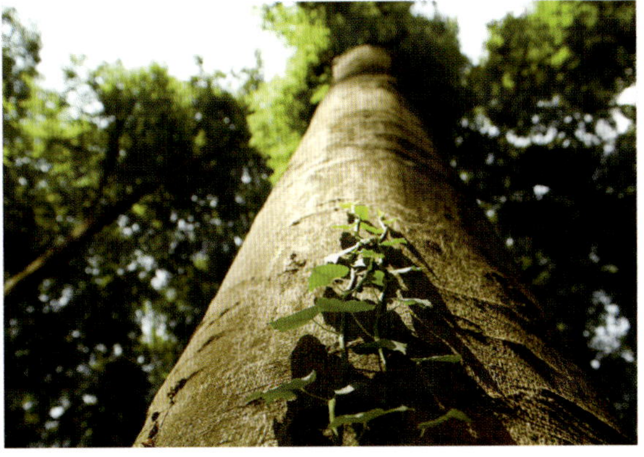

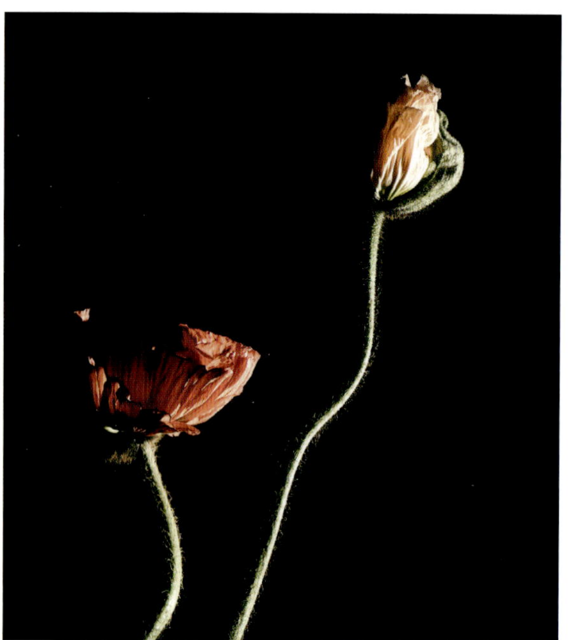

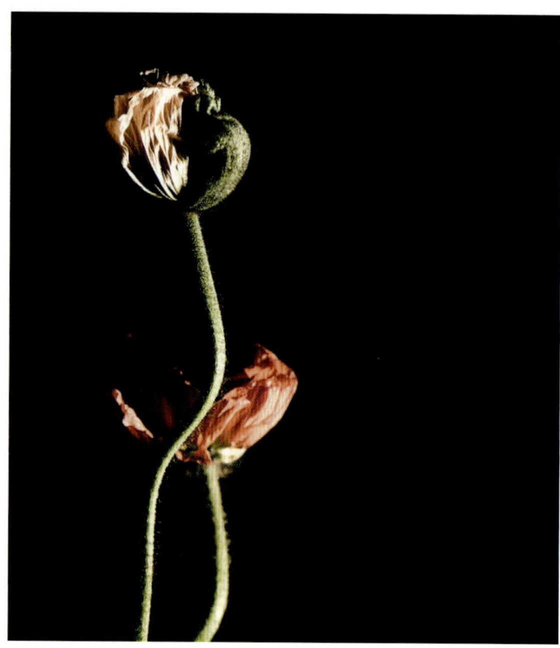

The black background robs these images of any spatial depth, something the sidelight can only partially resolve (left). When the flowers are arranged so they overlap, however, the image immediately takes on a clear depth and three-dimensionality (right).

to images that are relatively close to your camera; objects that are farther away will not be affected much by the same shift in your camera's position. You can also influence the proportions within your image by selecting a focal length and angle of view in a calculated manner, which is something we'll talk about later (page 111, 113).

Arranging and Overlapping

When you move on a horizontal plane in front of a subject you intend to photograph, you decide which elements to include in your picture and whether they should stand next to one another or overlap. Visual elements that are not obscured can be perceived separately from other elements. This creates a calm effect and a sense of clarity and distance. Just a simple sideways shift of your camera can be enough to visually separate elements from one another and give the impression that they were positioned deliberately.

Of course, it's just as easy to use sideways movement to intentionally overlap your subjects. Obscured elements lose their visual prominence because they are relegated to the background. The more layers of overlapped objects you include in your image (page 72), the more it will come across as unsettled and chaotic. However, extra layers convey more dimensions.

If you obscure one element to the extent that it's difficult to see, you will thoroughly irritate your viewers. People always want to know what they're seeing. At the same time, hiding a distracting detail is an effective way to increase the overall appearance of your shot.

Exposure Height and Perspective

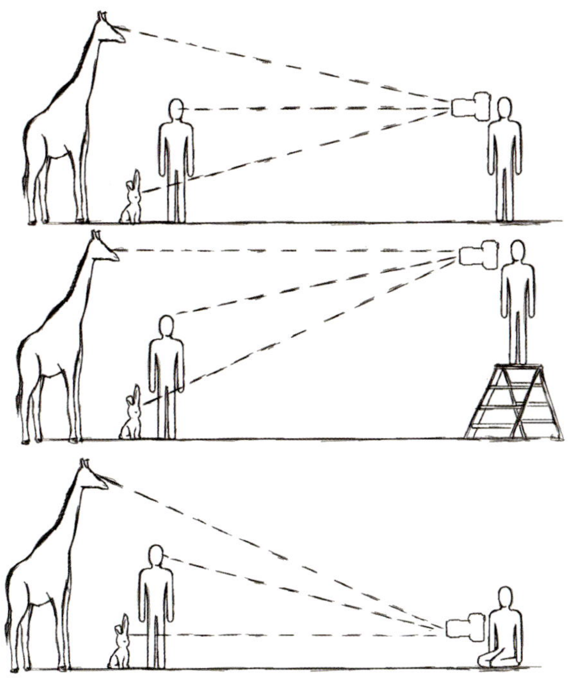

In addition to lateral shifts in perspective, you can adjust the vertical positioning of your camera by lying on the ground, kneeling, holding your camera over your head, or climbing on a chair, ladder, or other tall perch. If your camera has a swivel monitor and a live view mode, you can comfortably see your composition even with your arms stretched above your head.

As your camera height changes, your perspective of the subject will also change. Horizontal surfaces will appear narrower when viewed from below and wider when viewed from above, and your subjects will be distorted. In simplistic terms, there are three broad levels of perspective: eye level, bird's-eye level, and worm's-eye level. These terms are misleading because saying that a camera is at, above, or below a certain level doesn't take the size of the subject into consideration. Perspective can't be discussed in absolute terms because it's always relative to the camera and the subject. For example, if the camera is positioned just above the ground, it's said to be a worm's-eye perspective. If you take a picture of a person from this perspective, you'll look upward; if you photograph an ant, you'll look downward; if you take a picture of a toadstool, it will be at eye level. It's much more practical to use terms that consider the position of both the camera and the subject, rather than the camera alone, which is why we use the terms *normal view, downward view,* and *upward view* in the following pages. These terms describe the position and point of view of the camera—which is the same as the viewer's perspective—rather than the point of view of the subject.

The exposure height doesn't have any meaning by itself. Only when it is considered in relation to the subject's size does it indicate anything about perspective and the relationship between the camera (or the viewer) and the object that you're photographing. Holding your camera low can produce a normal view if you're taking a picture of a rabbit, just like an elevated camera position might be normal for a picture of a giraffe.

Normal View

A normal view amounts to a direct, immediate, and equal perspective of the subject. You and your camera will look at your subject, or the relevant part of your subject, from a level perspective. For example, if you're looking at someone directly in the eyes, you're looking from a normal point of view. If you gaze down at his or her feet, it's a downward view.

Looking at someone eye to eye is considered a normal view; the camera is positioned at the same height as the subject.

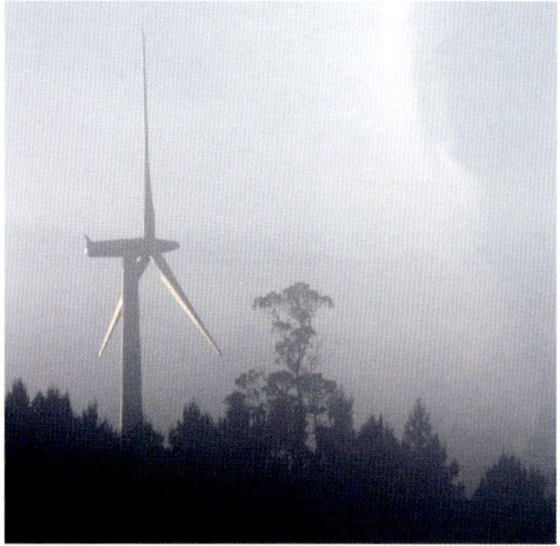
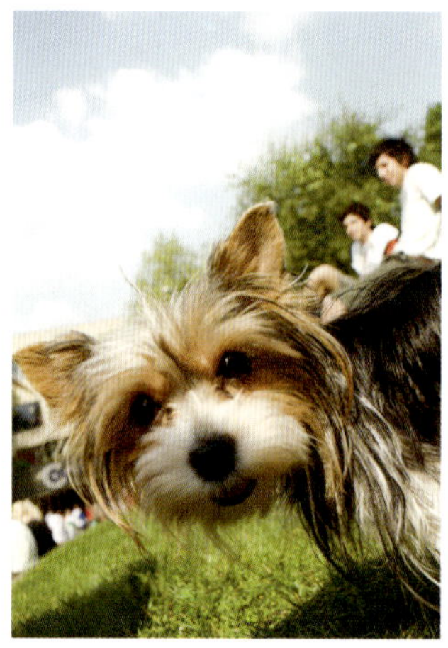
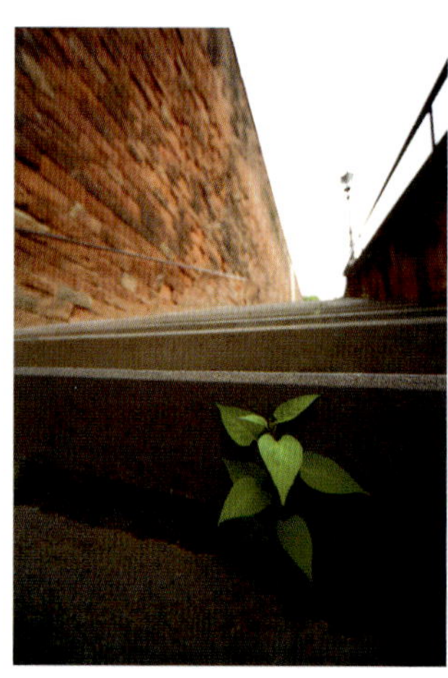

The normal view doesn't always lead to conventional images. Approaching the eye level of a very short or very tall subject is not common, so it creates an unusual perspective for the viewer. Images exposed from these points of view can have a stimulating effect.

If you photograph your subject from this perspective, the image will have an intimate, conventional, calm, and even a documentary quality that can easily become boring, depending on your subject. These qualities are common when you use this point of view by default rather than choosing it consciously to achieve your objective.

The normal view can be a truly exciting and eye-opening perspective for subjects that would normally be seen from below or above. If you use an eye-level perspective with smaller or larger subjects, you'll discover that images of your children or pets will be more exciting. Photographing subjects that we usually see from below, such as a giraffe, at a normal view will also reveal captivating perspectives. Images shot from the normal view force viewers to engage with your subjects eye to eye and view them as equals.

Downward View

Photographing subjects from above tends to reduce their size. It forces viewers to take on a more authoritative perspective, since they will look down on the subjects. The elements in an image shot from this perspective will appear unusually distorted and will come across as small and vulnerable. A downward view will also alter the proportions of your subject, especially when you shoot with a wide-angle lens. When you take a portrait from above, for example, your subject's forehead can become unnaturally and distractingly large.

Downward views provide an overview of a scene and show how the elements are positioned with respect to one another. This makes a downward perspective especially useful when you want your image to explain something, clarify relationships, or simplify connections.

Depending on your subject, a downward view can turn your image into a real eye-catcher. The view of a city from above may be an everyday sight for a helicopter pilot, but for most of us it's a novelty and will likely turn the viewer's head.

When photographers take pictures from directly above their subjects, the resulting images show an uncommon perspective. We may be familiar with this perspective for small things, but when it's used on larger objects the unusual and new perspective piques our interest. Shots from directly above also make it difficult for viewers to recognize the subject and make sense of the image. A downward view allows you to set up visual puzzles that force viewers to scratch their heads—and actively engage with a photo—while they're trying to figure out what each element is. This method is particularly effective when the visual element recalls a different object from the viewer's schema (page 24). When you apply this perspective carefully, you can lead the viewer on a visual journey.

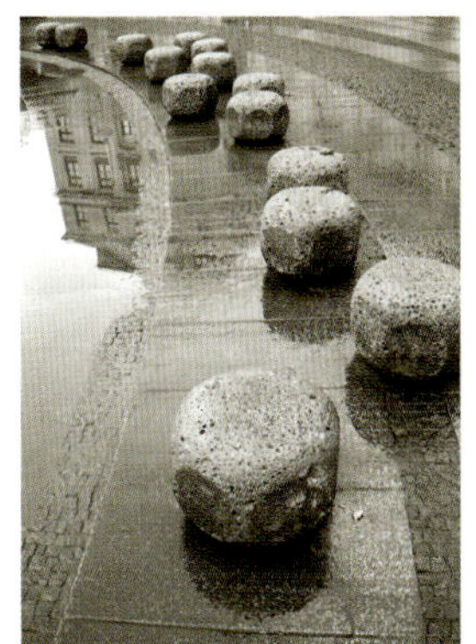

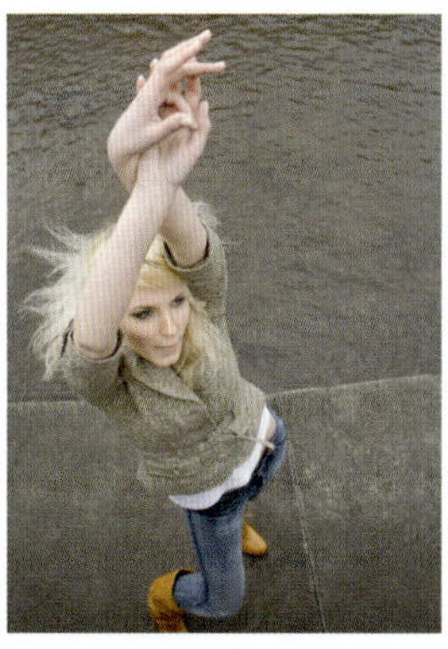

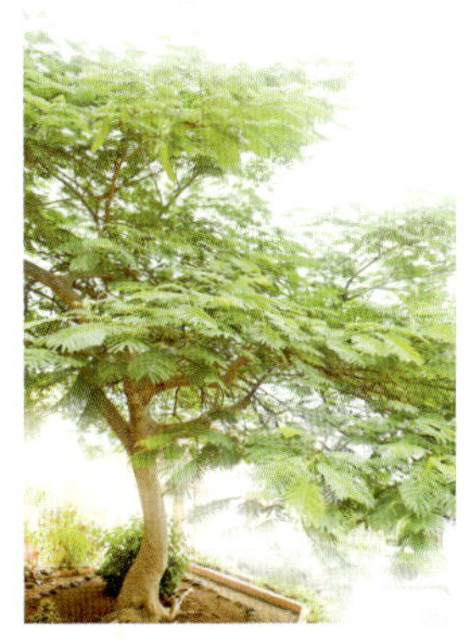

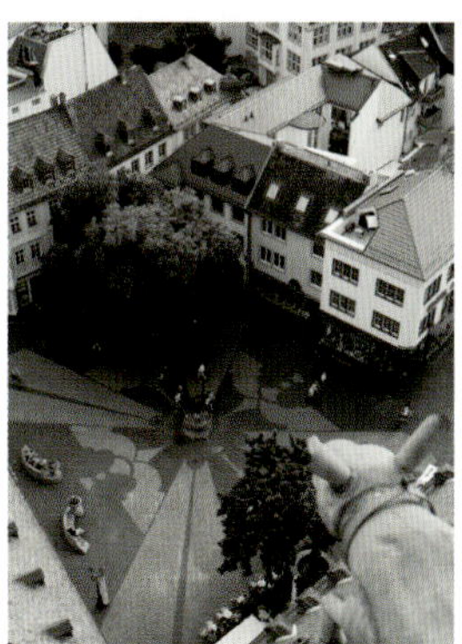

We're used to seeing objects from above if they are substantially smaller than us. The larger your subject and the higher your camera, the more jarring the downward view. The stones on this town square seem more familiar than the dancing woman. Looking at a tree or a city square from above can take the viewer to a new and fascinating place.

Upward View

The effects of examining an object from below are the opposite of looking at it from above. This upward view gives the subject a more powerful, dominant position, and the viewer is made to feel small and submissive. The viewer can't help but take on these qualities because the relationship between the subject and the viewer is established at the time of exposure. You can't change the point of view that was established by the photographer.

When we look at subjects that are larger than we are, we expect the upward perspective. But looking up to objects that are equal in size or smaller than we are is unsettling, and can add drama to images. Don't hesitate to crouch, sit, or lie down so you can point your camera upward. A swivel monitor will help you control your camera's point of view, but even without looking through the viewfinder you can use the upward view with a little bit of practice. Give it a try by manually setting a wide-angle lens to the minimum focal length and hold your camera in a bed of flowers with the lens pointed up. All of a sudden daffodils look like skyscrapers, and you're

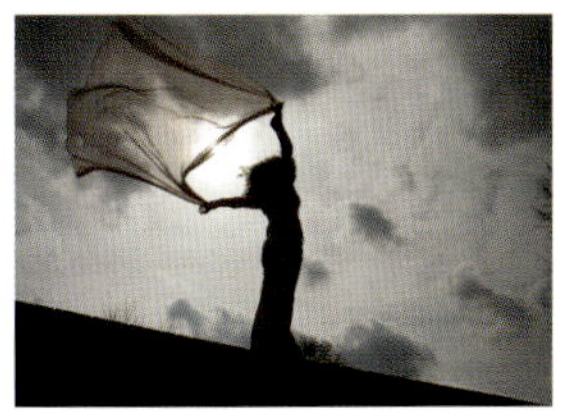

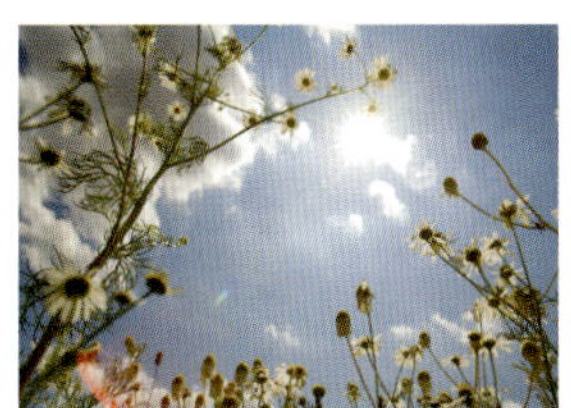

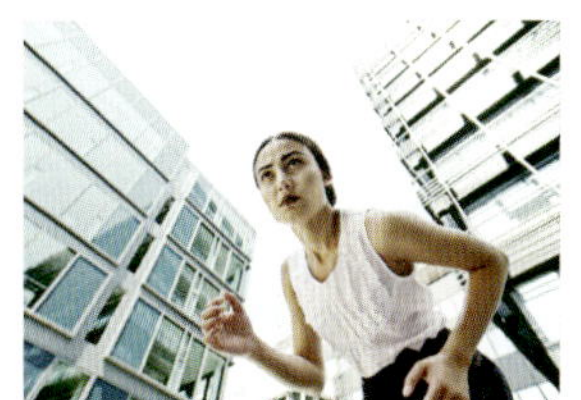

The upward view is familiar when you're looking at something that is larger than you. But looking up at another person or a wildflower is strikingly unusual. The upward view is enough to make these images interesting.

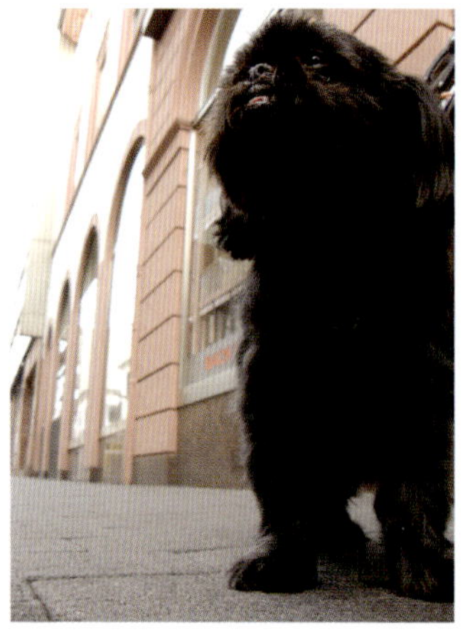

The extreme upward view turns a Pekingese mix into a big and dangerous dog that you might think twice about approaching. As a viewer, there's no way to undo this impression, even if you tell yourself that in reality, the animal is barely as tall as your knee.

guaranteed to capture an attention-grabbing image. An upward view makes it harder for viewers to understand what they are seeing. You should also be aware that upward views might not produce the most attractive images—nostrils, in particular, pose a problem.

In addition to these more extreme uses of downward and upward views, you can also apply finer shifts in perspective that viewers may not consciously notice. Even a tiny shift in perspective will place viewers in higher or lower positions with respect to the subject. Smaller adjustments are often more effective because the viewer subconsciously feels the change in perspective without rationally considering it. This is especially true with portraiture.

For this very reason, most photos designed for use in advertising feature a modest upward view, rather than a normal or downward view. This perspective makes models seem more self-confident, as though no one could look down on them.

Tweaks in perspective are especially effective with portraits. A slight upward view (left) or a slight downward view (right) results in a superior or inferior position, respectively. Since these nuances are so subtle, the effect often plays out on a subconscious level.

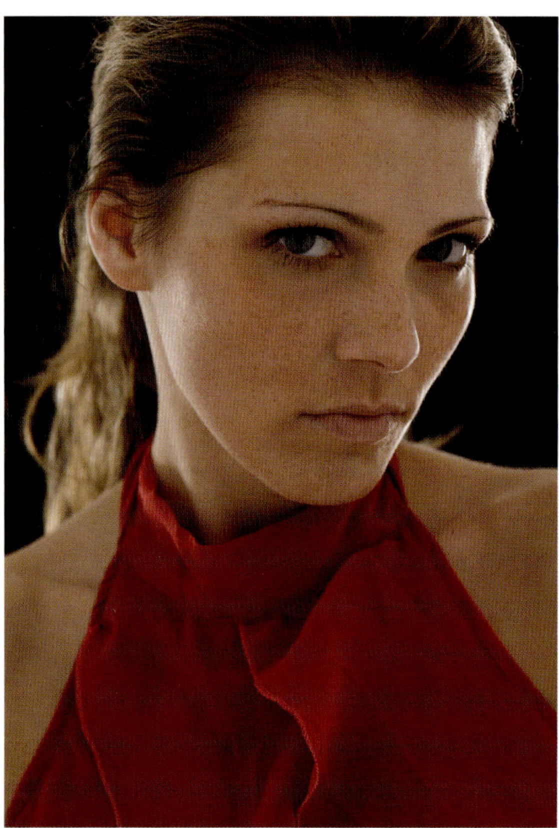

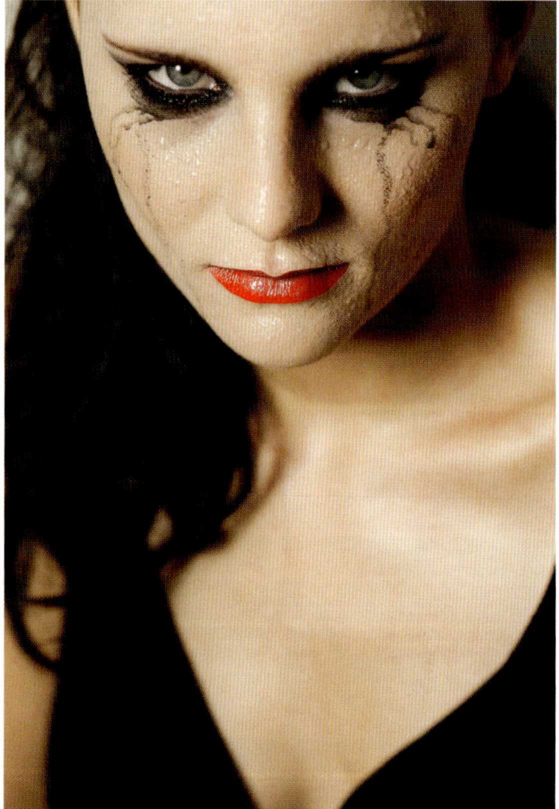

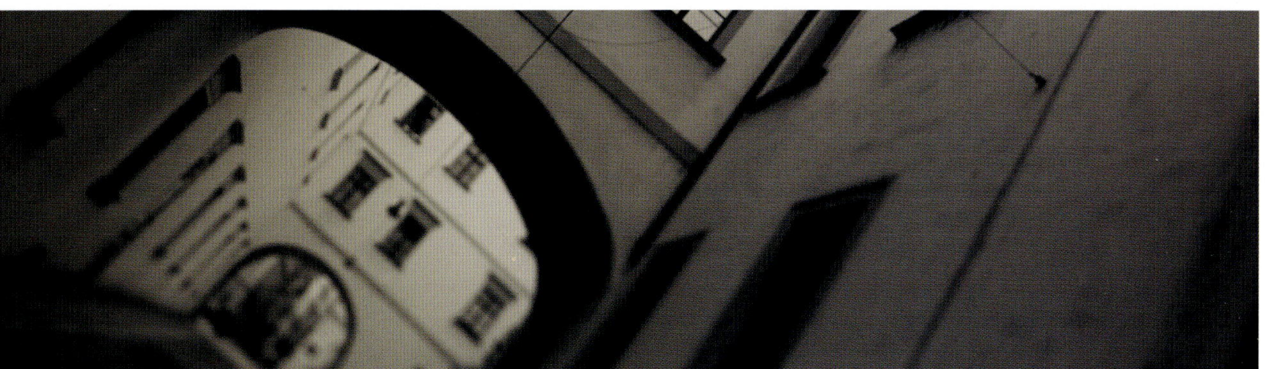

4.2 Lens Characteristics

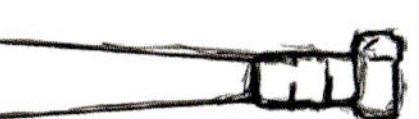

There's a lens for every occasion. Taking a picture of an animal, for example, requires that you stand a certain distance away so you don't scare it. A telephoto lens is ideal in a situation like this because you can fill up your frame with the subject, despite being far away from it.

In addition to determining a point of view, you also need to select a lens, which directly affects the elements that get included in your image. Different focal lengths exhibit different characteristics of subjects. As a design-conscious photographer, you can exploit these optical qualities to influence the look and feel of your images, as well as the way people perceive them.

Basics

A lens focuses light, aligns it, and produces a round, upside-down representation of the world on the image sensor or film. Because of the rectangular shape of the sensor, the image area is cropped to a standard image format (page 40). Lenses can be fixed to the camera body or they can be interchangeable, which allows for greater flexibility. Generally speaking, a lens can be a zoom lens or a fixed focal length lens. Lenses are also categorized based on the range of their focal length; wide angle, normal, and telephoto are the three standard classifications. Each type of lens has its own characteristics that make it suitable for different purposes.

The category of a lens is based on its range of focal lengths and speeds; zoom lenses have ranges, but fixed focal length lenses do not. In the following pages we will discuss the qualities of fixed focal length lenses, but everything we talk about can easily be applied to zoom lenses.

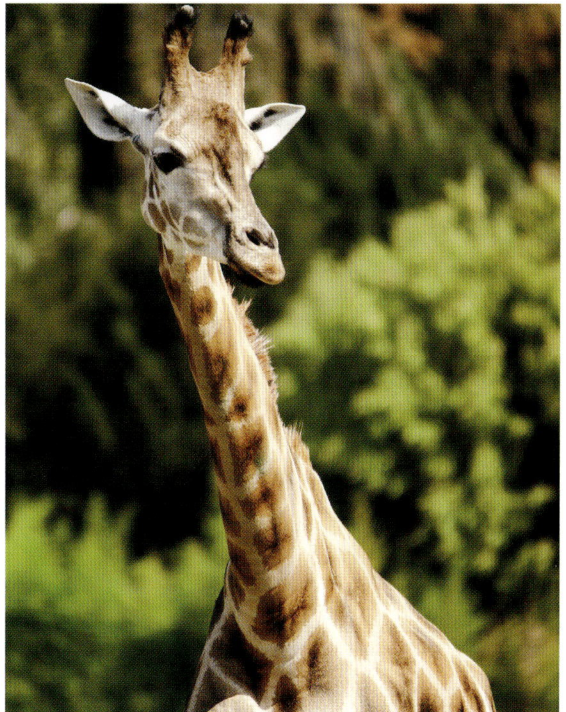

Focal length: 400mm

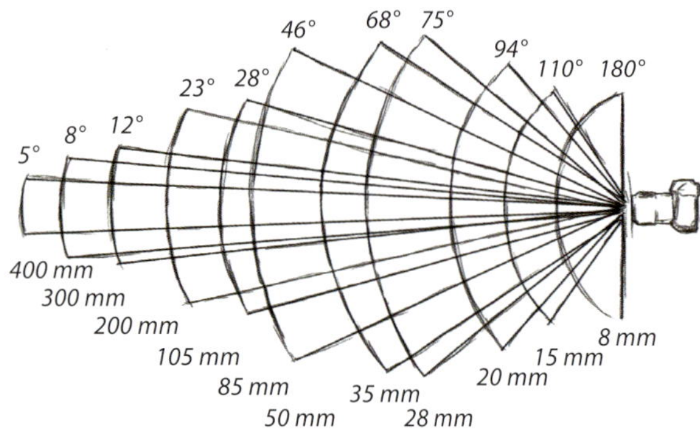

Angle of View

Angle of view is a variable that doesn't get enough attention despite the fact that it's at least as important as focal length and lens speed. Depending on its focal length, a lens can have a wider or narrower angle of view. The angle of view is one-half of the equation that determines what will appear within your image—the other half is the distance between your camera and the subject (page 48). Anything outside the angle of view won't be visible in your final photo. Assuming you keep the camera stationary, a smaller angle of view will encompass a narrower window of reality, and a larger angle of view will include a broader window of reality. To have a consistently sized frame for a picture, you need to be much closer to a subject when you use a lens with a wide angle of view than when you use a lens with a narrow angle of view. The angle of view is not only significant for determining how many objects will appear in your image (or which ones will be excluded), it also affects how far away you must be from the subject for it to fill the entire image area.

The focal lengths and angles of view indicated in the illustration apply to 35mm format systems. The longer the focal length, the narrower the angle will be.

Angle of View and Sensor Size

As a result of the widespread use of 35mm film, focal lengths are linked with certain angles of view in the minds of many photographers. A focal length of 20mm, for example, produces a wide angle. But a focal length itself doesn't actually reveal anything about the angle of view because the angle also depends on the size of the image sensor (more specifically, the diagonal dimension of the sensor). The smaller the sensor is, the smaller the angle of view. This sounds straightforward enough, but it becomes quite problematic in the world of digital photography, where different sensor sizes might not have focal lengths that are consistent with those in the world of analog photography. The angle of view and the resulting image area that the lens can capture varies for different cameras and camera systems. The only digital cameras that have optical characteristics identical to traditional 35mm film cameras are full-

The image on the left was exposed with a full-frame camera and a 105mm lens. The image on the right was shot with the same lens on a camera that has a crop factor of 1.6. The angle of view is noticeably narrower as a result of the smaller sensor. To capture the same image area as the picture on the left, the camera would need to be moved back substantially, or a lens with a shorter focal length of 70mm would need to be used.

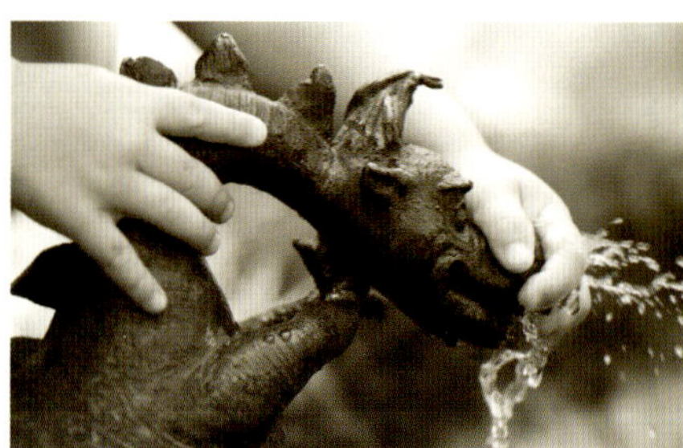

Focal length: 105mm

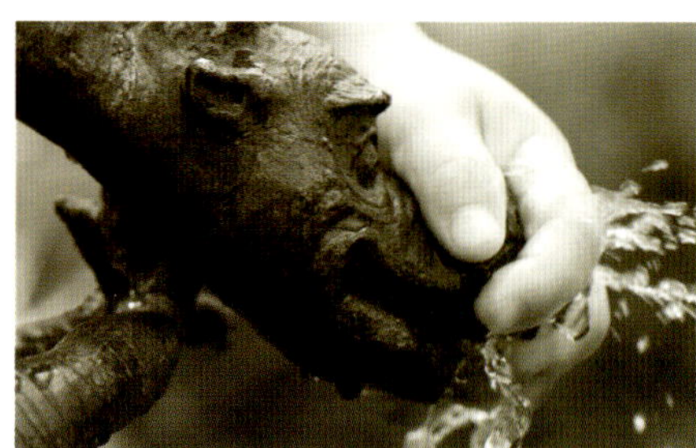

Focal length: 105mm with a crop factor of 1.6

frame cameras. People usually indicate focal lengths as 35mm equivalents. For the purpose of making comparisons and sticking with familiar practices, we follow this convention in all our books.

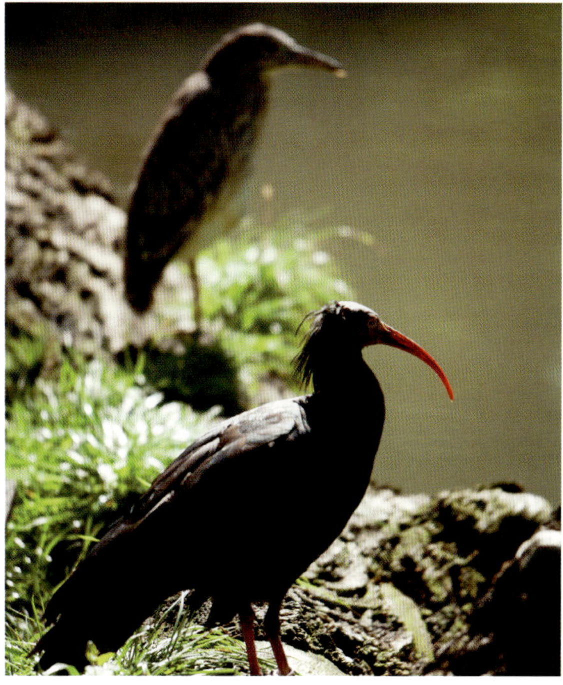
Focal length: 350mm

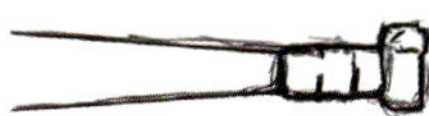
Sensors with a crop factor can show their better side when shooting a subject or scene that benefits from the use of a telephoto lens. As a result of the smaller sensor, only a portion of the image projected by the lens gets recorded, which results in a tighter field of view. The flip side of this is a limited ability to shoot with a wide-angle perspective. Full-frame cameras are better suited to circumstances that call for wide-angle lenses.

Designing with Small Sensors

If you are working with a camera that has a crop factor, it's important that you understand that your field of view will always be smaller than if you were working with a full-frame sensor. For example, if your sensor has a crop factor of 1.7 and you are using a 50mm lens capable of a full-frame sensor, your field of view will be the same as if you used an 85mm lens with a full-frame camera. The result is comparable to enlarging a cropped area of the image. Since imaging characteristics such as distortion and vignetting are more of a problem around the image borders, they can hardly be seen as a result of the reduced field of view. To use a 50mm lens and a crop sensor to get the same field of view as a 50mm lens on a full-frame camera, you would need to increase the distance between your camera and the subject. Shorter focal lengths require shorter distances between the subject and the camera to achieve the same field of view as longer focal lengths.

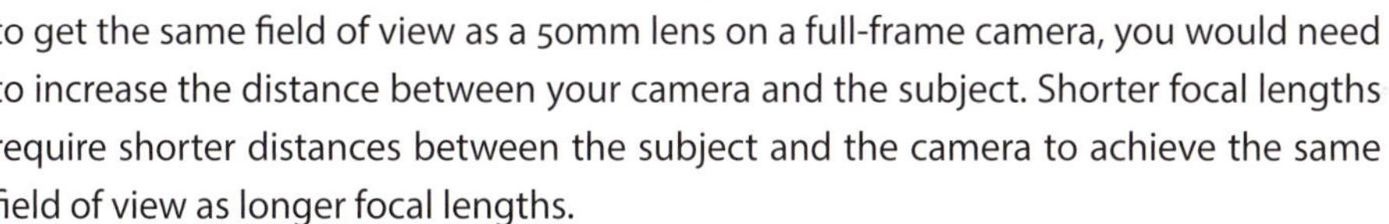

On a design level, this means that crop cameras need shorter focal lengths to establish a wide field of view. Conversely, they have a tighter angle of view with a conventional telephoto lens than you would get using the same lens on a full-frame camera, making it easier to capture objects that are far away. If your photographic style, preferences, and genres of choice lend themselves to telephoto shooting, or if you enjoy working with a large depth of field, a crop camera may be an ideal tool for you. Full-frame cameras are particularly well-suited for photographers who use wide-angle lenses. Full-frame systems also benefit from the faster and better wide-angle lenses that manufacturers are developing for crop systems.

Focal Length Ranges

Photographers generally categorize focal lengths into different ranges that are independent of the camera and that are based on the *normal* focal length. The focal length—depending on the sensor size—produces a field of view that corresponds to a person's natural vision. This natural field of view assumes that people can see clearly and optimally without turning their heads or moving their eyes, which

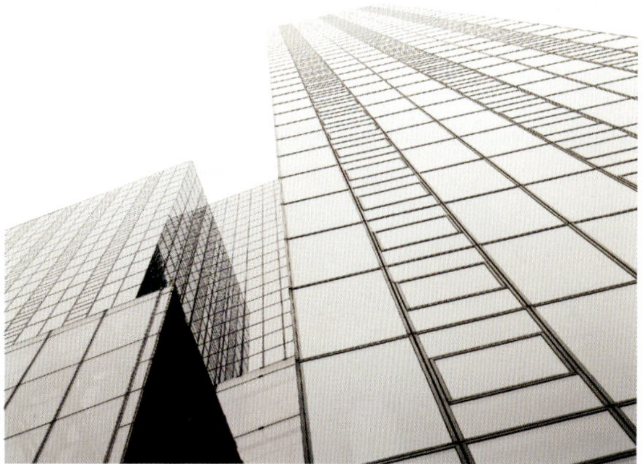

Focal length: 50mm

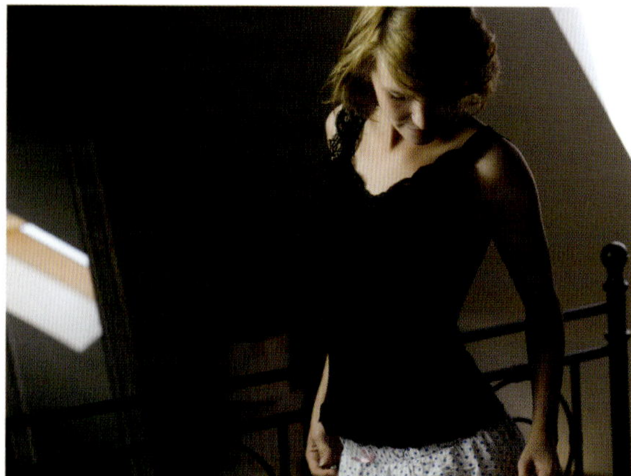

Focal length: 50mm

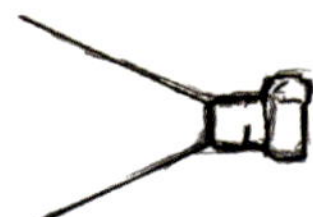

A person's natural vision encompasses a range of about 45 degrees. Any photo captured at this angle of view tends to feel familiar and regular, as shown in these two images. In these images, other design elements are required to capture the viewer's attention.

generally encompasses an angle of about 45 degrees. Another approach is to define the normal focal length based on the sensor's diagonal dimension, but this is less meaningful in terms of design than the familiar field of view that we consider normal.

With a 35mm camera or a full-frame camera, a 50mm lens produces an angle of view that approaches this 45 degree mark. This is also the dividing point between the range of focal lengths that are considered wide angle and those that are considered telephoto. Wide-angle lenses include all shorter focal lengths that reveal a broad angle of view, and telephoto lenses include all longer focal lengths that produce a tighter angle of view.

The dividing point shifts upward for cameras with a crop sensor and those with a larger format. For example, a camera with a crop factor of 1.7 produces the normal angle of view with a 30mm lens. A 6x6 medium-format camera will do nearly the same with an 80mm lens.

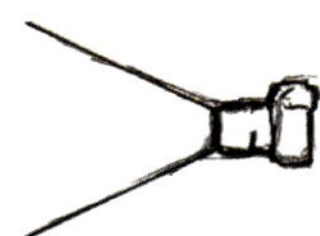

Normal lenses—which for the 35mm format, have a focal length of 50mm—have the unfair reputation of being boring. As with any photographic tool, you can use these lenses to design images that are exciting or placid, subjective or objective.

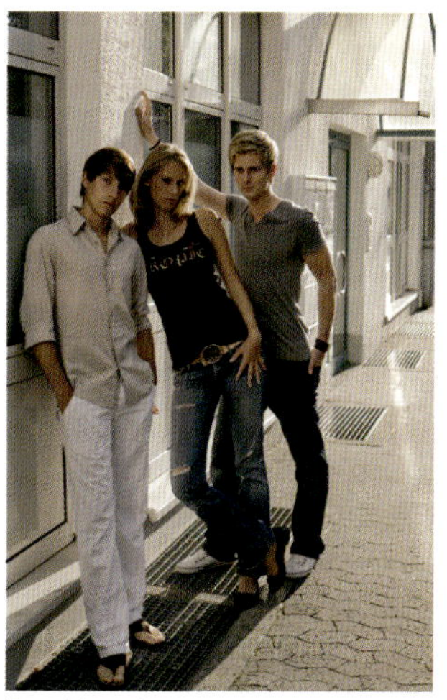

Focal length: 50mm

Normal Lenses

Since the view from a normal lens approximates the characteristics of our natural vision, photographs shot with this angle of view seem familiar, neutral, and objective. This perspective creates an authentic and documentary feel. These focal lengths lend themselves to photojournalism (regardless of genre) and all kinds of documentary work.

These lenses are also suitable for beginners and people who wish to be intentionally limited to a simple angle of view. Using these lenses forces photographers to concentrate on other photographic elements, such as technique (see *Learning to Pho-*

tograph Vol.1), purposefully designing the image, and creatively engaging with the visual content. Normal lenses often get labeled as boring, but they provide a clear and genuine look at a subject. There is one common motif, however, that doesn't work well with a normal lens: a human face that fills, or nearly fills, the image area. We perceive faces in a way that a camera doesn't—we focus on the eyes. A face captured with a normal lens looks unattractively flat and distorted.

Wide Angles of View

Angles of view that are wider than the natural human field of view allow us to see more without moving our heads. Since more objects are depicted in the same amount of space, they must be reduced in size. Wide-angle lenses can accomplish this because objects at different distances from the lens are represented with different proportions. Objects that are close to the camera look significantly larger than they really are, and those that are farther away look smaller. The shorter the focal length and the closer an object is to the lens, the more dramatic this effect will be. This can give rise to absurd, comical distortions, such as a dog with a huge nose and tiny ears or converging verticals (page 89). This characteristic of wide-angle lenses allows photographers to develop the dimensional space within an image and establish fields of view that seem subjective, unnatural, and even surreal.

The distortion in the foreground of this image is obvious. Everyone is familiar with the shape of a round manhole cover and knows what it should look like when viewed at an angle. The visual representation in this image, however, doesn't correspond to that expected view—stretched elements in the foreground and skewed proportions are indicative of a wide angle of view.

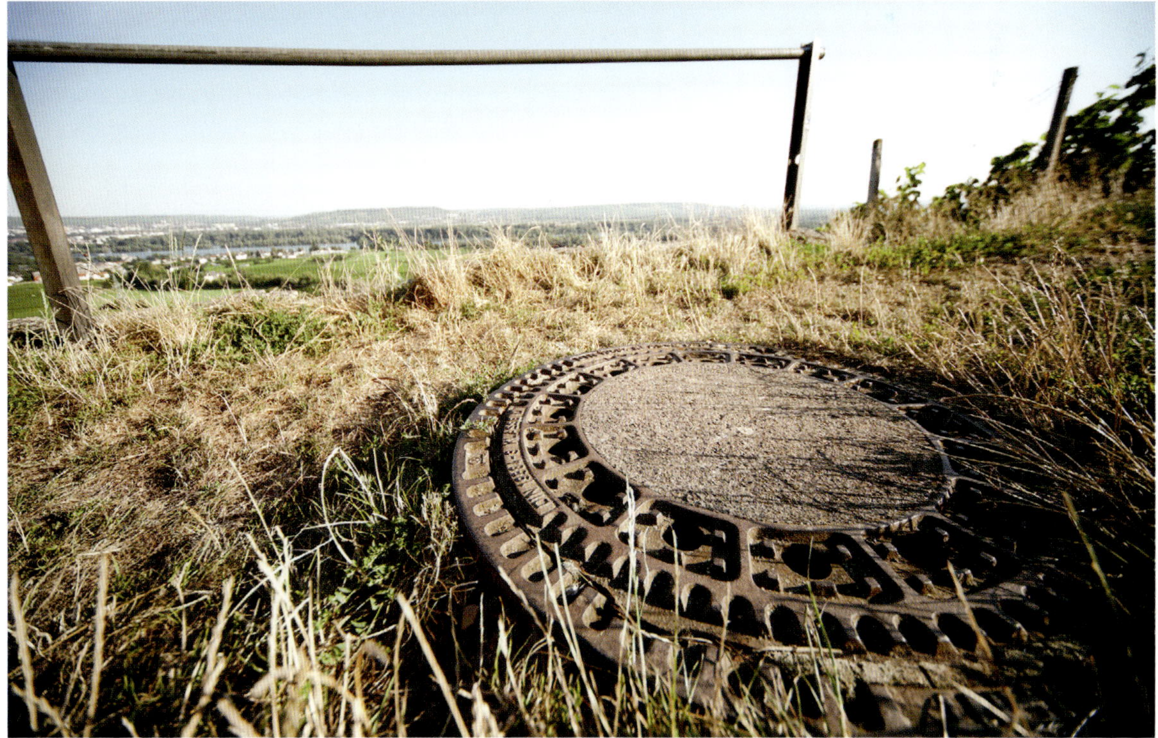

Focal length: 12mm

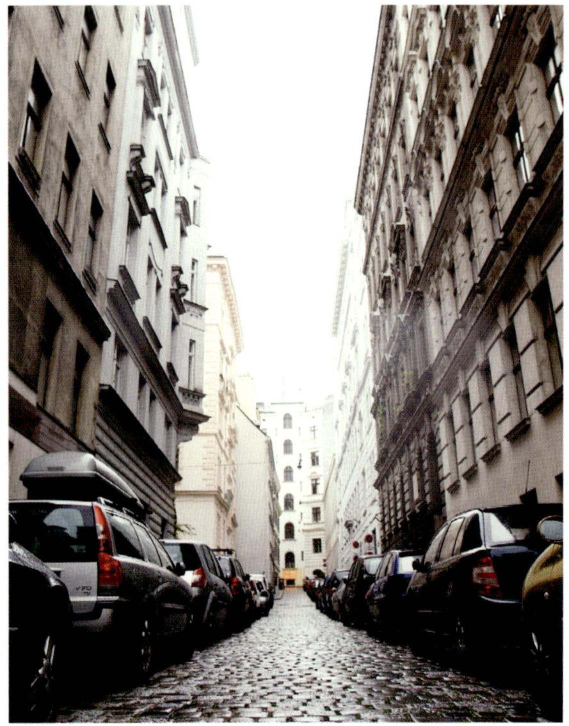

Focal length: 20mm

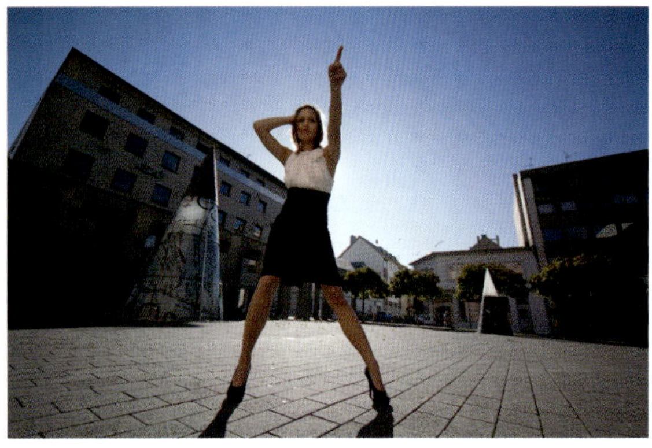

Focal length: 15mm

A wide-angle lens creates a dramatic stage in a photo and emphasizes all three dimensions. The image elements in the foreground appear larger than in life, the elements in the middle seem small, and those in the background become miniature.

If you intentionally use this effect, the subject will immediately become a dominant part of your image and viewers will feel like they're in the middle of the scene. Elements in the foreground seem to wrap around viewers. This perspective provides a direct, immediate, emotional look and feel, making it hard for viewers to resist. This effect can be so powerful that it's unnerving, and it may cause viewers to wish for more space.

Aside from making elements in the foreground substantially larger, wide-angle lenses generally allow you to work with a greater depth of field (page 179). They also make it easier to place objects however you want within the image, since so much surrounding area is also included. Depending on each individual shot, you can provide a substantial amount of contextual information. Photographers can exploit this characteristic of wide-angle lenses to depict complex relationships and vast amounts of information in a single image.

Be sure to check for distracting elements in the background because they will pull attention away from the main subject, especially if they fall within the in-focus depth of field (page 80). If you use this method effectively, you can create exciting, dynamic, and effective images that draw their potential directly from the wide angle of view.

Additionally, the significant curvature of the lens results in barrel distortion; that is, lines that are parallel to the border bow outward. The focal length determines the severity of this distortion, which is why it makes sense to test short focal lengths.

Depending on the genre, you're likely to find that some wide-angle lenses are ideal for your purposes, while others are too short or too long. Keep these points in mind when you select and use wide-angle lenses:

- People and animals can look distorted
- Converging verticals are pronounced
- Expansive shots with no foreground elements are usually monotonous

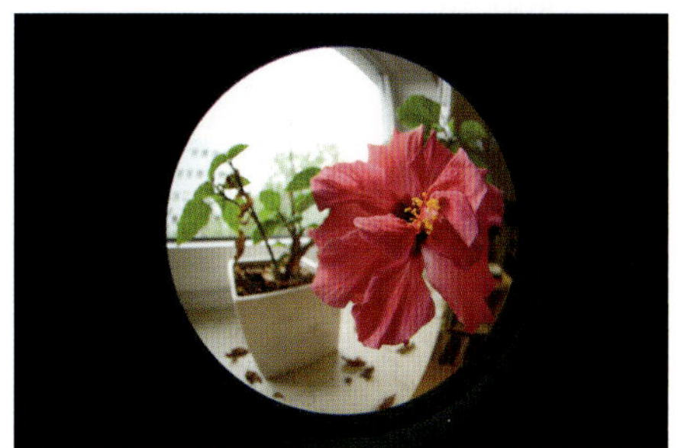
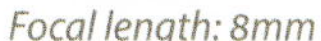
Focal length: 8mm

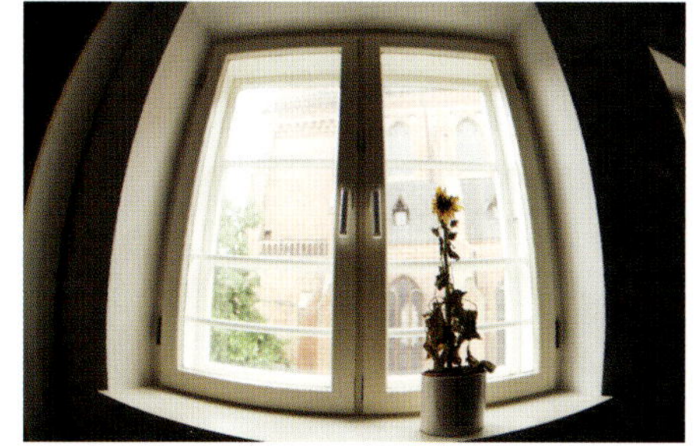
Focal length: 12mm

Fisheye lenses create unnatural and highly distorted images that exhibit a strong 3-D effect. No one expects realistic images from these lenses—they are used to create cartoony, exaggerated views of subjects in the image.

Telephoto lenses flatten the dimension of depth within an image by compressing visual layers. This causes objects to look like they are next to one another, even if broad expanses separate them.

Fisheye Lenses

Lenses with extremely wide angles of view are typically referred to as Fisheye lenses. This type of lens can capture up to 360 degrees, and they are generally divided into two groups: full-frame and partial-frame. Only full-frame lenses fill the entire image area. Partial-frame lenses create a circular image in the middle of an otherwise black surface. Both types of lenses, however, produce an immediately noticeable and very extreme distortion that grabs the viewer's attention. However, the Fisheye lens is a double-edged sword because the disharmonious effect can be tiresome. Viewers may ignore these types of photos unless you create engaging images. When you select a subject, remember that even large objects, at any distance from the camera, will look tiny in the final image. The horizon line will always be curved, and Fisheye shots usually come across as artificial. These features can help you convey a lively sense of emotion through unique and visually pleasing shots, even though they exaggerate the details of reality.

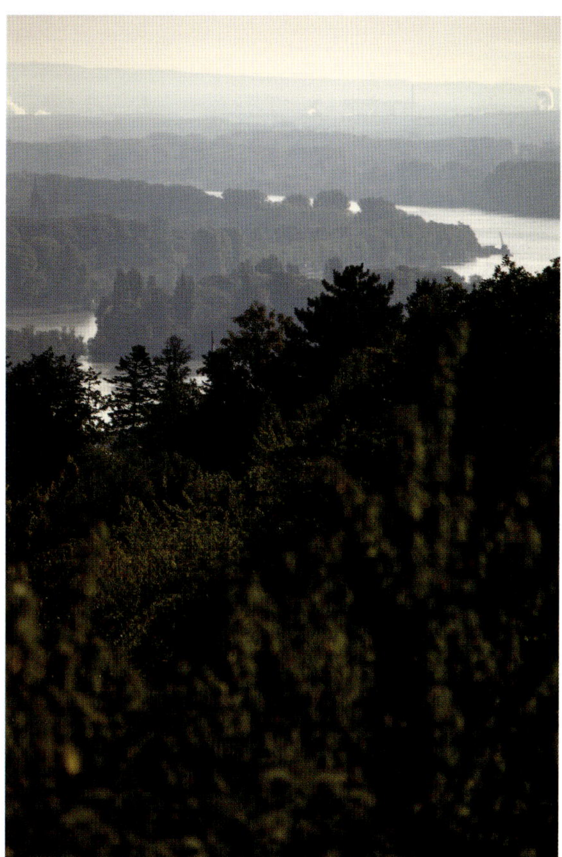
Focal length: 400mm

Narrow Angles of View

If a photo shows a smaller cross section of reality than we can take in with our natural vision, then the angle of view is smaller than our field of view, and was likely shot with a telephoto lens. Looking at images created with a telephoto lens is similar to looking through a magnifying glass or a telescope. The subject looks much closer than it actually is, even though it's obvious that the distance was optically collapsed. Telephoto lenses require a certain distance between the photographer and the

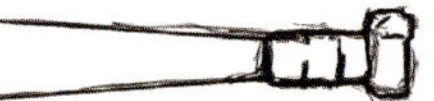

With a telephoto lens you often work with a narrow depth of field that extends only slightly in front of and beyond the subject. This makes telephoto lenses popular with fashion photographers because they can create images in which the models and their clothes are sharp while their surroundings and any potentially distracting elements are not. By carefully applying this principle, you can effectively isolate subjects even when they're in front of a busy backdrop.

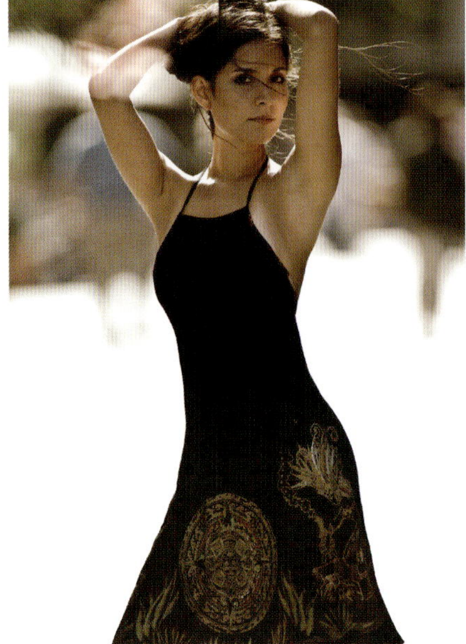

Focal length: 300mm

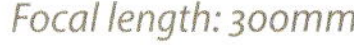

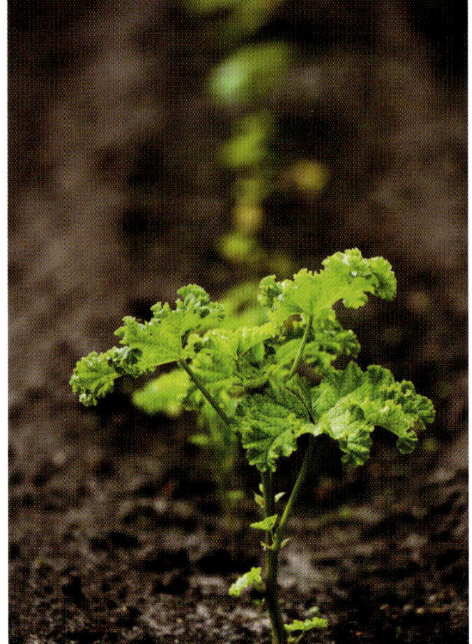

Focal length: 150mm

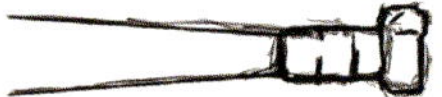

You can also create images with telephoto lenses that are in focus throughout all levels of depth. This is especially true when the subject is far away and there are a limited number of levels in close proximity. Despite the interesting shadows and the prevailing lines in this detail of the train station in Hamburg, Germany, the striking flatness of the image comes across first and foremost.

subject, which affects both the spatial and the emotional dimensions of an image. The distance depends on the individual circumstances of your shot, but the effect can be so pronounced that it gives your image a voyeuristic tone because the view of the scene seems unaffected by external viewers, including the photographer. The narrower the angle of view, the stronger this effect becomes. Telephoto lenses make it possible to depict subjects that viewers don't normally see up close, like wild animals or mountaintops, in fascinating and accessible ways, even when it's clear that there was a great distance between the subject and the camera.

The design applications of the telephoto lens are based on the impression of flatness it brings to images. The distances between individual elements seem to shorten, and the elements seem to be pushed together. Instead of producing images with pronounced depth and dimensionality, telephoto lenses create images that are striking, graphic, and sometimes abstract. Telephoto lenses create pillow distortions—at very long focal lengths, parallel lines near the edges of an image bow toward the center. At shorter focal lengths, this distortion is less noticeable. This is one reason telephoto lenses are preferred for taking pictures of people; this slight streamlining of the human form can have a pleasing effect. Longer focal lengths affect image sharpness because they typically yield a shallower depth of field. They allow you to isolate the subject from its surroundings and set it in a more general, less contextualized setting.

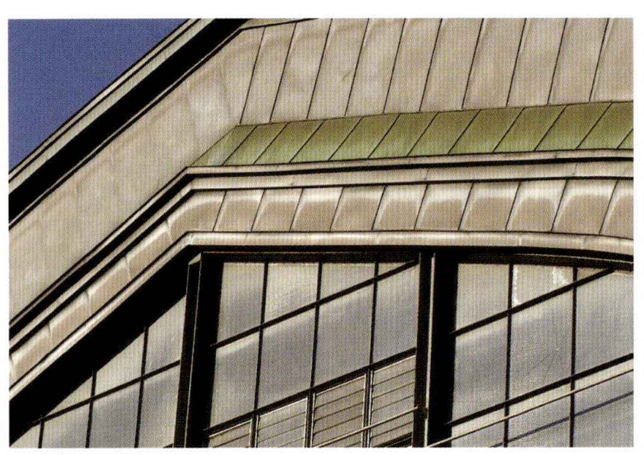

Focal length: 180mm

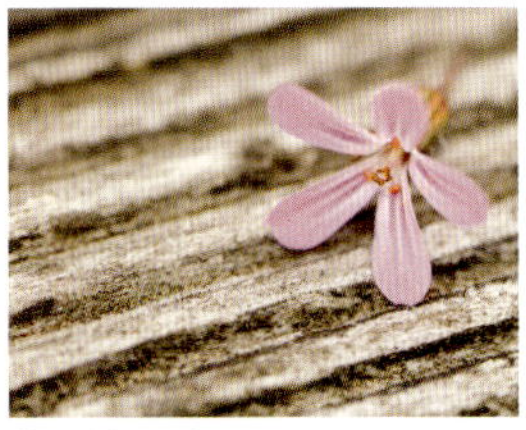
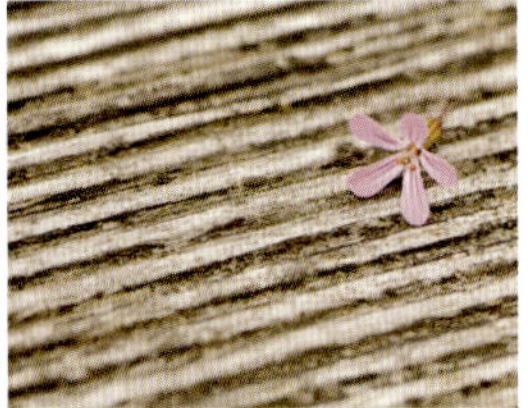
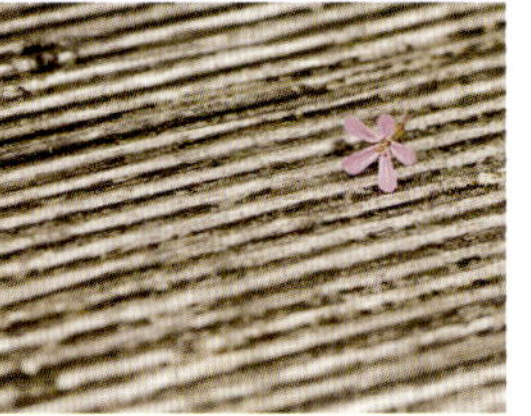
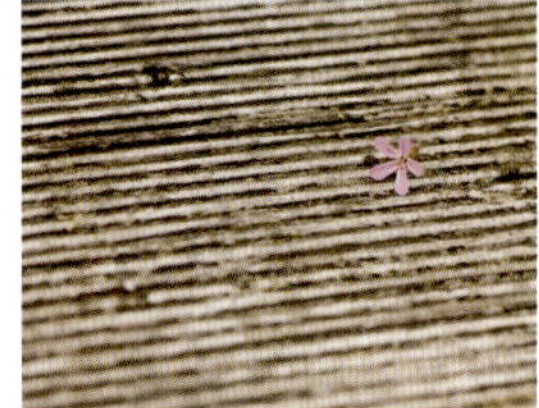

Focal length: 105mm macro

These four images were shot at four different levels of magnification: 1:1, 1:2, 1:3, and 1:4 (left to right). In reality, the flower itself is tiny and would normally be perceived as a part of a larger group of many such blossoms. At a magnification level of 1:1 you can see individual details within this flower that function on their own as visual elements. At the weaker magnification levels, it is reduced to a visual point that more or less functions to establish a contrast with the surrounding area.

The flip side of this particular characteristic is that you often end up with a lack of detail in the background of your image. This isn't a problem when you shoot subjects from a substantial distance because you can still create images that are sharp from front to back (page 179). This can produce interesting results with landscape and architecture photography. You can, for example, capture two buildings separated by hundreds of feet so they are both in focus and appear to occupy the same visual plane. A telephoto mirror lens has a long focal length in a compact case. From a design perspective, this type of lens poses some problems with circular, distracting bokeh (see *Learning to Photograph Vol.1*).

Macro

A macro lens—regardless of its focal length—allows you to shoot at an extremely short distance from a subject because the optics dramatically increase your focus range. There is virtually no requirement for a minimum distance between the camera and the subject. You can approach the subject as closely as you'd like and exploit the increased magnification to fill your image area with miniature objects. Macro lenses allow photographers and viewers alike to access a new world. You can photograph subjects that viewers cannot see with the naked eye. These images are often as surprising as they are fascinating.

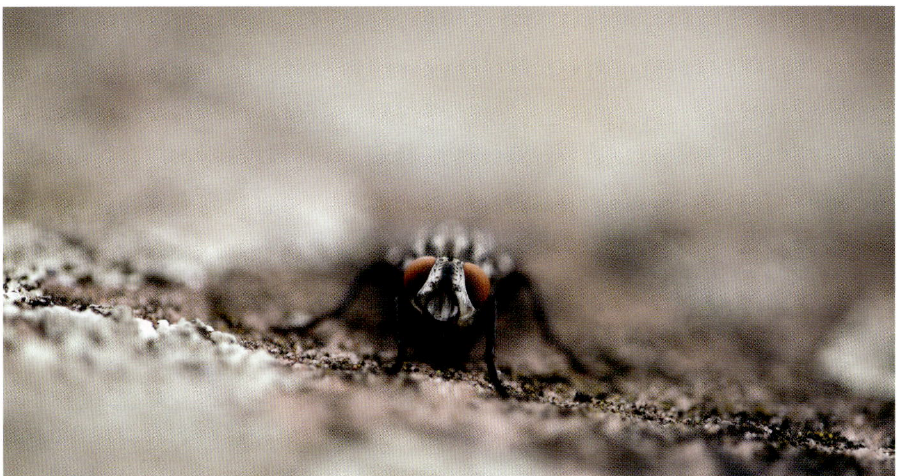

Focal length: 150mm macro

Powerful levels of magnification can turn subjects that are not usually interesting, such as this fly, into eye-catching winners. We would never be able to perceive the fly's faceted eyes and the detail in its face without the use of a macro lens. The magnification is a technical necessity here. It also produces powerfully engaging visual content.

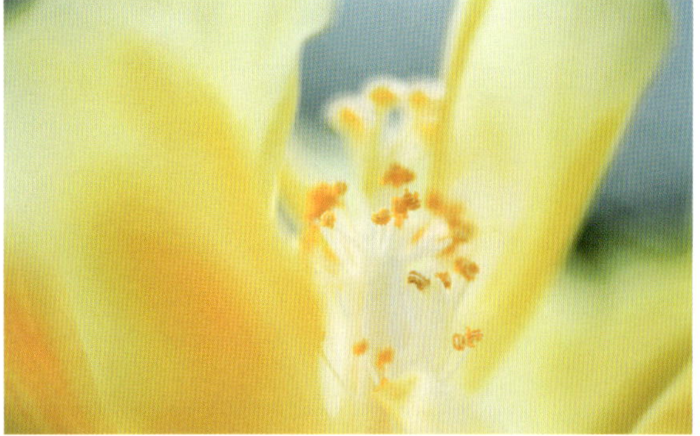

Focal length: 105mm macro

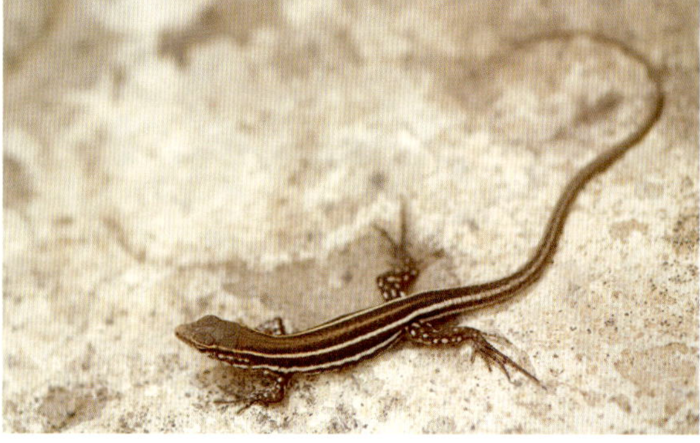

Focal length: 105mm macro

What viewers perceive as a macro image is thoroughly subjective, but it also depends on the subject. Viewers would immediately perceive the image on the left as macro because we always perceive pistils as a detail of a flower. This isn't the case with the gecko, though. Without a comparative point of reference, the viewer would have no way to know that this particular specimen is an especially small representative of its species.

The extreme closeness of the subject means that macro images exhibit exceptionally shallow depths of field. Macro images have a sharply defined plane of focus, which is where the viewer's gaze will settle. Objects positioned slightly in front of or behind this plane will be blurry, which often means that the sharp subject is surrounded by abstract, shapeless areas of color.

Tilt-Shift Exposures

Lenses with a shift function are popular in architecture photography because they can eliminate the effect of converging verticals. Images created with these lenses tend to seem clinical, tidy and artificial since they lack the converging verticals we are used to seeing with our natural eyesight. These lenses produce a journalistic or

It may take the viewer a bit longer to realize that the focal plane of this photo is not in parallel to the surface of the sensor. The feeling that something is unbalanced compels the viewer to engage more thoroughly with your photo.

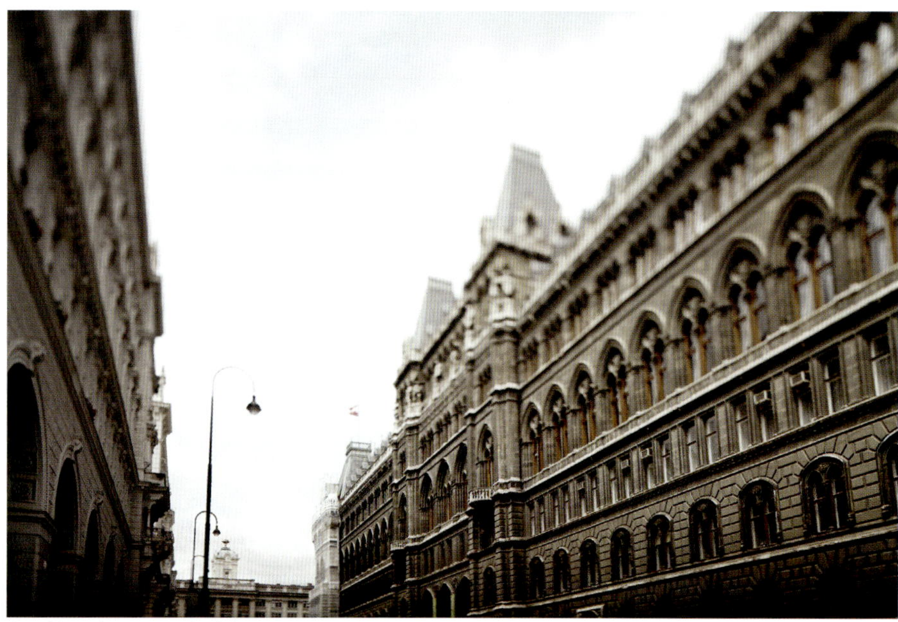

Focal length: 24mm, tilt-shift

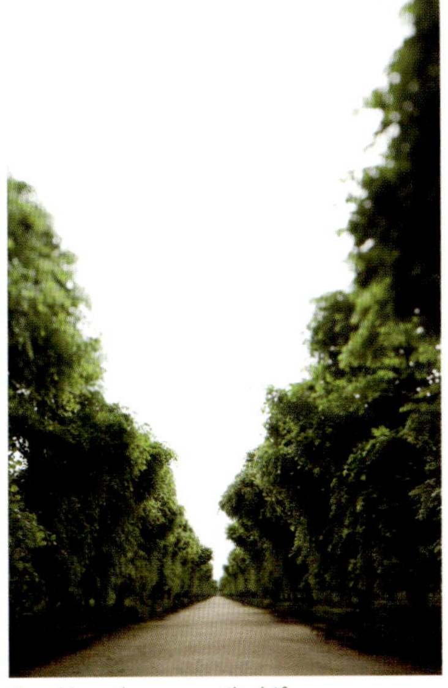

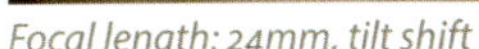

Focal length: 24mm, tilt shift

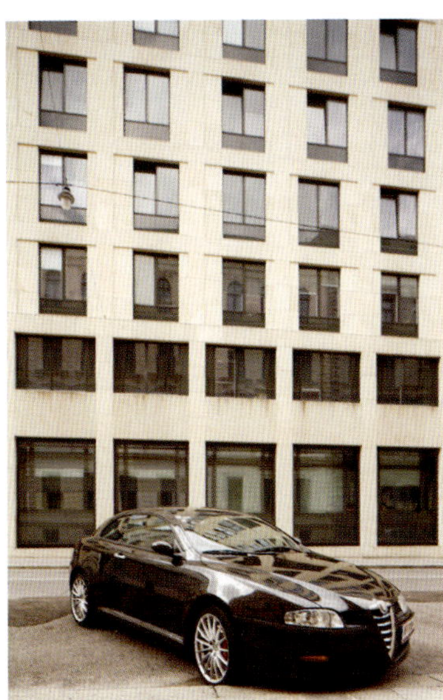

Focal length: 24mm, tilt shift

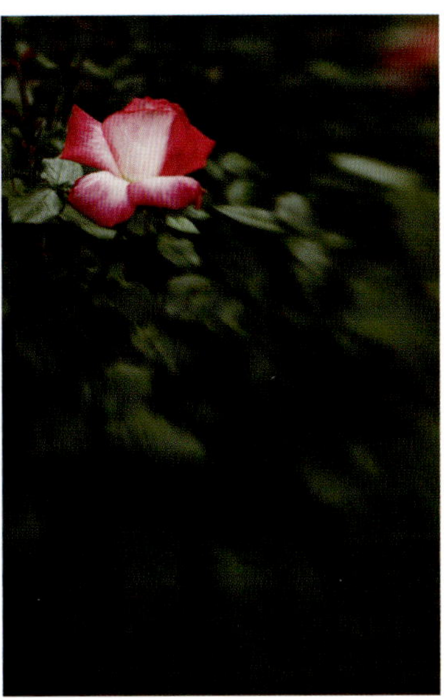

Focal length: 50mm, Lensbaby

The special exposure characteristics of tilt, shift, and Lensbaby lenses result in markedly different images. Tilt lenses are mostly known for their use in product or macro photography. Here a tilt lens trims down the magnificent scale of the park at the Schönbrunn Palace so it looks like a miniature landscape (left). The lines in this office building look straight and realistic because the effect of converging verticals has been neutralized with a shift lens; the car, however, looks like a small toy (middle). The blurred appearance resulting from a Lensbaby brings real movement and emotion into what would otherwise be an uninteresting shot (right).

documentary impression. Of course, using a shift lens can also exaggerate the effect of converging verticals instead of correcting it. This dynamic, exciting, subjective, and in many cases, chaotic design choice vastly increases the normal effect of converging verticals (page 89). Furthermore, shifting your lens laterally also gives you creative wiggle room—especially if you're shooting a reflective surface and you can shift yourself out of the image.

Shift lenses are generally combined with tilt functionality, which allows you to tilt the depth of field and create an unsettling visual effect that is unfamiliar to us because it doesn't exist in our everyday vision, or in most pictures we see. The unusual nature of this design technique feels very synthetic. Images shot in this way tend to exhibit an increased dimensionality when a left/right tilt is applied, and the viewer's gaze tends to remain in one spot or along one line when an up/down tilt is applied. In any case, using this type of lens is a sure way to guide the viewer's gaze, even though the means are unconventional. As with any design method, use a tilt-shift lens in a purposeful way that complements your subject.

The tilt effect produces images that remind us of miniature worlds because we most commonly see them in macro images created with a bellows in the world of product photography. Such images invite viewers to linger by giving them enticingly unusual perspectives.

Lensbaby lenses are similar to tilt lenses in that they allow you to adjust the depth of field within your image. They help create subjective, distorted, and purposefully flawed images that come across as experimental, artistic, and dynamic. As with many special effects, these results can quickly lose their appeal, and viewers will want to continue looking at these images only if they are combined with an interesting concept.

"Like language, when used effectively, [light] has the power to move people, viscerally and emotionally, and inform them." Joe McNally, US photographer

05 Light

Light is the central element of photography. In a purely technical sense, no image can be created without incidental light entering a camera. But on a more abstract level, light is among the most influential factors you can use to design your images. Light and shadows are subtle, versatile, and dynamic partners of image design, and the way they are applied directly determines the quality of an exposure. Light has many purposes in photos; it sometimes functions as its own element or as a subject unto itself, other times it seems like an animated object, and yet other times it flows around the rest of the visual elements like water. Subtle adjustments of light, through *exposure* or *light values*, can have much more impact than you might expect.

People inevitably resort to poetic language when they try to describe the look and feel of different kinds of light. This chapter serves as a starting point for you to consider the various ways to use light and shadows within an image. There is more to designing with light than simply making sure you have enough of it to properly expose your images. Foundational skills for designing with light also include controlling flash effectively, using light-shaping tools, and mixing in color. You can begin creating great artistic work with light only after you've learned how to use it to accentuate the strengths of your subject, obscure weaknesses, and elicit a highly emotional response from viewers. Even though this chapter appears in the middle of the book, don't forget that light makes or breaks an image—it is the heart of every picture.

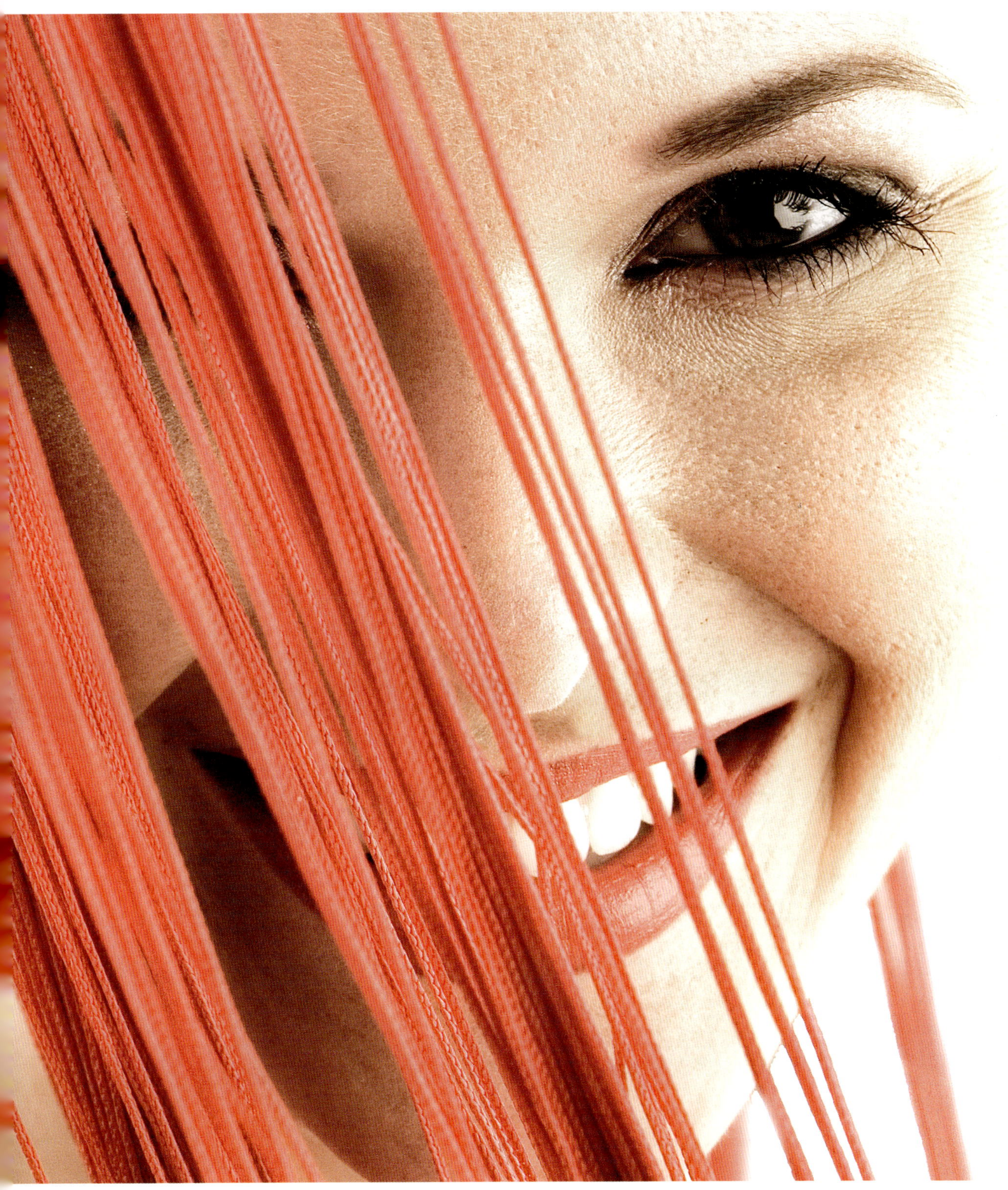

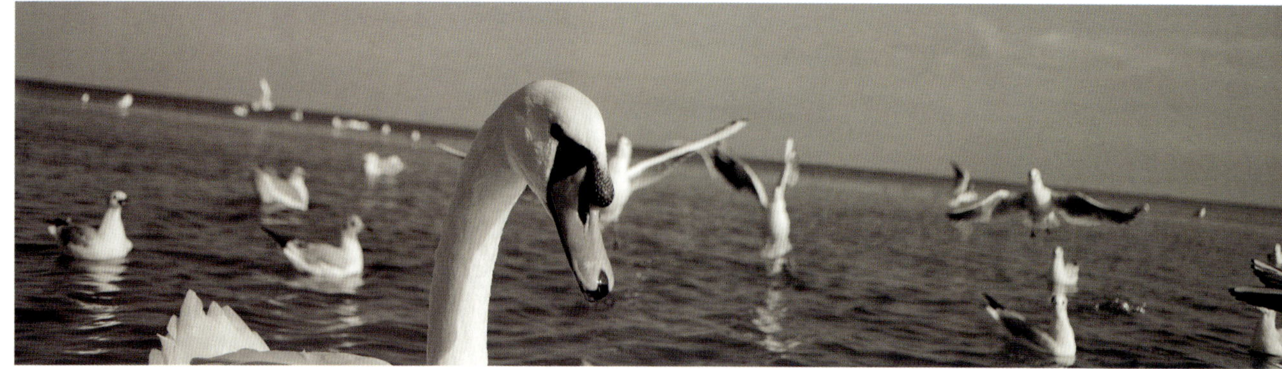

5.1 The Nature of Light

The overall effect the light has on an image is determined by its quantity and quality. Knowing when to use light to softly diffuse or smooth your image and when to allow it to harshly strike a surface is a true art that requires a good eye and a measure of intuition.

If you're working with natural light, you can influence it by shooting in the shade, adjusting your position with respect to the subject, or employing tools such as diffusers, reflectors, or light absorbers. With artificial light, you have additional freedom to combine any number of light sources to generate the exact light you want.

How Much Light?

The brightness of a subject in your image depends on the number of light sources and their output. This is obvious with artificial light—the more light sources you have and the brighter they are, the brighter the subject will appear. But daylight also varies dramatically in strength. This variable is beyond your control, and depends on the weather conditions, the season, and the time of day.

The human eye is capable of perceiving a very large range of contrast and can quickly move from bright areas to dark areas. We don't consciously register many gra-

The ambient brightness during an exposure not only affects your design possibilities, it also alters the overall feel of an image, independent of the subject. A lot of light recalls a summer day and creates a warm feeling, and a lack of light is associated with dimness and gloom.

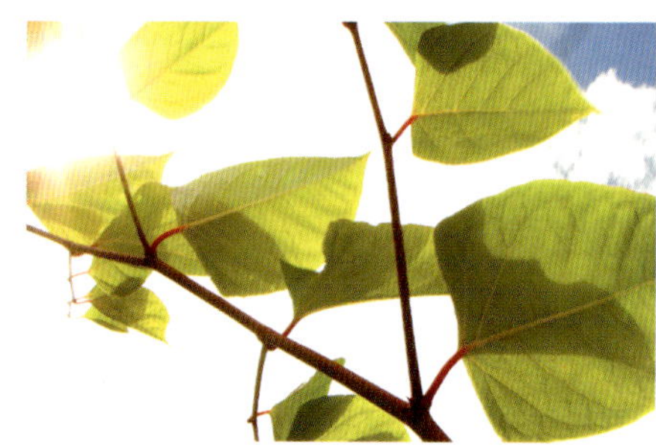

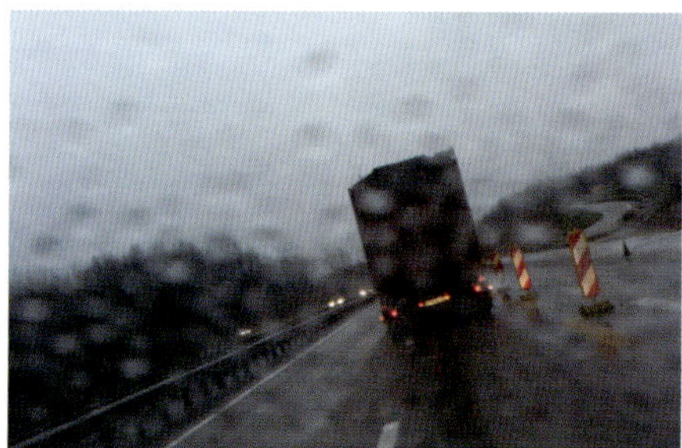

dations of brightness—only the most obvious differences catch our eyes. Cameras, however, absorb visual information in a much more limited dynamic range, which is why there may not be enough ambient light to expose an image properly, even if lighting conditions seem bright enough to our eyes.

A dearth of light will sometimes lead you to use your maximum aperture with a long exposure and an elevated ISO (see *Learning to Photograph Vol.1*). These parameters drastically reduce your ability to design an image, and lead to increased image noise and decreased image quality.

Too much light can overreach the capabilities of your equipment if you can't stop down your aperture any further and your shutter speed is already as fast as you can make it. But this situation is relatively rare and, as a rule, you're more likely to be in circumstances where you have to deal with too little light as opposed to too much.

On one hand, brighter images usually convey a warm, friendly feeling, since viewers associate light with the sun. On the other hand, when dark areas dominate your image, they intensify a heavy, ominous mood.

Harsh, Directed Light

The quality of light includes other dimensions besides brightness. These include the harshness of the light and its range of dispersion. If all of the light rays from a light source run parallel toward a subject, the light is described as harsh and directed. This kind of light creates obvious, sharply defined shadows with black interiors that look even darker because of high contrast.

The effect of this light may be dramatic, dominant, striking, masculine, inaccessible, or evil, and it tends to accentuate the graphical aspects of an image. If these shadows are combined with a generally dark scene, the dismal qualities come across all the stronger.

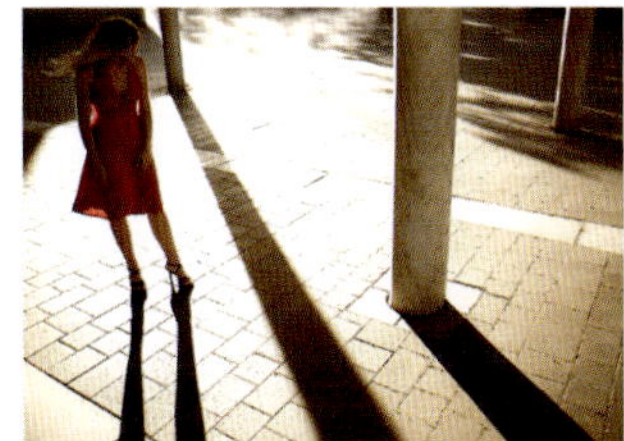

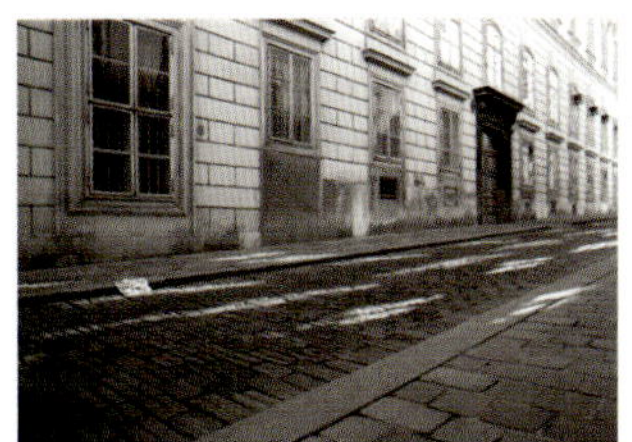

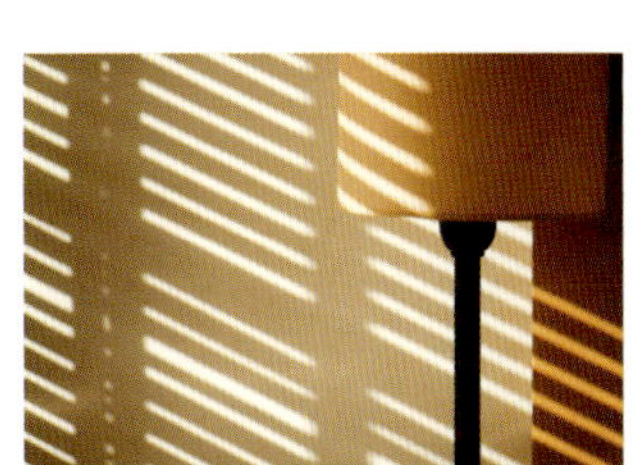

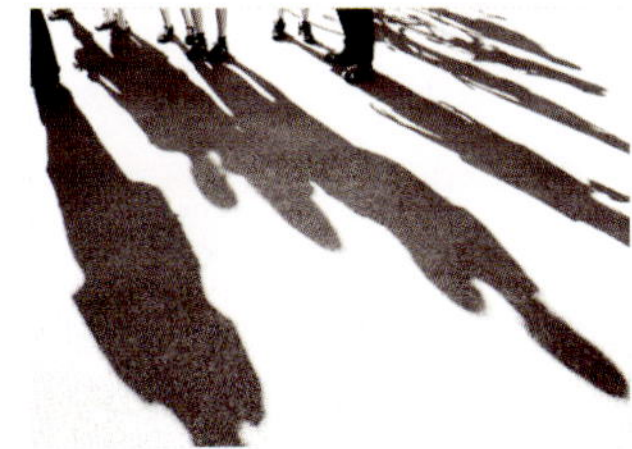

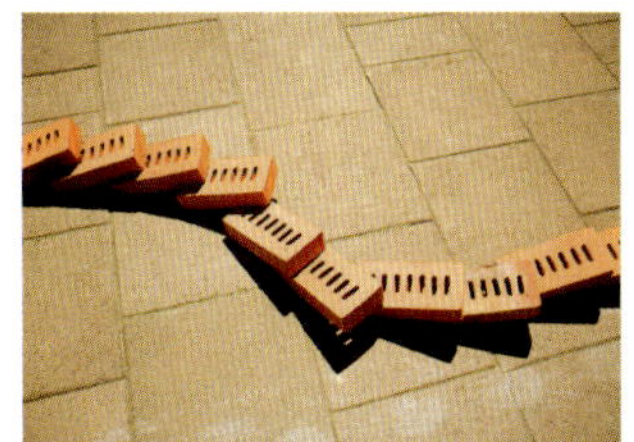

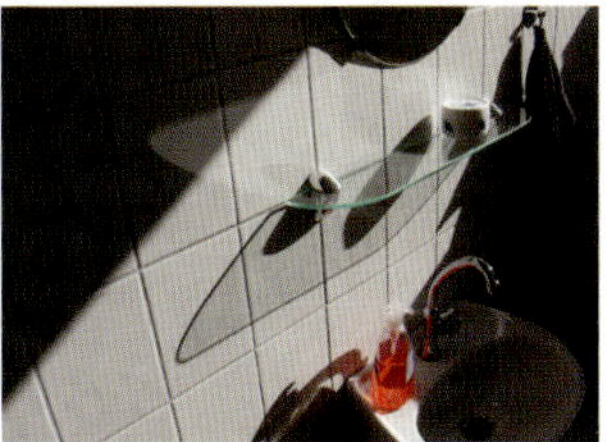

Harsh light creates clearly defined, conspicuous shadows and leads to a large contrast between the bright and dark areas of an image. Dark shadows will contract an image, but shadows with detail in them expand the dimensionality. Viewers associate especially long shadows with dawn or dusk, when the sun is low in the sky.

Soft light is gentle, and creates a discreet, contrast with barely perceptible shadows. Fine details are more visible, and no areas of the image are swallowed up in blackness. These lighting conditions don't come into the foreground—they are less striking and are more unobtrusive, allowing the subject itself, and any other design elements, to take center stage.

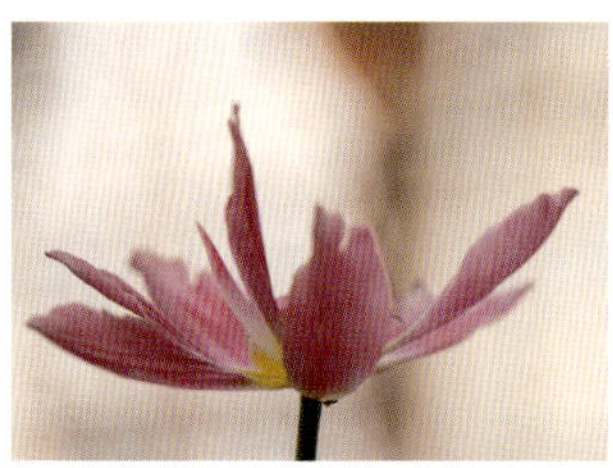

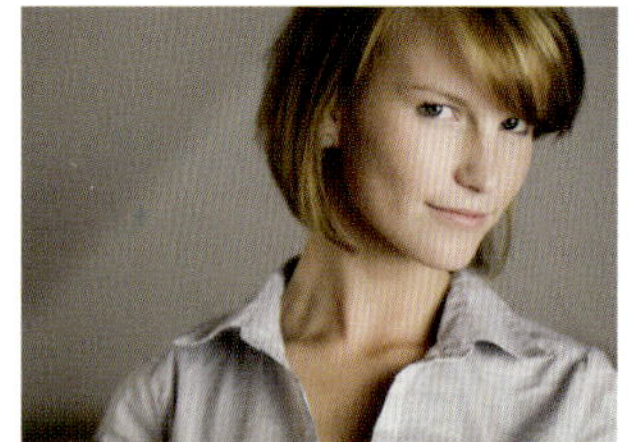

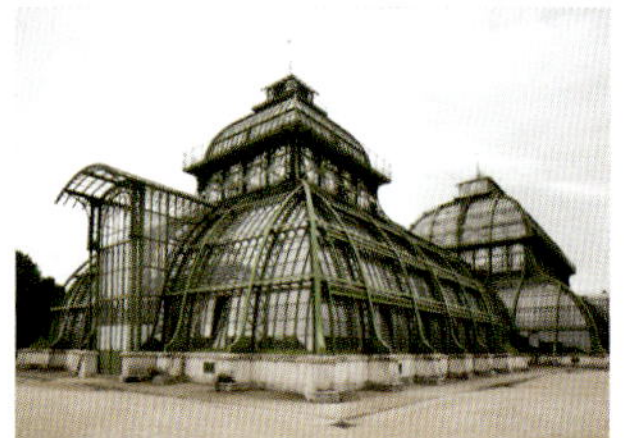

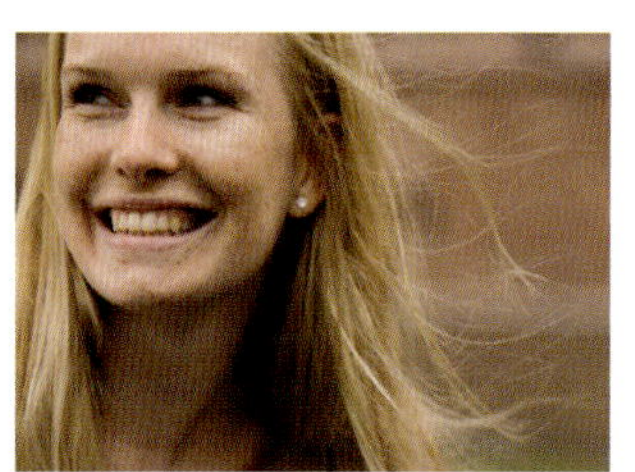

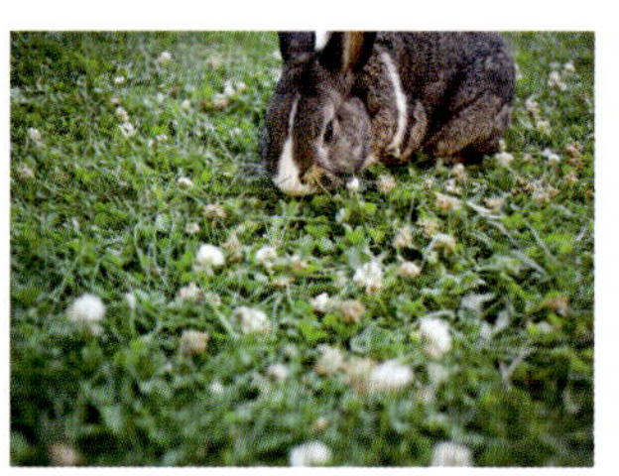

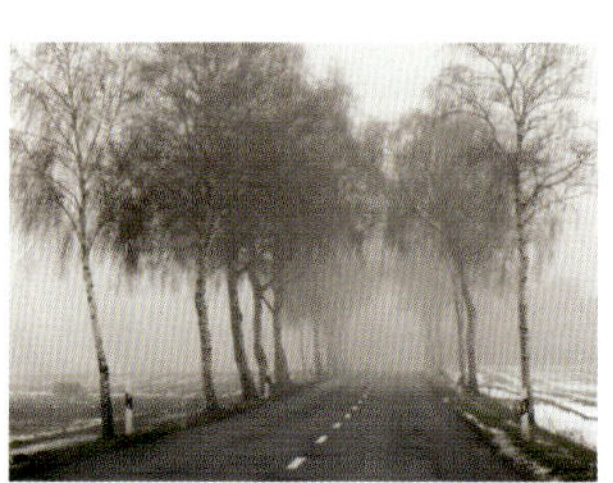

Since uniform, directed light doesn't produce stray light, you can determine the position of your light source based solely on how you want your shadows to appear. If more than one source of light is at play, the harshness of the light will be diminished and the general lighting of the scene will appear unnatural, like the lighting in a theater or on a concert stage. Harsh light sources can also be associated with the beginning and end of the day because they produce long shadows that seem natural when the sun is low on the horizon. To diminish the harshness of unwanted, distracting shadows that occur when a large distance separates the subject from the light source, you need a secondary source of light that is bright enough to illuminate the dark area. To avoid excess brightness that occurs by overlapping multiple sources of directed light, it often makes sense to use a combination of hard and soft light to create shadows that are still visible, but that don't increase the contrast of the image too much.

Soft, Diffuse Light

Light rays that become jumbled through diffusion or reflection shine on objects with soft light. Shadows are much less conspicuous with soft light since the definitions of the shadows blur and leave only the center of the shadow dark. The softer, brighter, and closer the light source, the less prominent shadows become until, in cases of extremely scattered light, they are barely perceptible. Images exposed with diffuse light and soft shadows appear rich in detail, feminine, calm, peaceful, gentle, harmonious, and, in exaggerated cases, even fantastical.

The prevalence of stray light in softly lit scenes makes it difficult to trace the light back to its original source. When multiple light sources are used, it can be particularly difficult to establish the ideal position for each source. At the same time, the direction of light sources becomes less critical as diffusion becomes more pronounced.

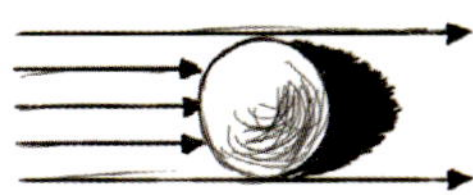

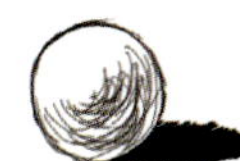

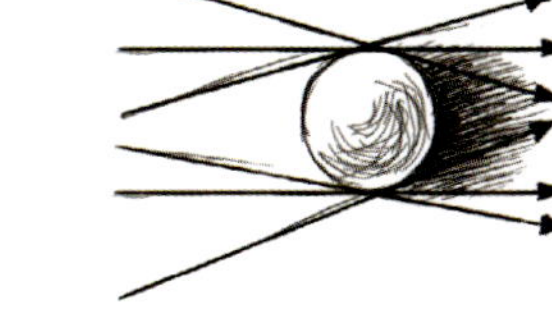

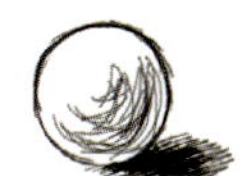

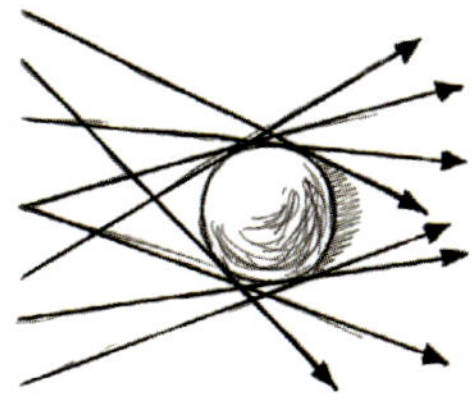

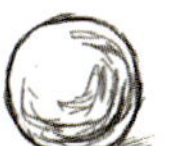

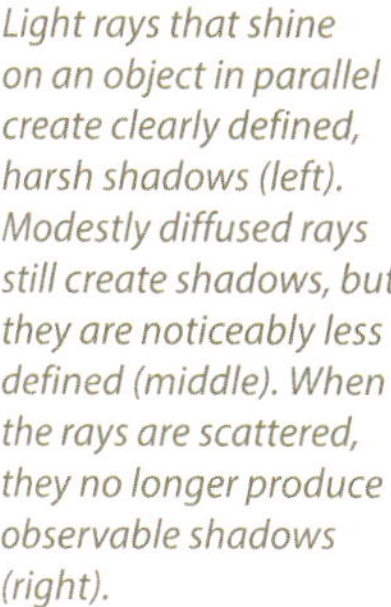

Light rays that shine on an object in parallel create clearly defined, harsh shadows (left). Modestly diffused rays still create shadows, but they are noticeably less defined (middle). When the rays are scattered, they no longer produce observable shadows (right).

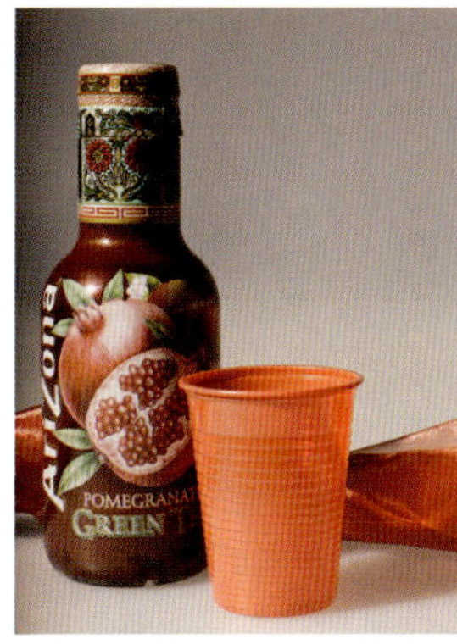

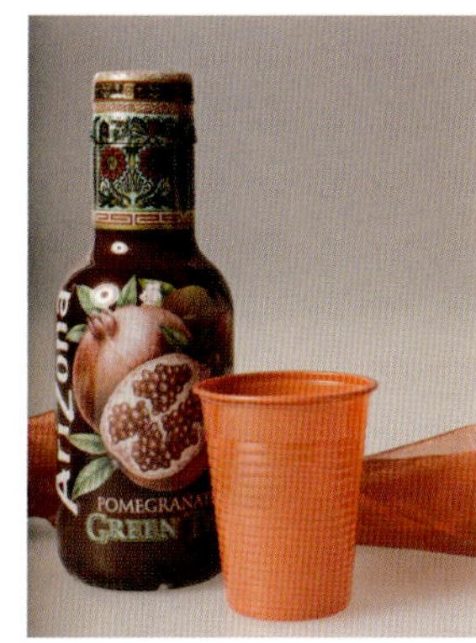

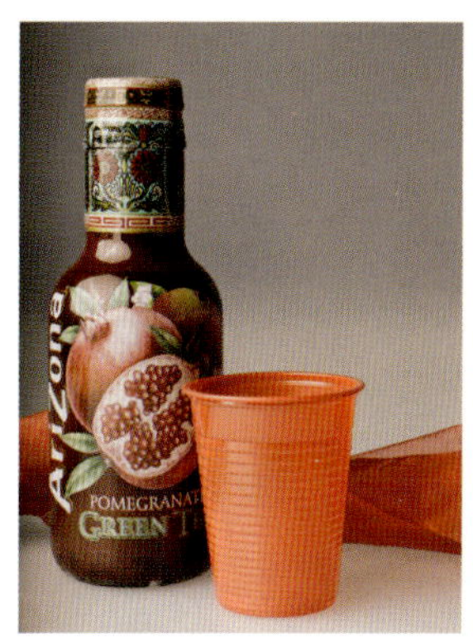

This example was shot in a studio with purposefully selected light-shaping tools. A spotlight was used for the left image, a beauty dish for the middle image, and a soft box for the right image.

An image will look especially gentle when there are no shadows within the image area. Photographers can accomplish this look by using multiple diffuse light sources in front of and to the sides of their subjects. This setup produces a shadowless scene that has the calmest and most balanced lighting. In these cases, the lighting is a supporting design element for more prominent design tools and the subject itself.

Diffuse backlight can produce a pleasant quality by creating a soft bloom of light around a subject. This effect comes across as natural and authentic.

Qualities of Natural Light

Daylight can take on any number of characteristics, depending on the nature of the clouds at any given moment. A sky without clouds produces harsh, direct light. Scattered clouds or a thin layer of cloud cover dilutes the intensity of the sunlight and the corresponding shadows. A heavily overcast sky produces a soft, diffuse light, which makes it possible to produce shadowless images. In other words, the thicker the clouds, the less light will fall on your subject. Dense fog has the same effect. A moderately dense layer of clouds is ideal for portraiture because it produces lots of light with soft shadows. Subjects that need more intense light should be shot with partially diffused light, or even direct light, so they don't lose their edge and become undesirably flat.

Qualities of Artificial Light

On a fundamental level, all unfiltered, artificial light sources used in photography—especially shoe-mount flashes—produce harsh, direct light that will create dramatic shadows. The wide variety of light-shaping tools, however, make it possible to modulate artificial light so it exhibits just the right amount of diffusion:

- **For harsh, directed light:** To direct unfiltered, harsh light toward your subject and retain control over its direction, you can use floodlights (wide beam), spotlights (narrow beam), barn doors (any lockable surface, including narrow strips), and all shapes of honeycomb attachments. When they are combined with other light-shaping tools, they minimize stray light and direct the rays of light more uniformly. To further intensify the shadows in your image and to reduce stray, ambient light, you can also use photographic light absorbers or black surfaces.

To shine harsh, direct light on your subject in the studio, you can use a floodlight with a honeycomb attachment to minimize stray light (left) or a spotlight with a tube to create a focused beam of light (right).

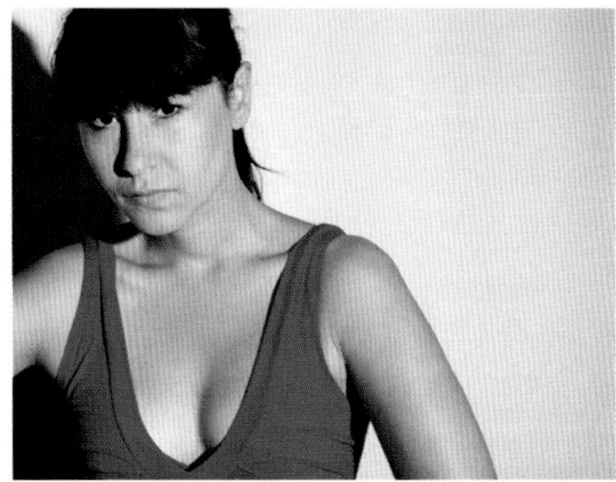

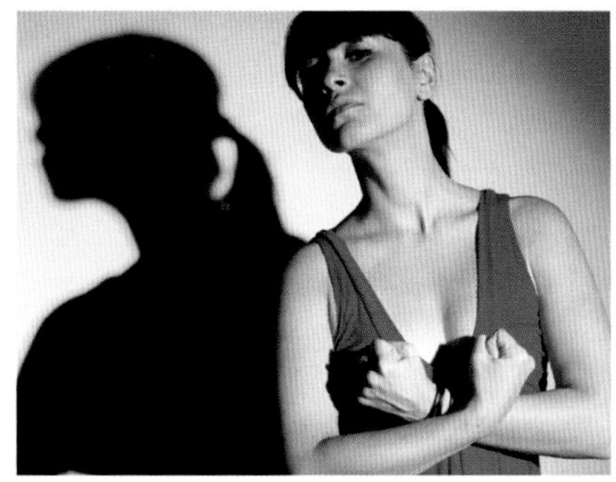

Soft and diffuse light results from light-shaping tools, such as all types of soft boxes (left) and diffuser umbrellas (right). In both cases, the light must pass through a semitransparent material, which causes the light rays to disperse.

- **For soft, diffuse light:** To increase the level of diffusion, you can either use soft boxes (ranging from narrow strip lights to various rectangular boxes to large octagonal boxes) or umbrellas, which either disperse or reflect light. Other reflectors make it possible to work with indirect light, which is generally more diffuse. Diffusers such as umbrellas and soft boxes are made of a semitransparent material and are placed between a light source and the subject.

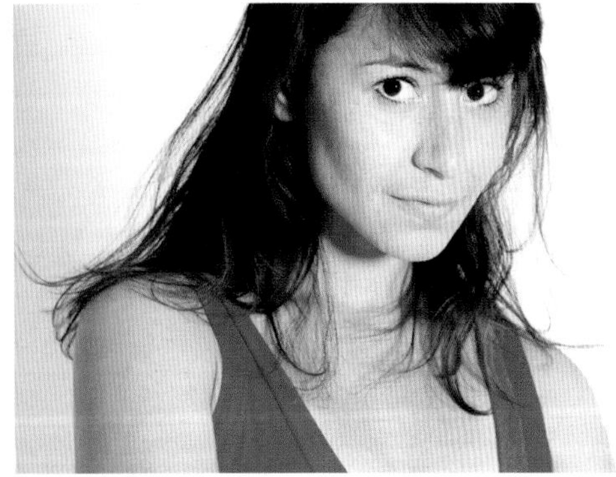

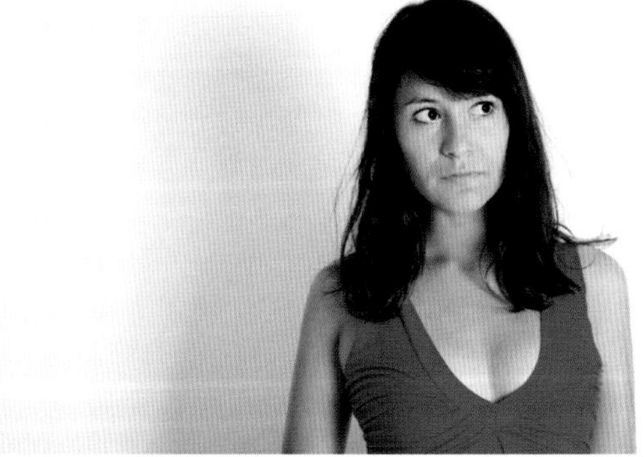

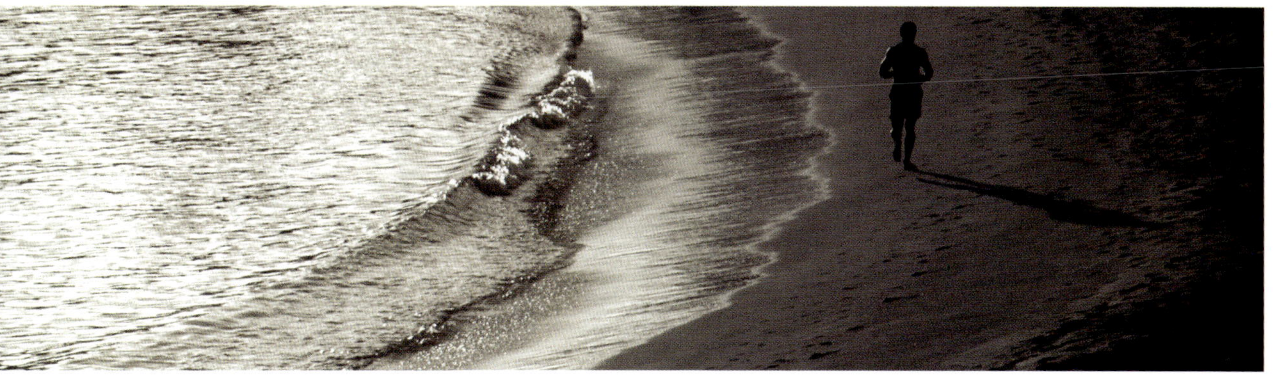

5.2 The Direction of Light

Designing the setup for a photo shoot starts with deciding on the alignment of the light. From which direction would you like the light to fall on your subject? Depending on the light source, you can move the light, adjust the subject, or move yourself. Try as many different directions of light as possible before deciding on the setup that best suits the subject and the concept behind your shot.

Front Lighting

If the light source is near the photographer and falls on the front of the subject, it is called front lighting. This uniform and equal illumination doesn't highlight any particular element. All of the details are clearly recognizable, and the image tends to lose some of its dimensional space. Visible shadows are limited, since they occur on the side of the subject opposite the camera. The contour lines in your image will be narrower with this type of lighting, and the borders between various visual elements (page 106) and levels (page 72) will be less noticeable. Other design tools, such as predominant lines, composition, and color, tend to be suppressed, but they play a bigger role with respect to everything else. This makes the image function significantly on a graphic level. Otherwise, front lighting gives images a neutral, familiar, and even documentary look that may be boring when it is poorly executed.

Front lighting is ideal when it is important to show everything about your subject. All of the granular detail is easily visible, and nothing is obscured

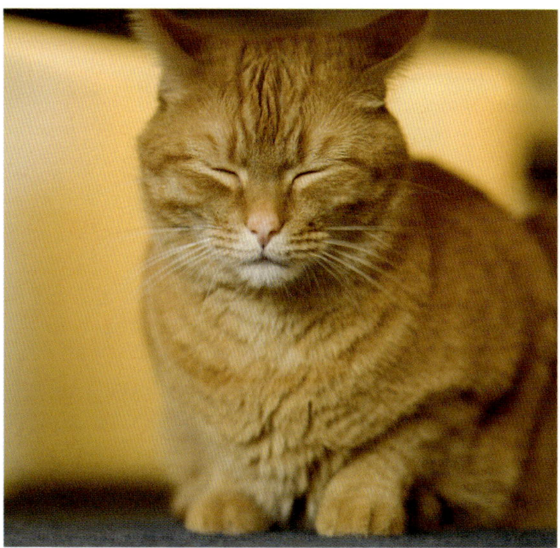

Light directed toward the front of your subject creates shadowless illumination that is ideal for showcasing fine details, such as the hair of this cat's coat. One disadvantage of front lighting is that it can blind the subject—not a problem for the cat, though, who chose to close its eyes.

Front lighting is used when photographers want to avoid shadows, which is often a goal of product photography. Shadows tend to give an object more weight, so if they are obscured behind the subject, all of the elements in the image can be weighted equally.

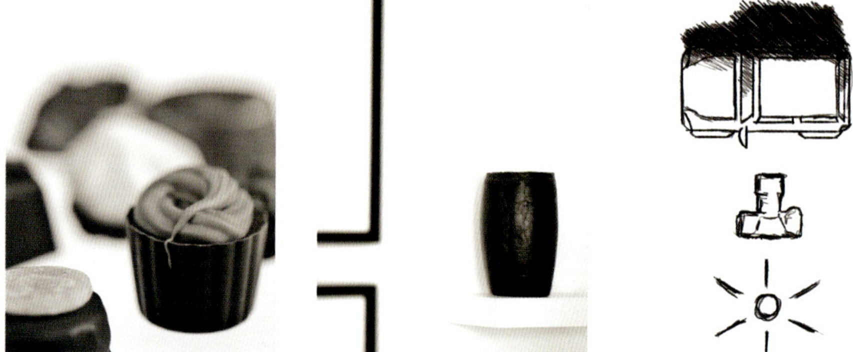

in shadows. For this reason, front lighting is particularly useful for product photographers, photojournalists, and anyone who needs to take a picture when the main objective is conveying accurate visual information, such as a passport photo. The visual authenticity of the subject is heightened with front lighting, and the viewer gets an objective, realistic impression of the subject.

Backlighting

If there's a source of light directly behind the subject, it will be backlit. In this situation, the backside of the subject is fully illuminated, shadows are cast in the direction of the photographer, and the details on the front side of the subject are dark. Subjects exhibit a stark contrast, which often extends beyond the dynamic range of the camera's sensor and makes precise light metering especially critical—spot metering is ideal. You need to decide whether you want to expose the foreground or the background correctly. If the foreground is exposed correctly, it means the background will probably be overexposed, and will show only rough structures and areas rather than specific details. Exposing the background correctly will produce details in that layer of the image, while the subject in the foreground will be underexposed or, in extreme cases, turn into a silhouette-like outline. This effect can work well for subjects that

Backlighting makes for an interesting but challenging situation for photographers because the contrast between the underexposed foreground and the bright background is often very marked. In this situation you have to decide which part of the image to expose correctly, and use a spot meter to help you. Adding fill light to the foreground helps reduce the contrast without robbing too much of the dramatic effect from the backlighting.

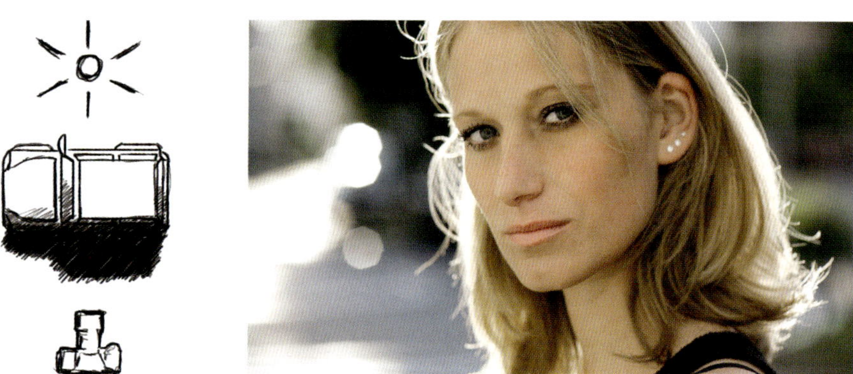

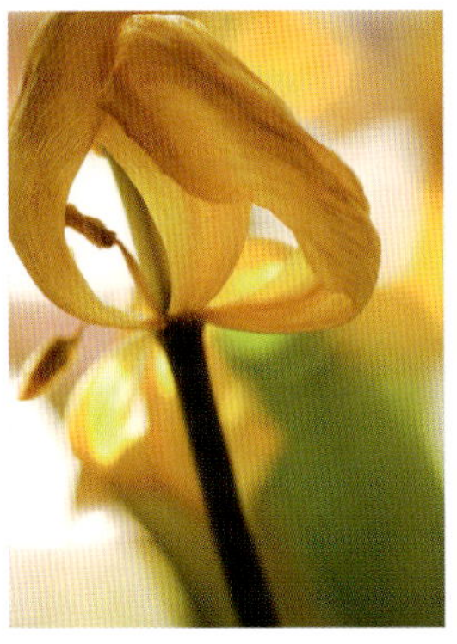
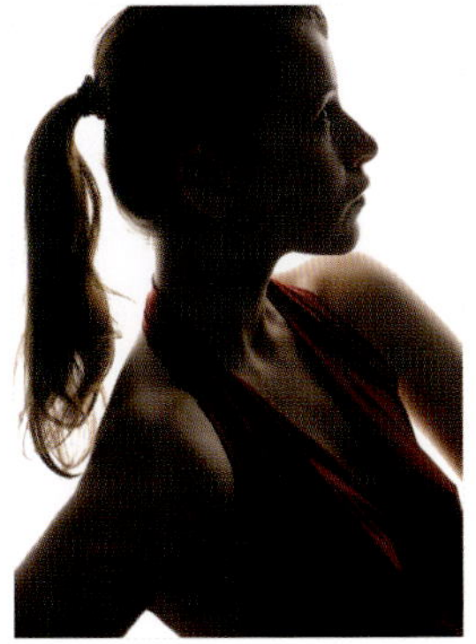
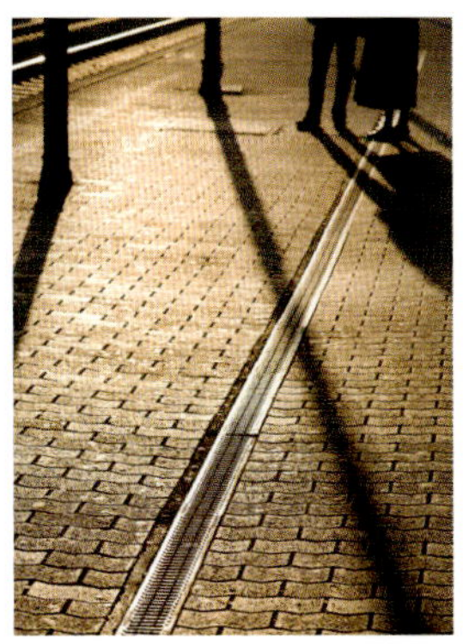
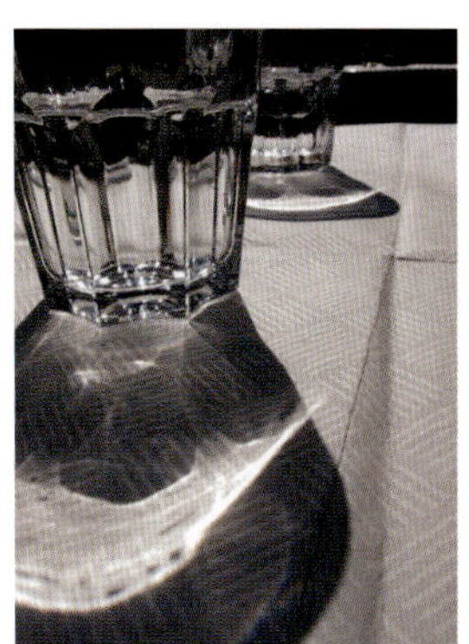

Backlighting can become an integral element of an image if it blooms around a subject or illuminates a transparent object. In other lighting conditions, all four of these images would be bland.

have distinguishable features despite the lighting conditions, but this is an exception to the rule. In most backlighting situations, photographers overexpose the background in exchange for a properly exposed subject.

If you have additional lighting tools on hand, such as a reflector or a source of moderate light, you can reduce the contrast in the scene by brightening the foreground without diminishing the effect of having the main light source behind the subject. Backlighting gives a dramatic and attractive look to an image. In extreme cases the high contrast created in backlit conditions can cause the image to look flat, but the contours of objects will be emphasized and transparent objects will be illuminated.

In fact, transparent and semitransparent subjects look best when they are backlit. Subtle structures, such as the veins in a leaf, are showcased. The colors look more intense, and brightly colored objects jump off the background like a paper lantern. When you shoot a transparent object, keep the background as dark as possible if you want to emphasize its luminosity and bring drama, vitality, and three-dimensionality into your exposure. You will see that backlighting is technically challenging, but it can substantially boost the attractiveness of your image.

Sidelighting

When light strikes an object from the left or right, the condition is described as sidelighting or oblique lighting. This style of lighting emphasizes the illuminated side of the subject and reduces the weight of

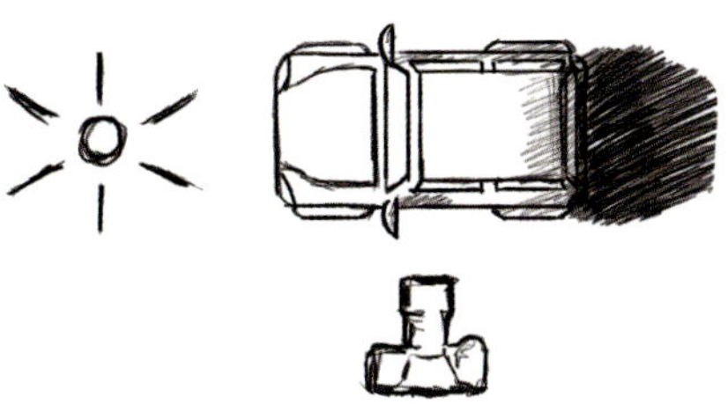

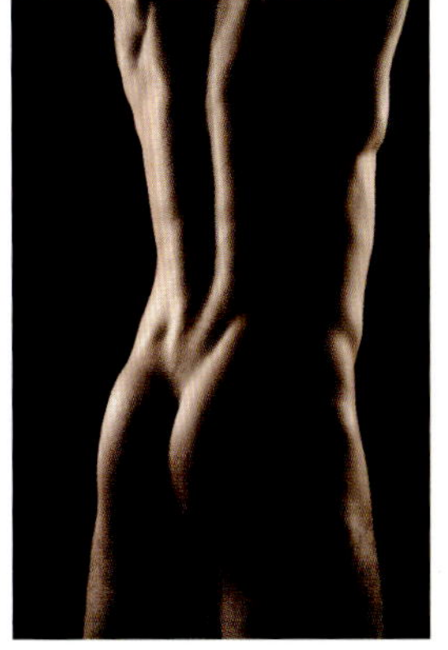
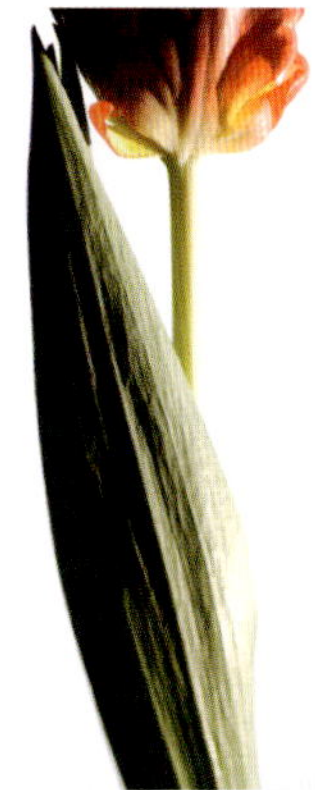

Sidelighting accentuates contours and structures and is often used when photographers want to draw the viewer's attention to specific aspects of a subject. In nude photography, for example, you often see some parts of the body in shadows while other parts are illuminated with sidelighting. The surface of the flower is shown in sharp relief as a result of sidelighting.

the opposite side. Sidelight casts conspicuous shadows behind any detail that stands out slightly, which greatly enhances the dimensionality of an image.

Sidelighting can be ideal for calling attention to the detail of a structure. The characteristics of cliffs, rock formations, and sand banks, for example, are most evident when they are illuminated with sidelighting. Clothes seem more real when viewers can tell that the material is three-dimensional; sidelighting is a must in fashion and beauty photography, and in many circumstances, for portraiture.

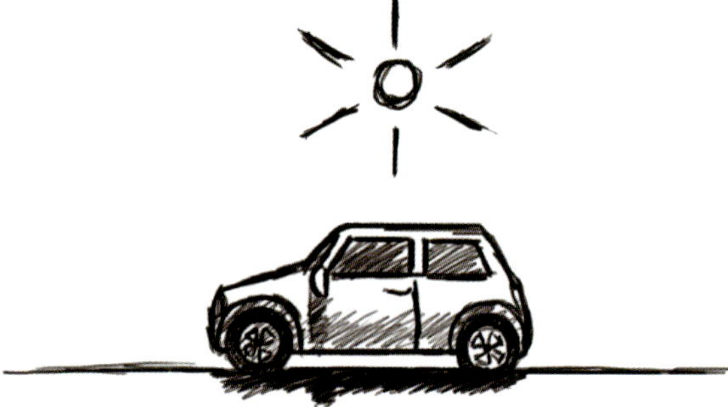

Top Lighting

Lighting from above is very familiar to us because of the sun's high position in the sky. When it is used to illuminate a subject, this type of lighting doesn't stand out, nor does it create an especially dramatic effect. Usually scenes illuminated with top lighting come across as quiet, natural, and conventional. Shadows fall directly downward, which may produce striking results depending on the subject and the point of view. If you're shooting from a slightly elevated standpoint, shadows won't appear in your image, but if you're closer to the ground, they'll be visible. Downward shadows are problematic when they obscure important elements within an image. In a portrait, for example, top lighting causes unwanted shadows in the eye sockets, under the nose, and under the chin. Even a slight backwards tilt of the head is enough to change the subject's relative angle to the light source and reduce or eliminate these shadows. Alternatively, reflectors or reflective surfaces, such as water, sand, or stone, may bounce enough light upward to take care of the shadows.

When large subjects are illuminated with top lighting, they cast downward shadows, which draw the viewer's attention upward. This effect can suit your needs perfectly, such as when you shoot a flower. But the side or front of many subjects reveals

Top lighting can either be a blessing or a curse, depending on your subject. In portrait photography it can create problematic shadows in the eye sockets if the light is too powerful and comes directly from above. Small reflectors are perfect in this situation to make the subject more lively and to ensure even illumination (left). Other subjects look fine when their shadows are cast directly downward. The shadows of the stones are very small and mostly inconspicuous (right).

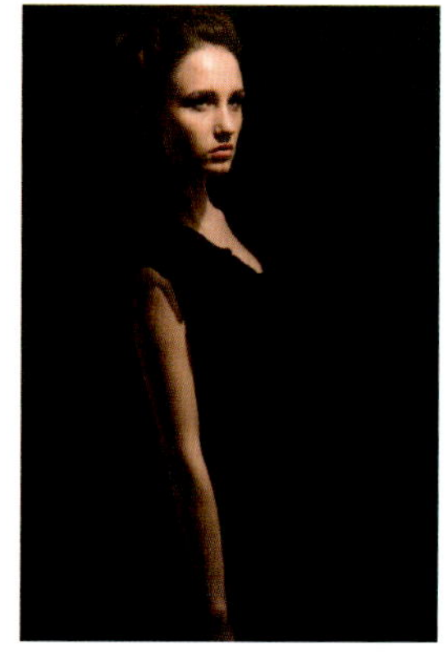

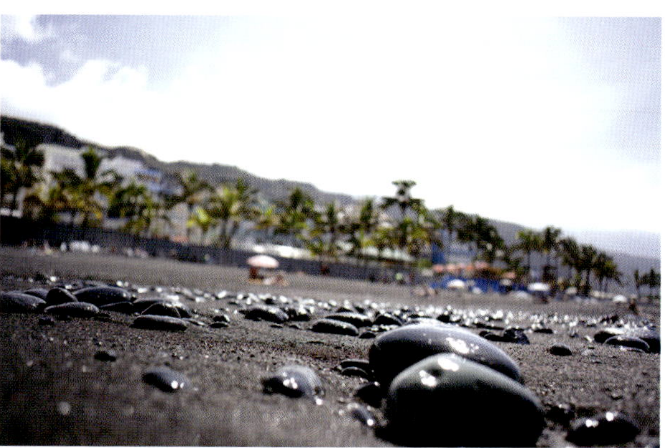

key details, so you should check to see how light from above shades these features. The most interesting part of an animal, for example, it usually its face, and the roof of a house is rarely as interesting as its front.

Bottom Lighting

Lighting an object from below is an unusual way to light a subject, so it draws a lot of attention. We're familiar with bottom lighting in nature only from reflected light, and we don't normally encounter it in daily life. Bottom lighting is used for performances in theaters and concert halls to create a dramatic and sometimes diabolical atmosphere. This method of lighting has the same effect when it is the main light source in a photo shoot. Use it carefully and only when it supports the idea behind your image.

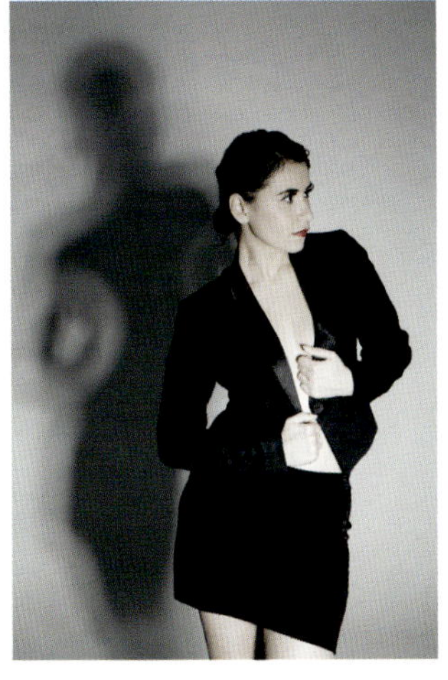

Bottom lighting is exceedingly rare, both in the natural world and in studio photography. In this example, light shines from below the model to create a larger-than-life shadow with an unusual and frightening effect. The bottom lighting underscores the dramatic tone of the image.

A reflective surface in the wrong spot is often enough to direct light in an undesired direction. You can counteract it with a secondary top or backlight to reduce the intensity of the shadows. This makes the contrast less dramatic and makes the overall quality of light more pleasant.

Undirected Light

If there is no obvious direction of light within a scene, it looks like the light is coming from all directions. This can be caused by multiple light sources or by a high level of diffusion. When photographers are working with soft, undirected light, they create shadowless, gentle, balanced lighting. Harsh light that lacks a prevailing direction produces chaotic, dramatic effects.

In these two examples, the direction of light can't be clearly identified. The lighting is uniform and unobtrusive.

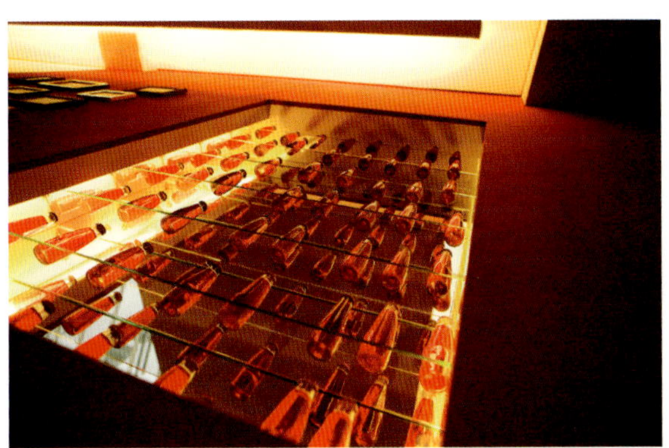

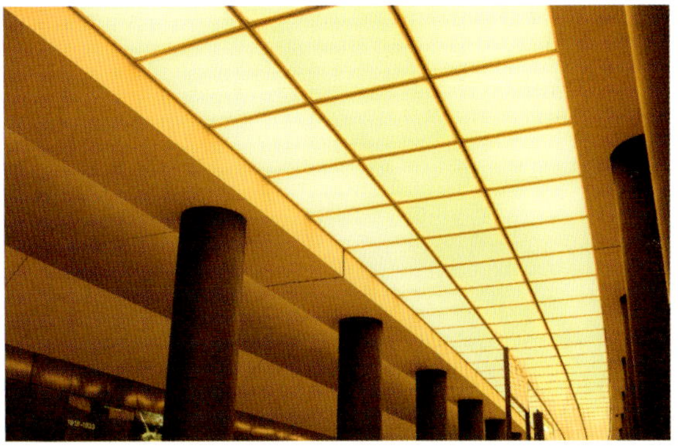

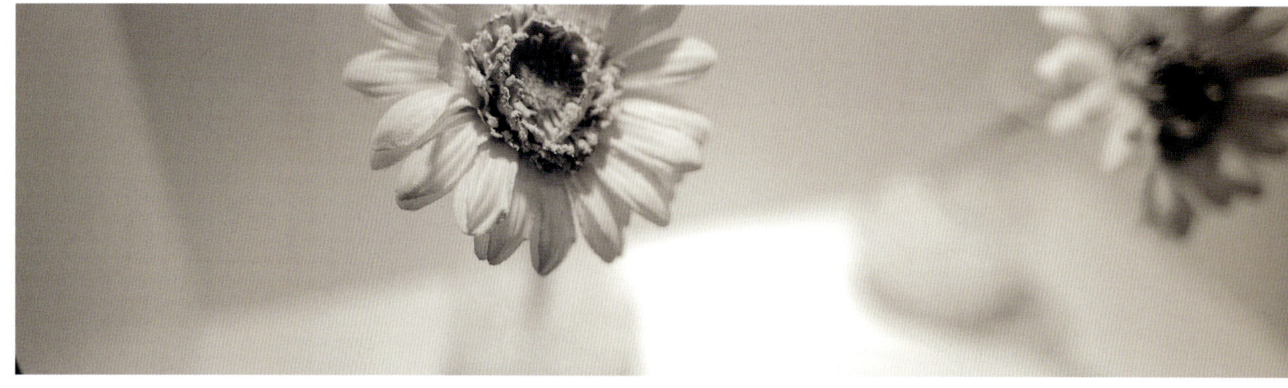

5.3 Light Sources and Their Colors

Even when we don't notice it, every source of light has a particular color that subtly influences the atmosphere and the emotional tone of the scene. The color of a light may look white, but you can sometimes see a strong color cast after it's been documented in a photo. Your camera's white balance setting allows you to compensate for the color of light by calibrating the colors in your photo. You can also correct it in post-processing.

As you can see from these photos, there is no straightforward answer to the question, What color is natural light? Natural light exhibits such a broad spectrum of colors that it never gets boring for photographers.

Natural Light

The color of sunlight changes throughout the day. In the morning, just before dawn, the light is blue, then it turns to yellow-orange, and eventually, at sunrise, it's a glowing red. In the middle of the day, sunlight takes on a bluish-white tinge before it melts into deep reds, oranges, and yellows at sunset. Just after the sun sets, the light turns deep blue before it disappears. At night, the phase of the moon produces either a pale yellow light or no light at all. Absolute darkness at night is actually quite rare.

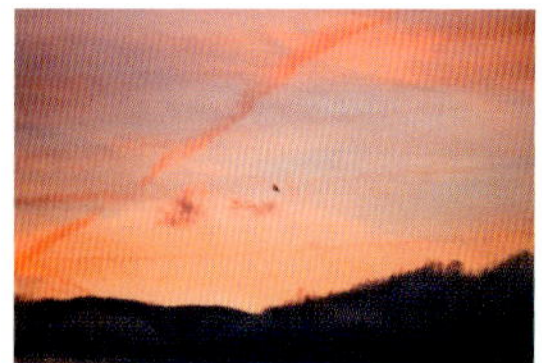
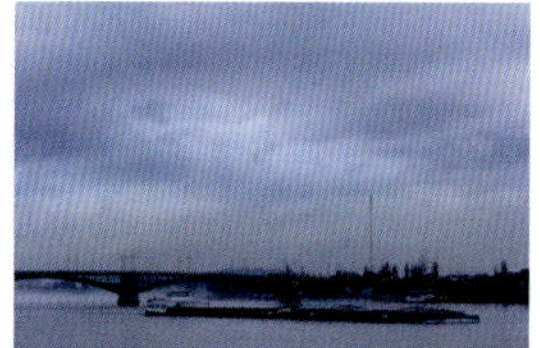
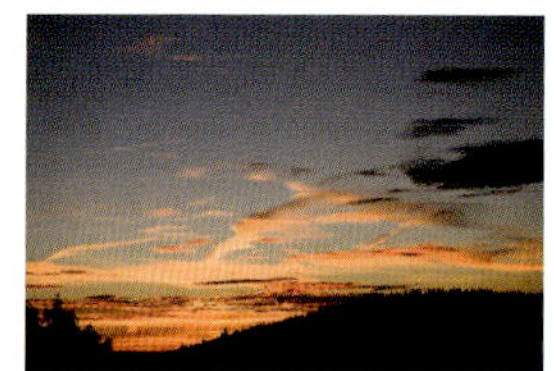
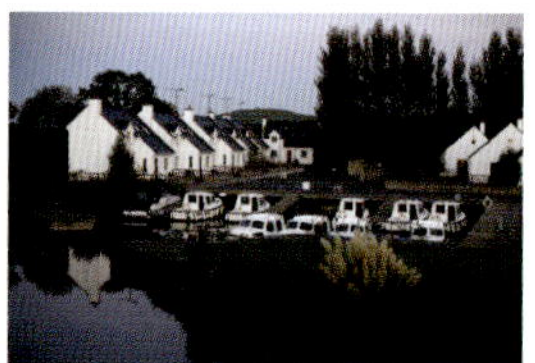
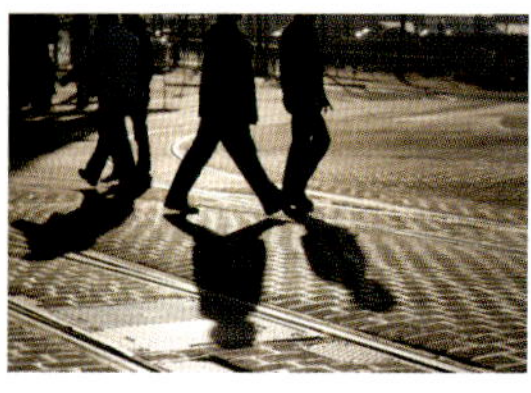
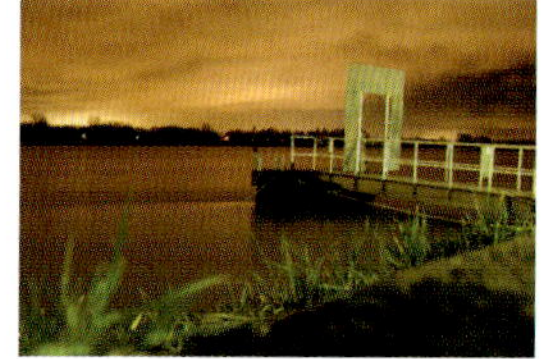
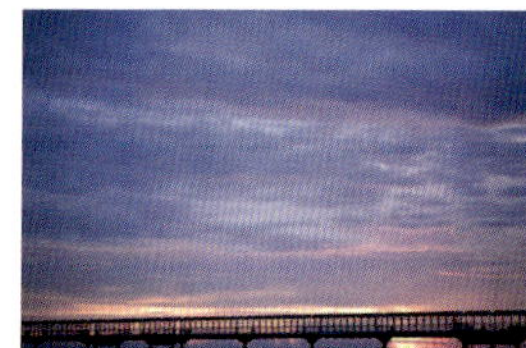
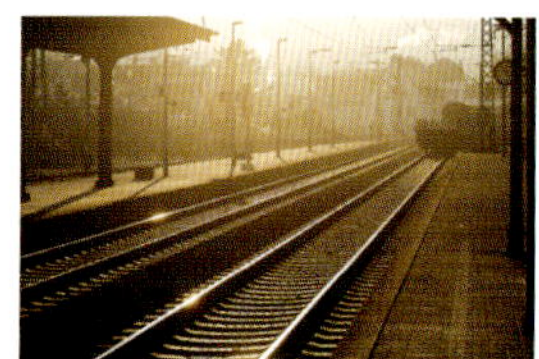

Artificial light sources give the impression that ambient light exists during the nighttime, as well.

An exposure taken with natural light will have a specific color tone and corresponding emotional depth, depending on the time of day. The bluish light of the so-called blue hour gives photographers an opportunity to create images that are gloomy, cool, and mysterious. The red light of sunrise and sunset produces a warm, glowing, and golden effect. In the middle of the day, colors are saturated and full, and during summer they are much brighter than during winter, when they look pale and dull.

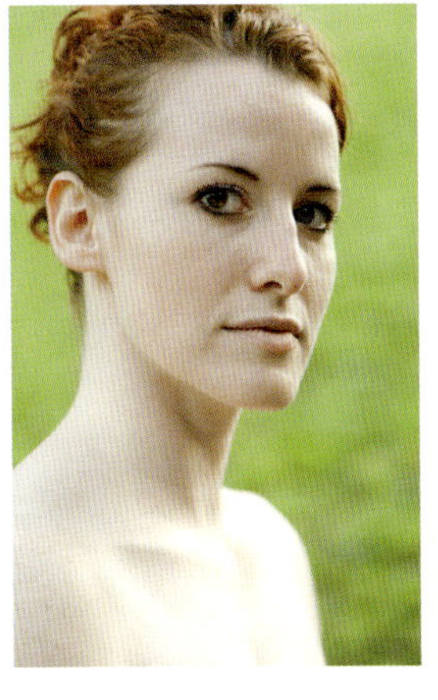

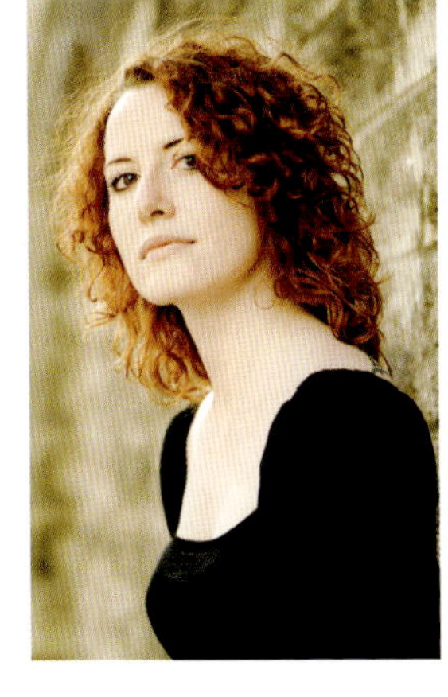

These two images were shot just minutes apart. They show how dramatically the subject's surroundings can affect the color of natural light. In the left image, the model stood beneath a cover of green leaves, and in the right image, she stood next to a yellow wall.

Take note of the time of day when you work with natural light, and examine the area around your subject to check for anything that may reflect or scatter the light and change its color. This is why, for instance, light that falls through a tree canopy has a green tint. Light reflected off the side of a house will be whatever color the house is, and affect your subject accordingly. Even small color shifts can have a subconscious influence on what an image communicates.

Artificial Light

Most often, the color of the light in an image allows the viewer to determine whether the light source was natural. It is possible, of course, to use artificial light in combination with color filters and white balance to simulate natural lighting conditions, but the common colors of artificial light sources are easily identifiable to the trained eye. Traditional light bulbs put off very red light; low-energy lamps produce white light that's becoming increasingly yellow and red; neon lamps produce green light and sometimes blue or yellow light. LEDs and halogen lamps emit cool blue light, and floodlights are known for their deep red light. It's important to note that the

Artificial light produces a rich variety of colors. These colors most often affect photography when sunlight alone is inadequate, since photographers who work in a studio generally use lights with uniform colors.

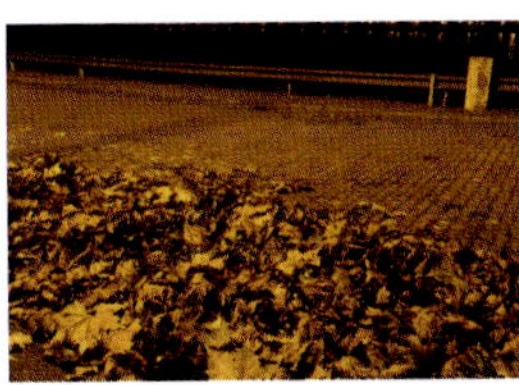

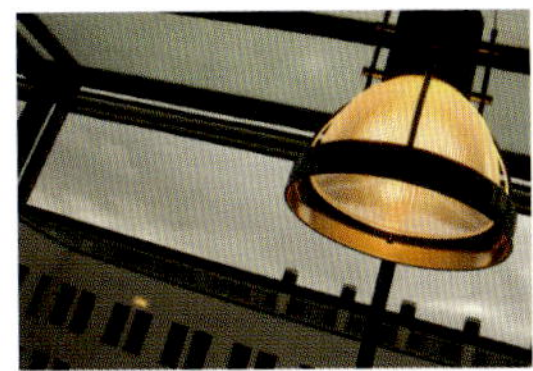

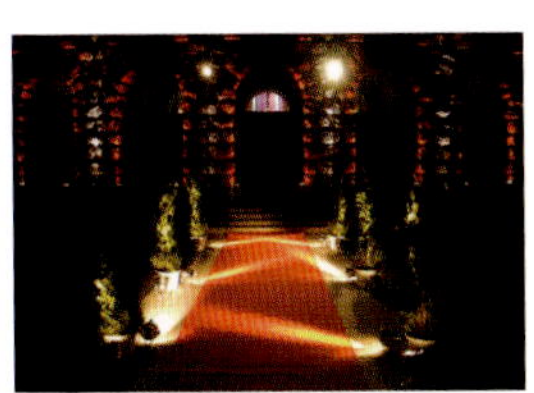

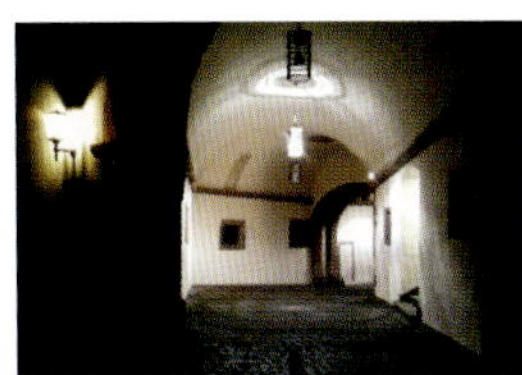

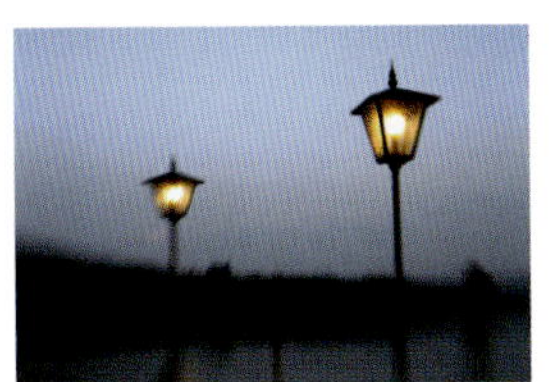

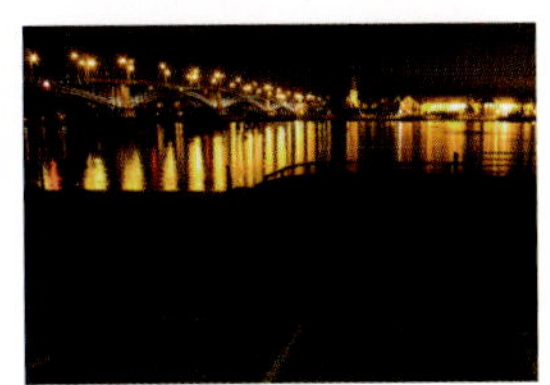

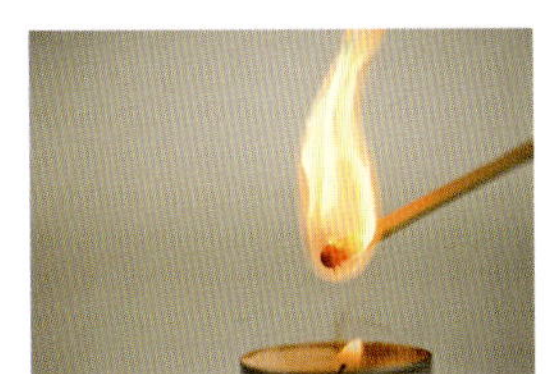

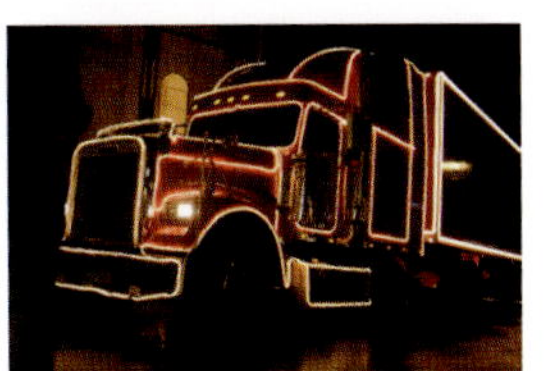

impression of a color cast depends on the subject. Viewers may assume that red-tinted subjects in an outdoor setting were shot at sunset, while the same lighting conditions in an enclosed space will make them think of incandescent bulbs or candles.

The prevailing light in an image works in the same way as other design elements. Viewers will make associations with different qualities of light based on their prior knowledge. Again, you have the opportunity to play into these expectations or lead viewers astray. For example, you can set up your light sources so they look like daylight, regardless of the actual conditions. Or, you can create an artificial look and feel by removing natural light and using very colorful light.

Flash Light

Of all the lighting tools that photographers have at their disposal, flash light plays a special role. It is a prevalent artificial light source, whether it's a handy, portable shoe-mount flash unit or a studio flash system with a huge power output. Flash light is white, very bright, directed, and does not continuously illuminate the scene—this is both advantageous and disadvantageous. The white light allows photographers to achieve neutral, realistic color reproductions. Photographers can use light-shaping tools and color filters to convert flash light to any type and color of light. Flash units generally have a strong output capacity, which means they have an exceptionally short operating window. This means photographers can examine the lighting conditions only after the photo has been shot. Studio flash units are helpful because they can produce a steady light for staging that automatically shuts off just before the flash fires. Since the light from a flash decreases in proportion to the distance it is from the subject, it is

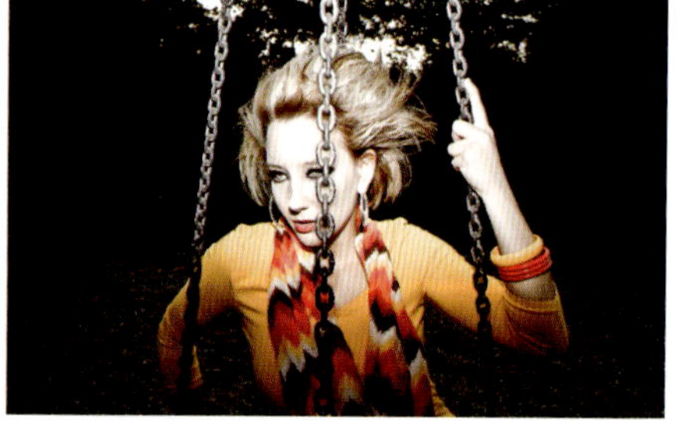

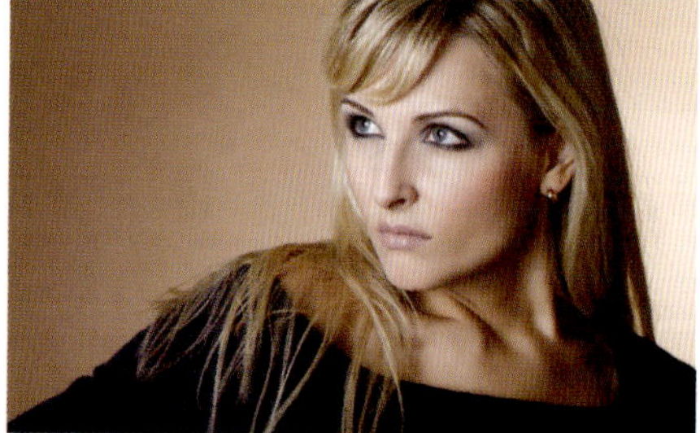

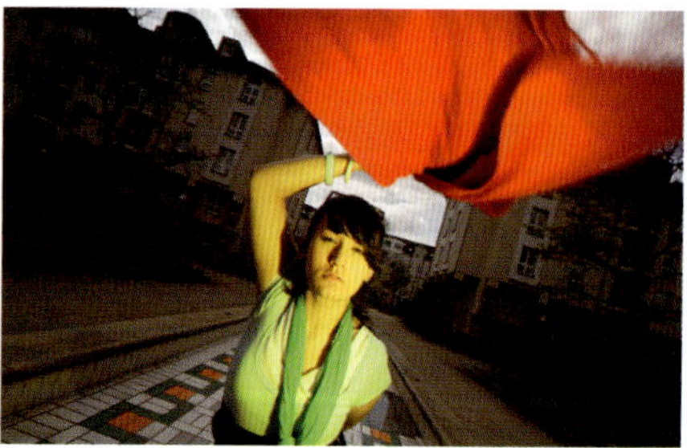

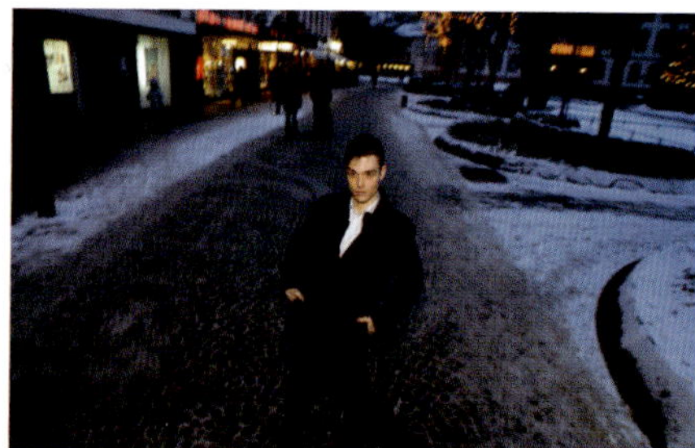

Anyone who only associates flash light with the integrated flash of a compact camera, which usually does more harm than good, is unaware of the immense design possibilities of this particular source of light. Whether it is used with light-shaping tools, colored filters, or by itself, flash light allows photographers to stage or simulate any type of light.

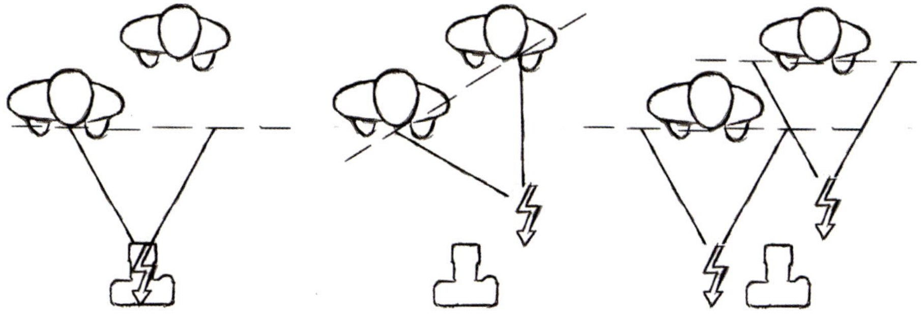

Flash light diminishes in proportion to the square of the distance that separates it from the subject. This means that an object twice as far from the flash will receive one-fourth of the light output. In this illustration, only the person in front will be properly illuminated (left). There are two ways to remedy this problem: the flash must be separated from the camera so both people are on the same plane in relation to the light source (middle), or the photographer must use two flashes to illuminate each person individually (right).

best-suited for objects that are positioned nearby. Otherwise, it can lead to a two-dimensional effect when only one layer of an image is properly illuminated. Any elements that are positioned in front of or behind that layer will be too bright or too dark (see *Learning to Photograph Vol.1*). Setting up multiple synchronized flashes that can be moved around to create sidelighting is an ideal solution for avoiding this two-dimensional effect.

White Balance

Whatever you decide to use for your light source, don't forget to set your camera's white balance for every image. This setting defines white based on fixed parameters and orients all other color tones to this value. Most cameras have presets for the most common light sources, and many of them have automatic white balance. Use automatic white balance with caution and take your subject into consideration because most of these automatic tools define the brightest area of an image as white, even when the brightest area is actually a different color.

It's best to set your white balance manually. This way you can account for slight color variations from different light sources, which is impossible with a preset white

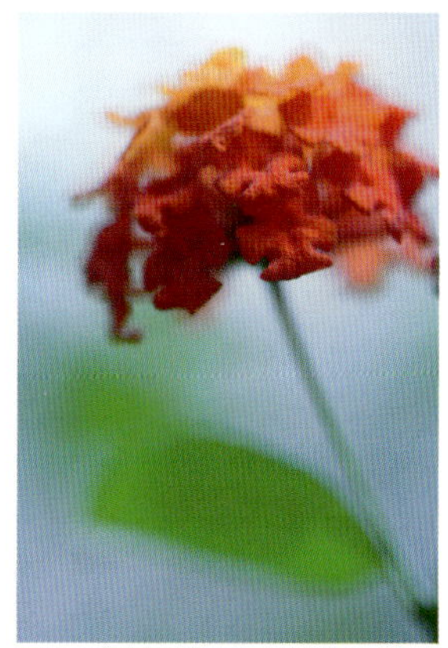

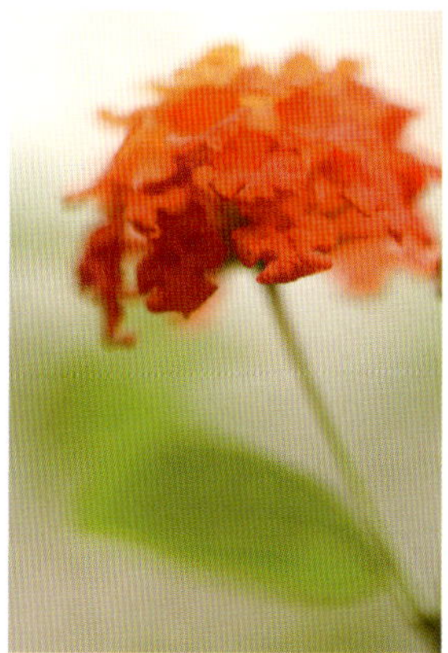

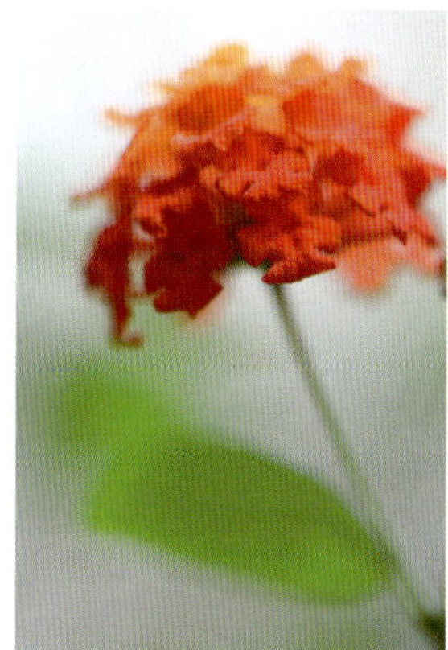

The white balance for artificial light (left) is vastly different from the white balance for daylight (middle). Trusting the white balance to an automatic feature of your camera doesn't always produce the best results because it will likely define the brightest part of your image, regardless of its actual color, as pure white (right).

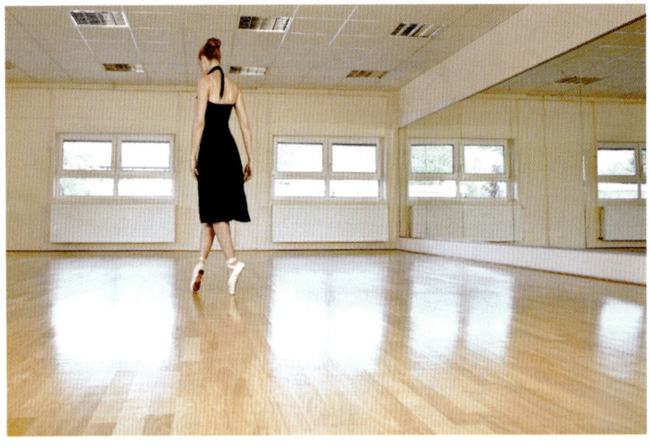

Combining natural and artificial light in the same image can lead to visible color shifts. It's not always possible to detect these color casts with the naked eye, but they often stand out in a distracting way in the final image.

balance. This is the only way to guarantee that the white balance will be based on a white object.

The most important reason to set the white balance is to achieve natural color tones (page 158). However, you can also manipulate the white balance for creative effects. By intentionally adjusting the color temperature in post-processing you can change the color tones in your image to suit your wishes. When you change the color temperature you give the whole image a specific coloration. This may come across as artistic and artificial, and the viewer might think the lighting conditions were different from how they actually were when the image was exposed.

If you work with your pictures in RAW format, you can adjust the white balance retroactively or even give it an initial definition. The JPEG format, however, requires the white balance to be set before you take a picture.

Mixed Light

Mixed light is when you have multiple sources of light that all have their own color characteristics. One potential problem with mixed light is it can cause unwanted color casts in an image, despite the presence of natural color tones. The white balance can be calibrated to only one source of light, which means that only some of the colors in an image will be authentically reproduced. It's up to you to decide which light source to use when you define the white balance, but it's generally a good idea to make sure that skin tones are as realistic as possible. Color casts can be especially distracting if skins tones are altered (page 158).

Aside from this problem, mixed lighting has its own charms. Photographers can showcase different colors of light without allowing this design element to completely take over the image.

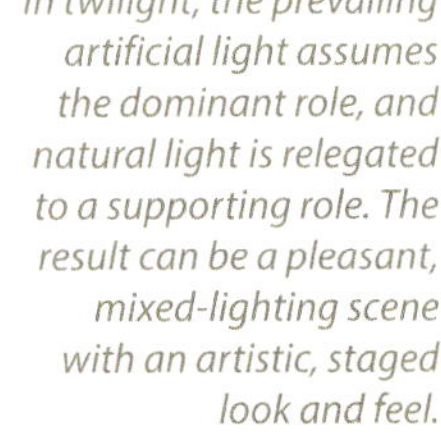

In twilight, the prevailing artificial light assumes the dominant role, and natural light is relegated to a supporting role. The result can be a pleasant, mixed-lighting scene with an artistic, staged look and feel.

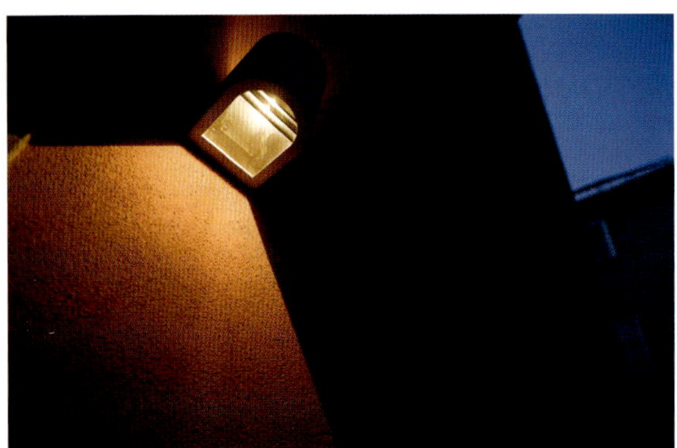

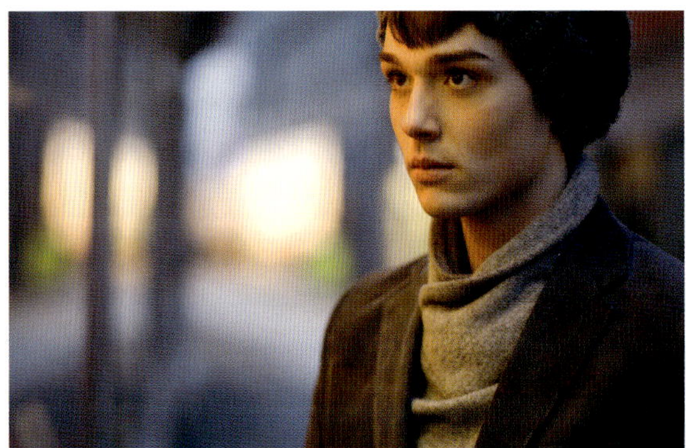

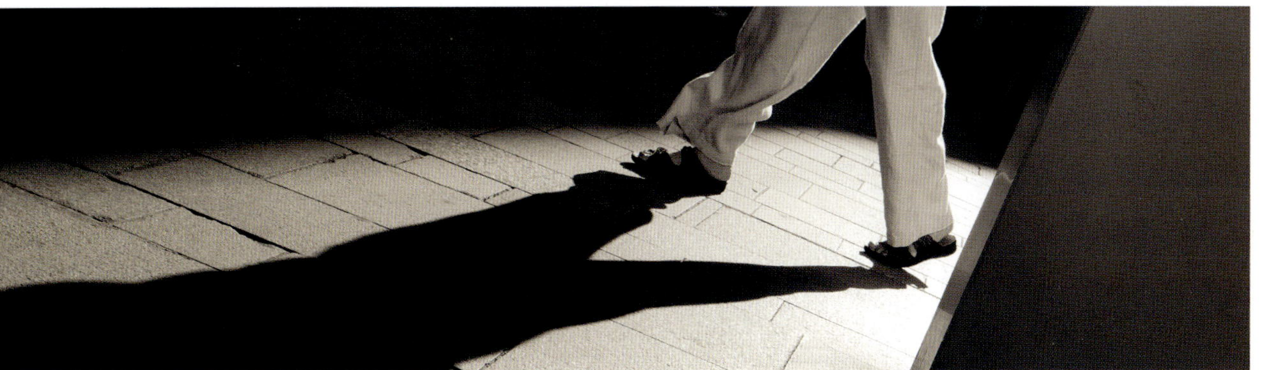

5.4 Shadows

Where there's light, there's shadow. If you consciously adjust the light in a scene to support your photographic objectives, you also influence the shadows. You should consider the presence of shadows when they play as significant a role in your image as light does.

Seeing Shadows

Elements hidden in shadows lose some of their weight because they are cast in darkness and are perceived only after viewers take in the well-lit elements. The human eye can adjust to different brightness conditions, and we perceive shadowy areas as brighter than they really are in order to see details. This is why viewers try to recognize what is hidden in the dark areas of an image. Since the dynamic range of the camera or the display medium is smaller than that of the human eye, the shadows can be too dark for viewers to decipher any details. When this happens, viewers perceive these areas as distracting.

This limited dynamic range means that even light shadows run the risk of looking pitch black in your image, so don't underestimate shadows when you take a picture. To find out how a shadowy detail will affect your image, fire off a quick test shot and examine the results on your

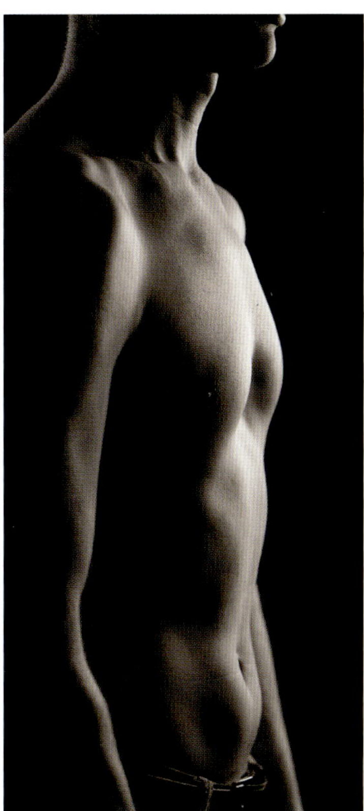

Shadows are a versatile tool for obscuring areas of an image that shouldn't be in plain sight. This goes for all subjects, but especially for nudes. Shadows can be used to hide any problem areas or the pubic region.

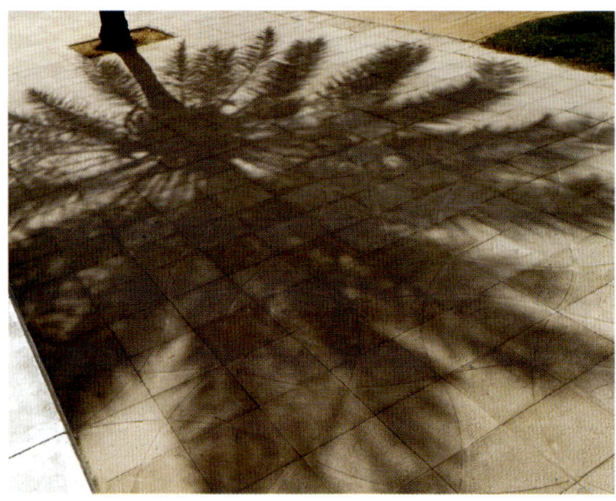

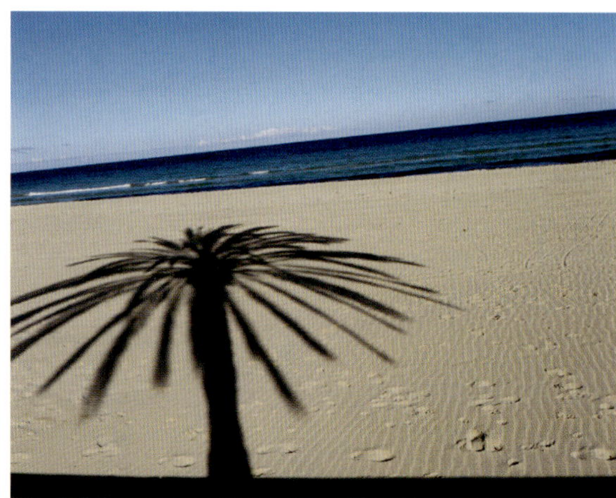

The dominance of a shadow depends on whether points of light break it up or if it's a dark, solid shape with clearly defined borders. The latter type is so attention-grabbing that it becomes a central element in an image. Softer shadows allow other elements to play a more prominent role. Shadows occur along a continuum from one extreme to the other in terms of visual gravity.

camera monitor. You can also squint to reduce the amount of light that enters your eyes. The cones in your eyes, which detect color, will be less activated than the rods, which detect differences in brightness. Even the slightest shadow could be distracting in your image. Use this quick assessment to decide how to deal with potentially problematic shadows.

Depicting Shadows

Since viewers are powerfully drawn to bright areas of an image, you can use shadows to help weight the visual elements, depending on what you want to convey. Shadows deemphasize less important parts of an image and make the critical areas more prominent. If you limit shadows to only the nonessential parts of a photo, they will produce a familiar, comfortable, and realistic effect. But if you obscure key parts of your image in shadows, viewers may be vexed. The shape, size, depth, and structure of a shadow

Shadows provide depth to an image and augment its content. They can form of a visual echo of a person's body (left), create a division between a model and the background (middle), or illustrate a leap by emphasizing the distance between a person's foot and the floor (right).

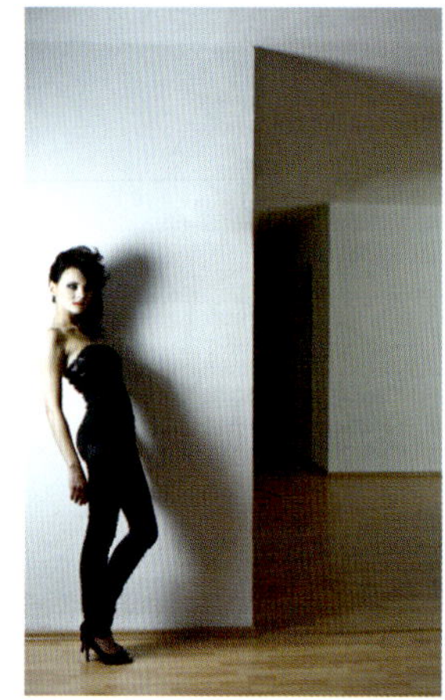

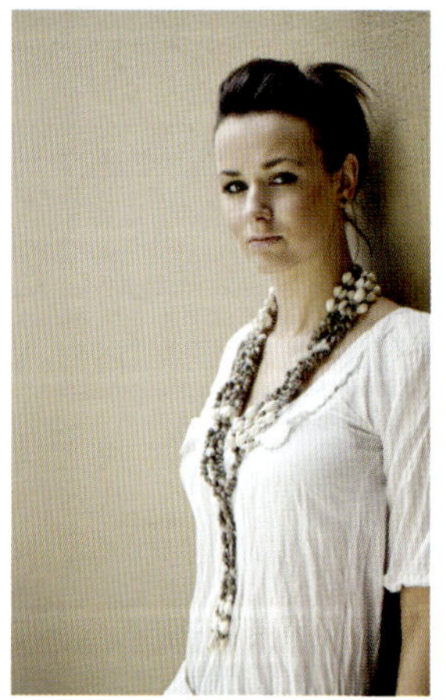

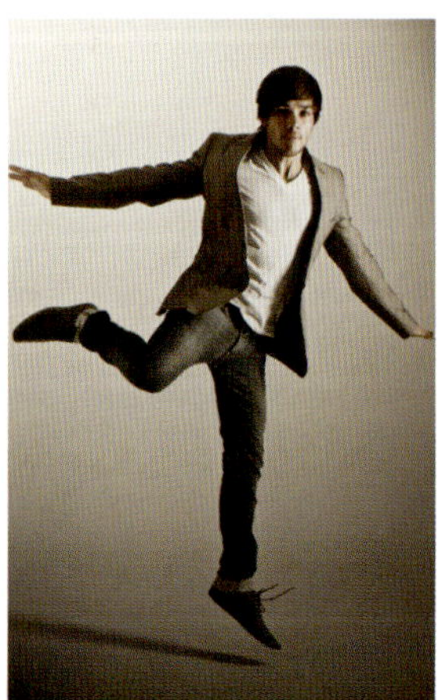

influences how it's perceived; smaller, lighter, or irregularly shaped shadows have less optical gravity than clearly defined, pitch black, or geometric shadows (page 96). When a light source produces direct, focused light on a far-away object, it creates hard, clearly defined shadows. Larger, diffuse light sources that are nearby produce softer shadows with blurred contours. When shadows occur, they always land on the next closest surface, and the distance and shape of this surface affect the appearance of the shadow. If the subject that casts a shadow is right next to the surface on which the shadow falls, the shadow will be sharper. If the surface is farther away, the shadow will be lighter, weakened by ambient light.

When you design with shadows, take care to position them so they don't detract from the dominance of the main subject. You can use shadows to hide or obscure distracting, less attractive parts of a scene. This is a common technique in portrait and nude photography.

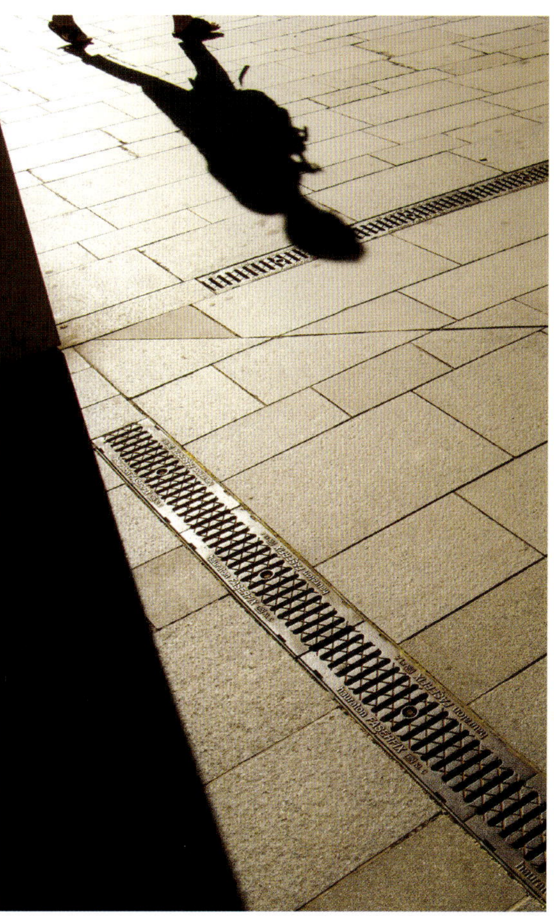

Sometimes shadows are the main subject. If this is the case, it's important to make sure the form of the shadow is recognizable.

Shadows as Subjects

Even though it may sound like shadows are a necessary evil, they can be fascinating subjects in their own right. Pay more attention to the shadows of objects. If a shadow itself is photogenic, it may make sense to include it in your image—with or without the object that casts it. When you include both the shadow and the object in your image, you may decide to crop through one of them. This leads to clearer and more decisive images. When the shadow is your main subject, this design method can lead to particularly unconventional results.

Including the shadow of your main subject gives the image a mysterious and peculiar effect because viewers are inevitably curious about the shadow. As with every visual puzzle, make sure to give viewers a chance to solve the mystery so they stay engaged with the photo. Make sure the outline of the shadow gives clues about the shape of the original object. Viewers often lose interest in abstract shadows because they don't provide enough information to tell a story about the object that created it.

The same goes for shadows that completely obscure the texture of the surface they fall on. Dark black shadows wipe out all details and work on a graphic level as striking, two-dimensional pictograms. Viewers don't spend much time looking at shadows like these unless the outlines provide easily recognizable details.

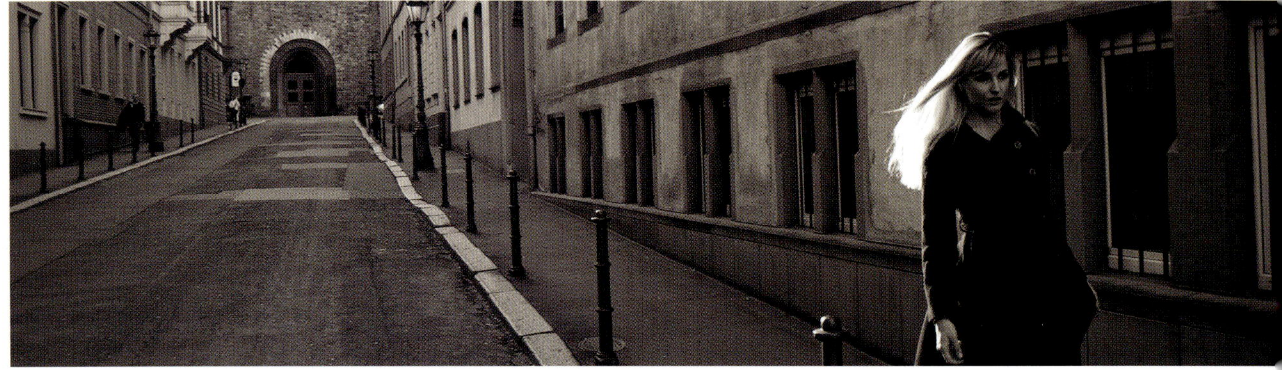

5.5 Light Management

Photographers have two main tools for directing the viewer's gaze within an image: linear composition (page 83) and light management. By dividing light and shadows, you deliberately weight the elements within the photo and clearly establish a sequence for viewers to follow when they explore your image. Both light and shadow should be consciously and purposefully employed—regardless of the light source—to support your intended visual message.

The viewer's eye is attracted to bright areas and skips over dark areas. Photographers can exploit these properties of light and shadows to guide the viewer's gaze throughout an image. In the illustration here, the viewer's eye follows the people as they hurry to catch the train.

Guiding Light

Light creates brightness, and viewers are naturally drawn to the bright areas of an image. Any object bathed in light will be perceived as important. Your job is to make sure the most important elements of your image are highlighted, and to prevent insignificant parts of the composition from becoming too bright. Brightness belongs where your main subject is positioned. For staged lighting, this may result in very different illumination depending on which individual contours or elements should receive the brightness they need to stand out within the composition. Image areas that don't contain important subjects or visual details should not be emphasized with light.

Portraits are a good example of how this process works. If the model is illuminated with sidelighting from a lamp that is in front of the camera, the viewer's attention will focus on her cheeks. If the model turns toward the light, her eyes, nose, and mouth will be emphasized, and if she turns the other direction, her hair will receive the most light. It's up to you to determine what the most critical aspect of your subject is and to make sure that your lighting matches your purpose. In a classic portrait, the emphasis is on the model's face, so the model should turn toward the direction of light, or the light source should be moved to a more frontal location.

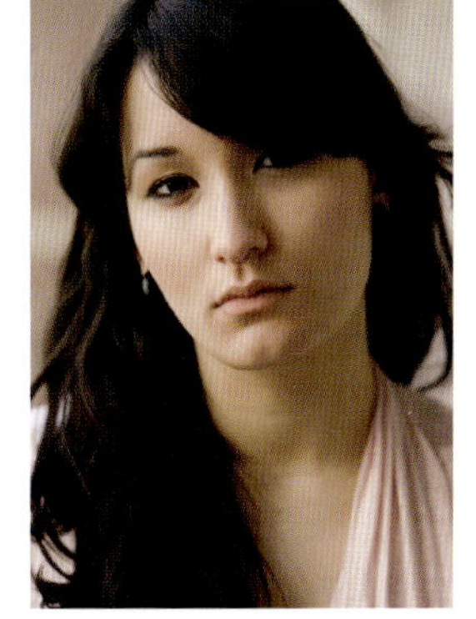

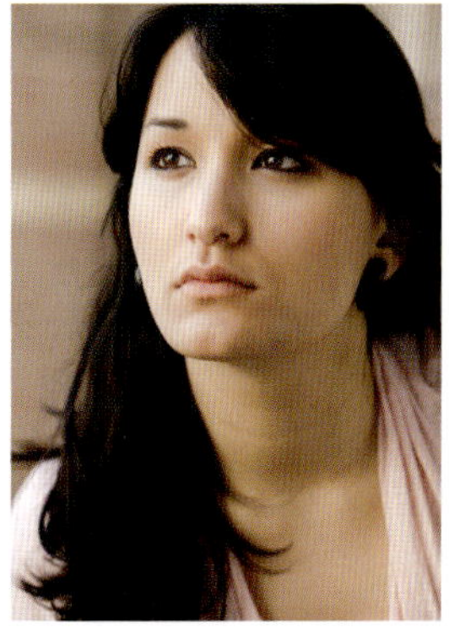

Even slight shadows can help add weight to visual elements because the eye distinguishes bright and dark areas. In the left image, the lighting conditions emphasize the left half of the model's face, her forehead and her hair; her eyes are played down because of the modest shadow. When she turns slightly toward the light source, both of her eyes receive more light, and her face and expression are emphasized.

Diverting Attention

Shadows reduce the visual dominance of subjects and can, in extreme cases, make them disappear entirely. This makes shadow control a vital part of designing with light—apply artificial shadows in post-processing, use light absorbers to intensify shadows, or brighten up areas by using reflectors or additional lamps for fill lighting.

Over- and Underexposure

Images that are too bright or too dark as a result of improper exposure settings have white or dark areas that lack visual detail. These solid areas of white or black attract even more attention than other bright or dark areas, which is problematic because they don't offer viewers additional information. The result is comparable to a hole that catches the eye and pulls the viewer's gaze. Depending on the size of blown-out highlights or clipped shadows, it can be very difficult to establish an optical counterweight to engage the viewer's attention. The one exception is when photographers deliberately use solid white or black backgrounds that feature zero detail to isolate the main subject and present it in front of a neutral backdrop. Otherwise, over- and underexposed portions of an element, especially the main subject, come across as undesirable.

Overexposure leads to a brighter, softer, pastel-like coloration in an image, while a lack of light results in dark, dull, and saturated colors.

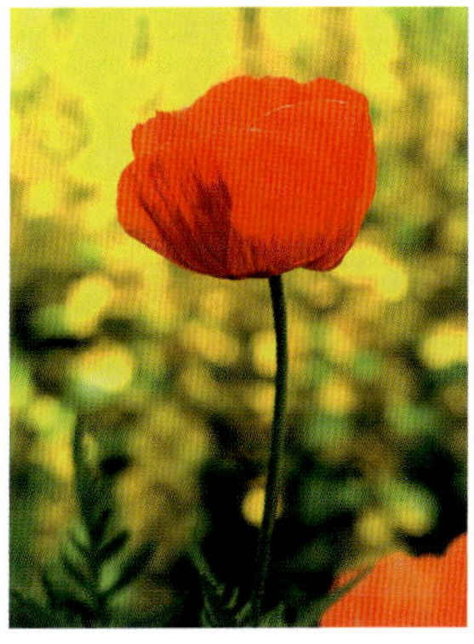

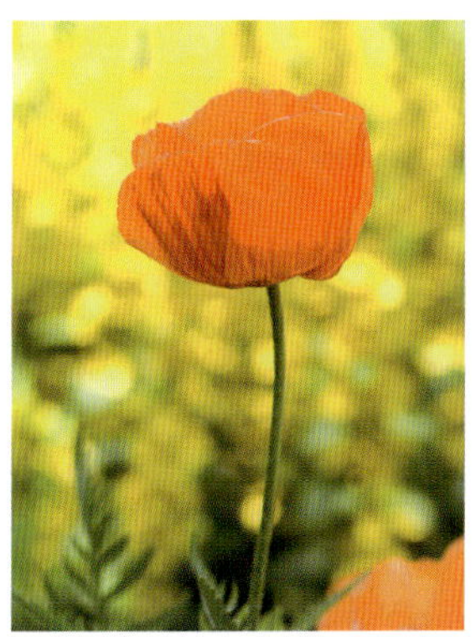

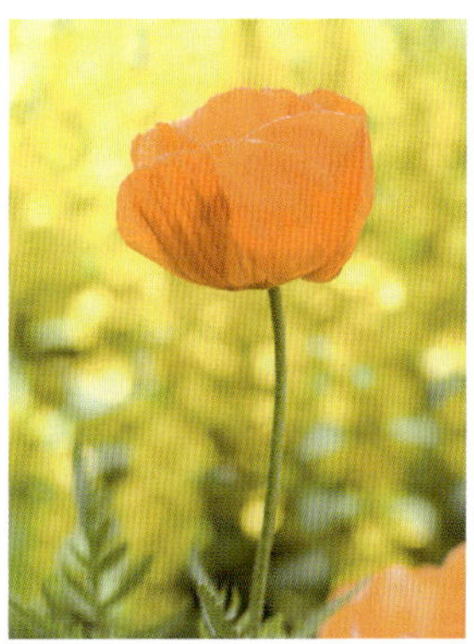

These three illustrations of an underexposed image (left), a properly exposed image (middle), and an overexposed image (right) demonstrate how colors are reproduced when they are cast in different levels of brightness. Less light saturates colors, and more light desaturates them.

"The impression that arises from the simple division of color, light, and shadow—that is the music of a painting." Paul Gauguin, French painter

06 Color and Black-and-White

With every exposure, you have the choice of introducing color or limiting yourself to the gray tones of a black-and-white image. In the age of digital photography, you don't have to make this decision before you take a photograph, nor does your decision necessarily impact the next 36 images you will capture. But the decision itself is just as important now as it was before. The choice to include or exclude color influences the overall effect of the image design. When you shoot in black-and-white, all colors are reduced to their brightness values, which tend to bring the graphic qualities of the subject into the foreground. Designing in black-and-white, in other words, means being able to think in gray scale before and while you expose an image.

In comparison, color exposures function on a very immediate, sensory level because every color arouses specific emotions—both conscious and unconscious—in viewers. This makes the selection of colors for your image, and the harmonization of multiple colors, a critical aspect of design. Some colors balance one another, but others form a strong contrast that influences the dominance and effect of the individual colors.

These aspects of image design are especially important for establishing the emotional impact of an image, and they influence how viewers will approach your subject. Thorough and attentive color management, as well as digital post-processing, help achieve your image design goals.

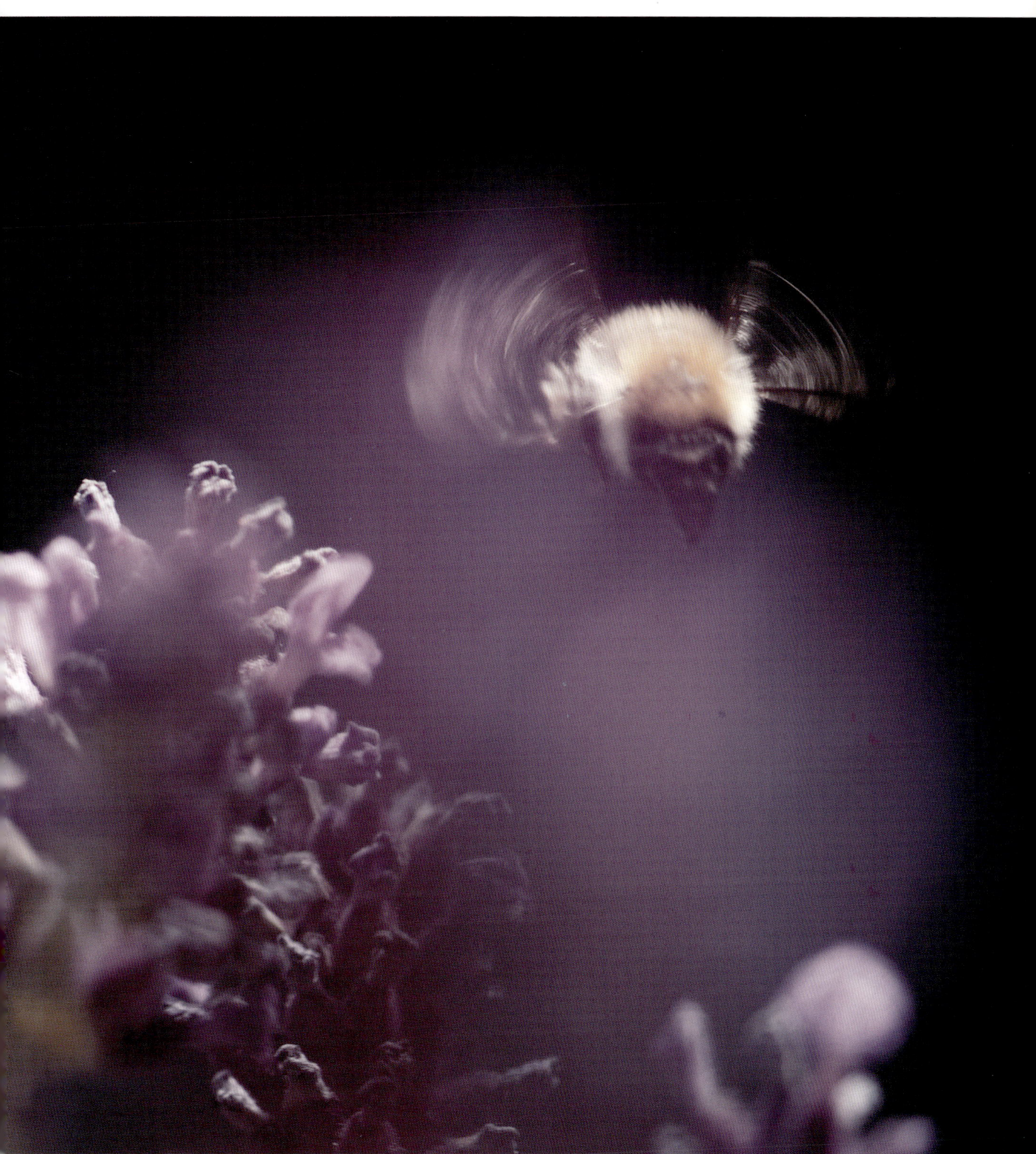

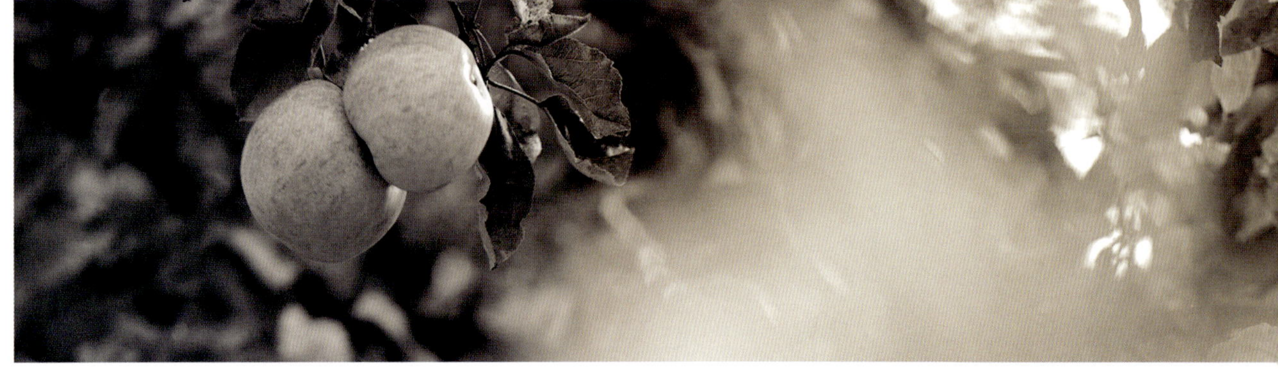

6.1 The Effects of Individual Colors

People have been fascinated with color for centuries. We've developed systems of organization for classifying, defining, and understanding the characteristics of individual colors tones. Despite different approaches, these theories tend to agree on some basic points: every color has a tonal value, a degree of saturation, and a brightness value. Depending on its application, each color achieves a different, very specific effect on the viewer.

The Color Wheel

Several organizational systems have been developed to catalog colors for the purpose of referencing them easily in our everyday lives. The harmonic color wheel is based on the three basic, or primary, colors: red, blue, and yellow. Mixing these colors produces the secondary colors: orange, green, and violet. These colors are arranged in a circle, and additional intermediate colors are generated from further mixtures of the neighboring colors. This color wheel includes 12 different color tones (red, red-orange, orange, orange-yellow, yellow, yellow-green, green, blue-green, blue, blue-violet, violet, and red-violet) and can be extended to include any number of intermediary tones to create a finely graded progression of colors that corresponds to the spectrum of visible light.

The 12-part color wheel includes mixtures of the primary colors red, yellow, and blue (middle). The first mixture level includes the secondary colors orange, green, and violet. These six tones can be mixed to produce more colors.

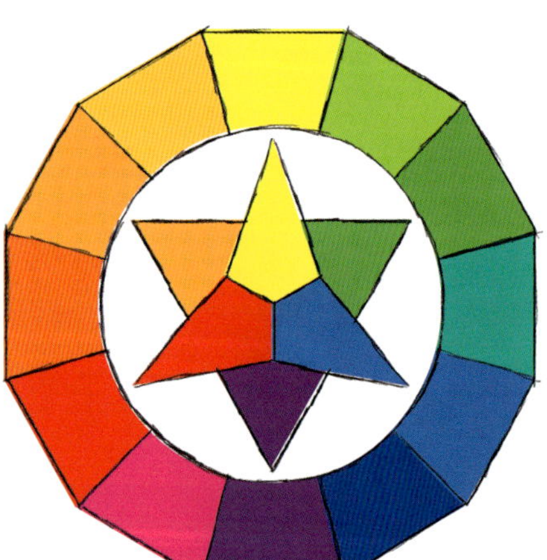

The Double Cone

Adding brightness and saturation as a third dimension to the harmonic color wheel results in the double-cone model. This model includes every imaginable combination of tone, saturation, and brightness.

The colors of visible light are represented by the circle in the middle where the two cones meet. Each color appears in its pure, saturated form at the outermost part of this circle. The vertical central axis encompasses all of the gradations from black to white, with every conceivable intermediate gray value. On the horizontal axis, the color saturation decreases near the middle as each color is infused with more gray (the outside edge is pure color, and the center is neutral gray). The brightness of the color changes along the vertical axis, depending on the addition of white or black (the top is pure white, and the bottom is pure black).

Every point within the double cone corresponds to a specific color. Points in the bottom are darker, points in the top are brighter, points on the outside are more saturated, and points on the inside are less saturated.

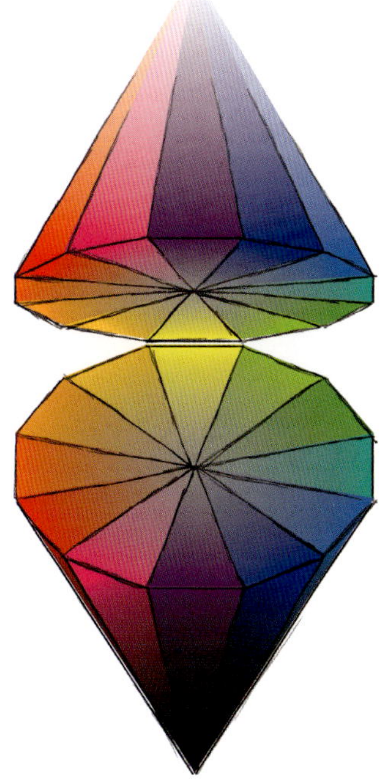

Every conceivable color can be found within this double cone, which is a complete color model. Its dimensions are based on three factors: tone, saturation, and brightness.

Associations and Emotions

Based on its appearance, every color has an immediate psychological effect that works on a symbolic, political, traditional, and creative level. We can't divorce these associations from colors because they are established at an early age and are profoundly internalized as we mature. This means that our personal experiences play a role in how colors affect us, and it is not possible to ascribe a universal meaning to a specific color. However, common meanings within cultural circles do exist, and photographers who understand them can purposefully use colors and their meanings in visual designs. The symbolic meaning of a color is learned more than it is experienced, whereas the emotional associations we have are more subjective and will not apply to everyone in the same way.

For example, not everyone associates black with death and mourning but we can generally assume that more people within Western culture associate death and mourning with black than with any other color. In Japan, however, most people associate white with death; in many African tribes, death

The effect and meaning of colors are based on social and cultural norms. We learn, at an early age, to link red with stop signs, restrictions, and danger. These associations affect how we respond to color.

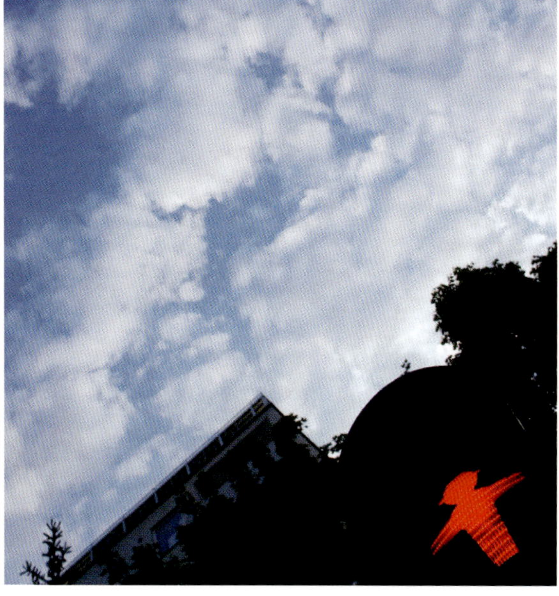

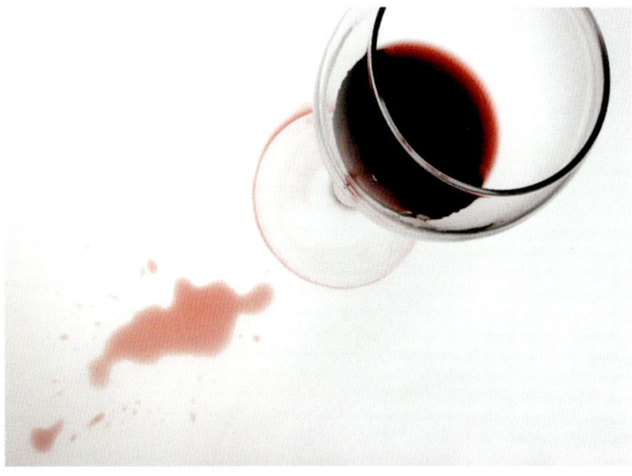

Colors take on meanings not only from social cues; they also assume characteristics of things they represent. We often refer to dark, heavy red as "wine red."

is associated with the color red. The meanings of colors or the emotions they elicit are deeply grounded in our cultural, social consciousness.

Objects that are traditionally a certain color tend to influence the way we respond to that color. Snow is white, clean, and cold. Clouds are white, light, soft, unapproachable, and far away. If we were to list our associations with white, we would likely come up with a similar list: clean, cool and distant, light, bright, soft, pristine, innocent, and pure. It's no coincidence that brides wear white to symbolize virginity and newly baptized children wear white to symbolize innocence. Our standard associations perpetuate themselves not only because we observe white objects in the natural world, but also because we see how white is applied within our society.

Warm and Cold Colors

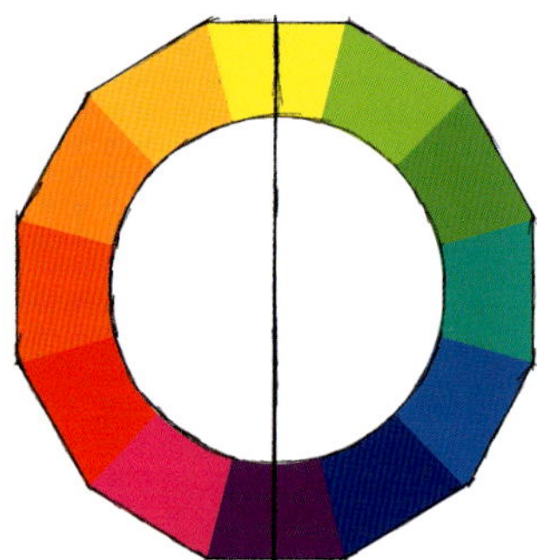

A color wheel split in this manner shows the division of warm colors (left) and cool colors (right). Yellow and violet sit on the fence because they are neither wholly warm nor cool; they can take on the characteristics of both warm and cool colors.

Regardless of the individual color tone and its associations, all colors can be fundamentally divided into warm and cold colors. This division is purely subjective, since colors aren't actually warm or cold, and it's mostly based on the common understanding that red, orange, and yellow tones are the colors of heat (fire, embers, sunlight), and that blue, turquoise, and green tones are the colors of coldness (water, sky). Taking a look at the color wheel from Johannes Itten, we see that a vertical line divides the colors into warm and cool palettes.

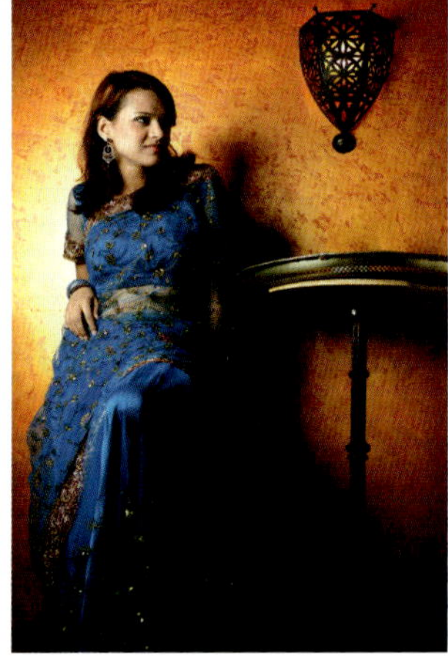

The combination of warm and cold tones in this image creates a fetching contrast that vitalizes the colors and makes them stand out to viewers. Color temperatures work strongly on a subconscious level and can have such a powerful impact on viewers who can feel the heat or coolness just by looking at the colors.

Warm colors elicit feelings of closeness, intimacy, friendliness, and comfort, which we may associate with sunlight, candlelight, or the yellow light of a conventional light bulb. Cool colors come across as distanced, reserved, and unflappable. These associations profoundly affect us, and even the slightest nuances of color don't go unnoticed during the process of perception. Even when an image is predominantly red and orange, if it shifts slightly toward bluish tones, viewers immediately register the cooler temperature and the image seems more distanced and serene.

Color Brightness

Every color tone exhibits a certain level of brightness that can be increased or decreased by adding more white or black, respectively. These changes in brightness produce different effects for viewers, who perceive bright, pastel colors as positive, gentle, subtle, and inconspicuous. These types of colors also convey a feeling of space and weightlessness that may translate to distance and aloofness. Dark colors, on the other hand, are perceived as negative, grim, and oppressive; also, depending on the context, they can seem closer and homier.

Parts of the image that don't feature much light come across as less friendly, more dangerous, and less clean than brighter areas, which viewers associate with kindness, vitality, and purity.

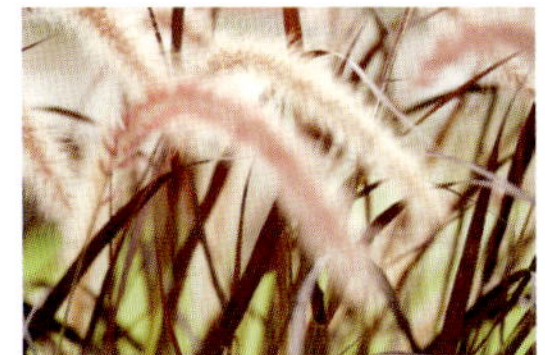

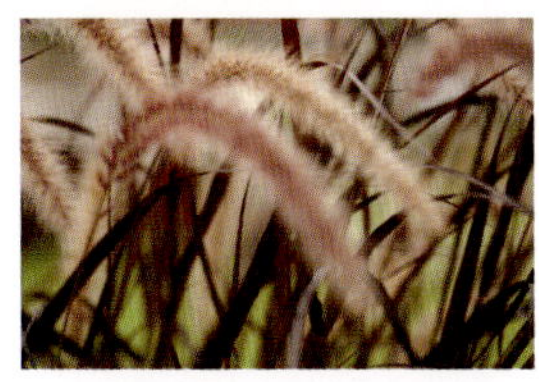

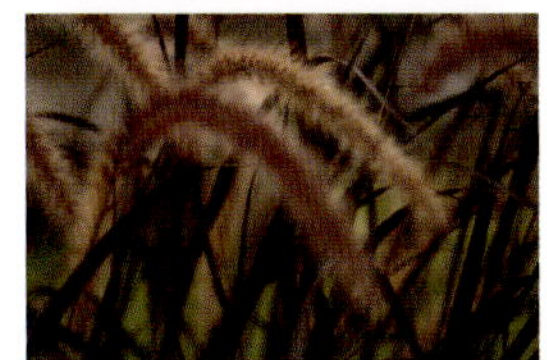

Changes in the brightness of a color have a strong influence on its characteristics. Bright colors seem to be illuminated by the sun, and dark colors seem to be cast in shadow.

Color Saturation

A color's degree of saturation is influenced by mixing in gray, the third variable of color. The more gray, the more diluted and subdued the color becomes. The intensity that's synonymous with highly saturated colors is lost with the addition of gray. Colors that are located in shadows within a photo are typically desaturated and have a much more restrained effect than colors that are brightly illuminated in sunlight, which appear loud, dominant, and happy.

A change in saturation also leads to a change in brightness. This is the case when objects appear in shadows. Dark, desaturated colors have a gloomier look than bright, desaturated colors. The latter conveys a sense of tenderness, distance, and reduced intensity. This is related to the concept of aerial perspective in painting, which describes the phenomenon in which colors in nature, when viewed from afar, take on a bluish tint. In the world of color tones, this means that more blue and gray get mixed in to create the illusion of distance.

Black and white, and all the gray tones between them, are considered achromatic colors. Since an achromatic color is added to a chromatic color to change its saturation and brightness, people refer to desaturated colors as achromatic. The term is applicable because desaturated colors are less dominant than chromatic, intensely saturated colors.

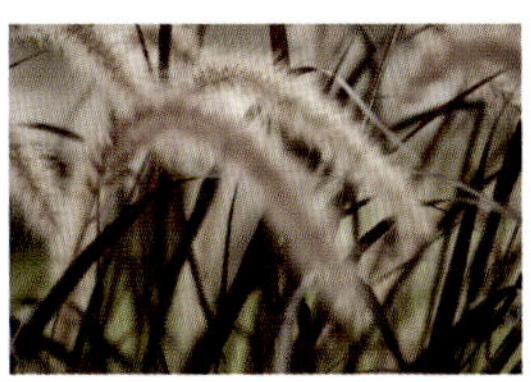

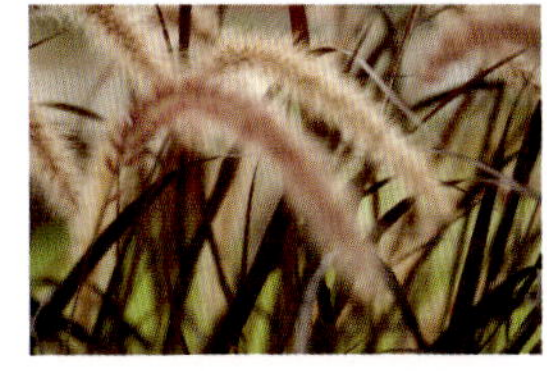

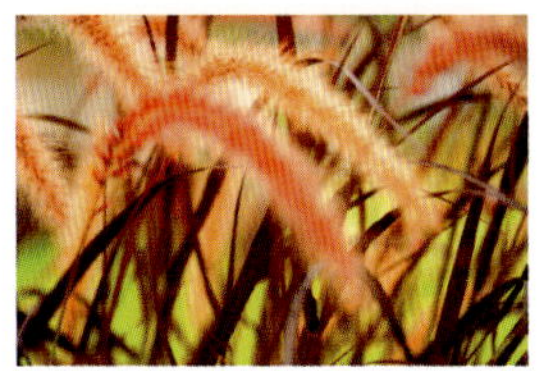

Saturation describes a color's intensity. Saturated tones are louder, brighter, and more colorful; unsaturated colors are modest and subdued—almost boring and bland. Intense colors have a stronger pull on the viewer's attention.

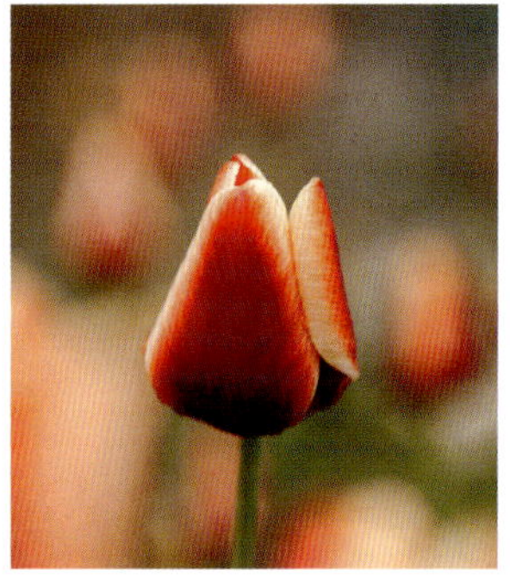

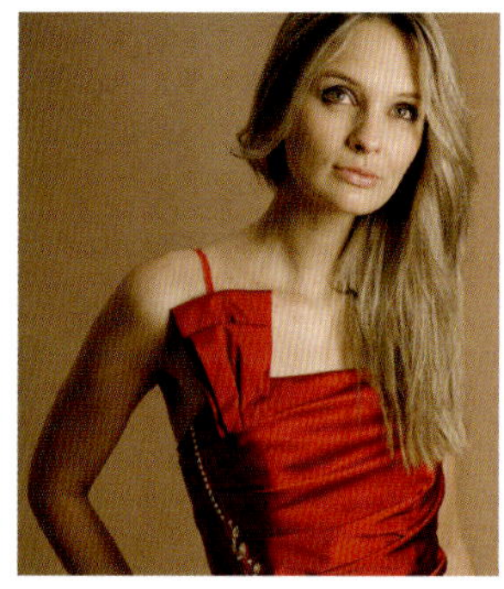

Color Tones and Their Effects

In the following discussion, we give an overview of individual colors, describe what these colors make us think of, why these associations exist (including figurative and symbolic meanings), and how they affect us. As we already mentioned, the effect of a color is, in part, a highly subjective response. Our response to color depends partially on personal taste and sensibilities. We don't all see the exact same color; slight differences in color perception can result in one viewer considering a color pleasant, while another person may consider it unattractive. There's no reason to argue about the effects and potential of color associations, especially when colors are displayed on different media. This is true of digital images because not all monitors are calibrated correctly.

The context of a color has a profound influence on its effect, which is clearly demonstrated in these two images that feature yellow, orange, and red tones. The colors are identical, but their effects are not. The context, the subject, and the additional green tones in the image on the left alter how the colors function in each image.

For the time being, we'll also disregard the context, which can result in contradictory color associations. For example, when red is framed by white and pink it functions as a sweet symbol of romance, but when red is flanked by orange and black, it appears angry, brutal, and violent. We will discuss the interplay of multiple colors in later sections.

Red

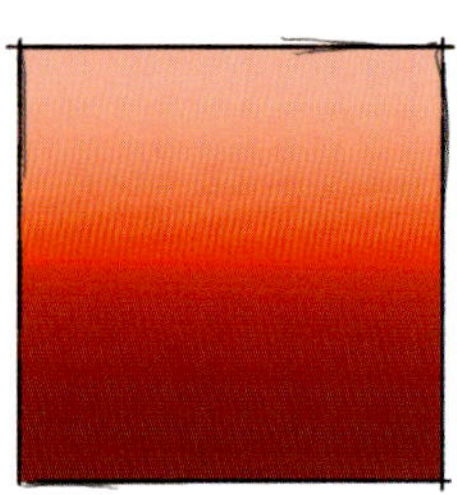

Red is the color of closeness and energy. Red objects generally appear to belong in the foreground and seem to exude heat. It functions powerfully as a signal, which is why it is often used for warnings. Red can also symbolize femininity, power, and prestige. In connection with brighter tones, such as white or pink, red can stand for love. With darker colors, such as black, orange, and yellow, red may stand for aggression, rage, and danger, but also for passion.

- Saturated red (fire engine red, blood red, traffic signal red)
- *recalls:* fire, blood, ripe fruit, traffic signals, traffic signs, warning labels, temperature displays, poppies, roses
- *feels:* warm, lively, exciting, moving, hot, angry, dangerous, erotic, vital, passionate, feminine, powerful, aggressive, sensual, dynamic, uninhibited

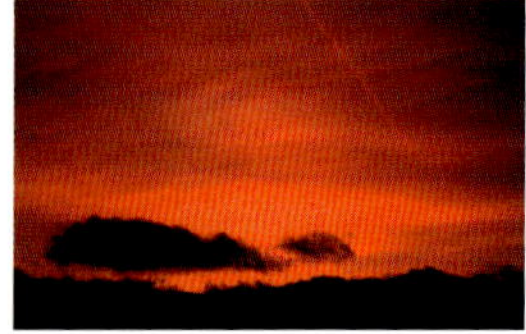

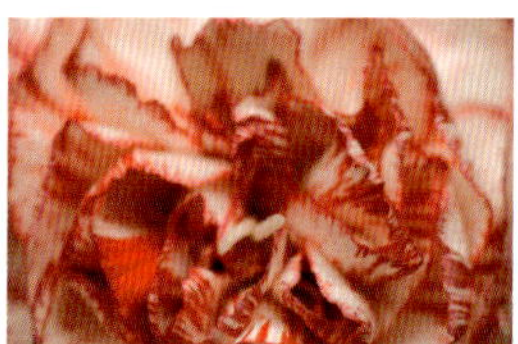

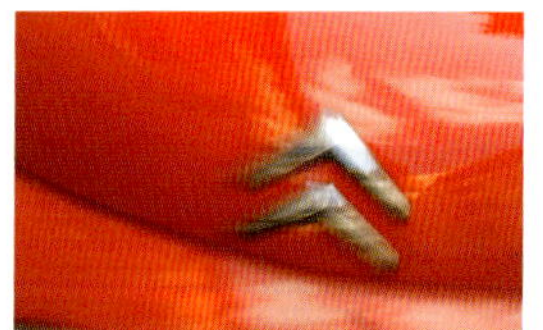

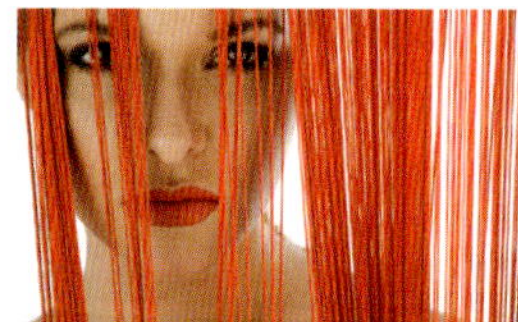

- Light red (pink)
- *recalls:* dolls, baby clothes for girls, cotton candy, flowers
- *feels:* tender, gentle, playful, girly, naïve, young

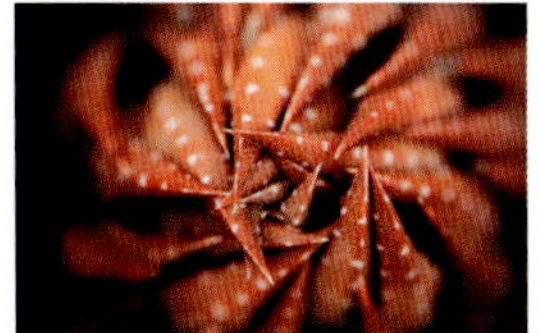
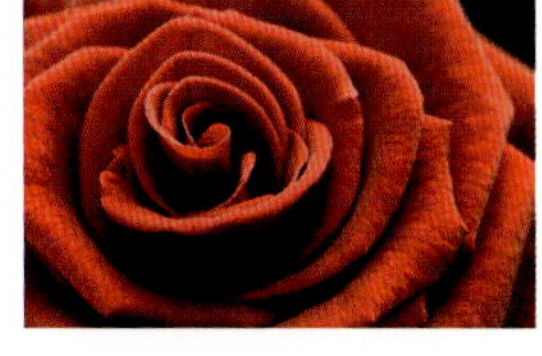

- Dark red (wine red, burgundy)
- *recalls:* red wine, velvet, church regalia
- *feels:* classical, traditional, dignified, soothing, calm, round, full-bodied, luscious, elegant, classy, expensive

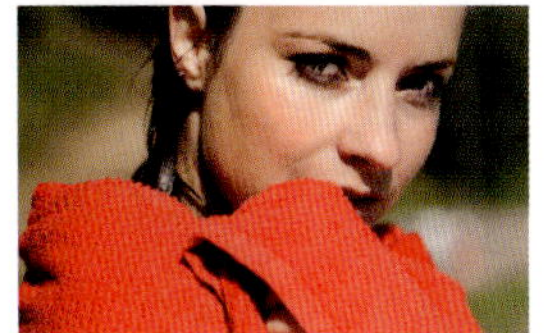
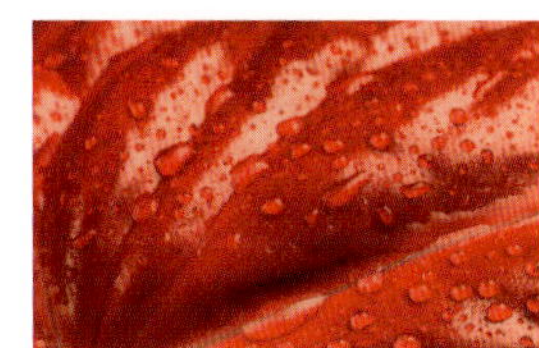

Orange

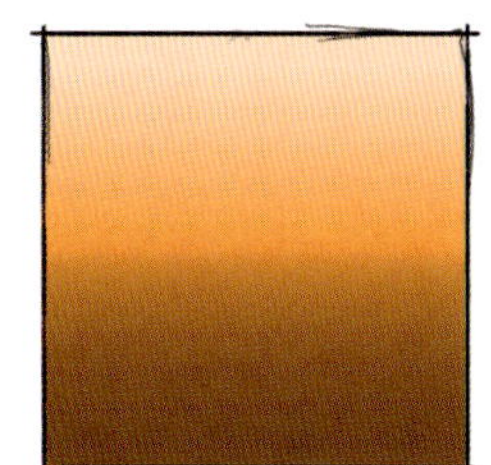

Orange is the color of having lust for life and it comes across as bright, radiant, and warm. At the same time, it has a strong religious meaning because saturated orange is a sacred color in many Asian cultures. Its association with a golden hue also contributes to this symbolism. As a mixture of yellow and red, orange is a flashy color that is often used specifically to attract attention, such as reflective vests and clothes for construction workers.

Bright orange tones lose their color quickly; beige tones have an almost monochromatic quality and suggest subtlety. Dark orange tones are browns that convey a warm and homey feeling, which is a universal quality for all shades of orange.

- Saturated orange (saffron yellow, dark yellow)
- *recalls:* sunrise and sunset, oranges, apricots, curry, robes of Buddhist monks, safety vests, tigers
- *feels:* cozy, warm, sweet, positive, spiritual, refined, fruity, lively

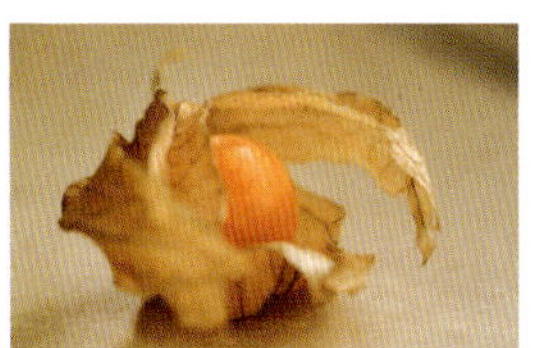
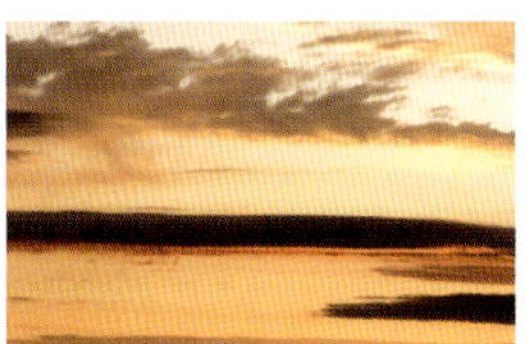

- Light orange (beige, ochre, light brown)
- *recalls:* earth, wood, sand, foliage, harvest grains
- *feels:* warm, stable, cautious, discreet, friendly, natural, Mediterranean

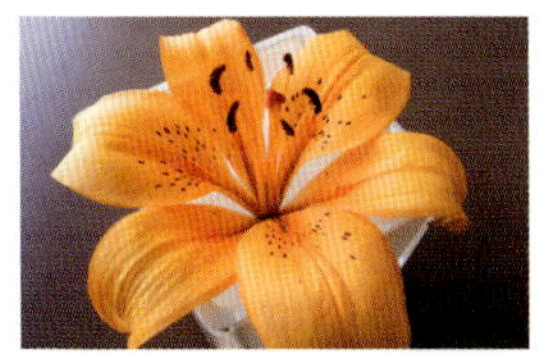
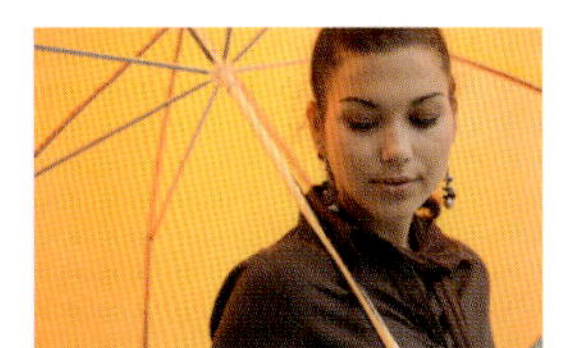

- Dark orange (brown)
- *recalls:* chocolate, wood, furniture, tree bark, soil
- *feels:* firm, stable, comfortable, calm, dirty, old-fashioned, organic, cheerless, expired, heavy, decayed

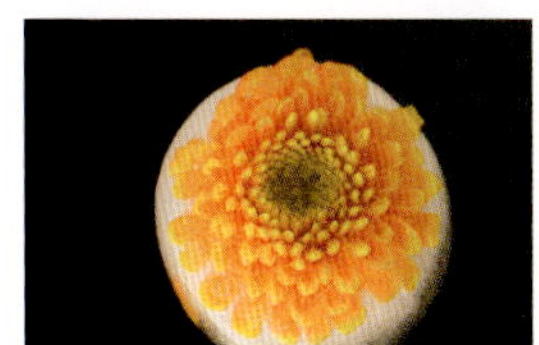
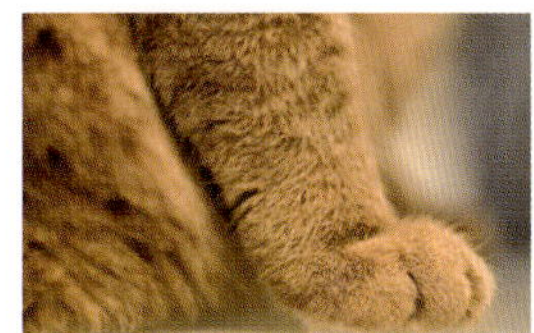

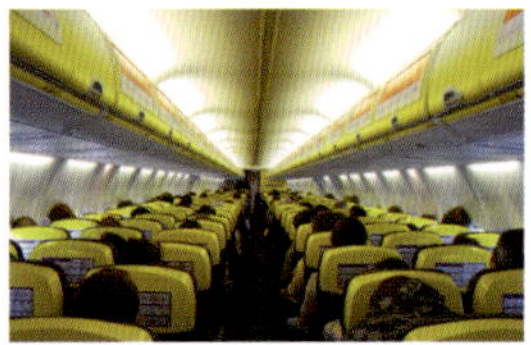
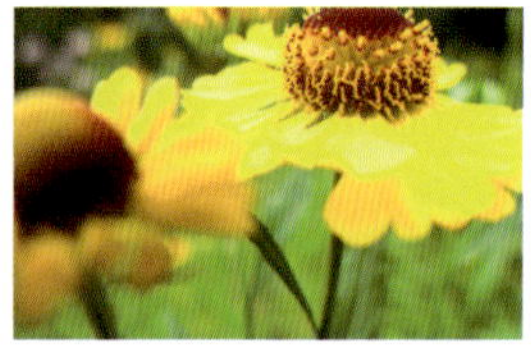
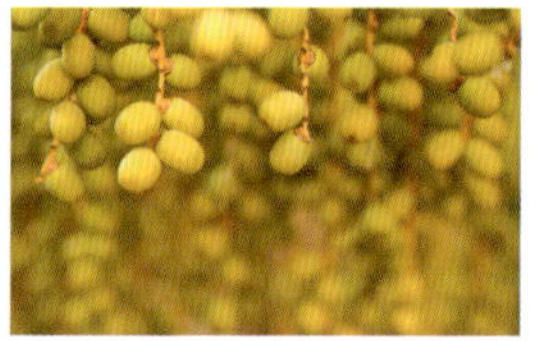
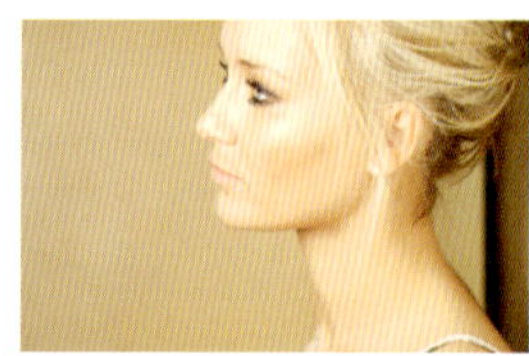
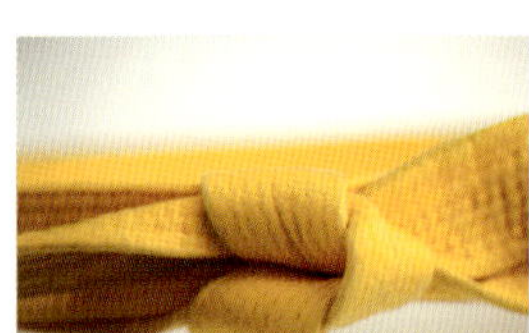
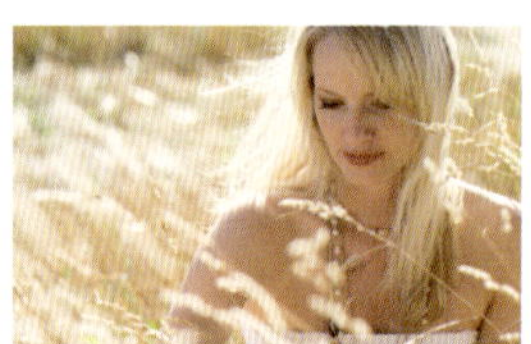
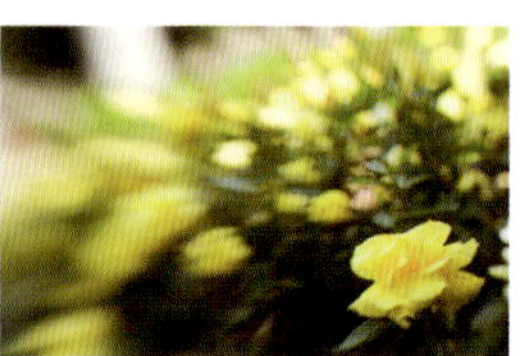
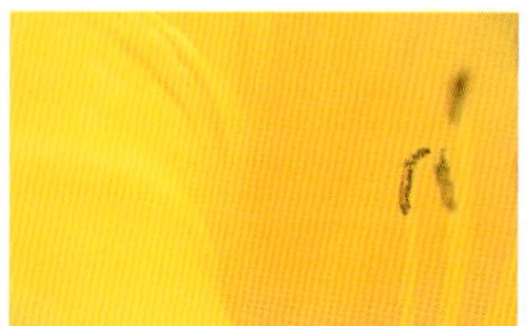

Yellow

First and foremost, yellow is the color of light. As soon as yellow is mixed with gray or black tones, it loses its character and becomes brownish or olive hued, which often comes across as unclean. In its true sense, there are only saturated and light yellow tones, which have an overwhelming, favorable effect. Yellow is very luminous; as its brightness is reduced, its brilliance hardly suffers, which is why it's the second most effective color for signaling information, after red. Yellow is especially luminous when it occurs in an otherwise dark setting. At the same time, since yellow is the color of lemons, it can also produce sour, biting, and even toxic impressions; it's significant that yellow is the color of envy in some cultures.

- Saturated yellow (sunshine)
- *recalls:* summer, sun, sunflowers, fields of wheat, canola, lemons, bananas
- *feels:* joyful, lively, cheerful, warm, good-humored, positive; also toxic, uncomfortable, jealous, cowardly

- Light yellow (lemon yellow, golden wheat)
- *recalls:* lemonade, sulfur, butter
- *feels:* fresh, sour, playful, cheerful, positive, tender, gentle, unripe

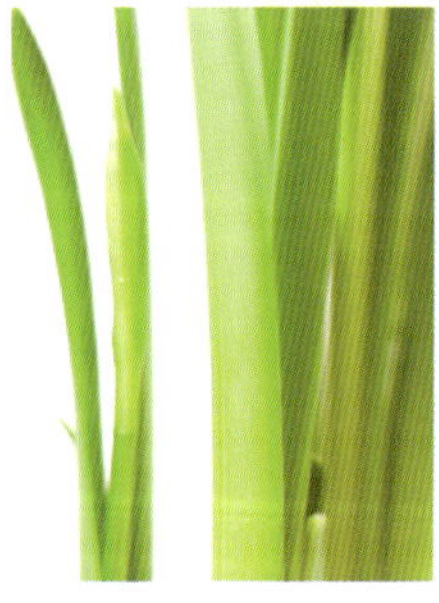
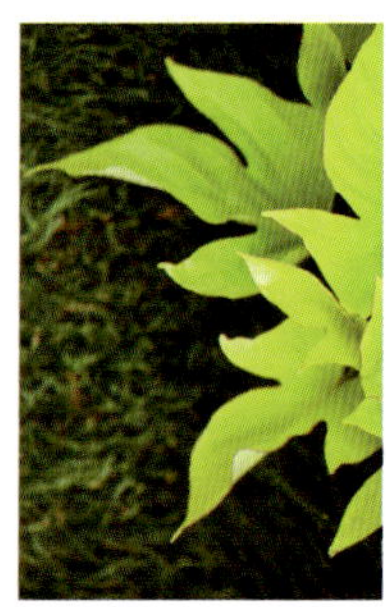

Yellow-Green

The mixture of green and yellow has an intense effect that can appear toxic and artificially loud. This color is often perceived as unpleasant, especially when it is not tempered by a dark tone. The coupling of yellow-green with chocolate brown has become trendy in recent years. Yellow-green has a fresh feel and can symbolize the springtime, since many new leaves exhibit this color before they develop more saturated green tones.

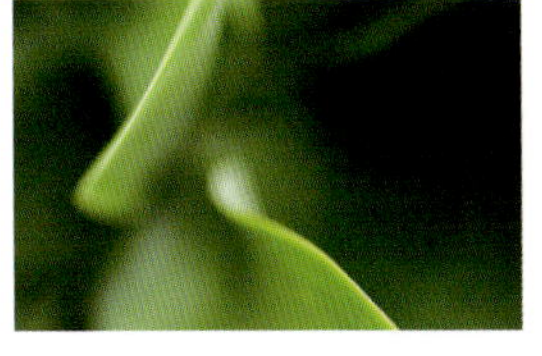
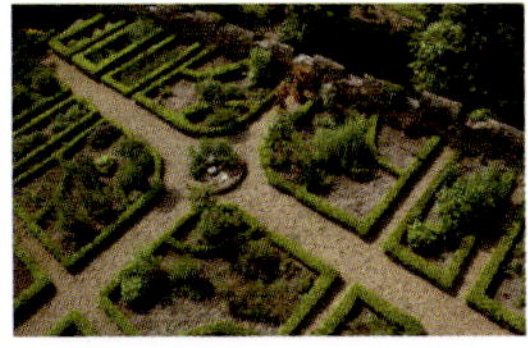
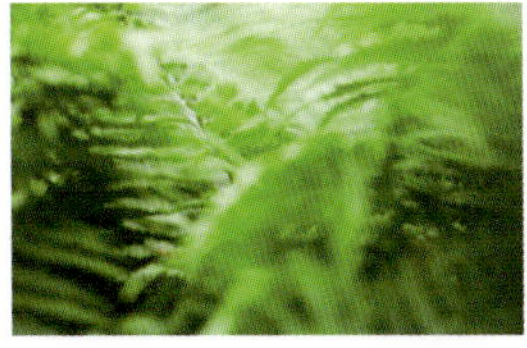
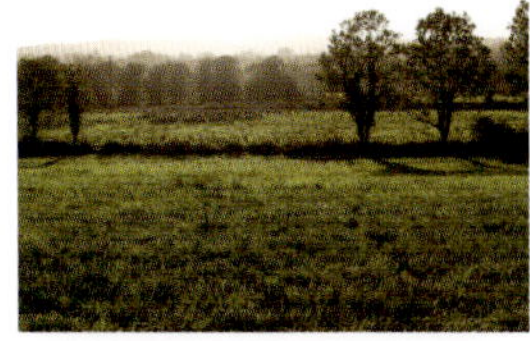
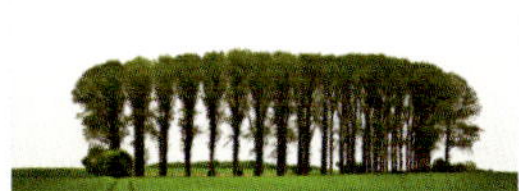
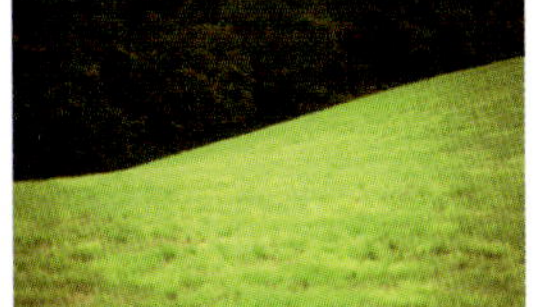
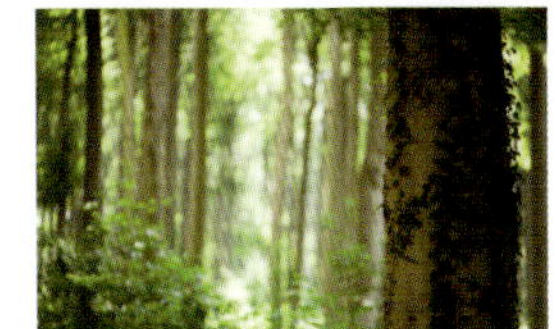
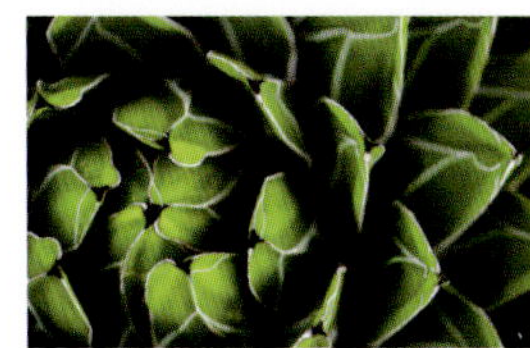

Green

Green is the color of nature and symbolizes life, youth, growth, and prosperity. It's associated with the concepts of hope, confidence, and optimism, especially when the hue is adequately bright. It recalls the botanic world of plants and leaves. Green can also be toxic and unripe, which is why it is so closely linked with jealousy.

- Saturated green (grass)
- *recalls:* meadows, leaves, plants, trees, soccer and football fields, tree frogs
- *feels:* lively, fresh, healthy, natural, new, growing, organic

- Light green (spring green)
- *recalls:* spring, unripe fruit, limes, apples, absinthe, new shoots
- *feels:* young, fresh, hopeful, sour, toxic

- Dark green (hunter green, olive green)
- *recalls:* evergreen trees, Christmas, olives, forests, military
- *feels:* quiet, thoughtful, welcoming, traditional, dirty, calm, dark

Blue-Green

A mix of blue and green is called turquoise, and we associate it with clear water near ocean beaches, which is generally why swimming pools are lined with turquoise. As a blended color of the CMYK color space, the term cyan is becoming more widespread. Bright tones of turquoise approach jade, and darker tones resemble teal.

The context of blue-green determines whether it has an artificial or a natural look, but it always seems to be matte and cool.

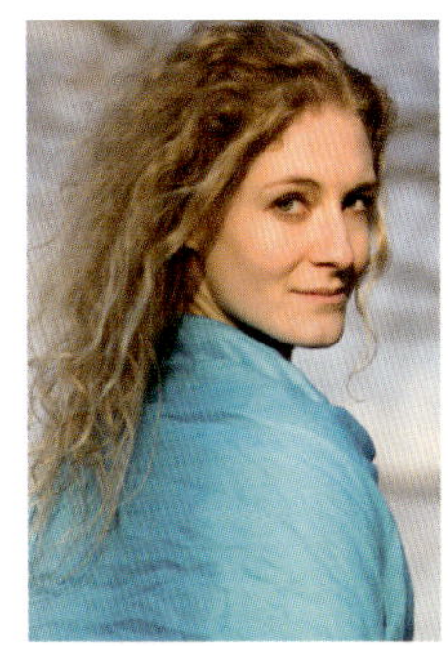
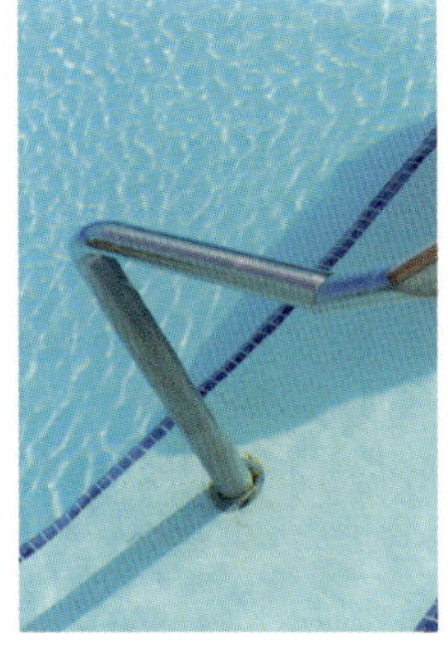

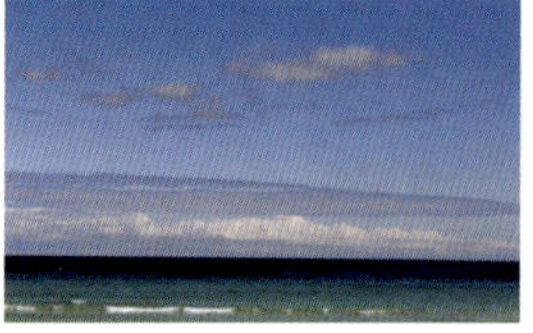
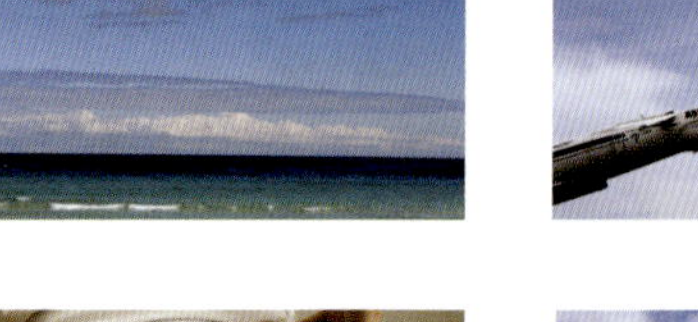
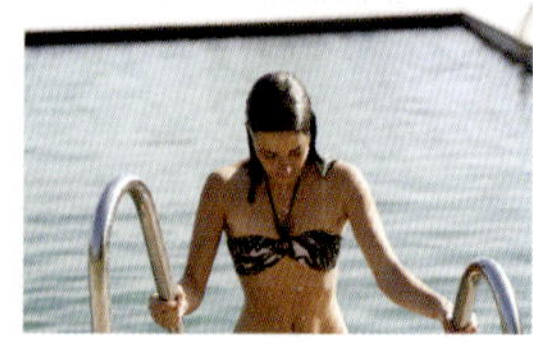
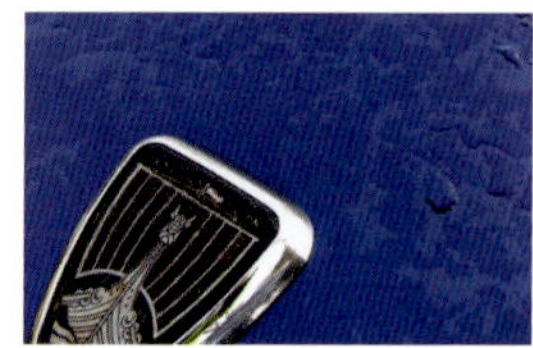

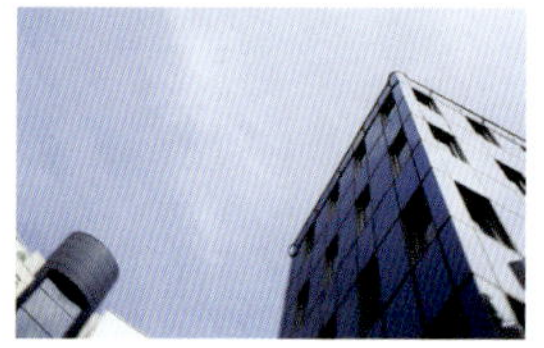
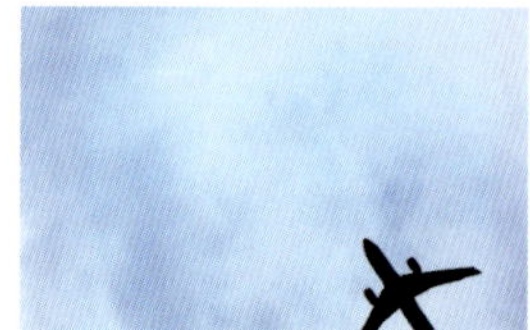

Blue

As both the color of the sky and water, many people name blue as their favorite color. In many respects, blue is the opposite of red because it symbolizes coolness and distance. Blue also stands for masculinity and strength. Blue feels quiet, passive, reflective, and introspective. As its brightness decreases, blue loses its substance and starts to appear pale, bland, and transparent.

- Saturated blue (cobalt blue, royal blue, cornflower blue)
- *recalls:* sky, sea, jeans, cornflowers
- *feels:* positive, cool, reserved, quiet, peaceful, relaxing, calm, modern, prosperous, closed

- Light blue (sky blue, steel blue)
- *recalls:* sky, water, baby clothes for boys
- *feels:* gentle, light, sweet, playful, relaxing, young, fresh, summery

- Dark blue (deep blue, navy blue, midnight blue)
- *recalls:* oceans, the blue hour, thunderstorms
- *feels:* fathomless, placid, tranquil, lush, thoughtful, traditional, exhausted, lacking in energy, depressed, noble, rich, understated

Violet

Violet is the color of religion and magic. We connect it with mysteries, the supernatural, enchantment, and the Christian faith. Violet often symbolizes wealth and luxury.

- Saturated violet (purple)
- *recalls:* violets, lilac, lavender, the Roman Catholic Church
- *feels:* floral, royal, religious, solemn, mystical, mysterious

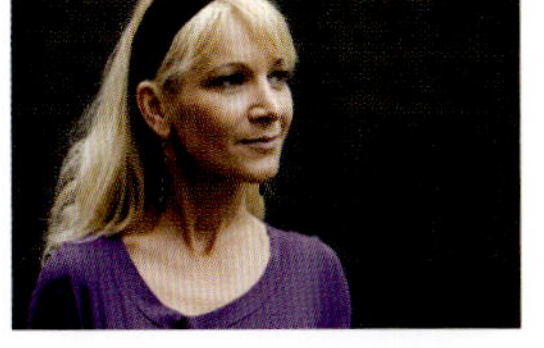
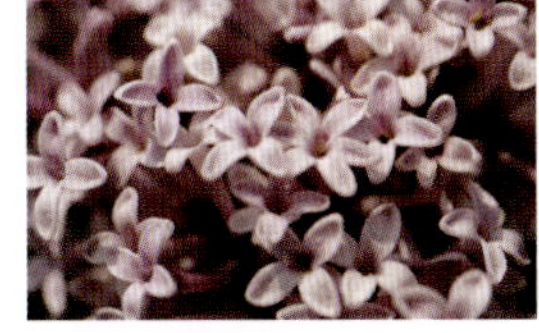
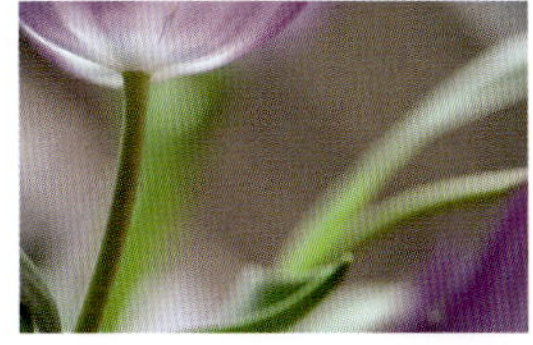
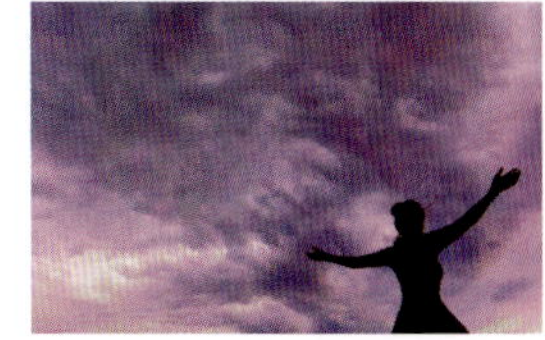
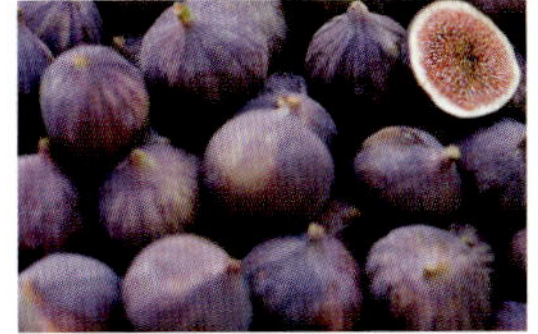
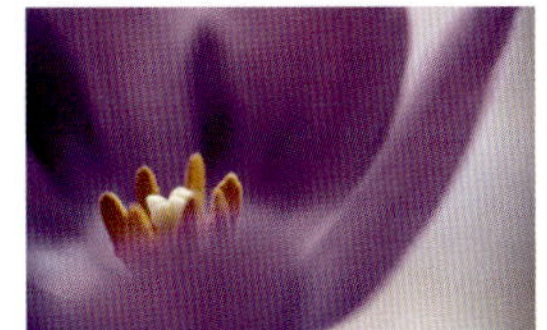
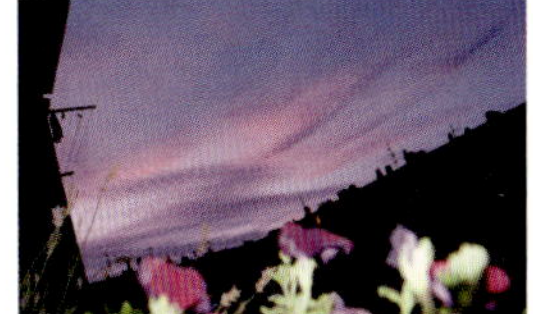
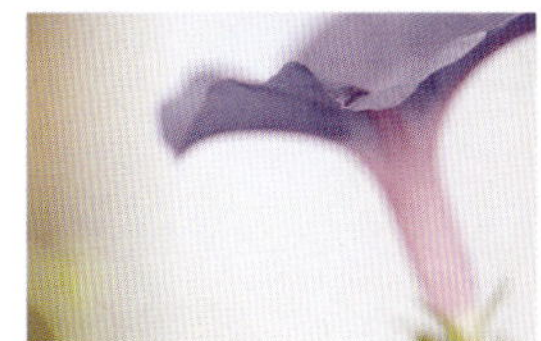

- Dark violet (aubergine)
- *recalls:* plums, eggplants, the first and last rays of the sun, black eyes
- *feels:* heavy, gloomy, listless, Mediterranean, dangerous

Red-Violet

A blend of violet and red produces fuchsia or magenta. When this blend also includes blue, red-violet recalls the majestic appearance of violets. When red or pink tones are added, this blended color recalls ripe raspberries and has an appearance that is lively, sweet, playful, bold, energetic, sharp, and sassy. This color tends to be intense and can border on brash and unpleasant. In terms of the CMYK color palette, the most common name for this blended color is magenta.

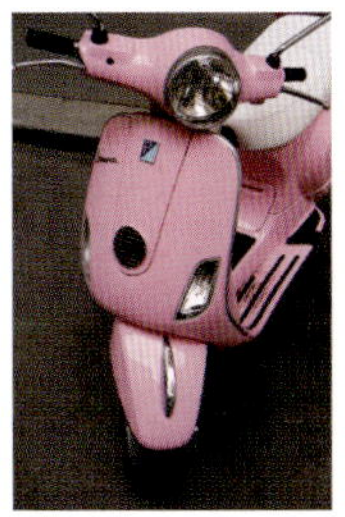
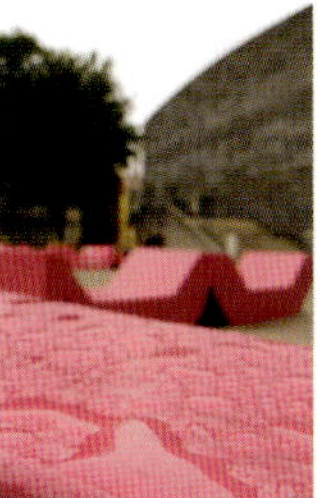
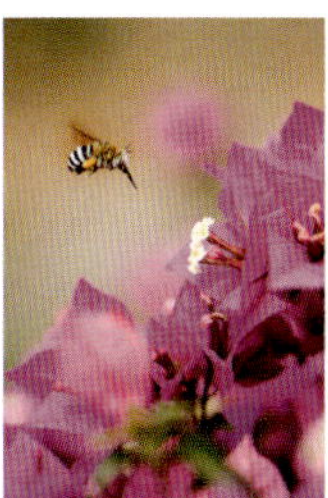

Achromatic Colors

White is the color of innocence and functions as the most neutral and cleanest color. White feels bright, cool, pure, pristine, and young; it also seems very still, like a sheet of paper or a canvas that is waiting for color. When they are set against white, all other colors show their true, unadulterated characteristics. White stands for infinity, peace, and freedom. No two shades of white are alike; the shades vary from cool snow white or lily white to a warmer linen white, which is almost a beige tone.

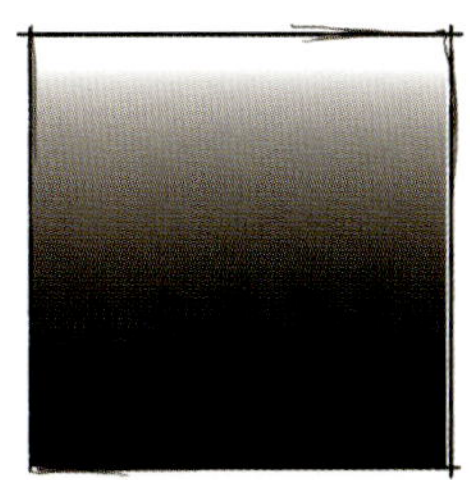

Black is the color of shadows; it symbolizes darkness and death. In our culture, it is the color of mourning, but it's also a stylish and understated fashion color that works for every occasion. When other colors are juxtaposed with black, they seem to have a heightened sense of intensity that can produce a telling contrast. For example, when

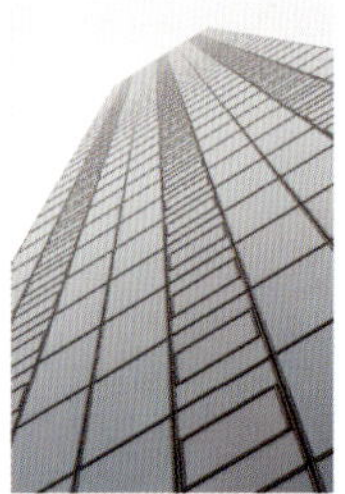

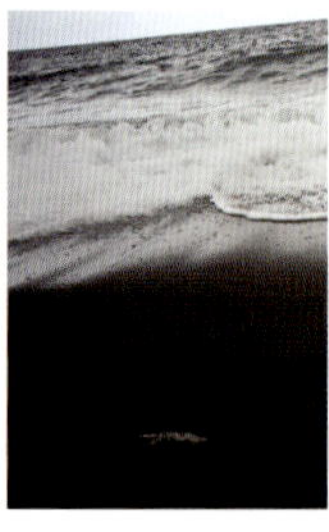

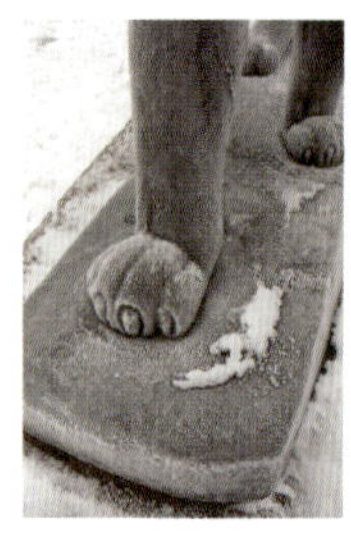

black and yellow are paired, both seem especially saturated. Black has a lifeless, heavy, gloomy feel, but it also comes across as neutral, unobtrusive, and discreet. Generally, any photo that features an area of pure white should also contain an area of pure black, no matter how small. Without a black counterweight, exposures quickly lose their sense of tonal contrast.

Gray is a versatile color because it can exhibit a near endless range of shades, and it encompasses all the shades between white and black. Gray feels neutral, distinguished, unemotional, and melancholy, but some shades of gray that are blended with a hint of color have more dramatic effects. Fully saturated colors tend to overpower isolated gray tones, and look especially vibrant. But grays can gain the upper hand in images; when they are paired with less saturated colors they can quickly turn a picture into a rainy, foggy November day—bleak, cold, and dreary.

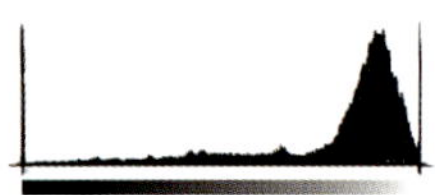

Predominantly light design elements and images have texture and detail, gentle shadows, and a small gradation of tones—these are the defining characteristics of high-key exposures.

High-Key and Low-Key

When a photo is dominated by achromatic colors, it is referred to as high-key (if white is the dominant color) or low-key (if black is the dominant color). This isn't the same as overexposed and underexposed images. High-key and low-key images have visual detail in the important areas of the photo, and feature other achromatic or chromatic hues. To create high-key and low-key images, it's best to use the histogram on your camera or in your image editing software. This will help you shift the curve of tonal values for your image either to the left or right, depending on which hue you want to dominate your image. High-key and low-key images often consist of gray tones or only one color (page 167), but they can feature multiple dark or light colors.

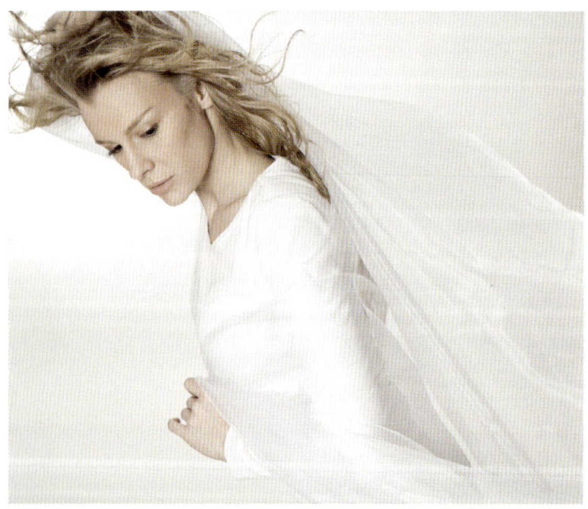

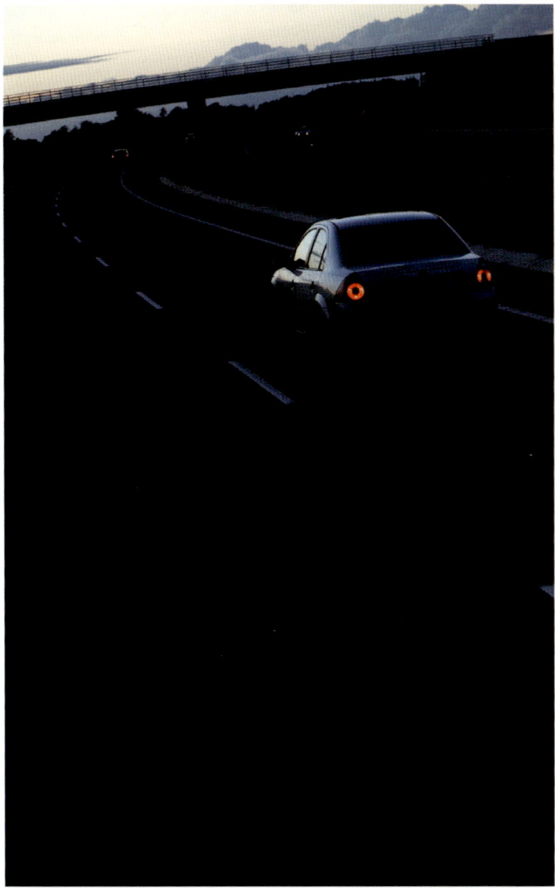

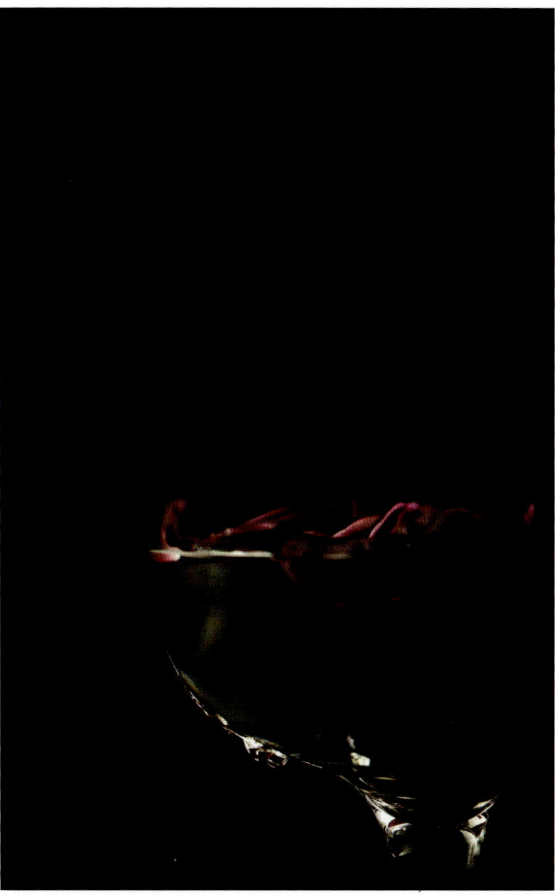

In a high-key image, not every tonal value will be bright or too bright, as with an overexposure—only the majority of the tones will be on the brighter side. These types of exposures have a sweet, airy, elegant, and unconventional feel. The more details that this type of photo reveals, despite its predominantly light distribution of color tones, the more interesting it will be for the viewer.

In contrast, low-key images feel heavy, dramatic, and mysterious, with an elegant, palpable atmosphere. Although dark tones dominate these images, lighter tones needn't be completely absent. The dark areas should contain enough detail to engage the viewer.

High-key and low-key images often feature a pure white or black background. White doesn't make these images less effective at all— solid backgrounds function as a canvas onto which the photographer can artfully position a few pixels from the opposite side of the brightness spectrum.

Aside from the formal, technical design aspects, high-key and low-key images must have appropriate content. The subject must be bright or dark to fit within the overall design aesthetic.

A low-key image exhibits predominantly dark tones, but it still has visual detail in even the darkest areas of the picture. Low-key shots also feature a limited number of brighter areas to contrast with the rest of the picture.

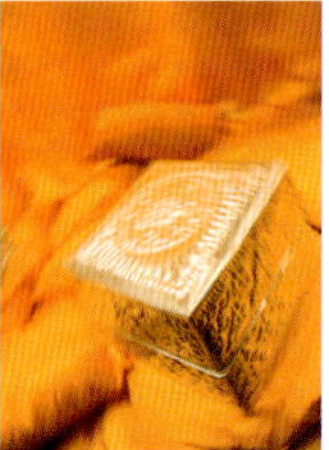
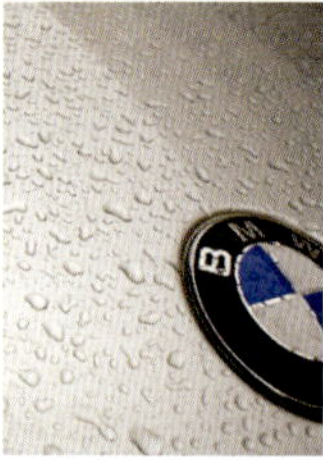
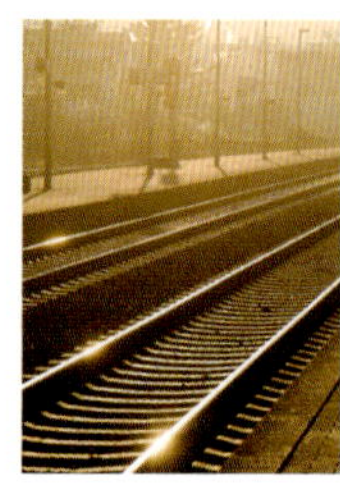

Metallic Colors

The main reason shiny metallic colors are so lively is that their tone changes depending on how light strikes them. We're most familiar with yellow, blue, and red metallic colors, and we associate them with the metals gold, silver, and copper. They often make us think of jewelry, money, treasures, and expensive ornaments. But because inexpensive costume jewelry is also available in these colors, we can associate these colors with objects that are cheap and gaudy.

Neon Colors

Garish, extremely bright colors remind us of highlighter pens and sticky notes, whose purpose is to draw as much attention to themselves as possible. They engage viewers, but they don't keep them interested for long. Regardless of their hue, neon colors have an exciting and flashy look.

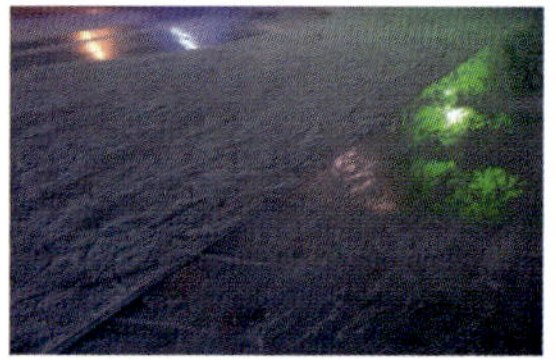
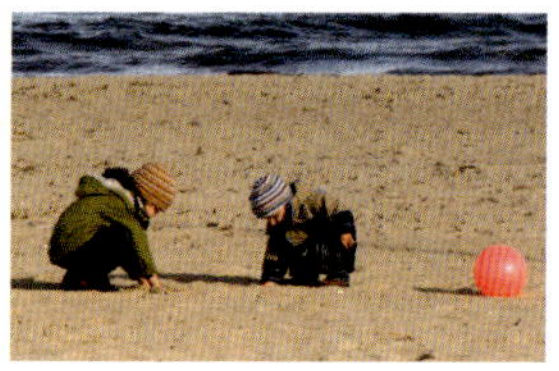
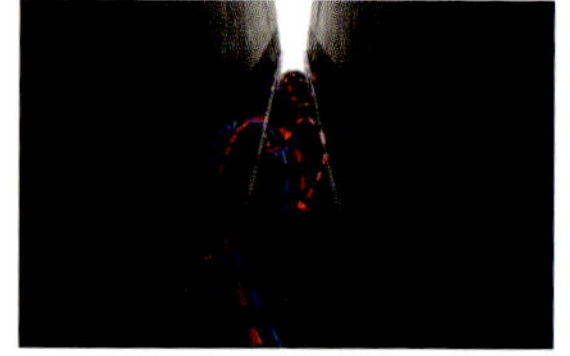

Memory Colors

Colors that are very familiar in their exact tone, brightness, and degree of saturation are considered memory colors. When they examine the colors in an image, viewers compare them to their memory colors and notice small discrepancies between what they see and what they remember. One of the strongest memory colors is the color of skin. Viewers immediately detect if it looks correct in an image or if it is tainted with a color cast. This is a major reason to prioritize skin tones when you set your white balance and edit your images.

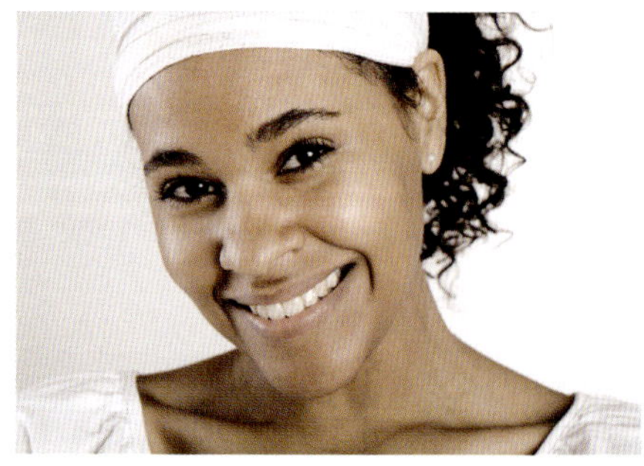
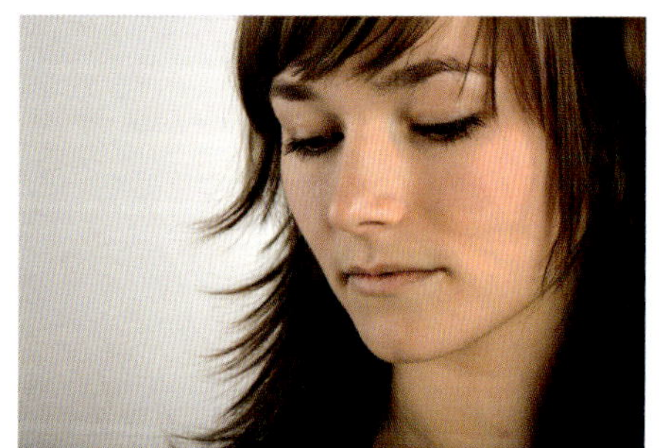

Skin tones are among the most important memory colors. We are immediately capable of detecting unnatural color casts on skin tones, even taking into account that skin tones themselves can vary.

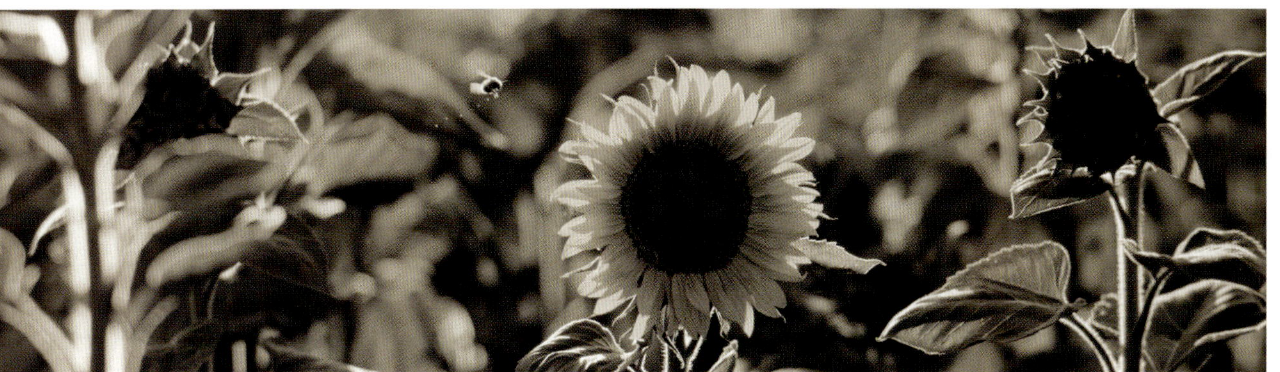

6.2 Color Combinations

If two or more colors are present in an image, they interact with each other and alter the individual characteristics of each. Depending on the specific colors, they may produce harmonious, discordant, or contrasting combinations. Harmonious color combinations have a pleasing effect on viewers; discordant ones are irritating and unpleasant. When colors contrast, they bring out the respective qualities and effects of each to a greater degree than if they appeared on their own.

Harmonious Colors

There are certain principles to follow when mixing colors to create a pleasant color palette in your images. These principles are based on schemes of harmony described by color theorists, which means they are highly subjective. In other words, the principles are flexible and there will always be someone who doesn't find a particular color combination pleasant. Harmony means the color combinations would normally be described as pleasant, agreeable, and undemanding.

On a basic level, colors that are similar to one another tend to harmonize well. This is one of the main reasons the following combinations appeal to viewers:

- Adjacent colors: Similar wavelength
- Different degrees of brightness within the same color: Same wavelength at different brightness levels
- Different degrees of saturation within the same color: Same wavelength at different levels of purity

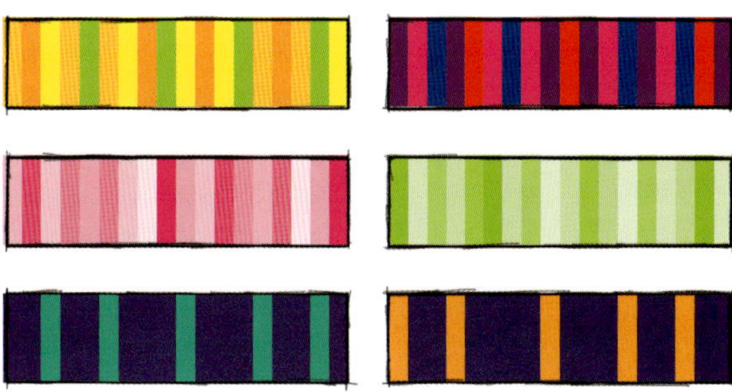

This illustration shows two examples of three different types of similar color combinations: adjacent colors (top), gradations of brightness (middle), and gradations of saturation (bottom).

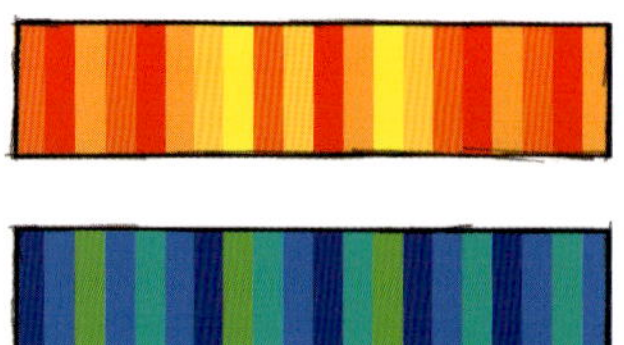

Warm colors and cool colors naturally go together because each group exhibits a similar color temperature.

- Warm colors: Similar degree of warmth
- Cool colors: Similar degree of coolness

When harmonious colors are presented together, their individual characteristics are strengthened, and together they enhance the overall effect. Multiple image elements that exhibit similar colors tend to grow into one large, dominant entity.

Discordant Colors

The opposite of visual harmony is disharmony, or dissonance. As is the case with harmonious color combinations, the perception of discordant colors is highly subjective. We develop these instincts culturally and through our own experiences. It is impossible to define color combinations as absolutely wrong, so we have not provided examples of discordant colors.

Dissonant color combinations are jarring and demand a high level of attention, which is uncomfortable for the viewer. These color combinations are called loud, garish, or bracing. Fully saturated and bright colors that are separate on the color wheel, without being complementary, are often involved in discordant color parings.

Color Chords

One principle of perception states that when we observe a color, our mental process also perceives its opposite color and creates a balance (page 163). This approach is another way to create color combinations. Here, balance means that when these individual colors are combined, their unique properties of tone and brightness produce a neutral gray. This theory assumes that the harmony resulting from matching colors has less to do with a pleasant, quiet effect on the viewer than it does a congruous, correct mixture that doesn't offend the eye. It is, nonetheless, loud in the sense that the marked contrast itself can be conspicuous.

Complementary color pairs, such as blue-violet and yellow-orange, are opposite on the color wheel. Together they produce a harmonious gray balance—when they are mixed together, they produce a neutral gray tone.

This gray balance can be produced by dyads (pairs), triads, or even tetrads of color—these chords of color must follow specific patterns on the color wheel. Color pairs are complementary colors that are opposite from each other (page 163), triads can be an equilateral triangle placed within the color wheel, and tetrads are in the shape of a square. The vertices of these geometric shapes indicate the three or four colors that differ in the same way. They add up to gray but must be combined in the correct proportion so no one color overwhelms the others. This proportion is based on the intrinsic brightness of each color, or on its quantifiable contrast (page 166).

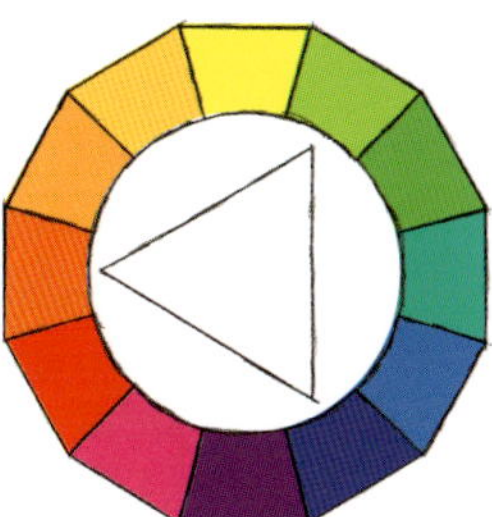

Musical Color Chords

Many viewers find musical three- and four-color combinations especially harmonious. These color chords are based on complementary color pairs and the balancing effect of colors located in close proximity to each other on the color wheel. Instead of using the two colors that are diametrically opposite one another on the color wheel, you you can replace one color with a pair of adjacent colors to create a musical triad. If you instead decide to replace both of the original colors with neighboring pairs, you have a musical tetrad.

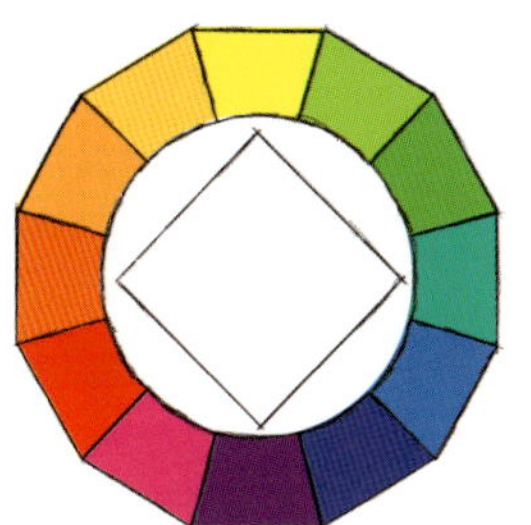

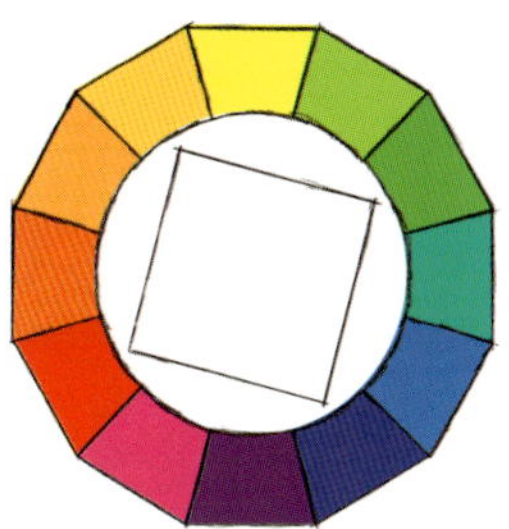

Triads or tetrads of color are indicated by the points of an equilateral triangle or a square, respectively, so they include colors that are separated by equal distances on the color wheel.

To achieve chromatic harmony with color intervals, the color tones need to be similar in brightness and saturation. Fully saturated color chords dramatically increase the potential an image has to attract a viewer's attention. Lighter, desaturated color chords don't have the same volume or richness, but they still produce harmonious results, albeit on a more subdued level.

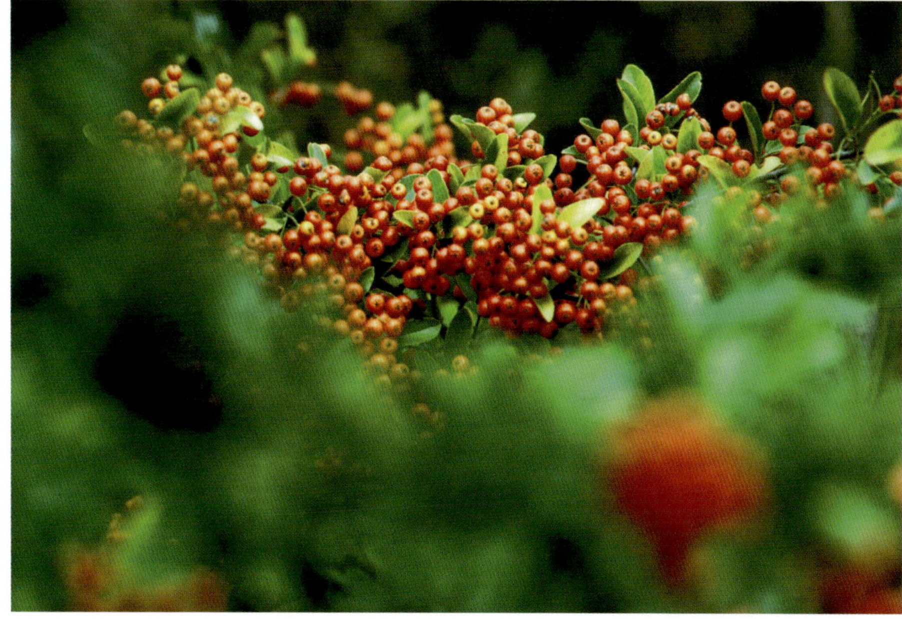

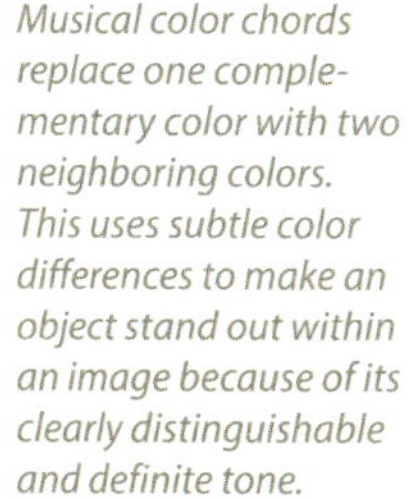

Musical color chords replace one complementary color with two neighboring colors. This uses subtle color differences to make an object stand out within an image because of its clearly distinguishable and definite tone.

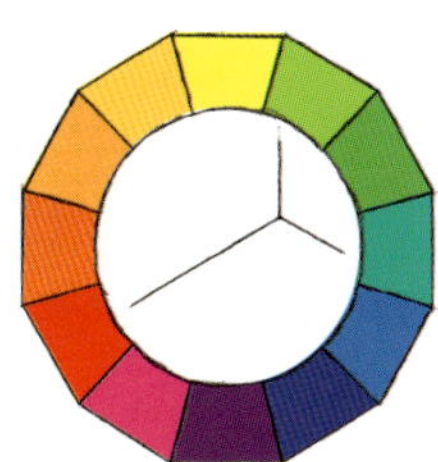

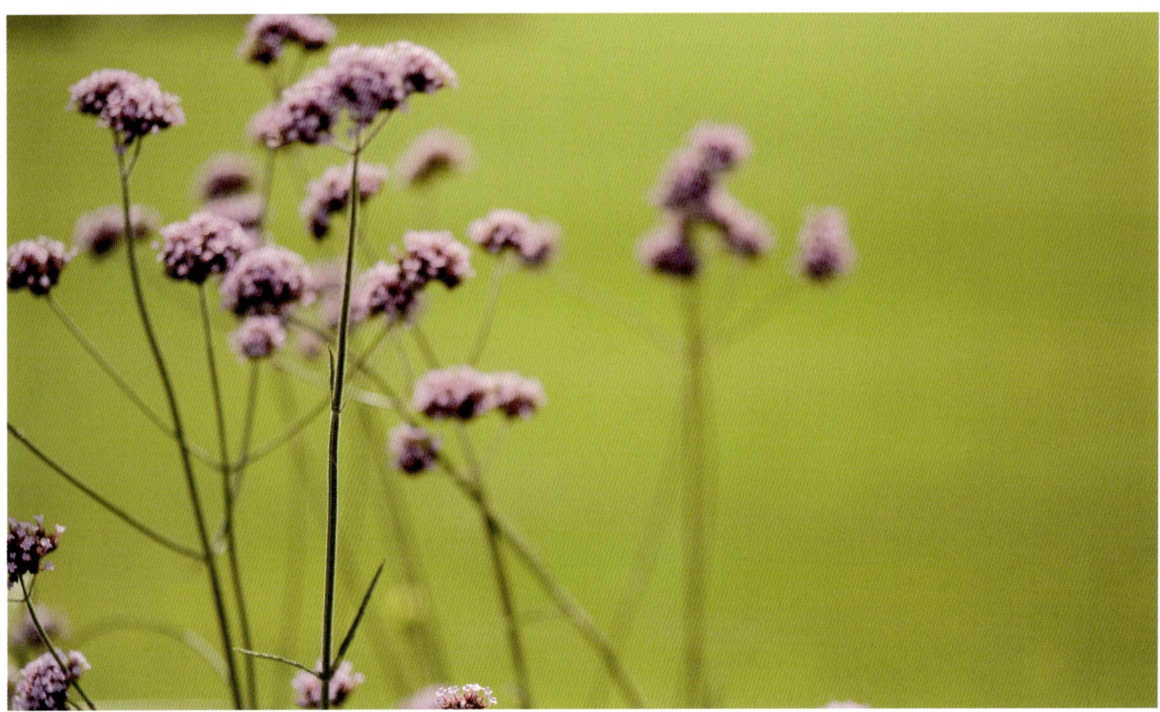

An image with a strong color contrast often works because of the contrast alone—other design elements fall to the background.

The more powerful the colors, the more sparsely they should be used. Excessive, bright, loud colors will all compete with each other for attention.

Contrasting Colors

When colors with different characteristics are present in the same image, they establish a contrast that increases the image's potential to attract attention. The presence of multiple contrasting colors brings out the individual characteristics of all colors more clearly. Johannes Itten identified seven types of color contrast that are based on various aspects of color combinations. It's rare for only one type of contrast to occur in isolation; usually multiple types are in play in any given image, and their effects can both complement and counteract each other.

It's important not to mistake contrast for the opposite of harmony—harmonious color combinations can also exhibit contrast. In fact, complementary pairs, triads, and tetrads of color function because of their balanced harmony and the contrasts among the colors.

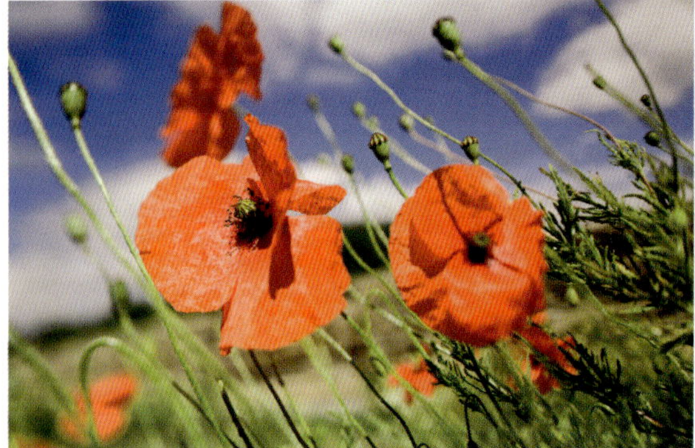

The Contrast of Color Itself

The more disparate two colors that appear near each other are, the more they contrast. This is the fundamental principle of this simple, almost purist type of contrast. If the colors in question are fully saturated, then the effect of their disparity is stronger and they will produce a loud, lively, folksy feel. The tones of

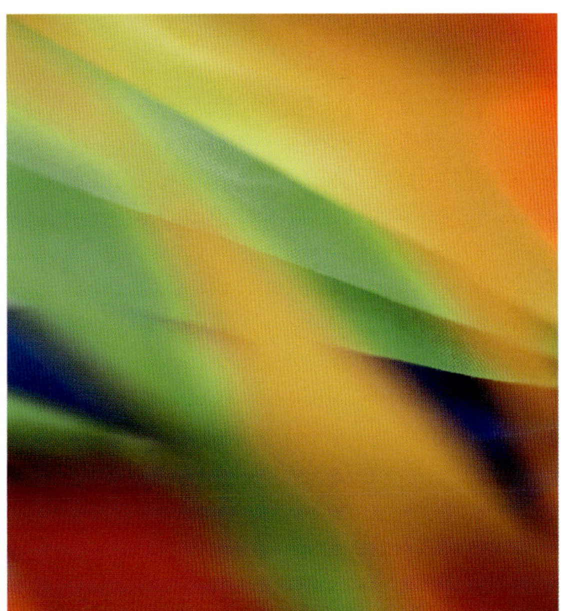

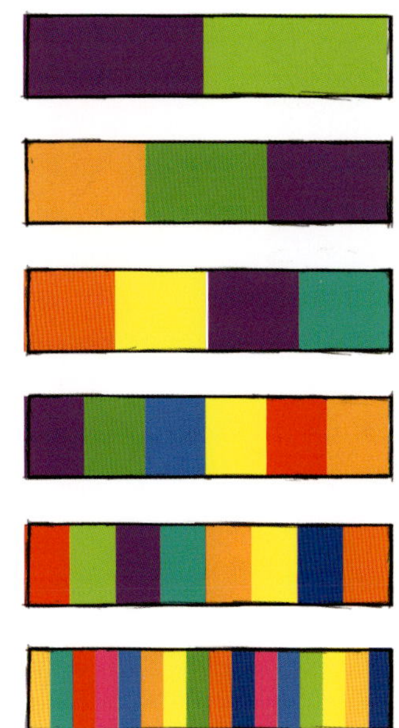

Color contrast is based on visual differences. A picture's sense of unrest and chaos increases with the number of dominant colors in the image.

the colors are highlighted with this type of contrast, which is one reason children are so drawn to combinations of strong colors. Images with very bright colors have a young, joyful, and relaxed feel. This type of contrast is particularly strong with a triad of the three primary colors: red, yellow, and blue (page 160). Other triads also produce colorful contrasts. Tetrads tend to appear less tidy. A combination of more than four colors results in an unsettling, chaotic mix of tones that, at first glance, doesn't appear to have a purposeful underlying design. The colors take center stage without helping the viewer to perceive the image.

Complementary Contrast

The arrangement of colors on the color wheel provides the foundation for complementary contrast, which occurs when an image contains a combination of two colors that are opposite each other on the color wheel. These colors produce a dyad (page 160), which is at its most effective when it includes a combination of primary and secondary colors, such as red and green, blue and orange, or yellow and violet. Subordinate blended colors can also be complementary, as long as they are located on opposite sides of the color wheel. These color pairs reinforce each other's qualities, and

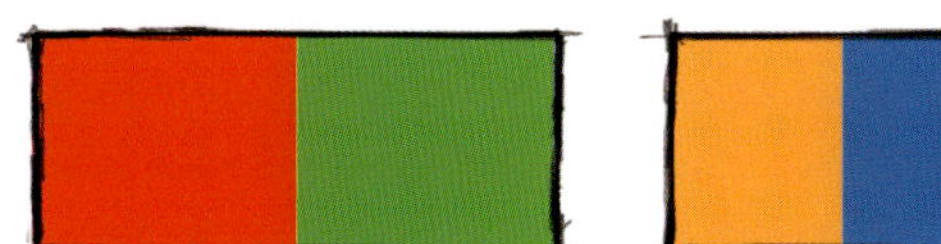

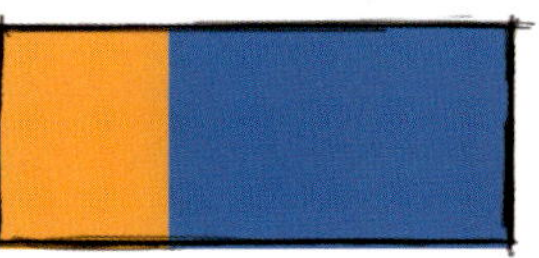

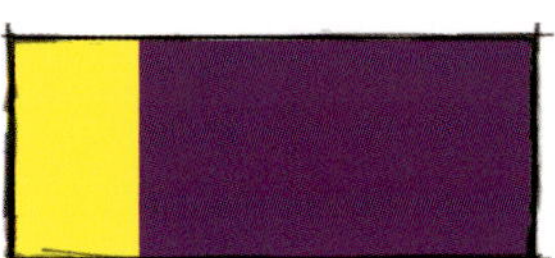

Complementary dyads are most balanced when the brightness of each color in the pair is taken into account. Red and green are balanced when their parts are equal; orange and blue are balanced in a 1:2 proportion; and yellow and violet are balanced in a 1:3 proportion. This means that a small yellow flower set against a violet backdrop has more visual pull than a violet flower on a yellow backdrop, for example.

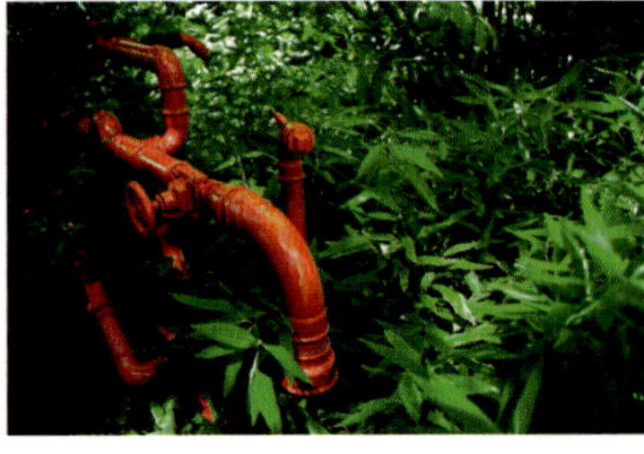

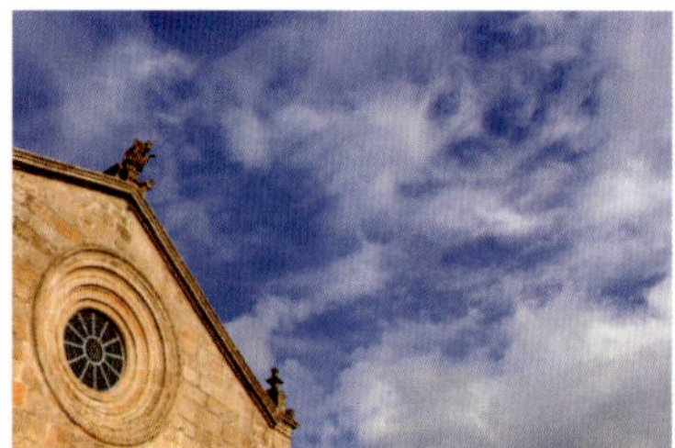

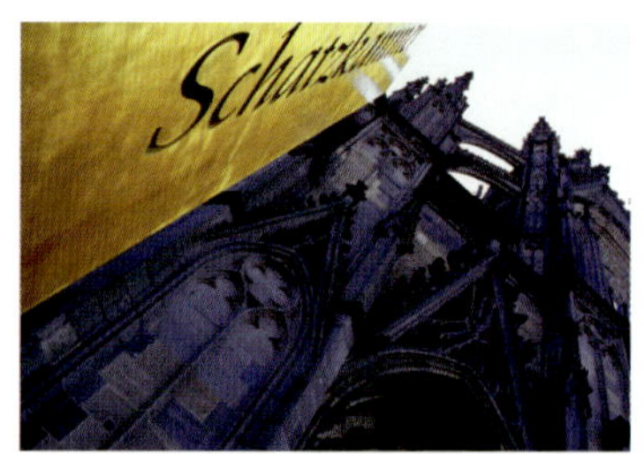

Complementary color pairs heighten the individual qualities of each color. Each individual tone appears more brilliant and has increased pull on the viewer's attention.

maximize brilliance and color tones. When perceiving color and brightness, people always see harmony when the tonal and color values add up to a neutral gray. This is always the case for complementary colors, which is why we're drawn to images that feature this balanced color design and why we find images like this composed and agreeable (page 160).

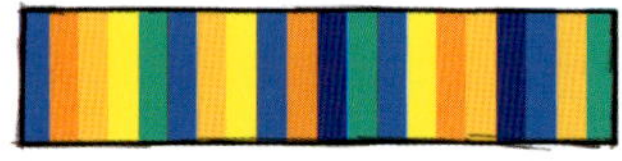

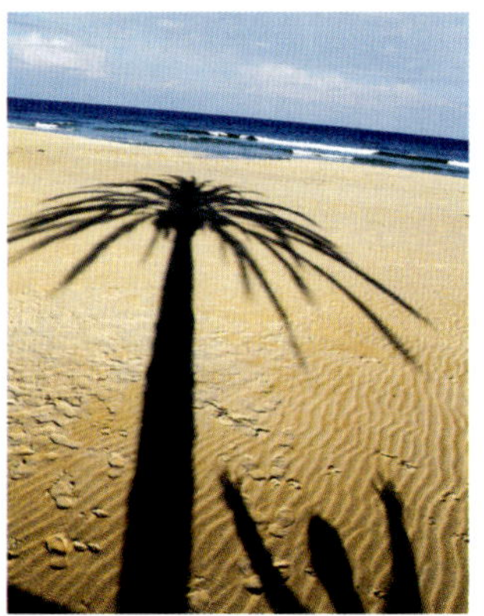

A combination of cool and warm colors pulls viewers back and forth between a pleasant, summery feeling and a chilly, distant one. This interplay tends to work more strongly when the color tones are intense.

Cold and Warm Contrast

When colors from both the warm and cold palettes appear within an image, it creates a warm/cold contrast. Such a color scheme can have an immediate, highly emotional effect on viewers, almost as if this particular contrast appeals to a kind of primal human sensibility. Bright red-orange and blue-green represent the warmest and coolest colors, respectively, and are inevitably interpreted in this way. All other colors can be drastically influenced by the surrounding colors—they can be warmed up or cooled down. A red tone set against deep blues, for example, feels cooler than the same red set against other warm colors.

In many cases combinations of warm and cool colors become subjects in an image because they represent concepts such as distance and closeness, shade and sunlight, stillness and movement, or air and land. Viewers make these associations when they view images with warm and cool colors, and these associations are influential enough to alter other levels of meaning in an image.

Brightness Contrast

Color tone is not the characteristic at play in brightness contrast. The varying level of lightness or darkness of each color establishes contrast with colors at other levels of brightness. This type of contrast is at its most obvious when achromatic colors of different brightness are juxtaposed; the shades of brightness are easy to see because they are manifested as different shades of gray (page 149). We also associate an abundance or dearth of light with color tones that exhibit different degrees of brightness. Brightness contrast has a strong affect on viewers, more so than most other types of contrast, since it's immediately perceived and helps viewers make sense of images. The division of light and shadow allows viewers to distinguish individual elements, grasp the spatial structure, and follow the prominent lines within an image. This is the type of contrast people are usually referring to in casual conversation.

Contrast of Quality

Quality contrast is based on the third aspect of color—saturation—and arises when colors of different purity levels are in close proximity to each other in an image. This type of contrast is very strongly felt, though not always on a conscious level, because we instinctively associate unsaturated colors with shadowy areas, the twilight hour, or scenes with backlighting.

The result of changing the saturation of a color is unique to each individual color—cool colors become lighter or darker, but warm colors take on a whole new character when you mix in achromatic colors. By mixing white into blue, for example, you end up with light blue. Adding white to red, though, produces pink. Similarly, mixing black into green creates a darker green, but if you add black to orange, you'll end up with a shade of brown.

Mixing in black, white, or gray causes colors to become less bright, intense, and colorful. For this reason, quality contrast is sometimes referred to as chromatic/achromatic contrast, which is comparable to the contrast of color itself when chromatic and achromatic tones are juxtaposed.

Colors exhibit more intensity when they are combined with white, gray, or especially black (left). When saturated and unsaturated colors are juxtaposed, the saturated ones take on added emphasis (right).

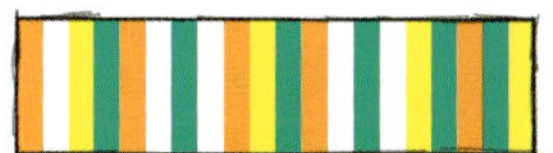
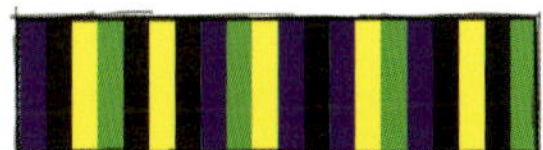
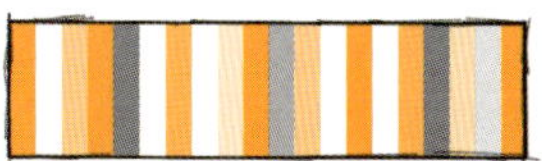
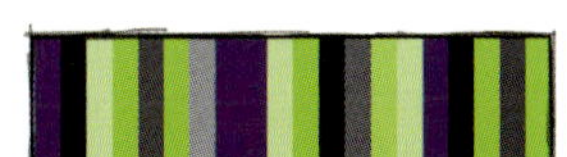

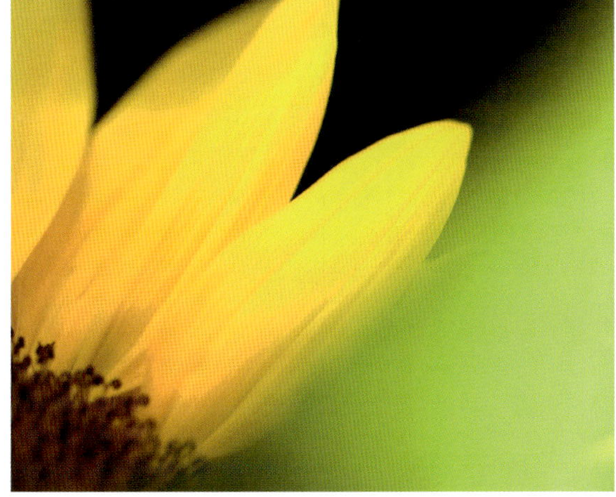

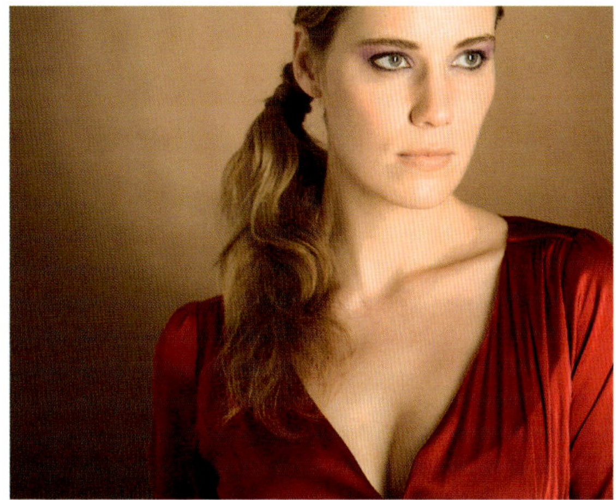

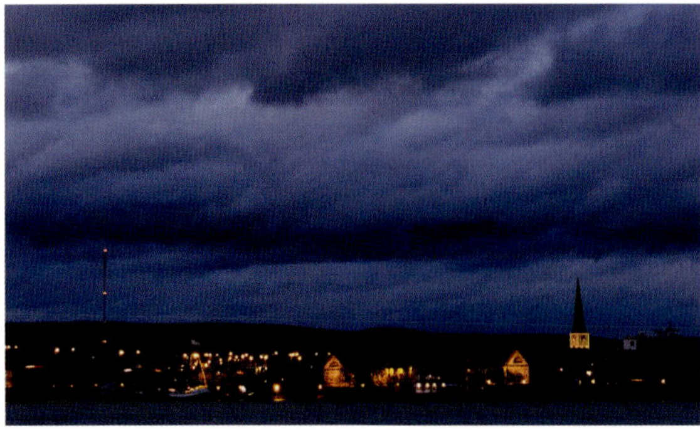

Bright colors, such as yellow or orange, can hold their own with substantially larger areas of darker colors (in this example, blue). The city lights, despite their relatively meager size, are dominant enough to avoid being overpowered by the blue sky.

Contrast of Quantity

The size of the color area affects the degree to which every type of contrast is perceived and how an image functions as a whole. If a small red flower is growing in a large green meadow, the two form a complementary color dyad, but they are not equal in quantity or size. To establish a balanced relationship between two areas of color, you must take the intrinsic brightness of each color into consideration. It's clear that the colors on the color wheel (page 146) lose brightness as you move downward—yellow, for example, is intrinsically brighter than violet. Goethe assigned the primary and secondary colors a brightness value (BV), which can help you analyze the contrast of quantity. Yellow (BV 9), the brightest color, requires only one-third the area of violet (BV 3) for the two colors to be balanced. Orange (BV 8) is twice as bright as blue (BV 4), but red and green (both BV 6) are visually equal when they are present in areas with similar sizes (page 163). The brighter a color is, the less area is needed to establish a contrast; just because a color takes up a lot of space doesn't mean it is the most dominant color. Similarly, a smaller, differently-colored area often has increased visual weight, which you shouldn't overlook when you design your images. A solitary red flower might be overpowered by a larger green meadow, but a yellow flower might be able to hold its own.

Simultaneous, Successive, and Shimmer Contrast

These types of contrasts don't result from colors or their particular qualities; instead, they concern faults in how we perceive colors. Simultaneous contrast describes the phenomenon that occurs when we see one color, but we also see its opposite color (i.e., its complementary color) and project it over the original color. This means that when we are surrounded by red, other colors will have a green tint; if we are surrounded by blue, other colors will have an orange tint.

Successive contrast is also based on complementary color pairs. It describes the phenomenon that occurs when we transport properties of a color we just saw to whatever color we are currently seeing. For example, if you stare at a red surface for a few seconds and then switch to a white surface, it will have a greenish cast. Successive contrast, in other words, doesn't have an immediate effect. Achromatic colors are also stored in our vision this way. When we first see a white area and then look at a dark area, we will see a trace of white in the dark area.

Shimmer contrast happens when balanced (usually bright and saturated) colors that are positioned next to each other vie for the viewer's attention. This causes the dividing line to shimmer or flicker. If the areas of color are narrow lines, or are arranged in a pattern with small repeating elements, the effect is even stronger.

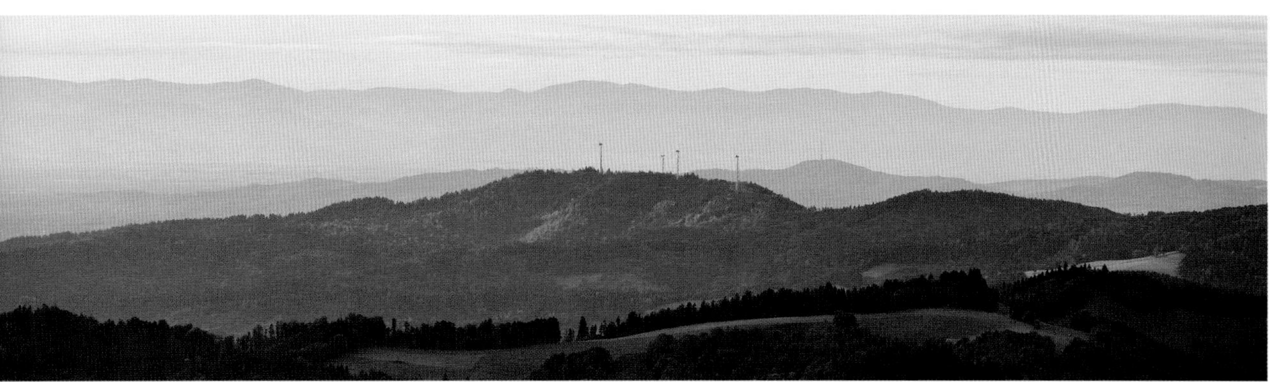

6.3 Shades of Gray

When you design a grayscale or black-and-white photo, the question of whether black, white, and the shades of gray in between them are colors or achromatic, or if they merely constitute different levels of brightness, becomes irrelevant. It's more important to understand the unique effect these images have, and to consider those effects when you design your image.

Colorless Reality

Historically, black-and-white images originated from the technical limitations of early photography, when it wasn't yet possible to create color photographs. Black-and-white-photography forces colors to be reduced to their brightness values—something that produces unusual, unnatural, and fascinating effects. The ability to photograph in color came about in the 1930s, but the charm and allure of black-and-white photography persists. In fact, viewers still consider black-and-white images to be elegant, high-quality, and special, which can certainly be traced back to world-famous black-and-white exposures of the 19th and 20th centuries.

Grayscale images rely more on graphical qualities than emotional ones. The prevalent lines and composition of a picture take on a more significant role. The subject is both defamiliarized and emphasized in a very particular way—since colors no longer give it weight, the subject is shown in a neutral context. Viewers need to concentrate more to decipher a black-and-white photo.

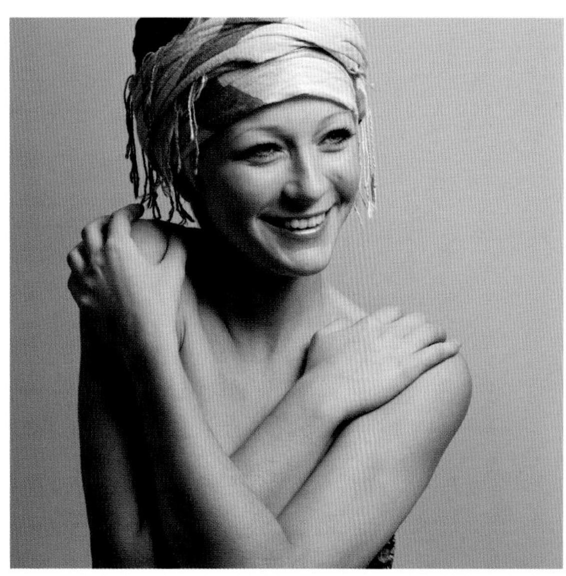

Without color, other visual aspects become dominant: the lines, shapes, and areas; the division of light and shadow; and the subject itself—here, the smile. There is nothing to detract from the subject and nothing to alter the viewers' emotional engagement like (even subtle) colors would.

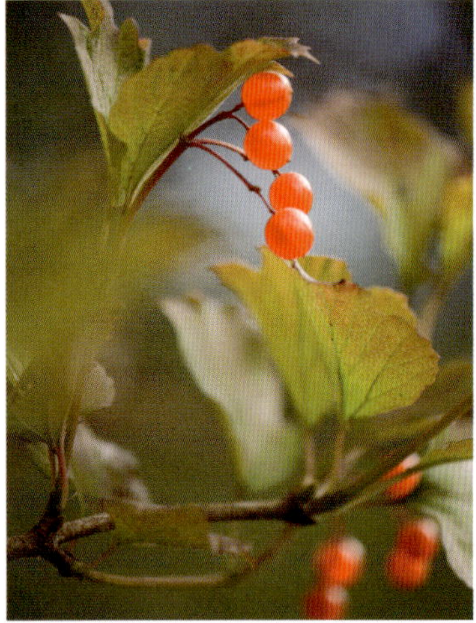

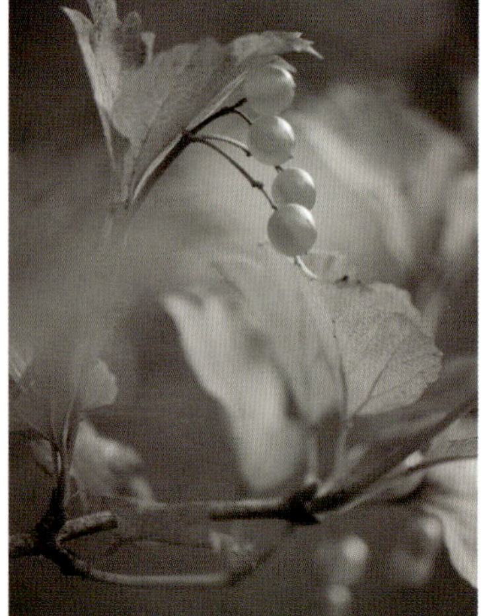

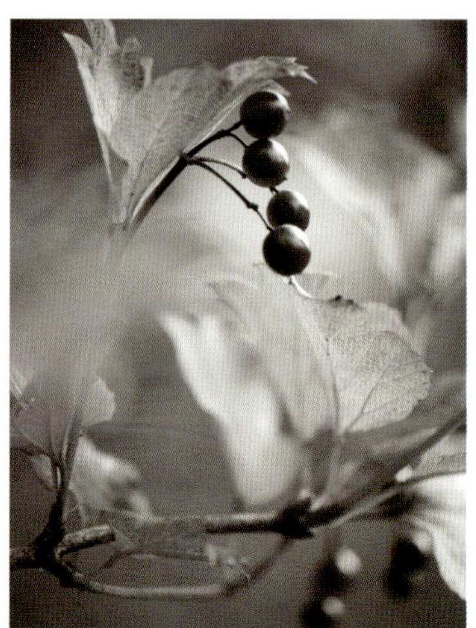

Colors that have similar brightness, such as red and green (left), can appear bland after being converted to standard grayscale because the color contrast is lost (middle). To retain a dramatic effect, the color contrast needs to be replaced with brightness contrast. The berries, in other words, still need to pop out from their surroundings (right) as they do in color. We achieved this particular result with a manual conversion.

Converting to Black-and-White

When colors are captured as gray tones, their brightness values are determined by the intrinsic brightness of the color tone (page 149) and by the amount of lighting. Using the double-cone color model, you can determine a color's intrinsic brightness by drawing a horizontal line from the position of the color to the gray axis in the middle. The higher the position of the line, the brighter the gray will appear in the image. If you're thinking that there are many colors located on any given horizontal plane of the double cone, meaning that the intrinsic brightness will be identical or similar for different colors, you've identified one particular challenge of grayscale photography. Distinguishing one element from another can be impossible as areas blend into one another and the defining details of structures dissolve.

The digital conversion process of color information to gray shades can also affect the final appearance of a black-and-white photo. To stick with our model, this means that the color tone would be shifted up or down along the middle axis. The exact process of conversion needs to be based on the content and intent of the picture at hand—there are no universal conversion parameters that will result in optimal gray tones in every case.

The effect of this color image is dramatically altered by converting it to grayscale. The physical characteristics of the wheat are emphasized. Subtle hues of color are lost, but they are replaced with rich tones of gray. Deciding which image works better is purely a matter of taste.

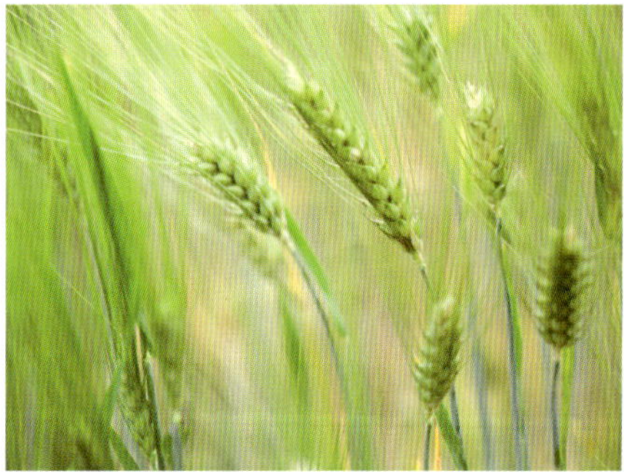

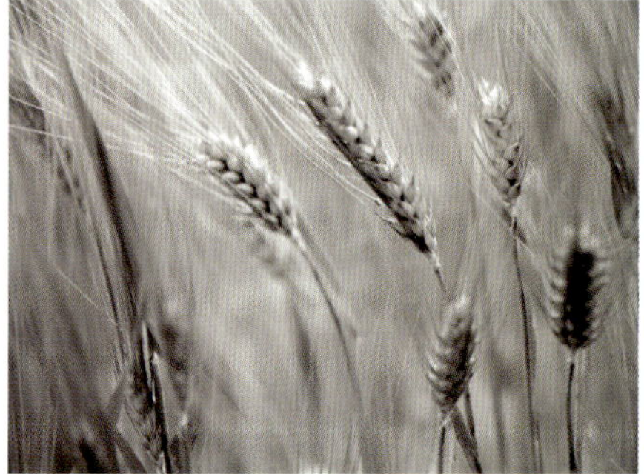

Controlling Contrast

In black-and-white photography, the only real color contrast is between black and white, or more specifically, between various shades of dark and light. When you design an image to convey a message, keep the following points in mind:

- More dark tones will cause the subject of your image to be perceived as darker, gloomier, and heavier.
- Light tonal values give an exposure a friendlier, more positive effect.
- The more gray tones in an image, the more likely viewers will see it as detailed, delicate, and elegant.
- To avoid a lifeless photo, the brightness values should range from light white all the way to dark black.
- Reducing an image to a few shades of brightness, or perhaps even to pure black-and-white, can create a striking result that, in extreme cases, results in a silhouette. This will initially pique the interest of viewers, but it won't retain their attention for long because the contours of the otherwise absent visual detail offer limited information.
- Lighter image areas tend to attract attention more than darker areas.

Not all grayscale images have the same look and feel. The number of shades in an image influences how harshly or subtly the effects of a black-and-white conversion are felt. Grayscale images can have a delicate and light feel if there is an even distribution of tonal values, or they can have a stark and contrasty look, such as in a silhouette.

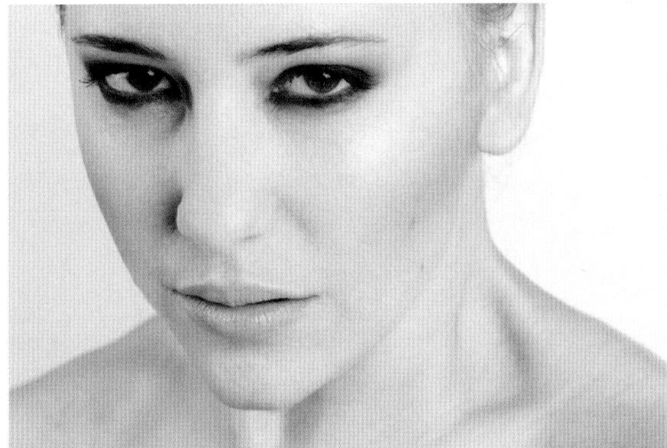

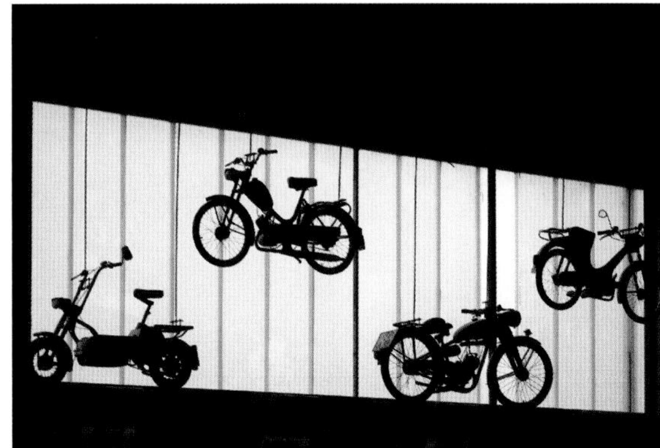

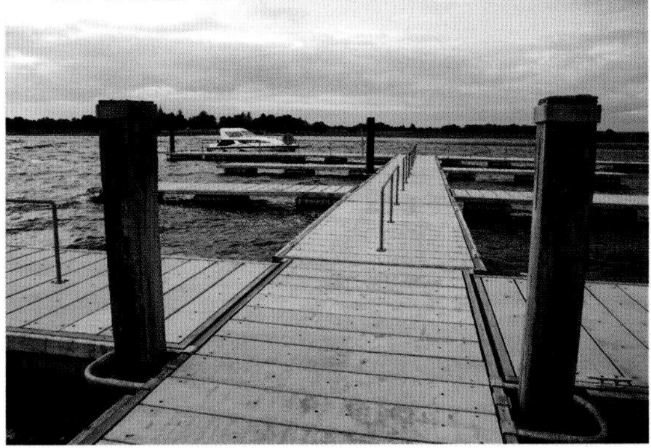

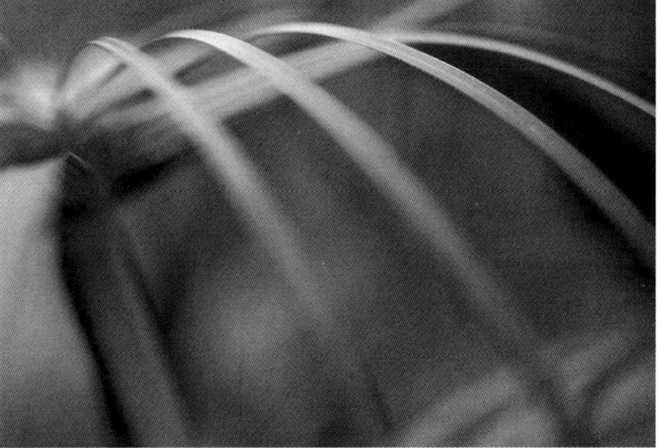

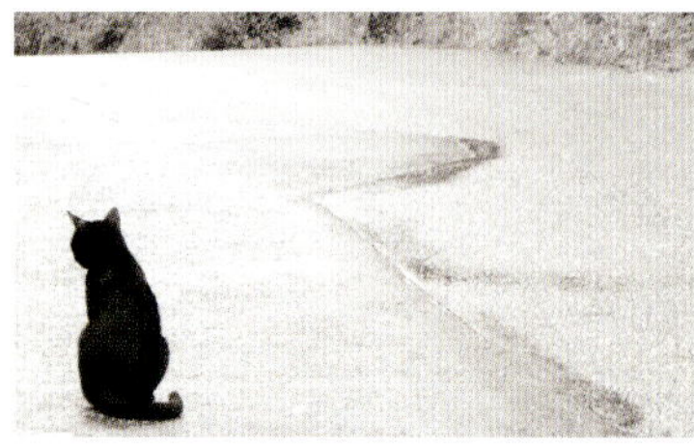

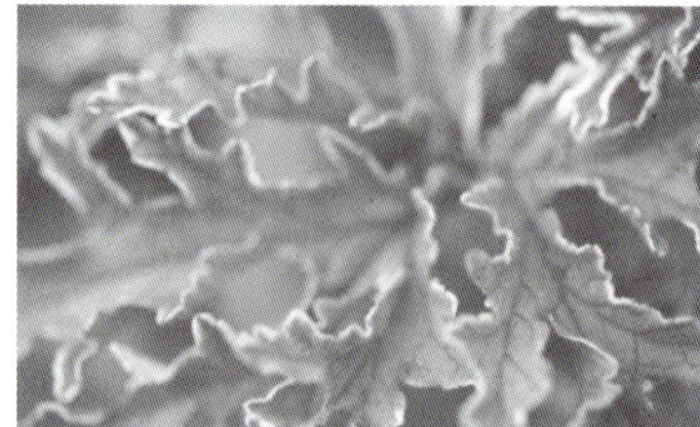

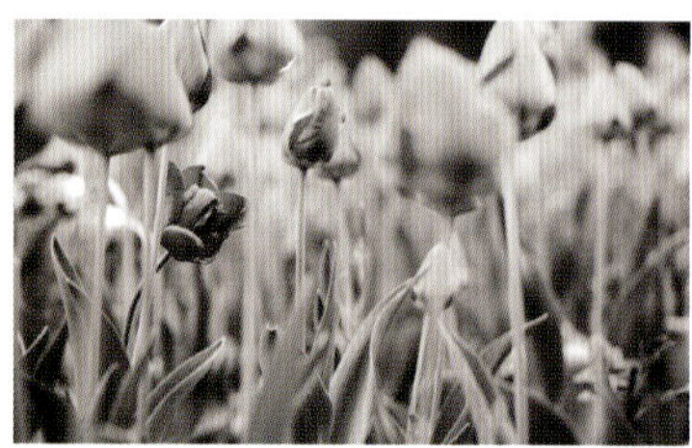

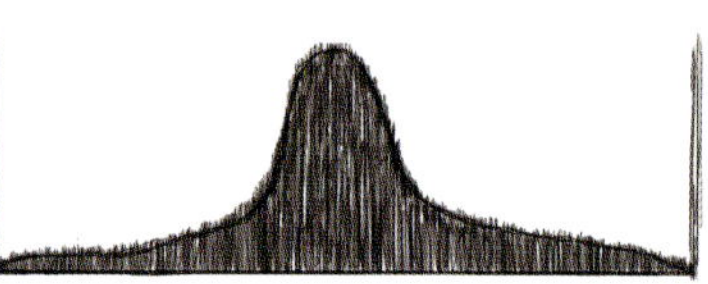

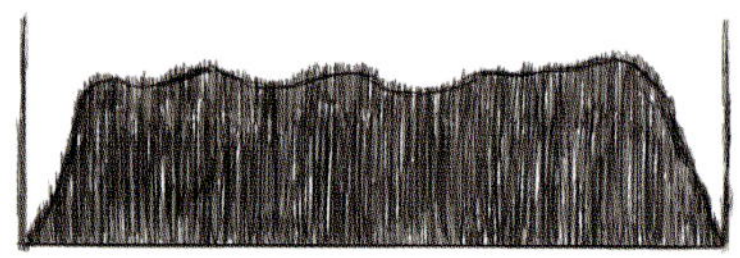

The histogram shows the distribution of tonal values in an image. If it exhibits two peaks at either side of the graph, the image has strong contrast (left). A single peak in the middle of the graph corresponds to weak contrast with lifeless tones (middle). A broad hump indicates an even distribution of grayscale tones (right).

With digital cameras, photographers can use histograms to evaluate and monitor the contrast within an image. The horizontal axis of a histogram represents the range of tonal values from black (on the left side) to white (on the right side). The vertical axis corresponds to the quantity of individual tonal values at any given level of brightness within the image; the higher the histogram plot, the more frequently that particular tone occurs. The plots themselves can take many shapes, but they should ideally approach the left and right limits to create images with the greatest range of values.

This method of monitoring contrast is substantially more convenient than the zone measurements required in the days of film photography.

Monochrome Images and Toning

A monochrome picture features shades of one single color. Grayscale pictures are monochrome, of course, but single-color images also fall into this category. The special appeal of a color monochrome image is that it functions similarly to a black-and-white picture, but it also offers the emotional complexity of a color image. These

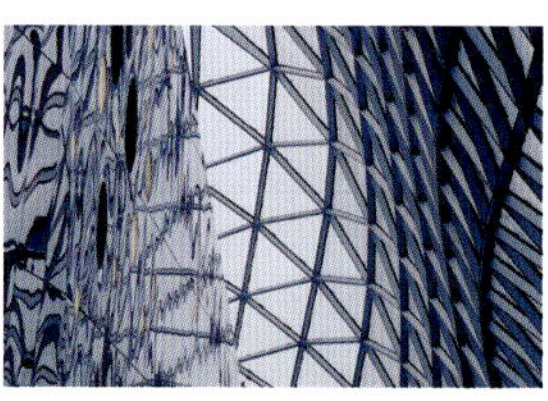

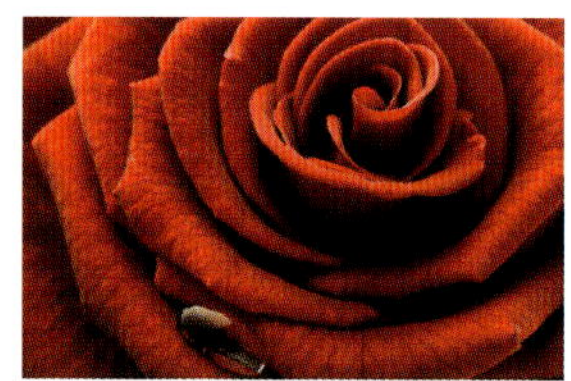

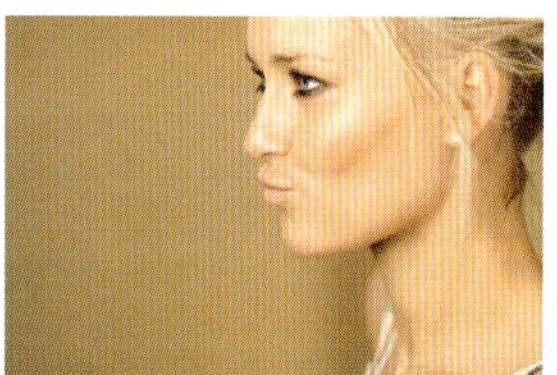

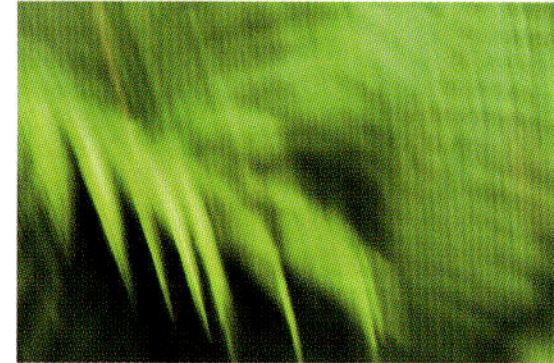

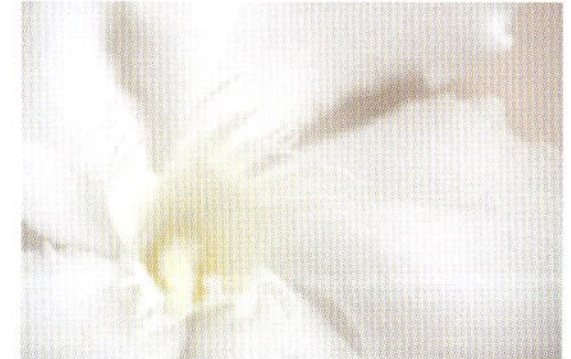

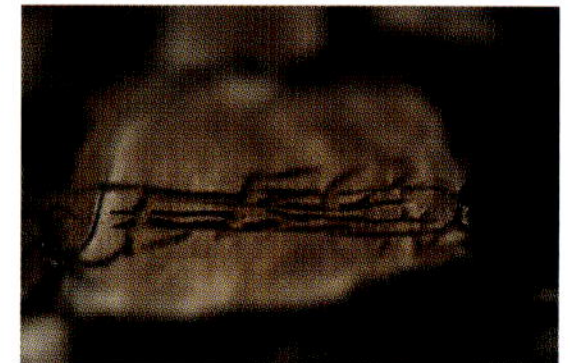

An image featuring only one color, and its various gradations of saturation and brightness, is considered a monochrome image, which can have a unique effect. As with grayscale images, the graphic elements of the image are underscored, but the emotional power of color is still active.

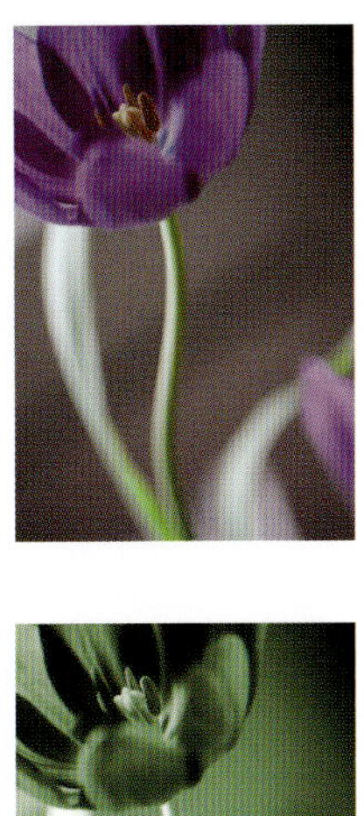

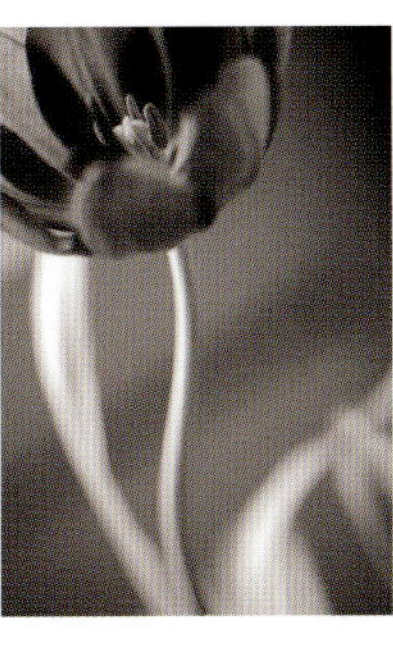

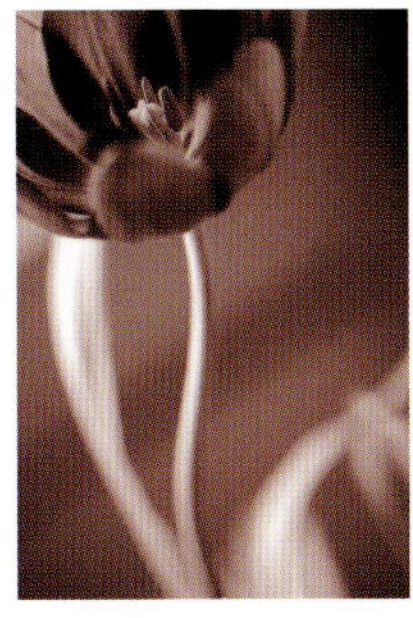

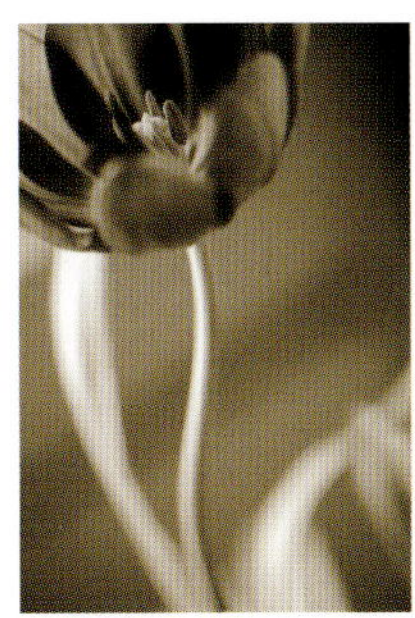

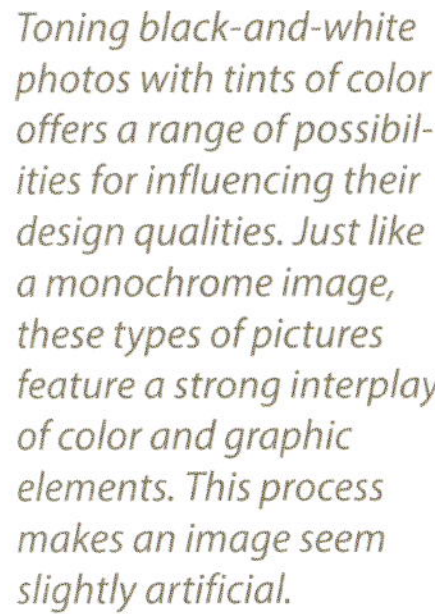

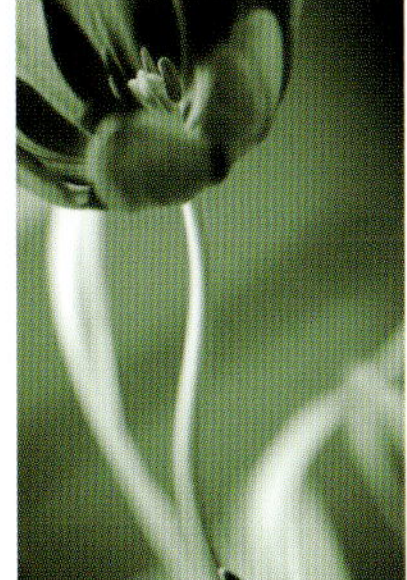

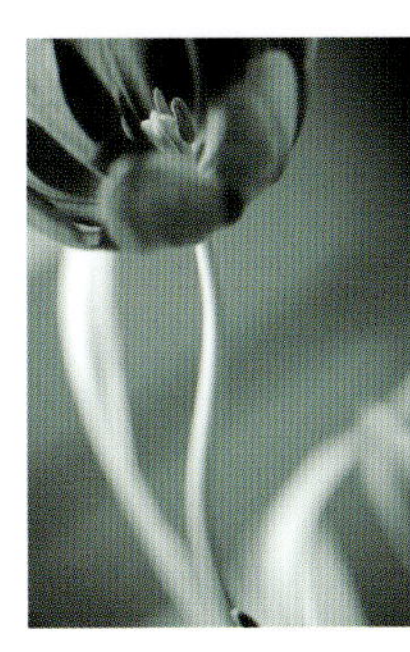

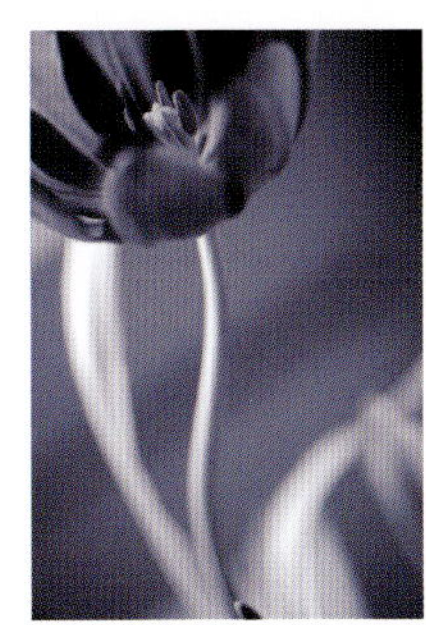

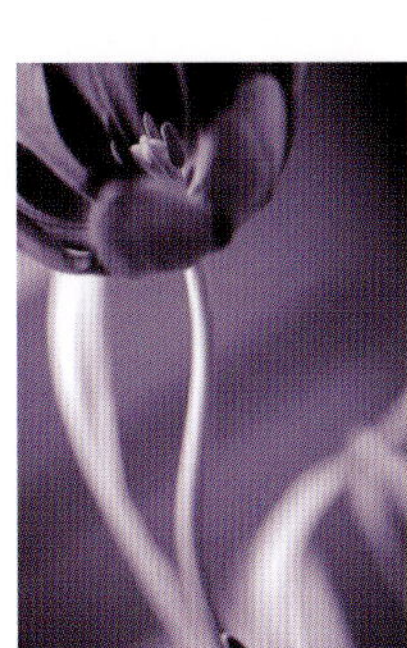

Toning black-and-white photos with tints of color offers a range of possibilities for influencing their design qualities. Just like a monochrome image, these types of pictures feature a strong interplay of color and graphic elements. This process makes an image seem slightly artificial.

images don't feature any color contrast; instead, they emphasize brightness contrast and graphic elements.

Adding color to a black-and-white image provides a range of creative possibilities for altering monochrome images. This treatment takes the aesthetic of a grayscale image and adds a color cast with digital post-processing. This color toning changes the look of the image and alters its emotional message. When the color tone is applied heavily, viewers will consciously register the image as monochrome; however, subtle application will still alter the emotional dynamic of the picture. Viewers may not consciously recognize a slight hint of color, but the color cast will nevertheless affect the viewer's experience on a subconscious level. The subject can be enhanced with a cool or warm, near or far, or positive or negative effect.

Even subtle color casts influence the emotional effect of an image and imperceptibly alter the viewer's response.

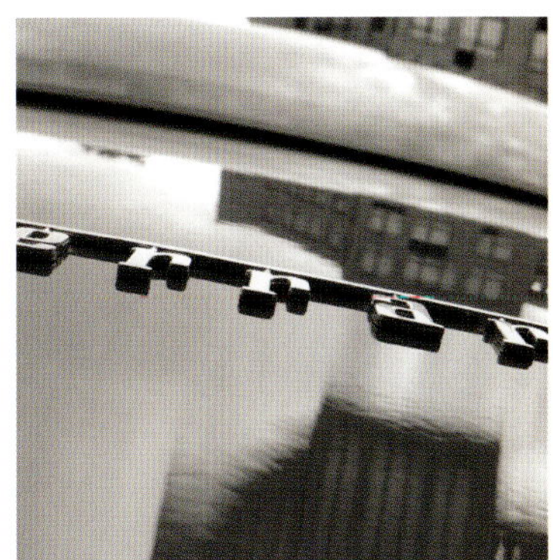

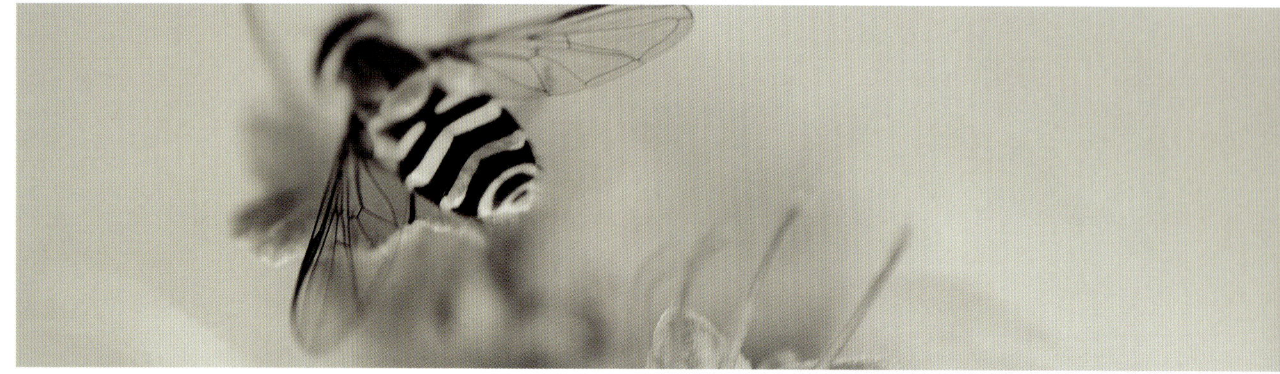

6.4 Colors in Practice

Given the powerful influence of color, you should avail yourself of these three techniques to control color design within your images. First, you can stage every aspect of the scene or subject you intend to photograph, including all visual elements, with color in mind. Second, you can document objects as they are, and rely on a specific, calculated perspective that includes colors within the image area to help you meet your photographic objective. Finally, you can edit the colors afterward with image editing software.

Monochrome image designs, very conspicuous colors, or dramatic color contrasts can take over the central focus of an image. Other subjects and design elements yield to them by forfeiting visual prominence.

Color as the Main Element

The more intense, saturated, and bright a color is, the higher its potential to attract attention, and the more likely it is that it will be the dominant subject of your image. Keep this in mind when you integrate loud colors into your shot. For example, a bright shirt can sometimes lure the viewer's gaze away from the subject's face. Of course, the increased attention that a dominant or loud color draws isn't always undesirable—it is often the goal of fashion photography to emphasize the garments more than the person wearing them. In detail and abstract photography, color can be a very effective way to give the viewer a clear path to follow through the image.

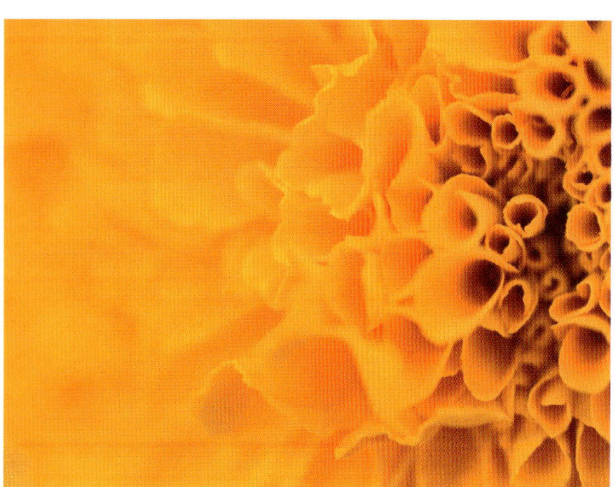

When you combine colors within an image, remember to select them carefully. Too many disparate colors can be distracting, and strong contrasts can be too loud. Harmonious color combinations are more gentle and effective. The more intense the colors, the more care you should exercise when juxtaposing them—which isn't to say that bright, loud colors placed side by side can't be charming. As always, your decisions depend on your subject and your image design. A loud color scheme can be reined in with an otherwise calm, predominantly graphic or abstract subject, and a conventional subject may be particularly photogenic when it has conspicuous coloring.

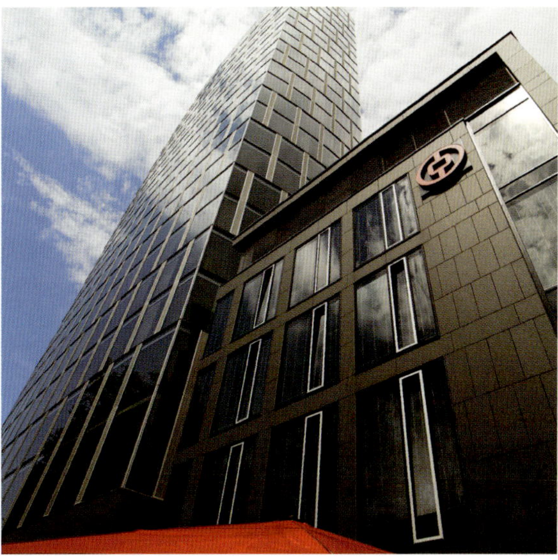

Colorful elements don't need to rely on size to influence a picture. A tiny sliver of a red awning along the bottom edge of this image and the red logo high on the side of the building succeed in giving this exposure more depth, an additional level of meaning, and a certain refinement.

Colorful Eye-Catchers

A colorful point that establishes a dramatic contrast with its surroundings doesn't need to be large to immediately draw the viewer's attention, which is why the red flower in the green meadow we discussed earlier isn't overlooked (page 78).

If the colorful element is in the background, however, and isn't part of the subject at all, its weight can throw your picture out of balance by stealing attention from the main subject. A blue traffic sign, a red car, or a bright green sweater in the background of a shot on a city street is enough to shift the viewer's attention away from the main elements, even if they are obviously situated in the foreground of your image.

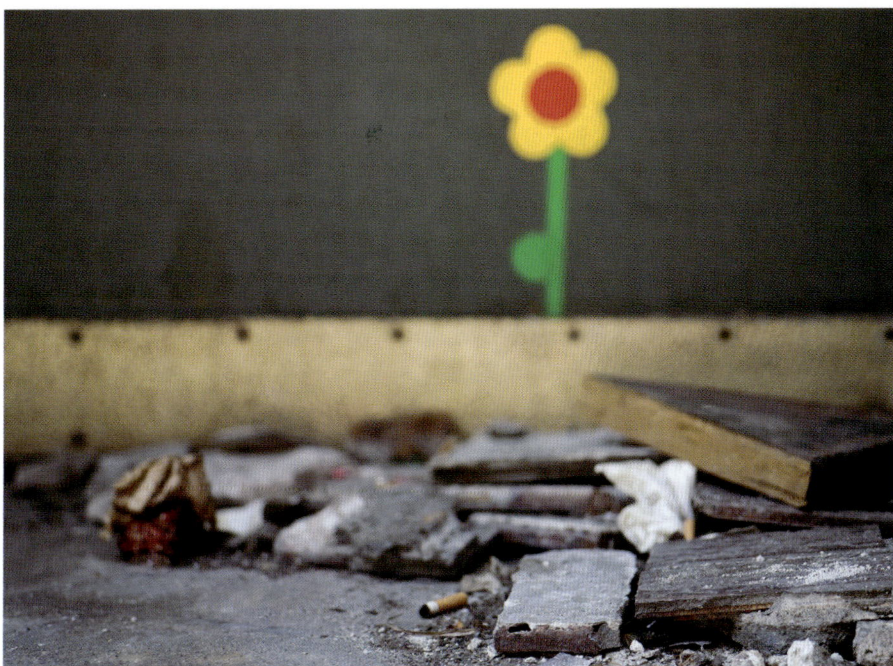

The contrast between chromatic and achromatic colors can help an image stand out from the masses. Without the color of this flower, the comedy of this scene would be nonexistent.

Colorful Side Elements

In most cases, the colors in an image are used to support the main subject, and don't play a primary role. To walk the line between restrained and perceptible colors, it helps to use only a few different, harmonious colors in your picture. A background with some color, a colorful eye-catching element, subtle toning, or a combination of similar color tones are examples of effective design choices that place color in a supporting role. One or two color families are enough to endow an image with emotional potency, especially when viewers find the colors pleasant, or when the colors establish an interesting contrast. Otherwise, the colors can overpower other design aspects of the image, and diminish the prominence of your intended subject.

Colorful side elements should not dominate an image or significantly influence it. These touches of color exist to establish emotion and atmosphere. Understated brown tones are capable of doing this, but so are more conspicuous blue-brown combinations. What's important in these images is that the subjects themselves don't exhibit much color.

The attention that saturated and bright colors command is easily underestimated; these colors can throw off the balance of a photo, even when the photographer doesn't plan it that way. To emphasize one particular element as the main subject, don't forget to use other design tools in addition to color. Give special attention to the color scheme when you stage a photo shoot, and avoid including too much color in general. When you shoot on-site, the selection of your image area and the position of your camera will help you avoid conspicuous areas of color. This will reduce the colors in the image to a supporting role.

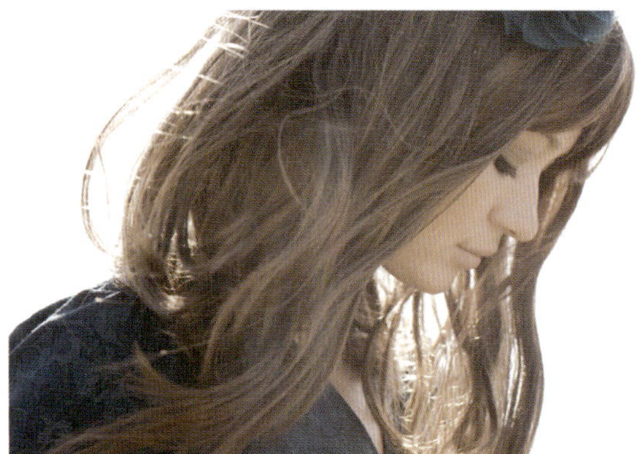

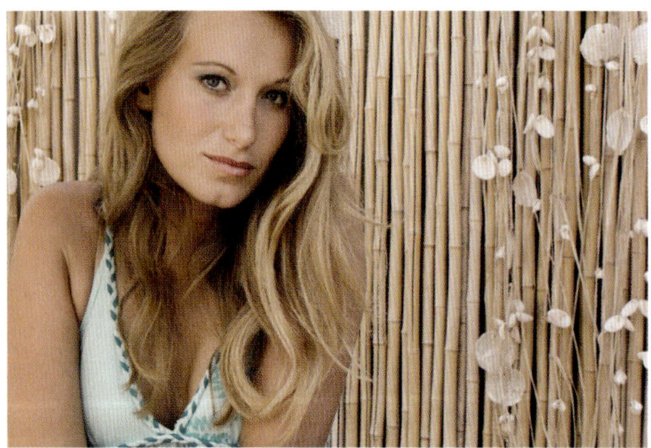

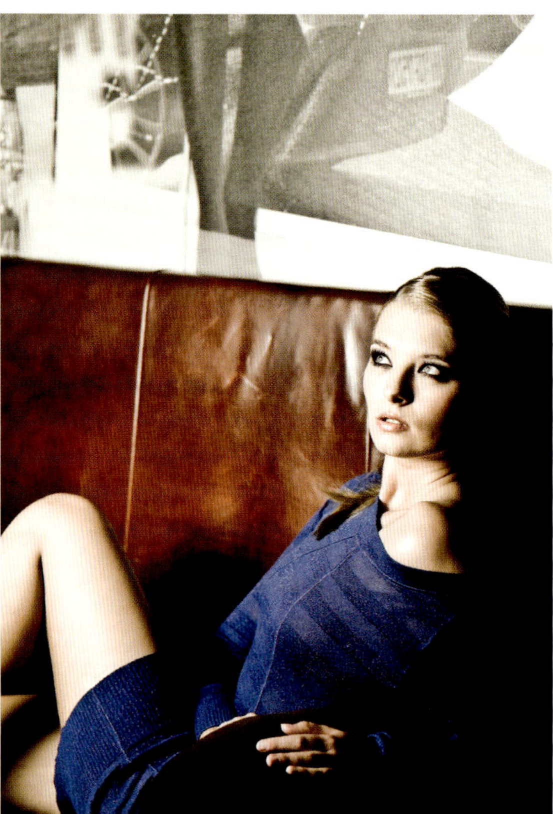

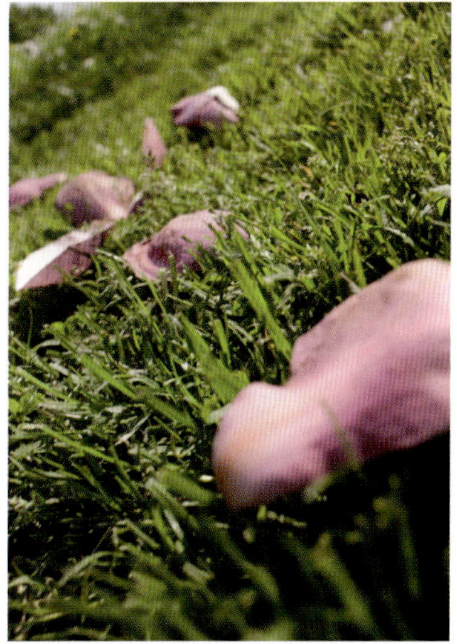

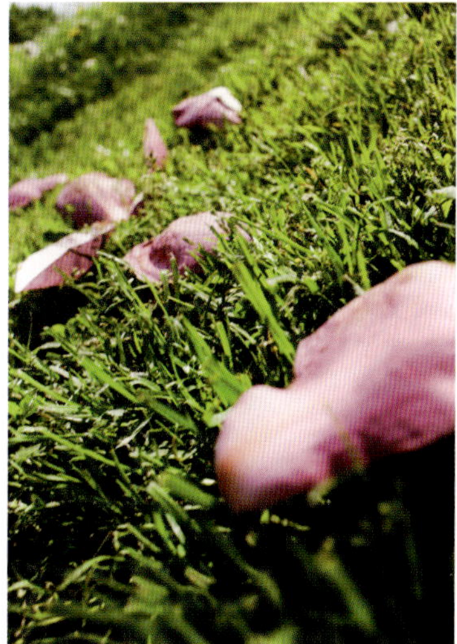

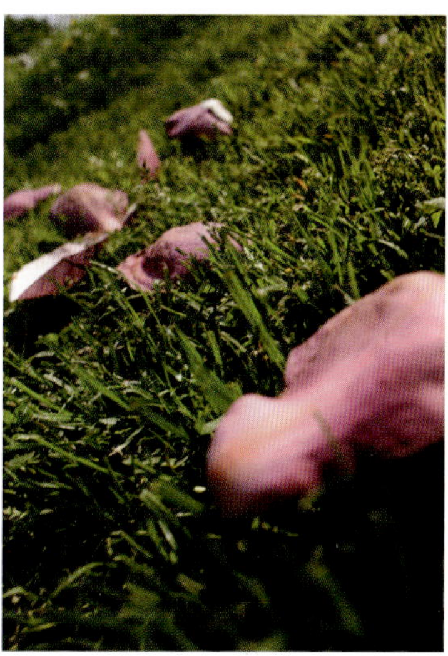

Post-Processed Colors

One of the big advantages of digital photography is that the colors within an image are relative. Your control over this begins with setting the white balance on your camera or your image editing software. This defines what will appear white for each individual image, and it allows your software to establish the other color tones in relation to this white point. You can shift the colors based on different lighting conditions or to achieve intentionally skewed, creative results.

It's not just the circumstances—plentiful or deficient light, clear or hazy skies—that determine how colors will appear in your final image. You also have digital post-processing to adjust the tone, saturation, and brightness of colors to support your visual message.

The possibilities of post-processing are what make digital photography so enticing. Among other things, you can adjust or manipulate the colors of your images to your heart's content. With little effort, you can shift the colors in your entire image, brighten or darken them, and increase or decrease their saturation. You can target a specific color tone, a range of colors, or a particular area of the image. You can partially or totally strip the color out of an image to produce a grayscale image; then you can tone or colorize it or alter its brightness values.

If you increase the contrast of the whole image, for example, the colors will shift. The higher the contrast is, the stronger the effect of the loudest colors will be. This intensified contrast can be a strong attraction for viewers. However, too much contrast will result in blown-out colors that exhibit distracting, unnatural symptoms indicative of heavy post-processing.

To prevent the colors from blowing out, you can alter the brightness of the image. A high level of brightness or overexposure turns colors into subtle, gentle, and desaturated pastel tones. Underexposed images or images with reduced brightness feature stronger, more saturated colors, but at a certain point they can start to look dark and murky.

All of this presupposes that you work on a calibrated monitor so you can be sure that the image on your screen has the same colors that viewers will see.

"The fact that (in a conventional sense) technically incorrect photography can be more emotionally effective than a technically flawless image will be shocking to those who are naive enough to believe that technical perfection alone constitutes the true value of a photo." Andreas Feininger, US photographer

07 Sharpness and Blur

When it comes to sharpness, everyone thinks of focusing, and slightly more experienced photographers also think of aperture. However, many other factors influence what appears sharp and what appears blurry. The subject of movement is not regularly addressed in this category of photographic design, yet sharpness and movement are two aspects of the same design method that have a tremendous variety of effects.

Focusing is usually and logically combined with the concept of depth of field because both primarily relate to unmoving subjects. With these particular design elements, photographers can emphasize specific subjects and areas with crystal-sharp clarity, guide the viewer's gaze to land on distinct objects or wander throughout the image area, and create striking spatial effects—sharpness, in short, is a multifunctional design tool.

In reality, movement is everywhere around us, but photography is an entirely static medium. What's captured in an image stays that way. Nevertheless, we photographers have many possibilities for depicting motion in our images. With the calculated use of sharpness and blur, photographers can create still images that allow viewers to see and sense movement or immobility—a unique and particularly substantive effect of this area of image design.

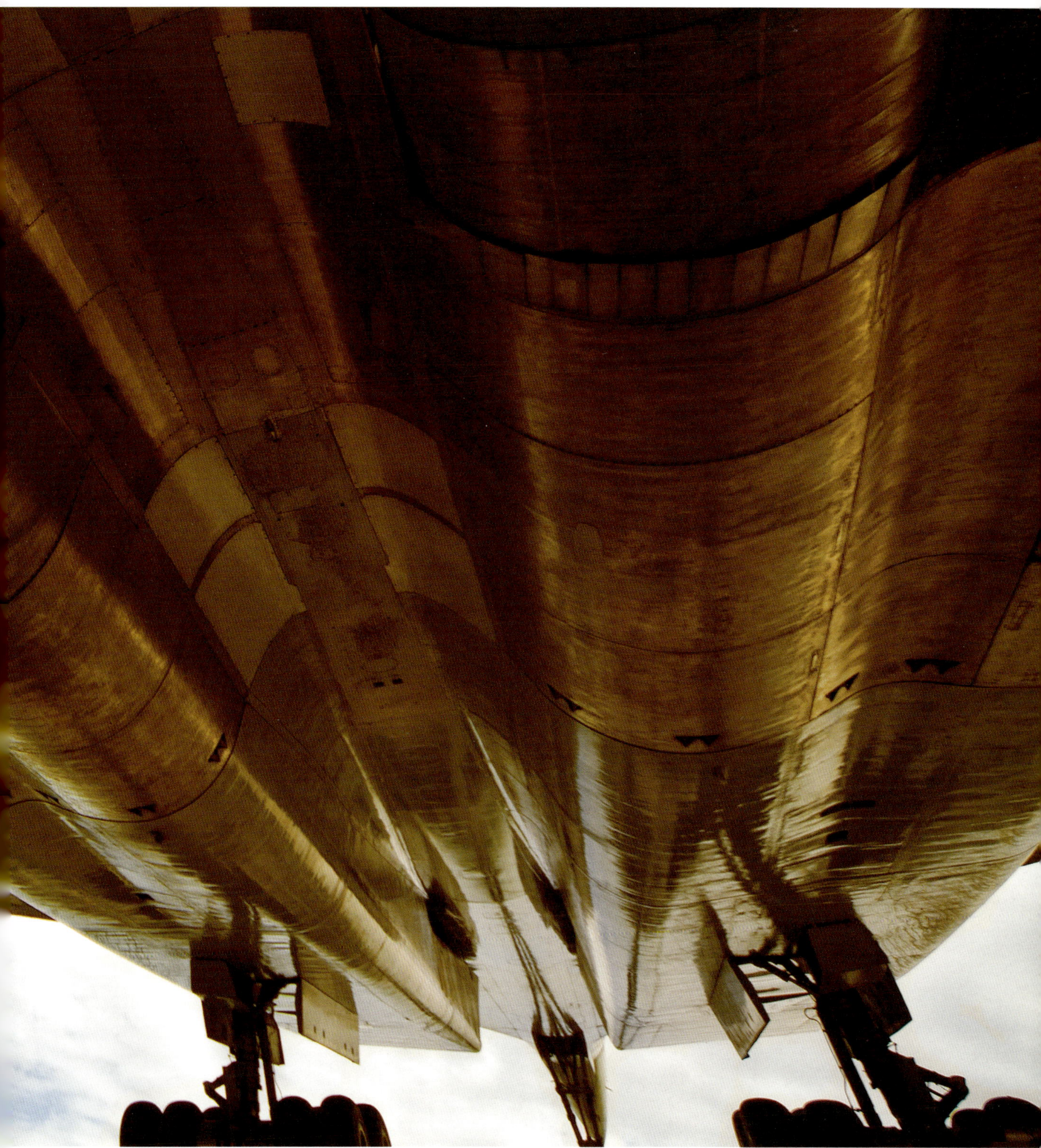

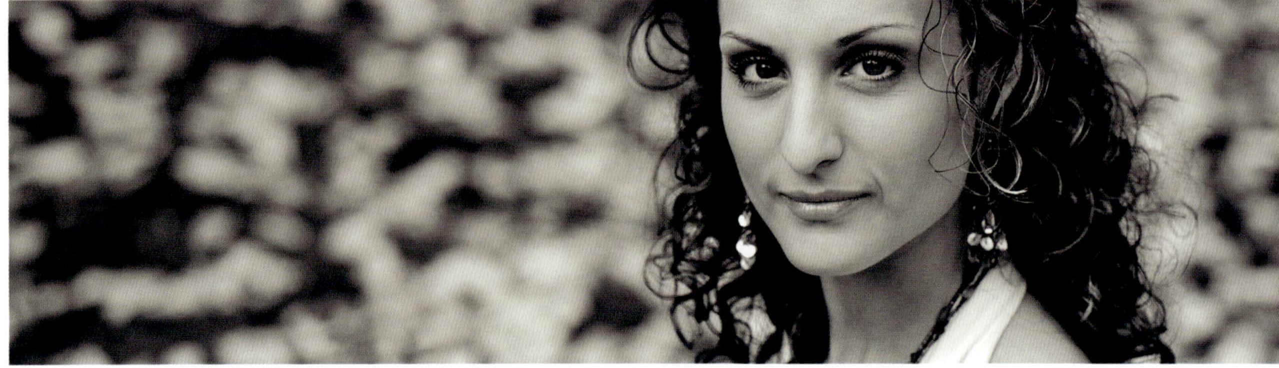

7.1 Establishing Sharpness and Blur

The impression of sharpness in a photo is influenced by a number of factors, including focus, depth of field, resolution and contrast. Managing these factors is the foundation of a conscious and decisive visual design. Before we go into the special visual effects of sharpness and blur, it's worthwhile to take a closer look at their individual building blocks.

Focusing

Establish the focus for your image with the help of your camera, either manually, by examining the image in the viewfinder, or by using the autofocus sensors. When you adjust the focus, you shift the distance of the focal plane until it reaches your desired subject. As a rule, the focal plane is parallel to the surface of the image sensor—the exception is lenses with a tilt function (page 120)—and all elements on the plane will be reproduced with the exact same level of sharpness. When only one element is positioned on the focal plane, the focus will appear at one point.

Cameras typically offer multiple autofocus modes that you can choose based on the circumstances of your shot. For stationary subjects, the focus priority mode is

Focusing requires that you make one of the most important design decisions about your image: which element will be perceived as critical. This is true even for images that have a large depth of field, though to a slightly diminished degree. In these shots of a poppy, you can clearly see how the focal plane shifts the main emphasis of the image from the blossom to the stem.

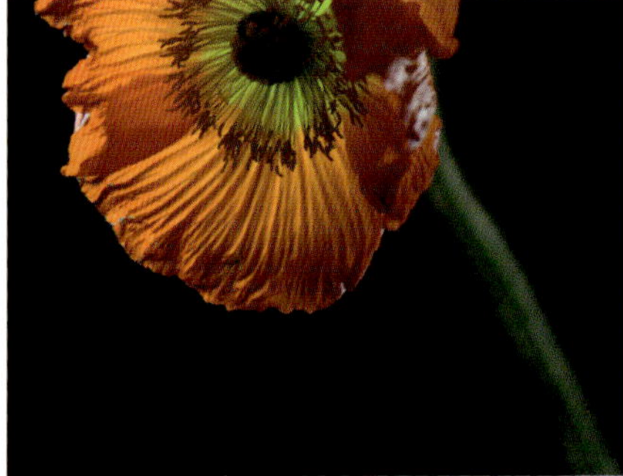

Aperture: 4

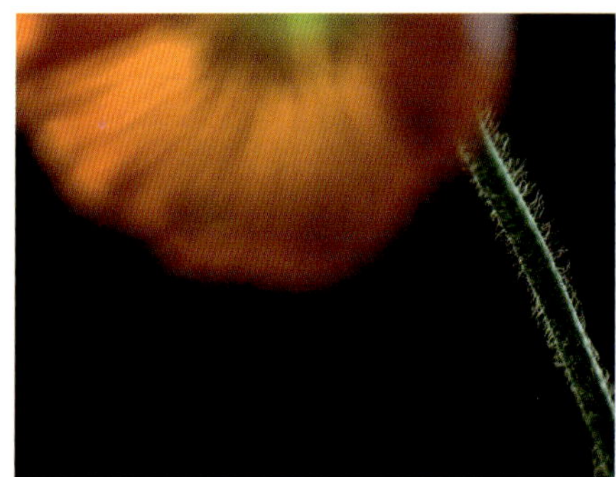

Aperture: 4

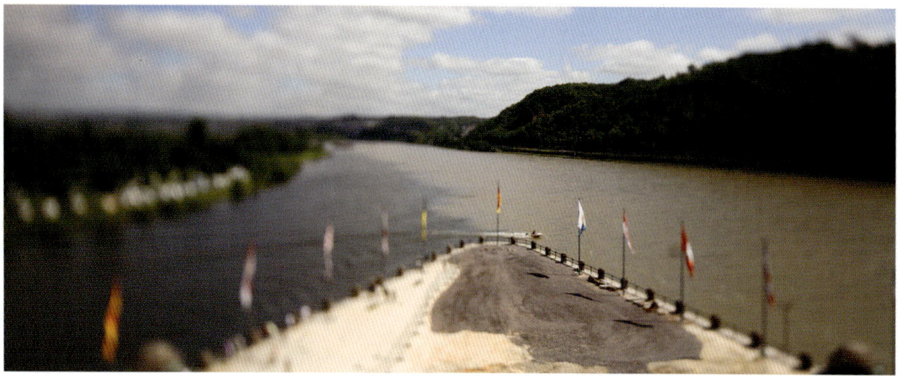
Aperture: 3.5

Normally the focal plane is always parallel to the sensor. Only with a tilt lens, Lensbaby lens, or bellows can you pivot the focal plane. In this image, the focal plane runs along the water's edge and out into space.

useful because it exposes the image only after the camera has successfully located a focal point. For moving targets, you should use the tracking or predictive autofocus option, which attempts to continuously and dynamically adjust focus. Releasing the shutter at just the right moment is of paramount importance, and the sharpness—depending on the quality of the camera and the merits of the automatic focus—will be as exact as possible (see *Learning to Photograph Vol.1*).

Depth of Field

Even though, in a technical sense, the focal plane is the only place where absolute sharpness is achieved, the limited resolution of human vision perceives objects to be sharp within a certain range in front of and behind the plane. This so-called depth of field is not always the same, and it depends on the distance between the focal plane and the sensor plane. In macro exposures, there is more depth of field in front of the focal plane, and with greater distances between the camera and the subject, the largest portion of the depth of field lies beyond the focal plane. The transition from sharp to unsharp image areas is gradual in both cases (see *Learning to Photograph Vol.1*).

The range in front of and behind the focal plane is called the depth of field. By adjusting the aperture we can directly influence how far this range extends. These images show the effect for a very close camera-to-subject distance.

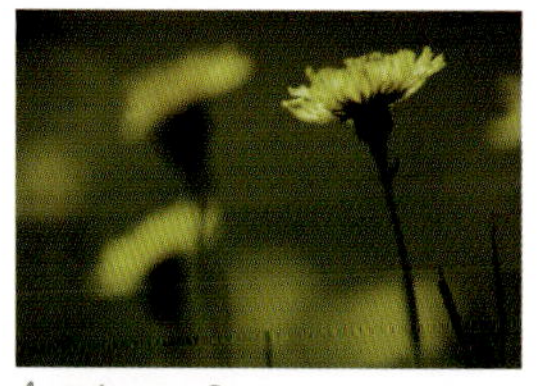
Aperture: 2.8

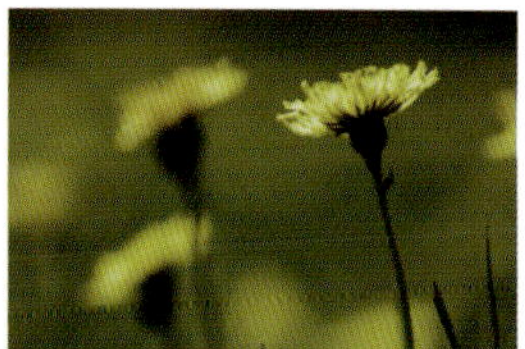
Aperture: 4

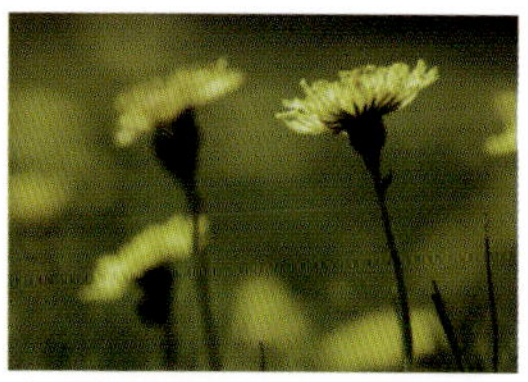
Aperture: 5.6

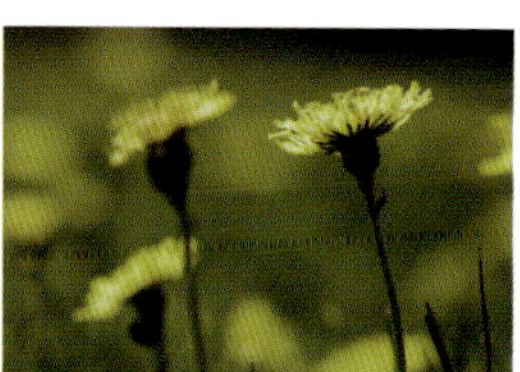
Aperture: 8

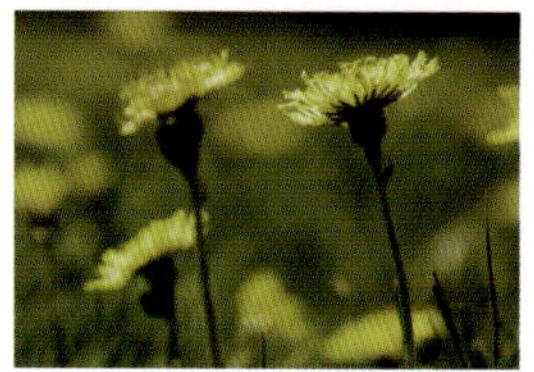
Aperture: 11

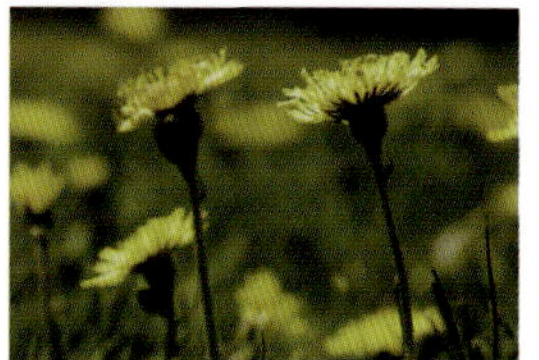
Aperture: 16

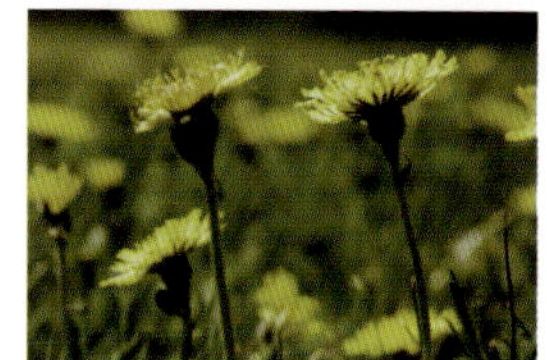
Aperture: 22

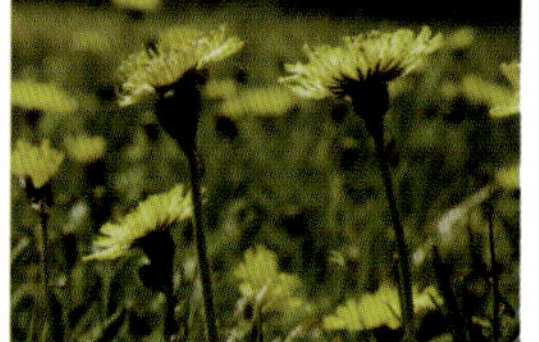
Aperture: 32

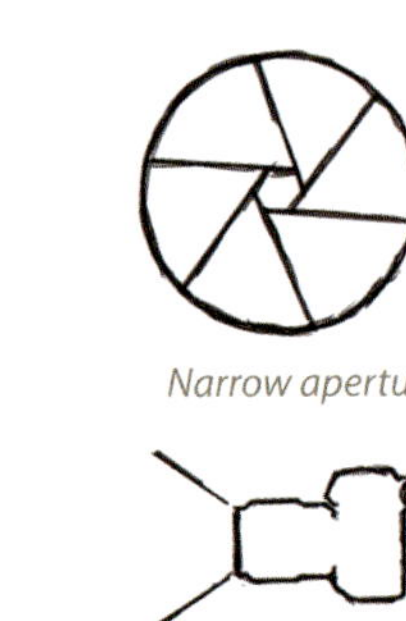

Narrow aperture

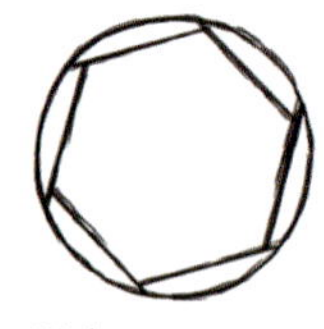

Wide aperture

Short focal length

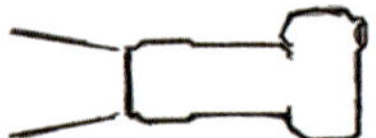

Long focal length

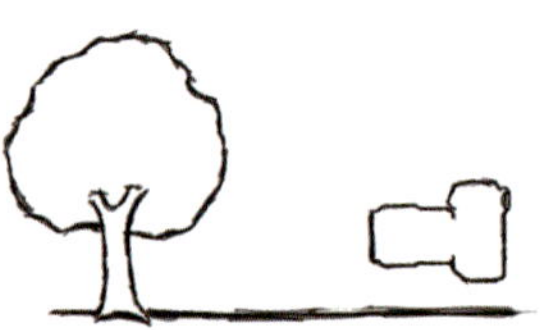

Large subject-to-camera distance

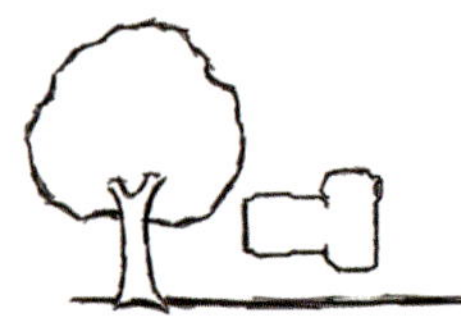

Small subject-to-camera distance

Small sensor

Large sensor

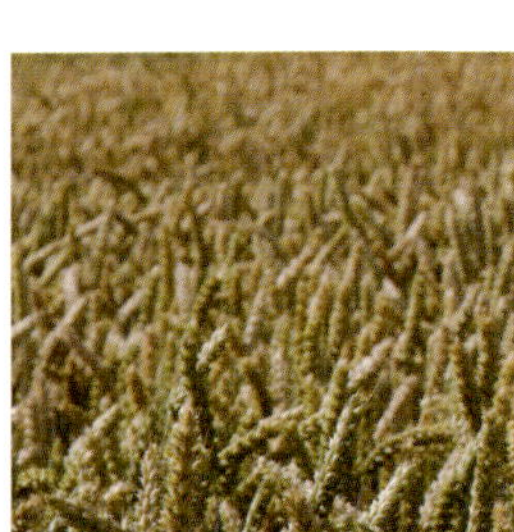

Aperture: 22

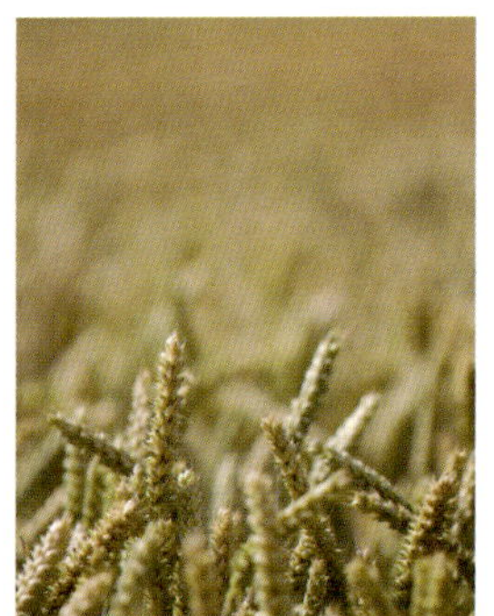

Aperture: 2.8

This diagram shows the four factors that influence depth of field—they each affect the image simultaneously. Depending on the circumstances of your picture, you can't always adjust all four factors.

The size of the depth of field is determined by four factors: aperture, focal length, sensor size, and the distance between the sensor and the focal plane. Combining these factors can increase, decrease, or negate their individual impact on the depth of field. Depth of field is increased by the following:

- Smaller aperture (i.e., larger number)
- Shorter focal length
- Greater distance between the sensor and the focal plane
- Smaller sensor

The opposite measures reduce the depth of field:

- Larger aperture (i.e., smaller number)
- Longer focal length
- Shorter distance between the sensor and the focal plane
- Larger sensor

It's worth noting that a particularly small distance between the camera and the subject causes the region in which objects appear blurry to become so large that it's not possible to compensate with the other three dimensions. This is why the depth of field is so tiny in macro situations, often just a fraction of an inch (page 186).

The Impression of Sharpness

When we examine a narrow focal plane and the areas in front of and behind it, it becomes obvious that the quality of sharpness within an image is not objective. The transition from sharp to blurry is gradual. Sharpness, in other words, is a matter of perception, and it describes the areas in an image that appear sharp.

There are three factors that determine whether we perceive an image as sharp or blurry. The first is the resolution of the image, which needs to at least match that of the human eye to appear sharp. Second, the highest possible brightness contrast for the entire image increases the impression of sharpness. Third, sufficient edge contrast (also known as *acutance*), or starkly demarcated transitions at the contours of the visual elements, influences the appearance of sharpness.

The distance between the viewer and an image also influences the appearance of sharpness. Images must have a higher level of sharpness at short distances than long distances. This is often the case for billboards, which generally have low resolution and look blurry when viewed from up close. Accordingly, the contrast and the edge sharpness for each image area are more critical for the viewer to perceive the overall image as sharp.

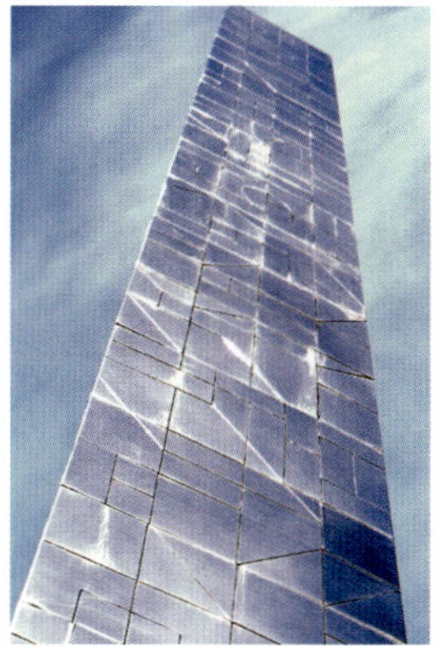
Aperture: 8

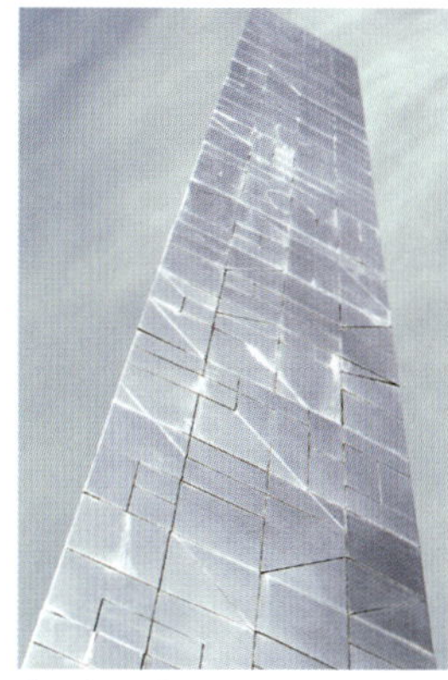
Aperture: 8

Increased contrast makes the image on the left appear sharper, even though it is otherwise identical to the image on the right. The editing is the same for each image with respect to gradation and color.

A Hazy Blur

Other forms of blurriness can affect the entire image and can't be addressed with camera settings or focus. A general haze, for example, can pervade your image and reduce the impression of sharpness and perception of quality. Haze can be put to good use to establish a spontaneous look and feel, a fairytale atmosphere, a retro look, or a snapshot quality.

You can achieve these effects by attaching filters to your lens, using a lens with poor optic qualities, or intentionally blurring your image with errant focusing. These techniques will result in a universal blur, and viewers will notice the blur itself. You can create haze by positioning a transparent substance between your lens and the subject, such as glass, fabric, water, steam, fog, heat shimmer, or mist. The closer you position your camera to this substance, the less perceptible it will be in the image and the stronger and more uniform the haze will be.

When water, fog, steam, dirty windows, or fabrics are in the foreground when you take a picture, the sharpness of the image will be diminished. Your subject, however, still may exhibit enough characteristic details, and the overall look of the image may be quite dramatic.

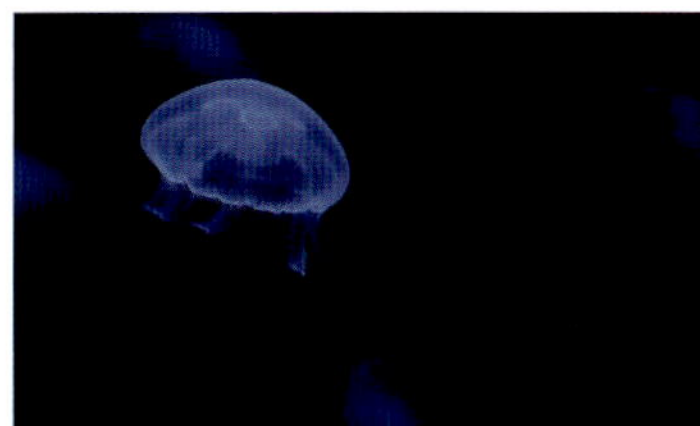
Aperture: 2.8

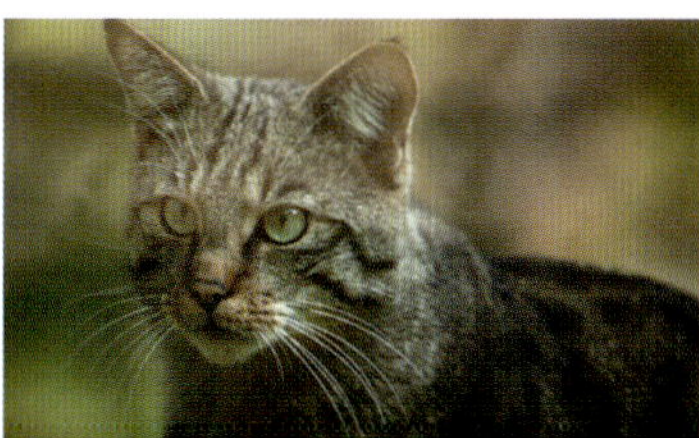
Aperture: 5.6

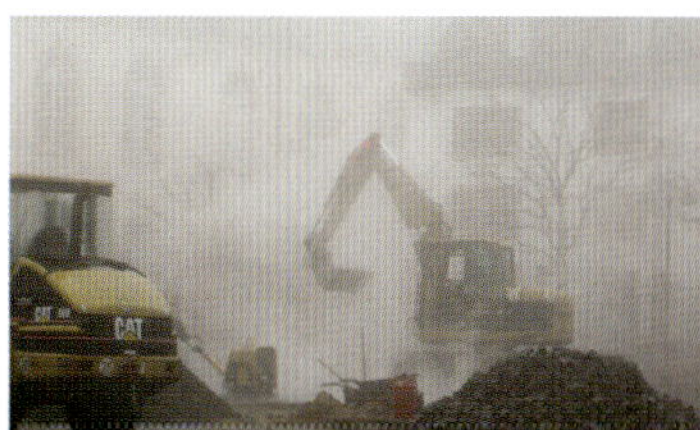

Aperture: 5.6

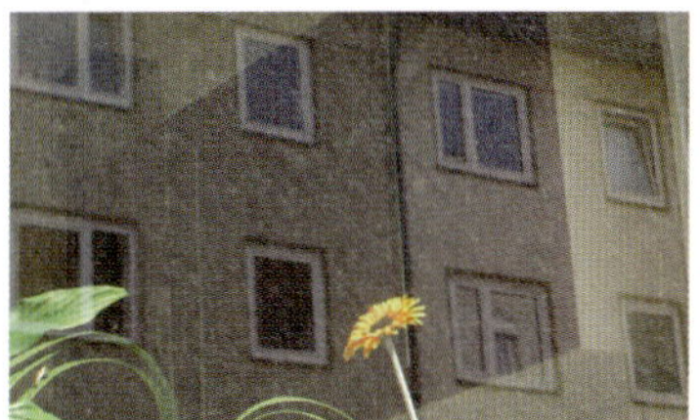
Aperture: 5.6

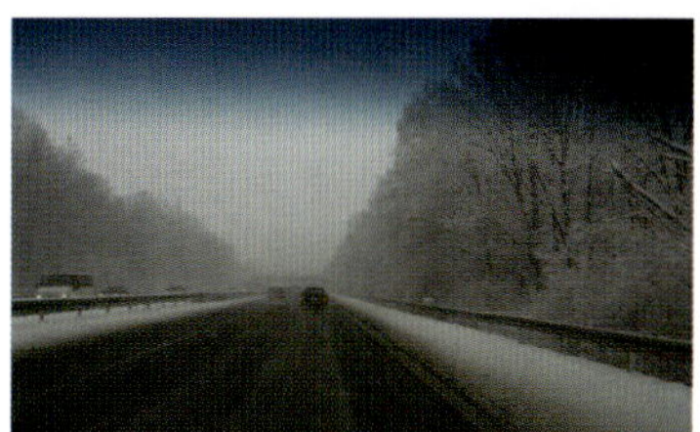
Aperture: 2.8

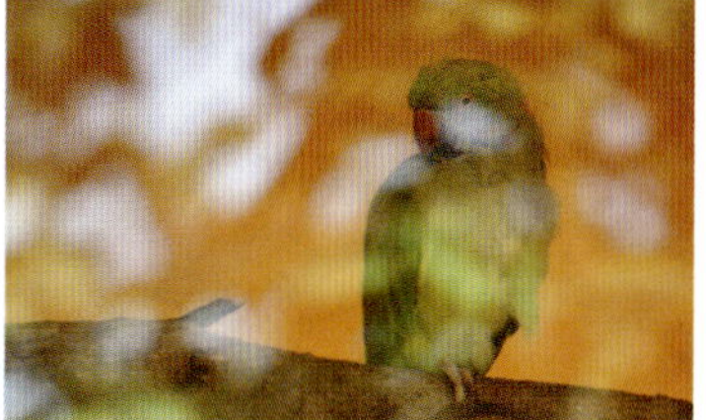
Aperture: 6.5

7.2 Designing with Sharpness and Blur

Purposefully exposing your images to feature some areas of sharpness and other areas of blur is a rich design method. Sharp areas inevitably attract attention—a fact you can exploit to catch the viewer's eye. You can use blur to deemphasize parts of your picture. A thoughtful design that makes use of both sharpness and blur gives depth to an exposure and separates internal layers.

Photos that lack blurred areas are challenging for viewers because details are present in all regions of the image. Determining which details are important is entirely up to viewers; they approach such an image like eating at a buffet—they must choose what to eat.

Sharp or Blurry?

The human eye constantly focuses and assembles individual areas of sharpness into a complete image. We're familiar with blur only from still frames, but we perceive it as common and normal as a result of intensive conditioning. Most viewers expect at least a small area of sharpness in an image—so the eye can settle and find repose—

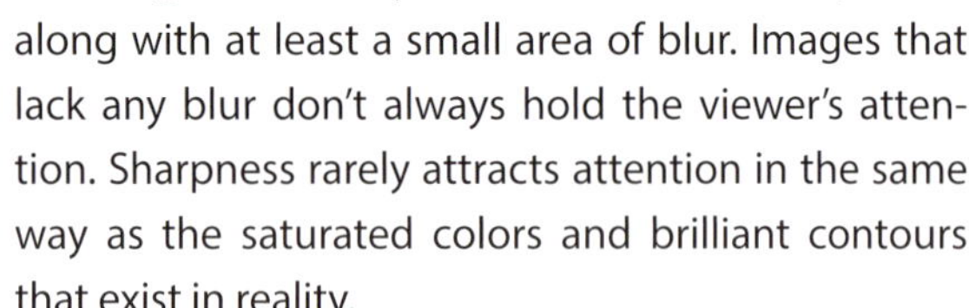

along with at least a small area of blur. Images that lack any blur don't always hold the viewer's attention. Sharpness rarely attracts attention in the same way as the saturated colors and brilliant contours that exist in reality.

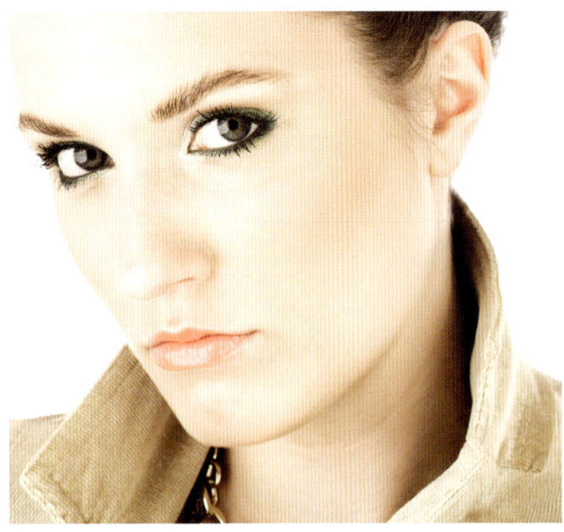

Aperture: 13

This doesn't mean, however, that an image absolutely must feature blur in some capacity, nor does it mean that there is a requirement for an image to contain at least one area of sharpness. An entirely blurry or sharp image can have a strong effect and a captivating look—sharp exposures have an objective feel, while blurry ones feel more artistic and experimental. Both demand the use of other evocative design elements, as well as subject matter that is interesting on its own merits, so viewers can look

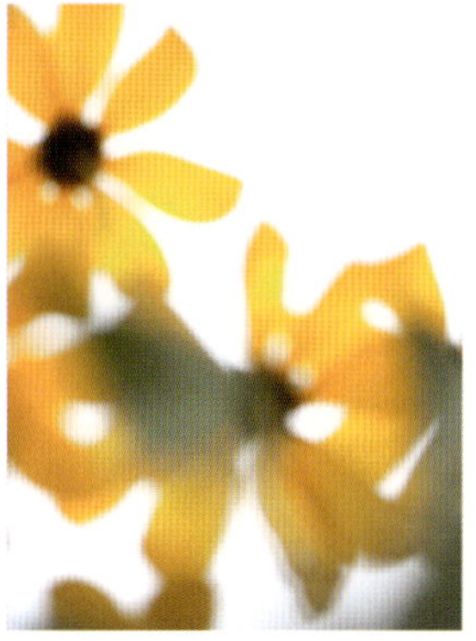
Aperture: 2.8

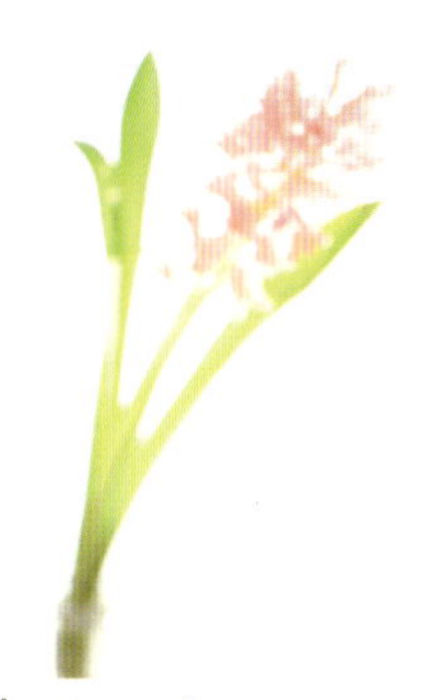
Aperture: 2.8

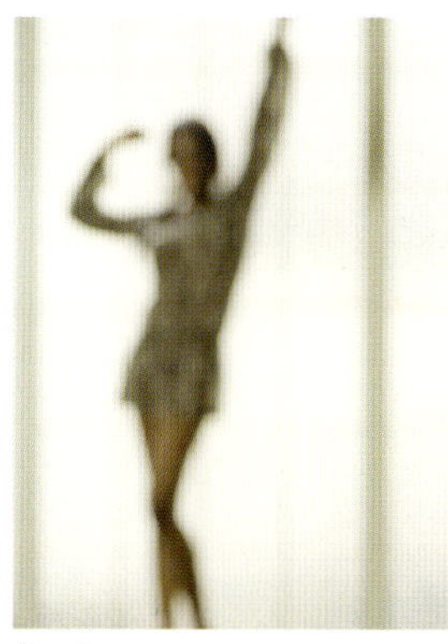
Aperture: 4

Images that are completely blurry have their charms, but they are not everyone's cup of tea. When you intentionally obscure the details in an image, make sure that no elements (including the ground) appear in focus. This will create an image that has an abstract, anonymous, general, and heavy effect, which may not hold a viewer's attention for long because it is devoid of any sharpness to act as an anchor point.

beyond the missing balance of sharpness and blur. The viewer's attitude is also a key factor in how an image featuring total blur is received—many photographers think of blur as a technical flaw or a grievous design mistake.

Depth of Field Preview

Most SLR cameras keep the aperture very wide to allow the viewfinder image to be as bright as possible; at the moment of exposure, it adjusts the aperture to the actual setting. SLRs often feature a depth of field preview button (see *Learning to Photograph Vol.1*). Pressing this button allows you to examine the depth of field in the viewfinder before you expose an image, but it causes less light to enter the camera, which results in a darker viewfinder image. You may need a bit of practice before evaluation of the depth of field becomes second nature; after that, the depth of field preview button will be one of your prized tools.

Large Depth of Field

A large depth of field is a natural choice for images that rely on an abundance of details and the excitement of discovery. Vacation, architecture, and urban images usually fall into this category.

The most common application of a large depth of field is to bring areas of sharpness and blur into an image. You can decide on the relative proportions of these areas depending on your preferences, what works with your subject, and what is necessary to achieve the desired ambiance. A broad range of sharpness demands a larger

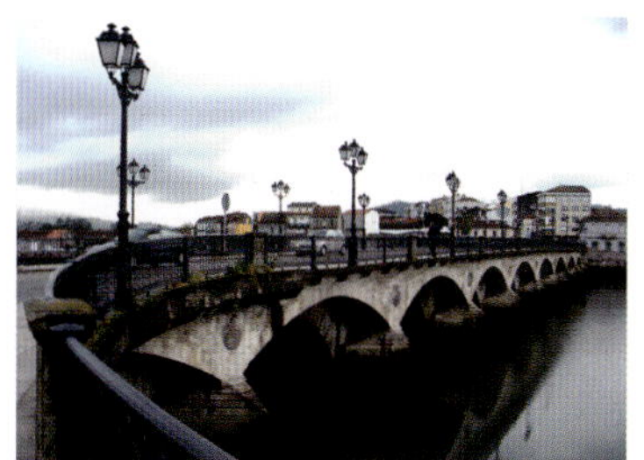
Aperture: 8

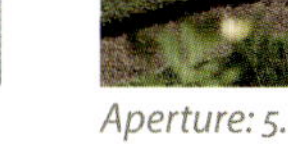
Aperture: 5.6

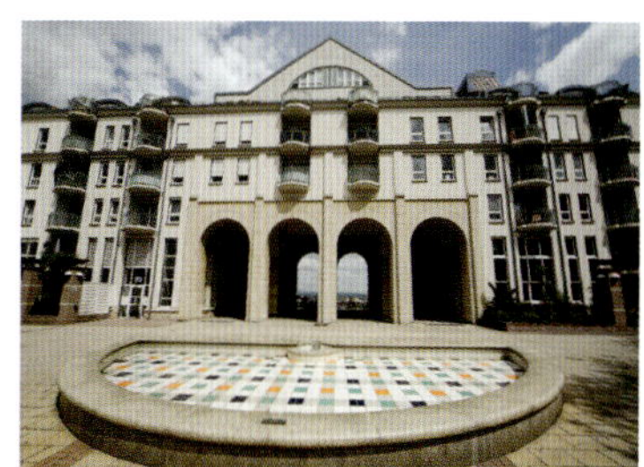
Aperture: 11

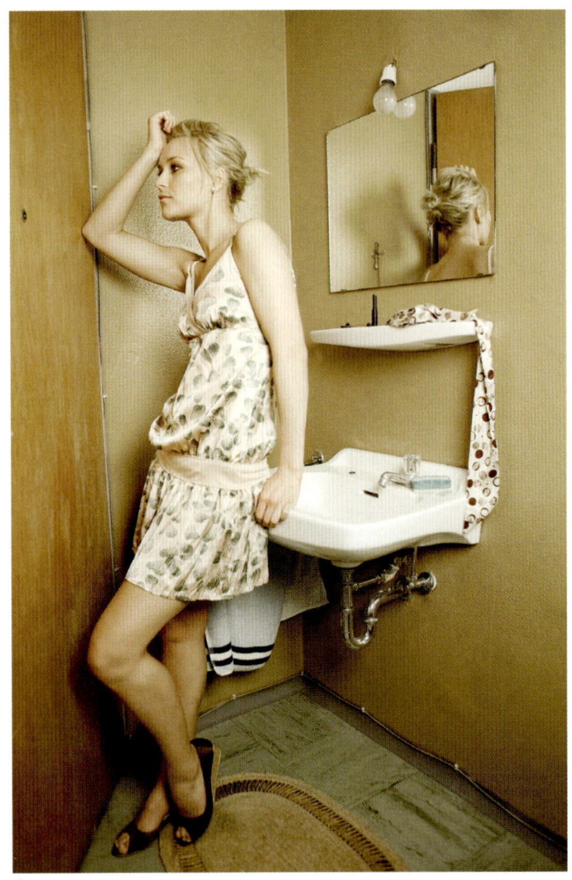

Aperture: 4

The depth of field in this exposure is highly effective because the eye can jump from one element to the next and take in every detail. The image is diverse enough to retain the viewer's attention.

depth of field, while a narrower depth of field (page 178) will yield an abundance of blur. A large depth of field opens up your subject and its surroundings in all their specific detail—a small portion of the image disappears in blur, but the majority of the image remains sharp and completely recognizable.

As a general rule of thumb, images that are completely in focus should also feature other design elements so it is clear that you selected the depth of field with a specific purpose in mind, instead of arbitrarily using a default depth of field due to limitations of your camera.

Images with a large depth of field are perceived as objective, two-dimensional, and rich in detail. They invite viewers to meander through the areas of the image since there is no focal point on which the eye can settle. With a large depth of field, viewers will either sense freedom or indecision, since the photographer didn't deliberately establish regions of blur and focus. This judgment is highly dependent on the subject matter; if the exposure offers enough interesting content, then a large depth of field is ideal. This is often the case with fashion and beauty photography, landscapes with a variety of vegetation, or even memento photos. A modest oversharpening of images that feature an exceptionally large depth of field can sometimes lead to a surreal look that attracts the viewer's attention.

Images that feature large areas without important details, or an exceptionally small subject set against a large and conspicuous backdrop, can use a narrower depth of field to deemphasize areas that are secondary to your photographic objective.

A shallow depth of field in the left image concentrates the viewer's attention on the front eye and causes the image to take on a subjective tone. In the right image, the same depth of field creates a much more balanced and even image because the eyes are equidistant to the camera.

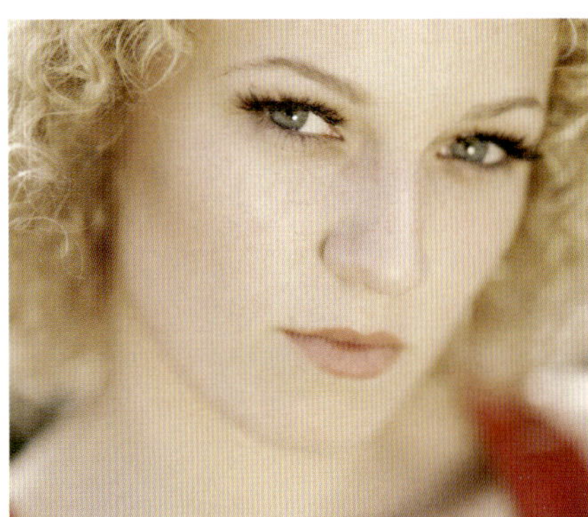

Aperture: 2

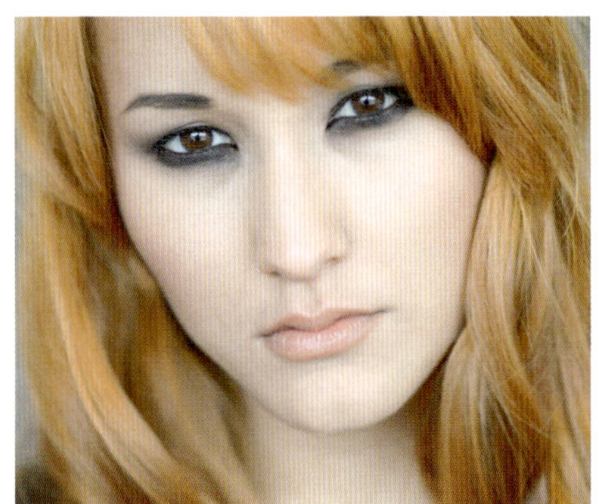

Aperture: 2

Aperture: 2

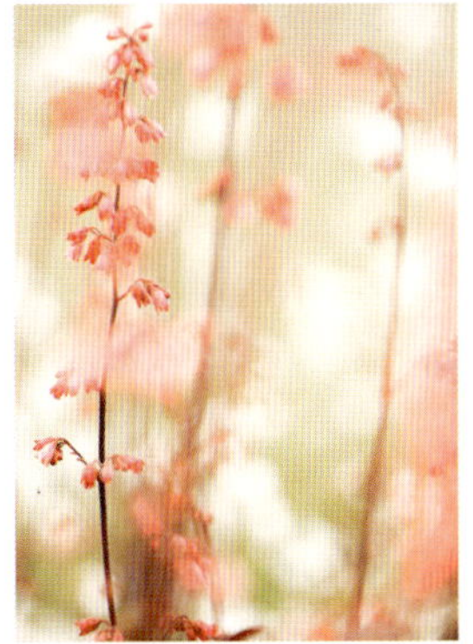
Aperture: 2.8

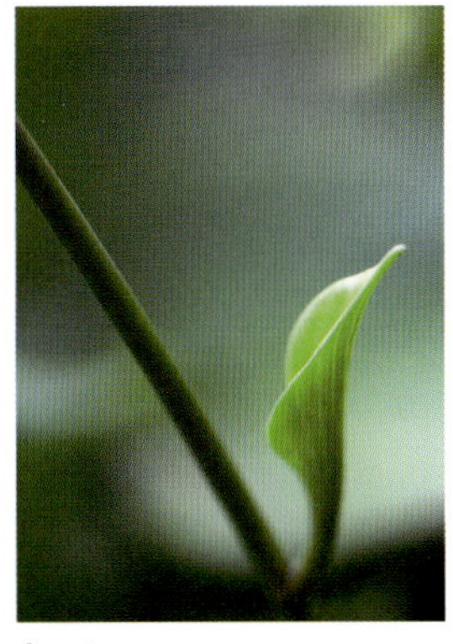
Aperture: 4.5

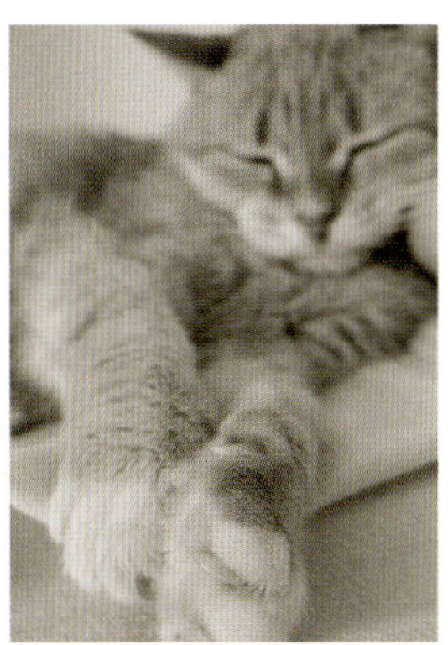
Aperture: 2.8

A very tight depth of field clearly demarcates levels in an image. The viewer is quickly directed to the most important element and can take in the core content of the image faster. These advantages come at the expense of lost details and don't hold the viewer's attention for long.

Shallow Depth of Field

Blurriness reduces the optical importance of a visual element because the viewer's gaze is pulled toward sharp areas rather than blurry areas. The shallower the depth of field, the stronger the effect; for truly tight depths of field, even large structures can be reduced to anonymity. Detailed textures and surfaces with a weak contrast are obscured with minimal blur. When large areas of an image appear out of focus, it makes it all the easier for viewers to detect the main subject based on its sharpness. The division of sharp and blurry areas also tends to underscore or define the visual layers within an image, causing an increase in the overall dimensionality (page 72).

Selectively applying sharpness to certain elements is a tried-and-true method of calling attention to them. You can highlight subjects that are part of a larger sequence or collection, such as a single flower in an entire meadow of wildflowers. An extremely shallow depth of field tends to make the in-focus areas look sharper. The contrast between the blurry and sharp areas reinforces the perceived level of sharpness, especially if this effect is supported by other types of contrast. Blurred elements can be featured in the foreground, middle, or background of an image, depending on where they best serve the subject. One particularly evocative image design occurs when you place a small, in-focus element on one plane (page 78) and a larger, blurred element on another. This optical balancing forces viewers to shift their gaze between elements.

If you are interested in playing with blur in your images, it's worthwhile to invest in a fast, fixed focal length lens, which will allow you to work with shallow depths of field even after you slightly stop down the aperture.

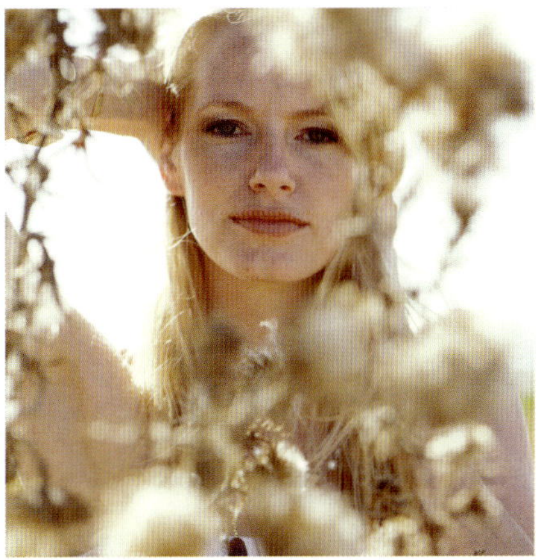
Aperture: 5

The focal plane doesn't always have to be positioned in the foreground of an image with blurred regions falling behind it. Placing blur directly in the foreground causes the viewer to search for the main subject. This engages the viewer and keeps the image interesting.

In macro photography, one of the four factors that determines depth of field is much more dominant than the others: the distance between the camera and the focal plane. The optics of a macro lens allow you to get very close to your subject. This results in such an exceptionally small depth of field that it must be measured in fractions of an inch. You can highlight very specific planes of an image because objects directly in front of and behind the focal plane will be extremely fuzzy. This is a useful way to create interesting abstract photos.

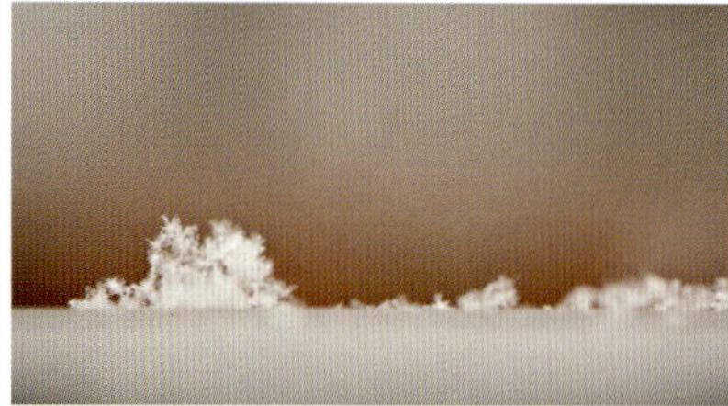

Aperture: 4

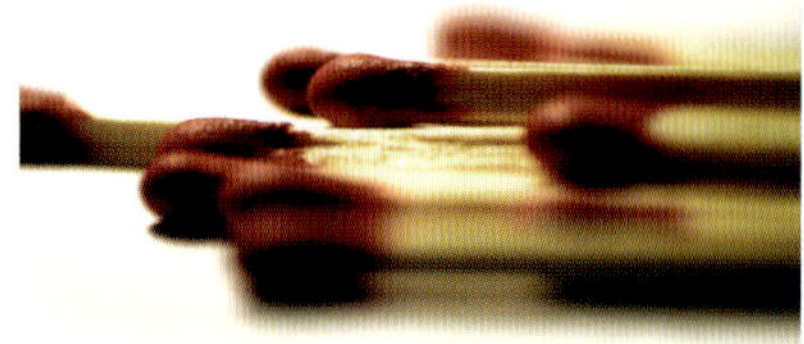

Aperture: 3.5

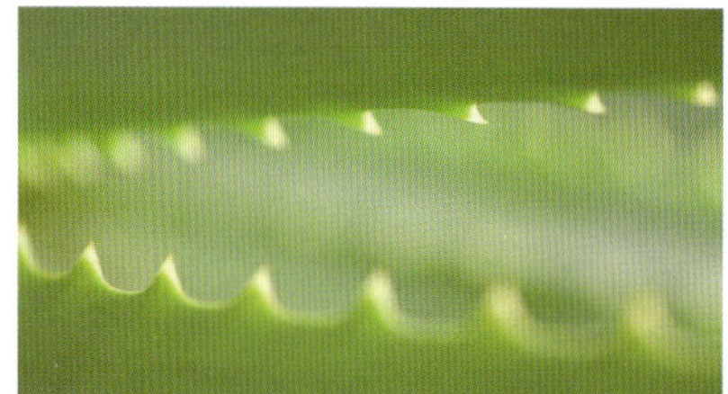

Aperture: 2.8

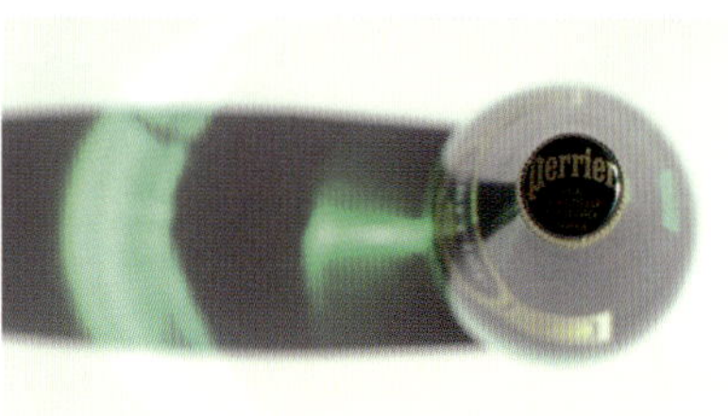

Aperture: 2

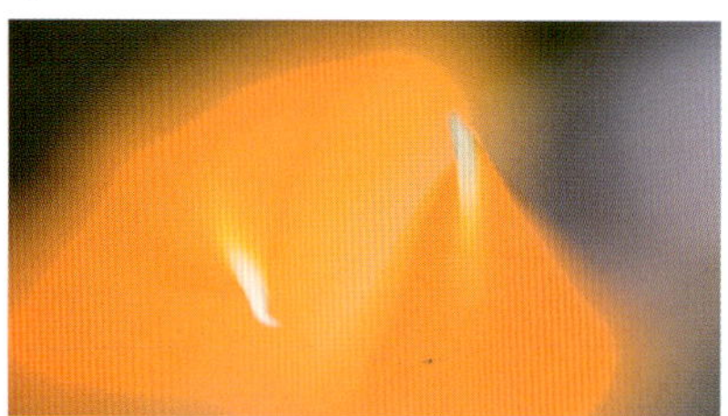

Aperture: 2.8

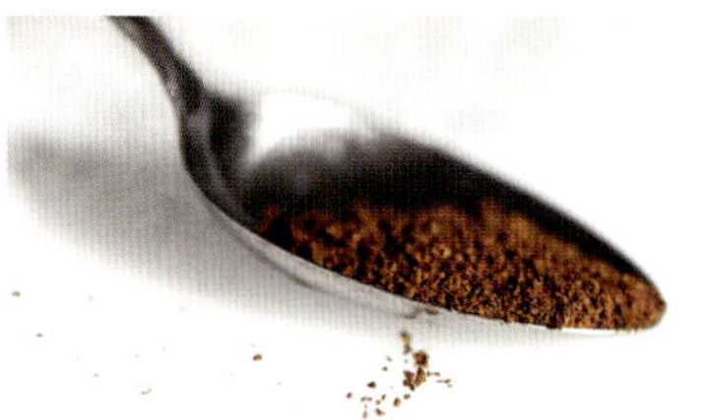

Aperture: 3.5

Sharpness in Macro Photography

Working with depth of field in macro photography can be a real challenge, since it's not easy to increase. Macro photography requires a very limited depth of field.

In macro photography, the area in which objects appear sharp is determined by four variables: focal length, aperture, subject-to-camera distance, and sensor size. There is minimal wiggle room to adjust each variable due to the extremely small distance between the camera and the subject. Work at the limit of your focal length and the minimum focusing distance of your lens, which is the shortest possible subject-to-camera distance. With shorter focal lengths, the minimum focusing distance is inherently smaller than with longer focal lengths. This means you can't change the depth of field by switching lenses. With shorter focal length lenses you will be much closer to your subject—partly because it would be otherwise impossible to create a concentrated representation of the subject with an even wider angle of view (page 117).

In macro photography, focal length and camera-to-subject distance can't be used to extend the depth of field. In theory, the sensor size could be changed, but it's not a practical option.

You can also alter the aperture to influence your macro exposures: the narrower the aperture, the larger the available depth of field is for image design. A smaller aperture requires a longer shutter speed—assuming otherwise identical exposure conditions. An increase in exposure time means a higher risk of camera shake (page 188), which is a good reason to use a steady tripod.

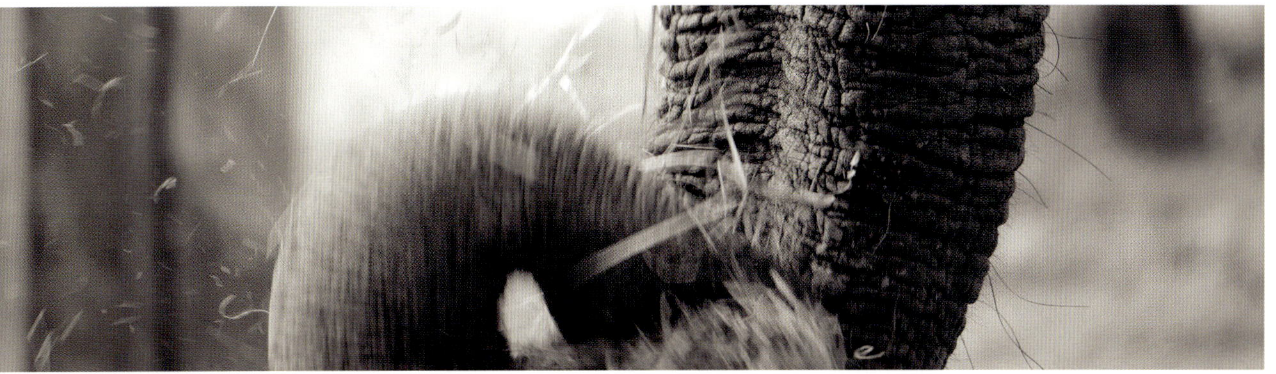

7.3 Movement

Aside from intentionally creating blur by adjusting the focus, the fact that nearly everything moves can be used to capture blur . Sharp focus requires that neither your camera nor your subject move, regardless of how long the exposure window is. If sharpness is not a consideration, the field size becomes a versatile tool to capture the motion of the camera or the subject.

Shutter Speeds

A camera makes it possible to document fractions of a second. The seconds during which the shutter opens and allows light to fall on the sensor are so short that they seem to lack a tangible duration. Nevertheless, a great deal more can transpire during these seconds than we are capable of perceiving with our own eyes. When a ball flies through a windowpane, we perceive only a quick motion, a crash, and the pieces of glass on the floor—for the camera, however, the process can be divided into many individual images.

Brief exposure times can freeze and capture fast movements and portray them in a way that the human eye wouldn't otherwise be able to see. Viewers find these subjects new, exciting, and dramatic.

The exact appearance of motion in an image depends on the camera-to-subject distance and the direction of the movement, but it is primarily determined by the length of the exposure in relation to the speed of the motion. Stars, for example, appear to be stationary in the sky, yet long-exposure images reveal their motion relative to the camera. On the other hand, rushing water can be frozen in time to look like sculptures of glass. Even if the subject doesn't move, as in architecture photography, a third type of speed that is often overlooked comes into play: the movement of the camera.

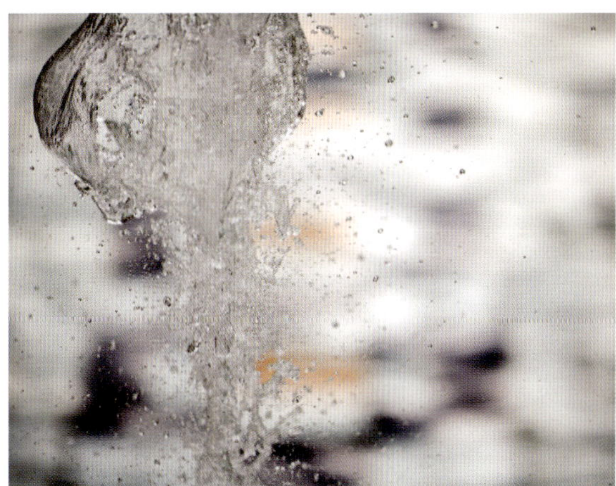

Shutter speed: 1/4000 second

These two images demonstrate the difference between frozen motion (right) and motion depicted as a blur (left). Neither image is more correct or better than the other. You can make this sort of judgment only when you start with a specific objective and decide on the desired effect.

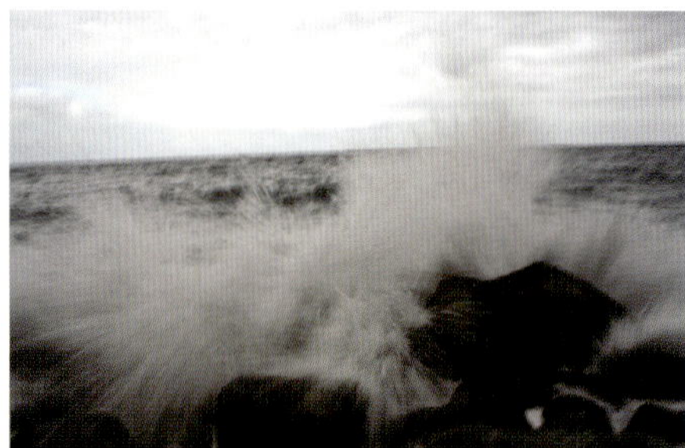

Shutter speed: 1/13 second

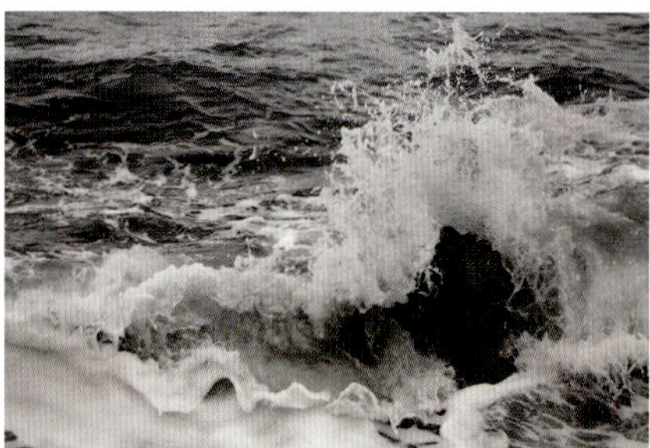

Shutter speed: 1/800 second

If the subject or the camera moves faster than the shutter speed, the image will exhibit visible signs of motion; if the movement is slower than the shutter speed, the camera will freeze the motion.

Camera Shake

One of the fundamental goals of most photographers is to create a sharp picture. Since no one is capable of holding his or her body completely still for an extended period of time, movements are transferred to the camera. The longer the shutter is open, the more the subject moves in relation to the camera. This gives rise to multiple representations of the subject that are slightly shifted, to produce a blurred image. The constant and slight trembling of our muscles causes these motions to occur in all directions, and viewers perceive images affected by camera shake as technically flawed, even if the flaw doesn't ruin the picture entirely.

Depending on the length of the exposure window, there are several ways to avoid camera shake. First, hold your camera properly. Use your left hand to hold the camera from below and support your left arm against your torso. Use your right hand only to stabilize the camera and press the shutter-release button. This way, you can typically manage to snap photos that are free from shake at exposures up to 1/125 second or even 1/60 second. This depends, in part, on the focal length: the longer the lens, the more ruinous small movements are. With longer lenses, the window of time during which you can hold your camera still enough to produce sharp images is shorter. The reciprocal of the focal length corresponds to the shortest feasible exposure time; for a camera with a small sensor, you also have to multiply the result by the crop factor.

At relatively slow shutter speeds, the small twitches of our muscles transfer to the camera and create blurred images. Normally photographers take precautionary measures to avoid camera shake because it detracts from the quality of an image. Only in rare cases do images turn out to be interesting despite this type of blur.

Shutter speed: 1/3 second

An optical image stabilizer lets you to shoot at exposure times up to four stops slower than you could otherwise, without camera shake. Optical stabilizers continually measure the movements of the camera and use the data to control small motors that negate the movements. This type of stabilizing device can be positioned within a lens where it can directly manipulate the optics, or housed within the camera body where it counterbalances movement by shifting the sensor.

For longer exposure times, it's best to use a support. Monopods hold the weight of heavy lenses and help you avoid unwanted movements, albeit only in the vertical direction. For a limitless range of exposure times, you need a tripod—ideally, the most stable one you can manage.

If you find yourself on-site without a tripod, set your camera on a stable object and position it so you have the desired image area targeted in your viewfinder. A final way to avoid camera shake is to control movement when you press the shutter-release button. You can use your camera's self-timer, which may have an interval of two seconds for this purpose.

Intentional Blur

You can intentionally exploit camera shake to produce creative results by moving your camera during a long exposure. Depending on the technique you use, shutter speeds ranging from 1/4 to 1/60 second are a good starting place for experimentation.

One technique is to hold your camera in an outstretched arm and bring your subject into focus. Press the shutter button halfway down and pull your arm toward your body in as even and steady a motion as possible while you press the shutter button the rest of the way. This results in dynamic stripes that lead from the slightly blurred—but still recognizable—subject. You can achieve a similar result by turning the focal length ring on your zoom lens during the exposure. Images produced in this manner recall the warp speed effect familiar from Star Trek.

Another way to produce intentional motion blur is to rotate your camera around the axis of the lens. Use one arm and rotate your wrist with a calm, steady motion. This produces an image with a heavy core surrounded by trails of concentric circles.

Another technique is to swipe or pan the camera in a specific direction. This is most effective when your subject has a marked contrast—either with respect to brightness or colors.

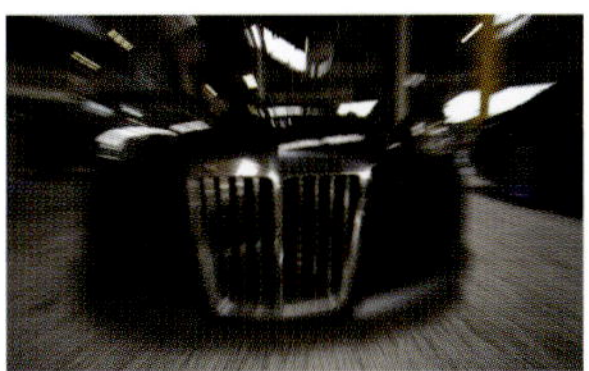
Shutter speed: 1/30 second

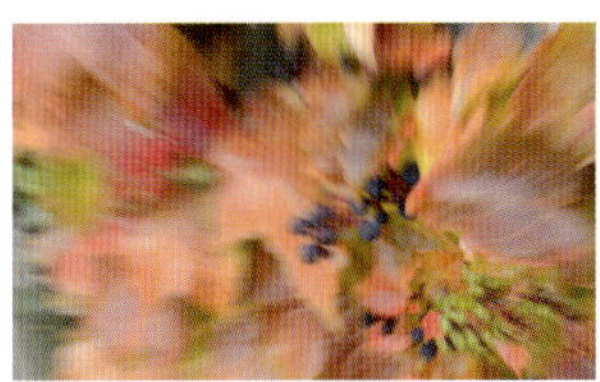
Shutter speed: 1/25 second

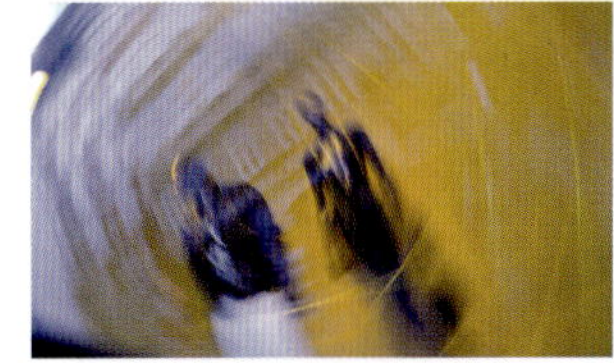
Shutter speed: 1/30 second

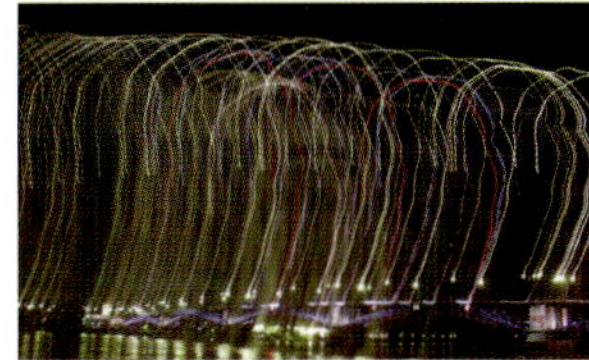
Shutter speed: 1/20 second

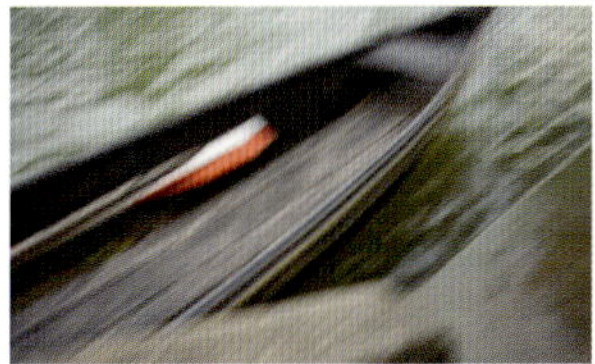
Shutter speed: 1/50 second

A combination of a highly calculated camera movement and a slow shutter speed produces smeared or blurred images. Under the right circumstances, viewers perceive these effects as purposeful. If you create these effects with a steady hand in a single direction, your intention will be clear. There are several different techniques to generate these traces of movement. The illustrations here were created in the following ways (top to bottom): adjusting the zoom during the exposure, thrusting the camera toward the subject, turning the camera with the wrist, moving the camera in a geometric shape, and sliding the camera in the direction of the subject's main contrast.

Rotating your camera around a specific axis is a fun trick that requires a bit of dexterity to make sure your images end up with a clear purpose. Scenes with uniform contrast and an interesting subject in the middle are ideal for this technique. As with every special effect, it must be warranted by the content and purpose of your shot. Without engaging subject matter, this design method quickly loses its appeal.

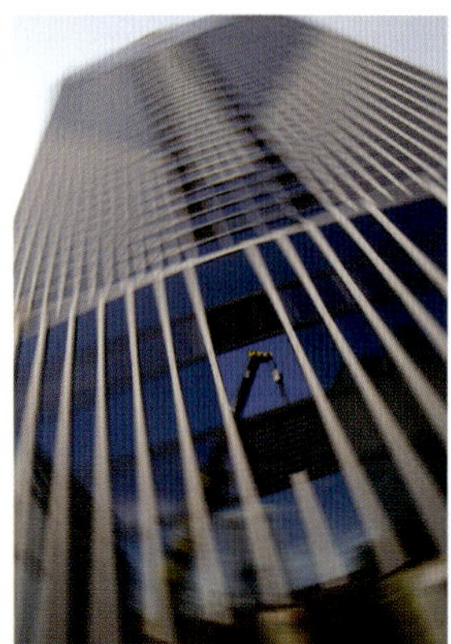
Shutter speed: 1/40 second

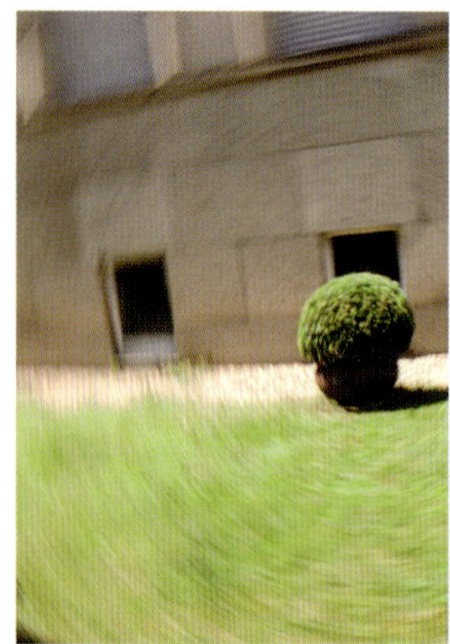
Shutter speed: 1/80 second

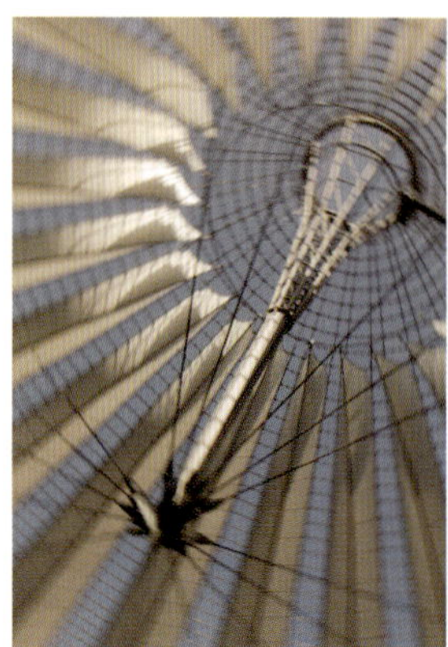
Shutter speed: 1/100 second

It's best to move the camera in the same direction as the prominent characteristics of the contrast, rather than perpendicular to them. Otherwise, you'll end up with blurred patches instead of dynamic traces of movement. Straight stripes don't need to be the only design you create with this technique; waves and shapes work well, too.

You can also combine this process with the use of a flash, which photographers usually synchronize to the second shutter. The extremely brief flash will capture a sharp image of the subject at the end of the exposure time, while the ambient light will illuminate the traces of movement throughout the duration of the exposure—an exciting combination.

You can pan the camera during an exposure and combine it with a flash, which results in a dramatic combination of blurred motion and a sharp subject. The flash fires for only a brief moment and freezes the subject. To achieve more natural results, synchronize the flash with the second shutter so the traces of movement lead up to the stationary subject, not away from it.

One thing to keep in mind with these creative techniques is that you should always move your camera evenly and in one specific direction, or in geometric shapes, to make sure your results look intentional. Otherwise viewers may think your images are faulty or unsuccessful. One exception here is the technique called tossing: especially brave photographers launch their cameras into the air with a spin while an image is exposed. Then, hopefully, they catch the camera. This creates the thrill of an image designed 100 percent by chance. That's one thing that all of these experiments have in common: chance, to some degree, influences each image and makes it impossible to reproduce the exact results.

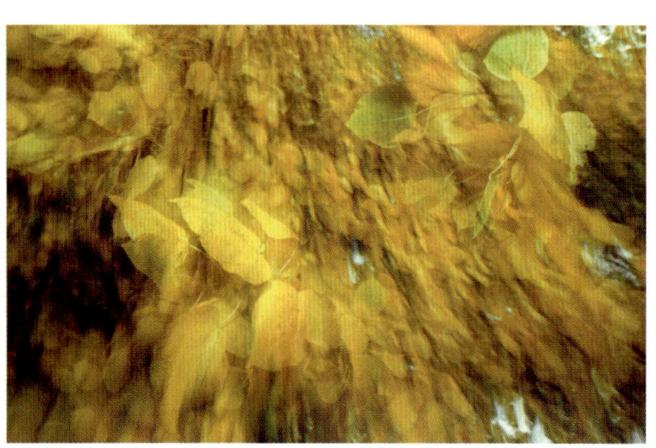
Shutter speed: 1/30 second

Producing photos with these techniques is fun, and you will be rewarded with interesting results that are lively, emotional, dynamic, and artistic. When you bring out these qualities further through dynamic post-processing work, you can produce images that abound with joie de vivre.

When you take pictures with these creative techniques, decide how much abstraction you're willing to accept. Long exposure times and fast camera movements can result in significantly blurred images with completely unrecognizable subjects. This sort of image captures the viewer's attention only when it features rich contrasts and colors. Dull images can't grab the viewer's attention if the central subject is no longer recognizable.

Motion Blur

It is both a similar and a different situation when the subject, not the camera, moves. The biggest difference is that only one specific part of the image is in motion instead of the entire area. Since the surroundings, the background, and other visual elements remain static, the same goal applies here as with stationary subjects: hold the camera as steady as possible. Motion blur is the photographic method of choice when you want to convey a feeling of movement in this totally motionless medium.

The shutter speed you choose is dependent on both the speed and direction of the subject's movement. A shutter speed of 1/500 second may be fast enough to capture a slow jogger without any noticeable motion blur, but if you are shooting a car race on a long straightaway, that shutter speed will produce nothing but a colorful stripe across your photo. The direction the object is moving also makes an enormous difference. The motion will be much more perceptible if it's moving perpendicular to the camera, and you will need a much shorter exposure to capture the same amount of blur as if it were moving parallel to the lens. The distance between the camera and the subject also plays an important role; the farther away your subject is, the less perceptible its movement will be.

With so many factors, there isn't a formula to achieve an exact amount of blur. It requires simple trial and error. For a one-off snapshot, you'll have to make your best guess. If you apply this design method more often, you can analyze the results on your camera monitor.

If a subject is moving, slow shutter speeds can permit a portion of your image to be in focus while other portions are blurry. For viewers to make heads or tails of your image, the central subject still needs to have a distinguishable shape, color, or structure. The appropriate exposure time depends on the speed and direction of the moving subject and the distance between it and the camera. The contrast between the sharp and unsharp elements in the image establishes the movement of the subject, not the camera.

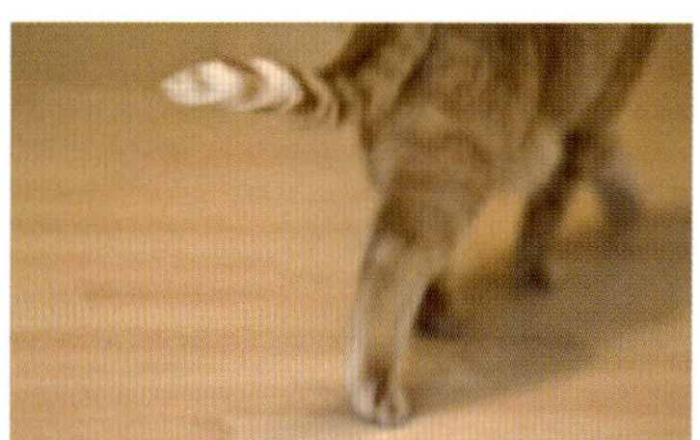

Shutter speed: 1/20 second

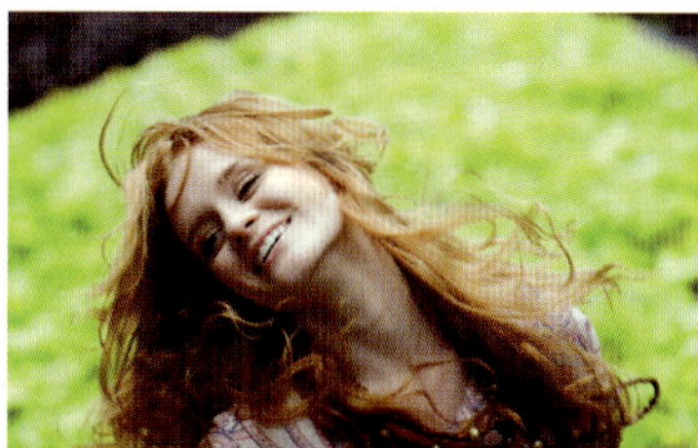

Shutter speed: 1/40 second

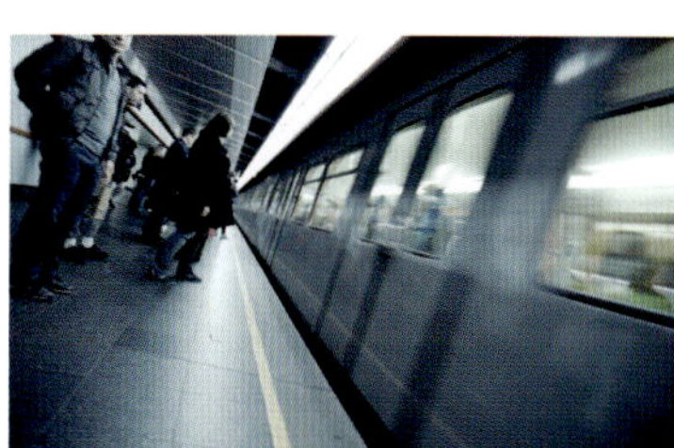

Shutter speed: 1/25 second

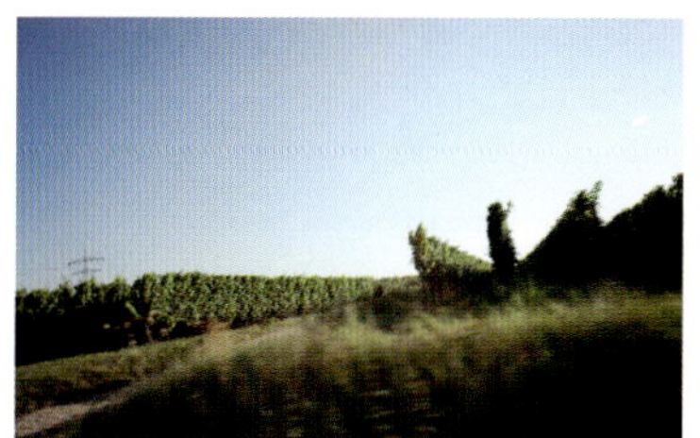

Shutter speed: 1/200 second

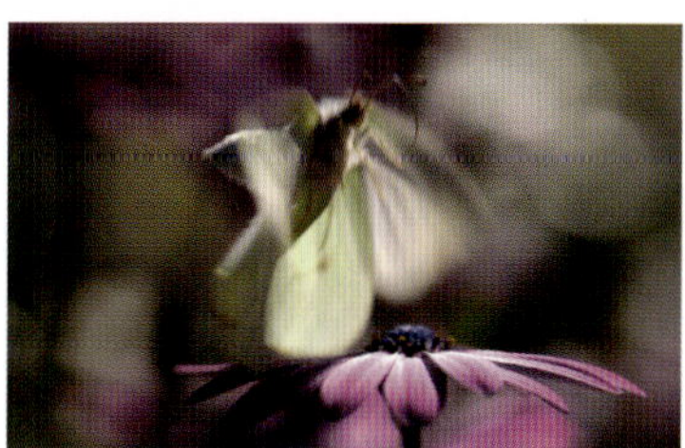

Shutter speed: 1/400 second

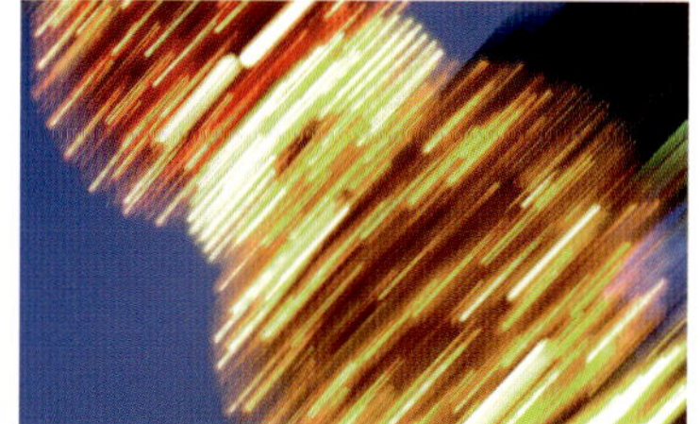

Shutter speed: 1/30 second

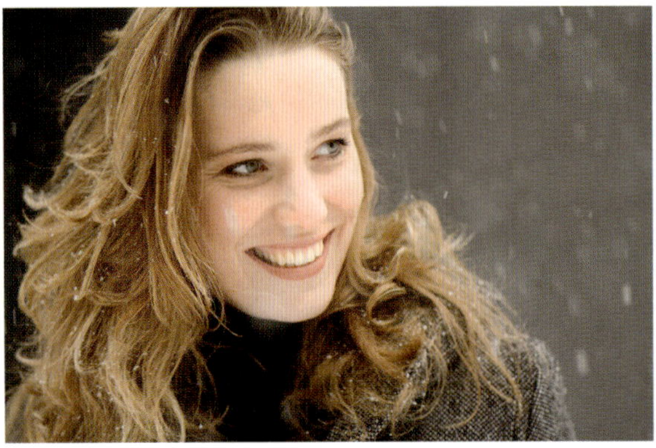

Shutter speed: 1/125 second

The snowflakes fall throughout the duration of the exposure and create little white stripes in the background. Without the flakes on the subject's hair and jacket, viewers wouldn't be able to tell whether it was snowing or raining. The length of the stripes is directly dependent on the exposure time. Choosing an exposure time that is ideal for your subject is purely a matter of personal taste.

The longer the exposure time, the stronger the motion blur effect will feel. How strongly to apply the effect is a matter of taste, but viewers should still be able to recognize what is in the photo so they can process the movement. If they can't recognize the context, they'll be looking at a blurry patch that will seem abstract, at best, and defective, at worst. A higher level of blurring can be applied to subjects that have distinguishing colors or outlines than subjects that depend on details for recognition. For example, viewers will quickly be able to decipher a person dancing, but the trace of movement following a monotone ball could be perceived as anything.

When you attempt to capture motion blur, keep in mind that not all parts of a subject move at the same speed. Points near the center of a moving body move slower than those near the outside. The arms and legs of a jogger will be more blurred than the torso—a horse's mane will exhibit the same effect. You can make use of this to add a touch of motion blur that hints at movement.

Success with this type of photography depends on chance and a degree of luck, since you can't plan every aspect of your shot. But you can and should take multiple pictures, ideally at different shutter speeds, and then choose the image that suits you best. This is easiest when you can shoot the same movement repeatedly.

The effect of images that feature motion blur corresponds to the way we perceive such movements. The human eye doesn't see all the details on a moving object, so this effect seems normal—in fact, it makes an image more credible. It also means that we tend to give these types of images less attention than if the motion were frozen, because we have a heightened sense of awareness for unusual details or scenes. Keep these factors in mind when you decide to expose an image with motion blur so you can be sure that your subject is well suited for this treatment.

Freezing Motion

The process is much different when you use a very brief exposure to capture one specific moment from a sweep of motion. The result is similar to pressing the pause button while watching a DVD; the subject is frozen in space, and instead of seeing the whole movement, you see an image that looks like a single pane of a comic strip. For this type of photo to work, the viewer needs to be able to infer motion from the pose or the context. Otherwise, it will look like a conventional snapshot. Movement is at play even in classical portraits, but we're not supposed to perceive it. A person's facial expressions change in fractions of a second, and the camera captures one specific expression of many. Nevertheless, we view a portrait in which the subject is

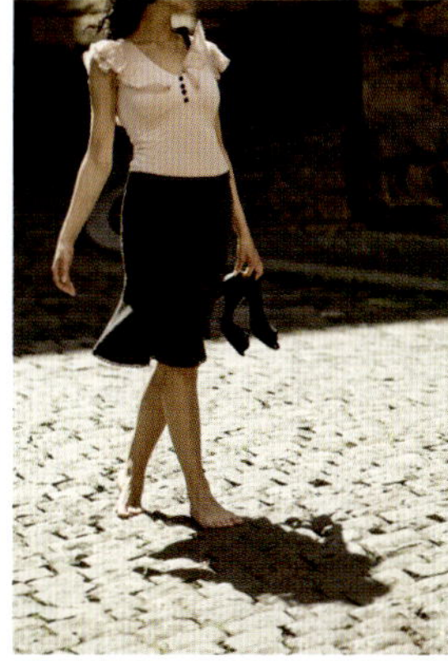

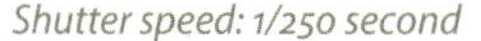
Shutter speed: 1/250 second

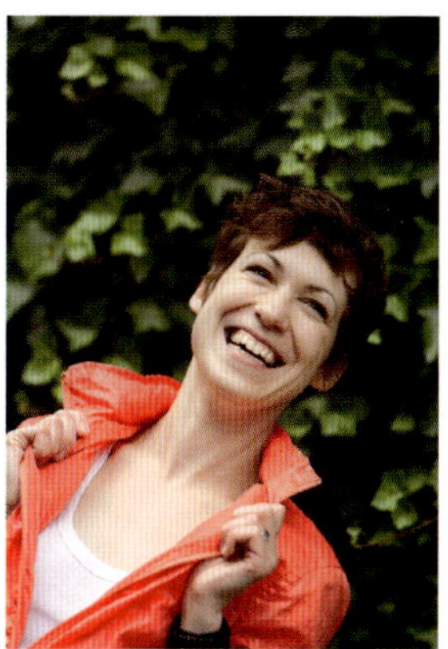
Shutter speed: 1/320 second

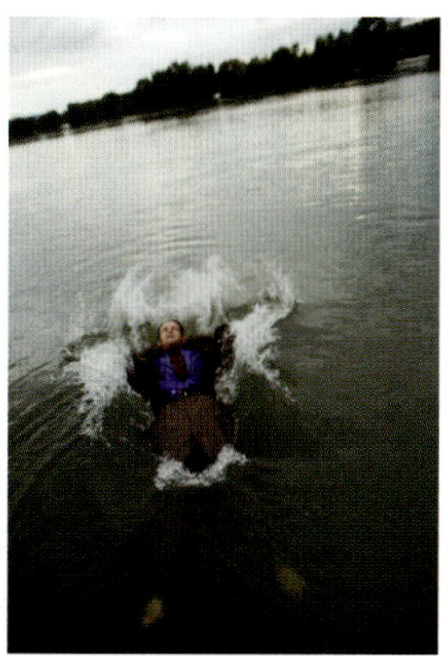
Shutter speed: 1/250 second

Frozen movements always seem somewhat artificial, since our eyes aren't capable of pausing real events. This makes it all the more exciting to study frozen movements and facial expressions.

not smiling as motionless. The art of portraiture comes from capturing the moment when the subject's expression represents a specific mood. Visually freezing a subject requires that you select a shutter speed that's faster than the subject's movement. Since the same factors influence the end result for portraits and motion blur images, you should experiment to get the results you want. It can be very difficult to expose an image of a moving subject correctly because fast shutter speeds require lots of light. The flash on your camera is ideal for this application, as are studio flash units. A flash emits very bright light at exceptionally quick speeds: 1/2000 to 1/60,000 second. This is fast enough to freeze the motion of a hummingbird's wings.

Focusing on fast-moving subjects is a challenge because only a few cameras have an autofocus that reacts quickly enough. If you can predict your subject's path of travel, it's often easiest to manually set the focus in advance. Use the smallest possible aperture for a large depth of field; this will compensate for focusing inaccuracies when the right moment comes.

Unusual images always attract attention, which is why a quickly moving subject that's frozen in an image is an eye-catcher—we can examine something that we can't see with our own eyes. Photos like these are truly fascinating. Viewers linger on them and absorb every detail so they can analyze the movement of the subject. The technical appeal of these images is strong. They come across as striking and artificial, in contrast to images that feature perceptible motion blur.

An image must include clues for viewers to understand that a subject was in motion at the time of capture. Familiar gestures, floating objects or people, typical situations that include movement, perceptible deformations, or an unstable composition can serve as clues.

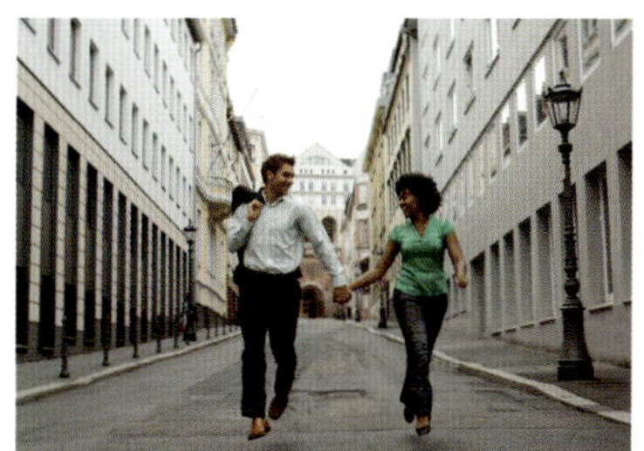
Shutter speed: 1/650 second

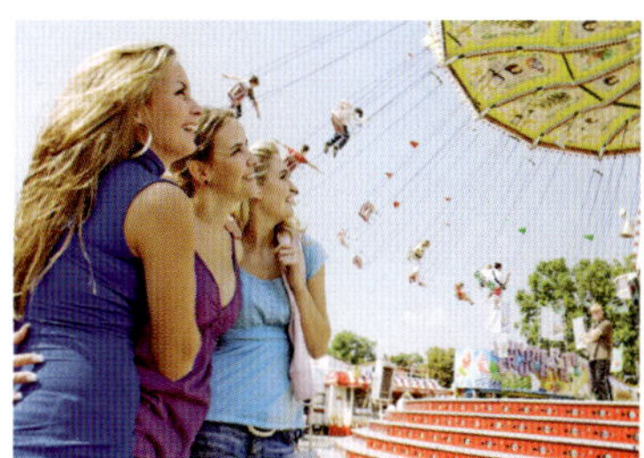
Shutter speed: 1/500 second

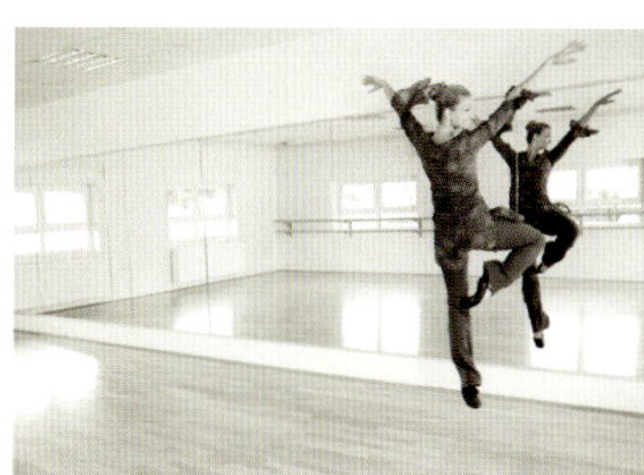
Shutter speed: 1/80 second

Panning is a complex technique that produces somewhat unpredictable results. The moving object should be sharp in front of a blurred background. The direction of movement must be parallel to the motion of your camera. (Photo: Werner Seeger)

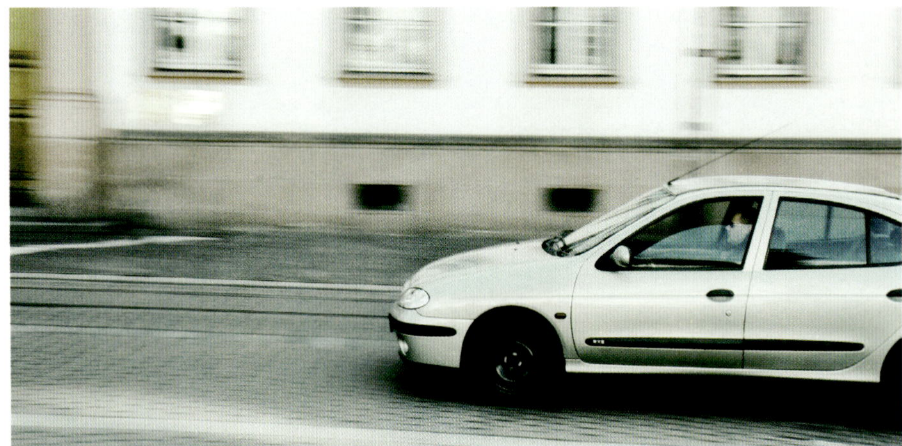

Shutter speed: 1/40 second

Panning with Motion

One design approach that mixes freezing and motion blur to achieve exciting results involves panning your camera parallel to the movement of your subject. Your subject needs to remain at a relatively constant distance from your camera for this technique to work. Exposing an image while you pan along with the subject keeps the subject mostly in focus in front of an evenly blurred and striped background. This unusual result commands attention. It is realistic because it functions the same way as our perception when we're sitting in a fast car or train. These kinds of images are particularly engaging because they convey both motion and speed.

The main challenge of this technique is smooth, even panning, to avoid unwanted movement. It requires practice and a steady hand. Make sure you have firm footing, and start turning your entire upper body before you press the shutter-release button to minimize any shaking.

However you decide to capture movement in your images, look for exciting subjects. Capture the fleeting moment and make it clearly visible, or experiment with long exposure times and introduce liveliness and chance into your images to create intrigue.

We're familiar with the general progression of many movements, such as throwing a ball. We don't need to capture every step of the process to perceive the motion. Here, three frames corresponding to different parts of the action are enough to help us visualize the entire sequence.

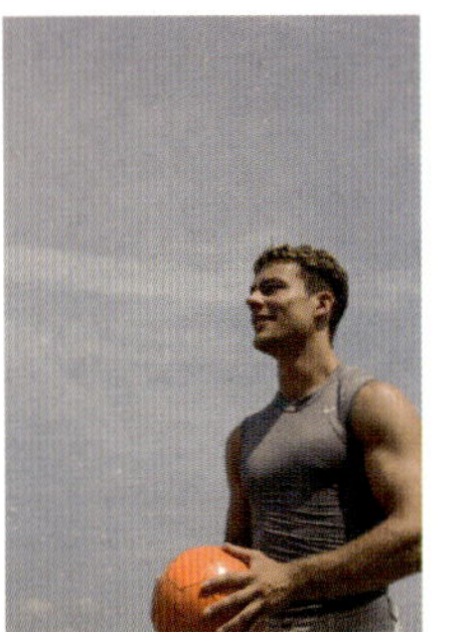

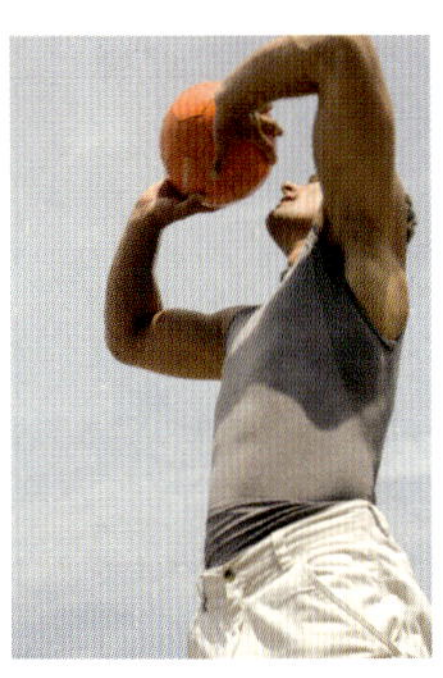

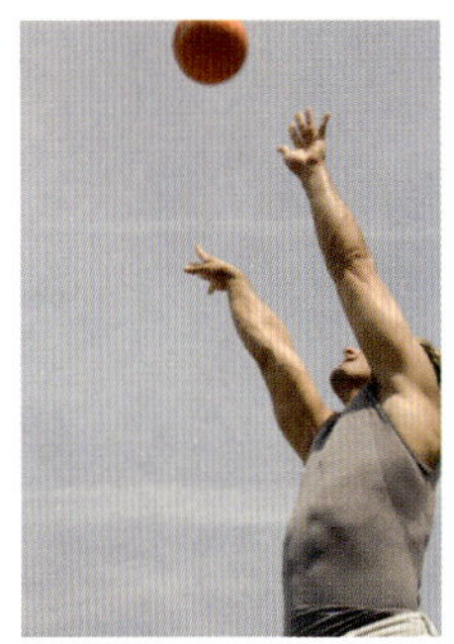

Shutter speed: 1/400 second

Image Sequences

If you don't limit yourself to a single frame, there is another way to capture motion: sequences. Collections of images are a unique way to convey a chronological process. Viewers can consider the movement within each image without being limited to a certain chronology—they can wander back and forth within the time frame portrayed by the series of images.

When you create an image sequence, the time frame is up to you. It may last only a couple of seconds, or it may be as long as days or months or years; the sequences can be designed to capture fast or slow movements. If your time frame is a matter of seconds, use your camera's burst mode, which allows you to expose several images in quick succession by holding down the shutter-release button. Longer spans of time likely require a tripod, which you can set up in exactly the same place each time to capture the identical image area.

The number of frames to include in your sequence varies. When it is done well, two exposures are often enough to convey an entire motion. It's more common, and often more interesting, to see sequences of three or more photos.

Video

Many digital cameras can record videos (see *Learning to Photograph Vol.1*), which is another way to capture motion. Time is introduced as a fourth dimension, and movement becomes the main focus. Single frames are briefly visible as frozen stills, but the entire, cohesive motion is the center of attention. This medium is much different than photography because it does not require special design methods to convey motion.

There are separate methods of design for video recording, such as time, sound, and editing. In a video, you can develop narrative suspense, which is not accessible with traditional photography.

The continuous shooting or burst mode on your camera allows you to capture more than individual steps of movement. When sequenced images are viewed one after another, they can tell a story in the same way that a video can. Georg observed this situation in Ireland; one person's hesitation leads to the amusing climax of this little comic picture story.

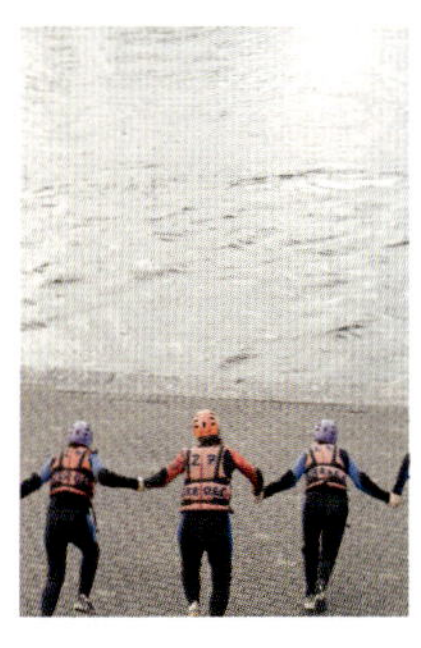
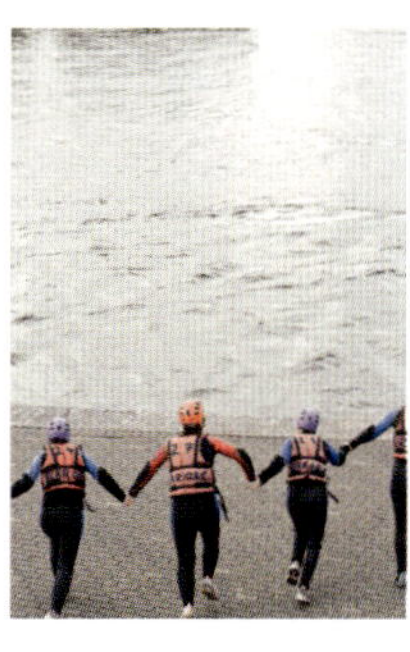
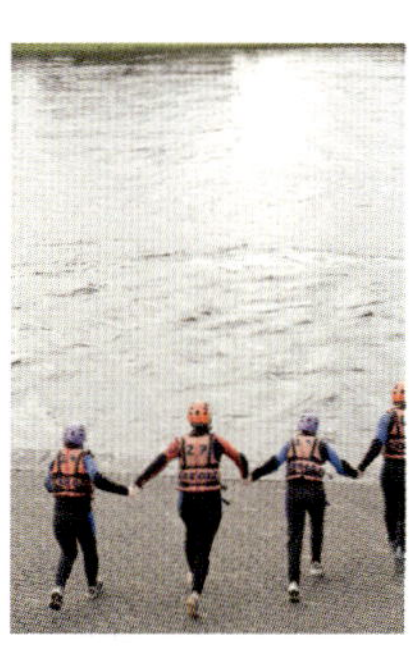
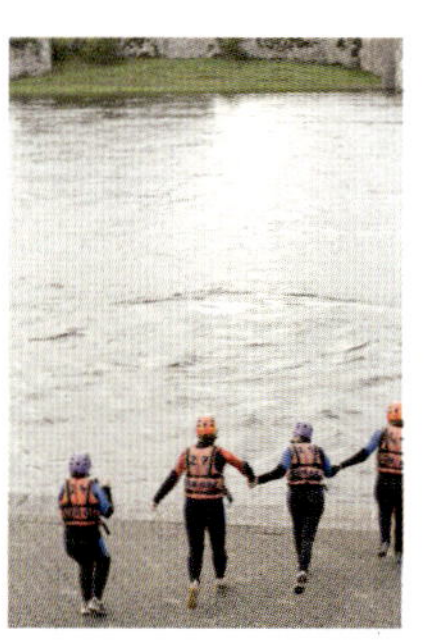
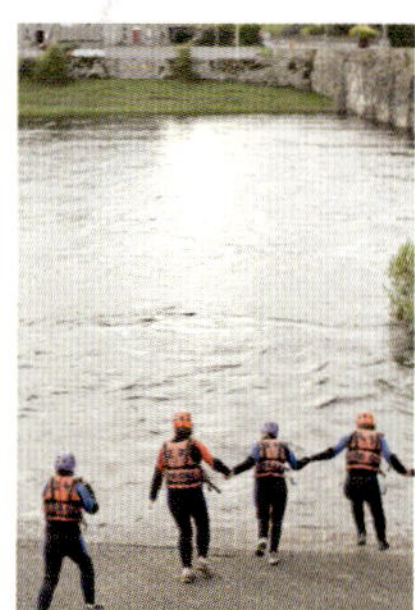
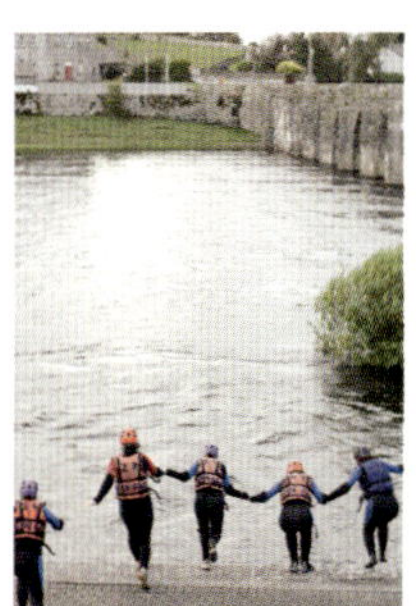
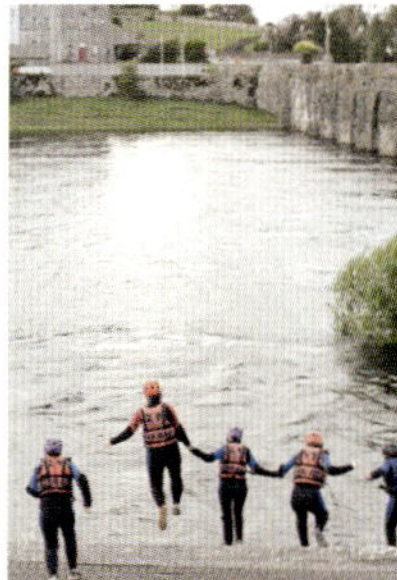
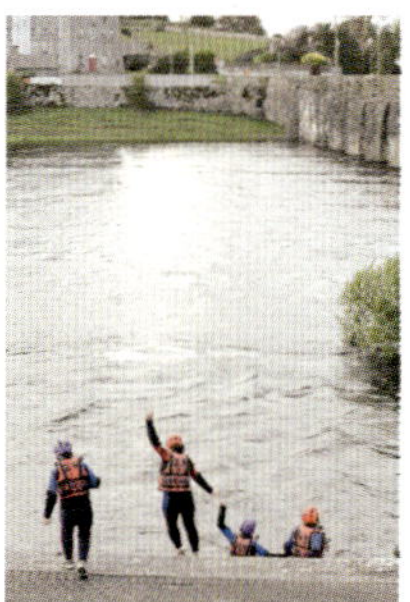
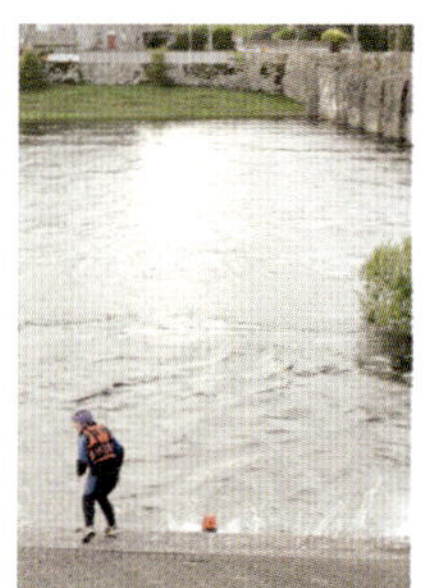
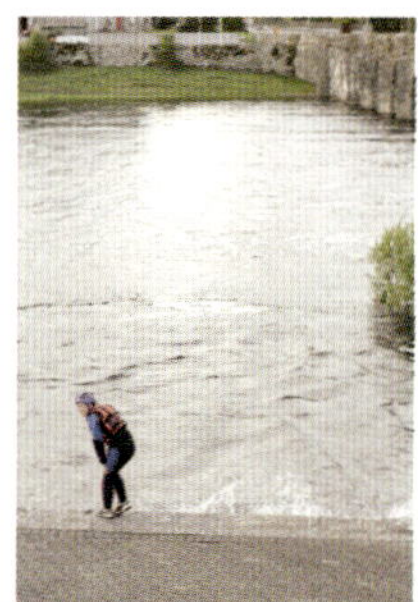

Shutter speed: 1/250 second

"A carefully planned photo will only be truly great when it leaves some room for chance." Jo van den Berg, Belgian commercial photographer

08 The Overall Effect

In the previous chapters we took a detailed look at the individual building blocks of image design. We considered all the applications for each method and analyzed how they work. To be as explicit as possible in our discussion, we assumed that, in any given image, only one variable would change while all others remained constant. This isn't how photographers work in practice, however; multiple design elements are usually in play at the same time, even when one particular aspect of a photo's design tends to dominate the others.

This chapter looks at the simultaneous interplay of all design tools. They don't always combine in the same way, and it's not possible to explain how a photo functions with any sort of mathematical proof; this can be done critically only on a case-by-case basis because it requires qualitative judgment. There are, however, various principles that help us analyze the overall effect of an image. These principles don't always give an image clear meaning—images are often ambiguous—but they do help us figure out what's at work in an image on a global level.

The presentation of an image also affects how it is received. When you expose an image, you can anticipate how and in what context it will be presented to help you decide on specific, targeted effects. In the end, it's all about how you employ different design methods to influence viewers. With time, you'll develop your own personal photographic style without even realizing it.

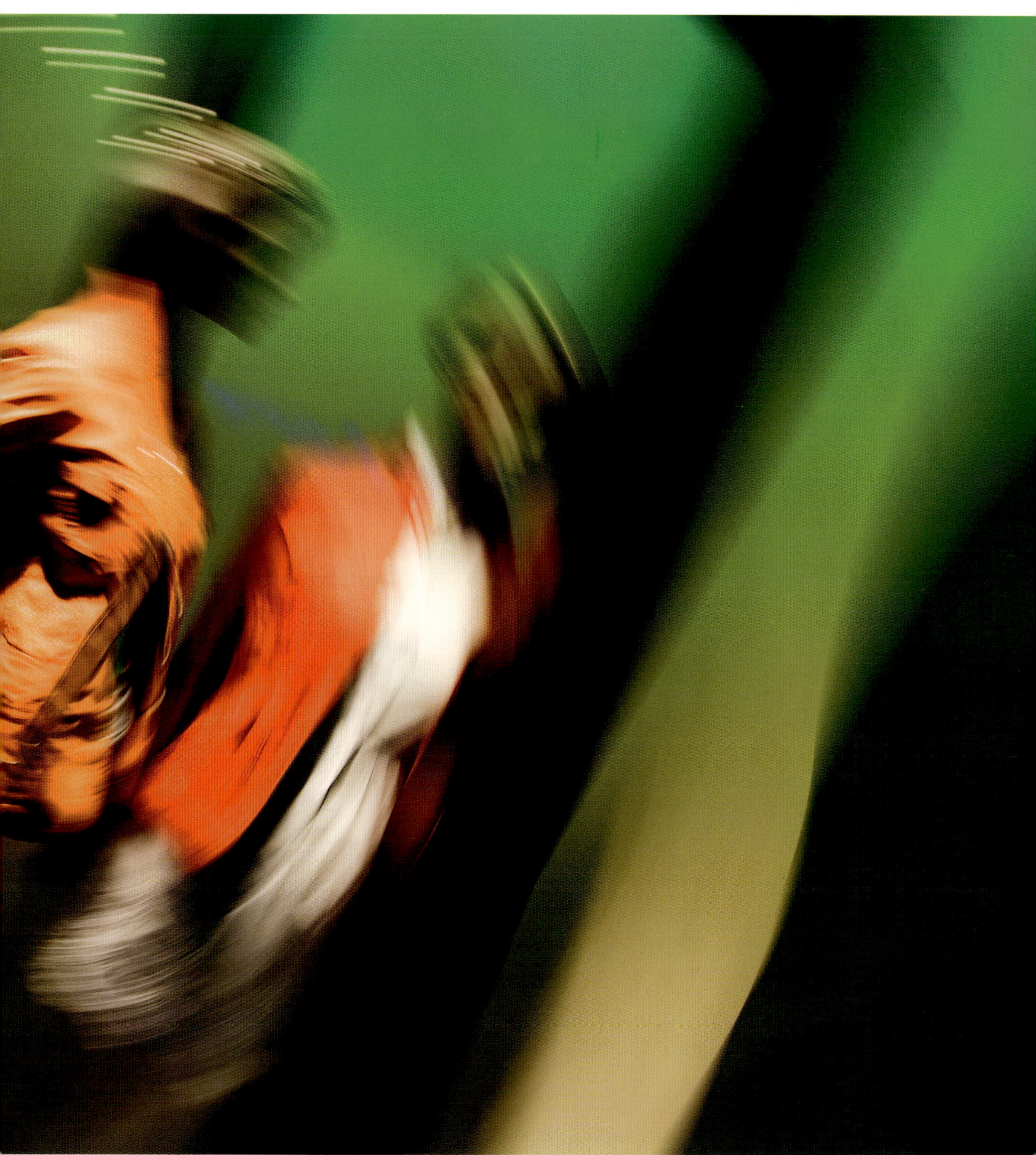

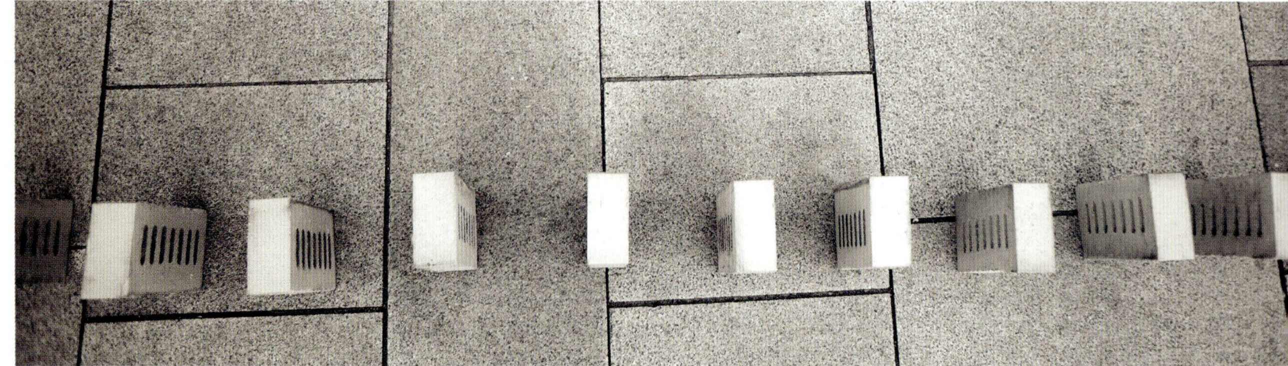

8.1 The Interplay of Design Elements

Every image exhibits all of the design elements on a basic level, even when some are much more prominent than others. Without a defined image area, an arrangement of elements, a certain level of sharpness, and a definite perspective, you don't have an image. The same is true if there isn't a clear and functional arrangement of lines in an image. Lines are required in the same way that colors are—even black-and-white images can be thought of as desaturated color.

This doesn't mean you need to make conscious and deliberate decisions about each building block for every photograph. You won't always have time for this sort of calculation; you may be shooting instinctively or for the purpose of documentation. The design elements in most images are determined subconsciously or by chance. Nevertheless, each particular design quality exists individually, and together they give rise to a very specific effect.

The Model of Visual Impact

Combined aspects of image design create a formal, comprehensive effect for the entire image. The individual pieces can't be simply added together because we're not dealing with mathematical values or quantifiable units; rather, they are qualitative characteristics. Every design element plays its own role within the overall impact of an image. The size of the role depends both on the nature of the design element and the power of the other elements. Consider a prominent line. If it is thick, long, and dark, it will make a stronger impression than a thin, light line would in the same position. If the image also features large areas of primary colors, a selective depth of field, and multiple circles, then even the conspicuous line would have a hard time competing for attention.

A universal formula is no help in identifying the most prominent design features of an image, and neither is ranking the impact of different techniques. Each individual

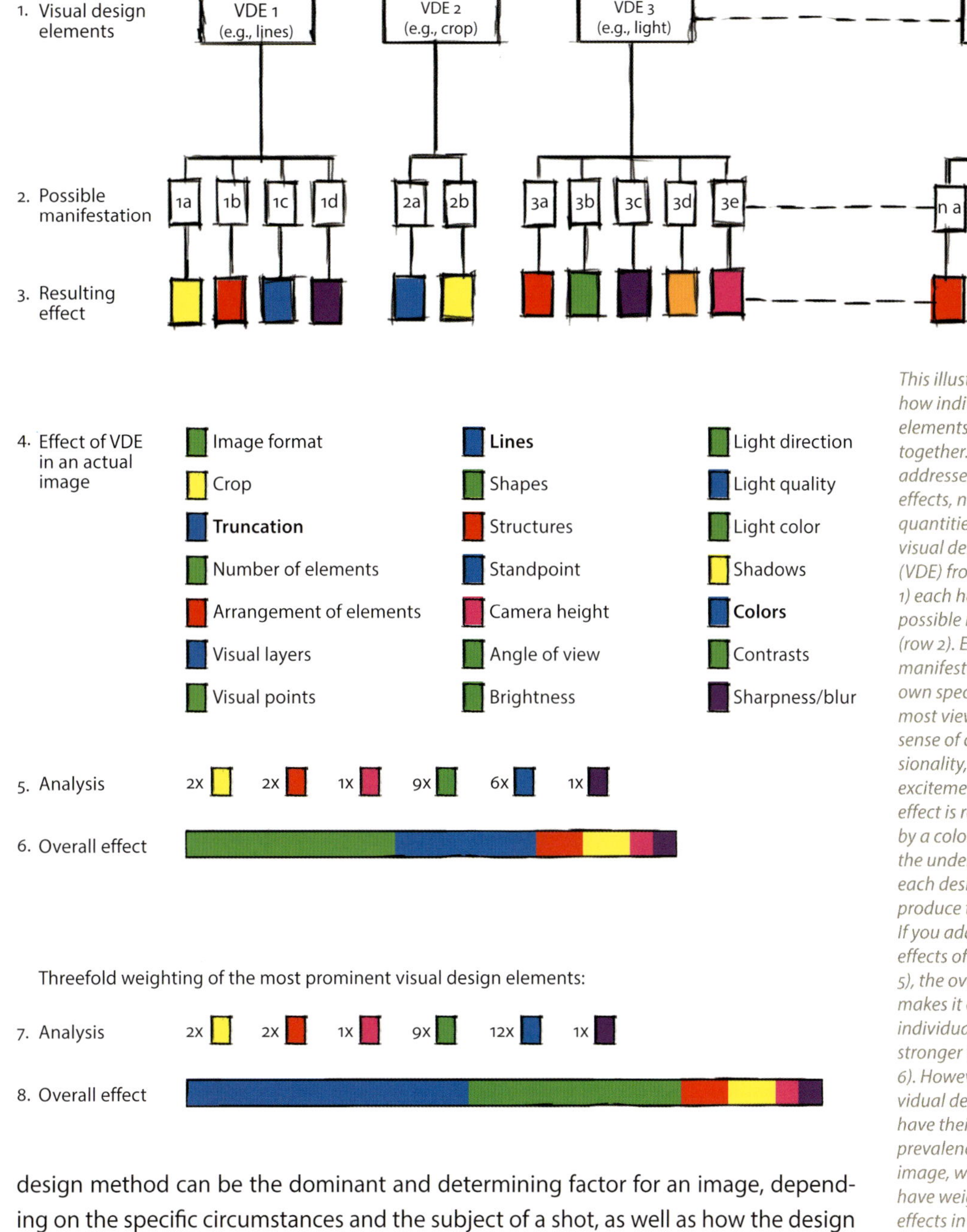

This illustration shows how individual design elements can work together. Note that it addresses qualitative effects, not measurable quantities. The individual visual design elements (VDE) from 1 to n (row 1) each have several possible manifestations (row 2). Each individual manifestation has its own specific impact on most viewers, such as a sense of calm, dimensionality, softness, or excitement. Every visual effect is represented by a color (row 3), with the understanding that each design method can produce the same effect. If you add the individual effects of an image (row 5), the overall effect makes it clear that some individual elements are stronger than others (row 6). However, the individual design methods have their own respective prevalence within the image, which is why we have weighted three effects in this example (row 7). This resulted in a shift in the order of the most dominant individual effects (row 8).

design method can be the dominant and determining factor for an image, depending on the specific circumstances and the subject of a shot, as well as how the design choice was applied. In a given context, any one characteristic, or multiple characteristics, may stand out more than the rest and be the dominant factor in how an image is perceived. Conversely, if the weight of the various design features is evenly balanced, no particular design attribute will dominate the image.

It's also possible—but not likely—that all of the design elements in a single image create uniform results, like a sense of calm or unrest, for example. Such a one-sided image would be monotonous and uninteresting. Most images exhibit at least a few contradictory qualities. Some elements may quiet an image while others escalate suspense or intensity. The relative weight of each individual element determines whether the overall effect is dynamic, balanced, or calm, since the individual effects both counteract and augment one another.

The overall impact of combined design elements needs to be analyzed and interpreted—it can't be objectively calculated or measured. Design elements work together in complex ways, and the subjectivity of our perception (page 22) and evaluation (page 218) makes it impossible for us to summarize them in absolute and universal terms.

Finally, the content of the image comes into play when you analyze the total effect of an image design. This is why, for example, you would be much more interested in, and much more likely to praise a photo of your own child than a picture of a stranger's child, no matter how the two images were designed. The same goes for all subjects; when viewers find the content of an image interesting, they are more likely to engage deeply with the photo.

There are many diverse and complex factors that influence the impact of an image, but this doesn't mean that every possible interpretation of an image is correct. A structured and thorough analysis will support a coherent and conclusive argument for each picture, which lends truth to the statement that a specific image works in a specific way for a specific group of people in a specific context. An image does not work in the same way for everyone.

Imagery research, which investigates how we perceive external images and how we generate, process, and store them internally, has led to some fascinating discover-

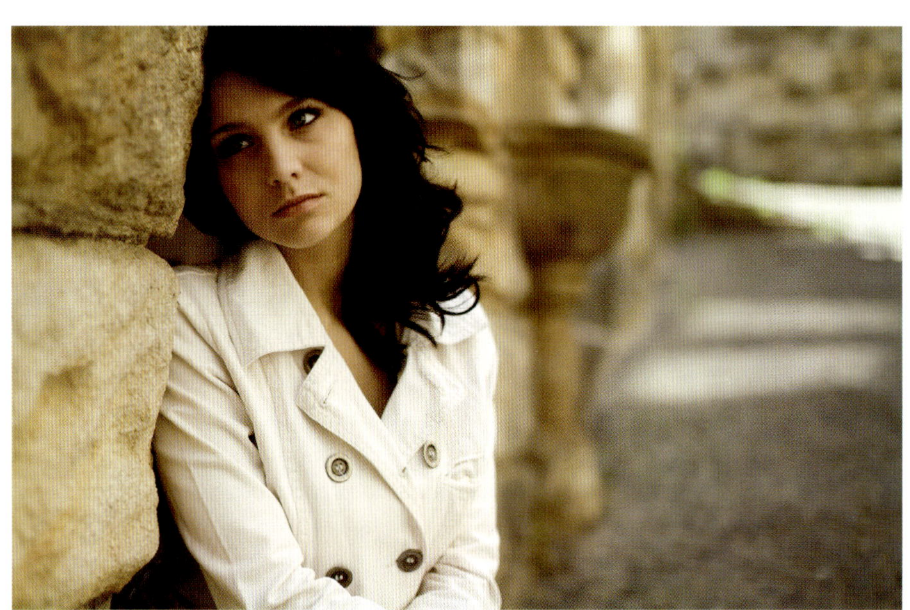

In terms of content, this image has a calm effect because the weight of the surroundings is reduced and nothing detracts from the model. Her expression is peaceful, introspective, and perhaps a touch melancholy. The formal design of the image, particularly the warm colors, allows the pleasant peacefulness of the scene to come to the foreground, rather than the cool, distanced loneliness that could be perceived based on the content alone. The distribution of sharpness and the strong chromatic/achromatic contrast clearly directs the viewer's attention to the model, who is framed by the sections of the wall in front of and behind her. Her hair functions as a frame for her face, which directs the eye to her facial expression and her bright eyes. The details of her coat and the interplay of light and shadow in the background encourage the eye to wander away from the model and take in the rest of the photo before returning to her once again.

ies that may help you with image design. Scientists have proven that images have more impact under the following conditions:

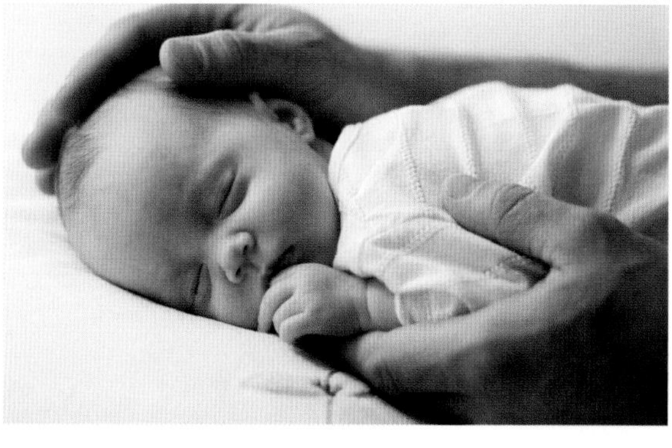

The content of some images appeals so strongly to viewers that the formal design aspects become a secondary concern. This is the case with babies and pets, for example. Rather than falling completely by the wayside, however, visual design in these types of images separates memento pictures from images that are interesting beyond their content.

- The content is concrete
- The content is emotional
- Specific emotions are revealed
- The content can be quickly processed
- The subject can be seen in its entirety
- The subject is large
- The level of complexity is low
- The image is in color
- The dominant lines are positioned horizontally or vertically
- The subject is oriented near the middle or the top of the image area
- The image is designed to stand alone

The Dimensions of Impact

Images usually have an impact on multiple continuums. For example, an image could simultaneously be classified between calm and tense, static and full of motion, tender and harsh, or natural and artificial. There can be many of these dimensions within a single image, depending on its content and the photographer's desired effect. Some examples are as follows: peaceful and disordered, natural and artificial, pleasing and jarring, still and in motion, tender and harsh, quiet and loud, heavy and light, credible and implausible, dynamic and static, near and far, exciting and boring, rich in contrast and monotonous, complex and simple, definite and ambiguous, chaotic and ordered, clean and confused.

Analyzing Impact

An image's design and content influence its overall impact in different ways. Images in which the design and the content are in agreement form an unambiguous message, and are easiest to understand. A little blonde girl in a ruffled dress standing in a meadow of wildflowers with bright light and gentle colors is just as coherent as a portrait-oriented, image-filling snarling tiger head with bright colors and sharp contrast—one image is fairytale-like and tender, the other is dramatic and dangerous.

It's much more rare for a photo to succeed at exhibiting multiple interpretive possibilities that require viewers to draw on their background knowledge and internal perspective. These images function similarly to optical illusions that reveal different subjects based on how viewers look at them. Portraits, in particular, are capable of rich ambiguity, especially when they are considered within a specific context; in one

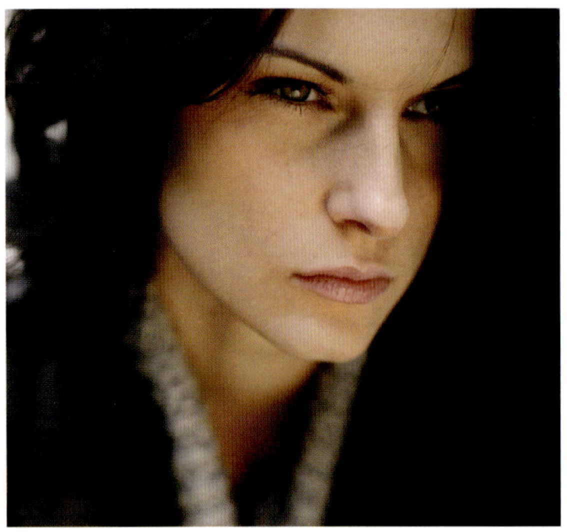

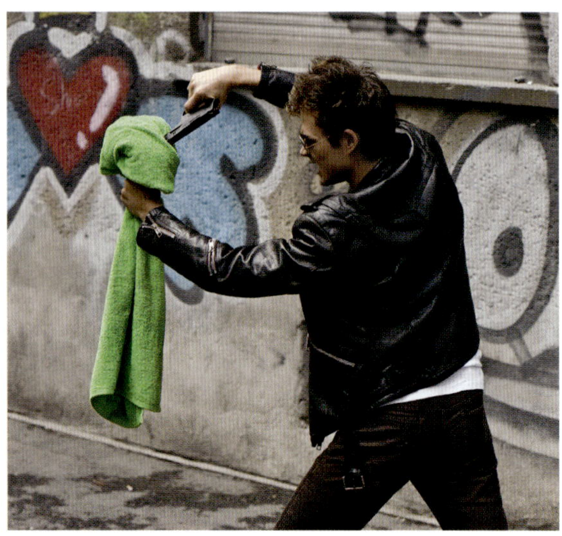

The expression of the young woman in the left image is not easy to decode because it doesn't obviously stand out as one particular emotion. There are hints of longing, sadness, vulnerability, and strength, which forces viewers to decide. The unsettled tone in the right image recalls the feeling of a snapshot and produces a sense of aggression and unrest that suits the violent gesture. Only after viewers recognize that the victim in the scene is a towel does their perception change—the image takes on an absurd tone.

image, a person may seem angry, introspective, and melancholy at once. It's more rare still for photos to succeed at exhibiting a coherent and balanced contradiction through its design elements. The individual aspects of the contradiction may seem equally matched, but on another level, they take on new meaning. This is similar to how you might think about the book *Animal Farm* by George Orwell. Animals can't talk, of course, nor can they work and build a social structure. But when you consider the story as a parable for the emergence of a totalitarian regime, everything fits together. Similarly, photography can exploit initially bewildering design elements to direct the viewer's attention to a hidden meaning or an additional level of content that is apparent only after deep engagement with the photo.

For images like this to work, they have to be well-balanced so viewers don't consciously notice anything at first. Their subconscious might detect that something doesn't fit, but the contradiction shouldn't be so obvious that they notice it immediately. If they do, chances are they will think the image was poorly composed and their perception process will break down (page 22). For example, imagine a photo of a man who's staring self-assuredly and arrogantly into the camera. Now imagine that the camera is positioned noticeably above the subject so he is forced to look up. His confident facial expression and his subordinate body position contradict each other, but a couple of possibilities can resolve this tension. Either he is so self-confident that he overcomes great obstacles, or his arrogance is a façade, and the view of him from above exposes his insecurity.

These types of photos generally don't offer a coherently whole effect. Often the visual design poses contradictions within itself, or the style doesn't mesh well with the subject. The majority of snapshots fall into this category, and, for the most part, viewers expect this lack of cohesion. This is why well-composed and unified images stand out from the masses.

Attention versus Credibility

On one hand, an image should capture the attention of viewers, draw in their gaze, and hold it as long as possible; on the other hand, the image should efficiently achieve a certain effect, tell a story, evoke emotion, and influence viewers. This is a cocktail of challenges, which presents a catch-22. The more likely it is that a formal image design will attract the viewer's attention, the less credible the image seems, and vice versa. Since objects and scenes that look natural tend to match our perception schema, they are more likely to affect us. At the same time, we pay less attention to these images and process them less fully. Conversely, visual designs that are new and potentially less credible are more alluring (page 22).

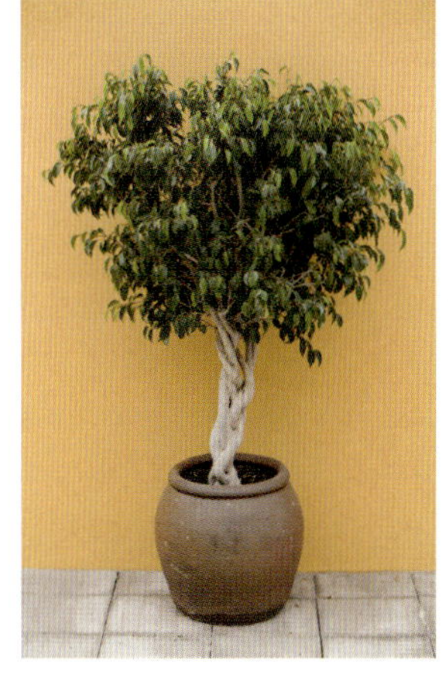

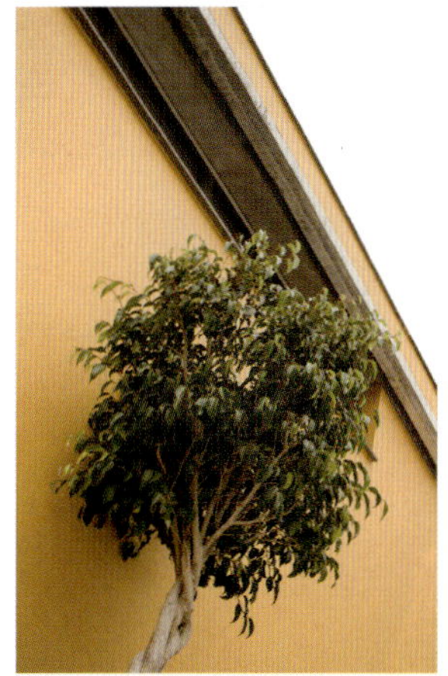

The image on the left is conventional and credible. It shows a tree in exactly the way that it appears in reality, which is neither interesting nor exciting. The image on the right, however, employs a creative design to boost the potential of the image to attract attention, but it gives up some of its authenticity. We don't assume that the tree is growing at a slant, but we can be sure that the lines of the building are actually straight.

The Interplay among Photos

If more than one photo is shown to a viewer at the same time—perhaps several or even an entire series of photos—an interplay of design and content will develop among the images, which will affect the message of each individual image. Images that stand out will dominate the others; they will not only attract longer and more frequent looks from the viewer, they will also be perceived as more important and will have a stronger overall impact. When various style or content consistencies exist among all or most of the images, the effects of the repeated characteristics are redoubled. This also means that dissimilar images presented together may weaken their respective effects, resulting in an unorganized, chaotic overall impression.

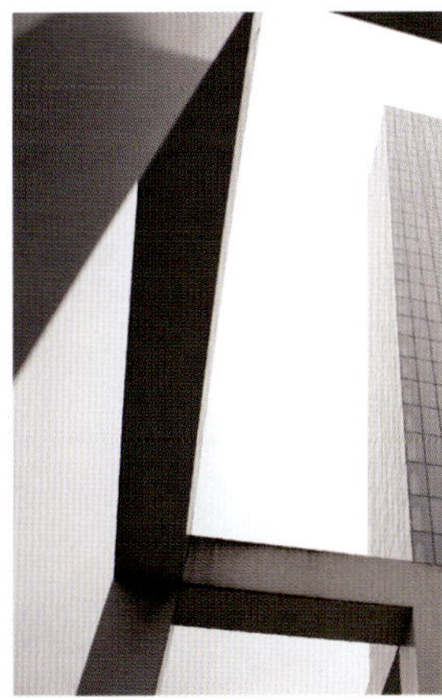

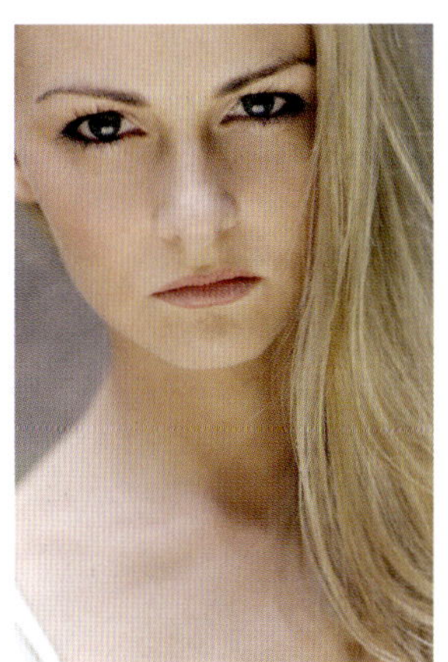

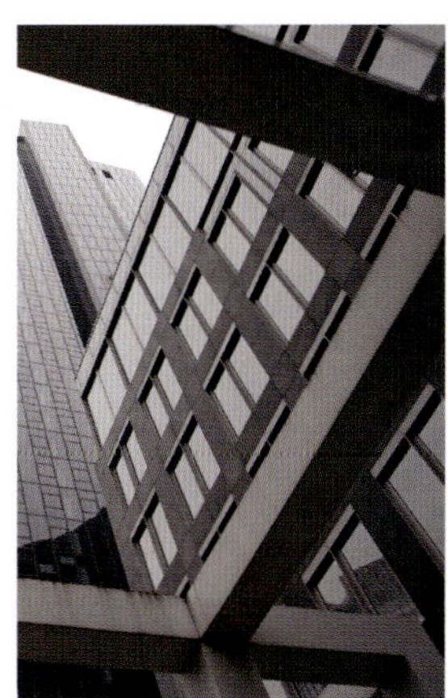

The model's gaze into the camera is cool and distanced. She looks pale, rational, and uninviting. The architectural motif surrounding her brings out the lines of her face; the colorlessness of the buildings also corresponds to her expression and overall look, and the extreme view from below makes her seem condescending and less emotional.

Regardless of if you're presenting two photos, a triptych, a series of images, an online portfolio, an exhibition, or a photo book, you should give thought to your collection. Try to achieve a relatively consistent image quality, or a weak link will stand out clearly and decrease the overall effect of the entire series. Similarly, exceptionally high-quality images will stick with the viewer longer, but they will also cast the rest of the images in an unfavorable light.

You also have to balance repetition and variety. Repeated motifs or design elements are essential to organizing images, establishing their cohesion, and presenting a unified collection. A similar or identical presentation for each image can also help. The more similarities there are among the images, the less likely your collection will surprise viewers with unexpected novelty. A dearth of variety makes any gallery of images monotonous, and the viewer will lose interest quickly. If there is too much variety, you'll lose the fundamental theme or characteristics that unify the images. The collection will be perceived as a motley group of single stills. The images in a collection need to have enough diversity to be perceived as individual works, but enough similarities to establish continuity and to convey the defining characteristics of the group. It's up to you to decide the balance based on your intentions.

Classical narrative techniques from literature and film become relevant when you combine several images in a group for the purpose of telling a story or illuminating various aspects of a theme. Overview versus detail, the type of shot, the arc of suspense, the narrative structure of comedy or tragedy—all of these devices apply to a photo essay. When you create conceptual images, devote some thought and planning to your series before you expose the first image. As in filmmaking, you can use a storyboard or a script to plan your photos.

When the same portrait is juxtaposed with gentle flowers, organic shapes, and soft colors, it looks much more tender and intimate than before. The red tones of the model's skin come out, and her complexion seems warmer even though the editing hasn't changed. The eye-level perspective seems less condescending, and the image has a friendlier look and feel.

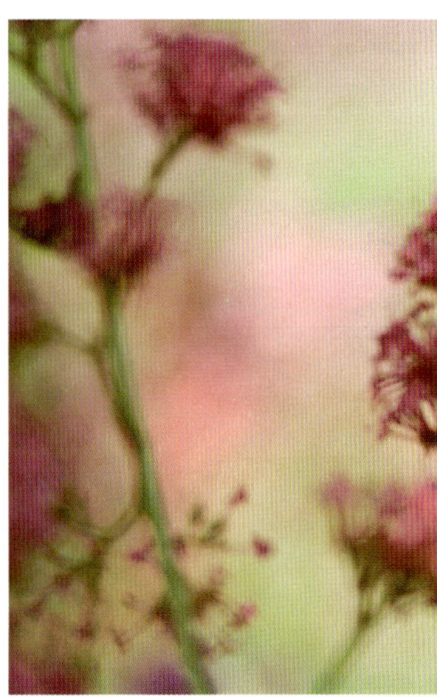

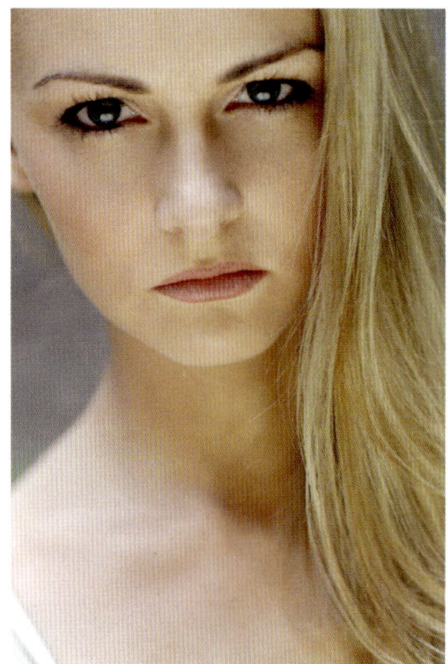

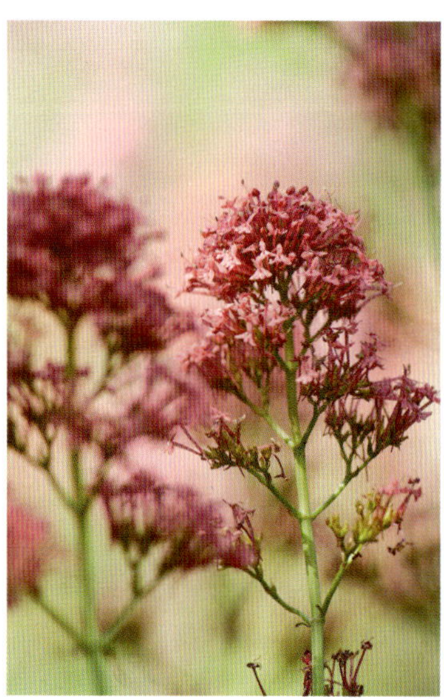

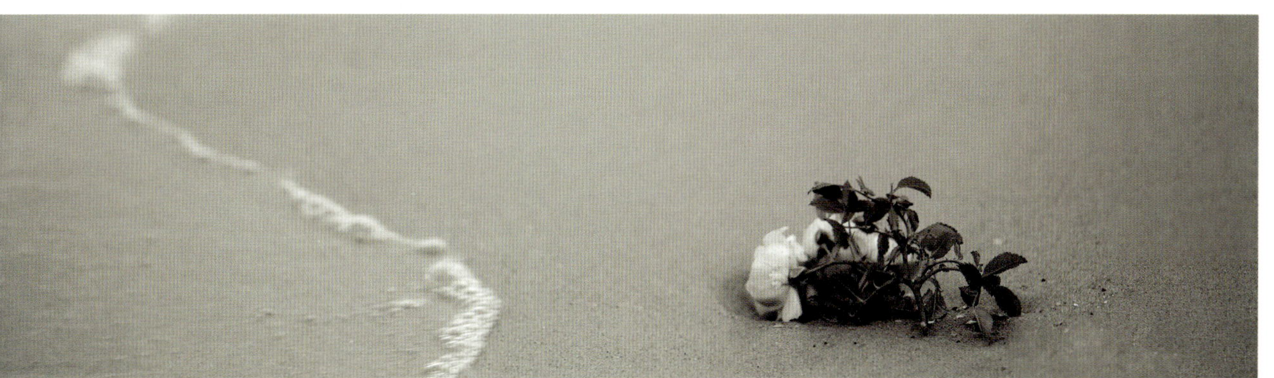

8.2 The Effect of the Setting

An image affects the viewer through its content and design—but that's not all. The way an image is presented and the thematic and situational environment in which the image is shown also influence how a viewer perceives a picture. The setting can influence a picture, even to the point of complete domination.

Frames and Matting

Trimming a photo with a frame or a mat enhances it. Even a snapshot seems elegant, high quality, and valuable if the photographer takes the time to frame it. It doesn't matter if the frame is made of wood or glass, or even pixels; frames and mats separate the image from its setting and allow it to function on its own. It is true, though, that a higher-quality frame will do more to enhance an image.

At the same time, adding a frame and a mat is akin to adding ornamentation to a photo. They elicit a response from the viewer and draw attention away from the image. This isn't too noticeable with simple frames, but more conspicuous frames can pull focus from the image, and in extreme cases, they can be the main attraction.

For these reasons, frames and matting should match your subject and your image, and they should also support your design. An ornate and gilded wood frame is just as incongruous with a modern portrait as a metallic digital frame paired

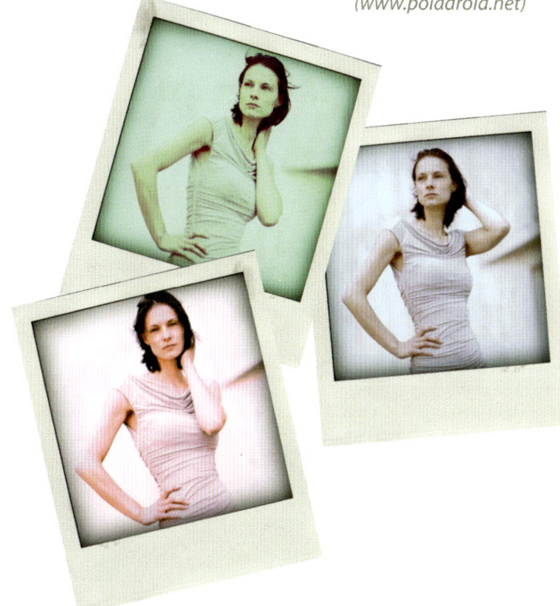

The presentation of these three images conveys a sense of spontaneity and imperfection because we can't help but compare them with Polaroid instant film exposures. The aesthetic is unmistakable—even when it's digitally reproduced. (www.poladroid.net)

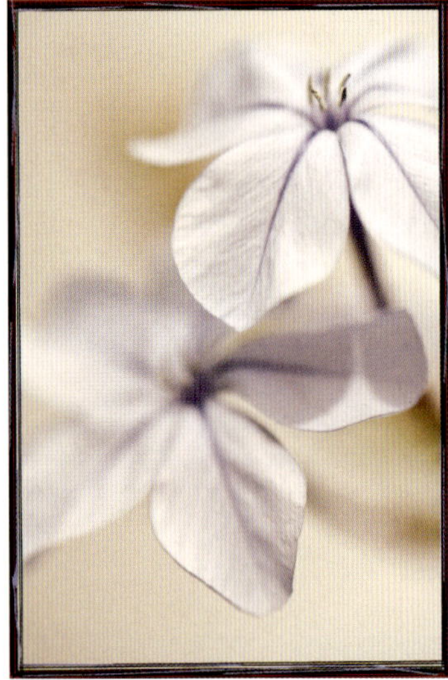
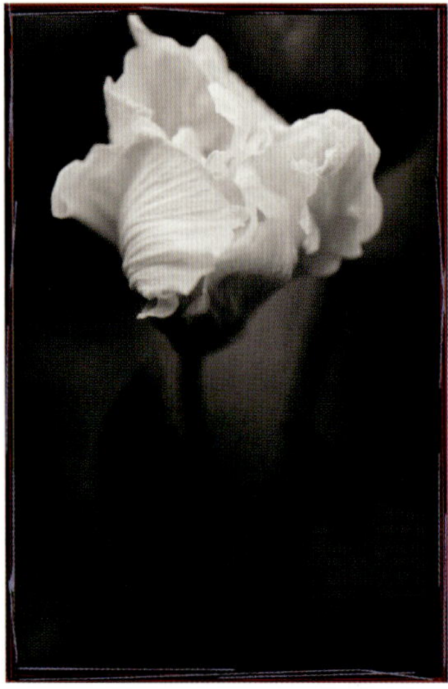
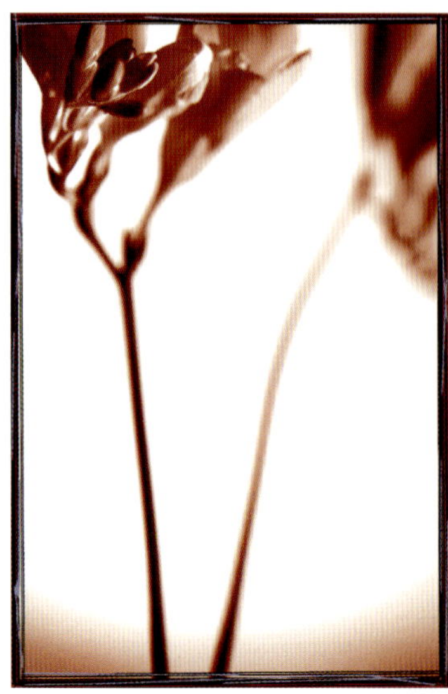

Every subject requires a unique treatment with regard to framing and presentation. For a more complex image, use an understated frame so it won't be a source of distraction. It is obvious from this illustration that the same frame doesn't work equally well with all photos.

with a classical landscape image. The use of frames is a matter of taste, and you can, of course, find plenty of forums on the Internet featuring heated discussions between purists and frame proponents. In any case, if you want to separate an image from its surroundings, an appropriate frame and a supportive mat can be useful.

Pay particular attention to the color of the mat. A white mat draws attention and tends to underscore the light tones of an image. A gray or black mat emphasizes the intensity of the colors in an image, but it can seem dirty, bleak, and small. Colorful mats emphasize similar colors in the image. They also bring out complementary colors and create a contrast with other colors (page 159). A colored mat for a black-and-white photo gives it an emotional cast (page 170) and can be overpowering.

Image Size and Viewing Distance

Every image has an ideal size that allows viewers to easily perceive and understand it. This ideal size depends on the complexity of the image, the amount of visual information, and the viewing distance. A close-up of a lemon against a dark background is suitable for a thumbnail or small image on the Internet, but it doesn't contain enough information to function as a poster. Keep this in mind when you select images for a specific purpose.

Presentation Medium

A photo's presentation medium has some bearing on how viewers will approach it. The most basic consideration is whether you're displaying the image on a digital screen or in print. Monitors not only offer an entirely different world of color through the extended RGB color space, they also illuminate those colors with backlight and produce very bright and vibrant colors. To achieve the most consistent color, you should calibrate both your image editing software and your monitor; you should also set up a color profile. With prints, the final appearance of the image depends profoundly on the printing process and the quality and surface of the paper. The range of contrast for digital and print presentations differs markedly.

Additional Information

The viewers' knowledge about the photographer or a specific image influences how a picture affects them and how they receive it. This may be background knowledge, or new information presented with the photograph. This information might include the title, caption, or accompanying text with the name and background of the photographer or the photo project, or an explanation of how and where the photo was taken, including technical data. Viewers can get additional information from the type of publication the photo appears in, medium and context of the display, or from other photos in the series. This information simplifies the process of orienting oneself to the image, and it also restricts the ways the image can be interpreted.

Selecting a title for an image is one way to make specific associations and to shape the viewer's expectations about the image. If the text above an image indicates it has won an award or was taken by a famous photographer, people are much more likely to take a closer look than if the same text indicated it was taken by a 12-year-old child or that its creation was a happy accident.

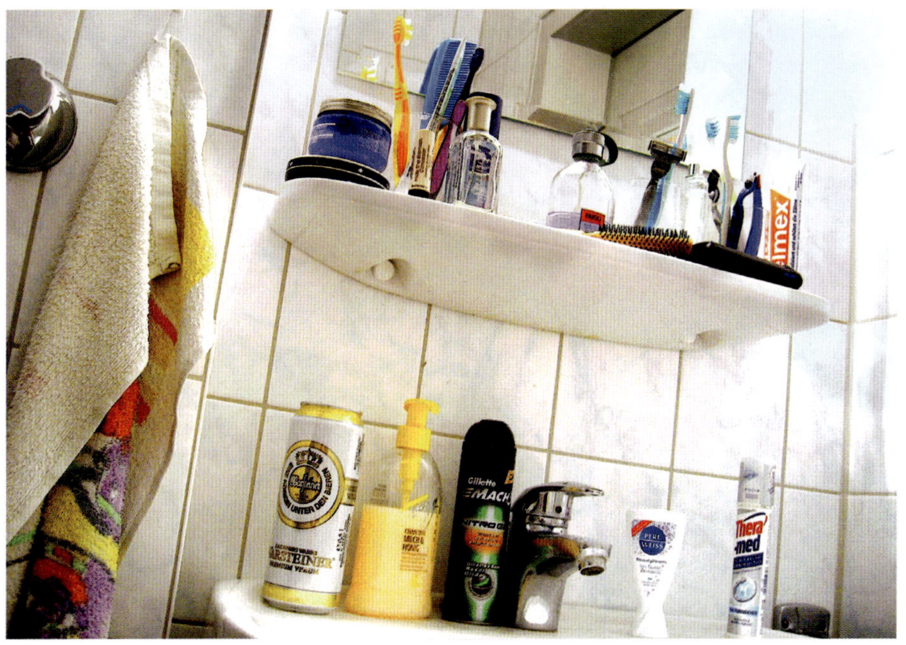

Title: »Nonfiction«

When you first examine this image, you wonder what the main subject is. Then you see the beer can and start to doubt the scene. If you believe the image title, though, then nothing here is staged.

Thematic Context

Aside from information that's communicated directly, we also gather information indirectly from our assumptions. Even with images on the Internet or in ads, we know much more than we think. We can deduce substantial information about an image, its creation, and its intentions from the way it is presented and its thematic context.

We can assume, for example, that an image used in an advertisement for a large company has not only been prepared for a specific purpose, it has also been professionally edited. We don't expect digital manipulation for an image with an article in a newspaper, but we can assume that even if the photo has not been doctored, it has been selected very carefully—a left-leaning newspaper will show different pictures than a right-leaning one. We assume that photographers put their best images on their websites, and we make inferences about their art based on what we see there. If we see an image of someone along with a report about right-wing radicalism, we make presumptions about his or her mindset and attitudes. In the same way, we view an art exhibition in a local bank differently than one in a gallery in an esteemed museum of contemporary art.

Depending on the presentation context, this photo might be read as an unplanned snapshot, a paparazzi photo, or a deliberate staging to highlight the woman's clothes and the feel of nightlife in the city. Without a context, it's up to viewers to interpret the photo.

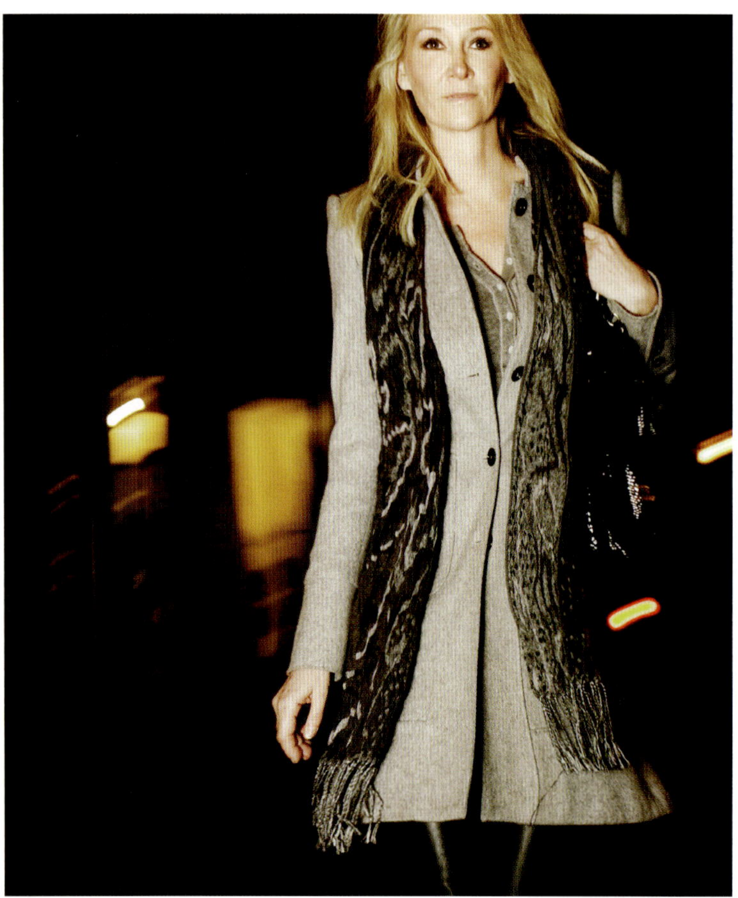

Play along with this experiment: Think of any nude image. Do you have one in mind? Good! Now imagine this image in a photography museum, printed in a large format, hung in a prominent location, and carefully illuminated. The context quickly establishes this image as art. Imagine the image in a new context and insert it into a photography magazine with an article about how to optimize your images. There are several notes surrounding the image that offer tips about various post-processing steps that would benefit the image. In this context, you would assume that the image needs improvement. Now imagine the same photo on a pornographic website. In this context, the image feels smutty. When you shoot and edit your images, consider the thematic context in which you plan to present them.

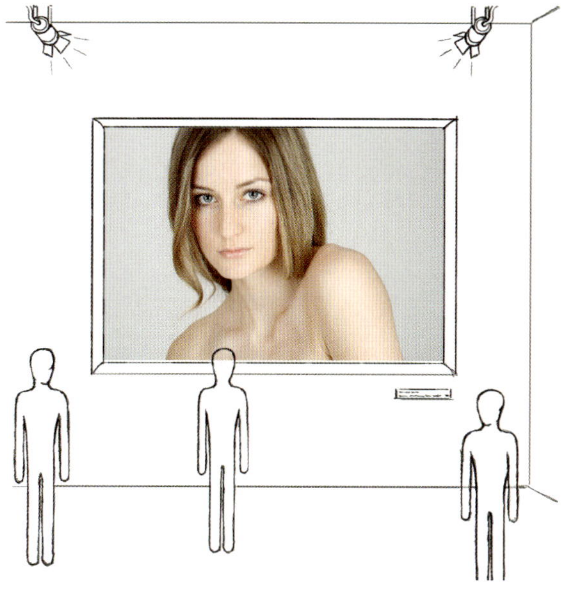

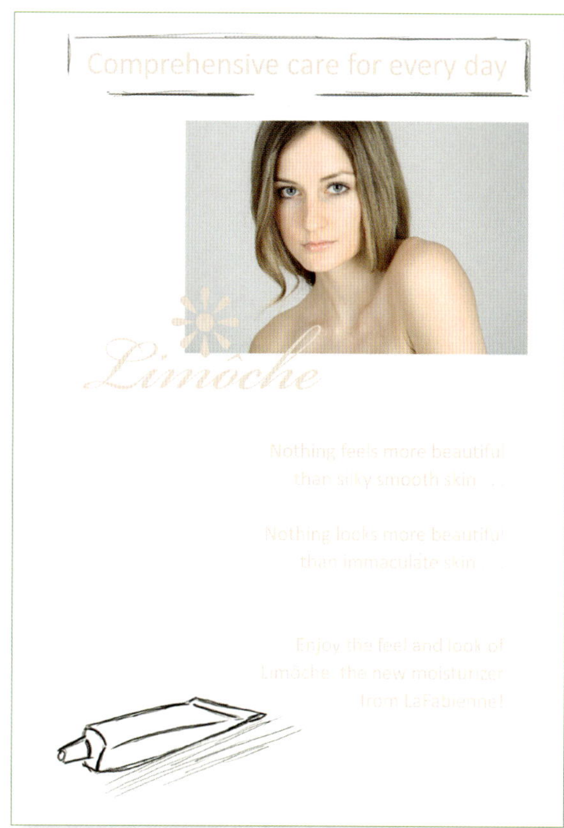

One image can function as a piece of fine art or as a simple illustration, depending on where it is presented. Amazingly, the context of an image changes our interpretation and our perception. On the left, the personality, expression, and emotion of the model are the focus of attention, but on the right, her attractiveness comes to the forefront.

The Context of Perception

Viewers are not always interested in and capable of perceiving an image thoroughly. When the viewer is distracted or preoccupied, or concentrating on something else, they are less likely to be affected by the image. If drivers see a billboard advertising a specific food while they are stuck in rush hour traffic, they will pay less attention to it than if it were in front of their parking space at the supermarket. The time that viewers have to examine an image is critical. You have more time to interpret an obscure image at a photo exhibition than when you're flipping through a magazine at a newsstand.

Similarly, the quantity and strength of external factors influence how strongly images can engage viewers. If an image has to compete with other images, objects, or attractions, it will have a diminished effect. Everyone tries to get his or her flyer to stand out on a bulletin board, which makes it difficult for any single one to succeed. A sophisticated black-and-white image tends to stand out more in a fashion magazine that features busy and flashy spreads.

The physical environment is not the only factor that influences how viewers engage with photos. Their state of mind positively or negatively influences how they respond to an image. Don't show your images to people when they are stressed or angry—wait for a more relaxed time.

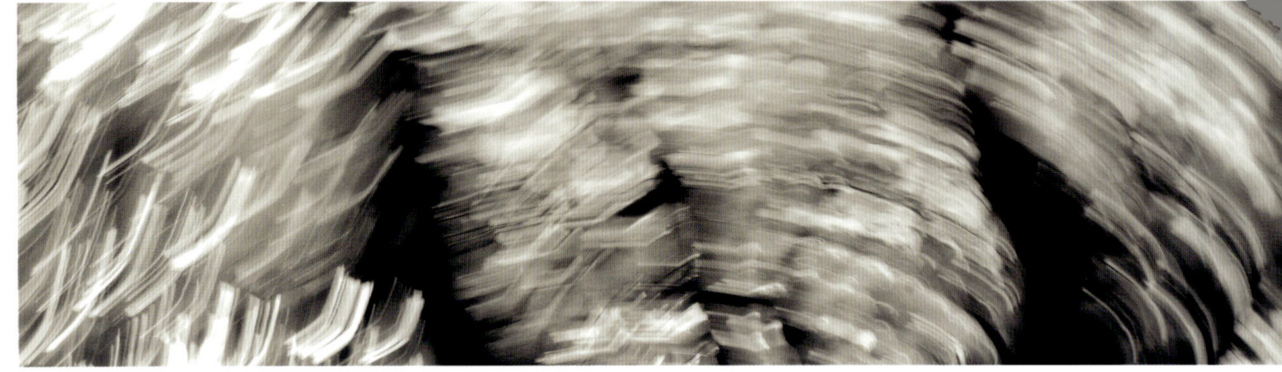

8.3 Visual Design and Language in Practice

All of the information in the previous two sections, and in the previous chapters, is extremely important and meaningful. It can help you photograph purposefully and decisively, to analyze images (page 219), to inspect a particular effect, and to select and evaluate images (page 223). Even if you can use all of the information in this book, you won't be able to put everything into practice right away. This is completely normal, since newly acquired knowledge requires trial and error before it can be used effectively. It's like learning how to drive—memorizing the driver's manual won't make you ready to navigate traffic.

Without practice, photographers can neither improve their own visual language nor develop their own photographic signature. Photographers require repetition in similar circumstances to get used to discovering—and eventually controlling—the details that distinguish their art.

Not all photographers approach their art with the same level of conscious deliberation. Every photographer is inspired by different subjects (page 31), and they all have their own way of seeing and capturing those subjects. Our experience, and the information we've gleaned from courses and other photographers, shows that consciously seeing your subject with a critical eye and making as thorough a plan as possible will grant you more freedom to concentrate on your creativity. We want to make a few suggestions for steps you can take to design your images more consciously and with a specific goal in mind.

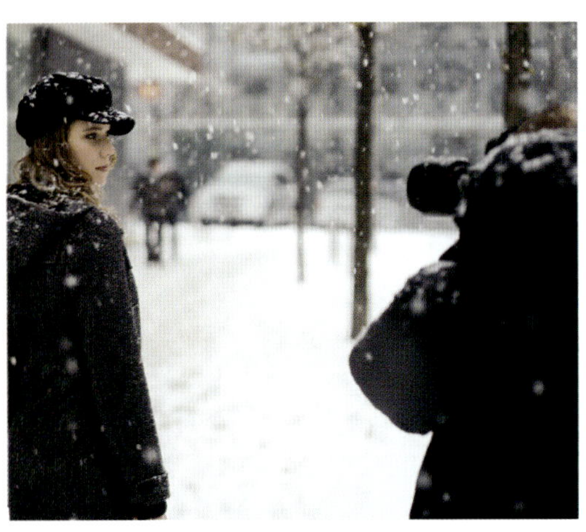

Practicing Design

As good as this sounds in theory, it's also a little farfetched. Photographers master their technique and consciously use it to design every last detail of an image. This includes determining exact crop, controlling the sharpness perfectly, capturing movement deliberately, and composing the image perfectly. For someone just learning to photograph, this sort of total control is hardly imaginable. Plenty of photographers don't make these decisions consciously; they rely on gut instinct and produce one breathtaking image after another.

Of course, some people have innate image design capabilities and intuitively see pictures without considering how and why something will work. Most of us, though, have to opt for constant learning and lots and lots of practice.

When you enter the cycle of photographic improvement, the speed of your progress depends on your diligence, your skill, and your talent. You can imagine that the stages of development form an infinite spiral since there's no such thing as an end destination—there's only progress and stagnation. A photographer's growth is not linear; it can be erratic and is unique to every person. Whatever the shape of your path, these key steps are unquestionably part of your journey:

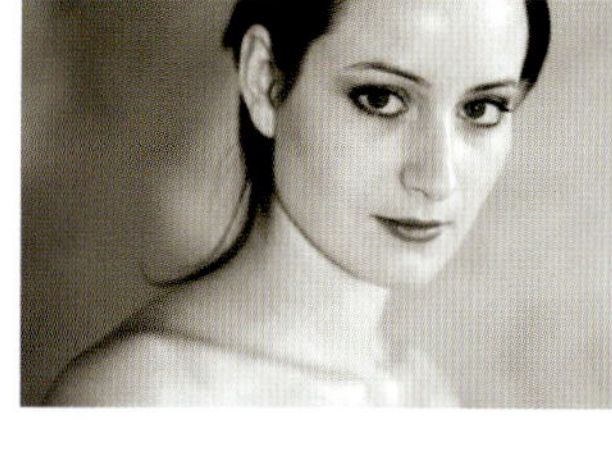

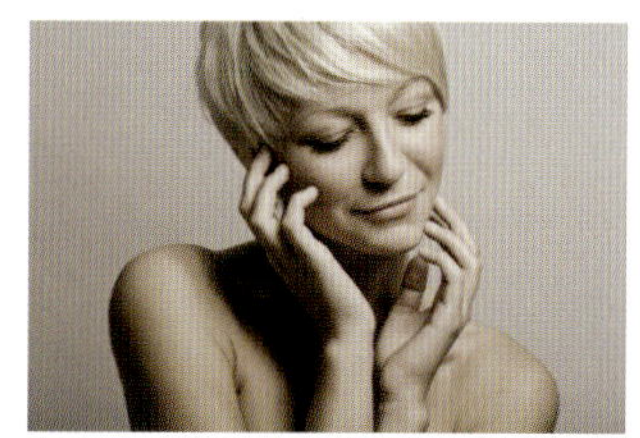

As the years pass, your images should improve, and you should become less and less satisfied with your older images. This will be evidence of your photographic evolution. The more mistakes you detect in your pictures, the more you can avoid them while you're working.

Six years of constructive discontent and critical thought about subject, light, technology, and editing separate these two images taken by Cora. In particular, the light and the color reproduction in the more recent image (below) are noticeably softer, less conspicuous, more pleasant, and better suited to the subject.

- **Accumulate knowledge:** Learn, read, and look at as many photos as possible. The more knowledge you have about methodologies and the connections between subject, design, and technique, the more consciously and intentionally you can improve your craft.
- **Set your objective:** Make sure you have a clear understanding of why you wish to take photographs and what you hope to achieve by doing so (see *Learning to Photograph Vol.1*). You can give direction to your development only when you have established this. If you're not quite sure of this yet, try shooting a variety of subjects and listen to your gut. Take pictures of what interests you and makes you happy—this will make it easier for you to stick with it. Quietly set your own goals about when and what to achieve.
- **Practice, practice, practice:** Without this step it's impossible to develop any sustained improvement. Only regular practice allows you to go through the motions and the decisions that will eventually become second nature. Just like musicians that practice scales and études for years before they tackle tougher pieces, the first years of photography rarely produce images that you will later count among your best.
- **Critique yourself:** Always take time to evaluate your skill as a photographer. An ideal time for this is when you select images for display (page 218). After every photo shoot, vacation, photo excursion, or family reunion, take time to examine and analyze your images. Which pictures please you and which ones don't? Why? Put yourself back at the scene and think about what you could have done differently to get a better result. This exercise will give you practical alternatives for the next opportunity.

- **Prepare for next time:** The next time you reach for your camera, take a few minutes to consider what you hope to accomplish. Examine images that have characteristics you hope to reproduce, and isolate their individual qualities. Think about the focal length, techniques, and camera settings you will need to use to get the desired result. Consider how to place different kinds of light. This exercise will prepare you so you don't have to make every decision in the heat of the moment. You'll be calmer while you shoot so you can concentrate on the subject, image design, creativity, and improvisational adjustments, since it's rare for everything to go exactly as planned.

Applying Image Design Purposefully

You will have to position each photo you take within the dimensions of design. For every exposure, try to pinpoint exactly what your subject is and if you are including too little, too much, or just enough to show exactly what you intend. Also consider what you want to achieve and what you want to say with your image, then think about which design tools will help you achieve those goals. Be conscious of your design choices and how you need to employ them to create an effect that fits your subject.

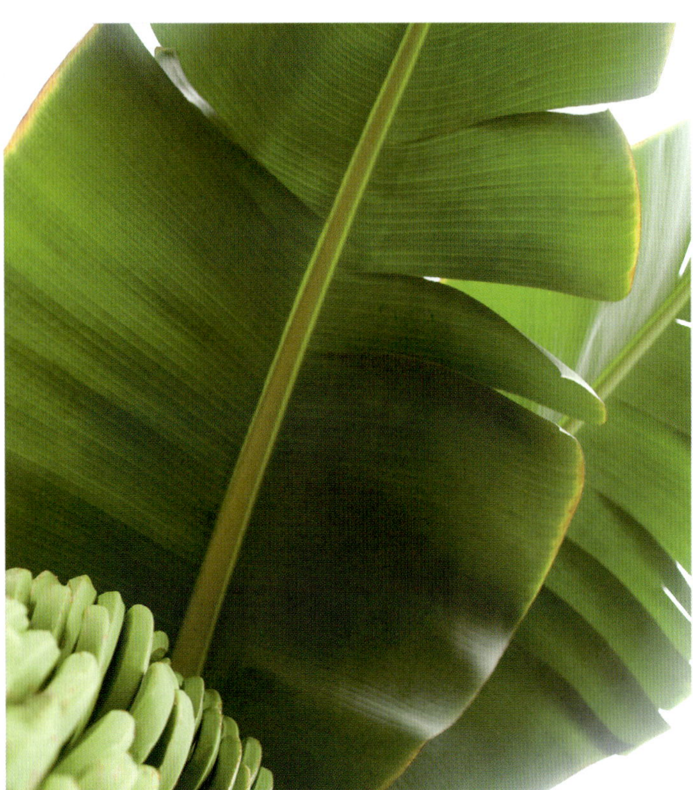

To reduce the complexity of the many different design methods, you might, for example, limit yourself to one constant light source—the sun—and a fixed focal length—here, 28mm. This still leaves you plenty of room for variation and for capturing your subject in unconventional ways.

This sounds arduous and complicated, but with a bit of practice the whole process can be as short as three or four seconds. When you can establish a suitable design within a matter of seconds, you might consider purposefully implementing an element of design that contradicts the overall effect of the picture. This will keep viewers on their toes, increase the attention-drawing capability of the image, and introduce something new to your photo.

Never forget that visual design is only a means to an end, and it should always be based on the intended message of the image. If the design does not support the purpose of the image—or worse, if the design works against it—then the design is unsuccessful. Often photographers dismiss a botched design by saying, "I meant to do that!"

The Principal Dimensions of Design

It's helpful to think about central or core effects that can be achieved through various design dimensions. Become familiar with these dimensions and use them deliberately when you establish the principal design of your image. The key dimensions are described in the following list, along with the various design elements that can be used to achieve them:

- **Simple/organized:** One main element; limited extraneous elements; blurred or monotone background; limited colors; limited but clear and dominant lines; central location for main element; narrow depth of field; landscape format; front lighting; normal view
- **Complex/chaotic:** Many visual elements; more than four or five bright colors; marked contrast of lines, shapes, areas, and color; large depth of field; downward or upward view

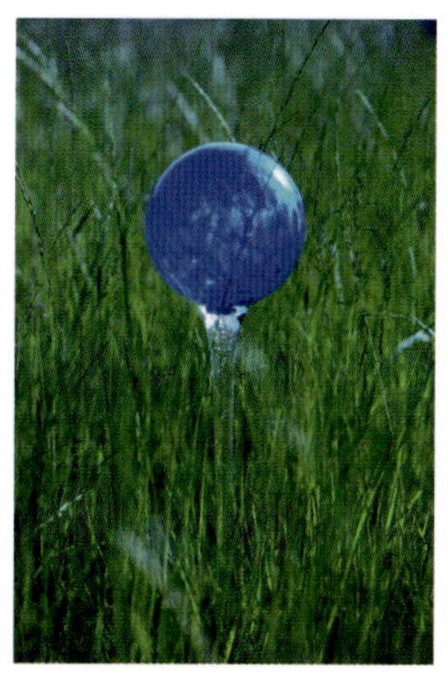
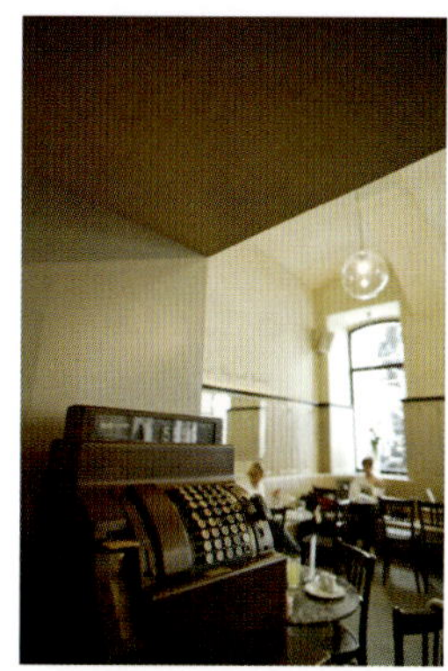

- **Positive:** Bright colors; many light areas; slanted lines from lower left to upper right; upward view
- **Negative:** Dirty colors; many dark areas; slanted lines from upper left to lower right; downward view

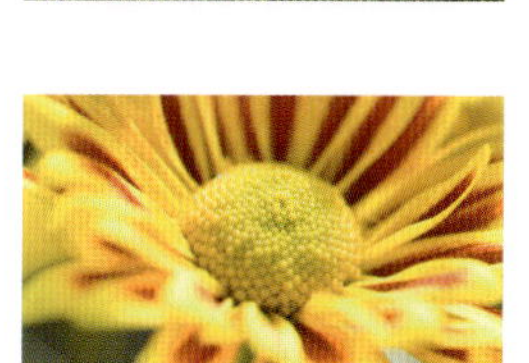
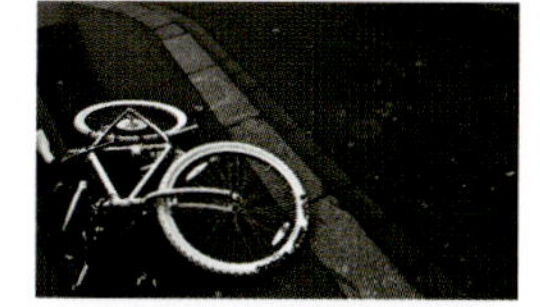

- **Spatial:** Multiple visual layers; vanishing point and lines; overlapping visual elements; saturated colors in the foreground with pale bluish colors in the background; large angle of view; sidelighting; converging verticals; various sizes for similar objects; shallow depth of field
- **Planar:** Parallel lines; single visual layer; no overlapping; similar objects are the same size; even colors; large, undistorted surfaces (right angles); tight angle of view; front lighting; large depth of field

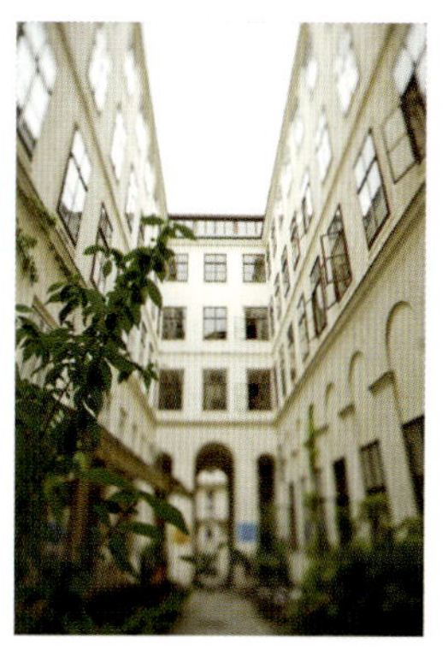
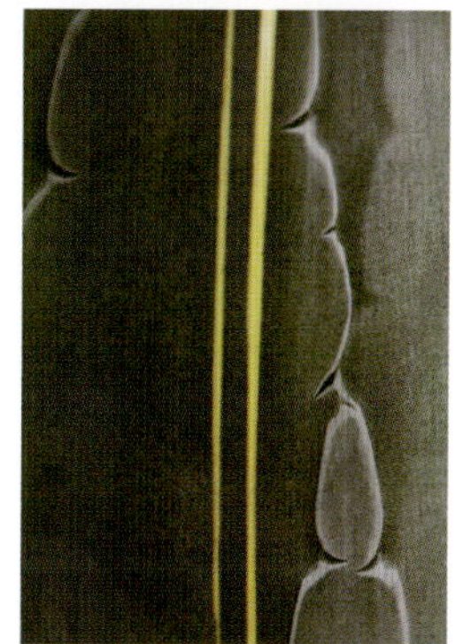

- **Calm/static:** Central positioning; large depth of field; square or landscape format; horizontal lines running parallel to the image border; soft, muted colors
- **Lively/dynamic:** Slanted lines; off-kilter camera position; motion blur; panorama format; converging verticals; bright colors

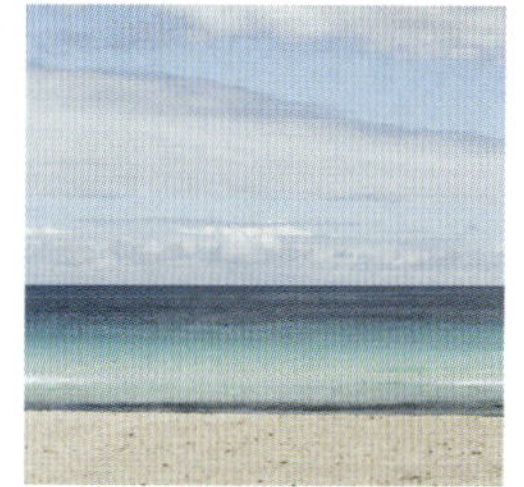
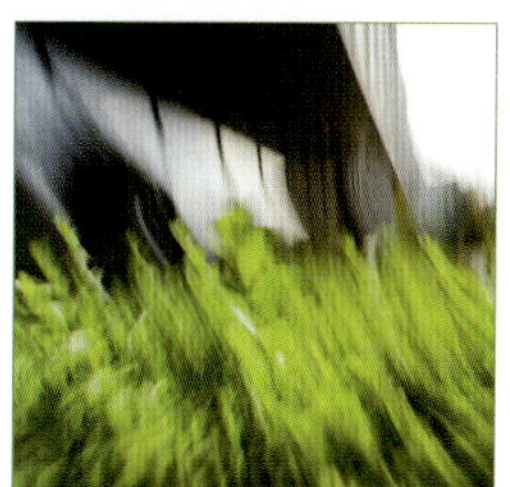

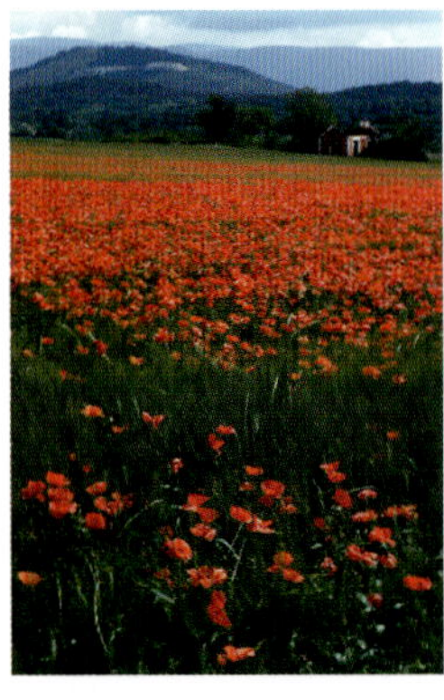

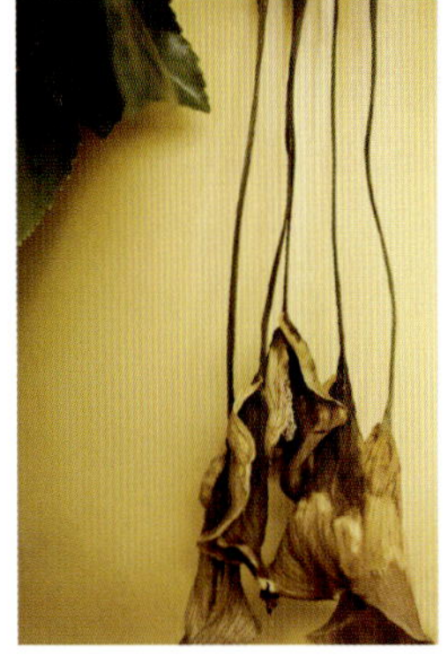

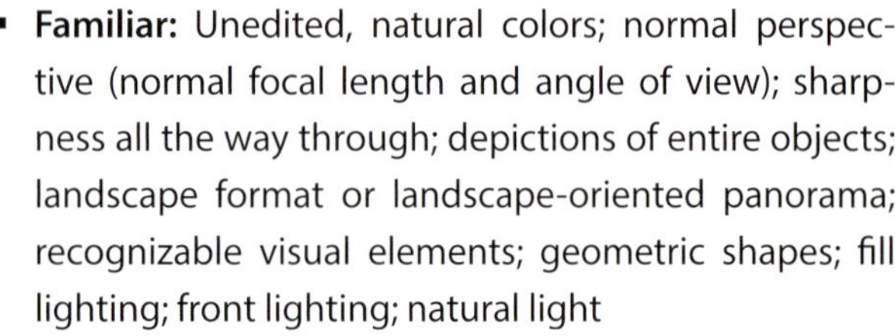

- **Familiar:** Unedited, natural colors; normal perspective (normal focal length and angle of view); sharpness all the way through; depictions of entire objects; landscape format or landscape-oriented panorama; recognizable visual elements; geometric shapes; fill lighting; front lighting; natural light

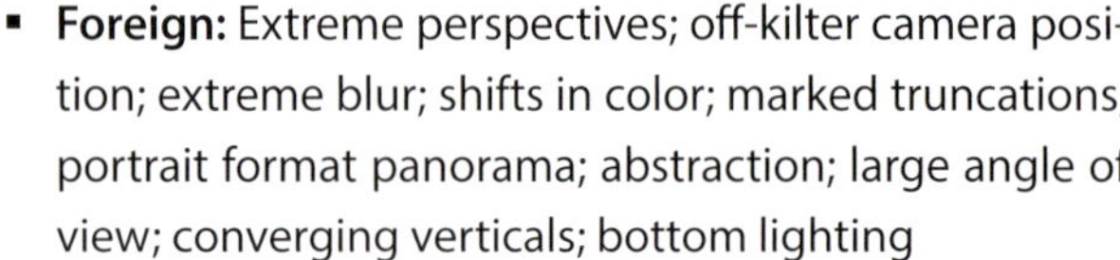

- **Foreign:** Extreme perspectives; off-kilter camera position; extreme blur; shifts in color; marked truncations; portrait format panorama; abstraction; large angle of view; converging verticals; bottom lighting

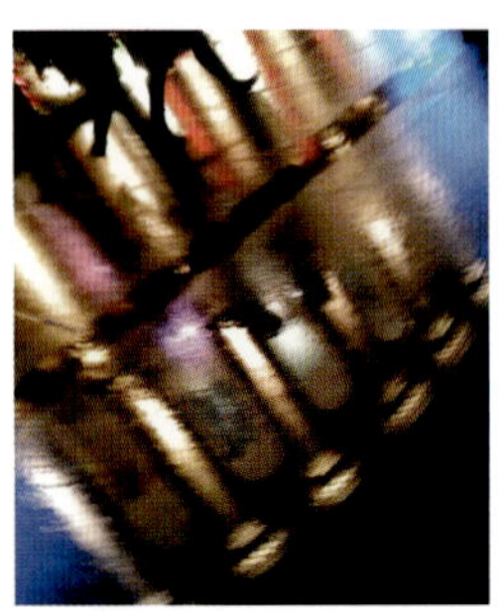

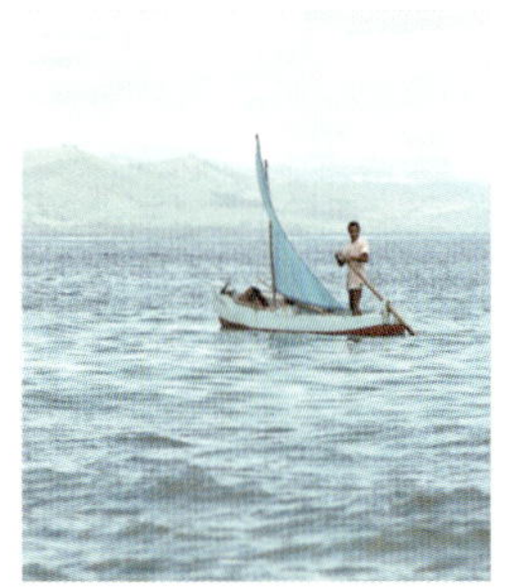

- **Exciting/stirring:** Objects positioned near the image border; off-kilter camera position; diverse, garish colors; marked truncations; backlighting; extreme perspectives; directed light; sharpness that gives certain objects additional significance; strong contrasts
- **Harmonious:** Golden ratio; limited, similar colors; landscape format; even weighting of multiple visual elements; front lighting; diffuse light; weak contrasts

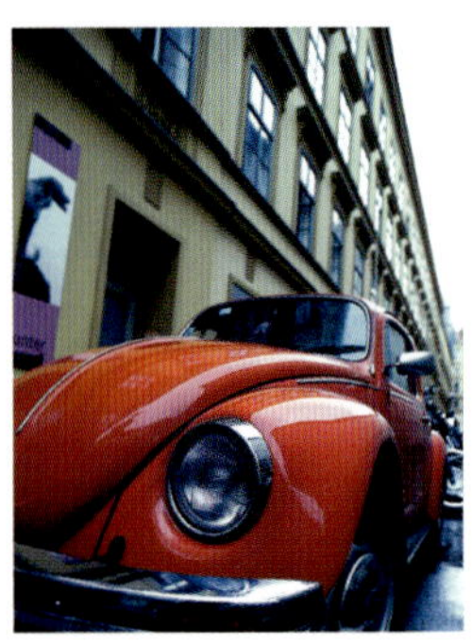

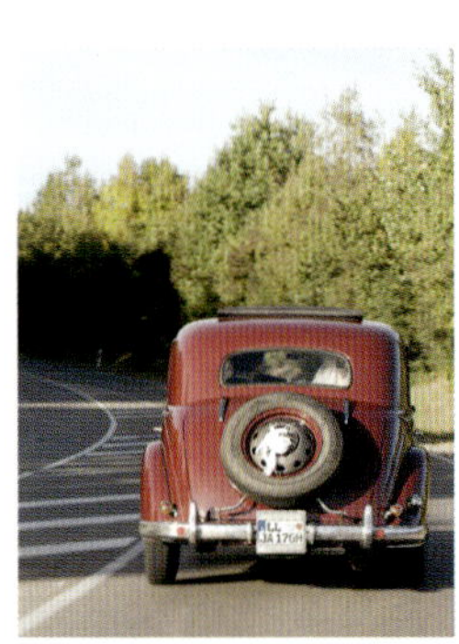

- **Subjective/emotional:** Truncations; shadows; backlighting; bright colors; abstraction; downward and upward perspectives; selective sharpness; blur; strong contrasts; large angle of view; closeness
- **Objective/neutral:** Complete representations of objects; front lighting; shadowless illumination; subtle colors or gray tones; recognizable visual elements; normal view; large depth of field; weak contrasts; small angle of view; distance

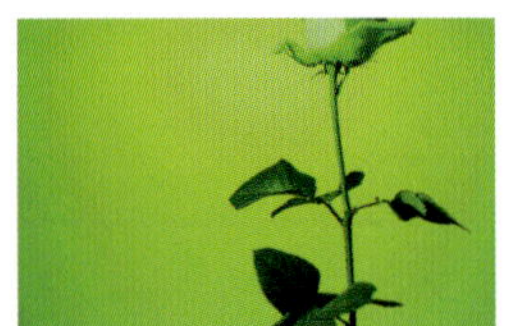

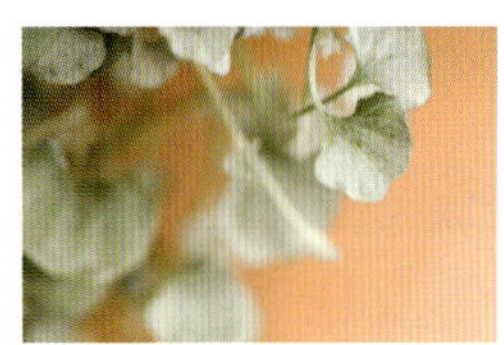

- **Loud:** Bright colors; tight cropping; harsh light; harsh contrasts; geometric shapes
- **Quiet:** Diffuse light; limited, similar colors; desaturated colors; limited contrast; golden ratio; organic shapes

Imperfection and Chance as Tools of Design

Despite all this planning and purpose-driven photography, it's important to not leave spontaneity and liveliness out of your images. While you're carefully planning your photography, always keep this idea in the back of your mind: not everything can be planned, and not every image is feasible. Nevertheless, you should always give it a try. Err on the side of taking one too many images than one too few; it's better to take an image when you have the chance than to miss the opportunity. You can always delete it later.

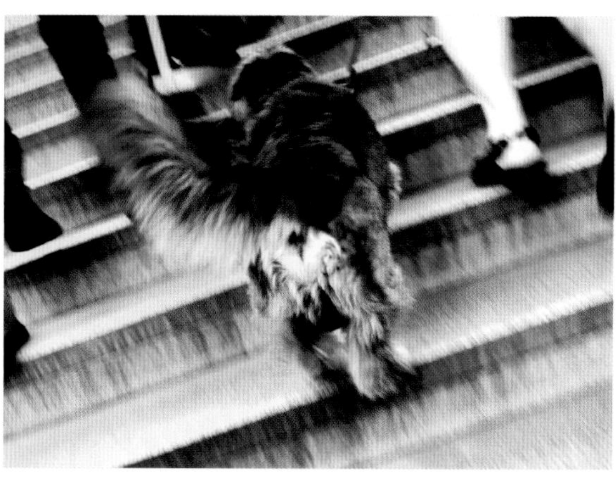

One of the simplest and most powerful ways to invite chance into your images is to shoot from the hip—literally. Not looking through the viewfinder or at the camera monitor, thereby forfeiting your ability to precisely define the image area, forces you to point your camera in the general direction of your subject. With a little practice, you'll get much better at flying blind, even if you can't get precise results. The charm of images like this comes from the potential for surprises and endearing imperfections.

Don't be afraid of imperfection. Many images are particularly strong because they feature what would normally be considered a defect. Small flaws give an image credibility; reality itself is never exact, precise, or perfect. Rough edges give subjects a certain charm and undeniable character. If they are too polished and perfect, pictures become boring and soulless. Minute imperfections don't substantively distract from the subject and the visual design. A portrait or a photo that accompanies a newspaper article can function perfectly well with a small blemish, but a product picture cannot.

Chance can also be a powerful design tool. Make use of creative techniques such as Lomography (page 54) and incorporating movement during long exposures (page 187). Experiment with your camera and invite serendipity into your images. You might unleash new perspectives and exposure techniques. If you stumble across something you like, repeat it and alter the subtleties of your new method to cultivate a specific style, then master that technique.

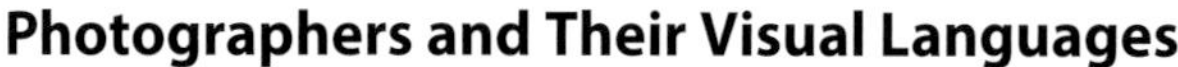

Photographers and Their Visual Languages

Image design can have an even more powerful effect when it extends beyond a single still frame. Photographers can cultivate a consistent emotional appeal and increase the recognition of their work by keeping some dominant design elements consistent throughout a collection of images. This consistency may provide coherence for a photo project, but for most of us, this regularity of style arises automatically with time. Photographers gravitate toward certain design elements, either consciously or subconsciously, and they become a visual hallmark. This is how photographers develop their recognizable signature—their visual language. Each photographer's visual language is similar to a dialect in spoken language that can be traced to a specific origin. A visual language—the consistent overall impact of design choices—can be characteristic of a specific photographer, project, company, or even an entire culture. Asia, for example, prefers a completely different visual aesthetic than Europe, the Americas, and the Middle East.

The Internet makes it possible for images and visual languages to travel quickly around the world. Nowadays this makes it extremely difficult to keep an individual visual language exclusive. Whether it's inspiration or theft, new visual styles and new visual ideas become widespread very quickly.

"The call for photographers to create quality images has a flip side—who creates quality viewers for the images?" Unknown

09 Image Analysis and Evaluation

Anyone can voice an opinion about a photo. However, if you need to select images critically, or constructively evaluate your images to move your photographic development forward, your judgments should be as rational as possible, if not totally objective. You must analyze an image in its entirety and probe beyond your emotional response to develop a neutral assessment. This assessment needs to include the content of the image as well as its design, the context of the presentation, and the intended audience. When you analyze an image, you assume the role of the uninformed viewer who knows nothing about technique or equipment, nothing about the specific circumstances of the exposure, and nothing about the emotional attitude of the photographer. Instead, base your analysis strictly on what you see in the final image.

In this chapter we will give you a template for analyzing and evaluating images so you can find the right words and expressions to discuss images critically. If you're considering your own images, it will take a little practice to become detached enough to evaluate them honestly. This process of self-evaluation is an integral part of improving your craft.

The end of the chapter features ten examples of image analysis to give you an idea of how to detect and describe the design of an image—in other words, to not only feel the overall effect of an image, but to understand it, too.

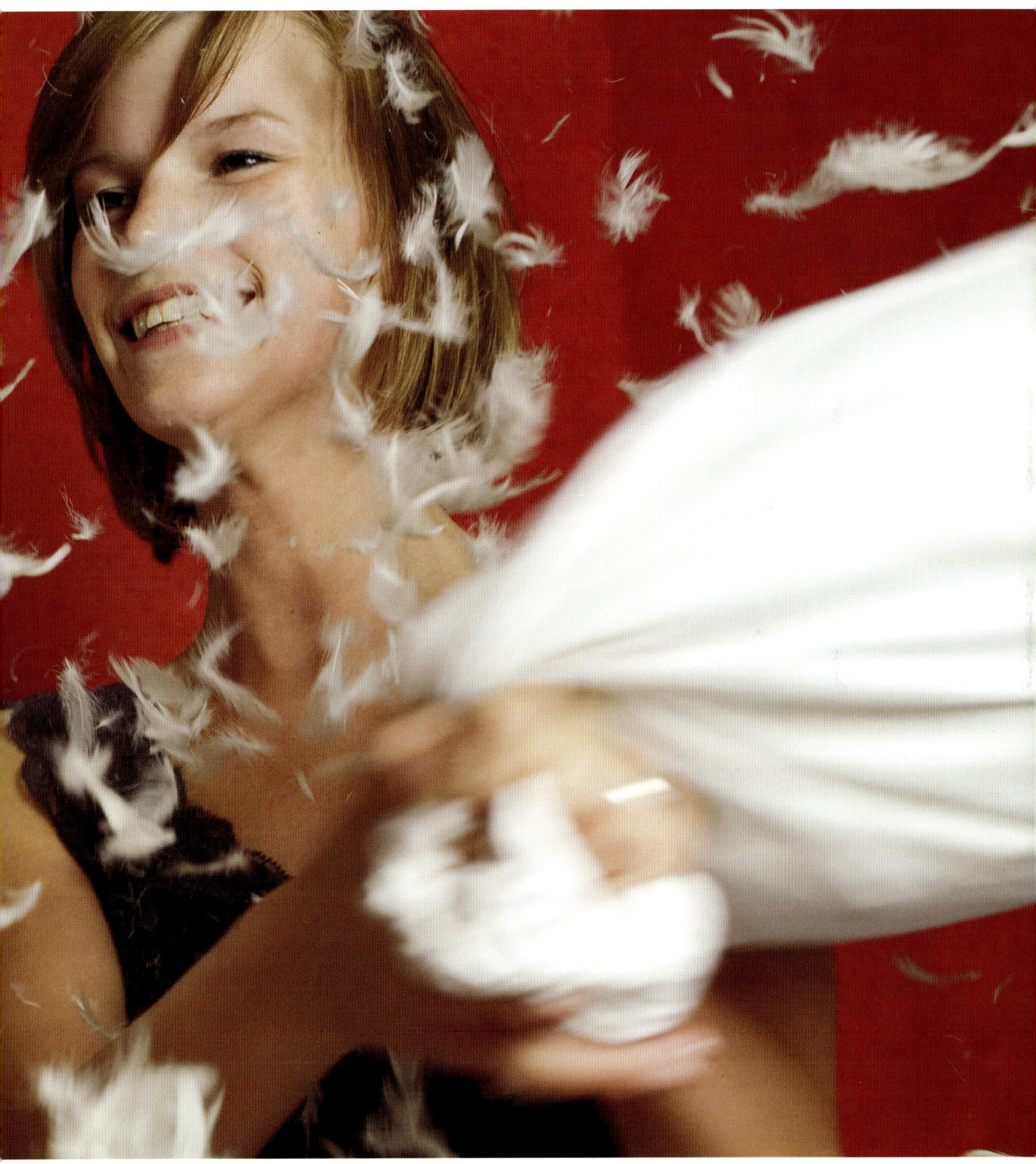

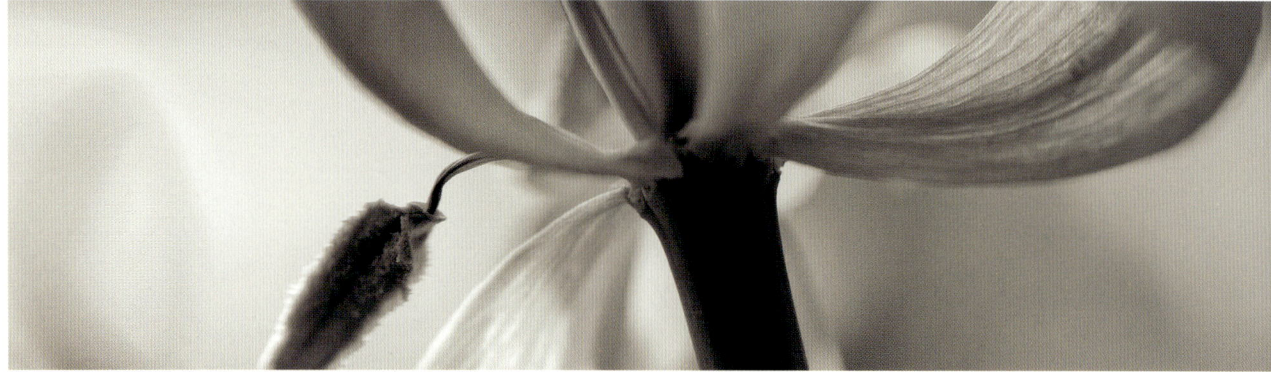

9.1 Structured Analysis and Evaluation

The stronger your emotional attachment to a subject in an image, the more difficult it is to evaluate the image objectively. For this reason, evaluating images independently of their content and setting is not an easy task.

Any time viewers look at an image, their first reaction is always a quick, subconscious evaluation (page 23) of whether they like it and whether or not it interests them. This snap judgment is based on preferences, beliefs, experiences, values, attitudes, moods, and learning; it's a personal opinion—nothing more, nothing less. Subconscious evaluations are unique to the viewer.

It's fascinating to hear a conversation about an image. Most people argue or defend their opinion. If people don't have the same opinion, the discussion is simply a matter of taste, and there's no point in arguing about that.

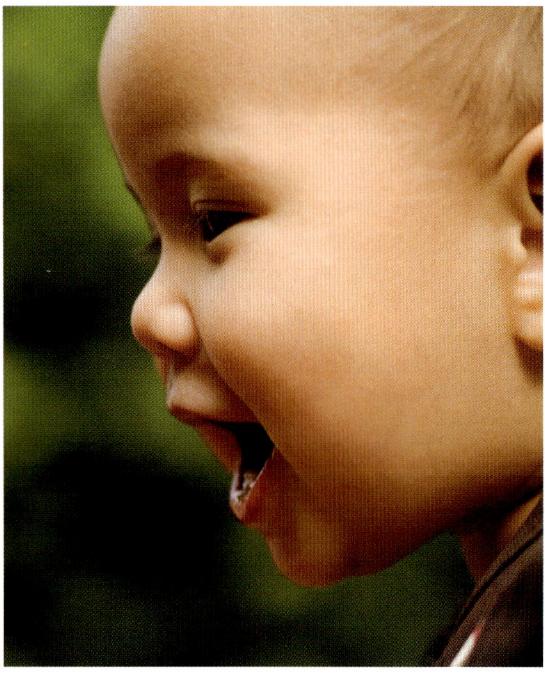

Focused Evaluation

By now it should be clear there are two different ways to evaluate an image: the first is personal and subjective, and the second is structured and purposeful. The conclusions of these types of analysis may be completely different and shouldn't be mixed in the same conversation. With practice, it will become easier for you to have conversations that are either based on personal sensibilities or on rigorous image analysis.

It's impossible to completely eliminate personal taste, especially since analysis and evaluation involve qualitative visual information rather than quantitative data. Despite this, analysis that is focused and structured can produce a more neutral, objective opinion of an image. It also becomes easier to discuss an image rationally and comprehensively after you consider it from different points of view.

Image Analysis

Analyzing images doesn't have to be a complex process. In fact, with some practice, all it takes is a few brief moments. Everyone can contribute to the analysis because there is no right or wrong opinion. An analysis evaluates the impressions and connections that an image conveys. There is still some subjectivity at play, but it concerns the way visual elements work, which are mostly—or even universally—consistent for all members of a cultural group (page 24).

Analyzing an image involves identifying its overall effect, and then recognizing individual aspects that produce that effect. Finally, analysis is about finding the right words to communicate these ideas about how the image functions. It's much easier to discuss images when people speak the same language.

Similar to textual analysis in the study of literature, image analysis begins with making a supposition, and then identifying support for the claim by investigating specific aspects of the image in a structured, logical way. The following topics are useful guides for analyzing all images:

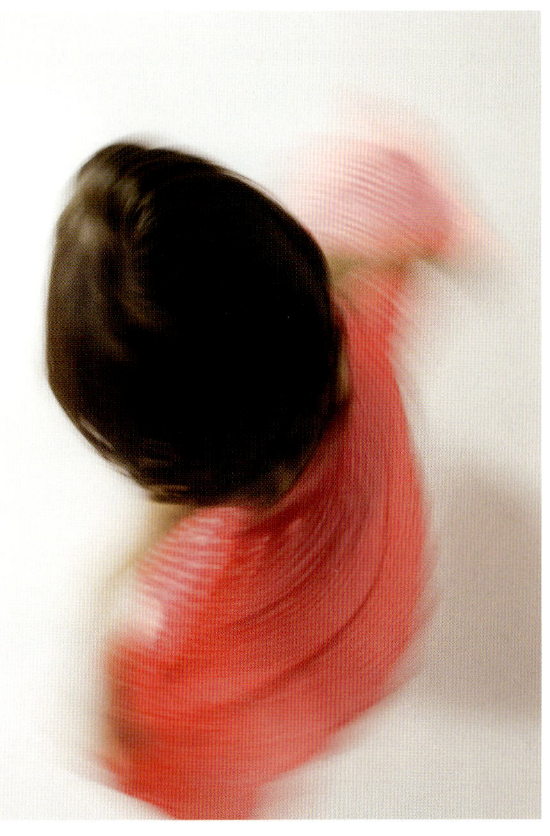

Not every subject is immediately recognizable to the viewer—but subject recognition isn't a prerequisite for the image to achieve its desired effect. In this image, for example, you first need to realize that the picture shows a spinning person captured from above. Then you discover that it isn't possible to identify the person or his or her age. What comes through clearly is the spinning motion.

- The subject
- The objective
- The intended audience
- The visual design
- The balance of the four previous points

The Subject

As banal as it sounds, every image analysis starts by determining what is actually present in the image. The following questions can help you sort through the visual content in a picture:

- What subject did the photographer choose and capture?
- What is visible in the image?
- Do you recognize the subject, or can you infer it with your background knowledge?
- Can you orient the subject within a specific time, place, or context?
- What other details are visible within the image area?
- How are the individual elements related to one another?

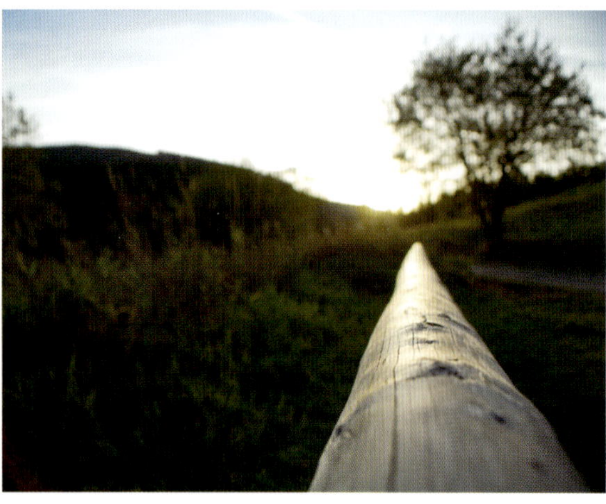

It's obvious that this image is a product of the fun of tinkering with image design. The focus is on the style, not the content, of the image. The landscape itself is insignificant because it's reduced to blur, and the sharpness of the wooden beam isn't enough to carry the image on its own. The clear and prominent lines and the emotional lighting make this image exciting.

- When taken together, what subject do these elements produce?
- What is the message of the image?
- What emotions does the image depict or evoke?
- What are the key stimuli that produce these emotions?

If you have trouble answering any of these questions, look for additional information, such as the title, caption, other related images, information about the photographer, technical data, the location where the image was shot, the presentation of the image, or its thematic context.
Even if no additional information is present, the subject should be your starting point because it will help you evaluate the photographer's objective, the intended audience, and especially the appropriateness and effectiveness of the design.

The Objective

A thorough evaluation always reveals an objective. Note that several objectives may be observed, depending on the context of the image and the reason you're analyzing it. The photographer, image editor, or an advertising agency might all want to achieve something different with the image; each of their individual objectives may be very different. Yet, the central question remains: what does this image attempt to trigger for the viewer? Additional questions that can help you pin down the purpose of the photo are:

- Why was this photo taken?
- Does the image fit the purpose?
- Who was the photographer?
- Who did the photographer take the picture for?
- What other types of pictures does the photographer take?
- In what situation was the image taken?
- Does the title or any additional text indicate the photographer's objective?
- Does the context provide any clues about the photographer's objective?

Of course, the photographer's thoughts about an image or the concrete purpose for which it was created are rarely documented next to the picture, so in most cases you need to make assumptions about the objective. Any information you have about the photographer, the story behind an image, or the context of the presentation can help you make this inference. Many images, for example, look like snapshots. Others clearly reveal more of an artistic purpose, which you would expect from an image displayed in a gallery, as opposed to an online photography forum. The subject, its surroundings, the presence of people in the image, the techniques used, the light conditions, and the post-processing can all help you form a hypothesis about why an image was created.

Identifying the purpose of photos used in advertising or journalism is generally straightforward. The image should portray a positive feeling about a product to encourage viewers to buy it, or the image should accompany an article to illustrate a point or underscore relevant themes. But the purpose for photographing an action, place, or object should also be clear from its context.

Intention is more difficult to pinpoint in an image by an amateur photographer because the image is rarely created with a specific presentation context in mind. In these cases we can usually assume that photographers primarily try to convey what interests them, or they try to illustrate their own perspectives and feelings. Amateur photographers may or may not be cognizant of their motives while shooting, but some reasons for taking a picture include standing out from the masses, drawing attention to an image or themselves, getting recognition and feedback for their work, and getting viewers to engage with an image for as long as possible.

These motives should be analyzed while keeping in mind the fundamental goals of every photographer: to capture and reveal a specific subject and present it to the viewer. Let's consider an example. In a photo spread in a fashion magazine, there are several pictures of models dressed in light summer clothes, cavorting in a flowery meadow. We can infer that the purpose of the photo is, first and foremost, to present the clothes. The design elements in all of the images support this purpose by showing the clothes sharply and in their entirety, except for one particular image that shows the face of a model with her eyes lowered, laughing with a strand of hair in her face.

This image does not reveal her clothing and doesn't support the original purpose we identified. Otherwise, its design fits in with the other fashion images, so it alters the whole series of photos. We can deduce that the photographer is not only interested in clothing; he or she also wants to convey the exuberance of summertime.

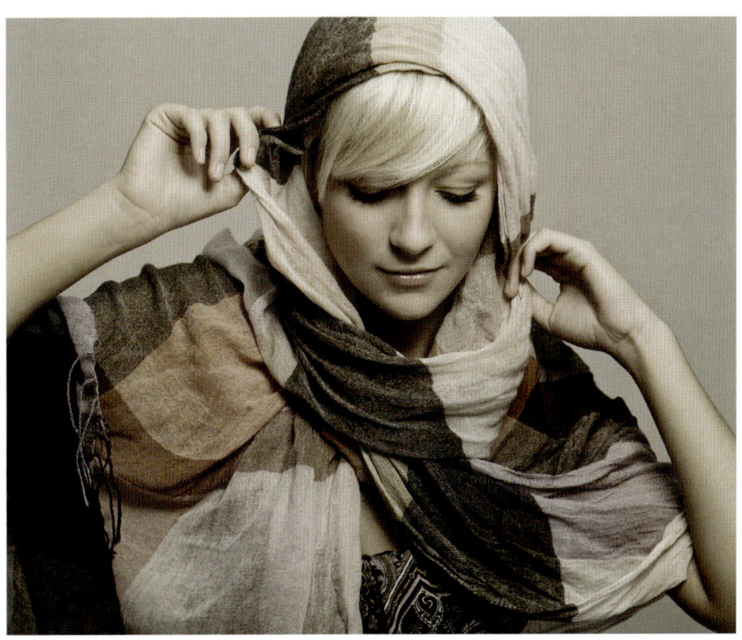

At a glance we can see that the purpose of this image is to flaunt clothing rather than function as a portrait. The face is critical to a portrait, so the fact that this model's eyes are so downcast indicates that something else is intended. The cloth draped around the woman's head and neck reveals it clearly. The limited color scheme also hints at a staged fashion shot.

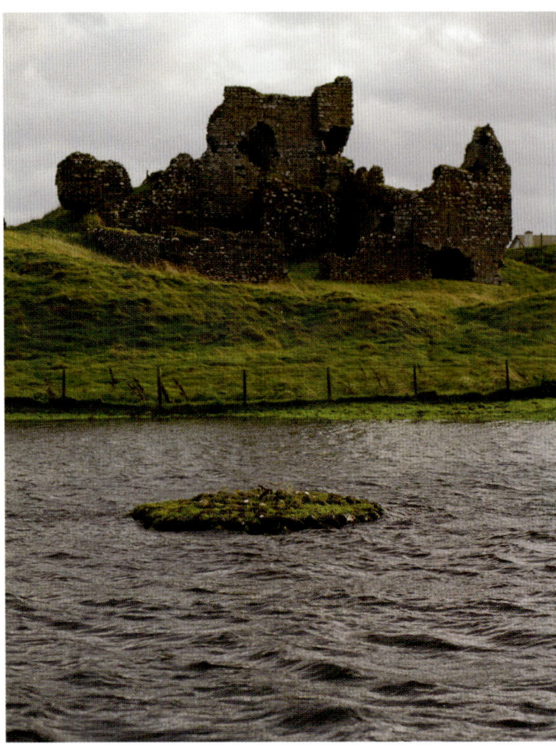

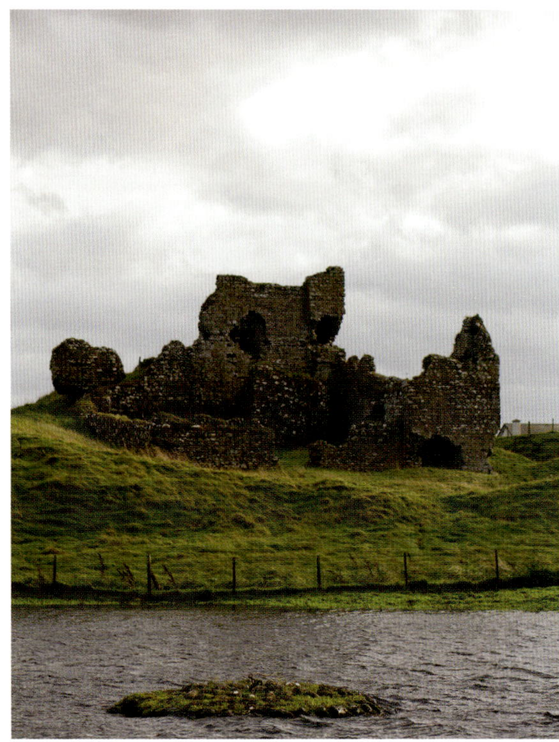

The first thing you are likely to notice in these two images is that the position of the horizon is dramatically different, which has changed the relative proportions of the sky and the water and caused other visual elements to shift. The shift is dramatic enough that the subject itself is different. The left image is more dramatic and emphasizes the water. The right image is calmer, more conventional, and is dominated by the sky.

The Intended Audience

You should also know, or be able to infer, who the target audience for a photo is before you evaluate how successful it is at eliciting a certain response. All of the clues within the image can help you identify a specific demographic or group. The intended audience is particularly important when a photographer chooses an image for advertising. Another example is when a photographer submits a photo to a competition; the selection process can be refined based on the cultural preferences at the location of the contest. When we see images in our daily lives, such as in a photography forum on the Internet, it's not always possible to define a clear target audience because the viewers come from diverse backgrounds. Depending on the general theme or bias of the forum, you can infer if beginning, intermediate, or professional photographers are likely to participate.

The Visual Design

The steps you take to figure out the subject, intention, and target audience are critical for image analysis, but the main concern is engaging with the visual design. Take a structured approach by considering each individual element separately and describing its use and influence on the overall visual impact. Some design elements will be intentionally emphasized, and some will be understated.

Examine the composition, lines and shapes, perspective, light, color, and use of sharpness and blur. Consider how these variables are manifested in the image. Think about how they work together and describe the overall effect (page 198), taking into account the exposure, the visual design, and any post-processing that is evident in the image.

Evaluating Balance

After you have critically analyzed the image, you are ready to evaluate it. This evaluation entails weighing the subject, objective, and target audience against the design and its overall effect. This balance test will help you determine whether the image can elicit the desired response from a specific audience. During the analysis, you gathered useful information to support your appraisal. Consider the following questions to help you evaluate the balance:

- Does the design suit the subject?
- Does the visual language speak to the target audience?
- Does each individual design element support the purpose of the image?
- Is the overall effect homogenous, or are some individual design elements incongruous?
- Do the incongruous design elements seem like they were intentionally used to surprise and engage the viewer?
- Do the incongruous design elements seem unintentional, and do they distract the viewer?
- Is the subject accessible to the target audience, and does it meet their interests?

These questions will help you formulate an exhaustive evaluation of the image instead of a snap judgment based on personal taste. You'll be able to decide if an image is producing a specific result. Because you considered the objective, you can critically evaluate whether or not the image is suited for its intended purpose.

Connecting the evaluation to a specific purpose is critical; a general assessment, such as deciding if an image is good, doesn't pass muster. A better conclusion might be that the content and style of an image go well together, so it will appeal to many different viewers. A more thorough evaluation is particularly warranted for detailed and nuanced images. A structured analysis will allow you to develop sound arguments, convince other viewers, and learn a wealth of new information that will help your own photography.

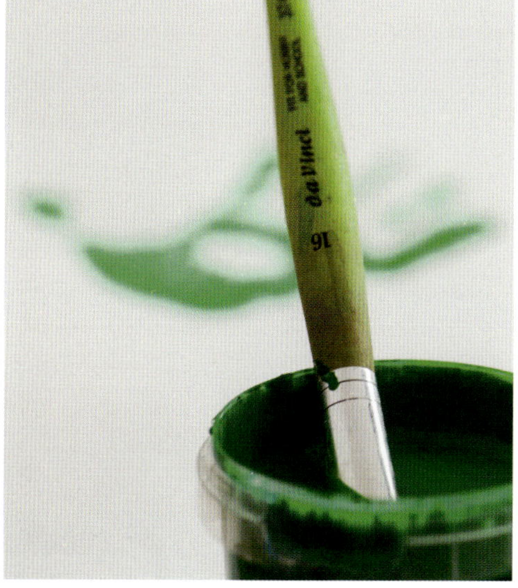

If this image were used in an advertisement for a paintbrush, you'd probably develop a negative impression. The brush is not shown in its entirety, the brand is not legible, the bristles are completely obscured, it is smeared with paint, and it is not being used. None of these qualities will appeal to buyers. If this image were on a website for a kindergarten classroom, though, it could work very nicely.

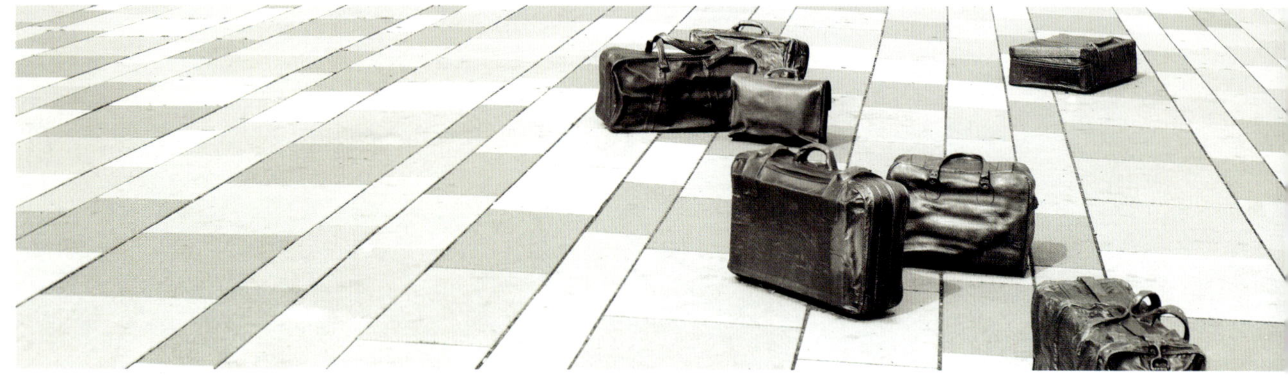

9.2 Applications

You won't analyze every photo you come across this thoroughly—such attention is hardly necessary on a regular basis. In many cases it's not important to understand how an image works, and it's enough to know that it works on an emotional level. In these cases it's enough to ask yourself if you like the image. But conducting an exhaustive analysis of photos you like and those that inspire your own photography can produce lasting improvements to your own personal style. Ask yourself at least the following questions:

- What is the subject of the image?
- What message is this image trying to convey?
- What are the dominant elements of design, and how do they influence the image?
- Does the overall effect support the message?

When you have multiple images of the same subject, the details distinguish the best ones from the rest. The two poses on the right are preferable to those on the left because of the model's hand position. The image on the far right is most effective because of the model's facial expression.

After Shooting

The technology of digital photography has made it possible for photographers to create many images. If you were to keep every single one of them, even the ones you never looked at, you'd quickly fill up your hard drive. It therefore makes sense to look at your images immediately after you shoot them—invest some time in your hobby and organize your photos. This is a perfect time to practice structured image evaluation.

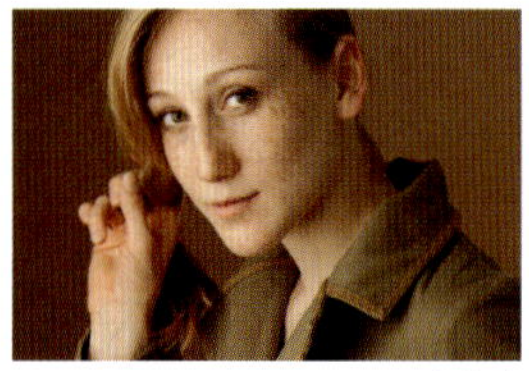

***

***

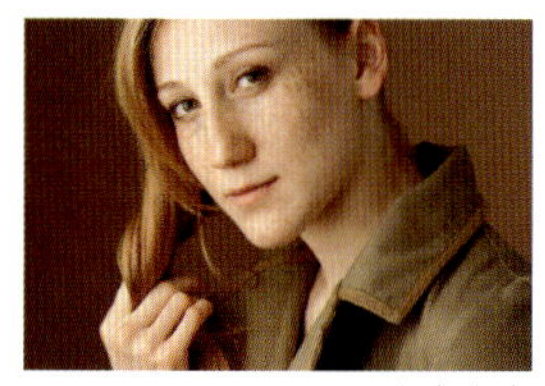

****

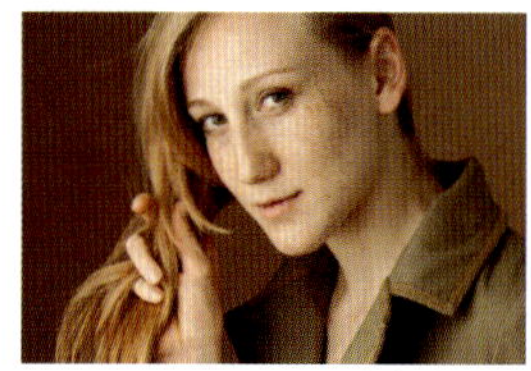

*****

On the first pass through your images, mark the ones you want to delete, including the inferior versions of any close duplicates. A great image will stand out more clearly in a small group of good photos than in a large group of good and bad photos. It can be helpful to compare similar images side by side to pick up on subtle distinctions. Pay close attention to the differences—they are often minor—and consider why you prefer one image to another. Maybe a line travels directly into a corner, or someone's eye is slightly more open in one version, or something in the background is either more or less visible. This is great practice for training your eye to notice details that can make or break your images. The time you spend on organizing and filtering your images is a practical investment in your continued improvement as a photographer.

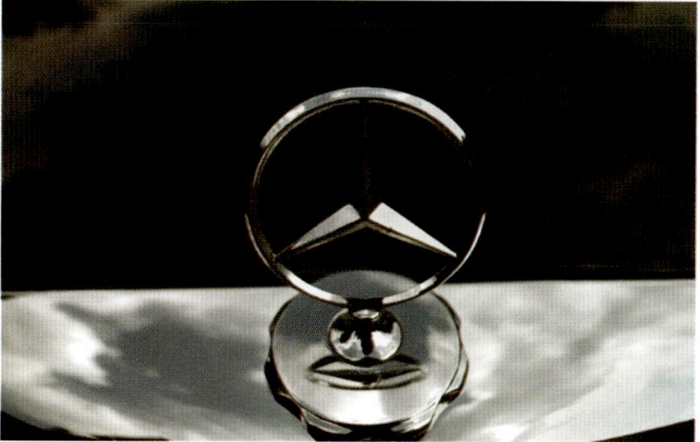

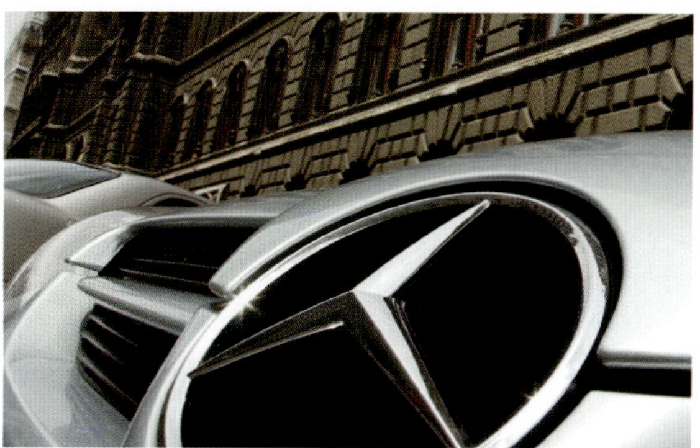

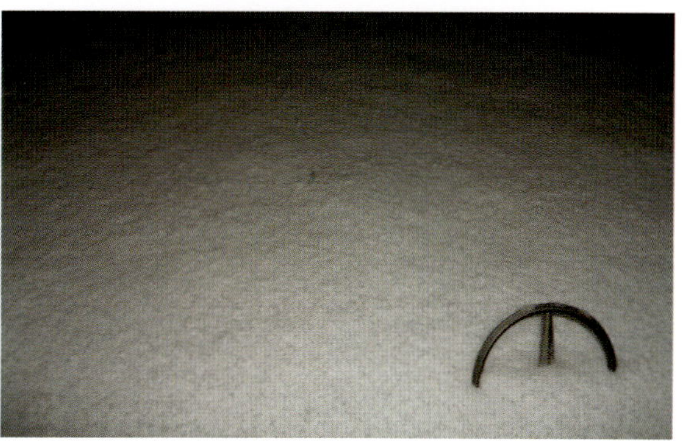

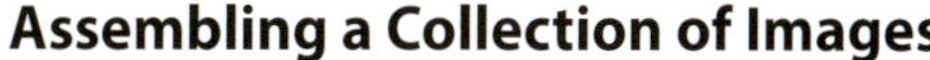

Assembling a Collection of Images

There is usually a purpose for taking photographs, whether it's a photo book, a slide show, an exhibition, or a selection of photos to attract attention on a website or online portfolio. Perhaps you're preparing an advertising pamphlet, a business report, or newspaper article, and you're researching images in an online stock photo agency.

Whatever the purpose, take the time to decide what the quality needs to be and how much similarity or variety you need. Establish criteria that will help you filter out unusable images and hone in on ones that suit your purpose.

The biggest challenge is adhering to your acceptance criteria, whether it's related to quality or something else. It's not uncommon to get attached to an image that doesn't meet your requirements, or for the stress of a deadline to force you to abandon your search for ideal images.

Keep your critical guard up as much as possible, even when it's a challenge. Don't settle for images that fail to meet your criteria; it's better to choose fewer pictures that are better suited for your purpose. After you've selected all of your images, analyze them one more time and ask yourself, and others with expert knowledge, if the selection truly reflects your purpose.

One reason to take your camera with you wherever you go is to build a collection of certain subjects. When you select images for a cohesive series, it's important that the recurring theme is easily recognizable. How similar the images in your series are to each other is a matter of preference.

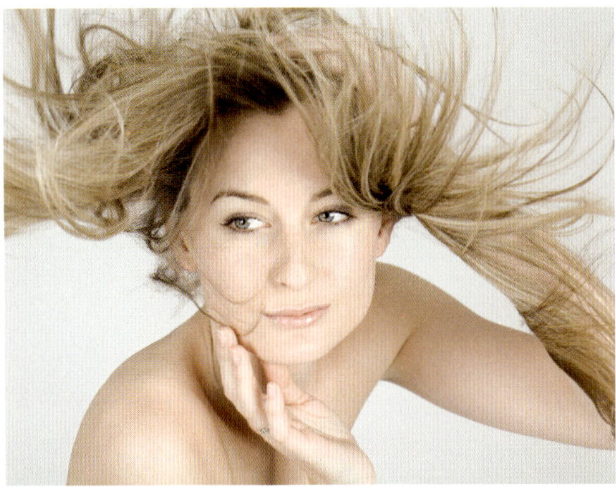

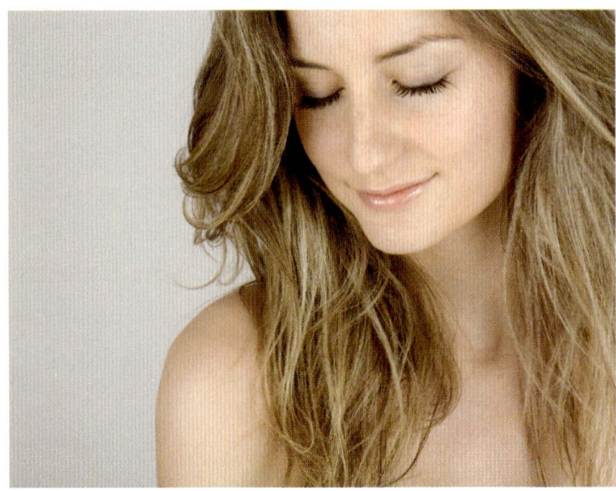

When you take pictures of people, the challenge is probing for something in the subject's character or finding and capturing a trait. The more time you spend shooting and evaluating photos, the more likely it is that you will discover the images that are convincing, well-suited to the model, and flawlessly designed. Whether you subject these images to the potentially bracing feedback of someone else is entirely up to you. There are times when you don't want to hear anything negative, even when it's warranted.

Self-Criticism and Continual Improvement

It's fundamentally easier to analyze other people's images than your own. Nevertheless, it's worthwhile to turn a critical eye on the entire body of your work independent of any specific projects you're working on. Take a step back, distance yourself as much as you can, and conduct as rational an analysis as possible. These questions can help guide your personal reflection:

- Are you satisfied with your photography?
- Are you making progress? How?
- Are you still interested in your subject matter?
- What specifically interests you about your subjects?
- What do you hope to achieve next?
- What steps are necessary to meet those goals? (see *Learning to Photograph Vol.1*)

Handling External Criticism

In addition to reflecting on how you feel about your own work, you should also solicit input from others. It can be especially difficult to come up with new approaches or ideas on your own. Another person will be less emotionally connected to your images and can analyze them more objectively. If the evaluation is positive, you'll generally welcome the feedback; negative feedback should be grounded in evidence and should be objective, argumentatively sound, and specific to your images. Deciding whom to solicit for feedback is always tricky.

If you trust the person you've chosen and think of him or her as a capable, well-versed photographer, you should take the criticism to heart—especially if it's negative, because the analysis will help you improve. This doesn't mean you should switch genres after a scorching review. Refrain from these common reactions when you hear criticisms of your images:

- **"I can't" or "The golden rules of image design":** When they are just starting out, many photographers are often thankful for feedback of any kind because they think they're not capable of taking good pictures or effectively analyzing them. This openness to criticism—no matter how experienced you are—can be very helpful. Advice from other photographers about how to improve your images, however, is often not specifically tailored to your work. If such criticism is valid for all images, recall the so-called rules of visual design that result in a one-dimensional visual language. It's much better to study the relationship between the design and the resulting effect of an image.
- **"Yes, but . . ." or "Most people like it":** The longer you take pictures and show them to others, the more positive feedback you'll receive. One reason for this is that your photographic skills will improve over time, but there are other reasons: your critics may want to avoid conflict, they might overlook shortcomings in your work, they might be hoping that you'll praise their work, they might be inexperienced, or maybe they've had bad experiences with offering critical feedback in the past. Some people would rather offer praise than criticism. When most of the voices around you are singing praises and only one person is offering criticisms, it can be tempting to ignore it. Praise is not only the soul's balm—it's also the photographer's reward. But don't ignore unpleasant criticism, because it may contain advice that can advance your practice.
- **"Aha-hmm" or "I wanted it that way!":** Photographers who are established in their careers and have long enjoyed success often turn a deaf ear to negative criticism; they don't want to hear it, let alone acknowledge it, even when it comes from experts. Their success—publications, workshops, or commissions—makes them immune to negative feedback. Their one approach becomes sacrosanct; they repeatedly use the same photographic methods and vary them only slightly rather than striving to improve. The boundary between standing still and developing your photographic signature is fluid. It can be helpful to solicit feedback from other esteemed photographers. Such feedback is often financially compensated to lend credibility to the process.

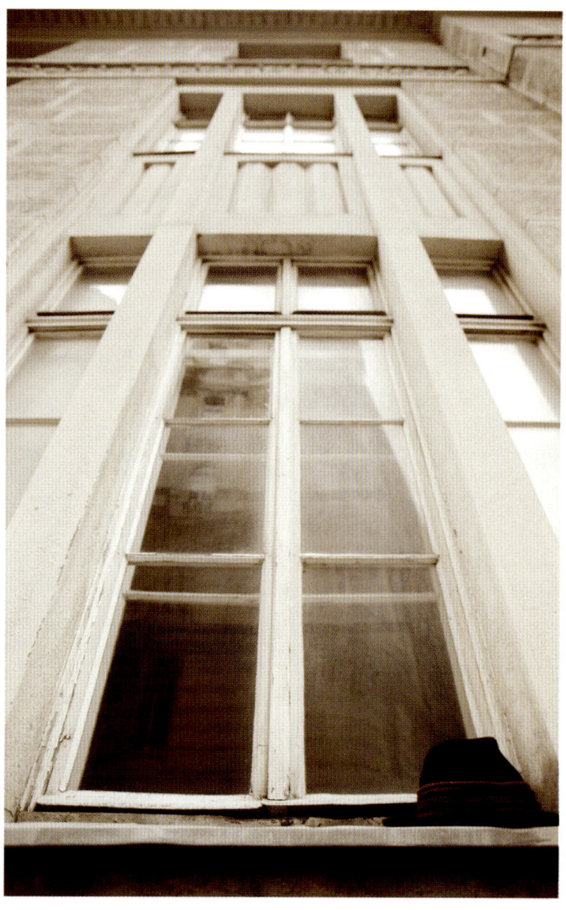

Just because you're fond of an image doesn't mean that viewers will be, too. The credibility of your critic will dictate how much you value the feedback. A well-reasoned critique can change your opinion of an image, sometimes immediately, sometimes gradually. All of a sudden, this cleanly designed picture that features a hat can become unremarkable.

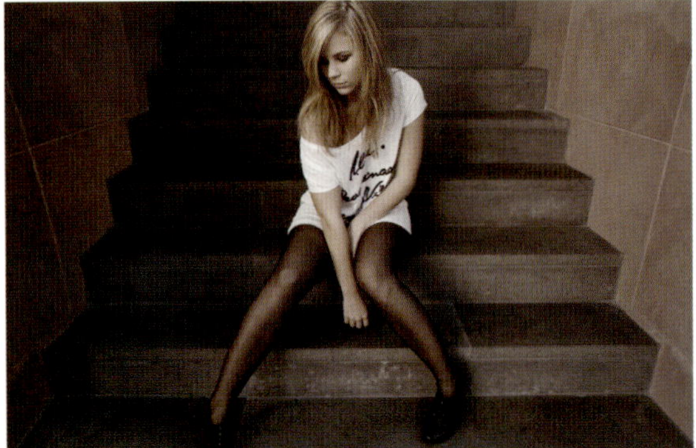

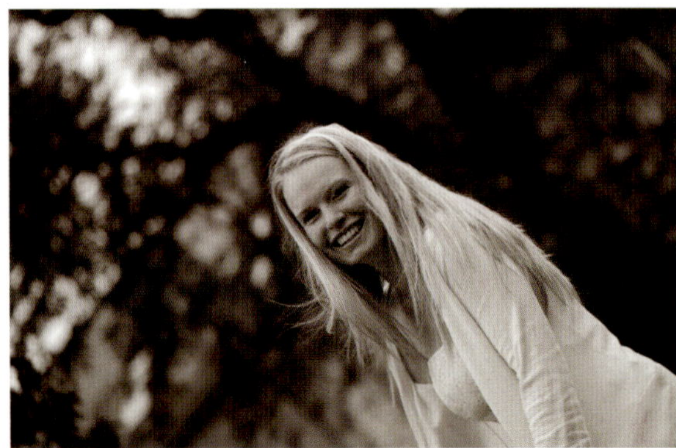

Making unconventional decisions about content and design can quickly polarize viewers. An objective conversation between the photographer and the viewer can often cause one of the parties to see the image differently. Admitting that you overlooked a way to interpret something or that you had a different perception of an effect can make a conversation constructive and worthwhile for everyone involved.

Playing the Critic

Not every critique of your work will be constructive enough for you to use. The old expression, "Do unto others what you would have them do unto you" applies here. If you want to receive constructive critiques of your photos, offer a colleague the type of criticism you hope to receive. You will improve your own craft by critically engaging with images because you'll learn how to look at pictures and find the right words to describe what you see. You should, of course, ask your counterpart if he or she wants to receive this sort of feedback. Keeping the following points in mind will help you structure your thinking and your response:

- **Content:** Determine the subject, the message, and the emotions in the image and briefly describe them. This way the photographer will know whether you have understood the image on a basic level.
- **Form:** Analyze the dominant design elements and their respective effects.
- **Exposure technique:** Determine if there are any irregularities due to the way the image was exposed.
- **Post-processing:** Look for irregularities in the way the image was edited.
- **Balance:** Assess whether the visual design, technique, and post-processing meld into a unified statement. Look for elements that don't fit with the overall effect.
- **Motivation:** Describe how the image is especially successful.
- **Suggestion:** Offer suggestions for improving the overall coherence of the image and how the photographer could accomplish those goals.

Remember that what you say isn't as important as how you say it. No one will feel attacked if you use tactful, friendly language supported by evidence, even when you are at a different stage of photographic development than your counterpart. A photographer might not understand your critique, and they'll use it as an excuse to deflect your feedback. But your job is to identify and describe the mistakes—you're not responsible for making them better. And it never hurts to have a jaw-dropping portfolio to give your feedback credibility.

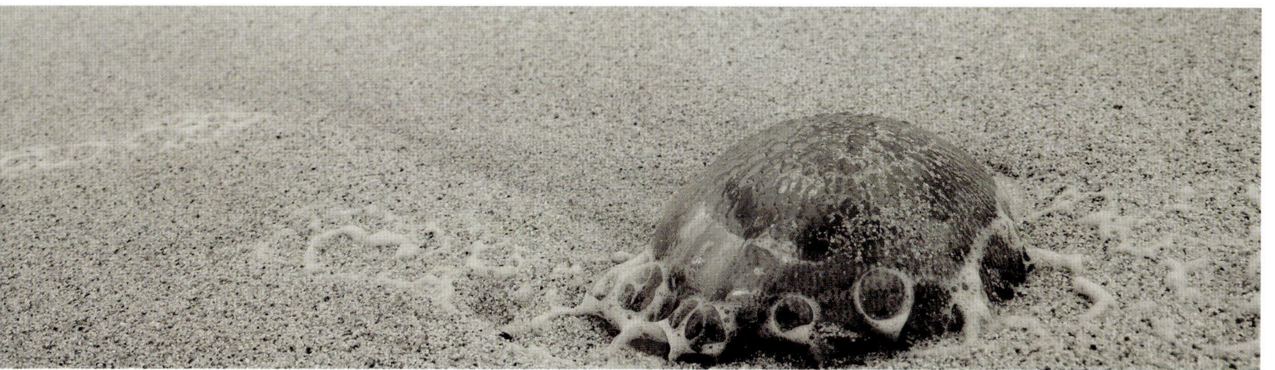

9.3 Common Design Mistakes

The goal of image design is to coordinate every aspect of a photo so it supports the intended message or concept. Since these intentions can vary dramatically, certain design decisions may be effective in one situation but not another. Take this into account when you evaluate images and understand that an element that does not work in one image may be effective in another.

There are specific aspects of visual design elements that viewers tend to dislike when they are used in certain situations, regardless of the subject. The following pages contain information about these design mistakes and how to avoid them. If you follow this advice, your visual designs will be more clear and coherent, and most viewers will interpret the results favorably. These guidelines are not absolute—they will help you avoid some problems, but they cannot guarantee convincing and interesting images.

When you want to take a couple quick shots it's often easiest to let your camera's automatic exposure mode determine the aperture, shutter speed, and ISO value. In low light conditions, such as early in the morning or late in the evening—or indoors, as in this picture of a cat—alarm bells should go off in your head telling you to pay careful attention to the shutter speed.

Camera Shake

The classic photographic mistake is using a shutter speed that's too slow. If you are shooting handheld in low light conditions with a fully automatic exposure mode, your camera may use a shutter speed that's too long to avoid unwanted blur. Camera shake is often hard to detect on the small camera monitor, so you won't see the mistake until you view the image on your computer.

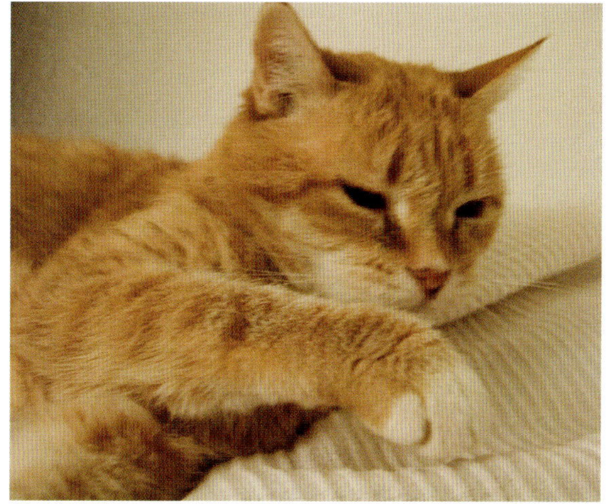

To avoid camera shake, expose your images in manual or shutter-priority mode. This allows you to define a safe shutter speed while the camera selects the aperture. Also, determine the maximum shutter speed you can use to get a sharp image. To conduct a simple test, look for a subject that has a small, uniform structure with a lot of contrast. Take a series of properly exposed images with shutter speeds of 1/30 to 1/500 second. Examine the results on your computer at 100 percent viewing size and note which speeds produced acceptably sharp images.

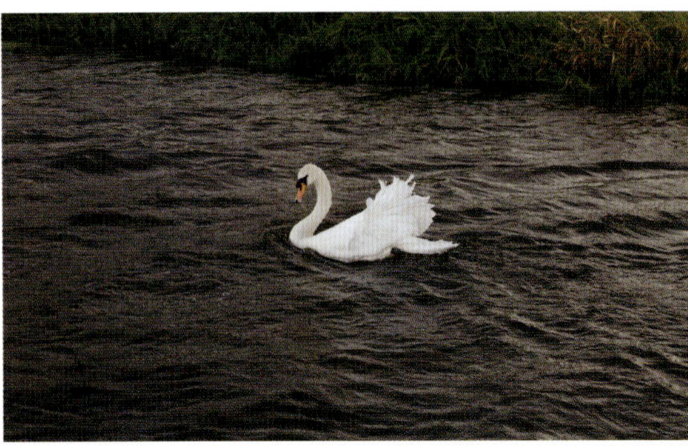

It's tempting to release the shutter immediately after you focus on a moving subject. With practice, it takes only a fraction of a second to press the shutter button halfway and then relocate your subject within the image area. You can compose the subject with the golden ratio if time is a factor.

Central Positioning

Inexperienced photographers often take pictures of their subjects without any deliberation. Positioning the subject at the center of the image area unambiguously highlights it as the most important element, but it also tends to waste a lot of space that could be used more effectively. There is often a large area above the subject that doesn't convey any information, and the subject may be unnecessarily cropped on the bottom. Also, when subjects are placed in front of a uniform background, they may not appear weighted in a meaningful way. The extreme calm created by this positioning improves the look of few subjects—most come across as boring.

One simple remedy is to focus on the subject first, then compose the shot and expose the image. Your pictures will seem livelier, regardless of how you position your main subject.

Overlapping Subjects

It's not uncommon to see images that have so many elements piled on top of one another that it's difficult to discern the main subject. Small structures and lines behind the main subject make it difficult to perceive its shape, and secondary elements in the background are also obscured. Our spatial vision allows us to separate objects better than a camera, which collapses all of the spatial layers into one plane. This is often more apparent in images than you would expect.

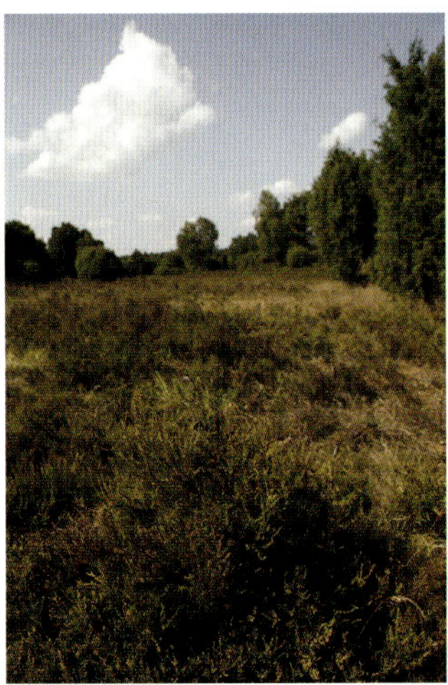

The background makes the subject, which is supposed to be the tiny fir tree in the foreground, nearly imperceptible. The more similar the overlapped elements are, the more confusing the image will be. In this case it would have been better to use an extremely low camera position so the outline of the fir tree would have stood out against the blue sky.

With a small adjustment to the camera position, you can eliminate this defect by shooting at an angle so the elements are side by side. This makes it easier to distinguish the contents of the image. With concentration and practice, it's easy to choose an effective camera position simply by looking through the viewfinder or at the display.

Chaotic Lines

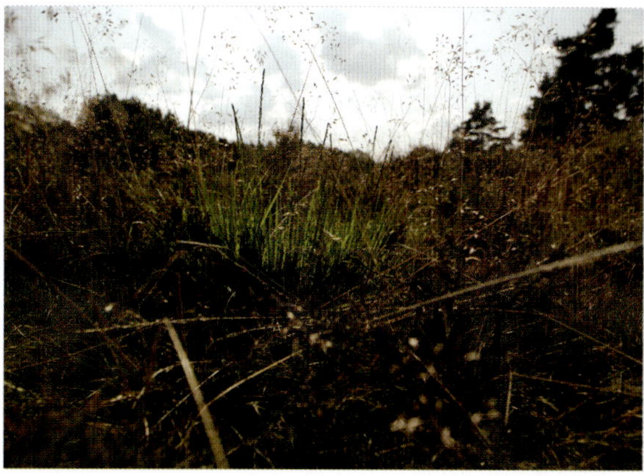

Pictures that feature too many lines pointing in different directions start to look like a maze. Viewers will follow each line briefly before switching directions to follow another line. The result is a hopeless mess that viewers will find chaotic.

Your only recourse is to be aware of and manage the lines in your subject. By carefully selecting the image area and your position, you can control which lines appear in your final image and which way they point. Arrange large lines so they are prominent and decisive, let conspicuous lines run out to the corners, and avoid or reduce portions of your subject that feature lots of small, unorganized lines. You can also turn on your camera's black-and-white mode; evaluating a scene without colors causes lines to look even more striking.

Each individual blade of grass creates a line. They all point in different directions without any recognizable order, which creates an extremely chaotic feeling. The viewer's eye can rest only on the large green area in the center of the image.

Harsh Light and Distracting Shadows

Due to the human eye's ability to adjust quickly, it can even out large disparities of brightness and deliver properly exposed images to the brain. Because our natural vision is capable of discovering detail in dark shadows, viewers often try to see details within the dark areas in an image, which is impossible. This is why clipped black areas are so distracting, especially when they have a conspicuous shape or when they obscure an important part of the picture.

Recognizing problematic shadows is the first step toward avoiding them. When you shoot in bright sunlight or with powerful lights, there will be shadows. Any shadows you discover with your natural eyesight will assuredly cause problems in your image. Squinting your eyes is one way to make shadows stand out (page 139), or you can expose a quick test shot.

You can also use fill light, diffusers, additional light sources, or light-shaping tools to reduce or eliminate shadows. When you're on location and don't have additional equipment, you can wait for the clouds to change, move into the shade, or turn the subject so shadows don't have a negative influence on your image.

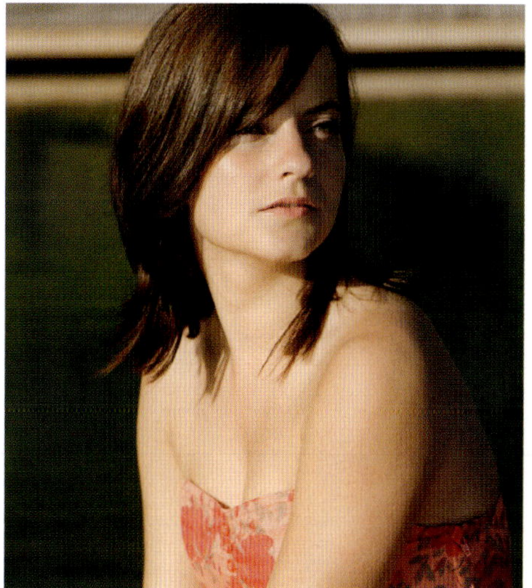

Shadows on a face can be particularly distracting, especially if they conceal the eyes, which are the most important part of the facial expression.

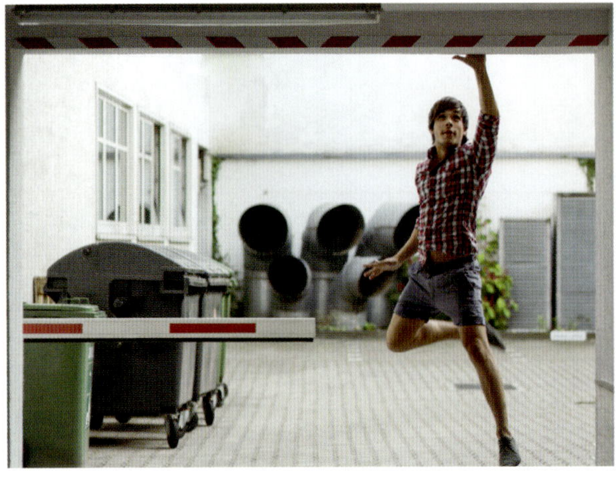

The subject in this image is a jumping man. The background, however, is so dominant and busy that the viewer's attention is scattered among the dumpsters, the windows, the exhaust pipes, and the metal boxes. Sometimes the background is anything but ideal for a picture.

Distracting Backgrounds

Since we tend to focus on the main elements of a photo, it's easy to forget about the background. Remember that distracting elements—such as a colorful or bright area, a geometric shape, a conspicuous structure, or a dominant line—can sneak into our pictures. They annoy viewers and detract from the main subject.

Take a moment to consider the background for every image. Choose your standpoint and image area to avoid distracting elements or hide them behind other objects. Be patient and wait for passersby to move out of the scene before you release the shutter button. Use a fast lens, and leverage sharpness and blur to weight different elements in your images. With the depth of field preview button you can check to see if the background elements are blurry enough or if they are still too sharp and distracting.

Too Many Elements

People see things differently than how a camera captures them. We can process one detail after another, distinguish visual elements, and concentrate on one specific element while everything else fades into the background. Since our vision naturally works this way, we instinctively try to capture entire scenes in our pictures—a practice that often results in too much information in the final image. Countless elements compete for the viewer's attention, and the most important details are hard to distinguish from the clutter. The result is a muddled and busy image that forces viewers to determine the relative importance of everything in the picture. This problem is common with wide-angle lenses because they capture a wider field of view than our vision.

With images that are this disorganized, viewers can't tell what the subject is. Only the tight depth of field suggests that the dragonfly on the lily pad is the subject, even though it's barely perceptible. The other elements, such as the circular leaves and the bright orange goldfish, detract from the insect. It would have been better to approach the subject more closely and crop out the other elements.

You must decide what to reveal in your photograph to make sure your subject is prominent. Try to depict your subject so it fills up most of the image area. It's generally more effective to isolate a specific aspect of a scene and take multiple images than to cram everything into a single image. If possible, shrink the distance between your camera and the subject. Remember, the saying Less Is More holds true in photographs. As Robert Capa said, "If your pictures aren't good enough, you're not close enough."

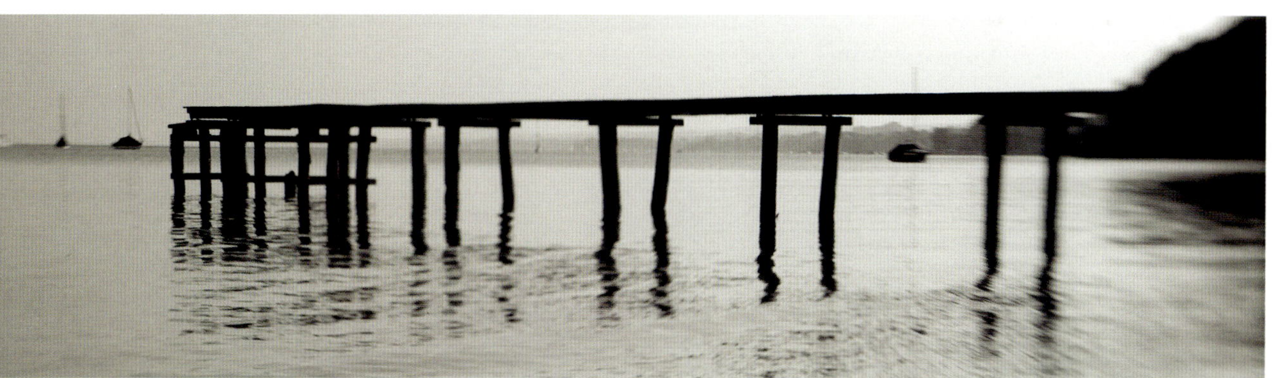

9.4 Analysis Examples

In photography there are two different perspectives for thinking about a picture: that of the photographer and that of everyone else. When photographers look at their images, they can think back to the circumstances of the exposure: what were they trying to achieve? How difficult was it to take the picture? Did the image turn out better or worse than expected? What are their emotional attachments to the subject? These factors can influence photographers' opinions of their own images.

Other viewers don't have this additional information. When they analyze or evaluate an image, they have to fall back on whatever is present in the image itself. They only have access to the final result; they can't see what the original image looked like before the edits were applied during post-processing. It makes no difference whether an image required elaborate planning and extensive editing or if it was a happy accident—the final result is all the viewer sees. This fundamental difference can lead to problems when photographers discuss their images with viewers.

To conduct a targeted analysis of your images, you have to base your assessment strictly on the photos themselves and suppress the knowledge you have as their creator. In the remainder of this chapter, we analyze ten images without background information that the photographer would have. We focus strictly on the final image.

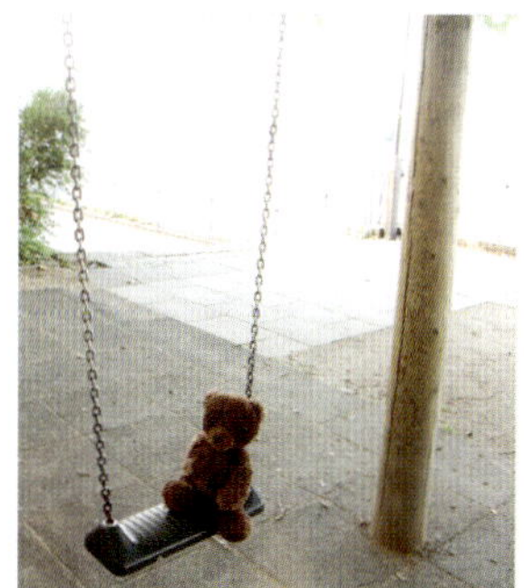

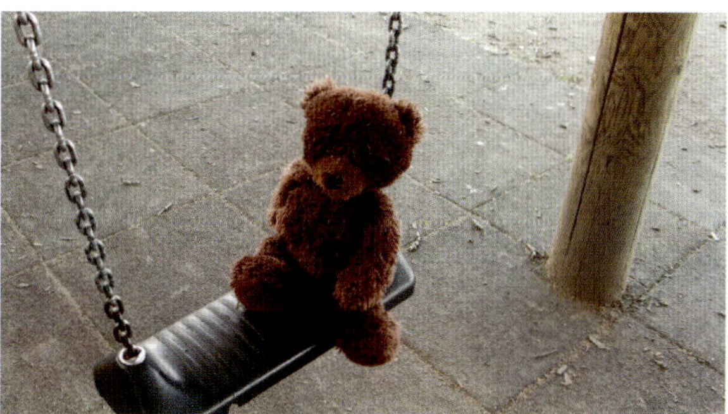

There can be a gap between what works best for the content and what works best for the design. The main themes of this scene feature a lost and forgotten toy sitting on a swing. It conveys loneliness and abandonment within a large, empty space. The wider angle of view supports the message better (left), but it causes the bear to be less recognizable, and the large white area in the background is distracting. The tighter angle of view (right) avoids these design problems and features lines that run out to the corners, but it does not convey the content as effectively.

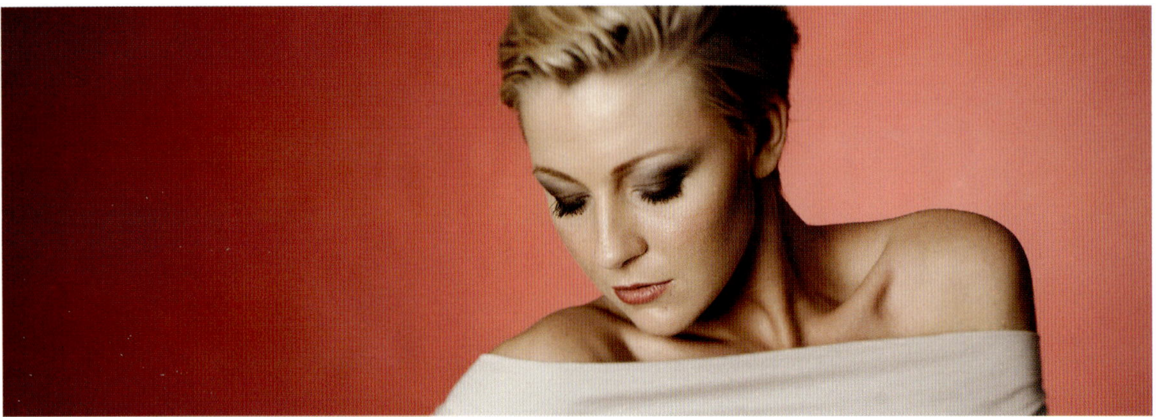

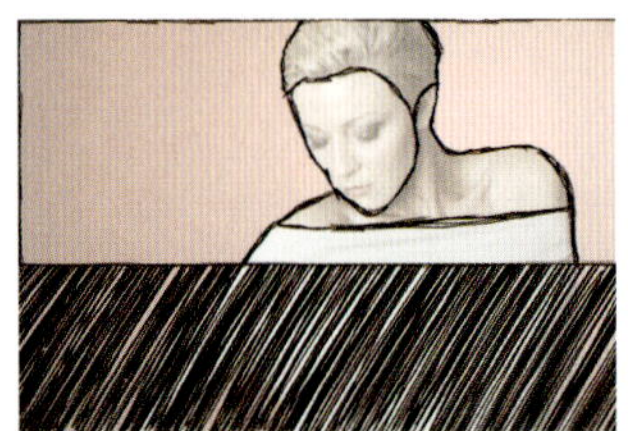

The drawing illustrates that this panoramic view was created with a crop. This was necessary because the loose garment took up a large amount of space and made the model's torso look bulky. The drawing also shows that the background is divided into two separate areas, which creates an exciting contrast. There are only six substantive areas in the image, but the lighting conditions make the picture seem spatial anyway.

Red Beauty

This image combines the genres of portrait and beauty photography. The makeup, hair, and dress make it clear that this is not a natural character portrait, but rather an emotional statement with the goal of fascinating the viewer with beauty and perfection.

Composition: Panorama format invites visual wandering; tight crop reduces hair and clothing and highlights the face; head and eyes are neither horizontally nor vertically centered, which is modestly unsettling; body clearly and dramatically shifted to one side
Lines and shapes: Lines of sight are directed downward, parallel to the arm on the left, bringing vitality into the image; same goes for the rising shoulder line; horizontal lines of the right shoulder and the neckline establish stability
Perspective: Normal view produces natural feel; classic focal length for portraits (90mm) produces familiar and pleasing proportions
Light: Structures emphasized with sidelighting; soft light from the front left for soft shadows; directed light against the backdrop produces vignetting; reduced lighting near the edges focuses attention on the model
Color: Red backdrop brings drama and life into the picture; lips echo this red and are emphasized; grays have natural effect; skin and hair tones are subtle; chromatic/achromatic and quality contrasts bring out red tones
Sharpness/blur: Sharpness emphasizes lips and eyes; focal plane is unusually bent in space with tilt-shift lens; blur prevents the fine structures of the model's hair from attracting too much attention

The absence of eye contact invites the viewer's eye to wander over the model's face and get lost in the details. The image produces an exciting but balanced mix of drama and stillness that creates a feeling of a calm before the storm. In this respect, the design works well in the beauty genre; it attracts the viewer's attention and holds it for as long as possible.

To the Corner!

The content of this image is straightforward: a leaping dog, a threshold, and a light blue patch we recognize as jeans. The actual subject of this image, however, is more developed; it includes the movement and the joie de vivre of the scene. There's enough here that viewers can imagine what's going on: it's a warm summer day, perhaps people are grilling, friends are coming over, or the dog is about to chase the neighbor's cat. Clichés and internal images can become part of a photo, even when they're not directly represented.

Composition: A modest panorama hints at a narrative quality; the crop through the dog conveys closeness; the crop through the tail fixes the dog at the top; the position of the main subject in the upper left creates tension; three levels create dimensionality
Lines and shapes: Dog's direction of movement creates a dominant line that runs left out of the image; bright areas give weight to the right side to create balance; the threshold guides the viewer's gaze to the right; jeans prevent the threshold from exiting the image
Perspective: Low camera position brings the viewer to the dog's level; modest downward view establishes an overview
Light: Bright, warm colors produce a summery feel; dark fur is an eye-catcher
Color: Very bright exposure leads to soft, desaturated colors; only three recognizable colors, which play a supporting role and add emotion
Sharpness/blur: Prominent blur conveys the dog's movement and direction; dog is still easy to identify; sharpness in the foreground pulls the viewer's gaze back and keeps it in the image

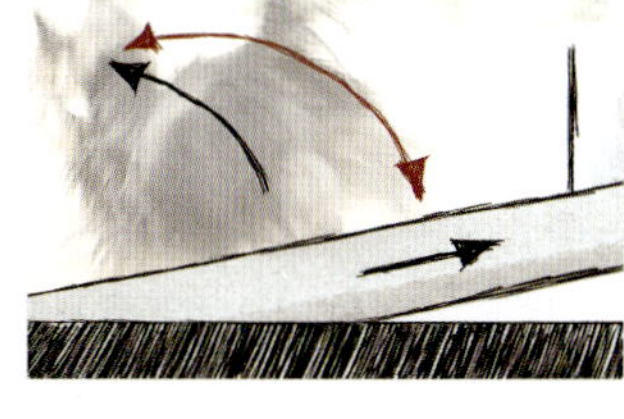

The dog's movement dominates the image, giving it the look and feel of a snapshot. Nothing stands out as artificial, so the picture seems authentic. The design supports the positive zest for life conveyed by the image and produces a strong vitality that holds the viewer's attention.

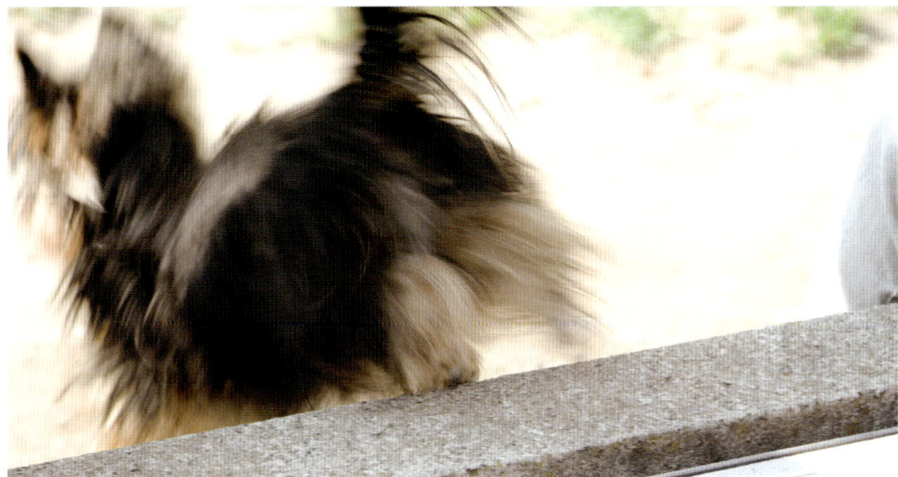

The direction of the dog's movement is the strongest force at play here, and it pulls the viewer's attention to the upper left corner. If the dog had been cropped any closer, the viewer's gaze would have been launched out of the picture. The bright areas, the sharpness, and the threshold's rising line keep the viewer engaged with the photo and direct attention to the right. A crop along the bottom was necessary to eliminate the heavy effect of the bright tiles, which don't convey any information.

Colorful Decay

This poor, wilted tulip without any water is a sad sight. Yet, because it appears in this unconventional way, it is also surprising, jarring, and new. We're familiar with tulips as upright, vivid heralds of springtime, so to see this particular one hanging limp over the edge of a vase is unusual and recalls the ideas of decay and transience. These concepts create a stark contrast within an otherwise clean and ordered environment.

The perceived motion in this image comes from the arrangement of elements and the prominent lines; normally a glass sitting on a slanted tabletop would slide off. The nearly round blossom functions optically as a stopper and as a pivot point around which the glass, and the entire image, spins. Its unstable shape supports the effect of the tipping glass—its top is wider than its base.

Composition: Portrait format conveys tension; crop reduces the prominence of the glass, which is optically fixed at the top left; limited number of elements produces a sense of order and concentration; three levels provide depth; contrast between the blossom and the remainder of the image produces tension

Lines and shapes: Clear lines give the image an artificial tone; organic shape of the flower stands out like a foreign body; all the lines are diagonal, which is unsettling and unrealistic but dynamic; bottom lines run near the corner to add excitement

Perspective: Off-kilter camera position provokes the viewer; modest downward view brings composure to the image; macro lens enables a feeling of closeness

Light: Weak backlighting from above creates contrast and tension; bright surroundings allow the dark tulip to stand out as an attention grabber; many spots of light open the surfaces and bring life into the picture

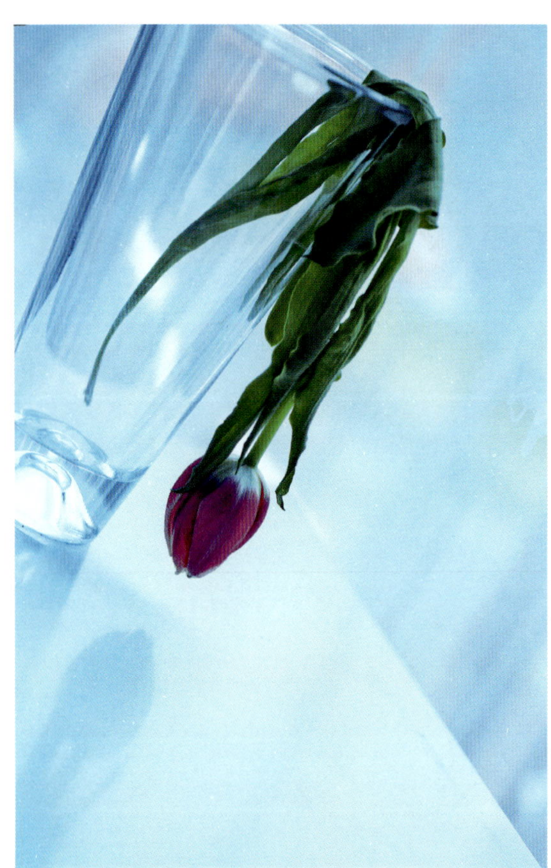

Color: Dark, bright colors dominate the image; triad of cyan, green, and magenta creates a strong contrast; combination of colors is disharmonious, arouses attention, and brings life into the image

Sharpness/blur: Selective sharpness isolates the tulip and emphasizes it as the most important element; heavy background blurring makes it difficult to situate the subject and makes the image more universal.

The design is extremely dynamic and edgy, which produces the feeling of movement even though everything is firmly resting on a table. The colors, above all, produce a fresh but artificial touch, which runs against the general grain of the subject. Decay is artistically exaggerated and aesthetically represented, which triggers confusion that will ultimately spur the viewer to engage with the picture even more.

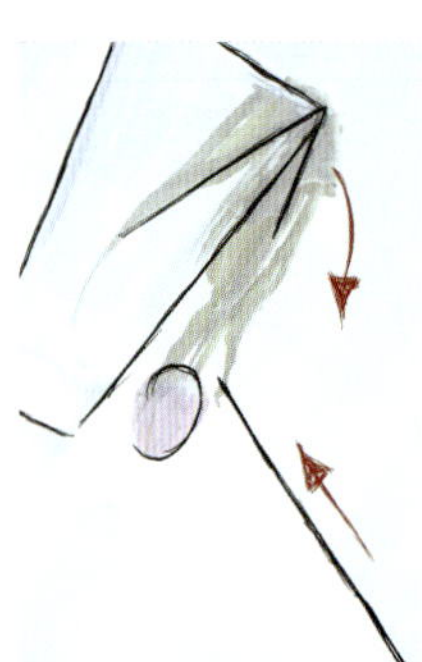

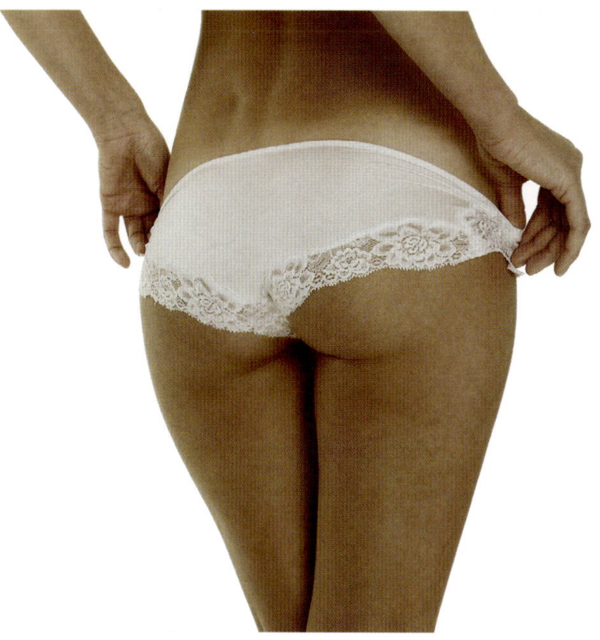

Feminine Curves

This image works primarily because of its content. Men and women alike are drawn to the smooth curves of a woman's backside here because this image is about perfection and aesthetics—it's not a sexually oriented representation. The lingerie gives the image excitement.

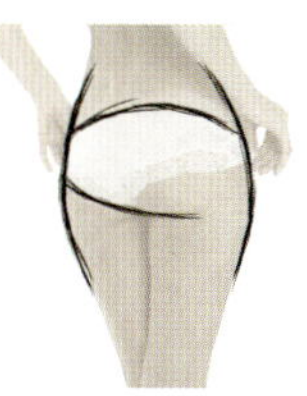

There are two primary pairs of curved lines in this image—together they produce a pleasant and natural effect. The model's hips and body look like two almond-shaped areas that are shifted in relation to each other, hinting at a smooth, cohesive, and harmonious unit. The other lines enclose this unity. The gentle, perfect movement of the lines highlights the delicate perfection of the female body.

Composition: Landscape format brings calmness and stability into the picture; crop limits the subject to the model's hips; arms and legs are reduced to insignificant elements around the border; truncations make the body anonymous; positioning at the right side increases the energy in the picture
Lines and shapes: Curved lines and organically shaped areas are feminine and natural
Perspective: Slight upward view increases and exaggerates the subject as something artificial and artistic; an absence of distortions augments the natural look and feel
Light: Soft, flattering light; sidelighting highlights the body's physicality
Color: Natural skin tones make the image feel realistic; pure white background releases the subject from any connections to other content; aesthetic, innocent, and pure
Sharpness/blur: Large depth of field allows the viewer to recognize all details and provides enough information to keep the viewer's attention; no distracting background

The overall effect of the image balances the almost supernatural representation of a perfect feminine ideal and the unaffected raw beauty that nature produces. The strong aesthetics of this subject support the overall content: a tribute to femininity.

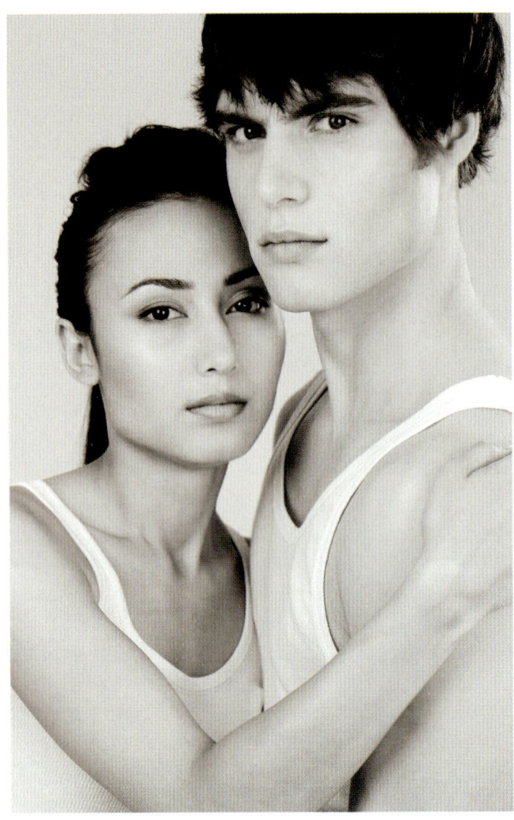

Alone Together

A man and a woman stand as a pair before the camera. Together they are unified, and typical roles and stereotypes are apparent. He stands firm and unshakable in the foreground, while she gently clings to him for protection. Their facial expressions are somewhat distanced—no unambiguous emotions can be inferred.

Composition: Portrait format, which is familiar for portraiture; tight crop and truncations produce a feeling of closeness; his face partially hides hers, which causes him to weigh heavier in the balance between them; her arm partially covers his and restores the balance; this overlapping creates a spatial effect; fragmented visual elements occupy the viewer's attention; most of these elements can be found in pairs, which intensifies their effect

Lines and shapes: Eyes, lips, and ears work as anchor points for the viewer; self-contained system of lines keeps the viewer's gaze within the image; angle, crop, and occlusion limit the area that the arms take up and avoid large areas that don't convey information

Perspective: Slight upward view exaggerates the emotion of the two people; facial features are natural and undistorted

Light: Gentle, diffuse light eliminates shadows and makes details visible; bright streak of light along his neck deflects some attention from their faces

Color: Black-and-white tones make the image less emotional, more artistic, and more elegant; the lines and shapes are emphasized

Sharpness/blur: Large depth of field reveals all the details and invites the viewer's eye to wander throughout the image; focus is on his face, making him the main subject

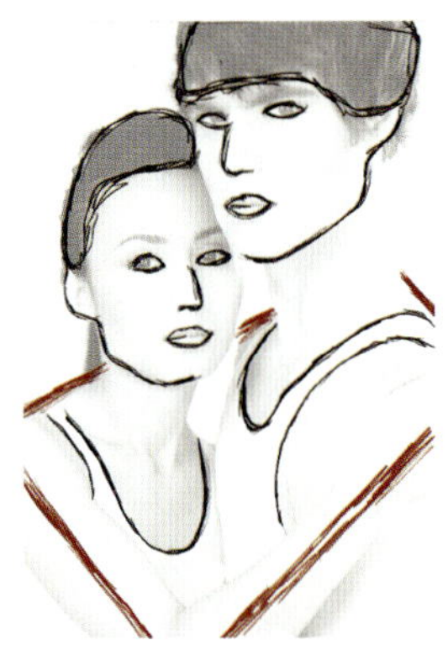

Each of the visual elements within the picture appear twice, and because the two figures have different sizes, these elements are staggered: hair, eyes, nose, mouth, ears, jaw, neckline, and shirt—each has an optical double. This repetition intensifies these particular elements and makes them work like a guide for the viewer's gaze. Since the figures are so close to each other, they almost merge into a single unit. The lines of the arms and shoulders produce a quadrangle, highlighting the closed-off effect of the image.

This image feels close, tender, and pure. It has an overall quiet effect, and no particular element of design takes the main role. The viewer needs to work out the main subject for him- or herself and make inferences from nuances in the image. This design is suited well for the subject, which reveals an intimate vulnerability between two people and doesn't exhibit any loud drama. At the same time, the people stare outward with their sphinx-like eyes, and their close stance makes the pair seem withdrawn, as though they are shielding their privacy.

A Splash of Color at the Edge

All there is to see in this image is a small portion of the belly and a foot of a bird; nevertheless, it's not difficult for the viewer to imagine the rest of the parrot. The human brain uses prior knowledge and experience to mentally complete images. Neither the bird nor the tree is actually present—the crop makes this image feel almost abstract.

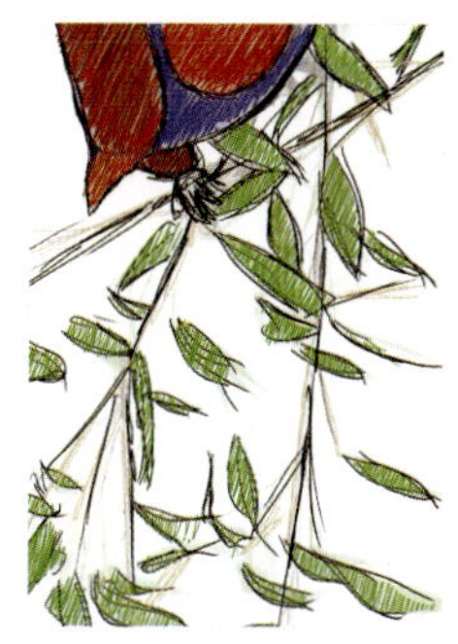

Aside from the radical crop directly through the main subject, the saturated colors are the key to this image. Saturated color tones contrast with a large white area and give them increased intensity. At the same time, the color contrast produces an immediate and striking effect.

Composition: Portrait format creates tension; daring crop makes recognizing the subject an obstacle and turns the image into a visual puzzle; crop reduces the parrot to colorful areas; position of the main subject and the red surface near the image border creates a high level of excitement; subtle darkening at the image border prevents the viewer's eye from leaving the image
Lines and shapes: Parrot's foot works as a visual point; colorful areas function as eye-catchers; green leaves guide the viewer's gaze from anchor point to anchor point throughout the entire image area; lines direct the viewer back to the colorful bird; intricate structures offer lots of information and invite the viewer to linger within the image
Perspective: Slight upward view elevates the subject and gives the parrot a lofty position; tight angle of view bridges the distance to the bird
Light: Extremely diffuse light eradicates shadows completely; most of the light illuminates the background, creating a monotone, bright surface that can often be found in a studio; gentle light allows the subtle shades of the colors to shine
Color: Color is the dominant visual design element; primary colors on the parrot's belly immediately attract the viewer's attention; high color contrast results from the bird's bright colors and the green leaves; white background intensifies the colors
Sharpness/blur: Focus underscores the bird's claws, thereby increasing the ease of recognizing the animal; sharpness pulls the viewer's attention away from the colorful areas and directs it to the lower parts of the image; shallow depth of field renders only a few leaves sharp, while the rest of the leaves are blurred

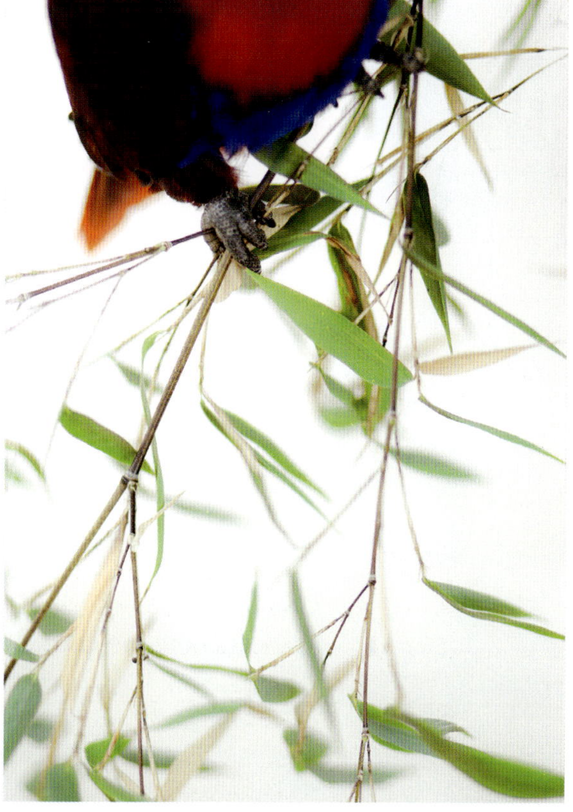

The overall effect of this image is bright, luminous, colorful, and cheerful. The lively colors and the fractured visual elements open the image, but the picture also stays static and motionless. The image has an abstract quality and seems artificial, almost like a watercolor painting. This design complements the unusual, anonymous, and somewhat baffling subject.

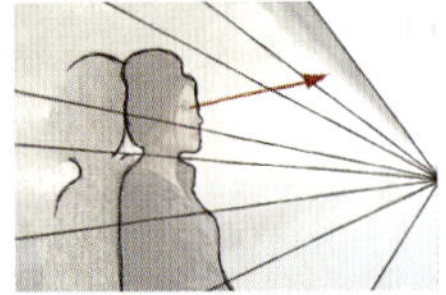

Even though the converging lines are very thin, they dramatically influence the dimension of the space depicted in the image. There is a small black point at the vanishing point that keeps the viewer's eye within the image area. The model's gaze produces a dominant line that runs against the others. Viewers involuntarily trace her line of sight with their own. When they discover that there isn't anything visually interesting in the right side of the image, they quickly return to the woman.

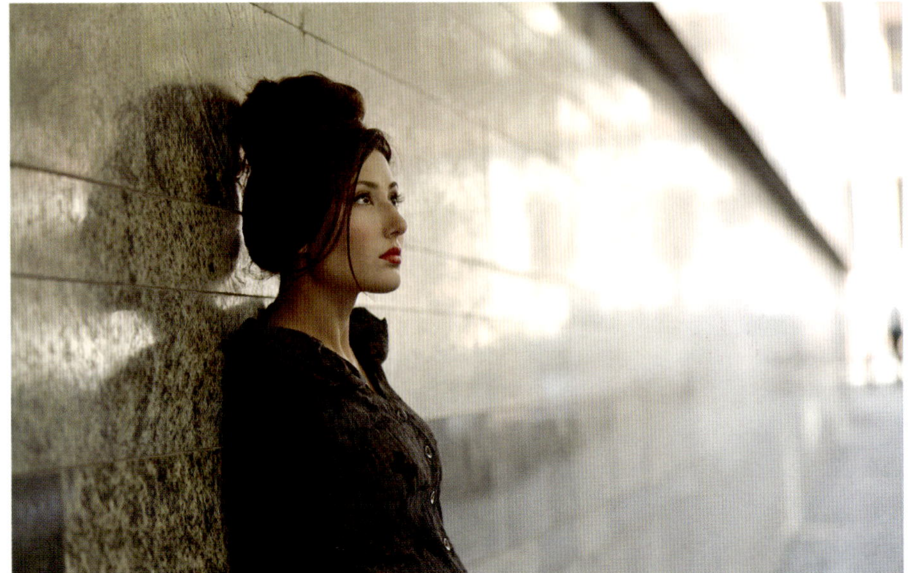

Fashion Lines

Fashion photographers attempt to show a piece of clothing explicitly or to create an emotional image that is representative of a brand. This fashion shot clearly belongs to the latter category. The subject is a specific type of woman and a specific atmosphere.

Composition: Stable landscape format supports the breadth of the image; the face and hair are shown in full; the clothes are partially cropped out and play more of a supporting role; position of the subject creates excitement
Lines and shapes: Smaller, organic area of the person contrasts with the geometric background; spots of light create slight unrest
Perspective: Slight upward view makes the model seem more important; enough distance between viewer and model to keep from disturbing her quiet concentration
Light: Backlighting establishes a stirring liveliness; indirect, reflected light prevents distracting, harsh shadows; direct light in background creates a big contrast in brightness with the darker areas in the foreground, which results in blown-out highlights that recall the bright, warm sun
Color: Concentration on one color family produces a monotone palette; bright sand and earth tones convey nature; red lips work as an eye-catcher
Sharpness/blur: Focus stresses the main element in a classic way; selective sharpness causes the person to stand out; background remains visible

In this image, the subject and the design work hand in hand to create a smooth, quiet, and understated tone. The result is pleasing both for its subtle, balanced design and the exotic beauty of the model.

Refreshing Colors

It's not difficult to recognize the elements within this image: a beer, a tree, a mug, a table, the beach, and the sky. The combination of these individual elements makes sense only when they are considered within the context of the exposure. In this particular image, the association between the objects is the subject.

The individual colors don't mix with one another—they form clearly divided areas. This emphasizes the shapes of these areas and causes each area to be perceived as a separate entity. It also causes the image to lose some of its dimensionality. The photo calls attention to the beer glass more than anything else because of its shape, striking color, complete representation, and position in the foreground. This emphasis allows the beer to hold its own with the dominant, bright background. The visual balance between the two elements causes the viewer's attention to move from one element to the other.

Composition: Portrait format produces excitement; truncated tree creates the feeling of closeness for the whole image; the crop reduces the tree; nearly central position of the beer makes it the key element and establishes stability in the image; outside placement of the secondary elements pulls the viewer's gaze outward, creating internal energy; four distinct levels do not create a three-dimensional feeling

Lines and shapes: Sand, water, and sky create three or four uneven areas, which makes for an unsettled background; horizon line close to the middle creates a balancing stillness; many disparate lines fail to produce a self-contained system of lines, conversely resulting in commotion and disorder; mixture of organic and geometric shapes is mildly disquieting

Perspective: Slight downward perspective establishes an overview; telephoto lens staggers the visual layers

Light: Separate lighting conditions for the foreground and background make the image appear synthetic; brightness in the background attracts the viewer's attention; front lighting makes the image seem flat

Color: Intense amber of the beer functions as a point of entry for the image and establishes a vivid chromatic/achromatic contrast with the desaturated colors of the background; subtle color gradients bring out details and entice the viewer

Sharpness/blur: Selective depth of field emphasizes the main element; background is still recognizable and has a large influence on the overall image; unfocused background has a flat look, like a mural

The overall effect of this image owes more to design than content. Nevertheless, it triggers associations with vacations, the sun, and the beach, while the bare tree and the stale beer bring some negative tones into the picture. The uncertain situation and the design, which conveys both stillness and tension, has a baffling but compelling impact on viewers who allow themselves to be drawn in by the picture.

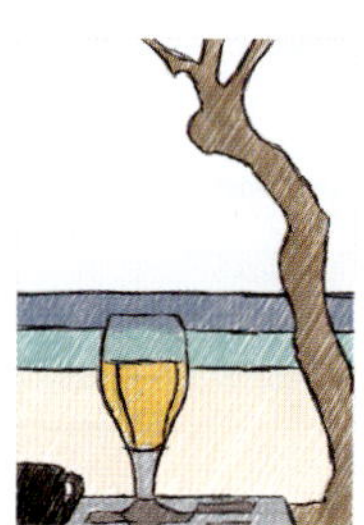

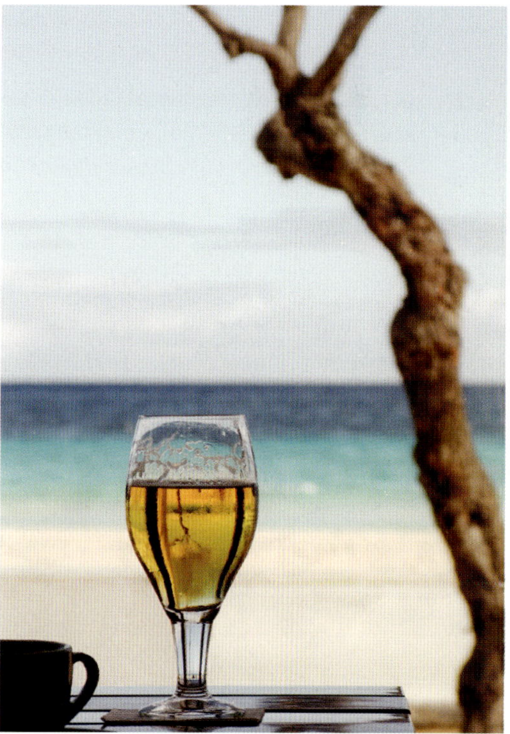

Clearly Confusing

This image documents a reflection in a painted glass façade—an incidental scene that appears exactly as it did in reality. There is no artificial staging here. The image area doesn't allow the viewer to establish an exact orientation or figure out exactly what's going on. The subject, in other words, is equal parts perplexity, coincidental arrangement, and visual puzzle.

Composition: Despite very dominant lines, the play of visual levels is the strongest design element; landscape format gives the unsettled subject an optical footing; tight crop makes getting bearings within the image a challenge
Lines and shapes: Red text is the primary attention grabber; light car establishes the second anchor point; soft texture of the pervasive white color reduces the optical dominance of the reflection, opens the image, and gives it an unnatural tone
Perspective: Normal view seems stable and familiar; perfect parallelism between the focal plane and the glass creates a striking, unreal effect
Light: Different lighting conditions divide the visual layers; large shadow area on the glass wall preserves all the fine details; front lighting without visible shadows on the beach make this layer feel very flat
Color: Desaturated colors lead to a subtle overall effect; characteristic colors in the background facilitate the viewer's understanding
Sharpness/blur: Focus is on the glass pane and emphasizes this layer; depth of field is sufficient so all details are distinguishable

Even though the individual elements are scattered about, the different layers give this image visual organization. Aside from their proximity, the contents of this picture have nothing to do with one another—which gives this image a puzzling and confusing quality.

The many visual elements lure the viewer's gaze throughout the entire area and provide ample details to keep the viewer engaged. Since the elements are evenly distributed, relatively small, and absent of striking color, none of them emerge as a dominant player. The lines divide the image into differently-sized rectangles, giving the image structure and creating tight boundaries. The contrast between geometric and organic shapes breaks up the rigid grid. Everywhere the viewer looks, there's something to see.

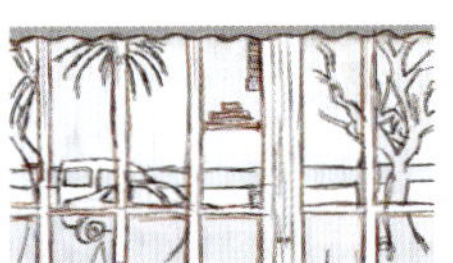

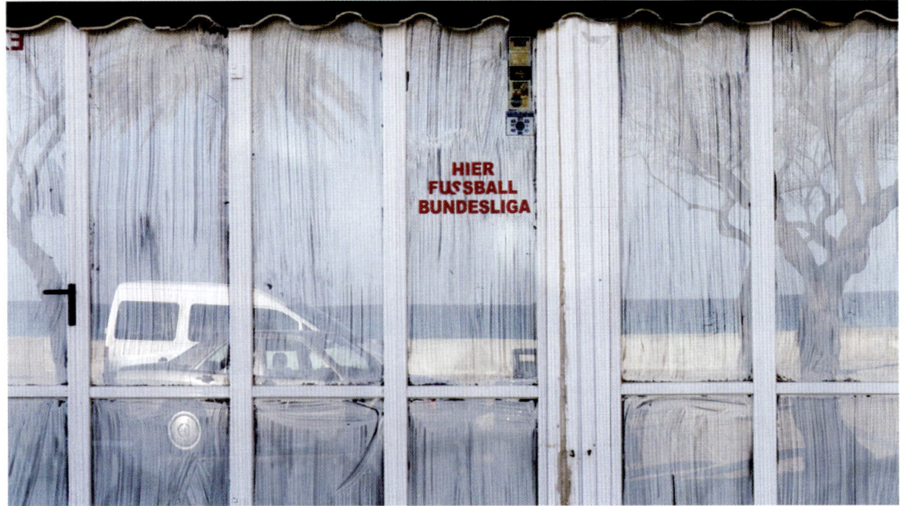

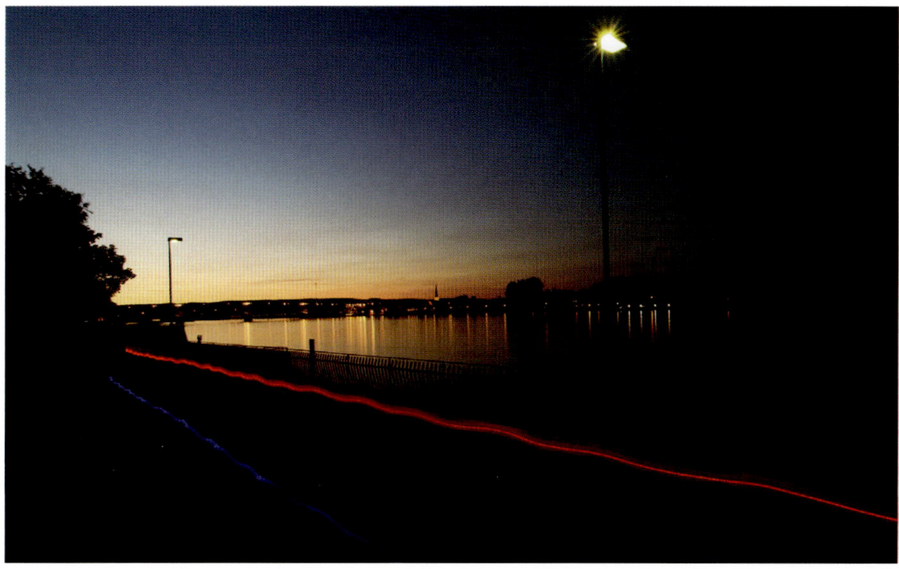

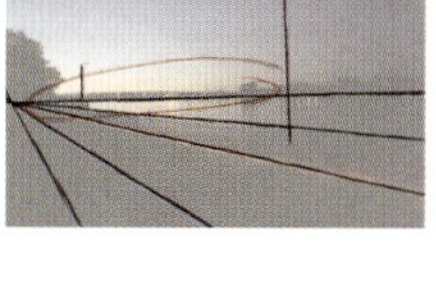

The lines of this image converge on a vanishing point off to the left, forcing the viewer to examine the image in the opposite direction of how we read. The repetition of the lights supports this visual direction. At the same time, the two lampposts create perpendicular lines that encourage the viewer to examine other areas of the image. In the large areas of the sky, the lights serve as anchor points that momentarily pull the viewer's gaze away from the sunset.

Traces of Light

This image combines three different subjects: the setting sun's play of colors, the lights on the waterfront, and the traces of light as a technical and artificial component.

Composition: Stillness of landscape format is strengthened by the centrally placed horizontal line; complete depiction of the scene establishes distance; large dark areas make it harder to decipher details and make the image seem flatter; several small secondary elements are distributed throughout the image area; no main element dominates the image, which allows the colors to come to the fore
Lines and shapes: A few clearly visible lines are a significant aspect of design in this image; vanishing lines create a palpable dimensionality
Perspective: Wide, downward view creates an overview of the scenery
Light: Two bright areas attract the viewer's attention; viewer's eye jumps back and forth between small, very bright lights and large, dark parts of the horizon; setting sun creates an evocative tone of light
Color: Cold/warm color contrast is repeated by the light traces; brightness contrast is also at play
Sharpness/blur: Depth of field allows all details to be visible; long exposure means moving lights produce two beams of color, which conveys movement and produces an artificial effect

The strong colors in this image appeal to the viewer's emotions and create a dramatic atmosphere. The specific characteristics of the location are obscured in the dark, which makes the image more universal. The light writing provides an artistic counterpoint to a familiar sunset vista.

Online Resources

The following online resources provide a range of information on the subject of visual design. There are undoubtedly great online resources that we don't know about, so this list makes no claim to be exhaustive. If you know of a useful website that could be of interest to our readers, or if you manage one yourself, drop us a line at the following email address: kontakt@artepictura.de. Thank you!

Blogs

In addition to maintaining a website, many photographers write blogs to regularly show their work and post articles on a variety of topics. A few of these blogs introduce highly accomplished photojournalists and publish interesting articles on the subject of image design:

fstoppers.com
froknowsphoto.com/blog
www.photoshelter.com/mkt/research
www.joeyl.com/blog
blog.chasejarvis.com/blog

Photography Platforms

Nothing trains the photographic eye better than actively, critically examining thousands of images. Exciting and fascinating pictures stay in your visual memory, and poorly designed ones show you what to avoid. The goal here isn't to base your work on what you discover at these links, but to use the images as inspiration and motivation to expand your horizons as a photographer:

www.fotocommunity.com
www.flickr.com
www.seenby.com
1x.com
500px.com
www.deviantart.com
www.selectedviews.de
photo-forum.net
photography-now.com
www.fotoblur.com
www.behance.net
www.photographyserved.com
www.boston.com/bigpicture
www.theatlantic.com/infocus

Notes

Some of the illustrations in this book are based on graphics located at
www.wikipedia.de

The quotes at the beginning of each chapter are originally from these websites:
www.best-quotes-poems.com
www.photoquotes.com
kwerfeldein.de

Since the main focus of this book is the visual design of images, and since each reproduced picture is intended to highlight one aspect of visual design, we decided not to include the complete technical parameters for each image.

Any focal lengths that are provided are 35mm equivalents.

We dedicate this book to our son,
who kept us in good spirits every single day despite the hard work!

Thanks . . .

. . . to our families and friends, who continually look forward to each and every one of our books and try their hardest to remember them all.

. . . to Darja Dewies for her swift pen that turned quick sketches into printable graphics.

. . . to the Technology Museum Sinsheim, the Opel Zoo in Kronberg, and the MyZeil in Frankfurt for the many wonderful subjects on-site.

. . . to Dirk Osterhoff for permission to photograph the natural pools of Bingen-Bingerbrück.

. . . to Anna Reußwig and Marco Hahn from SIGMA; to Thomas Hedler from Hedler Systemlicht GmbH; to Michael Willenborg, Thilo Röhrig, and Andreas Koch from SONY; and to Stephan Frahnert from GOSSEN Foto-und Lichtmesstechnik GmbH for their support.

. . . to Werner Seeger for loaning us an image exhibiting movement.

. . . to Fabian Quanz (quanz.me) for the English links.

. . . to our models Alica, Anja, Anke, Anna, Annekathrin, Anni, Annika, Antonio, Ava, Claudia, Daniel, Daniela, Darja, David, Dominic, Dwina, Ekaterina, Emma, Friederike, Hanna, Homa, Isabelle, Jana, Janine, Jasmin, Jenny K., Jenny R., Jette, Jochen, Judith, Julia S., Julia W., Katrin, Kira, Kristin, Larissa, Laura L., Laura S., Lena, Leyla, Lilli, Lisa, Lyutsina, Magdalena, Marc, Maria, Marina, Marion, Michael, Michaela, Moni, Nanda, Nelli, Nicole, Nina, Pamela, Ralf B., Ralf R., Rymma, Sarah, Saskia, Silke, Till, Tim, Tina, Ute, Verena, Victoria, and Virginie.

. . . to Gerhard Rossbach and Rudolf Krahm from dpunkt.verlag and to Matthias Rossmanith from Rocky Nook for their trust and commitment.

About the Authors

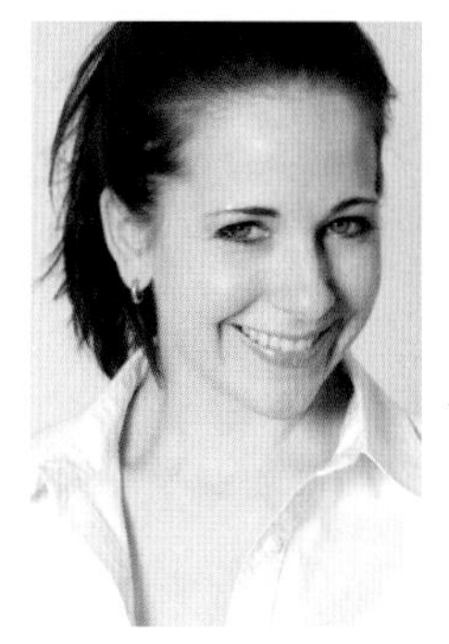

Cora Banek was born in 1981 and has been photographing since 2002. The unique aspect of her craft is that she almost always has the finished, edited image in her mind when she releases the shutter. She opts to shoot infrequently but with great intention and purpose. Cora's visual language is clean and quiet; she likes light, bright images featuring harmonious, subtle, and desaturated colors. She is a borderline perfectionist when it comes to designing her images. Her award-winning photography has been entered and exhibited in international competitions.

Cora's diverse photographic interests include portrait, beauty, fashion, nude, erotic, and floral photography. She knows Photoshop like the back of her hand and routinely optimizes, post-processes, and applies black-and-white conversions to her images. Top-quality color management is part of her daily craft, which she produces consistently for initial exposures, fine-art prints, and everything in between.

She is professionally trained in the cultural sciences and works as a freelance graphic designer and photo editor for exacting photography publications, such as the book you're holding in your hands. Together with Georg, she writes for magazines and book publishers and develops concepts for educational materials about photography. Her contract work focuses on stylish arrangements and ideal lighting for product photography and the post-processing of the resulting images.

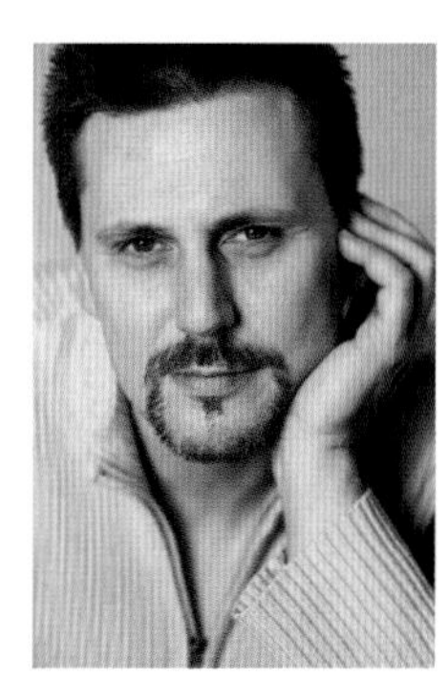

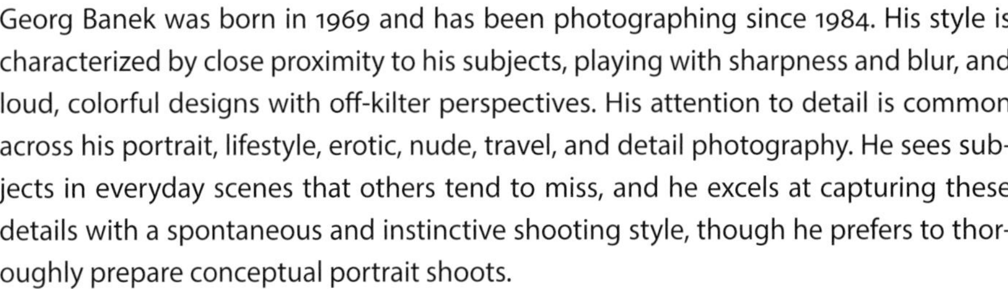

Georg Banek was born in 1969 and has been photographing since 1984. His style is characterized by close proximity to his subjects, playing with sharpness and blur, and loud, colorful designs with off-kilter perspectives. His attention to detail is common across his portrait, lifestyle, erotic, nude, travel, and detail photography. He sees subjects in everyday scenes that others tend to miss, and he excels at capturing these details with a spontaneous and instinctive shooting style, though he prefers to thoroughly prepare conceptual portrait shoots.

His contract work as a photographer centers on lifestyle images, everyday scenes, and employee and company profiles. For the past five years, he and Cora have written for photography textbooks and magazines. Georg studied economics and social education. As a management consultant, he pairs his photographic expertise with extensive experience in project and product management and sales to help corporate clients with their visual representation and professional image design needs.

Including the photography department at the college in Rhein-Main and the photography school at the university in Lüneburg, Artepictura Academy is the third structured course of photography study that Georg has devised and independently built. He is earning a teaching degree in Media Management in Wiesbaden and is responsible for the academy at Artepictura—information for which can be found at www.artepictura-akademie.de.

Index

W

Y

Z